Free Public Library
Dalton, Massachusetts

First opened, May 1861   **Accepted by Town, March 1885**

ALSO BY RICHARD M. KETCHUM

The Borrowed Years, 1938–1941: America on the Way to War
Faces from the Past
The World of George Washington
The Winter Soldiers: The Battles for Trenton and Princeton
Decisive Day: The Battle for Bunker Hill
Second Cutting: Letters from the Country
Will Rogers: The Man and His Times
The Secret Life of the Forest
The American Heritage Book of Great Historic Places
Male Husbandry
What Is Communism?

SARATOGA

SARATOGA

TURNING POINT
OF AMERICA'S REVOLUTIONARY WAR

Richard M. Ketchum

Henry Holt and Company
New York

973.33
Ket

Henry Holt and Company, Inc.
Publishers since 1866
115 West 18th Street
New York, New York 10011

Henry Holt® is a registered trademark of
Henry Holt and Company, Inc.

Published in Canada by Fitzhenry & Whiteside Ltd.,
195 Allstate Parkway, Markham, Ontario L3R 4T8.

Library of Congress Cataloging-in-Publication Data
Ketchum, Richard M., date.
Saratoga: turning point of America's Revolutionary War /
Richard M. Ketchum.—1st ed.
p.   cm.
Includes bibliographical references and index.
ISBN 0-8050-4681-X
1. Saratoga Campaign, 1777.   I. Title.
E241.S2K48   1997   97-2773
973.3'33—dc21   CIP

Henry Holt books are available for special promotions
and premiums. For details contact: Director, Special Markets.

First Edition 1997

Designed by Betty Lew
Maps by Jeffrey L. Ward
Photo insert designed by Jessica Shatan

Printed in the United States of America
All first editions are printed on acid-free paper. ∞

1   3   5   7   9   10   8   6   4   2

To Bobs, as ever,

*and to the memory of three friends
who understood that history is us*

*Bruce Catton
Allan Nevins
and my father, George Ketchum*

Contents

List of Maps

Preface

At Saratoga, the British campaign that was supposed to crush America's rebellion ended instead in a surrender that changed the history of the world.

Thanks to Saratoga, France entered the war as America's ally. Without the French navy, troops, and the financial and military aid so desperately needed, there is no telling what might have happened, but it is entirely possible that the unrelieved suffering and economic chaos brought on by three years of fighting might have led the Americans to negotiate a settlement with Great Britain—a settlement that could hardly have been on favorable terms.

So Saratoga was the watershed, the turning point. It meant that the fight for independence would continue and ultimately be won.

More than the Civil War or World War II, more than the opening of the West or the Great Depression, the American Revolution is *the* signal moment in our past. It was the event that gave birth to the nation, bequeathed a common purpose to the most varied of peoples, and ignited a beacon of hope that inspires the oppressed to this day.

A profound political and social upheaval, it was also a dirty, bloody, civil war as well as a struggle for freedom. John Adams described the Revolution in which he played such an important role as "the most complete, unexpected and remarkable of any in the history of nations." To loyalists, on the other hand, it was treasonable and frightening, this specter of a colonial people rising up against authority, this revolt by men and women of largely British ancestry against the patriarchal symbol of the British family, King George III.

No reporters covered that conflict, no camera captured the faces or actions of participants, so our image of the revolutionary generation depends entirely on letters and journals written by those who were there and saw the extraordinary events occur. It is impossible to read these documents without a sense of awe at the enormous hardships and suffering rebel soldiers endured—hunger, smallpox and other diseases, lack of food and clothing and blankets and shoes, deprivation beyond imagining.

What seems to have kept them going were four powerful convictions that recur in their letters like strands in a tapestry—reverence for their Maker, love of country, devotion to their family, and a deeply held belief in freedom. Four faiths—God, country, family, and liberty.

The chain of events that led two armies to their fateful rendezvous at Saratoga is a war story, to be sure, but in its unfolding it reveals much about the nature of Americans and the contest that ultimately produced the most powerful nation on earth. Never were the devotion and fortitude of those who stood up to the enemy put to a sterner test than during the terrible summer of 1777, when the chips were down and the outcome of the war for independence hung in the balance.

Richard M. Ketchum
Dorset, Vermont
March 15, 1997

SARATOGA

Chapter 1

The Secret Mission

He was bone-tired, painfully aware of his seventy years, and not at all sure he would survive the long journey that lay ahead. It was the second day of April in 1776, chilly enough to remind a man that winter was not yet over, when Dr. Benjamin Franklin and four companions stood on the Albany pier in New York's East River, watching their servants load the waiting sloop with baggage, food, blankets, folding beds, and a new saddle Franklin had purchased in Philadelphia.

This was an odd bunch—five men of disparate age, temperament, and experience, bound on a secret, highly sensitive mission to Canada on behalf of the Second Continental Congress. They had departed from Philadelphia on March 26, and a leisurely journey across New Jersey brought them to New York three days later. Assuming that the city would be crowded, Franklin had written ahead to an old friend, William Alexander—a burly, energetic major general in the Continental Army who laid claim to an earldom in Scotland and styled himself Lord Stirling even in these egalitarian times, and who was now in charge of preparing the city's defenses against an expected attack by the British. The general found lodgings for them and arranged for a vessel to take them to Albany, the first major stop on what promised to be a long and arduous expedition.

From where the travelers stood, the noise and smells of the bustling port were overpowering. The entire city of New York was contained within the southern end of Manhattan Island, and it was a hodgepodge of old Dutch and new English structures, fashionable brick residences standing cheek by jowl with mechanics' workshops, law offices, and the counting houses of merchants. Narrow streets, reeking of horse and pig manure, were crowded with boardinghouses, countless shops and warehouses, and a sea of trade signs, all surrounded by a forest of masts, intricate webs of spars and rigging, shipyard ways, ropewalks, breweries, a distillery, and grog shops—the innumerable ancillaries of a booming seaport. Buildings echoed with the blows of blacksmiths, gunsmiths, and joiners, with the shouts of hucksters and the man who arrived each day with a horse-drawn cart carrying a hogshead of fresh spring water for tea (yours for less than a dollar a bucket). The place had a bit of everything: it was a sailor's town, a wide-open town, a haven for smugglers supplying the Indian trade with contraband goods from Holland and for local merchants who bribed customs officers to look the other way when illegal shipments of tea were landed.

On all sides were the trappings of a great deepwater port that now rivaled Boston in the volume of foreign commerce landed at its docks. Nor was the water traffic all international: every day brought fresh shipments of corn and oats from Dobbs Ferry, cattle from Long Island, lumber, wheat, and precious cargoes of furs and skins from Albany—an incredible harvest of pelts carried by trappers and traders from the continent's vast interior.

Beneath the veneer of business as usual were layers of the city's deeply divided loyalties and the discontent they fostered. During his five-day stay in the city, Franklin called on a Mrs. Barrow, whose husband remained a loyalist. Since politics rarely if ever prevented the doctor from enjoying the company of a woman, he listened sympathetically as she spoke of her fears that she and her home might be mistreated by the Americans because of her husband's bias. He reassured her and later arranged with his friend Stirling to see that she was not harmed or harassed. But the incident suggested the rancorous ideological wall that separated acquaintances and friends and even members of the same family as the whirlwind of rebellion swept across America.* To Franklin's sorrow, his illegitimate son William, who gained the respect he craved by his appointment as governor of New Jersey, announced his intention to stay loyal to the crown—a loyalty that had him just now

---

*Paradoxically, as late as January of 1776 the officers at George Washington's mess were still toasting King George III.

under virtual house arrest and later took him to a Connecticut prison, where he remained for two years.

The doctor also had time to write Anthony Todd, an old friend in England, asking, "How long will the *Insanity* on your side [of] the Water continue?" before expressing his confidence in the outcome of the struggle. "The Breach between you and us grows daily wider and more difficult to heal," he observed, but "Britain without us can grow no stronger: Without her we shall become a tenfold greater and mightier People."

In the public house kept by Jesper Darkes, "zealous partizans in the cause of Liberty," as one habitué called them, met day and night, laying plans, discussing whether this man or that could be trusted or whether he was spying for the government, speculating on what could be done when the British military arrived, as it surely would. But other signs of the festering differences between America and Britain were out in the open, for all to see. Like Boston, New York had its Stamp Act riots in 1765, when the effigy of Lieutenant Governor Cadwallader Colden went up in flames along with his carriages. New York's Liberty Boys had held their own tea party, too, dumping the East India Company's hated cargo into the harbor—doing so, it was proudly said, fearlessly, in broad daylight, and without the Indian disguises worn by Bostonians.

In the spring of 1775, when news of the fighting at Lexington and Concord reached New York, members of the so-called patriot party seized City Hall, armed themselves, embargoed ships in the harbor that were loaded with arms for the British in Boston, and closed the custom house. And as a small detachment of redcoats prepared to march to the relief of Boston, the vigilant Sons of Liberty appropriated the arms and ammunition the soldiers were loading into wagons. Ever since the bloody affair at Breed's Hill in June of '75—a fight known ever after as the battle of Bunker Hill—the army led by George Washington had kept the British bottled up in Boston, but the rebels could do little more than that until a fat former bookseller named Henry Knox, who had a penchant for artillery, brought forty-three cannon and sixteen mortars over the mountains from Fort Ticonderoga on Lake Champlain, and work crews hauled them into position to command the enemy fleet, the shipping channels, and the town of Boston itself. That sealed the fate of the army under General William Howe: the British had nowhere to go but out—out of range of those guns and out of Boston harbor. And so they did, more than a hundred shiploads of them, redcoated soldiers and loyalist families, many of the latter leaving what they regarded as their homeland for the last time, bound for Halifax and England.

Two weeks before Benjamin Franklin and his party boarded the sloop bound for Albany, a New Yorker addressed an open letter to "Freeborn Sons of America," stating a proposition that was in just about everyone's thoughts that spring thanks to the powerful arguments for independence contained in the pamphlet *Common Sense*, written by Franklin's friend Thomas Paine. "The American separation and independence is now seriously thought of," the New Yorker wrote, "and near at hand, and reconciliation despaired of as a thing utterly impracticable. . . ." His object in bringing this out in the open, he said, was to provoke a dialogue that would lay the groundwork for "a more sound Constitution and perfect scheme of Government." As it happened, the same idea was receiving a good deal of attention behind closed doors in Philadelphia, where the Continental Congress was debating the most critical issue to confront the delegates. Describing these deliberations, John Adams, representing Massachusetts, wrote: "Objects of the most stupendous magnitude, and measures in which the lives and liberties yet unborn are intimately interested, are now before us. We are in the midst of a revolution, the most complete, unexpected and remarkable, of any in the history of nations."

At the same time, Congress received from George Washington the joyous news that the "Ministerial Army evacuated the town of Boston" on St. Patrick's Day, and the forces of the United Colonies were now in possession of it. Howe's departure to Halifax freed Washington's army to march to New York, where the American commander in chief assumed the British would go next. So Boston, which had been the focus of rebellion the year before, was now all but forgotten as advance units of the Continental Army began pouring into New York. Stirling was in charge here until Washington arrived; he ordered all able-bodied males to help fortify the city, and they and the growing number of American troops were doing a prodigious amount of digging—so enthusiastically, one of Franklin's companions noted, that two gentlemen unused to such labor shoveled until "the blood gushed out of their fingers." (Optimistically, Stirling requisitioned "intrenching tools" for ten thousand men, along with appropriate numbers of clothing, blankets, canteens, tomahawks, tents, muskets, and such items to a total of £26,000, prompting a poignant note to the New York Committee of Safety from the man in charge of these matters: "I have no cash.")

The city, one member of Franklin's party observed, "was no more the gay, polite place it used to be esteemed: but was become almost a desert [except] for the troops." Indeed, every day brought more of those rebel soldiers to New York, including a rifle battalion and five battalions of infantry under General William Heath, who were seen to be young and well armed, but without uniforms.* As fear grew among the populace—Tory and Whig alike—that the anticipated attack by British forces would be accompanied by a naval bombardment, thousands of residents fled—perhaps as many as 11,000 out of a population of 27,000.†

The island that Indians called Manahata, meaning "the place encircled by many swift tides and joyous, sparkling waters," had undergone considerable change since a small English fleet arrived in 1664 to take possession of New Amsterdam, its thriving fur trade, and its 1,500 inhabitants. Its contented burghers shed neither a blow nor tear but looked the other way as Governor Peter Stuyvesant stamped his wooden leg in futile protest. In Stuyvesant's day the dense forest north of the settlement's fortified wall was roamed by bears, cougars, bobcats, deer, wolves, and beaver; wild turkeys, passenger pigeons, and partridge were everywhere, as were saltwater birds, prolific shellfish beds, and fish in the island's freshwater streams. Beyond, the rivers were alive with otters, porpoises, and harbor seals.

By the time the uprising against Great Britain began, most of the wild animals were long gone; New York had 27,000 people and was, after Philadelphia (which was next in size only to London in the British Empire), the second-largest city in colonial America, with a superb port ideally situated for a base of British military operations. Despite the activities of its incendiaries, New York was not such a hotbed of rebellion as Boston; the city bristled with loyalists, and the entire Hudson Valley was full of conservative landed aristocrats—many of them Dutch, with pockets of Swedes, Scots, Huguenots, Germans, and Scotch-Irish who might be expected to support England against their rebellious neighbors.

And unlike Boston, New York dominated land and water communications and as such was *the* key city in America, gateway to the mighty Hudson River, that huge tidal estuary of the Atlantic. It was obvious to everyone—especially military planners in London—that New York, more than any other American city, was where the British *had* to be. The

---

*Almost immediately the puritanical New Englanders "Pulled Down some of the whore houses," according to one soldier.

†When the British *did* arrive in June 1776, so many more people evacuated the place that it was all but empty, with only about 5,000 remaining.

island was what one visitor termed a "centrical place," ideally situated on the Atlantic coastline. Surrounded by navigable waters, it could be protected and provisioned by the world's greatest fleet, which would have no opposition, since the Americans had no warships. New York, in short, was a superb base of operations for a military force that was dependent on its navy. From New York even the largest British ships of the line—those drawing as much as twenty feet—could sail up the Hudson, or North River, as it was also called, for more than a hundred miles, to within forty-six miles of Albany. At the very least, this meant that His Majesty's formidable navy could take some of the burden off his army by patrolling the lower reaches of the river, spotting and frustrating the movement of rebel troops and arms, while the army held strongpoints on the river's banks.

What were known as the Albany piers were located below the ferry slip where cattle from Long Island were landed, close by the fish market on Dock Street and Cruger's wharf at the foot of Wall Street—the thoroughfare that took its name from the protective wall bordering it, which marked the northernmost edge of the Dutch community. Here ships tied up after touching at major ports in the Atlantic and Mediterranean, as well as the West Indies and the coastal cities of North America. Flanking it on the other side was Whitehall slip, where ferries to and from Staten Island berthed.

By the time Franklin and his group had their gear stowed aboard the sloop it was late in the afternoon. The seamen cast off lines, ran up the sails, and the vessel slipped out into the East River, rounded the end of the island, and, after skirting the battery and barracks adjoining Fort George, caught a following breeze and headed upstream in the Hudson. Standing on deck, the passengers could see most of the landmarks on the west side of town—the tree-lined Bowling Green and the dozen or more houses of worship that suggested the cosmopolitanism of the place. Trinity Church, the Lutheran Church, both the Old and the New Dutch churches, the Presbyterian and New Scots meetinghouses, the Eglise du St. Esprit, and the Quaker Meetinghouse were all visible from the river. So were City Hall, Van Cortlandt's Sugar House (one of the three largest buildings in the city), and King's Wharf, site of the arsenal and royal storehouses. Beyond the ferry to Paulus Hook, where the road to Boston branched off from the Broad Way, were St. Paul's Chapel, King's College,* the poorhouse, the prison, and the powder house, interlaced

*Later Columbia.

with streets bearing the names of New York's leading citizens—Van Cortlandt, Vesey, Barkley, Murray, Warren, and others.

The last glint of a dying sun caught the rooftops of the elegant residences and grounds along the riverbank, belonging to the prominent George Harrison, Leonard Lispenard, and Abraham Mortier, paymaster general of the royal forces that had lately left town. Beyond, hidden now in the gathering dusk, lay acres and acres of farms, forest, and open lands with a scattering of isolated houses.

Thirteen miles upriver, the sloop docked for the night, and when the five passengers went ashore to cook supper they had their first real opportunity to size up their companions. Franklin already knew Samuel Chase, since both served in the Second Continental Congress, but he was less familiar with a Prussian officer who accompanied them, and had no more than a nodding acquaintance with two men named Carroll—Charles, and his cousin John, a Jesuit priest.

If the Carrolls had any doubts about the freethinker Franklin's tolerance for Catholics or his acceptance of them as associates, those reservations were quickly dispelled. He was by all odds the liveliest, most genial man in the group—"a most engaging and entertaining companion of a sweet, even and lively temper, full of facetious stories always applied with judgment and introduced *à propos*," wrote Charles Carroll, who was equally impressed with the old gentleman's boundless curiosity and broad knowledge of political, literary, and philosophical matters. Summing up his feelings, he added, "I am quite charmed with him."

Chase, who served so conscientiously as chef on the voyage that he once hurried back from an exploratory trip ashore for fear that a leg of mutton would be overcooked, was a delegate to Congress from Maryland. At thirty-five he was exactly half Franklin's age—a big, strong, beefy fellow known uncharitably as "Bacon face" for his florid complexion (and a choleric temper to match). He had studied law before his election to the provincial assembly, where he was a stone in the shoe of the royal governor and his loyalist friends, one of whom—the mayor of Annapolis—described Chase sourly as a "busy, restless incendiary, a ringleader of mobs, a foul-mouthed and inflaming son of discord and faction, a common disturber of the public tranquility, and a promoter of the lawless excesses of the multitude."

There was a coarseness about Chase that made him one of those men who are very popular with some people and intensely disliked by others, and his habit of criticizing those who didn't measure up to his political expectations did not endear him to his targets, many of them on his own side. At the time he instigated mob action against the Stamp Act he attacked those who were too timid for his liking by accusing them of skulking in their houses and grumbling in their corners, not daring to speak out while the real work of protest was carried on by others. Later, an annoyed Congressional colleague observed that he had "more learning than knowledge, and more of both than judgment."

Charles Carroll of Carrollton, another Marylander, was the antithesis of Chase except in his politics. He was said to be one of the three wealthiest men in America, along with George Washington of Virginia and Henry Middleton of South Carolina. At thirty-nine, he was older than any of the other passengers but Franklin and had an elegant, aristocratic look about him—he was slight, delicate, with deep-set, dark eyes and thin, almost ascetic features. His family claimed kinship with the ancient kings of Ireland, but a more direct reason for their eminence in Maryland was the friendship of Charles's grandfather with Lord Baltimore, as a result of which he had received huge land grants.

At the age of eight, Carroll was sent to France for a proper Catholic education, which was denied him in Maryland, and he spent twelve years there and another six in England, studying law. By the time he returned home in 1764 he was fluent in French and the owner of a ten-thousand-acre estate called Carrollton, a gift from his father. (He became known as Charles Carroll of Carrollton to distinguish him from his parent, Charles Carroll of Annapolis, and his son, Charles Carroll of Homewood.)

His fortune did not keep him from becoming a leader of the colony's patriot movement. He opposed the Stamp Act and what he called taxation by proclamation (by the governor) and played an important part in Maryland's own tea party, averting almost certain mob violence by persuading the owner of a ship loaded with tea to burn the vessel and her contents.

Despite Carroll's unfamiliarity with military matters he had an astonishingly prescient view of how the war for independence would be fought and won. Replying to a member of Parliament who predicted that six thousand British troops could march triumphantly through the colonies, he wrote: "So they may, but they will be masters of the spot only on which they encamp. They will find nought but enemies before and around them. If we are beaten on the plains, we will retreat to our mountains and defy them. Our resources will increase with our difficulties" until at last, he said, "tired of combating, in vain, against a spirit which victory after victory cannot subdue, your armies will evacuate our soil, and your country retire, an immense loser, from the contest." Much blood would be spilt, Carroll knew, but "we have no doubt of ultimate success."

Father John Carroll was under no illusions about his potential contribution to this undertaking. Having spent his working life in a calling remote from politics, he felt like a fifth wheel. It was his opinion, in fact, that men of the cloth who set aside their proper duties in order to engage in politics were deservedly objects of contempt, besides which, he took a very dim view of the mission's chance of success. His reason for accompanying the others was that Congress had done him "the distinguished and unexpected honour" of inviting him to do so.

In any society Benjamin Franklin would have been an uncommon figure, but as a product of what many Europeans considered a raw, uncouth, wild land peopled by renegades from civilized countries, he was looked on as a phenomenon. Which, to be sure, he was.

It was highly unusual for seventy-year-olds to become revolutionaries, but after striving for years to keep the ties between Britain and her American colonies intact, Franklin finally realized the hopelessness of his efforts and became one of the leading figures of the rebellion. He was, of course, far more—a man of such talents as is rarely seen and the embodiment of what would become the great American dream and its fulfillment, in which the bright, self-reliant youngster, through hard work, advances from rags to riches. Beginning life as the fifteenth child of a tallow chandler—a maker of soap and candles—he was apprenticed at the age of twelve to his brother, a printer, and at seventeen left home to seek (and find) fame and fortune in Philadelphia, and go on to become the most renowned of all his countrymen, an immensely creative figure whose life revealed how rich and varied human existence can be. His achievements even before 1776 boggled the mind: he was an essayist, master printer, journalist, publisher of the hugely popular *Poor Richard's Almanack*, and civic leader. He instigated programs to pave and illuminate Philadelphia's streets and founded the colonies' first circulating library, a hospital, the American Philosophical Society, a fire insurance company, an academy. He was the inventor of an efficient stove, the lightning rod, and, later, bifocal glasses. His interests were beyond all accounting: he studied eclipses, whirlwinds, ants, and the Gulf Stream, knew most of the prominent scientists and scholars of his day, became a farmer, and as deputy postmaster general established local mail delivery in the colonies. Although his formal education stopped at the second grade, he received honorary degrees from Harvard, William and Mary, and Yale, and a doctorate from the University of Edinburgh, after which he was always addressed as Dr. Franklin.

At the age of forty-two he retired from business with an income sufficient to support a variety of philanthropic careers for the rest of his life. As agent for several colonies—and as virtual ambassador for all thirteen—he spent eighteen years in England, returning in 1775, finally convinced that reconciliation with Britain was impossible, independence inevitable and essential.

European admirers regarded Franklin as the quintessential American. Part of this had to do with his homespun look: plain clothes, average height, benevolent appearance, thinning light brown hair that he brushed back from a high, wide forehead, steady gray eyes that gave the impression of having seen much of the world's follies and faults, a wide mouth that looked as if it might break into a grin at any moment. Part also was his ability to merge into his surroundings in such a way that he could appear the rustic, the diplomat, or the scientist, depending on the occasion. At heart he was a philosopher, a patient, wise, and immensely practical man with a delicious sense of humor and a rare facility for thoroughly enjoying almost everything he did. Thomas Jefferson wrote many years later, "I served with General Washington in the legislature of Virginia before the Revolution, and during it with Dr. Franklin in Congress. I never heard either of them speak ten minutes at a time, not to any but the main point which was to decide the question. They laid their shoulders to the great points, knowing that the little ones would follow of themselves."

John Adams, another of the doctor's Congressional colleagues, said of him: "Franklin had a great genius, original, sagacious, and inventive, capable of discoveries in science no less than of improvements in the fine arts and the mechanic arts. He had a vast imagination, equal to the comprehension of the greatest objects, and capable of a steady and cool comprehension of them." That from a man who was no particular admirer of Franklin because of his easy way with women, his habit of turning aside arguments with a joke, and his love of creature comforts that spelled lavish living to Adams's puritanical way of thinking.

Even before embarking on this trip, Franklin was exhausted from overwork in the Congress and in the Pennsylvania Assembly and Committee of Safety, his eyes so tired that he was often unable to write at night, yet he corresponded later with a friend about this period in his life, saying, "I do not find that I grow any older. Being arrived at seventy, and considering that by traveling further in the same road I should probably be led to the grave, I stopped short, turned about, and walked back again; which having done these four years, you may now call me sixty-six. Advise those old friends of ours to follow my example; keep up your spirits, and that will keep up your bodies."

The three commissioners—Franklin, Carroll, and Chase—appeared to have little in common beyond an abiding faith in the cause for which they were risking their lives and fortunes, but it seems likely that before they drifted off to sleep in their cramped quarters, with the waters of the Hudson lapping at the ship's sides, their thoughts turned to the mission and the question of whether it could possibly be consummated with any hope of success. The idea for their secret assignment had originally been suggested to Congress by Chase, and they had a flowery commission signed by John Hancock, the president of that body, endowing them with extraordinary authority. Their instructions, however, were as voluminous as they were improbable of achievement. Put briefly, the commissioners were to attempt to form a union with the people of Canada, Congress's hope being that Canada would become the fourteenth colony and fight side by side with Americans against the British crown, making a British attack from the north highly unlikely. The three men were given the widest latitude to bring this about: they were authorized to establish a free press, guarantee the Canadians religious freedom, encourage them to set up whatever form of government was most likely "to produce their Happiness," promote trade, resolve disputes between American troops and the Canadians, and exercise a host of other powers that would make Franklin and his group a *de facto* governing body of that country until "the pleasure of the Congress shall be known."

But there was a hitch here—several, in fact. Since 1774, Congress had been obsessed with the desirability of persuading Canadians to join in the conflict with Britain, but nothing much came of this until June of 1775, when the delegates decided to invade Canada if that proved practicable and "if it will not be disagreeable to the Canadians." The dubious theory behind this extraordinary idea was that the Canadians would be more likely to consider becoming a sister colony if the invitation was accompanied by a show of strength. So in the autumn of 1775, far too late in the season for any such notions, two hastily assembled American military forces had headed north—one jumping off from Fort Ticonderoga on Lake Champlain, led first by General Schuyler until poor health obliged him to quit and then by a former British officer named Richard Montgomery. That army was bound for Montreal. The other, under a tough Connecticut merchant named Benedict Arnold, who proved to be a superb battlefield commander, made one of the most heroic marches in history, traveling from Maine through 350 miles of unbroken wilderness toward Quebec. That city controlled the St. Lawrence River, which in turn controlled access to the interior of North America. A misguided venture from the start, the abortive two-pronged campaign was one in which just about everything that could go wrong did. Arnold arrived at Quebec with 675 ravaged survivors of 1,100 who had started on the dreadful march. Montreal fell to Montgomery, but when he joined Arnold he had only 300 men. Storming Quebec in a howling winter gale on the night of December 31, 1775, Montgomery was killed, Arnold badly wounded, and another exceptional officer, Daniel Morgan, captured. Even at that, the rebels nearly brought it off, but the British under General Guy Carleton had cannon, they were behind stone walls, and without leadership the rebel attack collapsed. Arnold was able to hang on through the winter, maintaining a siege of sorts outside the walled city, but he had a mere 500 effective troops against the 1,600-man garrison, and by spring of 1776 his supplies of food and weapons were almost gone and his soldiers crippled with disease and near the end of their endurance.

Not surprisingly, the Canadians who were supposed to flock to their liberators had no wish to join hands with the rough, tough rabble that first invaded their country and now made off with food and other property at every opportunity. But that was a minor factor compared to Canada's memory of the bigotry that characterized American reaction to the Quebec Act of 1774.

The Canadians were independent folk, subservient to no one, proud of their ability to endure hardship, and—with the exception of a few hundred British Protestants—Catholic. In 1763, when the Treaty of Paris ended the Seven Years War and ceded all of New France to Great Britain, the administration of the twenty-three-year-old George III was faced with the problem of managing the enormous territory won from France, and the job was made no easier by having to deal with a largely Catholic people who spoke a different language and whose customs and laws differed radically from those of their conquerors. Many of the defeated French leaders departed that year, but the French settlers— the habitants—remained, tilling their fields and tending their traps, and to their surprise were treated with kindness by two Britons sent to govern the territory—Generals James Murray and Guy Carleton. So satisfied did the habitants appear to be that Carleton was lulled into thinking he could count on them to enter military service in time of need. It was a miscalculation other British planners would make, to their lasting regret. The terms of the peace treaty had granted religious freedom to Canadians, but only "as far as the laws of Great Britain permit." That was not very far, as it turned out, since British law prohibited anyone but Protestants from holding public office.

But the British governor, Carleton, was an intelligent, perceptive, and tolerant man. He reasoned that England could win over the Canadians only if the French laws to which they were accustomed were restored and if public offices were opened to them. So he returned to England in 1770 and spent the next four years lobbying the government to adopt his far-sighted pro-Catholic plan, which was to be guaranteed by a Canadian constitution. The resulting Quebec Act was a triumph for Carleton and Canada, but to Americans—New England Protestants in particular—it was anathema. Not only did it recognize the hated Popish religion, it restored Canada's former frontiers, which stretched from the Ohio and Mississippi rivers to Hudson Bay and Labrador, thereby wiping out the western land claims of several colonies and a legion of individual speculators. To Americans who were already irate about London's colonial policy, this appeared to scrap everything for which the Americans had fought side by side with the British for so many years.

Speaking on behalf of the First Continental Congress in an "Address to the People of Great Britain," New York delegate John Jay predicted that a swelling tide of Catholic immigrants from Europe would "reduce the ancient free Protestant colonies to [a] state of slavery." He went on to express "astonishment that a British Parliament should ever consent to establish ... a religion that has deluged your island in blood and spread impiety, bigotry, persecution, murder, and rebellion throughout every part of the world."

Understandably, this did not sit well with the solidly Catholic land north of the thirteen colonies, and to make matters worse, three days later Congress had the gall to invite Canadians to adopt a constitutional form of government and join the United Colonies in their campaign against despotism, taxes, and arbitrary rule. The result of all this was what might have been expected—an extreme reluctance on the part of Canadians to fight alongside the Americans after the clashes at Lexington, Concord, and Breed's Hill, the enduring hostility of the Roman Catholic clergy in Canada, and what can best be described as a posture of guarded neutrality by the populace. And that is where matters stood when the commissioners were appointed to pick up the pieces, mollify the Canadians, and welcome them with open arms as the fourteenth colony.

As for the mission and the men Congress had nominated to carry it out, Franklin, it was thought, would bring to the negotiations considerable diplomatic skills and the prestige of an international reputation. Chase was a vigorous, outspoken champion of America's cause, deeply impressed with the importance of securing Canada, and a strong proponent of this diplomatic effort. Charles Carroll was thoughtful, highly intelligent, a keen observer, and, above all, a devout Catholic who spoke fluent French, and it was believed that he and his cousin, John Carroll, who had spent twenty-five years in France as a Jesuit priest, might be able to sway the powerful Canadian clergy. Finally, for reasons known best to Congress, a fifth man was included—a man whose appointment was as bizarre as the mission itself. His name was Frederick William, Baron de Woedtke, a Prussian officer who arrived in America along with many another European soldier to join the rebel army. Some of these men came with the most altruistic motives, others because they were unemployed adventurers seeking a job and an opportunity to make a name for themselves. Although de Woedtke was only twenty-six, he was said on somewhat shaky authority to have served a number of years under Frederick the Great, so two weeks before the group set off on their trip Congress made him a brigadier general and assigned him to the Northern Army, to serve under General Philip Schuyler in Albany.

The new brigadier joined Franklin's entourage while they were en route from Philadelphia to New York, and he made a lasting impression on Father Carroll, who described the meeting in a letter to his mother. "Though I had frequently seen him before," Carroll said, "yet he was so disguised in furs that I scarce knew him, and never beheld a more laughable object in my life. Like other Prussian officers, he appears to me as a man who knows little of polite life, and yet has picked up so much of it in his passage through France as to make a most awkward appearance." When he wrote that, the padre had not yet discovered that de Woedtke was also a very heavy drinker, though his cousin Charles had concluded that the baron "is not the best bred up by his Prussian Majesty."

April 3 was nasty, a cold, rainy morning with wind out of the northeast that kept the passengers uncomfortably crowded belowdecks in the sloop.

At 11:00 A.M. they found themselves off Frederick Philipse's manor on the east bank of the river, and this was their introduction to the Hudson Valley's pattern of huge landholdings. Charles Carroll was no stranger to large family estates, but nothing in Maryland had prepared him for the manorial tracts he was to see in this valley, such as the 700,000-acre Rensselaerwyck or the vast Livingston domain, which included most of the Catskill Mountains.

These baronies had originated with the Dutch patroon system, and were further sanctioned when England's royal governors made lavish grants of land, placing immense estates in the hands of a relative handful of families—Schuylers, Philipses, Livingstons, and Rensselaers among them. The idea behind this was to promote settlement of the colony, with the lord of the manor receiving his land in return for a promise to establish a certain number of settlers on it within a given period of time. He paid a nominal annual fee to the crown, while collecting rents from the tenant farmers who cleared and tilled his soil.

At Philipse manor the sloop was becalmed until five that afternoon, when a south breeze came up and gave them a run of forty miles to the Highlands, where violent gusts of wind off the mountains split the mainsail and forced them to anchor. For an entire day the crew worked to repair the sail while the passengers admired the wild, romantic beauty of the place and got to know each other better.

Underway again, they passed Cape St. Anthony's Nose and went ashore several times to inspect waterfalls and Fort Constitution, which by common agreement was in alarmingly "defenceless condition" (as they subsequently reported to Brigadier General William Heath, who was in charge of the Highland defenses). The British, they concluded, could easily take the place with sixty men and no cannon.

On April 5, Charles Carroll noted in his journal that "this river seems intended by nature to open a communication between Canada and the province of N. York by water. . . ." To inhabitants of the 500-mile strip of land that bordered the Atlantic seaboard between northern Massachusetts and southern Virginia, where the non-native population was concentrated in 1777, there was something mysterious and darkly threatening about the vast unknown world beyond. Settlements extended inland no more than 100 or 150 miles, where they were blocked by the Appalachians, and even though this long, thin slice of territory was the most densely peopled area of the continent, it contained an average of only eighteen individuals per square mile (outside it the figure ranged from two to eighteen). What Carroll saw as nature's intention had not gone unnoticed by Britain's military strategists. If the British succeeded in driving a wedge across this narrow ribbon of settled America and maintained their hold on it, they could split off the fractious New England colonies from the rest, squelch the rebellion where it had begun, and mop up any remaining pockets of resistance at leisure. The odds were that that would end the rebellion, for while the numerous large rivers emptying into the Atlantic were passageways to the interior, they were major obstacles to intercolonial travel because none were bridged.

As fortune would have it, geography had provided Britain with the ideal means for dividing the colonies, in the form of the great north-south water route that extended for four hundred miles—virtually without a break—from Montreal, entrepôt for the Great Lakes fur trade and Canada's second city, down the St. Lawrence River to the Sorel, or Richelieu, up (since its source is at the southern end) Lake Champlain, overland a short distance to Lake George, and thence to the Hudson River and New York. At each extremity of this waterway was an important population center, with Albany, a strategically significant settlement, roughly midway between. Since water transport was the only feasible way for an army to make its way through the great sweep of wilderness, this was one of the continent's most useful and most traveled natural highways.

For as long as Americans could remember, Canada—half tamed, half savage—had been the enemy. Frenchmen had adapted singularly well to wilderness ways; they were quick to ally themselves with the Indians and lived with, and like, them. Adopting the native style of warfare, they had swept down with raiding parties from the north to attack isolated English communities that had pushed out beyond the fringes of civilization, tomahawking and scalping some victims, carrying others off into captivity, to be kept or sold as slaves or ransomed to their families.

In 1759, proclaimed in England as "the year of miracles" because of the nation's triumphs on land and sea, Quebec fell to William Pitt's protégé, the thirty-two-year-old James Wolfe; while Jeffrey Amherst, another of Pitt's anointees, captured Fort Ticonderoga and Crown Point on his way north, then seized Montreal. All England was intoxicated with those victories, which determined that the far reaches of Canada would be ruled by George III of Great Britain, not the hated Louis XV of France.

During that bloody century when claim to North America washed back and forth between the nations of Europe on the tides of war, the Hudson-

Champlain passage was the continent's chief strategic military thoroughfare, and in 1776 it pointed like a long, vengeful sword at the heart of the renegade American colonies. What worried the Americans was the possibility that General William Howe might return from Halifax and seize New York, in which event the British would hold the southern as well as the northern anchor of the great water route. The notion of using that highway to sever the colonies was not a new one—had been around, in fact, for some time. Ten years earlier, Governor-General Guy Carleton had written to Thomas Gage, governor of Massachusetts and commander in chief of Britain's troops in North America, inviting him to consider the possibility of cutting off New England from the other colonies by locating "a place of arms"—a fort, that is—on Manhattan Island, along with "a citadel at Quebec, and the strengthening of the forts on the main line of communication" as the best way to stifle a potential revolt of the increasingly unruly Americans. One of Carleton's associates, the chief justice of Canada, observed astutely that Lake Champlain, Lake George, and their tributaries also made much of New England more accessible from Canada than it was from Boston—a fact well known to Indian warriors, who called the system of waterways "the gate of the country."

And in 1775, Major General John Burgoyne, who was then in Boston with the British forces, laid out for Lord Rochford, secretary of state for the colonies, a plan for subduing the continent by arms. Burgoyne recommended "a large army of such foreign troops as might be hired, to begin their operations up the Hudson River; another army composed partly of old disciplined troops and partly of Canadians, to act from Canada; a large levy of Indians, and a supply of arms for the blacks, to awe the southern provinces, conjointly with detachments of regulars." Those forces, supported by "a numerous fleet to sweep the whole coast, might possibly do the business in one campaign."

The American who probably knew more than anyone else in the colonies about the prospect of an attack from Canada, and who was also in the best position to see that it did not succeed, was the gentleman waiting at the landing in Albany when the sloop tied up at the dock on April 7—five days after leaving New York. Somewhat to the surprise of Franklin and his party, since it was seven-thirty in the morning, they were greeted by Major General Philip Schuyler and his "2 daughters (Betsy and Peggy), lively, agreeable, black-eyed girls," as Charles Carroll described them. The man who was to be their host for several days was tall and slender, with an imperious manner and an erect, commanding figure. He had a rather florid, expressive face, accented by the nose of an eagle, and his piercing eyes matched his dark brown hair. All in all, he gave the impression of someone who was very confident of his own superiority.

Carroll noted that Schuyler "behaved with great civility," as one might expect from a scion of the best Dutch blood in New York who was also one of its richest landowners. But during the next few days the visitors would become aware of a troubling fact about their host—his "infirm state of health," caused chiefly by extremely painful rheumatic gout, suggesting that the third-ranking major general in the Continental Army might not be physically up to the demanding tasks he faced.

Chapter 2

They Wish to See
Our Throats Cut

Franklin had written Schuyler from Philadelphia on March 11, informing him of the appointment of commissioners to Canada and asking the general to do what he could to facilitate and expedite their journey once they reached Albany. Schuyler commanded the Northern Department, which meant that he had under his wing all the posts and military activities between Albany and Canada. On top of that, he was expected to "watch the Movements of the Indian Agent," Colonel Guy Johnson, and somehow prevent him from using his considerable influence to prejudice the Iroquois League, or Six Nations, against the Americans. As if that were not enough, the general was to investigate the "Temper and Disposition" of the Canadians to see how their goodwill might be enlisted. All in all, it was a formidable job, a huge responsibility, and a task demanding extensive and rigorous travel.

In certain respects, Schuyler resembled General George Washington, with whom he had struck up a warm friendship after they met in 1775 and to whom he was indebted for his present command. Like Washington, he was wealthy, with large landholdings. He was a member of one of the oldest and most prominent families in the Hudson Valley and related to many of the others—the Van Schaicks, Livingstons, and Van Rensselaers, one of whom was his wife, Catherine.

He was about the same age as Washington, and like him had the executive experience and hands-on knowledge that came from managing a huge estate that composed a virtually self-sufficient community. He knew carpentry and construction, boat-building, and farming, and had been a merchant of grain and timber. He was a child of the frontier, knew the Indians, had considerable influence with them, was fluent in the Mohawk tongue, and had fought in the French and Indian War. But in two important respects, he differed from the commander in chief. Lacking the physical strength and toughness demanded by wilderness fighting, he was often sickly, and because he was frequently absent from his military duties on that account his enemies unjustly accused him of cowardice. A more important contrast between the two was that Schuyler lacked Washington's steely determination, his utter will to win, his resolve never to give up.

It was Schuyler's misfortune, despite his considerable abilities and experience and what seemed unflagging devotion to the patriot cause, to be intensely disliked by New Englanders. Some of the animosity was ethnic: his eastern neighbors of predominantly English descent considered him a Dutchman and thought that reason enough to hate him. Another factor was a polished, urbane manner that was often taken to be haughty, aristocratic, or downright snobbish. A Connecticut chaplain, writing to his wife, described the general as haughty and overbearing, noting that "he has never been accustomed to seeing men that are reasonably well taught and able to give a clear opinion and to state their grounds for it, who were not also persons of some wealth and rank." But resentment was rife among the Yankees because he had sided (naturally enough, it would seem) with the New Yorkers in their fierce boundary dispute with settlers of the New Hampshire Grants, which was to become Vermont. Although it was none of Schuyler's doing, New York's royal governors approved deeds to 328,000 acres of land in the New Hampshire Grants * during 1775 and 1776, two-thirds of which went to prominent loyalists. Small wonder that Ethan Allen wrote to two Yorkers stating that his Green Mountain Boys "will Not Tamely Resign their Necks to the Halter to be Hanged by Your Curst Fraternity of Land Jockeys who Would Better Adorn a halter than we. therefore as You Regard Your Own Lives be Careful Not to Invade Ours. . . ." This, of course, was the pot calling the kettle black: many of the Green Mountain Boys were land speculators who formed the Onion River Company and

---

*The term was originally used to describe the grants of land for townships west of the Connecticut River made by royal governor Benning Wentworth beginning in 1741.

were determined to defend their enormous landholdings against the claims of New York, which led that colony to declare Allen and his lieutenants outlaws.

Much of the opposition to Schuyler was familiar to Franklin and Chase, since it took but a mention of his name to set off a furor in Congress, where he had powerful detractors as well as determined supporters. Yet the civility Carroll had noted at the landing came as no revelation to his guests: Schuyler was known for the generous hospitality evident in the courtesies he and his family showed them after their arrival, entertaining them, John Carroll reported to his mother, "with great politeness and very genteely." On the carriage ride to the general's Albany residence Charles Carroll quietly indulged in his useful habit of observation. He was not only keeping a detailed journal of the trip but also writing long, newsy letters to his father, each addressed "Dear Papa" and signed "Ch. Carroll of Carrollton," and he noted meticulously that Albany's old fort was in ruinous condition without a single cannon in evidence, that the town was larger than Annapolis, and that most residents spoke Dutch (though the English "language and manners" were apparently gaining). The linguistic residue was hardly surprising, since Dutch control of the place had lasted more than half a century, until the British took it over, changed its name from Willemstadt to Albany (in honor of James, Duke of York and Albany), and immediately capitalized on the town's strategic location as an outpost against intruders from Canada and a depot for the seemingly boundless supply of furs coming in from the north and west.

The commissioners spent two pleasant days with the Schuylers before they, their host, and his family climbed aboard a wagon and set out for the general's summer home at Saratoga.* The trip was a nightmare: jouncing around in their conveyance over execrable roads, crossing two rivers by ferry, they managed to travel thirty-two miles between early morning and sunset.

Schuyler took them on a tour of his estate, whose bottomland and mills for grain, lumber, hemp, and flax were of particular interest to Charles Carroll, as was the prevailing system of rental agreements that proved so advantageous to the lord of the manor (which provided that the lease was to run "while water runs and grass grows," with the landlord to receive the tenth sheaf of all grain produced). Next day Schuyler bade farewell to his guests and he and Baron de Woedtke departed for Lake George with Brigadier General John Thomas, a fifty-year-old

---

*Now Schuylerville, New York.

veteran of the French and Indian wars and a practicing physician, who had just been named commander of rebel forces in Canada. Thomas and de Woedtke were heading to Quebec; Schuyler would remain at Fort George to supervise and expedite the transport of military stores and supplies for Thomas's troops.

On the morning of April 12 the weather turned cold, the commissioners were told that ice still made the lakes impassable, and when six inches of snow fell, Franklin began to fear that each day might be his last. He took advantage of the layover to write a few friends and say farewell, indicating that the exhausting trip was proving too much for him. But four days later he and the others were under way again, leaving behind Catherine Schuyler, her daughters, and the comforts of Saratoga for the harsh realities of a northern odyssey in wintry conditions. From Saratoga to Lake George their route took them overland past a series of forts, most of which had been key sites during the French wars but were now crumbling piles of rubble, their only occupants mice and bats and the ghosts of yesteryear—those thousands of English, French, provincials, and Indians who had passed this way as pawns of Europe's warring empires.

Fort Miller, built in 1755 as a palisaded blockhouse for Colonel Samuel Miller, was forty-seven miles north of Albany, at what was known as the Little Carrying Place on the Hudson. Beyond, eight miles and four hours later, after the travelers' bateaumen negotiated the river's rapids with extreme difficulty, sometimes dragging the boat by rope, they sighted Fort Edward. Situated at the confluence of the Hudson and a small creek, this outpost was at the southern end of the First, or Great, Carrying Place, where troops and supplies from Albany were landed for portage either to Lake George or to the head of Lake Champlain. Beyond Fort Edward the watershed of the St. Lawrence River began, since both Lake George and Wood Creek, which also flows into Lake Champlain, drain north into the Richelieu and, finally, St. Lawrence rivers.

The Champlain basin is believed to have been created when an enormous block of bedrock dropped into place between two mountain ranges with the collision of tectonic plates. The lake itself was a creation of the glaciers. Toward the end of the Pleistocene Era, when a fourth of the world's land area was covered with ice as much as two miles thick, the frozen sheets began their slow retreat but did so faster than the earth's crust—which had been crushed beneath the enormous burden—could rise in their wake. Meltwater that covered the crust joined the St.

Northern Theater

Quebec

Trois Rivières

St. Lawrence River

• Sorel

Richelieu R.

Montreal

• Longueuil
□ La Prairie
□ Ft. Chambly

St. Johns

Ile aux Noix —
Ile la Motte —
Cumberland Head —
Valcour Island —

Lake Champlain

St. Lawrence River

Ottawa River

Split Rock
Bouquet R. —
— *The Narrows*

Crown Point   **Chimney Point**

Mt. Hope   *Mt. Independence*
FT. TICONDEROGA —   **Hubbardton**
Mt. Defiance —
Sabbath Day Point   **Skenesborough**

Lake George   **Rutland**
Diamond Is. —   **Castle Town**
FT. GEORGE □ □ FT. ANNE
                      Pawlet   FT. NO. 4
FT. EDWARD □   **Dorset**
FT. MILLER □   **Manchester**   **Rockingham**
Saratoga   **Arlington**
Stillwater   **Bennington**
Half Moon   **Pownal**   **Brattleboro**
Albany   **Williamstown**

*Lake
Ontario*

Oswego

FT. STANWIX □
Oriskany   *Mohawk River*

Connecticut River

Merrimack River

Boston

Wood Cr.
Batten Kill
Hoosick River

Hudson River

Esopus (Kingston)

HIGHLANDS
□ FT. CONSTITUTION
□ FT. MONTGOMERY

Susquehanna River

Delaware River

Connecticut River

Manhattan   *Long Island*

Atlantic Ocean

• **Trenton**

0 Km   50   100
0 Miles   50   100

Philadelphia •

© 1997 Jeffrey L. Ward

Lawrence River to form a huge estuary of the Atlantic Ocean, and the valley between what became Vermont and New York was drowned, becoming a great inland saltwater sea in which whales once swam. Then, as the crustal surface beneath that sea continued to rise, the lake waters which once emptied to the south into the Hudson Valley began draining north into the Richelieu River.

The fort seen by Franklin's entourage was actually the third military establishment to be built on the site and had been a base for Robert Rogers's rangers and British forces marching to Canada. In its heyday it was a log-and-earth affair with walls sixteen feet high and twenty-two feet thick, surrounded by a deep ditch, with barracks for about five hundred men on the mainland and nearby Rogers Island. Now it was an inhospitable wreck, but fortunately the travelers found a decent inn nearby called the Yellow House, where Franklin and the others encountered two officers of a Pennsylvania regiment camped there—Colonel Arthur St. Clair and Lieutenant Colonel William Allen, Jr., whose family Charles Carroll knew.*

Next morning they had traveled about a mile from Fort Edward when word was received from Schuyler that the ice in Lake George had not yet broken up; he urged them to stay at Abraham Wing's inn, a quarter of a mile from the Hudson near a beautiful falls and about halfway between Forts Edward and George. A couple of miles to the north were the charred remains of old Fort Anne, where the sluggish stream known as Wood Creek led to Skenesborough and flowed into the narrow South Bay of Lake Champlain. Due west of that long-vanished fort was their immediate destination—Fort George, at the head of the lake of the same name. It was a post that had played host to some of the great names of the French and Indian Wars—Montcalm, Amherst, and William Johnson, among others—but now these were little more than memories, and what had been an important link in the chain of forts was merely a small, square structure faced with masonry, with room for perhaps a hundred men.

They saw at once that Fort George was in no better condition than any of the other posts along the way; in Charles Carroll's words, it was "in as ruinous a condition as Fort Edward." To be fair, the small wilderness outposts they had seen had been designed with a limited use in mind: to protect stores and ammunition from marauding Indians and serve as vital links in the northbound traffic of military supplies, affording wel-

---

*St. Clair was made a brigadier general in the Continental Army in 1777; Allen followed a different path and joined the British in July 1776.

come shelter after an exhausting day hauling tons of food and ammunition. In fact, the reason they were located roughly ten miles apart was that this was the average distance troops could march and haul supplies in one day's time. But these places were all but useless for European-style military actions, since they were incapable of standing up to artillery fire. All had once been held by the French or English (or both),* but after 1763, when they were in British hands, they were largely forgotten, sleeping in the depths of the silent forest and slowly decaying, their garrisons made up of a few invalid veterans who watched over ordnance and various other military supplies and eagerly welcomed the occasional traveler bearing news of civilization. During the hiatus between the wars, when no enemy threatened, the forts fell into advanced stages of decrepitude, which meant that all the putative strongpoints between Albany and Lake George were moldering away, forts in name only. This was most unfortunate for the rebels, since the assumption was that these wilderness outposts could safeguard and facilitate military travel while defending the crucial passage that extended from the port of New York to Canada.

In the wake of boats laden with heavy cannon and five hundred soldiers that left for Ticonderoga ahead of them, the commissioners embarked from Fort George aboard a bateau. These craft were normally used for carrying troops and were thirty-six feet long and eight feet in the beam, drawing about a foot of water when loaded with thirty or forty men and about half that with a lighter cargo. Routinely, Franklin and his friends put in to shore at night and camped, "making a cover of the boughs of trees, and large fires at their feet," John Carroll observed. But occasionally, he went on, "as we . . . had brought with us good beds and plenty of bed clothes, [we] chose to sleep on board." In honor of its eminent passengers the bateau had been fitted out with awnings that provided limited shelter from the elements for four beds, but awnings or no, it was not an easy voyage: they were frequently stuck in the ice and had to go ashore to warm themselves with a hot meal or tea. Nor were their spirits lifted when they learned that the snow in Canada was still three feet deep on the level and seven feet in drifts.

Negotiating the extraordinarily clear open water of Lake George, they

*Fort Edward was originally known as Fort Lydius, for the Dutchman John Lydius, a fur trader known to those who came out on the short end of his bargains as "Perfidious Lydius," who was active at the site in the early eighteenth century. Ticonderoga, called Carillon, was also named for a fur trader, and Crown Point was St. Frédéric. Lake George was called Lac St. Sacrement by the French.

admired the wild terrain on either side of the long, narrow passage—towering cliffs blanketed with hemlock and pine, which Charles Carroll described as fine deer country but not much good for anything else. On the 20th of April they reached Sabbath Day Point, the only settlement on the lake, near which they met the mail boat from Canada. Franklin, considerably overreaching his authority as postmaster, glanced through the mail, found a letter to Schuyler, and promptly opened it. Shortly afterward they were overtaken by the general himself, and since the only messages he was receiving from Canada these days were gloomy ones, such as the recent report from Benedict Arnold that 786 of his 2,505 men at Quebec were sick, and that the enlistments of 1,500 would expire on April 15, this communication cannot have been cheering. By now, the commissioners had begun to realize that the likelihood of military success in the north was "extreamly problematical."

Between the landing at the north end of Lake George and Ticonderoga, a distance of three and a half miles, the difference between water levels was two hundred feet. The bateaumen maneuvered the shallow-draft boat into the waterway known as the Chute, which connects Lakes George and Champlain, and planed along, often scraping bottom, for a distance of a quarter-mile. There, after the baggage was unloaded and put into wagons to avoid the spectacular waterfall that pounds through a gorge into Champlain, they had an exhibition of how necessity mothers invention. Their boat and others were lifted out of the water by a hoist and let down into a specially designed carriage, consisting of a long sapling, at each end of which were an axle and two wheels. Held in place by ropes, each boat was then drawn overland by six oxen to the open water of Lake Champlain, where thirty-five or forty men lifted it off the carriage and launched it. (The commissioners were made aware of the importance of this junction when they learned that fifty bateaus had been carried over the portage that day alone.) Along the way Franklin and his companions walked to a sawmill on the falls in the river and paused at the spot where Lord Howe—oldest brother of General William and Admiral Richard—was killed leading General James Abercromby's light infantry in a disastrous attack on Fort Ticonderoga in 1758.

About a mile from here they were given a tour of the storied fort itself. Near the southeastern point of a blunt, squarish peninsula that juts into Lake Champlain from the west bank, French engineers in the 1750s had laid up the local bluestone into an elaborate stronghold about 530 feet in width, with outworks on its two exposed sides. It was called Fort Carillon, the French phonetic approximation of the name of a fur trader, Philippe de Carrion du Fresnoy, whose seventeenth-century establishment here at the portage was known as "Carrion's trading place." Two-story barracks lined three sides of its Place d'Armes in the center of the bulwarks, and a bombproof structure of arched masonry, where stores were kept, was on the fourth side. On high ground half a mile to the northwest were the "French Lines," which dated to 1758, when earthworks consisting of huge piles of dirt covered with abatis (tree trunks with sharpened branches turned toward the enemy), making them all but impenetrable, were thrown up in forty-eight hours by fewer than 3,500 French defendants, who were anticipating an attack by a 15,000-man British-provincial force led by James Abercromby. For reasons best known to himself, the English general had not bothered to have his cannon brought up and ordered a frontal assault with small arms; the French held their ground against wave after wave of attackers before Abercromby finally withdrew with enormous losses.*

Sir Jeffrey Amherst succeeded Abercromby, and when he besieged Carillon with 11,000 men, employing the French Lines as offensive works, the outnumbered French blew up the fort and retreated. The British renamed the post Ticonderoga—a Mohawk word meaning "between the two great waters"—and restored it in makeshift fashion, but with the end of the French wars a frontier no longer existed between the thirteen colonies and Canada, the fort had no military role of any consequence, the ditches around it filled in with trash, and the works slowly deteriorated during the years the place was used merely as a way station on the route north.

In 1775, when Benedict Arnold, in uneasy partnership with Ethan Allen and eighty-three of his "wild people," known as the Green Mountain Boys, surprised the British in the distintegrating fort (Allen theatrically demanding their surrender "in the name of the Great Jehovah and the Continental Congress"), the entire garrison consisted of only fifty-odd men, many of them invalids, plus twenty-four women and children. Charles Carroll, seeing the place for the first time, was aghast and

---

*When a Pennsylvania colonel named Anthony Wayne saw this area in 1776 he found it infinitely dispiriting: he concluded that it must have been the last part of the world God made, and that He must have completed it in the dark. The Old French Lines reminded him of "the ancient Golgotha or place of skulls—they are so plenty here that our people for want of other vessels drink out of them whilst the soldiers make tent pins out of the shin and thigh bones of Abercrombies men."

described it with the same word he had used for the other forts they had passed on the way here—"ruinous"—with "a few pieces of cannon mounted on one bastion, more for show . . . than service." In its present state, he went on, it was "of no other use than as *entrepôt* or magazine for stores."

Recent American efforts to restore what were once imposing fortifications had improved them, to be sure, but it was a monumental task and tedious, hard work for the soldiers assigned to fatigue duty. For all their labors, the crown jewel of the chain of northern forts was in no condition to withstand attack by a professional army.

On April 24, feeling "heartily tired," the commissioners were under way down Lake Champlain, sometimes under sail, frequently with the oars out, passing a dreary, denuded landscape on the west bank, which for nearly a quarter century had been stripped of trees for firewood and timber used at Ticonderoga. Fifteen miles north they made their first stop at Crown Point, where the familiar story was immediately apparent—a once important fort and barracks in ruins, accidentally burned when they were still in English hands and then blown up when flames reached the powder magazine. With a sense of relief at putting the depressing scene behind them, they set out each morning at dawn, landing to build a fire when cold or hunger got the best of them, putting in to one of the numerous coves or inlets to sleep under shelters made of brush. Along the shore they could see the occasional lonely settlement, some with fields under cultivation, all of them embodiments of dreams— the longings of men and women for whom no hardship or sacrifice was too much if only they could have their own homestead in this place that must have been created for the gods.

A number of these windows in the forest had been made by paleo-Indians who moved into the area as the last glacier began its retreat. Small bands of hunters and food-gatherers, pursuing caribou and mastodon and the prolific fish populations of lake and streams, burned patches of woodland to open it for crops and game while enriching the soil. Thousands of years later the first adventurous white settlers arrived, clearing land around their house sites to reduce the risk of surprise Indian attack while supplying the wood for buildings, tools, fences, furniture, and warmth during the long winters.

Once past the Narrows and Split Rock, where the great inland sea begins to widen, Charles Carroll noted that the farther north they sailed on the lake "the mountains which hem it on the east and west extend themselves wider and wider and leave a greater extent of fine, level land between them and the lake on each shore." He was awed by the majesty of the distant snow-capped mountains—Adirondacks to the west, Green Mountains on the east—and was made aware of their great height when he saw them later from Montreal, at least eighty miles away. Carroll took the long view of things and had already concluded that an easy water passage could be opened at little expense between New York and Montreal. If America "should succeed and establish liberty thro'out this part of the country," he decided, the lands bordering Lake Champlain would without a doubt be very valuable, since they would participate in the great trade that was bound to be carried on between Canada and New York.

Beyond Ile la Motte the bateau rounded Pointe au Fer* and picked up the current that carried boats in a day's time to St. Johns, thirty miles farther down the lake; between those two landmarks was Ile aux Têtes, whose macabre name was a reminder of the heads of vanquished Indians which had been stuck on posts and left as evidence of a victory by a rival tribe. Here the current picked up speed and at a brush-covered waste called Ile aux Noix the Richelieu, or Sorel, River began, which led to the St. Lawrence. Nearby, a house owned by Colonel Moses Hazen revealed what the seesaw movement of troops up and down the lake could do to a man's dreams: "There is scarcely a whole pane of glass in the house," Carroll wrote. "The window shutters and doors are destroyed and the hinges stolen. In short, it appears a perfect wreck." Now it was a tavern of sorts, and wreck or no, they remained here after dispatching a messenger to Montreal to arrange for carriages for the last leg of their trip.

Across the river was a fort known as St. Johns, built by Montcalm in 1758 and enlarged by the British under Carleton. Here they learned that twenty bateaus carrying rebel troops to Quebec had recently passed this way, but unless those men and a great many others reached Quebec before the British garrison was reinforced, there was precious little hope that the city could be taken. Yet Charles Carroll was hopeful: the British, he believed, "have blundered egregiously hitherto and I am in hopes they will continue blundering on till they are driven quite out of this continent." Nearing Canada, the commissioners came face to face with the reality that was to overshadow all their efforts in the north. "Not the most trifling service can be procured without an assurance of

*Originally Pointe au Feu, or Point of Fire. Now known as Rouse's Point.

instant pay in silver and gold," they learned. At St. Johns they were only twenty-eight miles from Montreal, via La Prairie, but it was slow going and Charles Carroll had little to say for their trip through the flat, poorly drained land: "I never travelled thro' worse roads, or in worse carriages," he remarked of the two-wheeled carts the Canadians called calèches. When they reached La Prairie his spirits rose: here they were six miles from Montreal and caught their first view of the town and the great river, together with the houses on its east bank—a welcome prospect for weary travelers.

Four hundred miles due north of New York, embraced by the St. Lawrence River, the island-city of Montreal had been named by Jacques Cartier for the mountain that watched over it when he visited an Indian village here in 1535. More than a century after Cartier's appearance civilization arrived in the form of a group of French priests, nuns, and settlers, since which time the town had become a bustling center of the fur and hide trade, a staging area for the remarkable western expeditions of Joliet, Marquette, La Salle, Verendrye, and Duluth, and the destination of those tireless *voyageurs* returning with pelts from faraway places on the continent that no other white man had seen.

Within the high protective wooden walls of Montreal, lining its long, broad streets, were houses "very neatly built," as the naturalist-explorer Peter Kalm found them in 1749, mostly of wood with a few stone structures. Beyond the walls he saw "excellent grain fields, charming meadows, and delightful woods," and though Montreal might be the second city in Canada in size and wealth, he termed it "first on account of its *fine location and mild climate*."

When Kalm was not eyeing Montreal's handsome, "well bred and virtuous" women in their short skirts (imitating the Indian fashion, he concluded) and their powdered, elaborately ornamented coiffures, he noticed something that was to have a direct bearing on the success or failure of the commissioners' mission. "The difference between the manners and customs of the French in Montreal and Canada, and those of the English in the American colonies," he wrote, "is as great as that between the manners of those two nations in Europe." That difference was what the representatives of the American Congress somehow had to overcome.

On the 29th of April the travelers at last reached their destination, to find a surprise awaiting them at the landing. Benedict Arnold, a brigadier general now, had outdone himself, arranging for what John Carroll described as "a great body of officers, gentry, &c" to receive the distinguished visitors, welcoming them in grand military style with an artillery salute and full military honors. After this fanfare the commissioners were taken to Arnold's elegant headquarters, where a smaller group of well-wishers anticipated their coming. When that ordeal was over they were ushered into another room where they "unexpectedly met . . . a large assemblage of ladies, most of them French," all of them married to Englishmen friendly to the American cause. Then it was time for tea, another round of conversation, and "an elegant supper, which was followed with the singing of the ladies, which proved very agreeable, and would have been more so, if we had not been so much fatigued with our journey," the exhausted priest wrote.

His cousin was much taken with the French women, who were agreeable and lively, and had a "softness to their manner [which] is charming." More than that, he was greatly impressed with Benedict Arnold's polish and poise, saying that "an officer bred up at Versailles could not have behaved with more delicacy, ease, and good breeding." Yet for all the pleasant talk and politesse, such conspicuous gaiety must have astonished men who had been sent here to retrieve a situation that was exceedingly delicate, to say the least, and in the next days reality set in with a vengeance. They were confronted by a steady stream of angry creditors who had gone out on a limb in the expectation of being paid for supplies they had furnished to the American army and who now wanted hard cash, not more promises or paper money. (Franklin advanced £353 in gold from his own purse, for whatever help that might be, and the commissioners wrote at once to Congress requesting £20,000, without which they said it would be impossible to continue the war, much less effect a union with Canada.) Arnold emphasized that the rebel forces in Canada had no hope whatever of success without a major influx of men as well as money, since a British fleet bringing reinforcements for Carleton was expected at Quebec when the ice broke up in the St. Lawrence.

No sooner had they learned all this than the rebel military predicament became agonizingly clear: the army outside Quebec simply began to collapse. General John Thomas, who had preceded them from Saratoga to Canada to take charge of the troops there, informed the commissioners that nearly half of his men had smallpox, while one-third of the remaining able-bodied were preparing to leave because their enlistments had expired along with their enthusiasm. Powder was running short, provisions were on hand for only six days, and French residents in the vicinity were "much disaffected," meaning that it was impossible to obtain supplies from them. The inventory of disaster continued: shattering Charles Carroll's optimism that the enemy would not dare face Thomas's men in the open field and his conjecture that Carleton was about to pull out of the city, the masts of at least fifteen British ships were sighted entering the St. Lawrence on May 5, and the next morning—ten days before they were expected—five of them dropped anchor off Quebec and began disembarking troops of the 29th Regiment. A British officer inside the beleaguered walls wrote, "The news soon reached every pillow in town, people half-dressed ran down to the grand battery to feast their eyes with the sight of a ship of war displaying the union flag." The end of the star-crossed siege was immediately apparent when two columns of the enemy—perhaps a thousand strong— emerged from behind the walls to attack Thomas's pitifully small, outgunned force. It was simply too much for the discouraged remnants of the heroic army that had endured so much on the march and in the attack and siege of the city, and what should have been an orderly retreat turned into a rout of panic-stricken men, streaming down the roads as fast as they could move, pursued by the British for nine miles.

Attempting to convey the dimensions of this tragedy to John Hancock, the commissioners reported that all the rebel cannon, five hundred muskets, and two hundred sick men had fallen into enemy hands, that the flight of Thomas's army "was made with the utmost precipitation and confusion," with the result that "it will not be in our power to render our country any further services in this Colony." Realizing that the entire rebel army would be driven out of Canada (as it was a month later), Dr. Franklin decided to return to Philadelphia. He was still in poor health, suffering from boils and a swelling of the legs, and knew it was pointless to remain here, so he took a calèche to St. Johns, where he was joined the next day by Father Carroll, who decided to accompany him on the long trip home.

Although they had little hope of accomplishing much, Charles Carroll and Samuel Chase were reluctant to leave because of the effect it might have on the army's morale, and they remained for nearly three weeks. They had their hands full. In Montreal they were staying at the elegant home of Thomas Walker and his wife, who had become thoroughly unpopular with other Canadians because of their enthusiasm for the rebel cause. On May 11 the commissioners issued a laissez-passer so the Walkers could accompany Franklin to Philadelphia. That done, they made recommendations for the safeguarding of bateaus and canoes;

ordered the military to seize and hold hostage the principal citizens of Montreal if the inhabitants took it into their heads to attack the garrison there; wrote General Thomas suggesting that a gondola posted at the mouth of the Richelieu River might prevent British warships from moving up the St. Lawrence; asked him if men and military stores on hand were adequate for making a stand along the Richelieu; and told him to use force if necessary to acquire provisions, since it would "prevent the horrors arising from the licentiousness of a starving, and of course an uncontrollable soldiery." Perhaps this tough stance would have done some good earlier; now it was too late by far.

A garrison of four hundred Americans was surprised at a post called the Cedars and surrendered. At Chambly the two commissioners found "all things in much confusion, extreme disorder and negligence, our credit sunk and no money to retrieve it with." Things were so bad that Carroll and Chase had to pay a wagoner three silver dollars for the transport of gunpowder, since the officer in charge had not a shilling to his name. What remained of the army was turning into an undisciplined mob "without order or regularity, eating up provisions as fast as they were brought in." To make matters worse, John Thomas contracted smallpox, resigned his command, and on June 2, after suffering an attack so severe that he was blinded, he died.*

Thomas was succeeded by John Sullivan, a high-spirited Irish general from New Hampshire who had brought in some fourteen hundred fresh troops, but they, with the others, were soon in full retreat up the Richelieu, pursued by Major General John Burgoyne and Brigadier Simon Fraser, newly arrived from England, and four thousand British regulars, who were elated to see "the Rebels ... flying before us in the greatest Terror." The Americans barely managed to get out of Chambly before Burgoyne's advance guard entered the place. Fortunately, the sick and wounded had been sent ahead to Ile aux Noix, but only two men could be spared to row each boatload of them, and they had to pull against the current for twelve miles. The hand of death lay on this army, and everywhere men were crying out piteously for help. "It broke my heart," said a surgeon who was with them, "and I wept till I had no more power to weep."

---

*Smallpox was a terrible curse, and the question of inoculation was strenuously debated. Quarantine was essential because those inoculated ("by puncture in our arms") usually contracted a relatively mild case of the disease but could pass on a more virulent form to those who had not been previously exposed. In fact, citizens of Marblehead were so alarmed that inoculation would spread the epidemic that they burned the hospital.

By the time the survivors reached Crown Point their condition had worsened, if that was possible, and when John Adams received word of their plight he wrote, "Our army . . . is an object of wretchedness enough to fill a human mind with horror: disgraced, defeated, discontented, dispirited, diseased, naked, undisciplined, eaten up with vermin, no clothes, beds, blankets; no medicines, no victuals but salt, pork & flour."

Men were dying of smallpox at the rate of ten or fifteen a day, and a Connecticut officer who saw them at Crown Point said that the fragmented regiments from New Jersey, and Pennsylvania, New York, and New England were "not an army but a mob . . . the shattered remains of twelve or fifteen very fine battalions, ruined by sickness, fatigue, and desertion, and void of every idea of discipline or subordination." The scene was "the very acme of human misery"—a description echoed by Major General Horatio Gates when he arrived to take charge of "the wretched remains of what was once a very respectable Body of Troops." Another man described the scene as one of the most distressing of the entire war: of the 5,200 men who reached Crown Point, 2,800 required hospitalization, while those remaining were "emaciated and entirely broken down in strength, spirits, and discipline."

Even before the army's headlong flight, Charles Carroll and Samuel Chase wrote the official report of the commissioners to John Hancock. It was dated May 27, from Montreal, and its long inventory of disasters and ineptitude must have come as a stunner to members of Congress who had hoped first for a conquest of Canada and, failing that, a working partnership. Four sentences summed up the whole: "We cannot find words strong enough to describe our miserable situation: you will have a faint idea of it if you figure to yourself an army broken and disheartened, half of it under inoculation, or under other diseases; soldiers without pay, without discipline, and altogether reduced to live from hand to mouth, depending on the scanty and precarious supplies of a few half-starved cattle and trifling quantities of flour. . . ."

"Your soldiers grumble for their pay; if they receive it they will not be benefited, as it will not procure them the necessaries they stand in need of. Your military chest contains but eleven thousand paper dollars. You are indebted to your troops treble that sum; and to the inhabitants above fifteen thousand dollars." And so it continued in numbing detail.

The pity of all this was that anyone in Congress who had been paying attention could have learned essentially the same lesson four months earlier, from a letter written in January to General Schuyler by Colonel Moses Hazen, the man whose ruined house across the Richelieu River from St. Johns had sheltered the commissioners for a night. Hazen had acquired a seigniory, or feudal estate, thanks to the British, but as Montgomery's army came north in 1775 he had to choose sides and opted for the rebels. His reward was a colonelcy and a license to raise a regiment of Canadians, and at first his efforts met with modest success. Then he began to sense a disaffection, a fading enthusiasm for the American cause, and when he looked around him the reasons were not hard to find.

Hazen was at the time temporary commander in Montreal, and he began his letter to Schuyler by observing how cooperative and helpful the Canadians had been at the outset. But the change in attitude he detected had set in after the failed attack on Quebec and the death of Richard Montgomery. Now, Hazen suggested, the Canadians in Montreal could hardly wait for an opportunity to join the British. Local clergymen were unanimously against the Americans and "are now plotting our destruction." Peasants had been dragooned by the rebels—often at bayonet point—to supply wood to the garrison at prices below the going rate; their wagons had been seized and used without payment; and they were thoroughly sick of promises to reimburse them and certain the United Colonies and Congress were bankrupt. To cap it all, Hazen estimated that seven-eighths of "the better sort of people, both French and English . . . could wish to see our throats cut, and perhaps would readily assist in doing it."

So for the commissioners it had all come to naught. Simply to reach Canada they had endured twenty-eight days of grueling travel, and for their pains the mission was a fiasco, as a sensible Congress should have perceived before assigning them the impossible. But congressmen, then as later, had a talent for failing to look the truth squarely in the eye and recognize it for what it was.

On June 2 the thoroughly dejected Carroll and Chase sailed from St. Johns; even then the former, who had been unfailingly optimistic during his stay in Montreal, kept hoping that "our affairs in Canada may still take a favourable turn." But time had run out. At Fort Ticonderoga they picked up General Schuyler and traveled with him as far as Albany. This time, however, they went by boat to Skenesborough at the end of South Bay, bypassing Lake George in favor of the route that led up serpentine Wood Creek, then overland to Fort Edward, Saratoga, and Albany. Luckily, they found a sloop ready to sail, and on June 9 they were back in New York, spending the night at the estate of Abraham Mortier at

Richmond Hill, which George Washington was using as his headquarters. There they delivered their woeful account of Canadian affairs to three intensely interested listeners—the commander in chief and Generals Horatio Gates and Israel Putnam.

Franklin, of course, was already in Philadelphia by the time his fellow commissioners arrived at 2:00 A.M. on June 11. He had traveled from Albany to New York by post chaise, courtesy of the Schuylers. The doctor, understandably weary of water travel, had asked to borrow a sulky and drive himself to New York, but Mrs. Schuyler generously insisted that their man Lewis take him in a closed, four-wheeled carriage instead of an open two-wheeler. Since the road was stony and full of gullies, he wrote Schuyler, "I should probably have overset and broken my bones. . . ." Reaching Manhattan, he took the time to write to Charles Carroll and Chase to let them know what had become of him, showing that whatever his aches and pains, his gift for the pointed phrase remained intact. Mr. and Mrs. Thomas Walker had accompanied him to Albany, it turned out, and taunted him about the commissioners' failure in Canada. But he resisted quarreling with them, "landed her safe in Albany, with her three Waggon-Loads of Baggage, brought thither without putting her to any Expence, and parted civilly tho' coldly. I think they both have excellent Talents at making themselves Enemies, and I believe, live where they will, they will never be long without them."

When Franklin reached Philadelphia at the end of May he was worn out from his exertions of the past two months. As he wrote Chase and Charles Carroll, "I grow daily more feeble, and I think I could hardly have got along so far but for Mr. [John] Carroll's assistance and tender care of me." In addition to boils, edema, and what may have been psoriasis, he had developed gout and was slow to recover. His worried sister told a friend that "his Indisposition I believe Affected His Spirets, but He seems [a] little chearfull this morning."

Yet in spite of his ills, the faithful doctor accepted yet another assignment from his fellow members of Congress. On June 10 he was appointed to a committee that also included Thomas Jefferson of Virginia, John Adams of Massachusetts, Roger Sherman of Connecticut, and Robert Livingston of New York. After two days of debate, delegates on July 2 approved a resolution offered by Virginian Richard Henry Lee on June 7, "That these United Colonies are, and of right ought to be, free and independent States, that they are absolved from all allegiance to the British Crown, and that all political connection between them and the state of Great Britain is, and ought to be, totally dissolved." It remained for this resolve, expressing the American will, to be set forth in a declaration to the whole world, and that was the challenge for the five-man committee.

Jefferson, who had demonstrated his talent as a writer and had what Adams called a "peculiar felicity of expression," was chosen to draft the document, which he submitted to Adams and Franklin for comments. When it was complete, the assembled delegates took a hand at altering a word here, deleting a phrase there, to the intense discomfort of the thirty-three-year-old Virginian, for whom more than pride of authorship was involved. He had done his level best "to place before mankind the common sense of the subject, in terms so firm and plain as to command their assent, and to justify ourselves in the independent stand we are compelled to take." His heart and soul were wrapped up in the remarkable statement he had composed, and it was almost too painful to have anyone tamper with it.

The unquenchable Franklin, seeing his young friend's chagrin, told him a story about a hatter who was opening a shop and wanted a fancy signboard. He decided it should read, "John Thompson, Hatter, makes and sells hats for ready money." Surely, he thought, that and a painting of a hat would attract customers. Then a friend said the word "Hatter" was superfluous, so he eliminated it. Someone else considered the word "makes" unnecessary, since no buyer of a hat cared who made it. Still another said the words "ready money" should be omitted, since no one expected him to extend credit. That left "John Thompson sells hats," but he was told that nobody thought he would give them away. Finally, all that remained was his name, "John Thompson," and a picture of a hat.

Fortunately, most changes made by the delegates improved Jefferson's draft, and the final version, signed on July 4 by President John Hancock and Secretary Charles Thompson, was printed that night and proclaimed to a wildly cheering crowd in Philadelphia on July 8. By August 6, fifty members of Congress—including Benjamin Franklin, Charles Carroll, and Samuel Chase—had signed a parchment copy of the Declaration of Independence. The three commissioners to Canada had seen with their own eyes the horror and suffering brought on by war, but not even that could shake their conviction that the cause was just and worth any sacrifice it might take to make independence a reality.

On the eve of the signing, the impetuous Samuel Chase, who had waited so long and impatiently for this moment, wrote to Richard Henry Lee of Virginia to rejoice that the historic document would advance "Confederation between the united Colonies, in Making foreign alliances, & in adopting such other Measures, as shall be adjudged necessary for Securing the Liberty of America . . . *Jubeo Te bene valere* (I command thee to be especially strong)."

The phrases were aptly chosen, for if other measures should fail, making foreign alliances might prove the only way to ensure survival of the infant confederation.

Chapter 3

The Enemy's Plans Are Dark
and Mysterious

It was autumn of 1776 when General Sir Guy Carleton, newly knighted for his stubborn defense of Quebec, approached Ticonderoga, and his army was barely prevented from overrunning it by several twists of fate. To begin, he found he did not have enough vessels to carry troops up the lake in sufficient numbers to lay siege to the place, as a result of which he waited for weeks while a collection of ships and two hundred bateaus was assembled at St. Johns under the direction of a Lieutenant Shank. The lieutenant was an ingenious fellow whose claim to fame was the invention of the centerboard boat in 1774, and he got a remarkable performance out of the local shipwrights—who, despite their grumbling that "winter comes here early: nothing will come of the expedition this year"—took apart a square-rigged three-master known as *Inflexible*, hauled the pieces around the rapids on the Richelieu, and after re-laying her keel had her in action on the lake only twenty-eight days later. But even such miracles were not enough, and the delay was ruinous.

When Carleton's flotilla finally did get under way, it was met off Valcour Island by a patchwork fleet constructed by Schuyler and the resourceful Benedict Arnold and held up just long enough for the weather to turn against the enemy: for twenty days gale winds stalled the British ships. Carleton's spies informed him that the rebels at Fort Ticonderoga numbered twenty thousand (which they did not), and when he and his chief of artillery, Major General William Phillips, reconnoitered near the fort they judged that it was indeed too strongly held to attack; a protracted siege would be required. Carleton was a prudent man and he had experienced enough of the cruel Canadian winters to keep a weather eye on the calendar. He decided the opportunity for a siege was past: it was time to head north and retire to winter quarters. One of his officers, accustomed to the climate of England, explained the reason behind the general's conclusion: " . . . after the 15th November on account of the frost, which begins to set in with great violence about that time . . . Canada is as much shut out from all communication with the rest of the world as possible, particularly then, as the country from Ticonderoga was in possession of the enemy." No one could possibly know it at the time, of course, but the heroic engagement fought off Valcour Island by Arnold and crews that were made up mostly of landsmen completely upset Britain's timetable. It was regarded as a defeat for the rebels, but because of it, Carleton did not take Ticonderoga, which put off a northern invasion for another year.

William Phillips was an experienced soldier and a first-class artilleryman, but he was a stranger to North American winters and was outraged that his commanding officer would pull up stakes so readily. Canada might be shut off from the rest of the world, but at the very least, he argued, Carleton should hold on to Crown Point, which the British had taken without rebel resistance on their way south. A garrison there would give Carleton an advanced base, a springboard from which to launch an attack in the spring, but in view of the "languor which governs every movement," he complained, "I still fear a dreadful winter. . . . " Little did Phillips know how much weight would be attached to his opinion, once it became known in the government offices at Whitehall.

But Carleton was already laying the groundwork for a return to Ticonderoga, and perhaps beyond, after the coming of decent weather in the spring. When he withdrew to Quebec he left a crew of artificers behind at St. Johns, where they "stayed building ships, floating batteries, gun boats &c, two ships of 20 guns each, *George*, *Maria*, [and] *Carleton*, and a large floating battery carrying 16 guns, and several gunboats," according to a British soldier named George Fox.

That same autumn, General Philip Schuyler wrote a long letter to Congress detailing his department's urgent needs. Along with a list that included artillery, powder and ammunition, provisions for eight months, pitch and oakum for boats, wooden planks and boards, and—most critically—money to pay troops, he requested some 6,000 men for winter service, 2,500 of whom would be quartered at or near Ticonderoga when shelter could be provided for them.

Through no fault of Schuyler's, very little came of this until May of 1777, when reinforcements began dribbling into camp from the New England states. Some, from New Hampshire, headed for Ticonderoga after their militia colonels received an impassioned appeal from Josiah Bartlett, of that state's Committee of Safety: "Supose your House in Flames, your wife, your Daughters Ravished, your Sons, your Neighbours Weltering in their Blood. . . . " These calamities were probable, he said, unless men awake "from the Sleep they are now in." Long before those men arrived on the scene, Colonel Anthony Wayne, commanding at Ticonderoga, informed the general that he was unable even to post pickets for lack of men. Although conditions gradually improved as winter dragged on, Wayne was losing troops by the score to a malady that combined chills and fever, aching joints, nausea, and loss of appetite and was known as "camp distemper." Some men froze to death in their tents, and hardly a day passed without a fatality caused by exposure to the elements in the most primitive conditions. Short of staff officers, Wayne was obliged to serve as combination quartermaster, engineer, and commandant, and "worried with Wretches applying for Discharges or Furlows . . . until I am a mear Skeleton." Largely because of Congressional neglect, which spelled meager manpower and funds, the fort would be "an easy prey to the Enemy for want of proper Supplies to maintain an Army in the Spring—owing to a Supineness somewhere . . ." and he hardly needed to tell Schuyler that it was in Philadelphia.

No one ever accused Wayne—who came to be known as "Mad Anthony" for his fearlessness in battle—of timidity, yet the desperate situation of the post was a daily reminder of its vulnerability. On March 25, while seeking militia reinforcements, he reported to the Council of Massachusetts* that Indians led by a British officer had ambushed and killed a number of his troops and taken twenty-one prisoners. This happened at Sabbath Day Point, about fifteen miles south of Ticonderoga on Lake George, and it ensured that word of "the debilitated state of their garrison" would soon reach the British force rumored to be gathering at Montreal and St. Johns. The threat of attack was imminent, he warned the council, so "For God's sake rouze your field and other officers from their lethargy. . . . There is not one moment to spare."

---

*In Massachusetts, as in certain other states, the council was the upper house of the legislature. It also performed executive duties and had administrative powers.

Before joining up, Wayne had been a prosperous tanner, a surveyor, and a legislator in Pennsylvania. He had led a battalion to Canada in '76 in relief of the rebel army there and had fought against three-to-one odds near Trois Rivières. By the time the Americans lost half their men they were forced to retreat, pursued by Indians and Canadian irregulars, "almost devoured by musketoes of a monstrous size and innumerable numbers" as they struggled through the "most horrid swamps." When they finally reached the relative safety of Ticonderoga, Wayne got a lesson in handling a ragtag bunch of largely untrained, poorly disciplined soldiers at the farthest reach of an uncertain, shaky supply line.

Early in April of 1777 he wrote to John Hancock, predicting that the British would strike as soon as the melting ice permitted them to sail up the lake. To his wife he confided that he anticipated a "sudden visit from the enemy." And to Schuyler he admitted more than he had to either of his other correspondents. Now that the militiamen had gone home, he said, it was painful to report that "at least One third of the Troops now on the Ground [are] Composed of Negroes, Indians, and Children." Surely it was a "melancholy Reflection that we should be necessitated to Retain Indians and Negroes in our Ranks." And echoing Thomas Paine's scorn for the summer soldier and the sunshine patriot, he asked, "have we not White men? have we not freemen Sufficient without them?" and answered his own question: "we Certainly have."

He had some excellent troops, he added, who would give a good account of themselves, and if they were too few to hold out against the enemy, he would fall back toward the south with honor. The only hopeful note in his catalogue of gloom was a rumor that the British had neglected their naval force on the lake; Wayne judged that they would have at their disposal no more than ten ships and twenty-five or thirty flat-bottomed boats.

Somehow, despite omens of impending trouble, Wayne had convinced himself that wherever the enemy was, he would have at least eight weeks to prepare, and in that time he figured he could cobble together a fleet of his own, composed of a handful of vessels that had survived the battle off Valcour Island last year, plus new ones he would construct, if Congress supplied the manpower and money to make it possible. If he achieved superiority on the lake, he said (and that was a formidable "if"), he could easily defend Ti, as the fort was familiarly called, with two or three thousand troops (if only he could get the troops, of course), men who could "put the Enemy in Constant Alarm and Oblige them to keep a large Army of Observation in Canada." But with the exception of several small sailing vessels and bateaus that could be used to ferry soldiers here and there on the two lakes, the dream of a fleet remained exactly that.

As with Schuyler, Wayne's pleas to Congress and the states—to anyone who would listen—produced few results, and the garrison at Ticonderoga withered and all but died, leaving him to ponder the enemy's likely moves and pray that he might somehow be prepared when the time for action was upon him.

By the time Wayne was replaced (to his immense relief) the garrison had shrunk to 2,200 men—a number that varied almost daily as militia units came and went, and one that always included many sick. Continental regiments accounted for 1,576 of the total, and three militia regiments from New Hampshire were on hand, "engaged for no particular term and who go off whenever they please," plus two from Massachusetts, whose two-month hitches were nearly half complete.

In the Jerseys, some 275 miles south of Ticonderoga, the buds had burst, trees were leafing out, and the hillsides were dappled with the pinks and whites of dogwood and mountain laurel, the stream banks covered with the emerald green of countless skunk cabbages. Spring was the season of expectations, the promise of better times to come, but the expectations of the man known as the Commander-in-Chief of the Armies of the United States were that fine weather could only bring trouble. It was also the season for campaigning, and the British would soon be coming to get him.

After his astonishing victory at Princeton on January 3, 1777, George Washington led the worn, half-naked veterans of the Continental Army into winter quarters at Morristown, a New Jersey community described by Martha Bland, the twenty-five-year-old wife of a Virginia colonel, as "a very clever little village situated in a most beautiful valley at the foot of five mountains." Among the fifty dwellings, three houses with steeples gave it what impressed her as "a consequential look," but apart from two refugee families from New York she found little to choose from among the local folk. They were "the errantist rustics you ever beheld," she wrote her sister Fanny. The women she thought exceedingly pretty, although they were "the most inhospitable mortals breathing," and what was more, "You'd laugh to hear them talk."

Martha Bland was enchanted by Morristown and the nearby New Jersey communities, each with its steepled courthouse and church, beyond which lay fertile, well-tilled farmland that could sustain an army.

Yet she seemed oblivious to the fact that this was a war zone, where all winter Americans—notably New Jersey militiamen—had harassed the enemy, skirmishing with their foraging parties, snatching up supplies and the wagons and horses used to haul them, sniping at their pickets, nibbling constantly at the defensive perimeter. While the British retaliated by plundering and burning houses, this guerrilla warfare obliged the enemy to transport supplies by water from New York to make up the deficits of food, fuel, and fodder. Foragers had to be escorted by two or more battalions, while the miserable redcoats, many of them suffering from smallpox, were stuffed into cramped billets wherever they could be found in the small towns.

At the end of May, Washington's regiments left Morristown and headed south to Middle Brook, a crossroads village named for the stream that plunges through gorges in the Watchung Mountains, past the furnaces and copper mines of its namesake community, and on to join the Raritan River. It was a strong natural site for a camp, which Washington improved by building two redoubts. From here—especially from a prominent rock on the mountain behind the village, which afforded a spectacular view of the plain four hundred feet below—he could keep a close eye on the country between Amboy and Brunswick and the road to Philadelphia. That was the logical route for General Sir William Howe and the main British army to take if and when they left New York. Middle Brook had the further advantage of being situated on the edge of the Watchungs, to which the Americans could fall back if necessary, for the one thing Washington could not risk was a full-scale battle with Howe's vastly superior force.

As matters stood in May, Washington had Israel Putnam's troops stationed in Princeton, Nathanael Greene closer by at Basking Ridge, William Heath in Peekskill, New York, and Anthony Wayne at Ticonderoga. As long as these outposts were held, the lifeline between New England and the central and southern states would remain intact. Moreover, whether he remained at Middle Brook or returned to Morristown, he was in a position to attack Howe's flank if the British advanced toward Philadelphia, or march in support of the Hudson forts if Howe headed up the river. But whatever course Howe followed, Washington would have to find a way to deal with the enemy piecemeal, playing a game of cat and mouse, tempting the British general to detach part of his army, which the Americans might trap or catch off guard.

George Washington was now in his forty-sixth year, the prime of life in a day when a sixty-year-old was reckoned elderly. A head taller than the average American of that time, he stood six feet two inches and weighed more than two hundred pounds. His size, broad shoulders, and large hands, feet, and upper legs all gave the impression of great physical power. Yet for a big man he was surprisingly nimble and was, according to Thomas Jefferson, "the best horseman of his age and the most graceful figure that could be seen on horseback." A French nobleman observed admiringly that he always rode at a gallop, "leaping the highest fences and going extremely quick without standing upon his stirrups, or letting his horse run wild." Handsome in spite of a slight scarring of his face from smallpox, Washington had a large, straight nose, high cheek-bones, reddish-brown hair, light blue-gray eyes, and what can only be described as a commanding presence. In conversation, people noticed, he looked you straight in the eyes.

Despite a reputation for being serious and reserved and keeping people at arm's length, screening the inner man, all of which was true enough, in relaxed company he was affable, laughed easily at jokes, and amused listeners with wry observations on the affairs of the world. He was capable of blistering subordinates when his temper got the best of him, as it occasionally did when he was under great strain, yet he could charm men and women alike when in a mood to do so. Martha Bland, who visited his Morristown headquarters with her husband on numerous occasions, wrote her sister describing afternoon outings in the company of General and Mrs. Washington (who often referred to him as "the Old Man") and several of his aides, when "we often make parties on horse-back." There, "General Washington throws off the hero and takes on the chatty, agreeable companion. He can be downright impudent some-times"—and one can almost hear the soft Virginia drawl—"such impu-dence, Fanny, as you and I like."

George Washington had spent five harsh years soldiering on the western frontier, attracting a reputation for conspicuous bravery and leadership, before settling down to manage his Mount Vernon farms. The domesticity he loved so much was fleeting, however, especially after 1775, when he was sent as a delegate from Virginia to the Second Conti-nental Congress. Only a month after his arrival in Philadelphia, he was elected to command the American armies, then besieging the British in Boston. One reason Congress chose him was that his fame from the fron-tier days was still bright. But another, equally important motive was the realization by Massachusetts delegates of the crucial need to engage the support and influence of Virginia. The contrary Yankees on whose soil the fight had begun saw the appointment of Washington as surety that the South would join and stick by the North. What seemed like a horse trade ultimately made possible America's survival as a nation.

The man on whom so much depended was a gentleman who, despite being also a gentle man of moderate views, would fight a revolutionary war for seven years in defense of the freedom in which he believed so fervently. He was also a proud man, whose achievements justified pride. In Boston he proved that he could forge an army from the crowd of unruly volunteers he found there. Yet it was one thing to organize people from disparate sections of a vast country into an army; it was quite another to reenlist men of many different persuasions who had a boundless number of reasons to go home once the fighting was over in Boston. Washington's success in this almost superhuman task has no counterpart in America since that day, and the accomplishment reveals him as a man who won an enormous struggle against a determined enemy and against the natural disinclination of his own people to serve in or support a full-time army. As Lafayette was to say of him later, he *was* the Revolution.

He never had enough men or adequate food and shelter and clothing for them, let alone the weapons they needed or the money to pay them. His genius was in accepting that he was no match for the British and compensating for that disadvantage by leading the enemy into situations that gave him an edge. This meant curbing his natural tendency to impetuosity in order to wear out his enemies, slowly grinding them down, exhausting them and the government behind them until a foreign power intervened or the British decided that the war was too costly to continue. In practical terms, it required a war of attrition, a defensive war in which the Americans would be frequently on the run, just ahead of the pursuing redcoats. Whenever possible, it would be a war of minor battles: a general action would be avoided and major risks taken only if no alternative was in sight.

In December of 1776, Congress had conferred on Washington powers that could only be described as dictatorial, yet he never abused that power, never lost sight of the fact that ultimate control had to be in the hands of the civilian, not military, authorities, despite the infinite patience and understanding this demanded of him.

His soldiers spoke with awe and pride of Washington's imperturbability on the battlefield, his absolute lack of fear, his indomitable will, and those who believed that a power shapes the destiny of men could wonder if George Washington had been spared from near-death on so many occasions so that he might lead his countrymen in the fight they must win if they were to gain their independence. Yet from the time he took over the confused, disorganized mass of men who constituted the incipient Continental Army and tried to mold them into an effective fighting force, he was haunted by the thought that he would somehow be found lacking, perhaps forfeiting the reputation that meant so much to him. "From the day I enter upon the command of the American armies," he confided to a friend, "I date my fall and the ruin of my reputation." Behind the self-doubts were a "conviction of my own incapacity and want of experience in the conduct of so momentous a concern."

The liberation of Boston took place when a crew under Henry Knox hauled "a noble train of artillery"—some fifty-odd cannon and mortars captured by Arnold and Ethan Allen at Fort Ticonderoga—by oxen through the snow from Ti to Fort George, on to Albany, then across the Hudson and the Berkshire Mountains to Framingham, and afterward wrestled into position overlooking the British lines. And on St. Patrick's Day of 1776, after General William Howe, accompanied by nearly nine thousand soldiers, another twelve hundred men, women, and children attached to the army, and eleven hundred loyalists, finally sailed for Halifax instead of New York, where Washington had expected them to go, a grateful Congress had a gold medal struck in Paris and presented to the commander in chief. A new army, with its new general, fighting for a new nation, had won its first major victory, prompting many delegates to the Continental Congress to believe that this single campaign would be enough to achieve the goals of the rebellion. Defeated, frustrated in their attempt to quell the uprising, the king's troops would sail away, they assumed, and the government in London would yield to the Americans' demands. Only it did not happen that way.

When Howe sailed for Halifax he seemed to be following the script. But from that moment on, the record of Washington's army was abysmal—a succession of reverses and retreats beginning on June 30, 1776, when the masts of the Royal Navy's men-of-war and transports appeared in Lower New York Bay off Staten Island, making it clear that the British were not in the least discouraged by the events in Boston, were in fact determined to subdue the American colonies by whatever military might it took to do so. Howe had returned with some 31,000 professional soldiers, well armed and equipped, and in quick succession drove Washington's troops off Long Island and out of New York; Westchester was lost, and two strongholds opposite each other on the lower Hudson River—Forts Washington and Lee—were taken. During the agonizing retreat across New Jersey, Washington had reason to believe that some of his subordinates were disaffected, believing that another commander would be more decisive and do a better job of fighting Howe. Two of them were former British officers who favored the American cause and saw the possibility of advancement here as more likely than with His Majesty's forces. Washington was aware of the ambitious scheming of Major General Charles Lee, recently captured in New Jersey by his former brothers in arms; and he had already detected "symptoms of coldness and constraint" in the behavior of Major General Horatio Gates, another former British officer, symptoms which "increased as he rose into greater consequence."

At the same time, much of the commander in chief's reputation was redeemed in the wake of Trenton and Princeton and the winter just past, and his opponents began to see him in an entirely different light. A British officer, writing to his father, reported that the rebels had become "a formidable enemy," while an English traveler in America admitted grudgingly, if caustically, that "Washington is certainly a most surprising man, one of Nature's geniuses, if there is any of that sort. That a Negro-driver should with a ragged banditti of undisciplined people, the scum and refuse of all nations on earth, so long keep a British general at bay, nay, even oblige him, with as fine an army of veteran soldiers as ever England had on the American continent, to retreat . . . is astonishing."

A genius of Nature Washington might be, but just now, as he pondered where Howe would go when he finally emerged from winter quarters in New York, he had a lamentable shortage of soldiers for the job at hand, compounded by the fact that neither he nor his generals had anything like an accurate account of the number of troops likely to be on duty on any given day. Early in April, the commanding general wrote to one of his brigadiers, exaggerating only slightly when he said, " . . . the campaign is opening, and we have no men for the field." Congress had promised additional regiments for the Continental Army, but recruiting was maddeningly slow, so far producing only a few hundred new men. Bounties were offered for enlistment, but Congress often neglected to supply Washington with money to fulfill the commitments, and even when he did have the necessary funds he had to compete for recruits with the states, which offered enlistees larger inducements when the enemy threatened their borders. Some states cooperated with the commander in chief, of course, even volunteering to add their own funds to those promised by Congress, but this practice frequently caused Washington's troops to leave camp in order to go home and collect the money. Adding salt to the wounds, early in May, Howe let it be known that he would pay a bounty of twenty-four dollars to any American who would desert.

Human nature being what it is, the bounty system led to cheating, with men enlisting in several places for the money, and although Washington threatened the death penalty for anyone caught at this game, the practice continued. "I wish I could see any prospect of an Army, fit to make proper opposition, formed anywhere," he grumbled to Congress.

What passed for regular troops—the Continental Army, as distinct from state militia—constituted the force on which success would ultimately depend, and desertion among these soldiers was deeply disturbing. Month after month, men vanished, departing for home or to join the British, and while the figure may have been exaggerated, the enemy claim that three thousand deserters came into its camps between January and the end of May was not implausible.

After the most strenuous efforts to augment his army, on June 2 the commander in chief reported to Congress that he had a total of 9,200 men with which to counter a well-equipped, superbly trained force two and a half times their number. With almost 14,000 men in New Jersey alone, the British army under Howe not only was numerically superior, but thanks to the presence of a mighty fleet of armed vessels and transports could be moved at will—swiftly and secretly—to almost any destination along the Atlantic coast, or up one of the tidal rivers leading inland. "Their Fleet give them the most signal advantages, and opportunity of practicing a thousand feints," a frustrated Washington observed.

Nor was the weakness of the army his only cause for alarm. Again and again, he complained of lax discipline in the ranks, the shortage of good officers, and Congress's habit of handing out commissions to foreigners like Roche de Fermoy and Baron de Woedtke—some of them soldiers of fortune, the commander in chief observed bitterly, with "no attachments or ties to the country . . . ignorant of the language they are to receive and give orders in," and without "the slightest chance to recruit others." (The practice continued despite a commitment from Congress in mid-March: "No commissions should be granted to foreign officers . . . unless they are well acquainted with our language and bring strong credentials of their abilities.") Some of these newcomers were given commissions that meant they outranked American officers who had fought bravely and commendably for two years. Understandably nettled, several of Washington's best generals threatened to resign.

The jockeying of generals and colonels for higher rank was abetted by powerful cliques and individual members in Congress who wanted to see local or regional favorites advance. This was a source of bitter wrangles and enmities, threatening the unity of the states, the command structure, and the very cause for which these men were fighting. And the worst case of all centered on the Northern Department and a long-simmering rivalry between two major generals—Philip Schuyler and Horatio Gates.

The three commissioners to Canada had already assessed the patrician Schuyler, and Franklin and Chase could testify that Horatio Gates was cut from a very different piece of cloth. Fifty years old, he looked much older, because of a pronounced stoop, wispy gray hair, thick spectacles worn at the end of his nose, a double chin, and a habit of quoting time-worn adages to make a point, all of which prompted one soldier to describe him as "an old, granny-looking fellow," whereupon he acquired the nickname Granny Gates.

Although much was made of his lowly birth as the son of the Duke of Leeds's housekeeper, his mother's friendship with a woman who worked for Horace Walpole's mother led to his being made Walpole's godson, and that connection helped him obtain his first army commission. He was posted to Nova Scotia in 1749, was badly wounded during Braddock's defeat in 1755, and after holding several desk jobs returned to England to discover that further promotion (he was then a major) was out of the question, thanks to his lack of financial resources and the reversion of the British army to a peacetime footing. Bitterly disappointed, he retired on half pay and had plenty of time to contemplate and resent a meager pension and the evils of the English class system, while he was increasingly attracted to the radical political views then current in America. He became a rabid independence man and wrote to George Washington, whom he had known on the Braddock expedition, who helped him find a plantation in Virginia. At the outbreak of the Revolution he received a commission as brigadier general, and his very real talents as an organizer were put to use helping Washington bring order to the topsy-turvy mob of citizen soldiers outside Boston. A year later he was given his first opportunity to command a rebel army in the field, in what was called the Northern Department.

Since that command's primary responsibility was to block a British invasion from Canada, it was regarded by some members of Congress to be as important as George Washington's army. Moreover, the cold facts of geography magnified the normal difficulties of communication to the point where the region included in the Northern Department sometimes seemed as remote from the commander in chief's headquarters as a foreign land. Because Washington was preoccupied with a hundred concerns affecting his own army, he had little time to spare for what was occurring in Albany and points north. This untidy situation was much to the liking of certain members of Congress, with the result that Philip Schuyler, the man in charge of the Northern Department, while theoretically subordinate to George Washington, frequently received orders from Congress. All might have gone more smoothly had it not been for the New England delegates who had no use for Schuyler and wanted to replace him with Gates.

Gates was the darling of the New England legislators, particularly the Adamses, John and Samuel, who thought their interests would be better served by the former British officer and were certain that neither Continentals nor militiamen from their constituency would fight under Schuyler. In June of 1776, Congress directed Washington to send Gates to Canada to take command of the army there, but before Gates even left New York, what was left of that army was in full retreat down Lake Champlain with the British in hot pursuit. That left the general with no command.

Gates rode to Albany, where he and Schuyler argued long and heatedly over who was in charge, with the latter saying he could not imagine Congress putting him "under the command of a younger [by which he meant junior] officer, nor oblige him to be a suicide and stab his own honor." Hoping to resolve the impasse, Congress sent word that they had intended for Gates to command the army in Canada, but that they had "no design to vest him with a superior command to General Schuyler, whilst the troops should be on this side of Canada." This was the kind of ambiguous language that characterized many a Congressional resolution; it simply ignored the main issue of whether or not Gates was subordinate to Schuyler. To muddy the waters further, President John Hancock wrote to both officers, stating that Congress meant them to *share* the command. However that was supposed to work, it was clearly not going to foster a lasting peace between two proud, sensitive generals, each determined to be top dog. As a stopgap, during the summer and early fall of 1776, Gates took charge of the work at Ticonderoga and Schuyler remained in Albany, trying to round up militia reinforcements. Shortly thereafter, the two men did agree on one important departmental matter: in council with a group of other generals (including Baron de Woedtke, who died shortly thereafter from exposure and, as one man put it, *"la bile et l'eau de vie"*), they decided that the condition of the works at Crown Point was so terrible that the post could not be defended, and that all efforts on the lake should be dedicated to strengthening Ticonderoga.

This created an uproar: a score of junior officers, mostly from New England, petitioned to have the decision reversed. (Nathanael Greene, a man on whom Washington relied heavily, complained that abandoning Crown Point was "one of the most mad resolutions" imaginable—one that would "lay all the back parts of New England open.") Schuyler let the disgruntled officers know that relinquishing Crown Point was essential for a number of reasons, but with characteristic hauteur did not bother to provide the reasons. Finally Washington was dragged into the dispute and wrote a diplomatic letter to Schuyler making plain his regrets that Crown Point had been vacated. He had never been there nor to Ticonderoga and had no familiarity with the area, but from all he had heard he assumed Crown Point to be "of the utmost consequence to us, especially if we mean to keep the superiority and mastery of the lake." Then he wrote a considerably less diplomatic, more critical letter on the same subject to Gates, his former adjutant.

Gates responded with a reasoned defense of the council's decision, observing that none of the junior officers knew what they were talking about, since they were not on the scene, and Washington, irritated, told him he wanted to hear no more about the business. Unlike Gates, who thought it wise to forget the matter, Schuyler wrote Washington threatening to resign unless the commander in chief or Congress rebuked the young officers.

By this time Schuyler had been the butt of so much criticism that he was paranoid about it, seeing a sinister plot to get rid of him behind every slight. For some time, New England members of Congress had disparaged him in terms that made him out to be a coward, unfit to command, and now their criticism took the form of an attack on the operation of the Northern Department's commissary—a charge that cut Schuyler to the quick, for he regarded the supplying of the army as his most notable achievement (which it was), and one that had kept him so preoccupied he had been forced at times to neglect his strictly military duties.

Gates, finding himself an unemployed major general, was lobbying his supporters in Congress and in February 1777 was offered the position of adjutant general to Washington, which he had held before going to Albany and which he had no wish to return to, preferring a field command.

While Gates did not know it, his strongest ally in that quest was Schuyler, who had a talent for scolding Congress in waspish letters, complaining about slights on his character, and whose latest outburst led Hancock to slap his wrists for failing to respect the members' "rank and dignity." Nor was that all. Congress did not take abuse lightly and reacted by directing Gates to take charge of the army at Ticonderoga, as an independent command, with Arthur St. Clair as his deputy. Schuyler retaliated by demanding a Congressional inquiry (which he received), insisting on "absolute command . . . over every part of the army in the Northern department," and threatening once more to resign unless he had his way.

Like a bad play that seems never to end, Schuyler's friends now went on the attack, focusing on the absurdity of having Gates command *at Ticonderoga*, as if the British would restrict their operations to that spot. Congress was persuaded, and on May 15, 1777, recommended that Schuyler remain in command of the Northern Department and that Gates be offered his choice: either adjutant general under Washington, or a command "in the Northern department, under General Schuyler."

Now it was Gates's turn to play the injured suitor, and as he headed south for Philadelphia he was variously described as "extremely ill-used," "greatly chagrined," and "enraged" over what he termed his disgrace. He appeared on the floor of Congress, lost control of his temper, and engaged in a shouting contest with Schuyler's New York supporters before being ordered from the chamber.

Then, to complicate matters further, Schuyler announced his candidacy for governor of New York. Gates, assuming that his rival would win, enabling him to take over the department, was delighted. But neither seems to have focused on the good of the service, given the likelihood of an enemy attack on Ticonderoga. Eventually, to Gates's disappointment, Schuyler lost the election, ensuring that the dispute between the two major generals would continue to fester.

Along with trying to deal with the woes that plagued the forces under his command, Washington had to devise tactics by which his army might at the very least avoid defeat, in hopes that the government in London would weary of the war. He and most members of Congress were convinced that Howe would soon head for Philadelphia, where delegates from the various states conducted the nation's business. Washington's immediate concern was to prevent the enemy from taking the *de facto* capital of the new country while simultaneously avoiding a general engagement with Howe. But another, infinitely more damaging threat was that the British might contrive to separate the New England states from those to the south.

America's top general was not privy to Britain's military plans, but it required no leap of imagination to suppose that the enemy could seize the vital Hudson-Champlain passage. Washington did not like playing guessing games: a wrong guess could be fatal. But the British had him bewildered now, as they had on other occasions, leading him to mutter that they "have the best knack at puzzling people I ever met with in my life."

Washington's eye was fixed on Philadelphia and the likelihood that Howe would strike there, which turned out to be exactly what Howe had in mind. By April 2, in fact, the British commander had decided to recall his troops from New Jersey and move against Philadelphia—not by the overland route as he had originally intended, but by sea. The question was when Howe would get around to it, for haste was not his strong suit.

In seconding the forty-eight-year-old William Howe to Boston in 1775, George III may have hoped that some magic still attached to the Howe name. The general's brother, George Augustus, 3rd Viscount Howe, had been extremely popular in the colonies, and his death in the 1758 attack on Fort Ticonderoga was genuinely mourned by the New Englanders who served with him, who placed a monument to him in Westminster Abbey. William Howe was a kinsman, after a fashion, to George III, since one of his grandmothers had been the mistress of the king's great-grandfather. He was burly and coarse-looking, a six-footer with terrible teeth and the same swarthy complexion that led sailors to call his brother Richard "Black Dick." Years of self-indulgence had taken their toll, and one obvious manifestation was a midsection tending to softness. Howe had entered the army at eighteen and was a proven soldier, a skilled tactician, with a courage and élan in combat that made him popular with the men in the ranks despite what General William Phillips called his "damned vile disposition." Serving under Wolfe, he had stormed the Heights of Abraham at the head of the light infantry, playing a key role in the battle that ended France's dreams of American empire. He showed the stuff he was made of when he led his troops in a frontal assault on the rebel breastworks on Breed's Hill. There, after every one of his staff officers had fallen by his side, Howe, with his white breeches and silk stockings splattered with the blood of his men, tucked his sword under his arm and calmly dressed the redcoats' ranks for their final charge. More recently, Howe had been honored by a grateful monarch for his victories in and around New York. Yet the man charged with leading the greatest army ever sent out from Britain had made it known before his assignment that he opposed the government's colonial policy—had, in fact, condemned it to his Parliamentary constituents, saying he would accept no command in America. Since he was in need of employment and eager for preferment, he changed his tune, but in the eyes of his critics that did not necessarily make him an enthusiast for what he was doing and left him open to charges that his torpid campaigning was the result of sympathy for the American cause.

Howe was silent (some said inarticulate) and inscrutable, but whether or not he had lingering doubts about the rightness of the cause, his personal failings did nothing to improve his effectiveness as the general in charge of an army. Worse than ambivalence, they included the deadly sin of sloth, and it seemed as though the astonishing American victories at Trenton and Princeton had accentuated a natural indolence, making him keenly aware of the magnitude of his task and his own incapacity to carry it out.

Sir William loved his creature comforts and took them where he could find them. Often enough, according to the gossip, that was in company with Mrs. Joshua Loring, the handsome wife of Howe's compliant commissary of prisoners, who achieved considerable notoriety as his mistress. A popular bit of doggerel, from the pen of Francis Hopkinson, was relished by Americans:

> *Sir William, he, as snug as a flea*
> *Lay all this time a-snoring;*
> *Nor dreamed of harm, as he lay warm*
> *In bed with Mrs. Loring.*

The acerbic loyalist Justice Thomas Jones complained that the British could easily have driven the Americans from New Jersey during the winter, but "nothing could be done without the directions of the Commander-in-Chief, who was diverting himself in New York in feasting, gaming, banqueting, and in the arms of Mrs. Loring." The judge's tart comment on the arrangement between Howe and his commissary of prisoners was: "Joshua had a handsome wife. The General . . . was fond of her. Joshua made no objection. He fingered the cash, the General enjoyed Madam."

Snug and warm, the general hibernated in New York, indulging in too frequent gambling and too much alcohol while ignoring the existence of Washington's army only a few miles away. To be sure, distaste for a winter campaign was an accepted tradition of European armies, but it suited Howe's temperament admirably. He was accused by one American officer of being "too indolent and too ignorant for the command of such an army," but Major General Charles Lee, who was now Howe's prisoner, had harsher words, saying he was "totally confounded and stupefy'd by the immensity of the task impos'd upon him. He shut his eyes, fought his battles, drank his bottle, had his little Whore . . . shut his eyes [and] fought again."

Some years later, a fellow British officer wrote that while Sir William may have been fit to command a corps of grenadiers he simply was not up to the duties of a commander in chief. "His manners were sullen and ungracious," he went on, "with a dislike to business, and a propensity to pleasure. His staff officers were in general below mediocrity, with some of whom, and a few field officers, he passed too much of his time in private conviviality."

Howe was often criticized for orthodox handling of his army, a charge that is less than fair. To give him his due, he was an innovator in using light infantry as the most effective way to frustrate rebel snipers and prevent an ambush of the main body of the army. More important, the distance between England and America and the logistical problems that entailed demanded orthodoxy and would have been a crucial factor in any commander's calculations.

So Howe's would be a war of positions, a cautious, prudent war, and if the outcome proved inconclusive, less decisive than the total victory London expected, Howe was willing to take that chance. As for the length of time the army spent in winter quarters, his was an age when no one was in much of a hurry, when delay in all human affairs was normal, accepted by everyone. People whose activities were governed by weather realized that there was no overcoming nature, so it was expected that an army would go into winter quarters and hunker down until the roads were passable again and the sun dried out the fields on which battles would be fought. The reason Washington's attack in a blinding snowstorm on Christmas Eve had caught the Hessians so completely by surprise was that in Europe that sort of action simply was not contemplated.

Sir William knew as well as George Washington did that the side possessing the greatest strength at the decisive moment would win the war. Yet the American rebellion was quite a different conflict from any the government in London—or Howe—had experienced. Important as a general's success on the battlefield might be, what could tip the balance was the will of the people behind the lines. Short of foreign intervention, everything would hinge on how wholeheartedly the American populace supported the men on the firing line. Howe recognized this and as time went by spoke more and more often of how he would "raise the Provincials," by which he meant winning the active support of Americans who remained loyal to the king.

Howe's failure to act in that spring of 1777 was one matter. Quite another was his unwillingness to recognize that the capture of Philadelphia, beyond its potential psychological impact on rebels and loyalists, could not in itself determine the outcome of the war. In strategic as well as geographic terms, it led nowhere. To win, which is what London expected its commanding general to do in 1777, he must destroy Washington's army, and seizing a piece of real estate—no matter how valuable—was no way to achieve that.

So while the ultimate destination of General Howe's army was still far from clear, the several options open to the enemy preyed on Washington's mind throughout that spring. What nagged him incessantly when he wasn't worrying about Philadelphia was the fear that the isolated defenses far to the north on Lake Champlain might fall to a British force based in Canada. From his perspective, the enemy's ability to split the colonies in two hinged on whether the Americans could hold Ticonderoga and the several strongpoints in the Hudson Highlands. Even if Howe should head for Pennsylvania, Washington reasoned that he would leave enough troops in New York to push north and effect a junction with another army moving down from Canada, especially if no Americans on the Hudson or the lakes could stop them.

If George Washington was in a quandary it was simply because he had not a scrap of hard evidence to indicate what his opponents planned to do. Indeed, nothing reveals the American commander in chief's backing and filling on this matter more clearly than his correspondence during the first half of 1777. Late in January, a letter arrived at headquarters from General Philip Schuyler, voicing his fear that the British might attempt a winter attack on Ticonderoga over the ice. Washington was sufficiently impressed by this warning that he urged the authorities in Massachusetts, New Hampshire, and Connecticut to expedite the departure of troops to Lake Champlain, and on February 9 sent word to Schuyler, expressing the hope that these reinforcements would be adequate to stop Carleton.

A fortnight later his view of the situation changed and he wrote Schuyler again, predicting that Carleton "would not attempt to pass the Lakes until spring, if then. . . . " Mid-March found him speculating that the British would shift troops from Canada by sea to join Howe in an attack on Philadelphia, so he decided to concentrate at Peekskill the New England regiments recruited during the winter for duty at Ticonderoga. From that point, he figured, they could move in any direction where troops were needed and would be in a better position to support him against Howe.

Then he learned that an enemy raiding party had disembarked from ships in the Hudson and gone ashore at Peekskill, forcing the rebels there to burn their stores. Fearful that this might be the first of similar attacks aimed at taking the Hudson forts, in which event Ticonderoga could no longer be supplied from the south, Washington again called for reinforcements, only to discover that the New England regiments on which he was counting were at half strength or less.

On April 28, British raiders suddenly appeared in Danbury, Connecticut, destroying a number of buildings and a quantity of irreplaceable military stores, including almost seventeen hundred tents, the loss of which meant that the Ticonderoga garrison had to make do with old ones that were worn almost beyond redemption. Too late, the redcoats were driven off by militiamen and a few Continentals and harassed on their retreat by the ubiquitous Benedict Arnold and General David Wooster, who received a mortal wound. The immediate effect of this successful attack on a town that was supposedly too far inland to be at risk was to increase the New England states' reluctance to send their militia to Peekskill, let alone to Ticonderoga. Indeed, when members of Washington's staff heard reports that the British army in Canada was on the move, some of them shook their heads, certain that the post on Lake Champlain was doomed.

Washington began a March 12 letter to Schuyler with a brief catechism on strategy and a few admonitions, probably to make clear to the general in Albany that he was unlikely to get the men and equipment he wanted. Any "injudicious division" of the army should be avoided, Washington said. Further, it was manifestly impossible to guard against all the unexpected moves the enemy might make. Schuyler should be aware, however, that the commander in chief hoped to make "a capital stroke in the early part of the season," which would entail merging the New England troops with those of the other states. (Yet surely Washington knew that talk of "a capital stroke" was so much bravado, for within two weeks he was writing the President of Congress to say, "I have no men to oppose the Enemy's designs in any one Quarter, altho' called upon from every Quarter.")

Given his opinion that any attempt by the British to force their way up Lake Champlain to the Hudson was highly improbable, it would be fool-hardy to assemble too large a force at Ticonderoga, Washington argued, for if the enemy did *not* come that way, the troops would be of no use to anyone and the main army would suffer from their absence. Moreover, he informed Schuyler, "It will signify nothing to have our frontiers guarded, while the Enemy are ranging at large in the Heart of the Country."

Sometime before April 2, Washington's spies told him that the British were trying to locate pilots who knew the Delaware River, lending cre-dence to the possibility that they would move on Philadelphia by sea. Shortly afterward he learned that the redcoats stationed in and around Brunswick, New Jersey, had been stripping boards from buildings and cutting timber, probably to make berths for troops and stalls for horses aboard the transports. That prompted a warning to Major General Thomas Mifflin in Philadelphia, urging him to strengthen the city's defenses and those downriver. A further indication that Howe was bound for Philadelphia was the news that the British were constructing trans-port vessels and a pontoon bridge, to be supported by flat-bottomed boats, presumably designed for a river crossing.

Then, out of the blue, came word of an entirely new and unsuspected menace. Arthur Lee, who was working for Congress in Paris in an effort to bring about an alliance with France, had learned from an unnamed source that "Boston was certainly to be attacked in the spring, and that Burgoyne was to command." Lee had notified the Secret Committee of Congress of the rumor, and the committee informed the commander in chief and the authorities in Massachusetts, thoroughly alarming the latter and giving them second thoughts about sending troops to Peekskill or Ticonderoga when they might be needed at home.

Fortunately for Washington, the hearsay proved false, probably having been planted by the British in hopes of diverting attention from their real aims. It appears, however, to have been his first intimation that the man known as "Gentleman Johnny" Burgoyne might have a command in America.

May brought word that trouble was brewing in Canada, where an army was supposedly massing "to pass the Lake and attack Ticonderoga before our force is assembled to meet them," as Washington reported to Major General William Heath. "Whether it is authentic, I cannot say," the commander in chief observed to Major General Alexander McDougall in the Highlands, "but if [Carleton] means an attack on Ticonderoga, I am persuaded, Genl. Howe will not go to Philadelphia, but will endeavour to co-operate with him." He told McDougall to scour his neighborhood for provisions that would be needed if the main army had to march north, and warned Massachusetts legislators of "the necessity of straining every nerve," reminding them of "almost irreparable consequences" if Ticonderoga were to fall, leaving the road open for a strike into New England.

Washington's artillerist, Henry Knox, had yet another version of what was to happen. Writing to his friend Harry Jackson, he announced that Burgoyne, "with 10000 new rais'd Germans and 3000 British," would attack Boston while Howe moved against Philadelphia, to be joined there by Carleton, after he had dealt with Ticonderoga.

But the very next day, May 5, an officer who had left Albany on April 29 informed Washington that the rumors of a British advance were premature. Not even Anthony Wayne, commanding at Ticonderoga, was aware of such a move, he said. In fact, Wayne was so buoyed by the arrival of three thousand fresh troops, all but nine of whom were said to be in high spirits and health, that he vowed the fort "could never be carried, without the loss of much blood."

As May turned to June, intelligence from New York poured into Middle Brook every day, indicating that Howe's legions were stirring at last. A large fleet, upward of one hundred sail, stood out to sea, while eighteen transports disgorged what appeared to be foreign troops, to judge from their uniforms. Whether these men had arrived from Germany or Canada could not be ascertained, but the realization that Howe was receiving reinforcements was not reassuring. Meanwhile, wagonloads of redcoats from New York suddenly appeared in Amboy.

The only good news to come Washington's way was from Major General Horatio Gates in Albany. Gates had said nothing to his commanding officer concerning the purported British movement up the lake, but now he forwarded a report from Captain Benjamin Whitcomb of the New Hampshire rangers stating that enemy troops had been seen at Split Rock, but had then sailed back down the lake. It was Gates's opinion that the alarm over the enemy's approach to Ticonderoga was groundless.

June 20 was an unusually busy day in Middle Brook, with messengers leaving headquarters throughout the morning, clattering out of the village with letters from Washington to Congress, the Board of War, and Schuyler, and when the commander in chief was not dictating to one of his secretaries he reviewed court-martial sentences, approving seven convictions and a single acquittal.

That same day he received a letter from Schuyler suggesting that the enemy had changed plans, "or at least rendered them dark and mysterious," prompting Washington to order McDougall's and Glover's divisions to remain at Peekskill, while Putnam was told to have four regiments ready to march to Schuyler's aid if needed. On the commander in chief's own front, Howe was threatening, attempting three times within a fortnight to lure the Americans into battle, but Washington was too canny to risk falling into a trap.

Then Howe suddenly gave up, marched back to Amboy, and ferried his troops to Staten Island. For the first time in eight months, New Jersey was free of redcoats, yet for Washington, the maddening riddle remained: would Howe head north to join the Canadian army, or move on Philadelphia?

Chapter 4

To Effect a Junction
with Howe's Force

On December 3, 1776, an elderly American dressed in plain clothes and a fur cap and accompanied by his two grandsons—one who looked to be about seventeen, the other seven—stepped ashore at Auray, on the east coast of Brittany. They had arrived on the armed sloop *Reprisal*, which also brought two British prizes into Quiberon Bay, and although the old gentleman was so weak he could barely stand, he and the boys departed almost immediately by carriage for Nantes. The only bright spot in an otherwise miserable four-day ride through fields and woods infested with highwaymen was a passing glance the grandfather had of half a dozen pretty country women with white-and-red complexions, one of whom he described as "the fairest woman I ever beheld."

The observation was vintage Benjamin Franklin, and his sudden appearance in France was equally in character. He had been selected by Congress for yet another secret mission—this time to join Silas Deane and Arthur Lee as a commissioner, or emissary, to the court of Louis XVI, where, it was hoped, the three of them might pry loose additional money, arms, and military supplies and negotiate an alliance. During his few days in Nantes, wildly enthusiastic crowds of well-wishers and French friends of America, some of whom realized that Franklin would have risked being hanged for treason if the *Reprisal* had been captured by the British, paid homage to the famous philosopher and revolutionary and gave a dinner and a ball in his honor. Meanwhile, rumors of his presence on the Continent flew ahead, alerting Parisians who could hardly wait for his arrival in that city.

On the afternoon of December 9, the Monday after Franklin set foot in France, Major General John Burgoyne, following a six-week crossing from Quebec, landed at Portsmouth. He boarded a stage for London, was bounced and jostled over what a contemporary called "a curséd string of hills and holes," and at noon on the following day was in the office of Lord George Germain, Secretary of State for the Colonies.

This visit formalized the end of Burgoyne's second tour of duty in America, in both of which he served in subordinate roles—in 1775 under Thomas Gage in Boston and more recently with Guy Carleton in Canada. Now he wanted an important command of his own, and he knew as well as any man how certain things were made to happen in eighteenth-century England. At the very pinnacle of the power pyramid was the King's Household, which dispensed most of the favors, in the form of places, or positions, that meant additional income, social status, political leverage, and, above all, recognition at court. While some of these places were the most flagrant sinecures, the office held by Lord George Germain was decidedly not—not when you considered that he was responsible for Britain's immense colonial empire and, in this crucial hour, was in charge of the war in America. He was in fact one of several ministers of the king who could be said to control the nation's destiny.

The King's Household was a tight inner circle, an informal group that frequently met at dinner for important discussions. Once a decision was made, the minister whose responsibility it was had to plead his case before the king—not an easy task when the sovereign was intransigent and obstinate, not very bright, and absolutely certain that the authority of crown and Parliament was sacred ground, unalterable and unchallengeable. "I wish nothing but good," said George III, "therefore anyone who does not agree with me is a traitor and a scoundrel." If not white, black; it was as simple as that.

After the past summer's abortive campaign on Lake Champlain, Burgoyne had received permission from Guy Carleton to return to England because of pressing personal matters. Charlotte, his "invaluable partner" for twenty-five years of marriage, had died while he was in Canada, a shattering blow that had a serious effect on his mind and body. He was anxious to visit her grave in Westminster Abbey, where she had been laid to rest beside their only child—a daughter who died at the age of ten. Along with that, numerous family and financial matters demanded attention. But what brought the general to Whitehall on so urgent an errand was the knowledge that his reassignment would have to be reviewed and possibly argued with the king. The person to initiate and advance this advocacy process was Lord George Germain.

They made a curious pair, these two—the one vilified as a homosexual and a coward on the battlefield, now holding the reins that would determine the course of the war in North America; the other a popular soldier and playwright with a reputation for bonhomie, bravery, and risk-taking in combat, whose chances of getting an independent command rested in the hands of the man in whose Whitehall office he sat that wintry day.

A member of the powerful Sackville family, Lord George was the third son of the Duke of Dorset, and had come into a fortune upon the death of the childless Lady Betty Germain, who left him her estate on the condition that he take her name. So Lord George Germain he became.

At the age of sixty-one he was tall and still well-muscled if a trifle paunchy and "rather womanly," as one critic said, with blue eyes, an ugly beak of a nose, and a look of the melancholia that ran in the family: his oldest brother, who succeeded to the dukedom, was an eccentric loner; the next in line went mad. Germain gave people the impression of a cold, reserved, arrogant aristocrat, though it was said by those who knew him well that beneath the hauteur was an agreeable social companion and a good listener. He was without doubt an able administrator, though an irritable, impatient, unfailingly punctual one, a tough, demanding boss with numerous enemies, who was nevertheless much esteemed by his undersecretaries, one of whom noted that he had "no trash in his mind."

During his days as a soldier, Germain was wounded in action, cited for bravery, and promoted to major general during the Seven Years War. Money and powerful connections had facilitated a rapid advance, but his military career came to an abrupt and humiliating halt in 1759 in Germany, where, as leader of the British contingent at the battle of Minden, he misunderstood or misinterpreted his orders and refused to make a cavalry charge which might have turned a narrow-won victory into a rout. Prince Ferdinand of Brunswick, his commanding officer and a kinsman of the British monarch, rebuked him severely, and upon his return to England Germain was dismissed from the army. He demanded—and eventually got—a court-martial, which rejected accusations of cowardice and instead found him guilty of disobedience. The gravity of that charge was evident when it became known that the court narrowly decided against a death sentence, after which he was declared unfit to serve His Majesty George II in any military capacity whatever. The king, determined to punish him further, stripped him of his rank and ordered that the court-martial sentence be read to every regiment in the army. Notwithstanding the judges' decision, he was known thereafter as "the Coward of Minden," and even after George II's grandson, George III, who despised the ministers he inherited from his grandfather, appointed him as one of his principal secretaries of state, the Whig opposition in the House of Commons baited him mercilessly over the Minden affair.

Germain and young George III saw eye to eye on how to correct the situation in America: both wanted to go for the jugular. From the royal point of view, the great fear was that the rebellion in America would set off a reaction like the fall of a row of dominoes, with the West Indies becoming dependent on America and the Irish seeking independence, so that "this island reduced to itself, would be a poor island indeed." His Majesty referred frequently to the colonists as "my unhappy people," suffering from delusion and oppressed by daring, desperate leaders. If the rebellion was not put down, he said, "much mischief must grow from it," spreading to other, loyal colonies, to "the present system of all Europe," and with devastating effects on "the commerce of my Kingdoms." In a speech to Parliament at the end of October 1776 he expressed regret at the great expense that would be necessary to subdue the Americans but reminded his listeners that what was at issue was the honor of the crown and the rights of Parliament. His sole object, he went on, was to promote the true interest of all his subjects, who should realize that "no people ever enjoyed more happiness or lived under a milder Government than those now revolted Provinces."

On the eve of the conflict, just before the battles of Lexington and Concord, George III declared: "I am not sorry that the line of conduct seems now chalked out," adding, "Blows must decide." Lord George was in complete agreement. Not only did he applaud the decision to raise a large army to put down the uprising, he urged that the blow be swift and decisive. "As there is not common sense in protracting a war of this sort," he wrote, "I should be for exerting the utmost force of this Kingdom to finish the rebellion in one campaign."

Those were the sentiments of a majority of Britons, who had a hard time understanding the provincials' attitude. At the root of the dispute was money, of course: Great Britain's national debt was a staggering £150 million, largely caused by the Seven Years War, and the already heavily taxed Englishman felt that his American cousins, who had benefited hugely from the victory over France, should bear a fair share of the resulting financial burden.

A belief that the war to put down the rebellion would be quickly and easily won was an article of faith in most British military and political circles. A major on duty in Boston, writing home a month before the shots rang out on Lexington Green, stated confidently: "I am satisfied that one active campaign, a smart action, and burning two or three of their towns, will set everything to rights." That assurance was born of the generally low estimation of the American as a fighter; he was "a very effeminate thing, very unfit for and very impatient of war," according to General James Murray, who had once served as commander in North America. And the great General James Wolfe, before his death at Quebec, had pronounced the independent Yankees, who seldom took kindly to orders, "the worst soldiers in the universe." The unprincipled, inefficient Earl of Sandwich, who would direct the British navy during seven years of war, rose in the House of Lords to ask, "Suppose the Colonies do abound in men, what does that signify? They are raw, undisciplined, cowardly men. I wish instead of forty or fifty thousand of these *brave* fellows they would produce in the field at least two hundred thousand; the more the better, the easier would be the conquest; if they did not run away, they would starve themselves into compliance with our measures. . . . "*

Unhappily for relations between mother country and colonies, optimism begat more optimism, arrogance more arrogance. Germain's unbending conviction and his position as colonial secretary in this time of crisis soon put him second in importance in the administration only to Lord North, the prime minister, and it is worth noting that for as long as the war continued he alone would support the king's policy of coercion. North was at heart a dove, but Germain was never anything but a hawk on the question of how to deal with the colonies. He had been appointed to office because of his apparent ability at a time when the administration had few such men, and his very presence made it clear that British sovereignty would be upheld by force.

Early in 1776, when Admiral Richard Howe and his brother William, the general, were appointed commissioners to negotiate a peace with the rebel leaders, Germain disagreed vigorously, calling it a "sentimental

---

*Edward Harvey, the adjutant general who was acting commander in chief of the British army, did not agree. Before news of Bunker Hill reached England, Harvey wrote a fellow officer: " . . . it is impossible to conquer [America] with our British army. . . . To attempt to conquer it internally by our land force is as wild an idea as ever controverted common sense." To another he confided that "our army will be destroyed by damned driblets," and grumbled that "America is an ugly job . . . a damned affair indeed."

manner of making war," and insisted that the government refuse to begin talks unless the Americans first acknowledged the supremacy of Parliament, which was the concession above all others they were unwilling to make. He maintained, "It was necessary that the intentions of Parliament be complied with." And to no one's surprise the attempt at conciliation went nowhere.

Germain was responsible for grand strategy, which included the staggering logistical task of assembling supplies and transporting them to America, determining how Britain's resources would be employed and distributed to the various theaters of war, and appointing the field commanders. Unfortunately for the effectiveness of those commanders, Lord George regarded it as his prerogative to give them detailed instructions on how to conduct their campaigns. General Carleton, who was no admirer of the colonial secretary, would write in disgust that it was the height of arrogance and folly for ministers in London "to direct operations of war in a country at three thousand miles' distance, of which they have so little knowledge as not to be able to distinguish between good, bad, or interested advice, or to give positive orders upon matters which from their nature are ever on the change."

As the events of 1777 were to reveal, Germain had no real comprehension or appreciation of the distances and natural obstacles an army would encounter in America. By comparison, French awareness of the transatlantic wilderness was far more extensive than that of most Englishmen; one of Louis XVI's officers told Charles James Fox that a well-trained European army might well conquer the people of America, but the country of America was unconquerable. And France's foreign minister, the Comte de Vergennes, predicted in the summer of 1775 that "it will be vain for the British to multiply their forces" in the colonies; "no longer can they bring that vast continent back to dependence by force of arms."

The sixty-year-old Vergennes was indefatigable and persevering in his duties, loyal to the hopelessly slow-witted young Louis XVI (who happily did have the wit to put foreign affairs into more capable hands), and from the beginning of May 1776 he had been quietly sending money to the Americans. He was encouraged in this by Silas Deane, who arrived in Paris at the end of June and informed him that the colonies would soon declare independence. Curiously, the significance of that declaration seems to have aroused no fear on the part of Louis XVI's officialdom, no thought of what it might portend for the vast and gorgeous theater of Versailles, where he and his glittering courtiers were onstage, fluttering about like butterflies while the peasantry suffered and died in misery and squalor.

The salons of Paris, the fashionable world that was so captivated by Benjamin Franklin, had been entranced by the prophets of change—Voltaire, Montesquieu, Rousseau, and others—and embraced the American revolutionaries in a spirit of goodwill for humankind, never dreaming that catastrophe might lie ahead. As a titled Frenchman put it, "We walked on a carpet of flowers, unconscious that it covered an abyss."

Vergennes was keenly aware that everything France had lost by the Peace of Paris in 1763 England had won, and he and his sovereign were driven by an insatiable craving for revenge to regain their nation's prestige. (For all her military setbacks, France remained *the* power on the Continent, unrivaled by any other.) As it became clear that what had first seemed to be a short-lived squabble between Britain and the American colonies was becoming a serious conflict, Vergennes concluded that it would be greatly to France's advantage to aid the rebels secretly with the materials of war as well as money.

In this he was abetted by his secret agent, Pierre Augustin Caron de Beaumarchais, whose talents included watchmaking, undercover work for the monarchy, and brilliant satires on the privileges and foibles of the upper class—*The Barber of Seville* and *Marriage of Figaro*, each of which served as the basis of an opera. Beaumarchais set up a bogus firm called Hortalez & Cie. Financed by a million livres from France, a like amount from Spain, and yet another million from French businessmen, this was the channel through which aid would be funneled to the rebel armies in America.

Seldom was Britain's problem better described than by Edmund Burke in his final, most eloquent appeal for reconciliation: "Three thousand miles of ocean lie between you and them. No contrivance can prevent the effect of this distance in weakening government. Seas roll, and months pass, between the order and the execution; and the want of a speedy explanation of a single point is enough to defeat a whole system."

Yet never for a moment did Germain doubt the soundness of his plans or opinions, and on one subject he was adamant. Along with many others, he was convinced that the loyalists in America might constitute as much as half the population of the colonies, which suggested that if only they could be rallied in support of the cause which was theirs as much as their government's, victory would result. Shortly after arriving in Boston in 1775, General William Howe had expressed the opinion that "the insurgents are very few, in comparison with the whole of the people," and this notion was shared by the administration. It was an article of faith that loyalists would play an important combat role and would govern and preserve order as soon as the British put down the rebellion and pulled out. To give Germain his due, he realized that the Royal Army alone was incapable of subduing the rebellion; he knew it would have to be reinforced with foreign troops and loyalist legions raised in America.

Before launching an all-out punitive action, the king and his advisers had to be dead certain they could count on the support of the English people, and this was settled to the administration's satisfaction in the wake of George III's speech to both houses of Parliament on October 26, 1775, in which he announced plans to suppress the insurrection with military might. When the angry debate on the issue finally ended, Lord North's ministry had an overwhelming majority of the vote, largely because independent members, most of them country gentlemen, believed firmly that the colonials must be taught a lesson and put in their place. This was all of a piece with Germain's characterization of town meetings in Massachusetts as "the proceedings of a tumultuous and riotous rabble, who ought, if they had the least prudence, to follow their mercantile employment and not trouble themselves with politics and government, which they do not understand."

Few, if any, asked if the king and his ministers might be wrong; none seemed concerned with what would be best for the empire; so the harsh measures of the administration were set in motion, despite eloquent voices in favor of sanity and moderation that were raised in opposition. Those voices belonged to Whig leaders who were out of power and out of favor—Edmund Burke, Charles James Fox, the Earl of Chatham, and John Wilkes, among others—and for some years to come would prove futile. A discouraged Burke noted that "it was almost in vain to contend, for the country gentlemen had abandoned their duty, and placed an implicit confidence in the Minister." And so it was that after the battle of Bunker Hill the government took what appeared to be the easy way out and settled for war.

As far as Germain was concerned, a year and a half of fighting had produced spotty results. The British army had been chased out of

Boston; then Howe had waged a successful campaign in and around New York putting the rebels to flight across New Jersey. But an expedition against Charleston, South Carolina, planned by Germain's predecessor and undertaken by General Henry Clinton and Admiral Sir Peter Parker largely because the former royal governors in the south held out the will-o'-the-wisp of a loyalist uprising, was a miserable failure and a classic example of how the Atlantic Ocean and the distance between the two continents could make mockery of the best-laid plans.

And now here was Burgoyne, informing Germain—tactfully at first, in such a way as not to seem to be ratting on his commanding officer, then less so when it became apparent that Lord George shared his views—and making it unmistakably clear that Carleton had botched last summer's campaign when he had Ticonderoga all but in his grasp and then turned around and headed for Canada. Not only that: he left no garrison at Crown Point, which meant that the post would surely be reoccupied by the rebels and have to be taken again in the spring.

In a perverse way, the implications of this news were not altogether unwelcome. The colonial secretary's distaste for Carleton went much deeper than the disappointing events on Lake Champlain. Germain actively disliked and distrusted the general, in part because of a long-standing feud which may have had its genesis in Germain's conduct at Minden. One indication of Germain's animosity came after Thomas Gage, the commander in chief in America, was recalled from Boston in 1775, and Carleton was passed over in favor of William Howe. In August of the following year, Germain wrote Carleton, directing him to stay in Quebec while Burgoyne pursued the retreating rebels, but the messenger carrying the letter failed to get up the St. Lawrence before the river froze and returned to London without delivering the order. The result was that Carleton, unaware of Germain's wishes, led the operation himself. Burgoyne knew about that letter, knew that Lord George was looking to supplant Carleton again, and took pains to make it clear that he was the right man to take over the Northern Army. For his part, Germain was interested in his visitor precisely because he possessed many of the attributes Lord George found lacking in the man presently in charge in Canada—above all, fire in the belly.

Ambition was a driving force in Burgoyne's life, and he made no bones about it. When he wanted something badly and it looked as though he might not get it, he had not the slightest hesitation about suggesting that his wife's influential family connections could make life very difficult for anyone who stood in his path or failed to give his career a boost. He went so far as to remind two secretaries of war of his powerful friends—once when he was angling for a promotion, again when he wanted a chaplain, musicians, and an extra allowance for horses for his cavalry regiment—and in the end managed to have his way. In fairness, however, it must be said that this attitude was hardly unique to Burgoyne.

The British aristocracy was rich, it was powerful, and from its ranks, and its ranks only, had come the ruling class for as long as anyone could remember. Though this was changing, with many of the great entrepreneurs of the day—the makers of industrial revolution—clamoring for reform, it would be years before the programs they advocated took place. In the meantime the king's placeholders and the great landowners retained their firm grip on the army and navy, the church, and Parliament, behaving as if these were their rightful possessions by some sort of divine dispensation. Above all, they were against altering the status quo—which is why they found the upheaval in the American colonies so threatening.

The favoritism implicit in the system was particularly evident in the military, where a wealthy man could buy his son a commission, and even if the young officer never joined his regiment he drew his pay regularly and advanced in rank and seniority.

Burgoyne entered the army at fifteen and as a junior officer quickly acquired a taste for gambling, convivial drinking, and skill at card-playing that earned him a somewhat dubious reputation. By the age of twenty-two he was a captain with active service on the Continent under his belt and a certain notoriety as a womanizer and *bon vivant* in London, where he was an aficionado of the theater, knew most of the prominent actors and actresses of the day, and achieved a modest success as a playwright. In London, too, he met Lady Charlotte, the youngest daughter of the Earl of Derby, and they eloped because of her father's opposition to the match. Her parent was furious and unforgiving (probably because of the rumors of Burgoyne's illegitimacy, which may have been true), and Lady Charlotte and her husband suddenly found themselves with embarrassingly limited financial resources. Burgoyne was twenty-eight and his wife twenty-three—he a captain on pay that was inadequate to cover his gambling debts, let alone much of anything else. So he sold his commission, paid off some of his obligations,* and the couple sailed to France, where snobbish French aristocrats were delighted to entertain the daughter of an English earl and her dashing bridegroom. The Burgoynes remained on the Continent for more than six years before Lord Derby partially relented and grudgingly acquiesced in a reconciliation that ended their exile and brought them home.

Thanks to the renewal of his Derby connections, Burgoyne was able to purchase a captaincy in the 11th Dragoons in 1756, but the years abroad had cost him almost five years' seniority and he was acutely conscious that some of his former fellow officers were now lieutenant colonels. Eager for glory and recognition, he served in several abortive amphibious expeditions on the French coast, where he was favorably noticed for his composure under fire and his quick thinking and leadership, which averted one almost certain fiasco.

In 1759 he applied for command of the 16th Light Dragoons, and despite the opposition of Lord Barrington, then Secretary at War, the king approved his request, thanks to the backing of Lady Charlotte's family. That was the impetus Burgoyne's career needed, and the first move he made to raise a regiment in the neighborhood of Northampton suggests his imaginative and innovative approach to problems. Attracting officers was fairly easy, since a new regiment might open an avenue to a commission, but enlisting the rank and file was another matter altogether. Even in that heady year of triumphs there were few volunteers for service in the ranks, and the usual methods of rounding up recruits were bounties and impressment.

Burgoyne was nothing if not a promoter, he knew human nature, he was a serious thinker about military matters, and he hit on an idea that would be common practice more than two centuries later. Posters that were pasted up in Northampton and the surrounding villages evoked the glamour and excitement of service in a light cavalry regiment:

---

*Gambling, by rich and poor alike, was one of the curses of English society and the ruination of many a military officer. Excellent soldiers who were unlucky at cards were obliged to sell their commissions in order to pay their debts, often to be replaced by officers whose chief merit was that they had been more fortunate at the gaming table. Debtors' prisons were full of obsessive gamblers whose luck had run out; indeed, creditors hounded Burgoyne's father to King's Bench Prison, where he died. Burgoyne's friend Charles James Fox, a Whig member of Parliament, frittered away much of his patrimony at Brooks's Club, and General William Howe was a notorious gambler.

You will be mounted on the finest horses in the world, with superb clothing and the richest accoutrements; your pay and privileges are equal to two guineas a week; you are everywhere respected; your society is courted; you are admired by the fair, which, together with the chance of getting switched to a buxom widow, or of brushing a rich heiress, renders the situation truly enviable and desirable. Young men out of employment or uncomfortable, "There is a tide in the affairs of men, which, taken at the flood, leads on to fortune." Nick in instantly and enlist.

The quotation from Shakespeare and the breezy tone of the message were pure Burgoyne, and the campaign was a huge success, with so many recruits applying that two additional troops were authorized. Burgoyne quickly acquired the officers he sought, and promptly wrote for them a model code of behavior that was light-years ahead of its time.

Telling his junior officers that they should regard his instructions as the advice of a friend rather than as commands, he urged them to mingle and occasionally joke with the men in the ranks. In a total reversal of common practice, he suggested that the enforcement of discipline by flogging could be minimized if officers treated enlisted men as "thinking beings" rather than spaniels "trained . . . by the stick," and avoided cursing them for mistakes. His officers should read books about their profession, "write English with swiftness and accuracy," study mathematics, learn French (in which the best treatises on tactics were written), practice drawing, and get the hang of measuring distances by eye. And in what must have raised eyebrows in every regiment in the army, he advised them to learn the work of their grooms—"to accoutre and bridle a horse themselves until they are thoroughly acquainted with the use of each strap and buckle."

His troopers were soon calling him "Gentleman Johnny"—a term of genuine fondness—and the unit that became known as Burgoyne's Light Horse demonstrated the effectiveness of his training in 1762 as part of an Anglo-German force sent to assist Portugal in its war with Spain. Burgoyne led three thousand men, including his regiment, in a victory at Valencia de Alcantara and later surprised a Spanish force at Villa Velha, bringing off a number of prisoners and cannon. It was a brief and relatively unimportant campaign, but the gallant commander, who had been elected *in absentia* a member of the House of Commons thanks to a friend who owned several pocket boroughs, was greeted as a hero and received the gratitude of the House upon his return from Portugal.

In a day when an officer without money or influence might spend his entire career as a lieutenant, Burgoyne vaulted from captain to colonel in less than four years and was gazetted colonel of the 16th Light Dragoons, a lifetime appointment that was probably worth £3,000 a year.

A sure mark of distinction or money or—in this particular instance—upward mobility was to have your portrait painted by Sir Joshua Reynolds, and what the artist saw when Colonel John Burgoyne struck a pose for him was about equal parts good looks and panache. The foremost London portraitist of the fashionable painted his sitter in the regimental uniform of the 16th Light Dragoons—scarlet coat with gold piping and epaulets, mouse-colored waistcoat and breeches, a black stock at his throat, white lace at the cuffs. Heightening the drama on the canvas, the figure in scarlet stands erect against a background of threatening dark clouds scudding across a smoky battle scene in which armies are engaged on a vast field of combat. This is the warrior in his prime, an impressive, confident soldier of the king with dark curly hair and large brown eyes, holding one hand on his left hip while the other balances his saber. The face wears a serious, determined look, yet something about the expression hints that the colonel might possibly break into a smile. It is a clue that gives a lift to the portrait, a suggestion that here is a man of humor and understanding despite all the trappings of war.

During Burgoyne's first years in Parliament, the quarrel between Britain and her colonies became a festering sore that finally burst on April 19, 1775. As the tension rose, his was consistently a voice of moderation, urging restraint. (On the floor of the House and elsewhere he tended to be a rather pompous, prolix speaker; one of his orations prompted a fellow member to wonder if he did not belong "rather to the heavy than the light horse.") But shortly after news of Lexington and Concord reached England and the attitude toward the colonies hardened perceptibly, Burgoyne was hooted down in the House when he stated his opinion that "where the error of her ways was concerned, America could be convinced by persuasion and not by the sword."

He and William Howe were not the only military men reluctant to take the field against the rebels. General Jeffrey Amherst turned down an appointment as commander in chief on grounds of age, but the truth lay in his unwillingness to take sides; and Admiral Augustus Keppel flatly rejected any command that would require him to fight the Americans. "I cannot draw the sword in such a cause," he wrote.

When the triumvirate of generals—Burgoyne, Howe, and Clinton—were ordered to America in the wake of Lexington and Concord, each went with serious misgivings. Howe, after publicly informing his constituents that he would under no circumstance accept a command that forced him to fight the colonists, received word that he was to sail to America and asked if this was a request or an order. It was the latter, he was told, and off he went in the company of Burgoyne and Henry Clinton (who allowed years later that "I was not a volunteer in that war. I was ordered by my Sovereign and I obeyed"). Their departure was the occasion for an acid comment by the gossipy Horace Walpole: "Howe was one of those brave, silent brothers, and was reckoned sensible, though so silent that nobody knew whether he was or not. Burgoyne had offered himself to this service; but he was a vain, very ambitious man, with a half-understanding that was worse than none; Clinton had not that fault, for he had no sense at all." The event also provoked some merriment: "Our Generals may terrify the enemy," one wag declared; "they certainly terrify me." And when they arrived in Boston aboard HMS *Cerberus*, they were greeted by yet another piece of mockery:

> *Behold the* Cerberus *the Atlantic plow,*
> *Her precious cargo, Burgoyne, Clinton, Howe,*
> *Bow, wow, wow!*

Burgoyne's future involvement with those two colleagues and Guy Carleton had to be very much on his mind as he sat talking with Lord George Germain. Almost inevitably, an undercurrent of friction and jealousy marred the relationship between the four generals. The other three outranked Burgoyne, although he was older than any of them. Having replaced Gage as commander in chief, Howe was senior officer present in North America and certainly would continue to head the main army, since he was very much in favor in London on the strength of the string of victories he had won with relatively few casualties (news of Trenton and Princeton not having arrived yet in England). That made Clinton the most likely candidate to replace Carleton. And it meant that Burgoyne would probably return to America as deputy either to Howe or to Clinton, neither of which prospects he relished. His inferior position on his two earlier tours in the colonies continued to nettle him (he described his role under Carleton as "a secondary station in a secondary command"), and now he wanted to run his own show—an important one.

Burgoyne always maintained that he said nothing in his December 10 meeting or other conversations with Germain to undermine Carleton, but it stretches belief that he avoided criticism, direct or indirect, when his own interests were so intimately involved. He was energetic, vain, and pushy, with a history of promoting his claim to a higher position, often at the expense of the incumbent. Writing to Clinton in November, for example, he had expressed disapproval of Carleton's decision to abandon Crown Point, saying that the retreat to Canada had wasted "the fruits of our summer's labor and autumn victory." Then he added: "I must honor Carleton's abilities and judgement, I have lived with him upon the best terms & bear him friendship—I am therefore doubly hurt that he had taken a step in which I can be no otherwise serviceable to him than by silence." Those were hardly the words of a loyal subordinate, and there is no reason to suppose that he kept silent on this subject when he spoke to Germain.

Burgoyne had in his possession a letter from the aggrieved General William Phillips, artillerist on Carleton's expedition. Writing in October, Phillips reported the rebels in a panic, "the Royalists [i.e., the Tories] . . . all waiting with eager impatience for assistance," and what did Carleton do but abandon Crown Point and return to Canada for the winter. Whether or not Burgoyne showed that letter to Germain, the word he brought to the minister was that Carleton had thought it inexpedient to attack Ticonderoga and had vacated Crown Point. That was the sort of message that could influence the man in charge to consider another officer for the important northern command—specifically, an enterprising major general with experience in America and ideas about how the war could be won.

In addition to whatever innuendos he let fall concerning Carleton, Burgoyne doubtless reminded Germain of a memorandum he had written a year earlier. At that time, he submitted to the cabinet an impressive study with the title "Reflections upon the War in America." The paper advocated the use of mobile battalions of infantry and equally mobile artillery as a means of rooting out rebels from their hiding places in the woods and swamps and behind stone walls, in terrain where every American soldier was "his own general, who will turn every tree and bush into a kind of temporary fortress, from whence, when he hath fired his shot with all the deliberation, coolness, and certainty which hidden safety inspires, he will skip as it were to the next, and so on for a long time until dislodged either by cannon or by a resolute attack by light infantry." In short, the ordered, serried ranks customary in European-style fighting simply would not work in America—a lesson Burgoyne remembered all too well from the slaughter he had witnessed on Breed's Hill—and his characterization of the Americans' mode of fighting was as shrewd an appraisal as it was prophetic.

Burgoyne also brought to his meeting with Lord George a letter from Carleton, which the colonial secretary promptly forwarded to the king with a curt note: "Sir Guy Carleton's letter by which your Majesty perceives he has abandoned Crown Point." The king needed no reminder of his minister's hostility toward the general and at once warned Lord North that Germain was angling to recall or censure Carleton. He would not have that, he added; it "would be cruel." Nevertheless, he agreed with Lord George that the recent campaign had been conducted in too leisurely a manner and that the coming expedition from Canada should be in the hands of a more aggressive officer. "Burgoyne may command the corps to be sent from Canada to Albany," the king concluded.

The aspirant to that job knew nothing of this, of course. Christmas Day found him at Brooks's Club, in the company of his good friend Charles James Fox, and an entry was made in the club's betting book recording his wager of fifty guineas with Fox that he would return victorious from America one year hence. On New Year's Day of 1777—the Year of the Hangman, named for the series of 7's resembling the gibbets that would be active when the rebellion was crushed—Burgoyne wrote Germain, telling him he was leaving London for Bath on the advice of his physician, to take the waters and restore his health and state of mind. Before departing he had had an audience with the king, to whom he mentioned his holiday plans, and, on the assumption that arrangements for the next campaign might be discussed and perhaps decided while he was relaxing at the spa, "I humbly laid myself at his Majesty's feet for such active employment as he might think me worthy of." He hoped he had Germain's support, he added.

Not all Burgoyne's time at the spa was spent frivolously, mingling with the tony crowd. When he was not at the gaming tables or the baths he worked on a detailed position paper entitled "Thoughts for Conducting the War from the Side of Canada," which he intended to set before Lord George on his return to London.

As part of this new proposal he sketched out a plan of action that proved to be the basis of the campaign of 1777, recommending that an army in New York head north and join forces with an army moving south from Canada. This would capitalize on the relative ease of transportation afforded by the great Hudson-Champlain waterway while at the same time severing the New England states from the rest of the country. The plan was not original with Burgoyne, although he had mentioned it to Lord Rochford in 1775. Others had proposed the idea previously—among them Gage, Howe, and Lord Dartmouth. But what mattered now was that Burgoyne had several distinct advantages going for him. One was Germain's visceral dislike of Carleton. Another was Burgoyne's unquestioned drive and the likelihood that he would wage an aggressive campaign. Ambitious Burgoyne might be, but Germain knew it was a mistake to write him off as an adventurer and opportunist, as many did. He was also a serious thinker about military strategy and tactics, as could be seen from his "Reflections." Then there was his experience in America and his familiarity with Canada and the country around Lake Champlain. But what counted most, he was Johnny-on-the-spot. And if ever the signs were right for the campaign Burgoyne advocated, it was at the end of 1776, with New York and Canada firmly in British hands. The stage was set, but it remained to be seen what part Gentleman Johnny would play in the drama.

Meanwhile, Germain had received several letters from General Howe, written in the autumn of 1776, outlining his intentions for the coming year, and these were to have a profound effect on the 1777 campaign. The first was dated October 9 and repeated Howe's earlier notion of beginning the next campaign by "opening a communication with Canada," which meant taking control of the Hudson River. This, he went on to say, would be his "primary object," since it would enable him to attack "the heart of the rebellion" in New England, a move that was certain to please the king.

In a second letter, written on November 30, while George Washington and his army of ragamuffins were retreating across New Jersey, Howe requested reinforcements for the task ahead. In what came as a shocker to Germain he said he would need an additional fifteen thousand men, bringing his total force to thirty-five thousand rank and file, in order "to finish the war in one year." Ten thousand of them would be employed in what he apparently regarded as the key campaign—the advance up the Hudson, toward a junction with the Northern Army. Five thousand were to remain in New York. Another ten thousand, based in Providence, would attack Boston, while two thousand others would remain in Rhode Island for its defense. Finally, eight thousand were to cover

New Jersey, hold Washington in check, and "give a jealousy" to (by which he meant threaten) Philadelphia. It was, for Howe, an uncharacteristically dynamic strategy for a two-pronged strike—along the Hudson-Champlain waterway and against Boston—designed to end the rebellion where it began, in New England. Almost half of Howe's army would be allocated to New York and the Hudson, while the movement toward Philadelphia was envisioned as little more than a red herring.

Howe was a conniver—a political general who carefully assessed every plan, every move, from the standpoint of its potential effect on his rivals, real or imagined. By the time he wrote this letter to Germain he knew that Burgoyne was returning to England, where he would surely promote his own interests, probably angling for command of the Northern Army. That was hardly a prospect that Howe viewed with enthusiasm, and when he wrote again to Germain the letter was almost certainly motivated in part by a desire to prevent the dashing Gentleman Johnny from getting that post. Sir William preferred to have him in New York, where he could keep an eye and a short leash on him while Clinton—whom he despised—would be sent to Canada and be out of his hair.

By December 20, when he wrote a third letter to Germain, Howe had changed his mind. By then he apparently realized that his plan of November 30 was overambitious, his demands for reinforcements unrealistic and, since Washington had retreated beyond the Delaware, maybe unnecessary, since all Howe would have to do was march on the rebel capital and defeat Washington, who would be obliged to defend the city. "The opinions of people being much changed in Philadelphia," he noted optimistically, "and their minds in general . . . disposed to peace, in which sentiment they would be confirmed by our getting possession of Philadelphia, I am . . . persuaded the principal Army should act offensively on that side, where the enemy's chief strength will certainly be collected."

Implicit in this message was the chimera of loyalist strength, on which he would rely once he reached Pennsylvania, but the crux was that the British forces under his command—except those involved in the Philadelphia operation—would now in effect be on the defensive. It was a complete about-face from the strategy he had outlined on November 30, and it included a fateful aside that should have put Germain on guard: "We must not look for the Northern Army to reach Albany before the middle of September," he commented. "Of course the subsequent operations of that corps will depend upon the state of things at the time."

Those three letters were written before events, in the form of Washington's victories at Trenton and Princeton, upset Howe's calculations and his peace of mind. The battles in New Jersey had already been lost before his letters of November 30 and December 20 reached England, which meant that Germain could assess the several proposals only in terms of the conditions prevailing in America before rebel forces dramatically altered the situation. It should have been a stern reminder of Burke's warning of how the Atlantic's expanse dictated that months could pass between an order and its execution.

To exacerbate the time factor, Howe's letter of November 30 was lodged on Lord George's desk for two weeks before he answered it on January 14, and then his response was to reduce by one-half the general's request for additional troops. Germain's letter took seven long weeks to cross the ocean, and when Howe read it, he was furious. But far more significant than his emotional reaction was his assumption that since he would be reinforced only sparingly, he would revert to his December 20 proposal, which limited offensive operations to the attack on Philadelphia. When these intentions became public knowledge, Horace Walpole's comment to a friend was, "The conquest of America is put off to the millennium. It is hoped, and then supposed, that General Howe is gone to take some place, or beat some army. That is more practicable than dodging Washington."

While this was going on, General Henry Clinton was on his way home to London, and he, too, was angry at Germain because his failed attack on Charleston had been belittled by the press as a defeat. Following that action, he had been largely responsible for a brilliant tactical maneuver which made possible Howe's triumph on Long Island, and he had captured Rhode Island in a bloodless campaign. Neither of these successes, he believed, had brought him the praise he deserved.

Clinton was a study in morbid sensitivity, a victim of his own uncertainties. A small man with a banty rooster's eagerness to pick a fight when he felt his ability was being questioned, he was touchy, hypersensitive (a "shy bitch," he once called himself), easily depressed, irritable, petulant—afflicted, in other words, with myriad idiosyncrasies that made him few friends and numerous enemies. Clinton had been at Minden and was well aware of Germain's performance there, and he stood in no awe of the man. But Lord George was forewarned and forearmed: he had heard that Clinton would soon be arriving, and before the general could begin haranguing him or possibly even challenge him to a duel, he sent an aide to meet him at Portsmouth and deliver a letter ringing with praise for his performance in America and entreating him to return there, where his presence was badly needed.

Clinton was not so easily distracted from the motives that had brought him to England. He wanted atonement for the grievance he was nursing over the slurs on his handling of the Charleston expedition, and he was determined not to serve again under William Howe. Unless he was given an assignment commensurate with what he considered his due, he was thinking of resigning. Again, Germain was ready for him.

In an interview between the two, Germain glowingly described a conversation he had had with the king. His Majesty had not yet decided when or in what capacity Clinton should return to America, he reported, but wanted the general to know how highly he regarded his recent conduct there. Lord George said he had urged the king to take note publicly of Clinton's accomplishments, suggesting that "none [would be] so proper as the red ribbon." That was the Order of the Bath, which carried with it knighthood, and according to the general's record of the conversation, Germain emphasized that "my Family, Rank & Character intitled me to it." The two men parted company, he added, Lord George with "a thousand civil one two threes, & I as many polite four five sixes."

A deal had been struck, with Clinton agreeing to cross the Atlantic once again in return for the honorific "Sir" before his name. On grounds of seniority he had a claim to the command of the Canadian army, but to the relief of Burgoyne and Germain he did not press for it, possibly out of respect for Carleton. (As Horace Walpole wrote of the bargain, "General Clinton was pacified by a super-numerary red ribbon—a paltry way of retrieving his honor, which he had come so far to vindicate.") Surprisingly, until February 24, George III was under the impression that Lord George would nominate Clinton to command the army in Canada, with Burgoyne to serve as Howe's deputy—an arrangement the king endorsed—but the day after Clinton's meeting with Germain the cabinet made an astonishing about-face and gave command of the Northern Army to Burgoyne, obliging Clinton to serve once again as Howe's deputy. Almost certainly, this decision turned on Germain's assessment that since the king would not tolerate the removal of Carleton, a man of Burgoyne's energy and daring might supply the fire that was missing from Carleton's makeup, a flame that was so essential for victory. And he had contrived to arrange matters so that Carleton would have nothing to do with the campaign and might even resign.

Yet there may have been more here than met the eye. All things considered, it was probably lucky for Burgoyne's aspirations that Clinton *did* return home that winter, for he was so peevish, endlessly complaining, forever taking offense or sensing a slight, that the thought of his continuing presence in London may have been too much for the king and his colonial secretary to bear. Knighted or not, Sir Henry was his own worst enemy, and it is tempting to suspect that one complaint too many sent him back across the Atlantic as Howe's deputy.

On February 28, Burgoyne was back at his London house on Hertford Street and dispatched his "Thoughts" on the coming campaign to Germain. If he was aware of Howe's December 20 letter, which seems quite possible since Lord George received it on February 23, he ignored the ambiguities in it that were to dog his steps during the months ahead. Howe had mentioned that "there may be a corps to act defensively upon the lower part of Hudson's river," and that this corps would "facilitate, in some degree, the approach of the Army from Canada." He did not say he would join that Northern Army, only that he did not expect it to reach Albany until September. This could imply, of course, that he planned to rendezvous there, presumably after a quick conquest in the south. But the message was open to several interpretations, which is no way to win a battle, much less a war.

In his "Thoughts," Burgoyne put forward three options for consideration. The first conformed to what was by now established doctrine—securing the Champlain-Hudson line in order to divide and conquer the colonies. As Burgoyne saw it, an army of eight thousand, plus a thousand Indians and two thousand Canadians, including woodsmen and workmen, would head south at the earliest practicable moment, subject to weather conditions, leaving behind another three thousand for the defense of Canada. Up Lake Champlain the strike force would sail, seize Crown Point and Fort Ticonderoga by early summer, and use the fort as a base for future operations. If the administration decided that "the only object of the Canadian army [is] to effect a junction with [Howe's] force," the Northern Army should move toward Albany by way of Lake George, that being "the most expeditious and most commodious route," far preferable to an overland march over difficult terrain, which would be further impeded by obstructions the rebels could place across roads and narrow streams.

Meantime, to distract American attention, a diversionary force would march from Oswego on Lake Ontario to the Mohawk River, eventually joining the larger Canadian army and Howe in Albany.

An alternative scheme was for the army from Canada, after securing Ticonderoga, to march eastward to the Connecticut River, en route to a junction with British troops in Rhode Island. Since Howe had abandoned any idea of an attack on Boston, this suggestion was academic, yet Burgoyne may have included it since it would permit him to operate independently of Howe and perhaps, by conquering New England, to win the renown he sought so eagerly.

Finally, if the king and his ministers decided that the number of troops assigned to Burgoyne was insufficient to accomplish either objective, those men could embark on ships at Quebec and sail off to meet Howe.

In a marginal note, the king commented on these "Thoughts." After calculating rank and file in Canada as more than eleven thousand, His Majesty made several suggestions. "As sickness and other contingencies must be expected," he observed quite sensibly, "I should think not above 7,000 effectives can be spared over Lake Champlain, for it would be highly imprudent to run any risk in Canada. . . . Indians must be employed," and would have to be tightly controlled. Then, he went on, "As Sir William Howe does not think of acting from Rhode Island into Massachusetts, the force from Canada must join him at Albany." Sending the army by sea to meet Howe was not worth consideration, he added: "I greatly dislike that idea."

So the essential elements of John Burgoyne's first option were accepted virtually intact except for the number of troops he considered necessary. At last he was to have an independent command. He was to "force his way to Albany," where he and the task group moving east along the Mohawk would rendezvous and place themselves under Howe's command. Until then, he was to be on his own, acting as the situation and his judgment demanded.

In principle his plan was a good one, but in practice would be something else again, for it ignored or glossed over the unyielding obstacle of distance, not to mention the problems of three armies separated from each other by wilderness and terrible roads, and from their command center and source of supplies by the Atlantic Ocean. To anyone who knew the realities of the American countryside, it would have seemed all but impossible.

On March 10, Burgoyne dined with Clinton, with whom he had always been on friendly terms, and it is easy to imagine them speculating on what the future held in store, while raising a glass to their next meeting, quite possibly on the banks of the Hudson River.

Now it remained for Germain to give Sir Guy Carleton the humiliating news that most of the army under his command was to be turned over to his former deputy. Waiting until the last possible minute so that Burgoyne could carry the letter to Carleton, Lord George wrote what was essentially a rehash of his August 22 communication, which Carleton had never received. As a sop to Sir Guy's dignity and pride, he was directed to take more than three thousand men with him to Quebec, where he would oversee the defense of Canada; but he was to have nothing whatever to say about the selection of those troops—the units were all chosen for him. Further, he was to supply Burgoyne with some seven thousand men, about equally divided between regulars and Germans (again, with the decision on the composition of the force removed from his hands), together with "as many Canadians and Indians as may be thought necessary," while furnishing all the stores, artillery, and every other item required. Presumably Carleton was to do all this and send Burgoyne off with his blessing to Albany, where he would "put himself under the command of Sir William Howe."

As the ultimate slap in the face, Germain reminded Carleton of his "supineness" in not attacking Ticonderoga, rubbing salt in the wound by saying inexplicably that this had brought on the disaster at Trenton.

The letter to Carleton was prepared by a secretary in the carefully crafted, elegant script of eighteenth-century officialdom, with a fair copy for the file and one for Howe. According to William Knox, one of Germain's undersecretaries, his lordship was on his way to the country when he stopped by the office to sign his mail and was reminded that nothing had been written to Howe specifying what action was expected of him. Lord George was annoyed. His carriage was waiting, he did not want his horses to be kept standing, and his tolerance for frustration was just about nil. He made it clear that he had no intention of spending another minute at the office, so Mr. D'Oyly, who handled traffic concerning the war, said he would prepare an order for the general and enclose the copy of Germain's letter to Carleton. That was fine as far as it went, but since Howe later denied having received any instructions except the copy of the message to Carleton, it may be supposed that D'Oyly's "order" was nothing of the kind but at most a note explaining the enclosure.

Of considerably more importance than this "missing dispatch" is what Lord George neglected to tell Sir William. Given Germain's proclivity for giving his field commanders minutely detailed orders (of which the letter to Carleton was a prime example), it is incomprehensible that between March 3 and April 19—a period of seven weeks—he wrote eight letters to Howe and never once referred to the Burgoyne expedition or to what was expected from Howe in the way of cooperation. This meant that Howe's total knowledge of the joint operation was as described in Germain's letter to Carleton: Burgoyne was to "put himself under the command of Sir William Howe" and should "never lose sight" of the junction with Howe that was his "principal objective." If Howe failed to understand the purpose of the invasion from Canada, as he later claimed, Germain had no one but himself to blame.

Not for several weeks would Whitehall learn that Howe had changed his mind yet again. On April 2 the general wrote Germain to say that he was abandoning plans to march overland to Philadelphia. Instead, he would withdraw his men from their outposts in New Jersey, add them to his field army, pack the whole lot aboard ships, and sail to Philadelphia.

This was a momentous decision, one that profoundly affected Burgoyne's campaign and the course of the war, and for a number of reasons. For however long it took to sail to Philadelphia, the commander in chief of Britain's armies in America would be out of touch with the mainland and the fighting there. Any delays encountered in the ocean voyage would postpone by that much Howe's summer campaign, and the more that was put off, the later could there be any joint operation with Burgoyne. Perhaps worst of all, the main British force would then be immobilized occupying the rebel capital, leaving Washington's forces between them and their New York base, and between them and Burgoyne.

Nothing could have revealed Howe's concept of strategy more vividly than the movement on which he was about to embark. Unlike Burgoyne, who saw war in terms of mobility and maneuver, Howe had a chess-game mentality, which meant fighting a war of position, in the classic European pattern. But that was no way to do what was imperative, which was to destroy the enemy army—in this case an extremely elusive one—and Howe seems to have recognized the limitations of his plan, since he admitted to Germain that "my hopes of terminating the war this year are vanished."

In happy ignorance of this development, elated by the role he was about to play, and confident of success, General John Burgoyne departed London on March 27, 1777, for Plymouth, where he found a vessel that was about to leave for New York. After handing the captain the copy of Germain's letter to Carleton, to be delivered to General Howe on Manhattan Island, he boarded the frigate *Apollo* and saw to the loading of his personal belongings, including an ample supply of champagne, fine claret, and brandy. Five and a half weeks later the ship slowly made her way through ice floes on the St. Lawrence under the looming fortress of Quebec. It was Tuesday, May 6, 1777, the first day the river was navigable, when Burgoyne stepped foot once again on Canadian soil. The nucleus of his army was already here—had been for more than a year—and he and the troops he was to command were ready and eager for the great adventure.

Chapter 5

A Matter of Personal Interest
and Fame

It seems highly improbable that Stephen, 1st Earl of Ilchester, or his countess imagined in their wildest dreams that their daughter, Lady Christian Harriet Caroline Fox-Strangways, would one day journey to America aboard a troop transport. Yet there she was, twenty-seven years old, married for five years to Major John Dyke Acland, sailing off into the North Atlantic on the 8th of April, 1776, with the army Burgoyne would lead the following year.

The portraits Joshua Reynolds painted of the couple at the time of their wedding show them looking older than their years, both with sharp, pointed noses, and John wearing what almost looks like a sneer. Harriet, a popular young woman in London society who was considered "vastly pretty," was obviously as strong-willed as she was devoted to her husband, since she managed to overcome his objections to her accompanying him to war and, after leaving their two infant daughters with her mother, traveled to Cork, in Ireland, where six British regiments, including his, were preparing to sail to Quebec.

As unconventional and startling as this escapade was, it probably came as no surprise to Lady Harriet's family and friends, who from the beginning had regarded her marriage as a curious match. Not that John Acland was unsuitable: his family, after all, was one of the most ancient in Devon, having owned land at least since 1155, and they possessed large estates there and in Somerset, two of which John's father, a baronet, had given the couple as a wedding gift. The raised eyebrows had to do with Major Acland's political sympathies and opinions, few of which found favor in Lady Harriet's circle of Whig friends and relations. (Charles James Fox, the prominent MP, staunch friend to America, and Harriet's cousin, was one of the sharpest thorns in the side of George III, who remarked of him, "That young man has so thoroughly cast off every principle of common honour and honesty that he must become as contemptible as he is odious.") Acland, on the other hand, had the obstinate outlook of an old-fashioned Tory provincial, whose preoccupations were horses and hunting, and whose inflexible views against any form of conciliation with the rebellious Americans were those of an unreconstructed imperialist.

He took advantage of the seat he had purchased in the House of Commons to denounce Lord North for his reluctance to tax the colonists, predicting that any accommodation with them would bring about "a total convulsion of the British Empire." As colonel of a Devonshire militia regiment, he signed an address to the king, promising support against "Enemies of your Majesty's Government and this Constitution," and urged use of militia to support the regular army, pledging to raise as many as a thousand West Country men himself. (In rebuttal, Lady Harriet's kinsman Fox foresaw that the Devonshire militia would "alienate the King from the people, to imbue their hands in the blood of their fellow-subjects," and declared that such men ought not to be trusted with weapons.)

John Dyke Acland had an animal energy and a temper to go with it, and when he, his wife, his manservant, her maid, and their dog, along with five companies of his regiment, the 20th Foot, boarded the 709-ton East Indiaman *Kent*, bound for America, the major must have felt smug in the knowledge that he would be actively engaged in putting down the seditious rebels he despised. Although Harriet was the only woman of her class on the ship, she was not the only female passenger. The *Kent* sailed with a complement of wives, children, and a cow to provide milk; British army regulations permitted three women per company to travel with their men, to serve as laundresses, cooks, and nurses.

The vessel was part of a good-sized convoy—forty-two transports, escorted by two frigates—and the first day at sea provided landsmen with their first taste of what the North Atlantic could offer at this season of the year. Two hours out of Cork a strong northwest gale carried away the *Kent*'s mizzen sheet and the topmast of another transport, and Lady

Harriet could see soldiers on board the ship that carried her brother, Captain Stephen Strangways, leaning over the side, "very sick." The first week was cloudy, followed by another gale that overturned Harriet's bureau, smashing glass and china, and the next day huge swells caused the ship to heel over so far it was impossible to see the topmasts of vessels less than a quarter mile away. Squalls and more squalls, then a naval vessel appeared and spoke the commodore's ship, and the convoy suddenly turned south, baffling the passengers. The following day, in the vicinity of the Azores, the maneuver became clear when they spied another large fleet—said to be carrying troops from Germany as well as General John Burgoyne, making his second voyage to America—swelling the convoy to seventy-eight ships.

These transatlantic crossings were the stuff of nightmares. For the army officers, they were bad enough—harsh and uncomfortable—and in the case of Lady Harriet, certainly, they were a stark contrast with conditions to which she was accustomed at home, but to the common soldiers they were an unmitigated horror. Crowded belowdecks for six weeks and more, they had to endure the stench of vomit and unwashed bodies and the crudest sanitary facilities, with three men stacked in bunks in a space five feet high and seven feet wide, fed on the meanest rations— including water that was green with viscous algae and rock-solid hard-tack, crawling with weevils. Some suffered from scurvy or other diseases, some died, and on German transports it was reckoned that of every shipload of 900 to 1,000 men, 130 to 200 were ill on arrival in America, while thirty or forty had perished. Many passengers had never seen an oceangoing vessel before, let alone sailed aboard one, so along with acclimating themselves to shipboard life and the continuous, often violent motion, they had to face terrors to which even seasoned sailors never fully adjusted.

For landlubbers in these hostile circumstances the unpredictable fury of the North Atlantic was the most dreaded threat. As a German officer described one experience, he was about to fall asleep one night when he was awakened by a powerful movement of the ship, strong thunderclaps, and lightning, so he went up on deck to find that "a violent wind was blowing with a mighty roar and deafening noise, that suddenly became so strong that we could hardly furl our sails. . . . The sea rose violently . . . and rendered the wind's deafening noises even more terrible. Each foaming wave . . . resembled a fiery mountain in the dark night rolling forward with utmost speed and threatening to swallow up everything. . . ."

In the awesome swells and troughs of the angry ocean, ships were tossed about like toy boats, rolling from side to side until their spars touched the towering crests of the waves. Men vanished when tons of water crashed across the deck and washed them over the side. In cabins below, loose articles, including furniture, slammed from one bulkhead to another and bounced off the overhead. Ships collided in these titanic outbursts of nature, ran aground in shallow water, were driven off course and lost from the convoy, and always there was the risk of fire from coals used for cooking or from oil lanterns. Even in relatively calm conditions it was a near-miracle when the transports stayed together on dark, moonless nights or when visibility was poor, since the means of signaling changes of course were cannon shots, flags and pennants, or lanterns. When these voyages finally ended even the most unrepentant disbelievers might rejoice and give thanks for salvation from their Dantean ordeal.

Lady Harriet's journal records the long weeks of unstable weather—fog, fresh gales, clear and very cold days when they sighted porpoises, what she called penguins (which were probably puffins), and "mountains of ice." An epidemic of measles broke out, several men died of mysterious fevers, they had a brush with rebel privateers, and on May 10, in "thick weather," land was sighted—Cape Breton Island, still a long way from Quebec. The weather turned "monstrously cold," accompanied by snow and sleet, and three ships ran aground. On May 18 they entered the St. Lawrence River, where they saw whales "spouting water to a great height," and a week later the vessels in the convoy dropped anchor at their appointed rendezvous of Coudres, or Filbert Island, named by Jacques Cartier for the abundant hazelnuts or filberts growing there. The Aclands, with their servants and several officers, were rowed to shore, and in her journal Lady Harriet recorded almost lyrically her encounter with "the first American ground we had ever stept on. . . . It is easy to conceive how happy we were once more to feel terra firma under us, many of us having never been 3 days together at sea before. The hills rose immediately from the shore magnificently bold, clothed with the most beautiful trees, silver firs, larch, sycamore & many other plants with which we were unacquainted. . . . The variety & the luxuriancy of the verdure, & the strength of the vegetation . . . the neatness of a forest where no underwood but the clearest & most odoriferous plants could be seen, almost persuaded us that the scene was a creature of the imagination, or that we were walking on magic ground."

At eleven at night on May 27, seven weeks to the day after leaving the

Cove of Cork, the ships of the convoy dropped anchor in the basin below Quebec.

As the Aclands soon discovered, most of those thirty-six vessels that had joined them near the Azores were packed with what were known in America, then and later, as Hessian mercenaries. The great majority of those who came to Canada were not, in fact, Hessians,* nor were they mercenaries. Except for Colonel von Gall's Hesse-Hanau regiment (who *were* Hessians), all the German soldiers with the Acland convoy were from Braunschweig (Brunswick, as anglicized); they were generally called Brunswickers.

If by mercenary is meant a soldier who hires himself out for money, as a soldier of fortune, these unhappy fellows in no way deserved the description, and the reason could be found in the conditions of their employment. Almost from the beginning of hostilities, the government in London recognized the need for a large land force to put down the insurgents in America and to complement the work of the fleet, which was expected to isolate the colonists from outside supplies and assistance. But Great Britain had a deficit of troops that was not easy to fill. In addition to the regiments already in America, substantial numbers of regulars were on duty in Ireland, Gibraltar, the West Indies, and other outposts of empire; less than ten thousand remained in England and Scotland for home defense, should the French decide to take advantage of America's revolution and invade; recruiting was going very slowly indeed; and it would take time—too much time, in the king's opinion— to raise new units at home. So the decision was made to hire foreign troops, as the crown had done recently during the Seven Years War.

Initially, an attempt was made to obtain Russian levies from Catherine the Great, but either she thought it beneath her dignity to oblige, or she was pressured by Frederick of Prussia not to do so, leading George III to comment sadly that her response was "not . . . so genteel as I should have thought might have been expected of her." Fortunately for the king, more fertile ground existed in Germany, where he had strong

---

*Landgrave Friedrich II of Hesse-Cassel was the first German sovereign to provide troops to the British, and during the Revolution he furnished twenty thousand of them—far more than any other ruler—so it was natural for the Americans to apply the generic term "Hessian" to all the German soldiers.

family reasons to turn to Hanover, since he was the ruler of that state as well as king of England.*

In the 1770s, Germany was no more than a loose confederation of petty feudal principalities—more than seventeen hundred of them—many of which possessed few resources other than human beings, who were only too exploitable. Since all land was held in fief, the unfortunate subjects in the German duchies owed homage and service to their rulers, and service more often than not took the shape of enforced military duty. Some idea of the relationship between lord and vassal is indicated by the manner in which even high-ranking officers—in this case, Colonel Johann Friedrich Specht, whose regiment bore his name—addressed their masters. He wrote regularly to his sovereign and just as regularly his letters began, "Your Serene Highness, Most Gracious Duke and Lord," and might end with the phrase "I dissolve in utter devotion, Your Serene Highness, respectfully, loyally, obediently your servant, Specht." Men who greeted their monarch in such terms were unlikely to comprehend or sympathize with people who rebelled against authority.

It was the age of absolutism, and the posturing dukes, princes, landgraves, and margraves in their gingerbread castles, whether they were out to fatten their treasuries or avoid bankruptcy, were delighted to rent out the hapless, voiceless pawns who were their subjects. So avidly did they pursue this source of revenue that during the course of the war some thirty thousand German soldiers risked life and limb for George III in America. That less than half that number returned home was due to several factors—among them casualties in battle, disease, and desertion, abetted by a state of mind described by one of their officers. Painfully isolated in a strange land, where letters from home could take two or three years to be delivered, the Brunswickers, he said, "found themselves far from the Fatherland and kinfolk, and in an unknown country, in which they—with Englishmen, Hanoverians, Hessians, and other German troops, were to do battle for England's supremacy and wage a successful campaign against the native-born of the land, who were familiar with every road and lurking-place, and who were striving for their independence." It was not an enviable assignment for men who never wanted to be there at all.

*Thanks to the Act of Succession passed in 1714 by Parliament, if William III and Princess Anne (later Queen Anne) died without heirs, the throne of England would pass to Sophia, granddaughter of James I and electress of Hanover, or her heirs—*if* they were Protestants. There were no heirs, and as a result, Sophia's son George became the first of his name and line to rule England.

The case of the Brunswickers is instructive in another way. In 1775, Carl Wilhelm Ferdinand of Brunswick, son and heir of the duke and husband to George III's older sister, suggested to his brother-in-law that some of the duke's soldiers would be available to fight in America. A price was determined: for each soldier or his replacement, the duke would receive from Britain's treasury £7 4s. 4 1/2p.—the same amount being payable if he was killed. Half as much would be paid for a wounded man, and the unavoidable conclusion was that a man was worth more dead than wounded. Whether the war was to be calculated in lives or pounds sterling, it began to dawn on some members of Parliament that it was going to be very expensive indeed.

Nevertheless, contracts were drawn, and in February of 1776 the first division of Brunswick troops passed in review before His Serene Highness Duke Carl and their commanding officer, Major General Friedrich Adolph Baron von Riedesel, and with bands playing, flags snapping in the breeze, they marched out of Wolfenbüttel, tramping from one little town to the next to the cadence of their favorite hymns, sung as only 2,222 men who were bidding farewell to their homeland could sing. After a twelve-day march they were in Stade, where they were reviewed again—and carefully counted, man by man—by George III's agent before boarding ships bound for England and the New World.

After the torment of the long, harrowing crossing, the German and British troops who disembarked on Canadian soil in 1776 had the unexpected bonus of a relatively uneventful summer. Their arrival was a substantial addition to the force that had landed on May 6, lifting the siege of Quebec and putting an end to any hopes the rebels may have held for capturing the city. Although the harried Americans beat a disorderly retreat to the south, no major action could take place until Carleton moved his troops up the lake, and while he waited impatiently for a fleet to be constructed, his soldiers had a rare opportunity to enjoy the experience of sightseeing in this strange, wondrous land.

These Europeans, most of them young and impressionable, had the sensation of being dropped into a natural world totally different from anything they had known—a world virtually untouched and unspoiled by humankind. It was a place in which the laws of nature, not man, governed, in which man was the intruder and an alien being, unsought and unwanted, who survived only if he managed to accommodate to the environs. The humans who were already part of this ecosystem—the native

Americans—had found their niche, had taken their place in the scheme of things by learning the secret of nature, that each member has a part to play in the whole, and that he exceeds the limits of that role at his peril.

Briton and German alike were enchanted by the pristine beauty of the northern uplands with their majestic waterfalls and mountains, rivers and lakes, the almost uninterrupted forest, and an abundance and variety of flora and fauna that was extraordinary to them. Without exception the diarists among them echoed Lady Harriet's feeling of "walking on magic ground." They marveled at streams emptying into Lake Champlain that were filled with huge salmon; they found small, brilliantly colored birds that delighted them (though they missed seeing the nightingales and storks of Europe); and, to their intense regret, they met clouds of voracious mosquitoes "that almost devoured us," along with insects the French called *brûlies*, known to Americans as no-see-ums. One of the most perceptive observers among them was Julius Friedrich Wasmus, a Brunswick surgeon with the regiment of dragoons, who had said farewell to his wife and two children in February 1776 and was destined not to be reunited with them for seven and a half years. Wasmus, who admitted to being terrified of snakes, manfully recorded in his journal encounters with a seven-foot blacksnake and a four-foot rattlesnake with seven rattles, describing in detail the latter's color, teeth, poison sac, and terrible head and eyes. More to his liking were the wild animals, many of them unfamiliar to Europeans, such as moose (it pleased him, as a medical man, to discover a tame one in captivity that suffered from epilepsy) and beaver, which he portrayed at length, as well as black bear, bison, wolves, foxes, large wildcats, martens, turkeys, snowshoe hares, raccoons, woodchucks, and skunks, and passenger pigeons that darkened the sky when they flew over by the millions.

At the onset of the Germans' first winter in North America, the army was outfitted with snowshoes, called "raquets," enabling them to get around in snow that was already more than three feet deep in December, but the season, which Wasmus found "bearable" (whether in jest or not, the natives pronounced it the mildest in memory), was of less concern to him than the Canadian people. They were "our greatest enemies," he said, "they call us the German dogs . . . and would like to do away with us if they only could." Much of this animosity he attributed to Catholic priests and their fanaticism; they preached against the Protestants from Germany, saying that "if females were so unfortunate as to become pregnant from such heretics, they would bring all such types of animals into this world as wolves, dogs, cats, and the like." When the inevitable occurred and the illegitimate offspring proved to be "fair little boys and girls," it was a source of great satisfaction to Wasmus and discomfiture for the priests.

Unlike Wasmus, Lieutenant William Digby of the 53rd Regiment of Foot found the Canadians "a very happy set of people," and Lady Harriet took a liking to them from the moment she first set foot on land. Hers was a Rousseauan reaction: she imagined that she saw in them "the outlines of original society, excepting that being descended from ancestors who had lived in a polished country they had left behind them the barbarity which generally attends the first stages of primitive manners." She was impressed by their obvious good health, cleanliness, comfortable dress, self-sufficiency, and willingness to share food and drink with her party. But it was disappointing to find, when the food and drink were provided, that "the nature of man is everywhere the same," since "they asked 3 times the value of everything we wanted."

Wasmus and others noted with disgust that Canadian "men are the women's slaves inasmuch as they have to do all the work," and how, in the cities, the wives dressed extravagantly in the French or English fashion, "looking like high-ranking ladies." The men, he observed, worked outdoors and had strong, healthy constitutions, while the women, who spent their days inside, looked pale and sickly—as well they might, since they frequently had fifteen or sixteen children.

Like all Europeans seeing America for the first time, the soldiers were fascinated by the natives—the savages, as they were universally called— and Wasmus found himself wondering if they might possibly be descendants of the lost Jewish tribes, whom they resembled "in their ceremonies, positions, and gestures." (How the doctor became familiar with the habits of the ancient Israelites is not known.) In Quebec he saw a number of Hurons and Iroquois who had come to offer their services to the king, and quite a sight they were: big, strong, well-built men, whose color he described as a brownish yellow.

John and Harriet Acland went to watch a ceremony of Indians declaring war, called "digging up the Hatchet," which should have given them a foretaste of what was to come. It began with a French priest speaking to the tribe in their language, asking if they were willing to take up the hatchet. As he talked, a belt, some beads, and the head of an ox, split in two, were placed on the floor. After the Indians spoke to the lieutenant governor, saying they would consider his proposals but with the understanding that their wives and children would have to be provided for during the war, they went off for a meal and a council. Returning, the chief addressed the lieutenant governor and said that they had decided to take up the hatchet, upon which he picked up the belt and beads and, holding half of the ox's head by the horn, danced around the room "singing a most horrid war song & saying that was the manner in which they would treat the head of the Bostians."* A second Indian then picked up the other half of the head and did the same, followed by all the others, squaws and braves alike, dancing and shouting their blood-chilling war whoops. "Upon the whole," Lady Harriet commented, "it was a curious but a very horrible & disagreeable sight." Disagreeable was hardly the word. What they were seeing was the face of death.

The Europeans had no way of knowing what those Indians were like, only how they looked, and what they could see confirmed the worst stories they had heard of the North American savages. The thought that such wild creatures would be used by their army and turned against their fellow countrymen was deeply disturbing. They knew they would be employed as scouts and as a screen for the army as it moved south, at which tasks the Indians were known to be peerless, but it was the presence of another element that was so troubling. A certain code of honor existed among Europe's armies, and while war was war, that code did not include butchering your opponents after they had been taken captive. (The Indian warriors had *their* code of honor too—it happened to be very different from that of the white soldiers.) The redcoats and the Brunswickers were tough, and were familiar enough with the carnage of a battlefield, but this business of the Indians was something new, and deeply disquieting, not least because they suspected they might be out on picket duty or possibly lost, alone in the unfathomable forest, and who knew if these savages would forgo scalping a white man even if he wore a friendly uniform?

It was probably just as well that Lady Harriet was not present, as Lieutenant James Hadden was, at a "Congress of Savages" in Montreal. It was an eye-opener of another kind, which did little to dispel the growing anxiety about their native allies. The men were tall and well-built, wearing a tuft of hair at the back of their heads and very little else. In the hair a feather was fastened for each scalp they had taken. They wore rings and other decorative objects in their ears, which were slit, and a

---

*Bostonais, Bostonians, and variants thereof were the Canadians' generic terms for Americans.

silver ring hung from the nose. Their attire consisted of a blanket and breech clout, covering their private parts, but at important dances and on this occasion some were totally naked and had the head and neck of a handsome bird fastened at the end of the penis. Painted with vermilion and other brilliant colors, they were a fearsome sight indeed, especially when carrying their arms, consisting of a wooden ball fixed to a handle, a tomahawk or hatchet, scalping knife, and musket, all of which they used, Hadden said, with deadly skill.

The women were "far from tempting," the lieutenant noted, being covered with grease as protection against mosquitoes and flies. In contrast to the men, they wore no ornaments—only blankets and leggings or moccasins, with their long black hair tied in a club with red or blue cloth.

Absorbed as they were by the natives and their customs, Burgoyne's troops quickly learned that the Indians were inordinately fond of spirits, which was likely to make them berserk, and that they were "cunning and treacherous," constantly demanding gifts of such items as silver bracelets, gold-laced hats, and arms of all sorts, in which traffic the trader-interpreter invariably came out ahead. General Burgoyne was heard to say that "a thousand Savages brought into the Field cost more than 20,000 Men," and it was worth asking why they were used when the expense and attendant problems were so great. The answers, of course, lay partly in their legendary ferocity, which was a psychological weapon of considerable significance, what was to most whites an uncanny knowledge of the wilderness, and their ability to move silently and quickly through the most difficult terrain. As the European soldiers learned, these native Americans could travel hundreds of leagues through unbroken forest, scarcely deviating from a straight course, using trees, leaves, streams, and other natural features as guideposts. They could tell a man's nationality from his footprints and follow a trail through underbrush in the dark by their acute sense of smell. These skills made them incomparable scouts, serving as the army's eyes and ears, making them worth the trouble it took to deal with them.

It was sobering to learn, Hadden noted regretfully, that "the . . . most mischievous and treacherous Nations are those who are nearest & mix most with the Europeans: they acquire only our Vices & retain their ferocity."

Quartered in the homes of Montrealers and in a host of tiny villages on both banks of the St. Lawrence (the Germans alone were distributed in nineteen towns), the army hunkered down and tried to keep warm as the calendar of their first winter in North America tolled off a record of novel and memorable experiences—skating for miles on the frozen rivers; parading twice a day in the Champ de Mars ("a very bleak situation," Hadden called it); passing in review on the ice (on one such occasion, while the 21st Regiment dressed ranks and stood at attention for General Phillips, twelve men succumbed to frostbite); "carrioling," or sleighing, in a gaudily painted carriage on which the wheels had been replaced with runners, to travel like the wind over the snow or ice behind two fleet horses. At least once they had to dig a grave with crowbars in ground that was solidly frozen to a depth of six feet; they sighted wolves slinking out of the woods in search of food scraps; and at all times felt enveloped by a landscape in which "nothing but a melancholy white strikes the eye on every side," broken only by trees "which appear planted in the snow." As one Briton remarked, "The Winter passed in the most profound tranquility," with the monotony of garrison life broken and enlivened for the officers by balls and assemblies in Montreal and Quebec, where Governor Carleton lived "in a great degree of elegance, and as absolute in his government as possible."

December 31, 1776, was a day carefully orchestrated by Guy Carleton. Exactly one year earlier the rebels had been defeated at the gates of Quebec, and the general was determined to commemorate the anniversary of his triumph in proper style. All regiments that had chaplains were ordered to celebrate a solemn thanksgiving service, including the Te Deum Laudamus to be sung for the liberation of the city and Canada. That morning, in the damp chill of the cathedral, eight unhappy penitents, each with a rope tied in a hangman's noose around his neck, stood before the altar rail to crave pardon of their God, church, and king. These unlucky Canadians had joined the American assault on Quebec and been captured, and Carleton's purpose now was to humble them before he had the Roman Catholic archbishop forgive them in a gesture of magnanimity by the country's Protestant rulers.

A midmorning assembly was followed by a tribute to Carleton, a visit to the square in front of the Recollets' convent, where eight companies of Canadians fired cannon, lit bonfires, and shouted *"Vive le Roi!"* Then more religious services, the firing of guns from windows by enthusiastic local folk, and a dinner for sixty at three in the afternoon.

That evening officers of both armies filed through a lane of pine torches lighting the entrance to the *auberge* as jingling sleighbells signaled the arrival of Quebec's gentry, dressed in their finest and wrapped in furs, here for the banquet and fancy ball celebrating the city's liberation and the incoming New Year, when even more glorious victories could be expected. When General Carleton entered the hall he received a thunderous vivat, after which an original cantata was sung to him. But to the regret of many a British grenadier, John Acland and his popular wife were not present. The major had contracted a fever, and Lady Harriet had traveled "to attend him upon his sickbed in a miserable hut at Chamblee."

On January 18—the birthday of George III's queen, Charlotte—Carleton in the Castle of Quebec and Major General Baron von Riedesel in the Monastery of the Barefooted Friars in Trois Rivières each gave a magnificent dinner, ball, and supper, attended by officers from both armies as well as local ladies and gentlemen, and enlivened by what a German officer called "entertaining little chansons in the style of the region, which seemed quite displeasing to our ears compared to the beautiful voices and manner of German women." Yet for all the sangfroid exuded by these professional soldiers, behind the stylized embrace of the dance and the polite quiet laughter of the drawing room was the unspoken thought that some of these men—perhaps many of them—might be killed or maimed before the New Year ended.

Aside from these celebrations and a few other diversions, the army was wrapped within the silent cocoon of winter, through which news of the outside world filtered into the garrison only rarely. Brigadier Johann Specht noted that from mid-November until May 6 they were "completely cut off not only from every communication with Europe but also with the rest of our neighboring American provinces." What information they did receive he classified as "fly-news," or rumors, "whose truth and confirmation we had every possible reason to wish for. Unfortunately, they had been totally invented or were premature or exaggerated, so that they invariably had to be discarded after a period of time."

Early in April some hard facts circulated through the camps and reminded the men why they were here. Chronologically, the campaign of 1777 might be said to have begun with the skirmish that was so upsetting to Anthony Wayne, which was led by Captain Samuel McKay, a half-pay officer of the Royal American Regiment. McKay had no use for rebels or for the authorities in Connecticut who condemned him as a Tory and put a price on his head; he had already been captured by the Americans, broken his parole, and twice escaped from prison (once in the guise of a clergyman), and in March he was leading a scouting party of Indians near Lake George when a group of American recruits was spotted. At dawn

McKay's men surprised thirty sleeping Americans at Sabbath Day Point, tomahawked four of them, wounded their officer, and took twenty-one captive. Although McKay and his party were tracked down and attacked by Benjamin Whitcomb and his rangers on their way north, McKay returned safely to Canada to report—just as Wayne had feared—that the Americans were preparing for a British attack on Ticonderoga. That and a false rumor that Howe had taken Philadelphia were almost the only tidings to penetrate the winter fastness.

By April it was starting to thaw, the days lengthened, and by May 6, 1777, when Burgoyne came upriver after his third Atlantic crossing, the roar of the St. Lawrence was deafening, between the runoff and the thunderous collision of huge chunks of ice from the Great Lakes. The first order of business for the new commander of the Northern Army was to break the news to his former superior that he was taking his job, and some officers who didn't care much for Carleton held their breath to see how he would take it. Simon Fraser, a friend of Burgoyne's who was to be one of his brigadier generals on the campaign, commented that it came as a *coup de foudre*, a thunderclap, and required all Burgoyne's tact and understanding "to do business with a proud, austere, narrow-minded man, disappointed in all his views of ambition, environed by flatterers, Dependants & Sycophants, possessing for some time a degree of power not far inferior to that anciently given to a Roman Dictator." Whether or not Fraser misjudged Carleton, Burgoyne's assignment was a tall order, and despite his affability and Carleton's gentlemanliness, it must have been a hideously awkward moment for both. A lesser man than Carleton might have behaved very differently indeed, yet their meeting and subsequent relations were cordial and without a sign of rancor. What made the difference was that Carleton, who could have made life miserable for his former second-in-command and added immeasurably to the difficulties he faced, was the soul of cooperation, thanks to his innate courtesy and high sense of duty. He was enormously helpful, Burgoyne wrote to an army friend in London: Carleton "has received me and the orders I brought in a manner that, in my opinion, does infinite honour to his public and private character."

In accordance with those orders, the Northern Army was divided into three elements, of which Burgoyne naturally received the lion's share. Another detachment, consisting of about 200 regulars, 200 provincials, 300 to 400 Germans, and an expected 400 or 500 Indians—for a total of more than 1,200 effectives—was to be led by Lieutenant Colonel Barry St. Leger to Niagara, and from there across Lake Ontario to Oswego. From that point the force would march east against Fort Stanwix and, after taking it, proceed down the Mohawk River to join Burgoyne at Albany. The remainder of the troops—some 3,500 men including invalids in hospital—would remain in Quebec under Carleton.

Now the governor-general was nothing if not proud, and the news that Burgoyne—"an inferior officer"—was to lead the invasion army while he was relegated to defending Canada with a fraction of his former command must have been almost more than he could swallow. He was too good a soldier to question orders, so he retained his military office and confined his reaction to Germain's insulting terms by submitting his resignation as governor, stating that he had been treated with "Slight, Disregard and Censure," intimating that Germain was a fool to think large numbers of Canadians would volunteer for the campaign, and criticizing the colonial secretary's policy of employing Indians.

The official reason given for Burgoyne's appointment to lead the invasion army was contained in a statement by George III (undoubtedly written by Germain): "Whenever an army leaves the province in which it has been standing, the Governor of the Province shall not have the command over it outside his gubernatorial district even if he had previously commanded the army as commander-in-chief but shall surrender its command to the senior general under him." This was patently hogwash, and the troops knew it. Not that Burgoyne was unpopular—on the contrary, as one young officer remarked, he was "universally esteemed and respected," and most troops welcomed the news that he was to lead the expedition—but it was widely believed that the excuse given for relieving Carleton was "an unjust one." The reason Carleton had been "set aside," Lieutenant Digby said with asperity, was "his not attempting to reduce Ticonderoga the preceding season," but Digby, who had been with the general, knew he had acted wisely in returning to Canada when he did, "the season being so very severe and far advanced."

Before Burgoyne set foot on Canadian soil, Carleton had received a letter from Sir William Howe—one of the few that came his way for a year, although Howe, as general in charge in North America, certainly should have kept the man who was governor of Canada and commander of the Northern Army regularly informed about his plans. Yet only through the accidental capture of a letter from Washington to Benedict

Arnold did Sir Guy learn of Howe's victory on Long Island, and his frag-
mentary knowledge of what occurred at Trenton and Princeton came
from a prisoner taken by one of his scouting parties. Howe, in short, was
at his uncommunicative worst, and as a result rumors swirled about in
Canada, some true, some totally false, about his activities and whereabouts. Not until Carleton received this letter, written in April at the
time Howe informed Germain of his plans to take his army to Philadelphia by sea, did he have a clue to what was happening.

Unfortunately, Sir William was short on specifics and long on general-
ities, and he gave Carleton little more than hints. He would probably be
in Pennsylvania about the time the Northern Army approached Albany,
Howe announced, and his troops would have too much on their hands to
undertake a movement up the Hudson. The only hint that assistance
might be forthcoming was his casual mention of "a diversion occasionally
upon Hudson's River." Thus the commanding general in North America
indicated that he had no intention of coming in strength to meet the
Northern Army but, on the contrary, would either be at sea (and completely out of touch) or on land at a distance of some hundreds of miles.
It did not look as though General Burgoyne would get much help from
Sir William, although the planned junction of their two armies was
assumed by just about everybody. As one British officer noted in his
journal, "Lieut. Genl. Burgoyne arrived at Quebec from England, having
been appointed by his Majesty to the Command of a Detachment from
the Canadian Army to join that of Genl. Howe."

Complicating the situation further was the reply Lord George Germain had sent to Howe in answer to his letter of April 2. Speaking for the
king, Germain approved Howe's scheme of advancing on Philadelphia by
sea, but then went on to emphasize that whatever the general elected to
do, it was assumed that "it will be executed in time for you to co-operate
with the army ordered to proceed from Canada and put itself under your
command."

Unhappily for Carleton, Burgoyne, and the Northern Army, Germain
did not bother to send a copy of this letter to Quebec. If he had done so,
those generals might have realized that the witches' broth that was
about to be served up was a recipe for disaster. In the first place, Lord
George's instructions to Howe were ambiguous. Germain could have
consulted no authority, no veteran of the French and Indian War, say—
and certainly not a map—when he endorsed Howe's plan to move
against Philadelphia at the same time he was expected to cooperate with
Burgoyne. He was blithely oblivious to the great distances involved, the

enormous hardships to be encountered in moving an army through wilderness country across the most primitive roads, and the impossibility that Howe could sail from New York to Philadelphia, capture that city, and still have time to rendezvous with Burgoyne.

Lord George was not reckoned a stupid man, but he had the arrogance of one who knows it all, which may have been worse. Between that and his unaccountable failure to order Howe to follow the original plan instead of making a half-baked move on Philadelphia, he lost all control of what was going to happen. Without Germain's realizing it, the power to direct the course of events in America slipped irretrievably through his hands. From now on the two British armies would follow their own courses, with Burgoyne and Howe each pursuing his own self-determined goals separately, without any useful contact with the other.

It remained to be seen how Burgoyne would adjust to the drastic change in his "Thoughts for Conducting the War from the Side of Canada" and to his conviction that the object of the campaign was to "effect a junction" with the army under General Sir William Howe.

An important tenet of Burgoyne's "Thoughts" was that the campaign should begin as soon as the end of the spring runoff made it practicable to do so. Before the expedition got under way, moreover, he wanted magazines and provision depots established and all the vessels for transporting his impedimenta fitted out. Then, in a sentence that revealed as nothing else could his motivation for seeking this command, he observed that failure to make these preparations "will be sufficient to crush such exertions as an officer of sanguine temper . . . whose personal interest and fame therefore consequentially depend upon a timely set-out, would be led to make." Where personal interest and fame beckoned, John Burgoyne would surely follow.

He discovered very quickly, however, that almost nothing was going to go as smoothly as his "Thoughts" assumed. No sooner had he reached Montreal than he learned to his dismay that the plan of the campaign was public knowledge, bruited about "almost as accurately as if it had been copied from the Secretary of State's [i.e., Germain's] letter." Burgoyne had told no one on his staff and was confident of Carleton's discretion; he could only surmise, therefore, that someone in London had spilled the beans, though how that information could have arrived in Canada before he did is difficult to see.

Security was by no means his only problem. He found that the army would be "short of the strength computed in England" and would lack its quotas of "camp equipage, cloathing, and many other necessary articles." The deficit of equipment and, it soon turned out, transport could be laid at the door of an arcane supply system that had civilians responsible to the Treasury, not the army, arranging for procurement and distribution. A commissary general and his staff accompanied the troops to ensure that the army's needs were met, but even under the best of circumstances the lack of an adequate supply system proved a nightmare. Such essentials as wagons, for instance, had to be obtained locally, at prices set by wainwrights with an eye on the main chance. The corruption notorious within the commissary departments was exacerbated by the greed of local merchants, who had not the least compunction about gouging the military.

The supply line, after all, was not merely between Montreal and someplace on the way to Albany, though that was bad enough. It extended across three thousand miles of ocean, on which the westward passage could take as long as three months, prolonging by that much the delivery of men and matériel—not to mention the St. Lawrence River, which was often icebound for six months of the year. Every soldier and his weapons, every boot and gaiter, every button and musket ball, every article of clothing, not to mention immense quantities of food—everything from salted meat, flour, butter, and oatmeal for the men (each of whom consumed a third of a ton of food per year) to oats for the horses, since Canada's small, scattered farms were not equal to the demand—had to be carried to America aboard a ship. As costly as it was time-consuming, the process was also painfully wasteful, for ships blew off course or were lost at sea, supplies spoiled, and men and animals died. (Between 1776 and 1780, regiments sent from the British Isles to the West Indies lost a staggering 11 percent of their men on the transatlantic crossings.) And as hopeful as the administration was that the army in America would one day subsist without supplies from home by foraging for its food, that day never came.

The Admiralty bore the responsibility for finding and equipping transports, locating (often by impressment) the seamen to man them, organizing them into convoys, and providing naval vessels to ward off rebel privateers. Admiral Sir Hugh Palliser, sitting in for Lord Sandwich during one of the earl's absences from the office, was dismayed by the immensity of the task. Even before the Burgoyne expedition got under-way, the demands of the army in America, he complained, were "so great as to be thought impossible to furnish. If this is the case, what will it be when we have another army there?" No wonder, he said, that people were "astonished and staggered at the unexpected difficulties we are in."

Unhappily for the functioning of British strategy, the frailties of the supply line were not improved by the ultimate dependence of that system on Lord Sandwich, first lord of the Admiralty, a corrupt political hack who was cordially despised by Lord George Germain, and returned the sentiment. As a result, Germain, who was responsible for the war effort and whose handling of it hinged on a mutual understanding and complementary relationship with the navy, was continually at logger-heads with the one man capable of providing the shipping that was the lifeblood of the support system.

Considering the length of time Carleton had known that the expedition was in the offing (whether it was to be led by Burgoyne or himself), it is curious that he had done so little to arrange transport for the campaign. The enormously cumbersome field guns and ammunition required heavy-duty wagons and teams of horses or oxen to haul them, but as matters stood, not enough animals were available for the artillery, let alone to haul the mountains of supplies and equipment, tents and blankets and medical supplies. Even more puzzling than Carleton's lapse was the failure of Burgoyne to turn his attention immediately to this matter, on which his operation could stand or fall. Not until June 7 did he request another four hundred animals for the gunners and five hundred carts with teams for transporting everything else. The vehicle commonly used in Canada was a two-wheeled cart, since most roads there and those leading south—especially through the mountains—were all but impos-sible for a four-wheeled vehicle to negotiate, so because of time con-straints, the army's carts were jury-rigged affairs, constructed of raw, green lumber, including the wheels, many of which lacked iron rims. Those were hardly the vehicles to survive long journeys over deeply rutted wilderness roads. Adding to the problem, many of these rigs would be driven by civilians who were reluctant to expose themselves to danger and might hold back or desert if the going got tough.

To a degree, the failure to have a wagon train in readiness could be attributed to the assumption by both Carleton and Burgoyne that most of the transporting would be by water—up the Richelieu River to Lake Champlain and to Ticonderoga, then across a short portage to Lake George and up that body of water to its southern end, followed by a twelve-mile journey to the Hudson. Even so, the generals' lack of attention to wagons and draft animals was astonishing, since both were crucial. Because the route between the Canadian frontier and Albany—some two hundred miles as the crow flies—passed through dense forest, broken only by the occasional Indian trace or isolated settlement, the troops could not live off the land as they might in more settled country. Food for as many as ten thousand souls, including noncombatants, women, and children, would have to be carried, and when those provisions ran out would have to be replenished—again and yet again if the campaign lasted longer than everyone confidently expected.

The shortage of troops Burgoyne noted had to do with the auxiliaries, not the regulars. When he was not occupied with other urgent matters, Carleton had devoted some attention to recruiting during the spring, after the Americans fled, but instead of the two thousand men Burgoyne requested, he succeeded in forming only three companies of one hundred Canadians each, to be led by Major Samuel McKay, Captain René Boucherville, and Captain David Monin. The enlistees looked smart enough in their new green uniforms with straw-colored waistcoats and breeches, but from the first Burgoyne took a dim view of them. He complained to Germain that they were "awkward, ignorant, disinclined to the service, and spiritless" and showed "no promise of use in arms." The lack of enthusiasm he detected was corroborated one night when twenty of McKay's men and ten of Monin's deserted, leading Carleton to cluck righteously that "if Government laid any great stress upon assistance from the Canadians for carrying on the present war, it surely was not upon Information proceeding from me. . . ." Lack of enthusiasm among the habitants was altogether understandable. Canadians had been ordered to transport the army's provisions, ammunition, and baggage to St. Johns on the Richelieu River, and while great quantities of provisions had reached that destination during the winter, the rest of the process consumed the entire month of May, disrupting the planting of corn, oats, rye, and barley, and would most likely continue through the summer, keeping the farmers from tending and harvesting crops. As if that were not enough, the local people had to supply horses and carts and furnish two thousand men to repair the defensive works at Sorel, St. Johns, and Ile aux Noix. It did not take the Canadians long to realize that they were slated to be little more than porters on this expedition.

To collect the "hatchetmen and other workmen" Burgoyne had specified, Carleton was obliged to resort to the corvée—a form of forced labor so unpopular that the draftees deserted in droves, and the deficit had to be made up from the army's ranks. And as Carleton had predicted, loyalists failed to sign up in any significant numbers. Philip Skene, who had served as a brigade major with Amherst and had huge landholdings around the southern end of Lake Champlain, reassured Burgoyne with the promise that large numbers of American Tories were only waiting to be summoned, and would flock to the king's banner when called. With this in mind, two loyalists named John Peters and Ebenezer Jessup were provided with commissions to be handed out to enlistees at such time as their prospective commands reached two-thirds of battalion strength.

If you wanted a case study of American loyalists and their relationship to the British army, you could hardly find better examples than these two. Loyalists may well have constituted one-third of the population in the American states, as John Adams believed, but whatever their numbers they were not concentrated in any one place—indeed, rarely constituted a majority in a particular area—and were in most cases not experienced soldiers. Moreover, like the rebel militia, they tended to respond to crises in their own neighborhoods rather than going where the high command most needed them. But John Peters and Jessup looked to be the sort of men Burgoyne needed.

Born in 1740, Peters came from a well-to-do Connecticut family whose ancestors included Oliver Cromwell's chaplain and one of the regicides, who took part in the trial and execution of Charles I. After graduation from Yale, Peters settled first in Piermont, New Hampshire, and later moved to Moortown on the west bank of the Connecticut River, where he had large landholdings, a house, saw and grist mills, and a farm. Although the property was in the New Hampshire Grants, it was claimed by New York, whose royal governor appointed him justice of the peace, colonel of the militia, judge of probates, county registrar, clerk of the court, and judge of the court of common pleas. "Here I was in easy circumstances," he wrote, "as independent as my mind ever wished."

Then his troubles began. He was selected by two local counties as a delegate to the First Continental Congress, but as he traveled south and passed through his hometown of Hebron, he and his uncle Samuel were mobbed by "Governor Trumbull's Liberty Boys" because of their supposed loyalty to the crown. After much verbal abuse the two were released, having concluded that "the bankrupts, dissenting teachers, and smugglers meant to have a serious rebellion, and a civil and religious separation from the Mother Country." The experience was enough for his uncle, who decided to flee to England, but he persuaded his nephew to go on to Congress and take the pulse of the delegates there. John did, and after deciding that "nothing short of independence would satisfy them," he refused to swear that he would not reveal what went on in Congress.

On the way home he was attacked and mistreated by three mobs before he reached Moortown, where another gang threatened to kill him as "an enemy of Congress" under suspicion of dealing with Governor Carleton in Canada. On orders of Eleazer Wheelock, president of Dartmouth College, and three justices of the peace, he and a group of Church of England members were beaten and dragged through water and mud before being thrown in jail, where they were held until they sickened and several died. That was only the beginning of an increasingly painful saga; Peters was scorned and abused by his neighbors, and even his own father turned against him, saying that his uncle Samuel had "taught him bad principles." Finally John Peters got permission to go to Canada with some rebel troops, acted as a double agent there (he was with Benedict Arnold when Franklin and the other commissioners arrived), then was taken prisoner by Sullivan's men near Sorel, escaped, and after returning to Canada joined Carleton's army that pursued the Americans up Lake Champlain in the fall of 1776.

The following spring, two rebel deserters told him that his property in the Grants had been confiscated, that he was branded as an outlaw, that his wife and eight children had been turned out of their home and "sent off in a sleigh with one bed to Ticonderoga, 140 miles through the woods, snow storms, and bad roads," where they arrived more dead than alive. Anthony Wayne treated them kindly and in April sent them on their way to Canada, but they were conveyed to a deserted house and left there for eighteen days before being discovered by a passing British ship and taken to St. Johns—miraculously in good health, Peters added, "but naked and dirty." By the time he was reunited with his family and had taken them to Montreal, he was ready to seek revenge. That month he began to recruit men for a regiment and signed on with Burgoyne, who named his unit the Queen's Loyal Rangers.

Ebenezer Jessup was a New Yorker who had joined Carleton's army at Crown Point in 1776, determined "to conquer our enemies and re-establish civil government for the honor of the Crown and the true interest of the Colonies." The general regarded this as something of a mixed blessing, since he wasn't sure where and how these fellows fit into his army, not to mention how they were to be paid and outfitted. That winter, reference was made to this loyalist unit as "Jessup's Corps," and Carleton wrote Major General Phillips a starchy note saying, "I know no such thing as Jessup's Corps . . ." but then had a change of heart after

Burgoyne arrived in Canada and was casting about for more men. Jessup and his followers were now to be known as the King's Loyal Americans.

An indication of the loyalist attitude toward the war was Ebenezer Jessup's offer of lands on his New York estate to men who would serve in his corps, suggesting the importance he attached to recruiting his quota of men as well as his confidence that as soon as the British stamped out the rebellion the loyalists could return to their homes.

Regrettably for those individuals who felt strongly enough to support their king with their lives, neither these nor most other Tory outfits received from the British army the respect or recognition they felt they were owed, one reason being the regulars' disdain for people they considered provincials, plus the fact that too many loyalists had delusions of grandeur and considered themselves entitled to be officers.

Neither Peters nor Jessup came close to filling their ranks, and another serious blow to Burgoyne's plans fell when Indians numbering between four and five hundred instead of the thousand or more he wanted were brought in by the Chevalier St. Luc de la Corne and Charles Langlade. In New England's pantheon of devils, these two—particularly St. Luc—were at the top, and their presence here was a certain sign that Burgoyne's expedition to the south would take on a dimension beyond the normal progress of an army. As the regular troops moved up the lake, camping on shore each night, off on the perimeter, silent and unseen, Indians would ensure that no one came close enough to do the enemy much good, and they would pounce at any opportunity to take scalps and plunder. It was this aspect of the campaign—what seemed brutality for its own sake— that sent shudders down the spines of many a Briton or German, let alone Americans.

Langlade, a Frenchman who was a skilled forest fighter and interpreter, was notorious for having planned and executed the ambush and destruction of General Edward Braddock's army en route to the Forks of the Ohio in 1755. St. Luc was born in Quebec to a wealthy, influential family and had first gone into the western Indian country to fight the Sauks and Foxes at the age of twenty-one. From then on, the record of his participation in the frontier war was a catalogue of disaster for the English colonies. In a raid on Saratoga, he and his brothers burned every building at the garrison, taking a hundred captives. He was with a war party that torched all the isolated houses in Deerfield, Massachusetts, and took a number of scalps. He and members of his family raided Albany, Schenectady, and Saratoga, and once he surprised and destroyed a British wagon train, which yielded eighty scalps and sixty-four prisoners. In

Montcalm's army in 1757 he led eighteen hundred Indians and was in charge of escorting a number of English prisoners when the savages discovered liquor in a fort they captured, quickly got drunk, and erupted in an orgy of brutality, butchering upward of sixty-nine captives.

When he was not on the warpath he was deeply involved in commercial ventures, notably the fur trade, and saw to it that the portage routes and depots were protected from warring tribes. He bought and sold slaves and by 1760 was believed to be one of the wealthiest men in Canada. In all the frontier wars of his day he led French and Indians in battle, and his fluency in four or five native languages made him one of the most successful recruiters of warriors.

A miniature portrait of St. Luc, resplendent in uniform, has him glancing out of the corners of his eyes at the viewer, a sinister, Mephistophelean look on his face, as though he would just as soon turn you over to an Iroquois with a scalping knife—exactly what he did for four and a half decades. At the height of his powers, his domain reached from the Great Lakes to France, but even though he was now sixty-six, old for frontier warfare, he showed few signs of infirmity and his influence over the Indians was undiminished.

No matter the reputations and skill of St. Luc and Langlade, their followers were too few for Burgoyne's liking, and while more warriors from western tribes were expected, for now the general's slim complement of native Americans was yet another in a series of disappointments, and one that would at best prove a mixed blessing throughout the campaign.

In the final analysis, Burgoyne's hopes for success would rest on the backs of the veterans he could rely on—the professional soldiers from Britain and Germany who were reckoned among the best in the world. After a stretch of beautiful warm weather in the first days of June, the cantonments around Montreal—Batiscan and Grondines, Trois Rivières and Pointe au Lac, Yamachiche, Maskinongé, and a dozen other towns—came alive to the sharp yelps of command and the sound of marching feet. The planning, the drilling, the waiting were over, the men were healthy, rested, and as ready as they would ever be. Now it was time to go. The northern invasion of America had begun.

Chapter 6

A Theater of Glory

From the parapet the man in the blue uniform coat peered off to the north. On a fair day it was possible to see some three miles down the lake, and a breathtaking sight it was, white clouds scudding across the sky, the dark, silent forest mirrored in the water. But the beauty of the scene was the last thing on his mind.

It was the middle of June 1777, and the figure with the black cockade in his hat and a pink sash around his waist, indicating that he was a major general, was Arthur St. Clair—the man Franklin and his fellow commissioners had met near Fort Edward on their trip north a year earlier. The general had just arrived from Philadelphia to take command of the posts at Ticonderoga, and if it occurred to him that this was the loneliest outpost on the continent, despite the presence of some two thousand soldiers in the immediate vicinity, he was close to the truth. The fort and its outworks were on the far rim of the fledgling United States of America—whatever they might prove to be—with only the most tenuous connection to what his men called home. To the north were hundreds of square miles of forbidding wilderness, laced with streams and bogs and gigantic boulders deposited by the glaciers, with the mountains and their ancient underpinnings rank with vegetation that had been growing and decomposing undisturbed since the ice retreated, some of the trees grown to six feet and more in diameter—a primeval forest so dense in most places it was all but impenetrable by a man on horseback. To most white men it appeared vast and dark and threatening, yet by no stretch of the imagination was it a mystery to the people whose ancestors had come here thousands of years earlier, hunting with their stone knives and clubs and spears. They had split up into scores of tribes and subtribes over the centuries; the strong had grown stronger, the weak weaker, and much of this area now held scattered remnants of former tribal groups, subsisting in the forest because it afforded safety.

Beyond the ancient woods lay Canada and the enemy, and the only feasible way for an army to get from there to here was by water, which was why St. Clair was intent on what he might see as he took stock of his new command. Before he left Philadelphia, John Hancock, the president of Congress, had assured him that most, if not all, of Britain's soldiers who had wintered around Montreal and Quebec would certainly be dispatched by ship to join General William Howe in New York. In Hancock's words, there was "no probability of an active campaign." This prediction was reinforced by Major General Horatio Gates, St. Clair's immediate superior,* who claimed to have "the strongest assurances from Congress that the king's troops were all ordered round to New York, leaving only a sufficient number to garrison their forts" in Canada. And on his way through Albany, St. Clair learned that as of mid-May the enemy had made no preparations for an expedition, that "great uneasiness" existed between the Canadian and regular troops, that recruiting was extremely slow and clothing and provisions in short supply. Whether the congressmen or Gates or the Albany rumormongers knew what they were talking about was open to question, but St. Clair was sufficiently persuaded that he brought with him his eleven-year-old son, to give the boy a taste of military life and "to superintend his education." Yet there was reason to wonder if the general had made a mistake in relying too heavily on what might be sheer speculation.

In any case, he knew there could be no relaxing, not after he saw the deplorable condition of the fort itself and the outlying redoubts, batteries, and blockhouses when he arrived on June 12. Ticonderoga had been too long neglected, and while the signs and sounds of construction

---

*Gates was much impressed with his own importance and while nominally responsible for the fort, rarely visited there, preferring the more sophisticated ambience of Albany, where he could also keep an eye on his archrival, Major General Philip Schuyler, who commanded the Northern Department, and be in closer touch with his partisans in Congress.

were everywhere, there was no telling if the fort would be ready for any serious business ahead. He was the fifth commandant here in less than a year, and the place looked it. Fortunately, St. Clair was an experienced hand, a veteran of the 60th Foot or "Royal American Regiment" that brought him to America to fight with distinction at Louisbourg and the capture of Quebec, where he served in the light infantry under William Howe, when Wolfe took the city. At the end of the French and Indian War he decided to stay in the New World and, thanks to money inherited from his mother plus his wife's considerable fortune, bought some four thousand acres in the rolling hills of Pennsylvania's Ligonier Valley, becoming the largest landowner west of the Appalachians. The St. Clairs, an ancient family that emigrated from Normandy to Scotland in the eleventh century, had a long record of loyal service to their king. That loyalty had not always proved beneficial, since it caused them to share the humiliations of the House of Stuart, but it had been steadfast, and Arthur broke the family mold when he elected to side with the independence faction against George III. In this he was not unlike a number of other well-to-do men of property, including George Washington and Philip Schuyler, who had everything to lose—including their necks—by joining the rebellion.

After war broke out, St. Clair first became colonel of a militia battalion, then colonel of the 2nd Pennsylvania Battalion, which was involved in the Canadian debacle in 1776. More recently, he had fought under George Washington at the battle of Trenton, where he helped concoct a daring scheme to extricate the rebel army from a trap by making a night march that surprised the enemy at Princeton. So there was every reason to believe he was worth a great deal to the American cause, and on the strength of his proven leadership, courage, and judgment he was promoted to major general. He was then considered for an assignment consistent with his new rank. James Wilson, a Pennsylvania congressman, broke the news to him in a letter, saying, ". . . the important Command of Ticonderoga is destined for you next campaign. I presage it a Theatre of Glory."

St. Clair, whose name was pronounced "Sinclair," was a Scot by birth, a handsome forty-year-old with chestnut hair, penetrating blue-gray eyes, and a determined chin. With his tricorn hat cocked at a rakish angle and his mouth turned slightly down on one side, he had the look of a tough soldier who had seen much and was not about to take anything for granted. That was one aspect of the man; another came through in his literate, extremely articulate letters, which were likely to be sprinkled with references to ancient military campaigns and quotations in Latin from Horace.

Fortunately he was somewhat familiar with the fort and its environs, having been here the year before with the retreating rebel army, but he had a lot to learn about it during whatever time was granted him to prepare. It was axiomatic that an adequately manned stronghold could hold off superior numbers, as this very fort had in 1758, when the Marquis de Montcalm's small garrison cut to pieces Abercromby's frontal attack. But in two important respects the post known as Ti was now all but indefensible against assault from the north.

In the first place, it was oriented in the wrong direction. When the French built the stoneworks in the 1750s, France controlled Canada, and the star-shaped edifice named Fort Carillon was naturally sited on the southern flank of a peninsula so as to defend against the English approaching from that direction. Now the situation was reversed, and it was in exactly the wrong location to blunt an offensive from the north—an attack that would enable the enemy to portage to Lake George and sail south, or ferry troops through the narrow arm of Champlain as far as Skenesborough, whence they could march overland to the Hudson.

As Charles Carroll realized when he laid eyes on the place the year before, it was a dilapidated ruin; worse, it was presently so short of manpower, arms, provisions, and every item of equipment that it was absurd to expect defenders to hold out against a sizable military force determined to overrun the place. Yet should the unthinkable come to pass, the loss of Ticonderoga would be a shocking blow to morale throughout the states, a threat to the new nation's pride as well as its sense of security.

The retreat from Canada had made it clear that the sorry state and vulnerability of the outpost must be addressed at once, so in early July of 1776 two men—Colonel Jeduthan Baldwin, the army's engineer, and Lieutenant Colonel John Trumbull, deputy adjutant general—inspected the rocky bluff directly opposite Ticonderoga, known variously as East Point or Rattlesnake Hill, and concluded that it was more defensible than the main fort. It also had a good source of drinking water (the lake water was considered stagnant and unhealthy), and fortifying it would materially improve the chances of stopping an attack from the north.

The twenty-year-old Trumbull, a graduate of Harvard and a son of Connecticut's governor, had a talent for drawing and a keen eye for terrain. He made some sketches for the visiting generals Philip Schuyler and Horatio Gates, who were then rowed across the quarter mile of water to Rattlesnake Hill to size up the situation for themselves, and they concurred with the young lieutenant colonel's opinion.

As Trumbull saw it, a low area on the north side of the promontory afforded a good landing place for boats from Ticonderoga. Fifty to seventy-five feet above it, surrounded on three sides by steep cliffs, was a level plateau suitable for batteries, redoubts, barracks, a hospital, and other buildings. To the east a road with an easy grade to the plateau could be constructed. It would take work—a lot of it—to make the place ready, but when completed its guns would have a clear field of fire down the lake to the north, blocking passage of ships through the narrow neck of water between Rattlesnake Hill and Ticonderoga. Those cannon would also cover the old stone fort across the lake, which Trumbull dismissed out of hand, labeling it on his map "Old Fort & Redoubts, out of Repair," while the new post's location on the east bank made it accessible to troops and supplies coming overland from the New England states. All in all, it was ideally situated for a defensive position.

Trumbull also came up with an interesting idea, which he set forth at Gates's table one evening with all the principal officers present: he was satisfied, he said, that the distance from the mountain known as Sugar Hill, just south of Ticonderoga, was such that guns there would command the fort *and* Rattlesnake Hill on the opposite shore, since both were within range of most cannon. What he got for this "new and heretical opinion" was a great deal of ridicule, but the general gave him permission to fire on Sugar Hill from both points. In each case, the shells landed close enough to the top to indicate that it was certainly possible to achieve the same result in reverse. And to see if artillery pieces could be dragged to the top of Sugar Hill, he and two other officers who were there at the time—Anthony Wayne and Benedict Arnold, gimpy leg notwithstanding—scrambled up to the peak and agreed, yes, it could be done. But the warning went unheeded, and no defenses were built on Sugar Hill.

On the 18th of July, 1776, fatigue parties were clearing Rattlesnake Hill and building a road up to the plateau when word arrived from Philadelphia of a momentous proclamation signed by members of Congress declaring the "united States of America" free, emancipated from all allegiance to the British crown. On July 28 the troops were paraded, the inspiring words were read to them by St. Clair, and three "loud huzzahs" went up, followed by a salute of thirteen guns—one for each newly independent state—after which the bluff with the homely name Rattle-snake Hill was enthusiastically rechristened Mount Independence, while Sugar Hill became Mount Defiance. Two weeks later a newspaper reached the outpost with an account of how Congress, on June 14, had "resolved that the flag of the United States be thirteen stripes, alternate red and white; that the union be thirteen stars, white in a blue field, representing a new constellation." But at the moment the chances of that constellation surviving to light up the skies looked very dim indeed.

At the time St. Clair took command of the post, he found meat for seven weeks on hand, but he did not dare call for more militia for fear they would ruin him by eating all the spare provisions. Work crews scavenging firewood had denuded both shorelines of the lake for miles, and even the abatis—those piles of trees felled in such a way that the branches faced outward and upward like a porcupine's quills, to impale enemy attackers—had been burned during the winter, which meant that no stockpile of wood was on hand for cooking or warmth. The fort's stone and earthen walls and its important wooden structures and redoubts were in horrendous condition; tents were in shreds; the magazines were in such wretched repair that fifty pounds of powder was found damaged each week. As for weapons, the colonel of a Massachusetts regiment, Thomas Marshall, complained that "many of our guns are broke," having been damaged when a cart on which they were being hauled through the woods overturned. Other muskets had been lost from a boat that capsized, while some were "stole on the Road by the Torys which abound in these parts." Nor was that the end of this tale of woe. When the troops turned out on field days a third of them had to carry spears instead of firelocks, and not more than a fifth of their arms were equipped with bayonets.

So while the average American may have regarded Ticonderoga as an impregnable bastion against invasion from Canada, and its capture in 1775 by Ethan Allen and Benedict Arnold cause for jubilation and pride, anyone on the scene could see that its reputation was hugely overblown. The popular vision of an imposing stone fortress that blocked invaders from the north was a figment of the imagination with no more substance than King Arthur's Tintagel.

The reality was a grim, malodorous, unsanitary campground for several thousand men, many of whom were afflicted with measles, dysentery, and lice, who left the fort's works at their peril: a few days after St. Clair took over as commandant, two unarmed men strolled down the road to go fishing and were set upon and scalped by Indians.

If the men in the garrison were lonely, homesick, and worried about what the future held in store for them, it was no wonder. The only communication between this godforsaken place and the outside world was by letter, and mail was so uncertain and so long in coming that many of them despaired—writing repeatedly and pathetically to family and friends saying that they had heard nothing since leaving home. In the normal course of events, what passed for a postal system meant that a soldier from Acton, Massachusetts, would hear of a militiaman who had been discharged and was going home to Worcester, and the Acton man would give him a letter to carry to his family. When the militiaman reached Worcester he had to find someone else who was going to Acton, which might take another week or more. So it was at best an extremely haphazard arrangement, one that made for correspondence that was lost or interminably delayed, especially since addresses could only be described as sketchy: Brockholst Livingston, for instance, sent letters to his sister addressed "Miss Susan W*m* Livingston, near Morris Town, New Jersey." And it was not thought strange that a letter written from Peekskill, New York, took thirty-six days to reach Providence, Rhode Island.

These difficulties were exacerbated by the frequent scarcity and high cost of paper, quill pens, and ink. In some states these items were standard issue for soldiers, but sutlers did a thriving business, especially in powdered ink, which was easily carried by troops in the field and could be mixed with liquid when needed.*

Their letters and journals were pervaded with signs that they and the army of which they were a part were improvising, meeting new and unfamiliar situations daily, doing their best to cope. And probably without realizing it, in those documents they wrote history as they made it, recording events, day by day, in homely words and phrases (as often as not in maddeningly abbreviated accounts), putting words to paper in spidery Spencerian script or mere scribbles, jotting down a record of their thoughts and experiences on whatever piece of paper came to hand.

---

*Known as iron gall ink, it was made of ferrous sulfate, or copperas, and galls from the bark of oak trees, which contain both tannic and gallic acid. These two substances were mixed with gum arabic from the Middle East, which gave body to the ink and kept it from flowing too fast; the ingredients were then reduced and sifted through cloth to make a fine powder. Before writing a letter, the soldier only needed to add rainwater (the preferred solvent, and readily available) or white wine or beer.

For the better part of a year, responsibility for almost every aspect of the planning, building, and repair work that would turn this squalid place into an outpost that was militarily sound and reasonably habitable had fallen on the capable shoulders of the engineering officer, Colonel Jeduthan Baldwin, and it was appropriate that he should take St. Clair on an inspection tour of the works shortly after his arrival—a tour as dispiriting as the fog and rain that greeted the general. This man Baldwin was the solid stuff of which the American Revolution was made. He had already played an active role in the movement that fostered independence, and he would fight for seven weary years in the war that had to be won if freedom was to be achieved. The rebellion had its share of sansculottes, to be sure, but Baldwin and his likes were inherently moderate men. More to the point, they were the ones who stuck it out through good times and bad (mostly bad), providing the stability and responsible leadership the Revolution had to have if it was to survive.

The colonel was a man of action, continually in motion, an engineer who was happiest when he was building and had no use for the casuals who slouched around camp with too little to do. Each day he entered his commonplace doings in his diary, and there is not the slightest indication in those pages of anything but work, except for the times he shared a meal or a bottle with a friend, or when he was sick with the camp distemper in the fall of 1776.

As a civilian, he had prospered in his hometown of Brookfield, Massachusetts, married and fathered four children, and decided, somewhere along the way, that he had an obligation to serve his country. That service took a variety of forms, not all of them military, though his first appearance on the public stage was as captain of a militia company in the expedition against French-held Crown Point in 1755, where the word quickly got around that he was no quitter. In the fighting, he was badly wounded in the leg, and was advised by surgeons that they would have to amputate, whereupon he hauled himself up on the cot, reached for his bayonet, and said he would run through anyone who tried to hold him down for an operation. When he departed this life, he said, he planned to go out the same way he came into it.

Like Benjamin Franklin, who was until 1776 deeply loyal to king and mother country and once dreamed of an Anglo-American empire, Jeduthan Baldwin and others of like views gradually became convinced that nothing would be done to redress their grievances or fulfill their hopes for reconciliation. Even so, the path on which they embarked was a dangerous, unsettling one that meant abandoning loyalties that had tied men and women to monarchs for as long as two thousand years—an ages-old set of traditions that had been at the very heart of society. No one knew where this revolution would take them or what lay ahead for them and their families, but in Baldwin's case each successive public task he took on saw him drifting ever more surely toward alienation. At the last, the man who had served his king throughout the French and Indian War realized that the only hope of securing "our dear bought rights and privileges" was to break with England and fight for his beliefs.

In 1773 he was a member of a citizens' group that protested importation of tea bearing the hated Townshend duty, and the committee's manifesto reads as if it might have been written by a man who held off a surgeon with a bayonet. After expressing loyalty to King George and his government, the Brookfield men declared their "utter abhorrence of the ... most detestable scheme, in the introduction of Tea from Great Britain to be peddled out amongst us, by which means we were to be made to swallow a poison more fatal ... than ratsbane would be to the natural body."

Baldwin was elected town clerk, selectman, member of the town's Committee of Correspondence, and delegate to the Provincial Congress, and in 1775 he hauled provisions to Boston for the relief of those "suffering the severity of ministerial vengeance." His ultimate estrangement from king and country came about on June 17, 1775.

Perhaps it was true, as John Adams believed, that the Revolution was "in the minds of the people, and this was effected from 1760 to 1775, in the course of fifteen years before a drop of blood was drawn at Lexington." Certainly the wounds had been festering for a long time, especially after the end of the French and Indian War, when the elimination of France from the continent fostered a growing sense of security and self-sufficiency. Yet for many Americans (and for Britons as well, to be sure) the breaking point came at the battle for Bunker Hill, which demonstrated that it would take a war to settle the differences.

Jeduthan Baldwin helped build the redoubt the Americans threw up on Breed's Hill, forcing the British attack, and his brother Isaac was killed in the wild melee that followed. From that moment on, for the next seven years, even when he was overcome with black despair and doubt, he worked tirelessly and fought for the cause he believed in. He planned fortifications for the siege of Boston, followed General Washington to

New York, and was heading for Canada when he met the retreating remnants of the army at Sorel, on the Richelieu River.

A week after arriving at Ticonderoga in July 1776, all his clothes, money, papers, and surveyor's compass were stolen, and he fumed as he scribbled in his diary that he was "heartily tired of this Retreating, Ragged, Starved, lousey, thevish, Pockey Army in this unhealthy Country." But the clothes were found, the thief (a deserter) was caught, and the momentary despondency passed. He spent much of the rest of the year in poor health and left for his Brookfield home early in December, but by mid-February of 1777 he was back in Albany, from which he traveled by sleigh down Lake George (noting that he made it across two dangerous cracks in the ice), and returned to Ticonderoga carrying elaborate orders from General Schuyler that included building a bridge to connect the fort to Mount Independence.

By the time he conducted St. Clair around the post, Baldwin could point with pride at an extraordinary array of achievements: he had designed and built or repaired ships and sawmills, batteries and redoubts, a wharf, two guardhouses, a boom of logs across the lake to impede enemy vessels, an artillery park, campsites, a huge storehouse, hospitals, and a bakery. He had laid out for Dr. Jonathan Potts a vegetable garden (one of several totaling twenty-five acres), located a source of drinking water on Mount Independence, and supervised construction of what he justifiably called the Great Bridge. (An awed German officer later termed it one of the seven wonders of the modern world.) Following Schuyler's instructions, he had twenty-two timber caissons, each twenty-four feet square and thirty feet tall, built on the frozen lake and partially filled with rocks, so that when holes were cut in the ice his "cassoons" sank to the bottom. Once they were in place, further work began. As described by Surgeon James Thacher, the spaces between the caissons were "filled with separate floats, each about fifty feet long and twelve wide, strongly fastened together with iron chains and rivets." On the north side of the planned bridge was a boom of large timbers, tied together by riveted bolts, and alongside it was a double iron chain made of metal an inch and a half square. All in all, Thacher said, it was "admirably adapted to the double purpose of a communication, and an impenetrable barrier to any vessels that might attempt to pass our works." Unfortunately for the progress of this project, no draft animals were available, so all the timber had to be hauled out of the woods by hand, and it was tedious, backbreaking work.

As a stopgap until the span was completed, Baldwin installed a footbridge alongside the caissons to connect the two posts. Back and forth across the narrow neck of water he went, sometimes three or four times a day, checking on this redoubt or that building, now and then traveling by boat, more often on the slippery, floating bridge of logs that were fastened to each other with iron and held in place by anchors. He also erected a crane on Mount Independence for hoisting provisions from the lake to a fort he built there, and even constructed a house for himself. All this while recruiting, managing, and paying what amounted to more than two hundred artificers, whose axes, hammers, and saws created even more noise than that made by the family of Jeduthan's biblical namesake with their cymbals, psalteries, and harps.*

Along the way, Baldwin received some skilled help from Colonel Thaddeus Kosciuszko, a volunteer from Poland with solid engineering experience, who became his assistant and took over the direction of the fatigue parties on Mount Independence, but the help was a mixed blessing. Kosciuszko's interest was less in Baldwin and his projects than in promoting his own agenda with General Gates, to whom he wrote fawning letters seeking a staff position while belittling Baldwin's efforts. "I say nothing of what unnecessary works have been carried on," he wrote in May, "you will be a judge yourself, my General. We are very fond here of making blockhouses & they are all erected in the most improper places. Nevertheless we'll conquer, headed by your Excellency."

With or without Kosciuszko, it was quite an accomplishment, but the work was still far from complete in mid-May when a new topic began appearing in Colonel Baldwin's diary. Now, along with notations about how the work was progressing, the pages echoed an increasing drumbeat of rumors and reports about the enemy.

From the moment the ice went out of the lake and it was again open to shipping, Arthur St. Clair had to assume—despite reassurances by Congress and General Gates to the contrary—that the British would be heading his way. Whether they intended a siege followed by a full-scale assault or a more modest campaign, he could not know, but neither

---

*An idea of the complexity of his task is suggested by Baldwin's list of skilled men working for him in 1776: "House & Ship Carpenters, the Smiths, Armourers, Roap makers, the Wheel and Carriage makers, Miners, Turners, Coalyers, Sawyers & Shingle makers. . . ." He also directed hundreds of men in fatigue parties working on his projects, with the result that "I have my hands & mind constantly employed night & Day, except when I am asleep & then sometimes I dream."

could he believe that they would repeat last October's performance, when they turned back because of the lateness of the season. No, this time they would surely take advantage of the long summer days, the best time for campaigning, and one of these mornings sails would appear on the horizon he was watching so intently—the vanguard of a fleet coming up the lake.

As St. Clair took stock of his situation he realized how much would depend on several factors. One was the location of the defensive works and the lay of the land (and water) around them and how much of an advantage that gave him. Another was whether the building and repairs that had been going on for a year could possibly be finished in time. Finally, he had to ask how much importance was attached to Ticonderoga by General Washington and Congress, on the one hand, and by the British on the other. The answers to this last question would determine how much outside help he could expect to receive and the size of the force that would attack him.

On June 8, a warm, pleasant Sunday, the Reverend Enos Hitchcock had chosen for his text Psalm 119, the 150th verse—"They draw nigh that follow after mischief: they are far from thy law"—and five days later, when St. Clair took command of the fort, it looked as if the man of the cloth had been in touch with higher authority.

Two prisoners were brought before the new commandant for questioning on June 13. Captured on the Onion River, near Colchester, by a scouting party and led into camp the previous day, they divulged enough information about British preparations to justify all the uneasiness that had troubled the sleep of Anthony Wayne and Philip Schuyler. Now St. Clair could begin worrying in earnest, for if this news was accurate the enemy was indeed drawing nigh, and with more than mischief in mind.

One of the prisoners was named Adams, the other Amsbury, and what they had to say was that General John Burgoyne had definitely arrived in Canada and assumed command of most of Carleton's army. Even now his troops were "assembling as fast as possible" at St. Johns on the Richelieu River, near the outlet of Lake Champlain, from which point a British fleet would transport them up the lake to attack Ticonderoga. Already the light infantry under General Fraser had reached Pointe au Fer, and the prisoners predicted that the redcoats would reach the fort in force within two weeks. Another contingent, they said, with a party of Iroquois Indians under the command of Sir John Johnson was heading from Oswego toward the Mohawk Valley to join Burgoyne near Albany.

Something about this smelled fishy to St. Clair. For one thing, he was sure Amsbury was a spy. The fellow was carrying a British pass and an unusually large sum of Continental money, gold, and silver, plus letters from Montreal to people in the states. What better way for the enemy to deceive him, St. Clair mused, than to send these two with what purported to be an accurate picture of British preparations in Canada, along with letters from friends of Americans, and in this way gain admission to the fort and discover what was going on at Ticonderoga. He suspected the information they gave him was phony.

Amsbury was a slick one, and St. Clair wanted him interrogated at Albany rather than at Ticonderoga: the last spy brought to the fort had been allowed to escape, and the officer guilty of this offense had been acquitted by a court-martial. So Amsbury was sent under guard to Schuyler, who got him to talk about his mysterious errand. Amsbury had made the mistake of hanging on to a note intended for British troops on Ile aux Noix. Written by a brigade major with Burgoyne's army, it stated that the bearer was on "secret service" for the general, that his journey was not to be "interrupted," nor was he to be searched. In addition to what he had told St. Clair, Amsbury admitted to Schuyler that the British had built numerous carts for transporting baggage and ammunition; they were sending a great many horses overland, down the west side of the lake; they intended to cut off the rebels' communications between Mount Independence and Skenesborough and between Fort George and Fort Edward.

As if that were not enough to clinch the case against him, Amsbury had left a canteen with a false bottom with a soldier at Fort George and when it was retrieved and opened by Schuyler it proved to contain a curious letter from Peter Livius, a New Hampshire loyalist who was now chief justice of Canada, to Major General John Sullivan, who succeeded to the command of the Northern Army after John Thomas died, urging him to recant and "exert himself for government," by which Livius meant for Sullivan to rally men from New Hampshire, his home state, and bring them over to the British.

What to make of this? The letter to Sullivan was strange, to be sure, but more ominous by far was the news Amsbury brought, indicating that Burgoyne and a sizable army were advancing up the lake. Other bits of intelligence appeared to corroborate the prisoners' story: for several weeks scouts had been reporting the movement of vessels at the other end of the lake, a British schooner was now within four miles of Crown Point, and what was thought to be the enemy army's morning gun had been heard in the distance.* St. Clair and Schuyler concluded that they had better act as though the information was accurate and prepare for the worst. Schuyler dispatched an express to Washington urging him to send reinforcements at once.

Long before Amsbury's tidings reached Schuyler in Albany, Ticonderoga was abuzz with the news. At last all the camp rumors seemed to be confirmed: the enemy *was* coming after all, and the reaction was generally one of relief and excitement. This confidence was astonishing, to say the least, in view of a report that Burgoyne's force was reputedly ten thousand strong, outnumbering them four or five to one, but many of the rebel troops were green, they were cocky, they had not seen the face of the enemy or been on the receiving end of a murderous volley by massed British regulars, and of course they had heard from old-timers how Montcalm had routed five times his numbers at this very fort. No one, they figured, could beat them as long as they were protected by these walls.

George Washington had had experience with amateur soldiers such as these and believed he knew how to get the most out of them. "Place them behind a parapet, a breastwork, stone wall, or any thing that will afford them shelter, and from their knowledge of a firelock, they will give a good account of their enemy. . . ." he said, adding, ". . . but I am as well convinced, as if I had seen it, that they will not march boldly up to a work nor stand exposed in a plain." For these reasons, Washington said, "I have never spared the spade and the pickaxe."

Neither had the engineer at Ticonderoga, for that matter, but if what Amsbury had told St. Clair and Schuyler was true, these old walls and the men behind them would be put to the test before long.

---

*It was not the army's morning signal. British troops were too far down the lake for their guns to be heard; the boom that echoed at Fort Ticonderoga almost certainly came from a ship's cannon in the vicinity of Split Rock.

Chapter 7

The Scalping Knife
and the Gospel

Major General Friedrich Adolph Baron von Riedesel was feeling the strain of long hours and heavy responsibility. Already working to the point of exhaustion, in Trois Rivières he made the mistake of sleeping with the window open and came down with a bad cold and a fever that left him weak and depressed.

Shortly after Burgoyne's arrival, the two officers dined and had a thoughtful discussion in which the English general outlined the goals of the campaign. Their mission, he said, was to drive the rebels from Lake Champlain and Lake George and open communications with Sir William Howe, from whom he would receive further instructions. He planned to head up the lake as soon as provisions for six weeks were on hand at Chambly, with adequate transport available for the army and its provisions. Meanwhile, St. Leger would be moving in on the rebels from the west to cut their supply line.

Despite Burgoyne's reassuring words, the baron was uneasy. For one thing, the recent change in command was unsettling. Writing to Duke Ferdinand of Brunswick, he described General Carleton as "very indignant at being replaced," which was to be expected under the circumstances, yet "God knows what [Burgoyne] will do with the ... army which has already been a whip to his ambition."

Several weeks later, by which time Riedesel had an opportunity to size up the expedition's commander, he decided that "he judges somewhat hastily." Burgoyne's impetuousness differed sharply from the temperament of his predecessor, who worked carefully, not making a move until he was convinced of a plan's safety and likelihood of success. Well, all one could do was wait and see, the baron decided: "The result will show who was right in the first place."

After Burgoyne divided his army into three units—an advanced corps; the right wing, consisting entirely of British regiments; and the left, with all the Germans—Riedesel personally shepherded his troops safely across the St. Lawrence. Up the sluggish Richelieu the men of Brunswick and Hesse-Hanau traveled by bateau as far as the falls at Chambly, site of an old French masonry fort that had been burned by the retreating Americans the previous year and was now reconstructed. Here they disembarked to drag the boats along the portage around the rapids. In Chambly sailors, shipwrights, and soldiers pressed into service were readying everything that might float for the trip up the lake. Although bateaus were flat-bottomed and, according to a British officer, "quite ungovernable when it blows hard," they were to be the workhorses of the amphibious operation, each carrying about thirty-five men. They were designed to be rowed, but frequently a single mast was stepped with a square sail to take advantage of a following breeze. These boats were loaded onto newly made carts, miserable vehicles that reminded the Germans of those used in the Harz Mountains for drawing coal from the mines, and onto large wagons made of logs (half of which broke down on the portage). Larger sailing craft were disassembled and hauled to St. Johns, to be rebuilt and launched.

The Specht Regiment set out at eight one morning with its gear in fifty carts; once arrived at Ste. Thérèse the baggage was unloaded and the carts sent back to repeat the business for the von Rhetz Regiment, but in spite of the spell of fair weather the road was dry only on the surface and horses and wagons floundered in a spreading sea of mud. Boats were dragged with ropes pulled by the straining, cursing men, and it was slow, frustrating, dangerous work, with bateaus snagged repeatedly between gigantic boulders or in the branches of fallen trees. When they reached St. Johns at last, they found a village of some eighty houses, an artillery park jammed with small cannon and mortars, hundreds of waiting bateaus, numerous gunboats, and—riding at anchor in the harbor—Great Britain's proud Lake Champlain battle fleet. At best it could be described as a motley lot of vessels, the largest of which were the *Royal George*, 384 tons, carrying twenty-six guns, that had recently been built here at St. Johns, and the *Thunderer*, an ungainly craft known as a radeau. Square, blunt, and armored, the *Thunderer* embodied the story of this northern frontier: it had been built by the French, sunk by the Americans, and raised by the British to be remade as a floating battery for the anticipated siege of Ticonderoga.

The *Inflexible*, a three-masted ship carrying twenty-two guns, had been brought down from the stocks at Quebec and rebuilt at St. Johns. The schooners *Maria*, named for General Carleton's wife, and *Carleton*, fourteen and twelve guns respectively, had both been taken down at Chambly, carried over the portage, and reassembled. The gondola *Loyal Convert*, seven guns, had also been brought overland, and the *Washington*, *Lee*, and *Jersey* had been salvaged from Benedict Arnold's unlucky fleet. The last three were destined to be turned into transports when it became known that the rebels had no ships to oppose them on the lake, since all the supplies—countless tons of food for hungry men and horses, powder and shot for the guns, and everything else the army would need, packed in thousands of barrels and boxes—were to be ferried to Crown Point and stockpiled in the depot that was planned there.

By the time Baron Riedesel reached St. Johns he was more feverish, upset that his private stock of food and wine had not yet reached him, and suffering the familiar pangs of homesickness even though he knew now that his baroness was on the way to America. He was thirty-nine years old and deeply in love with his wife, and ever since leaving Wolfenbüttel he had been writing a stream of letters to her, pouring out his loneliness and his love. He had promised she could join him as soon as she recovered from the birth of their third child, but their separation had been prolonged for sixteen months because the ship on which she was supposed to sail from England in the autumn had left without her, dooming her to a frustrating, expensive winter in London, during which she often despaired of seeing him again. Theirs had been an arranged marriage, but it was clearly a love match between the beautiful Frederika Charlotte Louise von Massow, daughter of a Prussian general, and the dashing cavalryman Riedesel, an aide-de-camp to Duke Ferdinand of Brunswick.

A portrait of the baron at the time of his marriage might be taken for an elegant wind-up toy soldier decorating the wedding cake. He was then twenty-four years old (his bride was sixteen), a wisp of a man with the face and figure of a child, standing casually with one hand on his hip, holding his richly braided blue cap, the other on the hilt of his saber. The white fur edging his cape matches his powdered hair, his blue jacket is a mass of gold braid from neck to waist, his sash and skin-tight riding trousers are bright red, and he appears the very essence of the aristocrat-turned-soldier.

Riedesel's father had hoped he would study law, but instead he joined the army and was one of the Brunswickers who fought under their duke at Minden in '59. The baron had begun to add weight since that wedding portrait was painted, but his years as a cavalryman kept him active and alert, and he was still a handsome man. Known for his intellect, charm, and tact, he became one of the duke's favorite staff officers, and because a great deal of authority had been delegated to him he was actually more experienced than Burgoyne at commanding an army. He had a sharp eye for terrain, a real talent for intelligence work, and was much admired by his troops for the way he looked after their health and comfort. Although he spoke some English, he and Burgoyne communicated with each other in French, as did most British and German officers in the campaign.

At Minden he had been promoted to captain after the stupendous battle fought in the classic European manner. On the great level plain, where 37,000 allied troops confronted 44,000 French, the battle began with the British infantry marching in silence, directly toward the enemy across three miles of flat land. Then, suddenly, to the steady, insistent roll of drums, ranks were dressed, the gun teams deployed into line, and scarlet-coated foot soldiers—three ranks deep, with senior regiments on the flanks, junior units between them, colors flapping overhead—pressed forward in perfect step toward the waiting French cannon while 7,000 mounted cavalrymen waited for the order to charge. It was the romantic and beautiful stuff of heroic paintings—or was, until the French artillery opened fire, tearing jagged holes in those neat scarlet lines, shattering 30 percent of the redcoats' total strength in the four-hour battle. Yet it was their incredible discipline that made possible the victory.

It was unlikely that anything remotely resembling the battle of Minden would be seen during Burgoyne's campaign, but discipline and drill were the very fiber of the British and German units that would carry the fighting to the rebels, and on June 13 their training was put on display in a tribute to General Guy Carleton. The previous afternoon and evening had been devoted to an elaborate banquet laid on by Major General William Phillips, who commanded the right wing of the army. All the other generals were present—Carleton, Burgoyne, Riedesel, and the brigadiers—and it was a festive occasion, with the madeira, Rhine wines, and champagne flowing freely before the port was served. It was also a moment of mixed emotions: a number of these officers were extremely fond of Carleton, believed he had been treated shabbily, and were genuinely sorry to see him left behind; but the mood changed with the arrival of a messenger bringing word to an ecstatic Riedesel that his wife and three daughters had finally arrived with a convoy from Portsmouth that was also carrying reinforcements and supplies. "The whole company showed general joy and drank a good toast to your safe arrival," the baron wrote in a note sent posthaste for delivery to his baroness when she landed.

An eighteenth-century army was nothing if not superbly drilled, exquisitely versed in the ritual of the review (especially the Brunswickers, who were often accused of dressing ranks so often they could not keep pace on the march), and it was a pity so few spectators were on hand in St. Johns to see the spit and polish of disciplined soldiers passing in review for General Sir Guy Carleton. A knowledgeable onlooker would have noticed the British wearing uniforms that were definitely nonregulation. This was an unintended tribute to an American privateer: the previous fall a British transport carrying uniforms for sixteen thousand men, plus thirty thousand shirts and thirty thousand pairs of shoes and stockings for the army in Canada, had been seized by a rebel ship. As a result, the soldiers had been ordered to cut off the tails of their scarlet coats for patches. Now they all wore short jackets and had trimmed their cocked hats into caps, in the style of the light infantry, clothing that was much more practical for the rough wilderness fighting ahead.

The Brunswick dragoons had also undergone a facelift of sorts. Since they had no mounts, they no longer wore the heavy jackboots that came halfway up the thigh, or leather breeches and gloves. They still carried sabers and carbines, but the latter had been modified to accommodate bayonets, and to replace the leggings they left behind in Canada, they now wore canvas trousers.

With the bands playing and regimental flags snapping in the breeze, Carleton took the salute from what was to have been his army for the last time, and he made the most of it. He had the German regiment of dragoons march past in platoons and files; then he went to the riverbank to watch the Specht and von Rhetz regiments disembark from their bateaus and come on the double to camp, where he reviewed them once again, after which he complimented their officers and recommended them to General Burgoyne. Back in barracks German bakers were removing loaf after loaf of bread from the ovens, while out in the stream the royal standard of Great Britain was run up the mainmast of the *Thunderer* and saluted by the flotilla of British ships lying at anchor. Ordinarily flown only when a member of the royal family was present, on this occasion the standard was meant to inspire loyalty to the king as if he were actually on the scene. The banner displayed the three golden lions of England, the red lion of Scotland, Ireland's harp, and, as a curious anachronism, the fleur-de-lis of France, whose throne the kings of England had claimed since the fifteenth century—all symbols of the might that would be unleashed against the rebellious Americans.

Carleton's last official act was to order rum distributed to the troops (at the rate of a quart for every sixteen men it would not go far, but it was a welcome gesture—except to the Germans, who were accustomed to whiskey). Then he departed for his elegant quarters in Quebec, where he could sit and wait and curse his luck, envying his successor's inevitable triumphs over the rebels. The next day Burgoyne, now with the rank of lieutenant general which was to be his during his service in America, received a fifteen-gun salute as he boarded the *Maria*, and the army, carrying provisions for two weeks, cast off, bound for Ticonderoga.

The plan was for the regiments to head out at regular intervals, one after another, so that each successive unit would occupy the campsite its predecessor had used the previous night, and the entire army was to rendezvous at Cumberland Head on the west bank of the lake. Until the army reassembled, there was theoretically a risk that the separate units would be vulnerable to piecemeal attack, but Burgoyne had no worries on that score, since Commodore Skeffington Lutwidge had ample force to prevent any rebel vessels from approaching.

In the early days of May, before Burgoyne arrived, Major General William Phillips had ordered Brigadier General Simon Fraser to have his men sweep the area between the St. Lawrence and St. Johns. Men from the light infantry were to "enter the woods and make their scout in a half circle so that the woods toward the rebels may be explored ten or twelve miles. . . ." Phillips was taking no chances: he was familiar with the rebel practice of sending two or three men out on patrol, and he wanted no word of British movements or their strength to get back to Ticonderoga.

With no fanfare other than a review by Burgoyne, the campaign began in earnest when Fraser and his advanced corps broke camp and left Canada at the end of May. This elite outfit consisted of Fraser's own regiment, the 24th Foot, led by Major Robert Grant; a grenadier battalion under Major John Acland; and light infantry commanded by another young major, Alexander Lindsay, 6th Earl of Balcarres. In addition to these regulars, Fraser had about 150 reluctant Canadian woodsmen in tow; Ebenezer Jessup's King's Loyal Americans; the Queen's Loyal Rangers under John Peters; and a company of rangers from Canada led by his nephew, Captain Alexander Fraser.*

John Acland may not have been aware of it, but Balcarres had a chip on his shoulder because of him. The Scot had written in February to General Carleton, requesting that he—not Acland—be permitted to purchase a lieutenant colonel's commission that was to be sold. It was unthinkable, he submitted, that preference in this matter should be given a man who was junior on the list of majors, younger in age, and "under no particular description of Distinction superior" to Balcarres in terms of "*Service, Family, Zeal,* or *Attention* to his Duty." Corresponding with his mother, Balcarres explained his predicament: he was "fourth major in the army" with no immediate hope of promotion, which meant that the purchase of a commission of higher rank was his only hope. He had no expectation of being "a very splendid Peer or . . . a very rich one," and knew that the army offered the best chance of advancement; in fact, it was "the only way by which a man in my Situation with a small Fortune & no Connections can insure to himself the Respect that is due to him." That being the case, he asked her to see that a credit of £1,500 be arranged in the event an opportunity came his way to purchase a lieutenant colonelcy.

In the British army of that day, an infantry company numbered sixty men at full strength, with ten companies to the regiment. Eight of the ten were made up of ordinary foot soldiers, and were known as battalion companies. On the flanks, which were considered the positions of honor, were a company of grenadiers and one of light infantry. The latter were carefully chosen for their physical ability and were posted on the left flank, serving as skirmishers and scouts. The grenadiers (who no longer carried the grenades from which they got their name) were the tallest, strongest men in the regiment, whose bearskin hats, in the case of the British, or tall, miterlike caps, in the case of the Germans, gave them the appearance of even greater height. They were on the right flank and were usually the first to be engaged in an attack. Fraser's command—a formidable little army in itself—was made up of ten grenadier and ten light infantry companies drawn from the regiments traveling with Burgoyne, plus three from those that had remained with Carleton.

While Burgoyne was still in London, planning the campaign with Lord

---

*General Phillips had taken a shine to this young officer. "I never took more liking to any man than Fraser," he wrote to the captain's uncle. "He is a sensible, cool, civil, plain man. I daresay a most excellent officer. . . ."

George Germain, he had selected the regiments he would take on the expedition, and he had chosen well. His army, on the whole, was composed of sound, seasoned outfits that were uniformly well officered, for he had picked the commanders with special care. It was a measure of his high regard for Simon Fraser that he wrote him on May 6, the day he arrived from Europe, saying he had a large parcel of letters from Fraser's family and friends which he would deliver personally. In the meantime, he informed Fraser confidentially, he was about to relieve Carleton—a touchy situation he described as "critical and delicate"—after which "the military operations, all directed to make a junction with Howe, are committed to me." Nothing could have indicated more clearly how Burgoyne interpreted his orders.

No one stood higher in his esteem, he went on, than Fraser, and he had done his best while in England to see that the Scot was held in the same regard "in the [King's] Closet and with the ministers"—a broad hint that promotion might be forthcoming. Promotion or not, Burgoyne was going to lean heavily on Fraser, who would be his most trusted adviser as well as a good friend, and the brigadier's advanced corps, as its title suggested, would be out in front of the army, on the march and in battle, inevitably with the toughest assignments. Even before hearing this from his new commanding officer, Fraser had received hints of the coming operation and his role in it. A friend in London had written to say that Burgoyne was coming to "cross the lakes so as to afford Sir Wm. Howe some assistance in putting an effectual end to the rebellion in this ensuing campaign," which was sincerely to be hoped, since "the expence is enormous." And from the same source had come word that Germain agreed with Burgoyne that Fraser should have an important command.

This man who was expected to be one of the key figures in the campaign was forty-eight years old and had spent most of his adult life in uniform, fighting in the Low Countries, where he was wounded at the age of eighteen, in Germany, and in America, where he served with the 78th Highlanders under Amherst and Wolfe. Along with a wealth of experience, Fraser was a competent, accomplished officer. As it happened, he and Baron Riedesel were old comrades-in-arms, having fought together during the Seven Years War, and he got on famously with Phillips, with whom he had worked closely in 1776, learning a great deal about American scouting parties and how best to cope with them, using Canadians and Indians as guides and trackers. Fraser had also developed corps of a hundred marksmen in each regiment—men "chosen for their strength, activity, and being expert at firing ball." Each man was furnished with the best available firelock and was expected to practice marksmanship regularly, to learn exactly how much powder was required to fire accurately at maximum range and then to make up his cartridges accordingly. This was innovative stuff, as was furnishing the marksmen with tomahawks.

Major General William Phillips, commanding the British right wing, was made of the rock-solid material that has held successful armies together since men began organizing to make war on one another. Big and beefy, as tough as he was outspoken, he was a no-nonsense officer whose vocabulary did not include the word "failure." (Some years later, Thomas Jefferson paid him the dubious compliment of being "the proudest man of the proudest nation on earth.") The fact that he was an artilleryman says a great deal about his appointment as Burgoyne's second-in-command, since engineers and artillery officers were generally regarded with scorn by line officers and were actually prohibited from field command by royal order, to which Burgoyne was granted a temporary (and grudging) exception in Phillips's case.

A big mark in Phillips's favor was his familiarity with this area, since he had been actively involved in the '76 campaign. He was about of an age with Fraser and had thirty years' experience as a gunner—notably at Minden, where he was said to have broken fifteen canes over the backs of horses to spur them into a gallop and get his cannon into position. For this unheard-of haste and the superlative performance of his artillery, he—like Riedesel—received a battlefield promotion and was personally commended by Duke Ferdinand of Brunswick, who also presented him with a purse of a thousand crowns.

Like Burgoyne, Phillips was a member of Parliament. More to the point, he was a superb gunner and a man of great energy (along with a terrible temper), and he approved of using Indians on the expedition, having learned the necessity of employing them in this forested country in lieu of cavalry to screen the army's advance and serve as its eyes and ears. He and Fraser seem to have had an unusual insight into the fears of raw, inexperienced soldiers, and he praised his fellow officer's practice of exposing his men gradually to their foes, saying that "it learns the officers and men to know that troops may look at an enemy without an absolute necessity of fighting and that going near and retiring may be a demonstration and not a retreat."

When Burgoyne's critics in London learned the size of his artillery train, they were scornful, complaining that it was far too large for a wilderness expedition, but the general had no intention of repeating

Abercromby's fatal mistake in 1758 of relying solely on small arms to attack Ticonderoga, and besides, the memory of Bunker Hill was still green in Burgoyne's mind. Furthermore, it was a given in the eighteenth century that a strong fortress like Ticonderoga was vulnerable to three methods of attack. One was mining, which meant tunneling beneath the walls and blowing them up; another was bombardment by heavy artillery until the walls were breached; the third was protracted siege, to starve the garrison into submission. As the British knew, mining was out of the question in this instance because the fort was built on bedrock. And Burgoyne, having witnessed the tenacity of Americans when they were protected by earthworks, was convinced that the only way to dislodge them from behind the stone walls of Ticonderoga was by overwhelming firepower and, probably, a prolonged siege. This was one reason for his reliance on the artilleryman Phillips, and it was why his train included 138 guns, ranging in size from twenty-four-pounders to 4.4-inch mortars, and required the services of 250 British and 100 Hessian gunners, plus another 150 British recruits. According to the *Annual Register* for 1777, "the brass train that was sent out on this expedition was perhaps the finest and probably the most excellently supplied as to officers and private men, that has ever been allotted to second the operations of any army."

After the festivities and the reviews at St. Johns, Phillips's right wing set sail: following in the wake of Fraser's advanced corps came the First Brigade, under Brigadier General Henry Watson Powell, consisting of the 9th, 47th, and 53rd Regiments; and the Second, led by Brigadier General James Inglis Hamilton, which had the 20th, 21st, and 62nd Regiments.

These outfits were followed by the left wing under Riedesel, who was known to irreverent Cockneys among the British rank and file as "Red Hazel." Riedesel's First Brigade was commanded by Brigadier General Johann Friedrich Specht, with the von Rhetz, von Riedesel, and Specht Regiments; the Second was under Brigadier General W. von Gall, who led the Prinz Friedrich and Hesse-Hanau; plus an advanced corps under Lieutenant Colonel Heinrich Breymann, made up of jägers—or riflemen— under Major von Barner; an unhappy lot of horseless dragoons under Lieutenant Colonel Baum; and grenadiers under Breymann himself.

Even on the water these units were expected to maintain a sort of parade-ground perfection: each corps had four boats in the van and on the flanks, with enough room between to accommodate the oars of boats in the center, and whether sailing or rowing they were to "endeavour to keep the same Order."

On June 20, 1777, the armada got under way after two guns were fired from the *Maria* and a Jack was hoisted from her foretopmast head, and if ever an army exuded confidence, with every reason to do so, it was this one. Thomas Anburey, who was accompanying the expedition as a volunteer, wrote that "if good discipline, joined to health and great spirit amongst the men, with their being led on by General Burgoyne, who is universally esteemed and respected, can ensure success, it may be expected."

In numbers, British and Germans were more or less evenly divided, with 3,981 of the former and 3,116 Brunswick and Hesse-Hanau troops, for a total of more than 7,000, including artillery. They were similar also in a preponderance of tough, disciplined, experienced troops: the regiments had long traditions of valor and skill, and the Germans were led by officers who had learned their trade under Frederick the Great and Duke Ferdinand of Brunswick. In training and weapons, there was not much to choose between them, but most Germans were severely handicapped by their inability to speak English, which meant that communication was largely between officers, and in a sort of pidgin French. Most unhappy of all were the unfortunate dragoons, who, lacking the horses on which they were trained to fight, would have to traipse through deep woods and abominable roads wearing ridiculous plumed hats and carrying long, straight broadswords that were as useless as they were a hindrance.

In almost all respects, the force at Burgoyne's disposal was a superb tactical instrument. In battle, the British infantry was rated at or near the top of the major powers' armies, as was the artillery, and firepower was the essence of that superiority. The foot soldier was not expected to be a marksman: what was required of him was that he point his musket in the general direction of the enemy and load and fire on command about fifteen times in the space of four minutes. When this was executed by ordered ranks of men who were thoroughly drilled in the close-order volley, it could shatter and paralyze an enemy, and was usually followed by the bayonet charge, so feared and hated by the rebels. Burgoyne's officers were under orders "to inculcate in the men's minds a Reliance upon the Bayonet," on grounds that while men half their bodily strength— even cowards—might be their match with the musket, "the onset of Bayonets in the hands of the Valiant is irresistible."

If there was a major flaw in the arsenal of these British or German units, it was their dependence on enormous baggage trains, but as long as they were capable of being supplied by water that might not be a problem. What would happen when they began traveling overland remained to be seen.

Burgoyne had directed Fraser to proceed from St. Johns to Pointe au Fer to the south end of Cumberland Bay, a place called Pointe au Sable, where the Ausable River flows into the lake, after which the entire army would assemble at Cumberland Head. Arrangements had been made in Canada to lead strings of artillery horses overland (the general added that officers would have to assume the expense of moving and feeding their bât-horses, as the animals that carried their personal baggage were called). Burgoyne also had the Indians on his mind: some were coming by canoe, some on foot, and when they arrived at Pointe au Sable he wanted Fraser to have them camp on Ile la Motte, where they would be "at hand for a council as soon as I arrive at Cumberland Point." That was to be an important occasion, and the general was preparing carefully for it.

Fifteen miles from St. Johns the invasion flotilla passed Ile aux Noix, a mile-long, humpbacked strip of low-lying land commanding the entrance to the Richelieu, bristling with barracks, magazines, and blockhouses. Once past the little island, they were in Lake Champlain, no more than a mile and a half wide here, where they saw "some miserable dwellings in ruins on the west shore," including a large sawmill owned by a Colonel Christie that had been burned by the rebels. At Pointe au Fer, where two hundred Iroquois Indians led by Captain Fraser were seen shoving off in their birchbark canoes, a loyal Englishman had built a fortified house of stone overlooking the superb terrain of the headland, and it too had been burned down to the masonry walls. Mute casualties such as these would be the pattern as the army continued up the lake—tiny apertures of what had passed for civilization in the surrounding gloom of the forest, clearings and little huts—some built under a French king, some under a British monarch, most of them now destroyed by rebels or Indians as the frontier wars waxed and waned.

One day the troops in their bateaus might make nine miles, the next fifteen, seldom more than twenty, and the soldiers who were new to this lake were struck, as everyone always was, by the quantities and varieties of its wildlife—"pike of an incredible size," salmon and bass and muskellunge, prodigious numbers of passenger pigeons so exhausted from their flight across the lake that they fell or were knocked off the limbs of trees with clubs to make "the most delicious eating." The men saw bison and moose, bears and wolves, fox, beaver, wildcats, eagles, and turtles weighing as much as eighty pounds.

Each night they went ashore to the dreary routine of clearing brush, collecting firewood, digging latrines, swatting the voracious mosquitoes and no-see-ums against which their only defense was to build fires and be nearly suffocated with smoke and to sleep with hands and face covered while trying to endure the torture. "If anybody could have watched us," one soldier wrote after a night of agony, "he would have thought the whole camp full of raving maniacs." The Germans, having finished off their supply of bread, were equally unhappy to learn that the British commissary did not supply troops with the staff of life—only flour, with which the men were expected to bake their own loaves in hot ashes. General Burgoyne might express pleasure that "some corps have got the art of making Flour cakes without ovens, which are equally wholesome and relishing with the best bread," but the hard, heavy product was not to the Germans' liking. Almost as bad, they missed the whiskey and tobacco that were part of their rations on duty in Europe.

Below Ile la Motte, a wild, uninhabited place some six miles long, the banks of the lake were faced with cliffs and rocks, inhospitable campsites, and the soldiers had a long, difficult passage across open water before they reached the rendezvous at Cumberland Head. It was not a good choice. It was, in fact, a "miserable place," according to Surgeon Wasmus of the dragoons, with swampy ground and thick woods swarming with the dreaded *brûlies* or no-see-ums. Little wonder, the men thought, that Burgoyne remained aboard the *Maria*, anchored offshore, though there was some suspicion that the woman who had been seen with him might have something to do with his preference for the ship. On June 19 the general did come ashore long enough to inspect those regiments he had not yet reviewed, and orders were passed to shove off the following day. Every man was issued ten ball cartridges, causing Wasmus to note, ". . . the affair is becoming serious." The army also received instructions to be followed if it was necessary to get under way immediately (tents were to be struck at once and stowed in the bateaus with knapsacks, blankets, provisions, and ammunition). If the situation demanded a sudden movement by land, they were to leave tents standing and form up, ready to march. Each man was to make up one hundred cartridges; regiments were to have two days' provisions cooked; and above all, the men were prohibited from selling liquor to the Indians, under pain of death.

At 4:00 A.M. on the 24th the order for the general march was beaten. The troops clambered aboard their bateaus and rowed out of Cumberland Bay as the sun was coming up, to be treated to a sight few of them would ever forget. Approaching the widest part of the lake, they could see off to the east, silhouetted against the rising sun, the peaks of the Green Mountains. To the west the craggy Adirondacks loomed dark and mysterious, dappled now with soft light that first caught the rims of ridges and moved slowly down their flanks, transforming the shadows from minute to minute. These were the oldest mountains on the continent, whose foundations had been laid a billion years earlier, and as the sky lightened, tier after tier became exposed, each dimmer and more distant until they vanished beyond the western horizon.

It was a glorious morning, bright and clear, and the water that reflected the mountains suddenly mirrored the entire army, spread out in a grand cortege of boats. Out in front were the Indians, as many as forty of them seated or kneeling in each birchbark canoe, their brilliant war paint, feathers, and jujus contrasting with the white and black of their graceful craft that were as swift as swallows. Then came the advanced corps—regulars in scarlet coats, white breeches and waistcoats; light infantry in black leather caps and red waistcoats; grenadiers distinguishable by their heavy black bearskin hats; and Canadians in Indian costume, followed by the gunboats, carrying artillerymen in blue.

In their wake the *Royal George* and the *Inflexible* moved ponderously through the water, towing large booms intended for service near Ticonderoga: reaching from one side of the lake to the other, they would prevent any rebel vessels from heading north. Astern of these ships came the dark-hulled *Maria* and *Carleton*, then the first British brigade—more scarlet coats, some faced with bright yellow, others with red or white. Three pinnaces, or cutters, were next in line, each bearing a general—Burgoyne, Phillips, and Riedesel. The second British brigade followed, oars flashing rhythmically, then the Germans—infantrymen in dark blue coats, white breeches and waistcoats, jägers in green with red cuffs and facings, the officers wearing plumed hats. Unlike the British grenadiers, their German counterparts were outfitted with tall caps with shiny metal plates, and by now these fellows had become accomplished boatmen, having discovered to their joy how much easier travel was by water than tramping overland. Bringing up the rear of this extraordinary procession came the sutlers and camp followers of all kinds.

Accustomed to the measured tramp of feet on a dusty parade ground, the British and German soldiers had seen nothing like this before—

could never have imagined the sight of a whole army, more than seven thousand men, costumed as colorfully as songbirds, with brass and steel and silver glinting in the sunlight, and the entire tableau doubled by the mirror images in the water. Off in the distance little rebel watch boats could be seen, hurrying down the lake as close as they dared, then darting back to relay the sobering news of this force to Arthur St. Clair at Ticonderoga.

The breathtaking panorama of the British armada was a matchless setting for the next scene in this unfolding drama. The army was in high spirits, confident in itself and its destiny, and no small factor in the collective state of mind was the popularity of its leader. Soldiers liked his bluff, hearty manner; he was quick to laugh and had a bonhomie and panache that caught their fancy, prompting Lieutenant William Digby to comment that he was "the soldier's friend" and was "idolized by the army." General John Burgoyne had written the scenario for what was now taking place, and there is every reason to believe that he saw himself playing the leading part—the actor on whose shoulders the entire production hinged. The role was that of Jack the King's Commander, as a wag once called him, and Jack was to have all the best lines, lead the charge, and reap the applause and the rewards when the final curtain fell on a superb performance.

Only it was not necessarily going to play according to the script. When a large ego is involved, as one certainly was in this instance, the possibility exists that the ego will outrun reason. From the moment Guy Carleton departed, leaving the stage to Burgoyne, the campaign took on a character that was a direct reflection of the latter's personality, and the first indication of this came on June 20, with the army camped on both banks of the Bouquet River.

Burgoyne had spent several days preparing a document to be widely circulated through New England, where it was intended to strike fear into the hearts of "the harden'd Enemies of Great Britain and America" (whom he considered to be one and the same), while offering open arms, restoration of their rights, and security to loyal subjects of the king. On the face of it, that was more or less to be expected of any army commander in his shoes, but Burgoyne had a penchant for the histrionic and the pompous that defeated his purpose. A single sentence suggests the whole: reciting the arbitrary imprisonment, confiscation of property, persecution, and torture inflicted by revolutionaries upon loyalists, much of which was true enough, he stated, "To consummate these shocking proceedings the profanation of Religion is added to the most profligate prostitution of common reason, the consciences of Men are set at naught and multitudes are compelled not only to bear Arms, but also to swear subjection to an usurpation they abhor." Even in an age when the prose of official pronouncements tended to be high-flown, this was not going to have much appeal for the average American farm boy.

He went on to legitimize his proclamation "in consciousness of Christianity, my Royal Master's clemency, and the honor of Soldiership," apparently unaware that the tone of boastfulness and the turgid rhetoric guaranteed that his manifesto would be as much ridiculed in Britain as in America. But the real shocker came in the form of a threat no American could mistake. "I have but to give stretch to the Indian Forces under my direction, and they amount to Thousands . . ." he promised, adding that the king's enemies could now expect to meet "the messengers of justice and of wrath . . . devastation, famine, and every concomitant horror."

Several days later, copies of this document were carried to the east side of the lake by Fraser's men, where they were handed out to local inhabitants who were selling cattle to the British for "hard coin." In no time at all, news of the general's pronouncement spread to the south and east.

Predictably, Horace Walpole greeted the news of Burgoyne's proclamation with derisive remarks about the "vaporing Burgoyne," who was able to "reconcile the scalping knife with the Gospel," and observed that even "if he was to overrun ten provinces" his manifesto "would appear too pompous." Just as predictably, the reaction from the rebels in America was about equally divided between ridicule and anger. Long after the event, Burgoyne maintained that his proclamation was intended only to intimidate his enemy, and not as a promise. Whether that was true or not, a speech he delivered the following day left no doubt in the minds of the rebels or anyone else as to the course he intended to take.

This occurred at the "Congress of Indians" Fraser had arranged for him beside the falls on Gilliland's Creek.* Men of the advanced corps had arrived here a week earlier, thoroughly worn out from their exertions, and established what Fraser called "a pleasant & a safe post . . . the most pleasant Camp I ever was in." While he was waiting for the main body to appear, some Indians joined him, and he sent them off on a scout toward Ticonderoga with orders to bring back one or two prisoners.

*The Bouquet River.

This resulted in a raid near the fort on June 17 in which two Americans were attacked and one captive taken who was no part of the garrison, as the Indians supposed, but who turned out to be of inestimable value to the British. This was James MacIntosh, a Scot, a retired British soldier who had lived in the shadow of the fort for a long time and was intimately knowledgeable about Ticonderoga and its outworks, the positions of its cannon (which were the main strength of the post), the number of troops on hand, and just about everything an adversary might want to know about the place.

By extraordinary coincidence, when his captors brought MacIntosh into camp, he recognized Brigadier General Simon Fraser as his onetime commanding officer in the 78th Regiment of Foot. During a tedious four-hour interrogation, the "very sensible, cunning sagacious highlander," as Fraser described him, revealed in minute detail the number of troops, workmen, and wagoners (about four thousand all told) and the number and description of ships (two galleys mounting twelve six-pounders each, the sloop *Betsey*, with the same armament, two "Scooners, very small," each with four four-pounders, a gondola carrying two nine-pound guns, and about fifty usable bateaus and thirty that were useless because the rebels lacked pitch with which to caulk them).

He described the small, incomplete naval force on Lake George, estimated the quantity of provisions at two months' supply for the garrison, and furnished the particulars of Ticonderoga's construction, its outworks and batteries, and the location of each. Not far from his house, he said, where the lines turned southward and faced west, there were no cannon—the Americans were confident that this stretch could be defended with small arms.

The flood of information that spilled from MacIntosh's lips included everything from the construction of bombproof powder magazines to the sawmills and their daily activity; from the minutiae of redoubts, block-houses, and breastworks to those of abatis, palisades, and "Picquets made of Seasoned white oak very Sharp pointed, planted very thick each leaning different ways, the whole about two foot wide supposed to serve instead of Crows feet."

The loquacious Scot was less knowledgeable about Mount Independence, across the lake from his house, where many of the works were still under construction, but he did know that a French general (Fermoy) and what he thought to be a French engineer (the Pole, Kosciuszko) had arrived there five or six days earlier. He was also able to inform Fraser that most rebel reinforcements came by way of Fort No. 4* on the Connecticut River, to Castle Town in the Grants,† or Skenesborough‡ at the head of Lake Champlain, usually in parties of ten or twenty, and never more than a hundred. He was convinced that the rebels were having difficulty finding enough hands to man the works.

Asked for his opinion on which way the Americans would retreat if it came to that, he thought it probable that they would travel overland by way of Mount Independence to Castle Town and Skenesborough.

Based on this mine of information, Fraser had a drawing made of the two posts and their immediate environs and urged that no time be lost in moving against the rebels, laying siege to their defensive positions and cutting off their supply lines.

By the time Burgoyne came ashore at Gilliland's Creek, more Indians had appeared, making about four hundred Iroquois, Algonquian, Abenaki, and Ottawa braves who were on hand to hear the general invoke the name of "The Great King, our common father" and urge them to go forth and "strike at the common enemies of Great Britain and America, [those] disturbers of public order, peace and happiness, destroyers of commerce, parricides of state."

Now, if anything, this bluster was even more florid than the proclamation to Americans. It was the pompous Burgoyne at his worst, and the Indians loved it, undoubtedly assuming that his instructions concerning the taking of scalps were only so much embroidery. With extraordinary naiveté, the general insisted that no blood of civilians was to be shed, that aged men, women, children, and prisoners "must be held sacred from the knife or hatchet, even in the time of actual conflict," and that while the Indians would be paid for prisoners taken, they would be "called to account for scalps." Explaining this last to an audience captivated by his oratory (who probably paid little attention to substance), he recognized that it was their custom to take scalps as "badges of victory," but under no circumstances were they to scalp anyone who was still alive, even though wounded or dying. (Since it was only the promise of scalps and booty that brought many of these Indians hundreds of miles to join the king's commander, it suggests that that commander was being disingenuous, to say the least.)

This was followed by much cheering from the assembled braves—

*The present-day Charlestown, New Hampshire.
†Now Castleton, Vermont.
‡Now Whitehall, New York.

"Etow! Etow! Etow!"—and an enthusiastic response by an aged Iroquois chief, which Burgoyne and the other officers present took as affirmation of the conditions, and after shaking hands with the elders of the various nations, Burgoyne left, trusting that his native allies would serve him well, and on his own terms.

Like his proclamation, his speech to the Indians crossed the Atlantic and created a major stir among the opposition in the House of Commons. Edmund Burke compared the absurdity of it with what might occur at the menagerie of the Tower of London if a riot occurred. "What would the keeper of His Majesty's lions do? Would he not fling open the dens of the wild beasts and then address them thus? 'My gentle lions— my humane bears—my tender-hearted hyenas, go forth! But I exhort you, as you are Christians and members of civilized society, to take care not to hurt any man, woman, or child!' " Upon which, it was said, tears of laughter streamed down the chubby cheeks of Lord North, who may have forgotten that the impetus for using Indians was in part his doing.

That policy was like a bomb with a long fuse planted in a fast-moving carriage. No one knew when or where it would explode or what the damage would be. Burgoyne was keenly aware of the risks, and despite his cautionary words to the tribes he was uneasy. The idea was not his: it had been prescribed by George III and his prime minister, Lord North, to put teeth in the king's threat to "distress" America. And while it was true that the rebels also used Indians, the difference was that Burgoyne would be turning them loose not only on enemy soldiers but on the civilian population as well, with consequences beyond all reckoning.

Burgoyne was in most respects an able man and a competent, knowledgeable soldier, much admired by the men he led and respected by most of his fellow officers. His plan for the campaign was a sound one (setting aside the question of whether Sir William Howe intended to cooperate), and his goal of reaching Albany in tandem with St. Leger's force was both reasonable and feasible. But the general's love of the theatrical had no place in a military operation.

It was all very well to write and produce an elaborate theatrical like *The Maid of the Oaks* for a nephew's wedding festivities, or a farce like *The Blockade of Boston*, ridiculing the rebels, to entertain British officers and loyalists in Boston, but it was a grievous error to confuse playwriting and acting with strategy and tactics. Along with that, there was something phony and contrived about these recent effusions, something that almost smelled of the mountebank and quackery, that was plainly done purely for effect and in the long run was bound to diminish him as a soldier, making him less a man to be respected or feared than a figure of ridicule and contempt.

Equally serious, his posturing and threats may have led to a development reported by Captain Alexander Fraser to his uncle. Returning to camp on Putnam's Creek, the young man told the brigadier he had caught no cattle. There were none to be found. The inhabitants of the country through which he had marched "were exceedingly disaffected" by Burgoyne's proclamations and had driven their livestock away, out of reach of the advancing British. For an army that might have to live off the countryside, this was not a good omen.

Chapter 8

The Scene Thickens Fast

March had come on cold this year—so cold it brought work on the Great Bridge to a halt at times; April had been as fickle as ever, May wet and chilly with high winds, on one Sunday evening gusting so badly that it "broke the Boom & Bridge" just as Parson Hitchcock started to preach from the cheerless 25th verse of Isaiah ("For thou hast made of a city an heap; of a defensed city a ruin"). Now here was June, wearing a promise of real spring and warm, sunny days, a godsend after the six months just past. Spirits were high and the men of Ticonderoga confident of victory, itching for the enemy to appear, despite a widespread shortage of essentials. Colonel Thomas Marshall wrote a friend in Massachusetts requesting sole leather for shoes; for lack of it, he said, his men were throwing away their badly worn footwear and "the greater part of them are barefoot. . . ."

Reporting the latest news to his father, the governor of New Jersey, Henry Brockholst Livingston explained that the garrison was now manned entirely by men from New England. (It was perhaps as well that it was, since one of the worst problems that had plagued the army retreating from Canada in '76 was the bitter animosity between soldiers from different regions. At the time, a Pennsylvania captain, contemplating the imminent arrival at Ticonderoga of New England troops, growled, ". . . unless they are better than the greater part of those that all have been here before them, they had better stay at home. No man was ever more disappointed respecting New Englanders than I have been. They are a set of dirty, low, griping, cowardly rascals.")

It is difficult to say whether Livingston's remark was one of consternation or relief, since it was often said that Pennsylvanians would as soon fight the Yankees as the British. At any rate, he said, the New England regiments were so slow in recruiting and traveling to Ticonderoga that the post was much weaker than Congress realized. Yet even though the army here was not as strong as it had been in the 1776 campaign, most of the men were now healthy and "determined to maintain this post till the last extremity." To reassure his family, he indicated that the British had received no reinforcements for a year, their Canadians and Indians were not to be relied on, and should Sir John Johnson attempt to attack from Oswego, as was rumored, a "very respectable garrison at Fort Schuyler" would be there to meet him.

More heartening news arrived in the form of three Continental regiments of New Hampshiremen, led by Nathan Hale,* Joseph Cilley, and Alexander Scammell, who came into camp in late May after marching more than a hundred miles over roads so soddened by rain they were all but impassable. These troops were here in response to a summons from George Washington to the New Hampshire Committee of Safety in February, ordering the regiments to Ticonderoga as soon as they were recruited. Despite the inducement of bounties to men who would enlist "for the war or three years," there were not many takers, and most New Hampshire towns were slow to fill their quota of Continentals or militia. Josiah Bartlett of the Committee of Safety did his best to promote recruiting with frantic appeals to militia colonels: "The Enemies Army is moving on all quarters—for Heavens sake! for your Countrys sake! for your own sake! exert your self in getting your Men & sending them forward without a Moments loss of time." But results were disappointing, and St. Clair was lucky to get as many men as he did.

Understandably, the recruiting process took time. Officers appointed by Committees of Safety were authorized to enlist men for three years or for the duration of the war, and an officer received no commission until he filled his quota. Not only were the recruits to sign up for a lengthy hitch, they had to furnish their own "good effective Fire-arm, with a Bayonet fixed thereto, a Cartouch Box, Knapsack and Blanket"—all this and their service for twenty shillings a month. Recently Congress had second

---

* Not the man who was hanged as a spy by the British in 1775 after declaring, "I only regret that I have but one life to lose for my country."

thoughts about that stingy arrangement and authorized a twenty-dollar bonus for privates and noncommissioned officers who enlisted for the duration, adding the promise of one hundred acres of land at war's end. A bonus of another kind consisted of a suit of clothes, two linen shirts, two pairs of overalls, a long-sleeved leather or woolen waistcoat, a pair of breeches, a hat or cap, two shirts, two pairs of stockings, and two pairs of shoes—these to be given to every soldier unless he furnished his own, in which case he was to receive twenty dollars.

Initially, John Stark, a proud, prickly character if ever there was one, had figured that he was entitled to the rank of brigadier general and command of the New Hampshire regiments. His claim had a lot to recommend it: he had recruited more men than anyone else in his state, because he was much admired, and his two years in the army included a heroic performance in the battle for Bunker Hill. But Congress decided otherwise and gave the rank and the command to Enoch Poor. Stark quit in a huff, so the three New Hampshire contingents set off for Ticonderoga under Poor.

No one could know what lay ahead for these newly minted Continental soldiers who kissed their wives and children and sweethearts good-bye, mustered in tiny hamlets all across New Hampshire, and marched bravely down a dirt track to the tootle of fifes and the rat-a-tat-tat of drums, but a sense of high adventure was certainly in the minds of many. A few were veterans of the French wars; others had been in the dusty, smoke-filled redoubt on Breed's Hill when Howe's scarlet-coated regulars climbed toward them in precisely dressed lines, and they recalled for initiates how they aimed at the crossed white belts on the bloodybacks' chests. But a majority were raw recruits, amateurs fresh from the farm who needed heavy doses of discipline and drill before they could be considered proper soldiers.

Rookies they might be, but they had the smug satisfaction of being *Continentals*, from which vantage point they could look with disdain (touched occasionally with a little envy) at militiamen who signed up for a couple of months and vanished when their time expired. One of the worst drawbacks of the American military establishment, if it could be dignified as such, was the manner in which troops were recruited and employed. The militia companies were *ad hoc* collections of men—mostly farmers, since that's what a majority of Americans were—and often a good many members of those companies were related, since they came from small communities. They were called to duty by the states when emergencies arose, but usually for a fixed period of time that might expire at the least propitious moment, leaving the general in charge of fewer troops than he thought he had.

The militia system had its genesis in the "training bands" that had been a Massachusetts institution for the common defense since the founding of that colony. It was understood that able-bodied men, except those whose consciences prohibited them from fighting, plus college students, professors, and ministers, who were also exempt, would serve in time of danger. And if the danger happened to be acute, older men were organized to be ready.

By and large, the companies were voluntary associations of neighbors who tended to have an easy, loose-jointed way about them, and if discipline was often lax it was because they stood in no great awe of their captain or colonel, who was, after all, the farmer who lived down the road. Even the privates expected to participate in decisions—and did, sometimes to the embarrassment of the captain they had elected to lead them. Naturally, the militia companies were regarded with scorn and amusement by the British, who saw them in their homespuns and floppy hats, carrying weapons that might have been in the family for a century. "It is a curious masquerade scene," one observer wrote, "to see grave sober citizens, barbers and tailors who never looked fierce before, strutting about in their Sunday wigs with muskets on their shoulders ... if ever you saw a goose assume an air of consequence, you may catch some faint idea." What the British perceived as laughable amateurism had to do with the fact that the Americans were fighting a war for which they had almost no preparation, no real support structure provided by existing institutions.

But they made up for their ignorance of the manual of arms and the mysteries of close-order drill by a knowledge and skillful use of their weapons,* marksmanship that could be superb, and a talent for mobilizing quickly with astonishing results.

Their performance in battle was erratic, to say the least, but when they were fighting on their own turf, close to home, they could be ferocious competitors, as the redcoats had learned to their sorrow in the outskirts of Boston. They were not professional soldiers by any stretch of the imagination: they were simply dedicated individuals who believed their cause was just and worth fighting for, and they went off to war knowing it was a dirty business, but one that had to be done. And if they

---

*This in spite of the old saying that if God had meant men to shoot muskets He would have given them three hands.

were commanded by such a man as John Glover of Marblehead, they learned very quickly what this war demanded.

"We must and shall all share the same fate, either freemen or slaves," he wrote. "Every man who has the good of his country and posterity at heart ought to put his shoulders to the burthen, and bear part of the weight.... There's no man, let his abilities and circumstances be what they will, but is able to do something (in this day of difficulty and distress) for the good of his Country."

Their officers, who were appointed by civilian authorities or elected by the men in their outfit, might or might not have any particular experience or skill leading men in battle. One of the likeliest claims to rank was to bring in more recruits than anyone else, which meant that a captaincy sometimes had more to do with popularity than military competence. Privates and officers alike, often poorly armed and trained, frequently lacking in discipline and therefore more likely to panic, probably deserved the comment of General William Howe, who once remarked unkindly that it took two of them to equal one British soldier on the battlefield. Yet some of these rebel irregulars now had two years of sporadic service behind them and were beginning to get the hang of soldiering.

None of this is to suggest that the part-time men were lacking in courage; when properly led, they could make an attack with the best of them, and on occasion—as the British (including Howe) discovered at several critical moments during the long war—they were capable of assembling so rapidly, suddenly appearing from thin air as if by magic, as to turn the tide of battle and provide the margin of victory. They had come together in such a manner at Lexington and Concord (where "it seemed as if men came down from the clouds," one eyewitness wrote), at Bunker Hill, and at the battle for Princeton, and they would do it again when the need arose.

Useful as the militiamen might be, however, they could not be relied on for the simple reason that one never knew for certain when they would answer the call to arms, or if they would return to their farms or shops in the middle of a campaign, often on the very eve of battle. One cause of this reluctance, it must be remembered, was that prolonged military service by farmers could mean hunger at home as well as a shortage of food for the regular army, and as General Arthur St. Clair was beginning to realize, the constant comings and goings of militia companies depleted badly needed supplies while adding little to the effectiveness of the fighting force. Another was that the American economy couldn't possibly support a large army even if the men were available. And yet another was the inherent resistance of Americans to regimentation.

A generation earlier the Massachusetts Assembly had explained it this way: ". . . our people are not calculated to be confined in garrisons or kept in any particular service; they soon grow troublesome and uneasy by reflecting on their folly in bringing themselves into a state of subjection when they might have continued free and independent." This was a society unlike any other in the world, in which people placed great value on their status as independent individuals, beholden to no man. They were suspicious of standing armies and impatient of discipline, and while they realized the need to resist the enemy, they preferred to do so on their own terms at a time and place of their own choosing. It did not make for the kind of army on which generals could pin great hopes.

Largely because of the vagaries of the militia system, in 1775 Congress faced up to the necessity of raising a hard core of troops—a national, "Continental" army of men who could be counted on to be present when needed because they had enlisted for a long period and whose skills would improve with training and experience. Initially, their service was to last for one year; in 1776 it was revised upward to three years or the duration of the war, despite the complaint of one delegate that "long enlistment is a state of slavery." George Washington, who was more acutely aware than anyone of the necessity for long-term service, urged that men be required to sign on for the duration, but not enough did, so he had to settle for the three-year hitch and was lucky to get that. (On Christmas Day of 1776, for instance, five men from Cornish, New Hampshire, signed a document certifying their willingness to "voluntarily inlist ourselves as Soldiers to serve in the Continental Army at New York or at such Place or Places as we may be Order'd to, until the first day of March next"—in other words, for two months and six days, much of it to be used up marching to and fro.)

At times the recruiting process was ludicrous. A Brimfield, Massachusetts, official who tried to send off fifteen hundred men to Ticonderoga ran into an unusual problem. Some men hired others to enlist in their place, only to find that they were drafted to march "while the men they hired are rioting at home on their money, unconcerned about the fate of this country. While the one is quitting his family, his farm and husbandry, to reinforce at Ticonderoga, the other is sporting from house to house and from tavern to tavern, spending the money the honest farmer has earned with the sweat of his face. . . ."

Obviously, the Continental Army had its laggards, its ne'er-do-wells and deserters—men who had not made much of themselves in their communities. The pay was poor (and in the days to come it was usually in the form of increasingly inflated Continental paper currency) and the life was cruel, but the hard core they were intended to be became just that—men who believed in the cause, endured every kind of adversity, and fought on doggedly in what were surely the most desperate circumstances imaginable.

Years later, when they were old men to whom nothing much mattered but the memories they chose to keep, they would forget the hunger and fatigue, the mud and disease, the cold and drenching rains, the lack of decent clothing or shoes or a tent, the horrors of what passed for a hospital, and remember instead the camaraderie in a remote camp on Lake Champlain and the excitement of waiting for the enemy to show his face.

Through the lengthening days of June the area around Ticonderoga bristled with activity—companies drilling, carpenters sharpening tools, work parties heading off to one or another of an endless list of projects to which Colonel Baldwin assigned them, convalescing measles victims strolling with the walking wounded in the spring sunlight. On Mount Independence, Kosciuszko had 100 men building batteries and forming an abatis; Baldwin supervised another 150 who were sinking caissons; a fatigue party was carrying stores from Lake George landing; Udney Hay had charge of a number of black freemen drafted from Continental regiments who functioned "as a constant fatigue, independent of the daily detail"; and two regiments, also exempted from other garrison duty, were cutting timber for the caissons. When the sounds of all this activity finally subsided for the night, out of the darkness came the rustle of creatures in the woods, the *hoo-hoo* of an owl, the howl of a wolf, the scream of a dying rabbit, and from the marsh and lake the chatter of peepers and frogs, the mad cackle of a loon.

When the men were off duty they foraged for food in the ways of soldiers before and since, and fortunately for them the area abounded in fish and game. The Reverend Enos Hitchcock filled his journal with references to pickerel and other fish, venison steaks, roasts, and soup—even "Radishes for breakfast," presumably from the post's big vegetable garden. (The parson not only relished his food but was an inveterate gambler, a regular purchaser of lottery tickets with his friend Moses Greenleaf, though the evidence is lacking that either of them won.)* Twenty-two-year-old Captain Greenleaf of Francis's Massachusetts regiment was a big man—near six feet tall with broad shoulders, straight as a ramrod—and along with playing the lottery continually he too was a world-class eater, to judge from a diary brimming with references to food, including teal, meal after meal of beef and peas, stewed and fried pigeons (one day he and another officer netted twenty dozen of them), and a heavy intake of chocolate at breakfast.

Since many of these New Englanders were little more than boys whose horizons extended only a few miles from home, seeing the world and soldiering was a heady, exciting business. For some it began almost as a lark, this journey into the unknown, crossing rivers and mountains to enter a jungle of trees darker and deeper than most of them could recall, an unfamiliar world with stops along the way that opened their eyes to how families on the outer edge of the frontier lived. The previous autumn the Reverend William Gordon had traveled from Boston to Ticonderoga, sleeping on pea straw in barns when he could find no other place to rest, riding through forests in the Grants that seemed endless and reminded him of a boy who was asked by a gentleman, "How far through the woods?" The boy replied, "When you have rode twelve miles, you will come to a tavern, and then they begin again."

Along the route military men almost always found hospitality of a sort, for which they expected to pay. "Entertainment," as they called the meals they were served, varied from delicious to just plain terrible. One night James Gray of Byfield, Massachusetts, stopped at "a poor man's house" because no tavern was nearby and was astonished to be served a loin of fine veal that was obviously the family's dinner (he "paid him well for the entertainment," he reported). But Gray and others frequently found it difficult to find hay for their horses and filled their diaries with reminders of food and lodging, good and bad, for humans and animals, of distances between towns, in case they or friends should come this way again. On May 19, 1777, the Reverend Enos Hitchcock passed "thro part of Williams Town to Pownal . . . oated Tracey's, 6 miles, 10 o'clock—Roads tolerable—Land good a pleasant River—dined at Capt. Billings Benington 8 m. . . ." And the next day he continued northward after spending the night in Bennington, rode through Shaftsbury to Manchester, where he "oated [his horse] at Frenchs," then he "Lodg'd at

---

*Lotteries were fairly common at the time. The states permitted them for various enterprises, and the Continental Congress used them as a means of raising money.

Manly's in Dorset, 6 m—oated at Smiths Ruport [Rupert] 5 m—dined at Latherbees Powlett [Pawlet] 5 m, oated at Hickbees 5 m . . ." and two days later reached Ticonderoga—at 6:00 P.M. on a fair day, he was careful to note.

A majority of these men came on foot, slogging through rain and cold on unbelievably bad roads and trails, enduring days when they saw no sign whatever of human habitation, and they suffered with smallpox and measles and diarrhea, not to mention blisters and boils and insect bites, bedding down at nightfall with no more cover than a blanket and some bushes. It was a rough experience, but then so was the camp life at Ticonderoga, especially for those unused to regimentation and unwilling to adapt, though in some respects no one was worse off here than at home. They were accustomed to the rigors of a New England farm and the savagery and duration of northern winters, where the punishing struggle to survive was the order of every day and never really ended. They were handy with tools, adept at an extraordinary range of tasks that included carpentry, masonry, shoeing horses, butchering animals, digging trenches, and cutting trees, and hard physical toil—the Puritan work ethic—was accepted as the way of the world. On a typical homestead the workday was longer, if anything, than it was in the army, and because chores were often performed alone, without help, that existence was probably more difficult than it was in camp. Here a man was part of a self-contained community on the edge of wilderness, with everyone in the same fix, sharing hopes and fears along with the grumbling and tall tales and jokes that are the common currency of military life.

Which is not to suggest that it was always easy or pleasant. It was a day of harsh physical punishment for infractions of the rules, for transgressions large and small. For enlisting twice and deserting, a private in Marshall's Massachusetts regiment was required to sit on the gallows for a half hour, presumably to count his blessings for not being hanged, after which he received a hundred lashes. Another man, from the 2nd New Hampshire Regiment, was given seventy stripes and sentenced to serve on the frigate *Raleigh* for the duration of the war. (This was a sure sign that recruiting for the Continental Navy was going slowly. Service on any naval vessel was as tough a job as might be imagined, but at least aboard a privateer it could be monetarily rewarding, since the crew shared in the prize money. A sailor on a government vessel, on the other hand, endured the same hardships but received only his pay, and not much of it at that.)

A strong streak of Calvinism was evident in these Yankees. The rough edges of that unbending faith had not worn off, even after a century and more, and many a soldier recorded in his journal or in letters to family and friends what he had heard at divine services—repeating chapter and verse of the biblical text plus his own comments on the quality of the sermon. Usually the clergymen drew inspiration from the Old Testament, stressing that failure was sin (and vice versa) and would be punished by an unforgiving God. Meek and strong alike were predestined to go to Heaven or Hell after that grand sorting out on Judgment Day when the "chosen" would be selected from all the others. So when Parson Hitchcock read from Isaiah, "That there is no peace, saith my God, to the wicked," a man might judge for himself what lay in store for him.

From Exeter, New Hampshire, in late March of 1777, Colonel Alexander Scammell had written a tender love letter to Nabby Bishop, imploring her to marry him in spite of the "cruel Fate and a more cruel war [that] has thrown an Obstacle in your way." But love, he reminded her, "overlooks small obstacles," and he hoped to hear before marching to Ticonderoga that she would accept his proposal. Now it was June 8 and he had been at Ticonderoga for three weeks after marching a hundred miles "through the woods in an excessive miry Road, wet, rainy weather accompanied with Snow and Hail." And here he was, still asking for her hand in a letter he began two weeks before completing it.

He would have written sooner, he said, but he had been presiding at a general court-martial, trying several men for desertion and some Tories who were accused of spreading smallpox among the troops. He was fortunate to have an able group of officers under him, and while the privates of his New Hampshire regiment were undisciplined, unused to rigorous duty, sick, and poorly sheltered, they looked up to him as a father and were in good spirits, ready to meet the "british Villains" and avenge "the blood of our murdered countrymen." Scammell was homesick for his dearest Lovely Girl, pleaded with her to write, and concluded with the hope that the time would come when he might send his regards to her parents, calling them "by the tender Name of Father & Mother."*

---

*Scammell was one of those heroic figures of the Revolution who receive little attention in the history books. A Harvard graduate, he taught school and worked as a surveyor before leading his New Hampshire regiment to Boston with the first alarm in April 1775. He fought in Canada in 1776 and served with distinction throughout the war—including some time as George Washington's aide-de-camp and adjutant general of the army—only to be captured by one of Banastre Tarleton's troopers at Yorktown in 1781. After he was made a prisoner, he was reportedly shot in the back by one of his captors and mortally wounded.

During the fortnight between installments of Scammell's letter to Nabby, hardly a day passed without a new sign that those "british Villains" were coming closer all the time, as evidenced by the unusually large number of Indians now in the vicinity. Clearly they were being used to screen the enemy's movements from the Americans, and doing it with a cold-blooded efficiency that had a corrosive effect on morale at the garrison.

About noon on June 17 two men from the 2nd New Hampshire Regiment, John Whiting and John Batty, strolled out of camp toward the sawmills on a road traveled every day by soldiers as if they hadn't a worry in the world, and were attacked by some thirty Indians less than a mile from the lines. Eighteen-year-old Whiting—"a likely lad," it was said—was shot in the head, stabbed in the throat, neck, and stomach, and then scalped. His companion, Batty, was wounded in three places and somehow survived the excruciating experience of playing dead while an Indian stripped off his clothes and scalped him. When the enemy disappeared into the woods he hobbled toward the lines, streaming blood and screaming for help, and was carried to the hospital.

This gruesome reminder of what the Indians could do occurred near the home of James MacIntosh, whose interrogation by Simon Fraser had yielded invaluable data about Ticonderoga. A small detail sent out to avenge Whiting and Batty failed to overtake the Indian raiders, and within hours, as luck would have it, the same war party ambushed Lieutenant Nathan Taylor and twelve scouts, who were returning to the fort from a mission down the west side of the lake. In a brisk engagement one American was killed and scalped and Taylor was wounded in the shoulder. Several Indians were thought to have been killed and carried off by their companions; another rebel soldier was missing and believed captured.

The first word to reach camp, when Taylor returned with only two of his men, was that all the others had been killed or taken prisoner, but the next morning eight came in, one of whom swam across the lake. The unfortunate Whiting and Batty had been tentmates, and a day later another man from their mess—a soldier with a wife and three children—was resting his chin on the muzzle of his gun, talking with his brother, when the musket went off accidentally and "blew out his brains against the side of the House," as Massachusetts militiaman Jabez Colton graphically described it in a letter to his pastor back home. "Thus God in his Righteous Providence is pleased to snatch suddenly some out of the world as a warning to the living," Colton concluded piously. He was perplexed that "such things seem to be little noticed," but clearly the incident had its effect on him, and he began to wonder if his outfit would be allowed to leave Ticonderoga when their time was up.

A squad of St. Clair's scouts spotted a large body of Indians on the east side of the lake, about four miles above Crown Point, causing the general to wonder yet again about the enemy's intentions. He found it hard to believe that they would disclose their proximity by permitting the Indians to take prisoners within sight of the fort, yet on the other hand he could not imagine that the savages would be so bold unless an army was close behind, to support them.

St. Clair sent scouts out continuously, but still he lacked solid information about the enemy beyond reports of vessels moving around the lower lake—nothing about the army, its size or composition. On the one hand, he was sure the British were moving closer all the time; on the other, he still didn't dare call for more militia, since he had received no supplies of meat, salt or fresh. More important, he had reached the unhappy conclusion that he did not have sufficient troops to defend both the fort and the extensive works being constructed on Mount Independence. As St. Clair described the dilemma, "Had every man I had been disposed of in single file along the lines of defense, they would scarcely have been in reach of each other's voices," and Generals Schuyler, Gates, and Poor had already expressed the opinion that ten thousand good soldiers were required for the job. Because the two posts were dependent on each other, it would be risky to abandon either, but St. Clair finally decided he would have to take that chance and concentrate his force at a single location. He informed General Schuyler that he would hold on to Ticonderoga as long as possible, and then retreat to the Mount.

On the 18th of the month, Schuyler came up from Albany to see for himself how matters stood, and was dismayed by what he found—much of the work incomplete, especially the obstructions in the lake to hinder enemy shipping; not enough artificers; insufficient reinforcements; and the garrison "miserably clad and armed . . . many are literally barefooted, and most of them ragged," without blankets (and, he might have added, bayonets—some had spears, others merely "sharp pointed poles"). Even their huts, which had been built the year before, had been razed and burned for firewood during the winter. Two days later he held a council of Generals St. Clair, Roche de Fermoy, Poor, and Paterson. (Fermoy was one of the "Frenchmen" MacIntosh had seen around the fort; he was an adventurer who arrived in America in 1776 wearing a

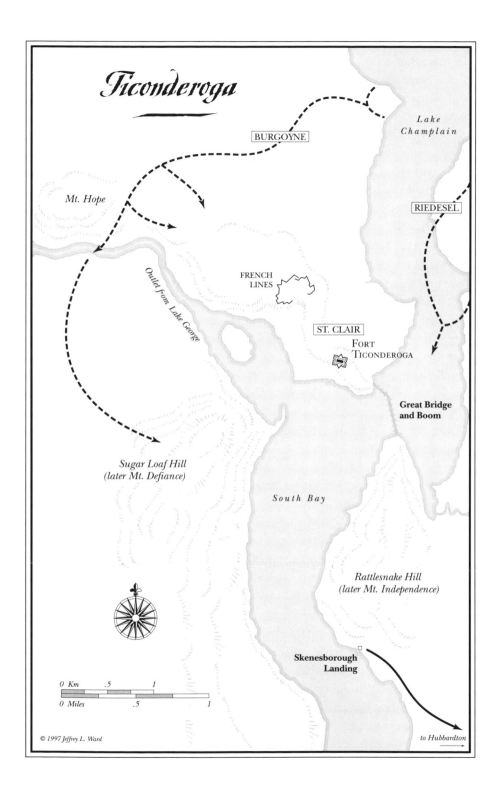

Ticonderoga

BURGOYNE

Lake Champlain

Mt. Hope

RIEDESEL

Outlet from Lake George

FRENCH LINES

ST. CLAIR

FORT TICONDEROGA

Great Bridge and Boom

Sugar Loaf Hill
(later Mt. Defiance)

South Bay

Rattlesnake Hill
(later Mt. Independence)

Skenesborough Landing

0 Km   .5   1

0 Miles   .5   1

© 1997 Jeffrey L. Ward

to Hubbardton

medal and claiming to be a colonel of engineers. Unfortunately, like the hapless Baron de Woedtke, he was also an alcoholic. Put to work, he had led a brigade creditably in the attack on Trenton in December, but he quickly acquired a reputation for unreliability by leaving his post and botching his assignment to delay the British advance toward Princeton. Recently he had been handed to Schuyler, perhaps on the theory that he might be useful at Ticonderoga.)

Considering that the garrison consisted of slightly more than 2,500 effective rank and file, that the safety of the troops, cannon, and stores was paramount, and that only thirty-nine days' supply of meat was on hand, the officers at the council of war decided it was "prudent to provide for a retreat" and if that last resort proved necessary, everything on the Fort Ticonderoga side would be evacuated, after the guns and stores had been moved to Mount Independence. Meantime, work on the fortifications and lines at the latter place were to have top priority: Kosciuszko marked out the lines where fascines—great bundles of sticks bound together—were to be laid. The accelerated construction was to be handled by brigades, with every officer and man not on duty expected to pitch in, and one task that was quickly accomplished was felling twenty acres of trees on the sides and bottom of the mount. Completion of the obstructions in the lake—which meant the boom and footbridge, Baldwin's Great Bridge having progressed no further than caissons sitting on the bottom—was to be accomplished "with all imaginable dispatch." The best guess was that this would take at least six weeks, and it defies belief that any of those present thought the enemy would grant them that much time.

On June 23 one of St. Clair's most reliable scouts, Sergeant Heath, returned from a mission down the lake to report that the Indians were as thick as the area's famous mosquitoes. Near the mouth of Otter Creek he had seen five British ships, as well as encampments on both sides of Gilliland's Creek, forty-two miles north of the fort, and he had spoken with a local resident who said the enemy first appeared at Gilliland's aboard "a vast number of batteaux and some gondolas" and had been there for four or five days, waiting for additional shipping and the arrival of stores. This disagreeable news convinced the general that "we are infallibly ruined" unless reinforcements arrived, and he began to wonder if even a retreat—let alone a defense of the forts—would be possible.

Nothing revealed the efficacy of the screen of Indians so graphically as Heath's failure to get closer than six miles to Gilliland's Point, and across the lake from it at that. On the occasions when scouts skirmished with the Indians, they were invariably routed, and the frequent bloody ambushes within sight of the fort were so unnerving that few men wanted to risk going beyond the lines. Every day scouting parties—often selected from Major Benjamin Whitcomb's corps of rangers, who were experienced in this line of work—went out, and every day they returned with little to report beyond what was already known. The woods, one rebel officer said, "were so infested with savages as to render it exceedingly hazardous to send small parties . . . and the force of the garrison was too weak to justify . . . detaching a large number." In the face of such difficulties it was not easy to be sanguine about the future; as St. Clair put it, "The scene thickens fast."

By June 28, when a three-man party of Whitcomb's best men failed to return, the general was so desperate for intelligence that he thought seriously of sending out Whitcomb himself, risky as that would be, since the chief of scouts was a marked man. Whitcomb was in his thirties, tall and thin, with a rough, pockmarked face and brown hair pulled back and tied in a queue. His usual outfit was a sleeveless jacket, leather trousers, gray stockings, and shoes, with a gold cord tied around a broad, turned-up felt hat. It was said he could move through the woods as silently and as swiftly as a cat, and like an Indian, he knew how to survive in the woods for days or weeks at a time and how best to take advantage of the concealment afforded. He and others like him were progenitors of a new breed of American known as the Long Hunters for the length of their stays in the wilderness: loners, with the unmistakable mark of the frontier forever on them, they were always on the move, insistent on their own way of life, which might be described as total, unfettered freedom. They endured hardship and disease, prolonged periods without food, and encounters with Indians and wild animals, and even in a strange countryside their instincts were such that they were seldom lost. The one thing they could not tolerate was what passed for civilization.

Benjamin Whitcomb was a master of the type of warfare so unfamiliar to the British and so abhorred by them. The year before, he had traveled from Crown Point to St. Johns and Chambly, where he hid in the forest and fired on a redcoated officer who rode by. The officer happened to be Brigadier General Patrick Gordon, whose rank made the offense the more heinous to the British, and when Gordon died of his wound a few days later, the incensed Guy Carleton offered a reward of fifty guineas to anyone who brought in the assassin Whitcomb dead or alive, preferably the latter, since the British wanted nothing so much as to hang him. The incident made an indelible impression on a German officer, though not for the same reason that had infuriated Carleton. He was thunderstruck at the way Whitcomb and five of his men "stole into the very center of our encampment" and he couldn't imagine how they could "make this long march of forty leagues through deserts and dense woods and carry, at the same time, rations for fifteen days on their backs."

The Indians also had reason for wanting Whitcomb. Two days after the skirmish between Lieutenant Taylor's detail and the Indians, Whitcomb came into camp with several trophies taken from the body of a chief who had fallen in the battle. The rebels had found him, according to Major Stevens, "with all his Ornaments on, of which they strip[p]ed him, as well as his Scalp which were carried in triumph through our camp."

"No army was ever in a more critical situation than we now are," Arthur St. Clair wrote to Schuyler. But lacking the kind of intelligence Whitcomb might provide, and despite the presence of seven ships anchored off Crown Point and troops seen landing across the lake at Chimney Point, he could only speculate that the enemy was either "in full force or very weak," and chances were it was not the latter.

A hopeful sign that warm weather might last was an order moving the troops out of barracks and into tents, but they remained on alert, lying on their arms by night, rising at the morning gun to hustle to alarm posts, where they remained until sunup. About 150 fresh troops from Massachusetts arrived at Mount Independence, and on June 27, St. Clair decided that his need for more help outweighed the problem of what quantity of stores the reinforcements would consume—and in any case a number of cattle had been brought in from Pawlet, easing the situation somewhat, so he sent Colonel Seth Warner to the New Hampshire Grants to round up all the militia he could locate. Meantime, Jeduthan Baldwin noticed that the Indians were "very thick" and the pressure mounting, with more men being killed and scalped near the mills. Someone else reported war parties moving against Skenesborough, presumably to cut off communication with that settlement, as Amsbury had predicted to Schuyler.

For two days the sense of foreboding intensified as cumulonimbus rumbled in from the Adirondacks—towering thunderheads propelled by some giant, distant wind, darkening the sky and weighting an atmosphere that was already stifling. The dark surface of the lake, lit by shattering cracks of lightning, boiled with waves and the sheets of rain that kept Burgoyne's army huddled in tents. Finally, on June 30, the main body of British and Germans was established eleven miles north of Ticonderoga at Crown Point (which a squad led by the Earl of Balcarres found abandoned by the rebels). Here Burgoyne issued a general order to his command. Unlike his proclamation and the speech to the Indians, it was a model of brevity, and it brimmed with the confidence of a man who knew he held all four aces:

> The army embarks tomorrow, to approach the enemy. We are to contend for the King and the constitution of Great Britain, to vindicate Law, and to relieve the oppressed—a cause in which His Majesty's Troops and those of the Princes his Allies, will feel equal excitement. The services required of this particular expedition are critical and conspicuous. During our progress occasions may occur, in which, nor difficulty, nor labour nor life are to be regarded. This Army must not Retreat.

The gusts shifted to the south and for a week and more favored the rebels, holding up the British fleet. But the wind, as everyone knew, was fickle and could change suddenly, without warning, bringing those vessels up the lake on the first fair breeze. A succession of alarms put the garrison on guard, making the men more alert than usual, and one sentry's vigilance was rewarded one night when he saw movement in the darkness, fired, and heard a body fall, but the victim proved to be a cow foraging for food.

From various inhabitants on both sides of the lake scouts picked up for the first time some fairly reliable eyewitness assessments of enemy strength. The approaching army was believed to include eight thousand regulars and fifteen hundred Indians and Canadians, plus a detachment of about five hundred men that was reported heading up Otter Creek toward Rutland, where the New Hampshire regiments had left their stores. The threat implicit in such numbers was enough to persuade St. Clair to send his eleven-year-old son off to a safer haven at Fort George.

At seven o'clock on the morning of June 30 a warning shot was fired from one of the rebel guard boats patrolling the lake, and within the hour St. Clair and the two thousand Americans* in his command saw the vanguard of the army they had awaited so expectantly.

---

*The number of men in the works at any one time was often a matter of conjecture. For instance, on June 13 St. Clair told Schuyler he could count on no more than 2,200 effectives; on June 20 it was "under 2,500"; and on June 25 "little more than 2,000." On May 25, however, Dr. Jonathan Potts had reported that the garrison consisted of 3,400, with more arriving every day.

Burgoyne had split his force into its two wings, with Riedesel and his Germans advancing up the east shore of the lake toward Mount Independence, while Fraser, who was already at Three Mile Point (the name indicating its distance below the fort), was followed by Phillips and his regulars up the west bank toward Ticonderoga. Out on the water, only a mile and a half from the rebel lines, the armada's pennants flapped in a light breeze while regimental bands played brightly and "contributed to make the Scene and passage extremely pleasant." Twelve artillery bateaus formed a cordon between Fraser's and Breymann's advanced corps, with the *Royal George* and the *Inflexible* anchored nearby. Between the two large ships and the shoreline floated the boom that had been towed here, constructed of beams linked by chains, to prevent rebel fire ships from reaching the bateaus. With the lake blockaded, the army could go about its business without fear of interruption, and the soldiers began wading ashore on the west bank. Now the regulars were close enough to the fort to "distinctly discern the enemy's whole situation" and observe with some amusement that only a few defenders were in uniform. Most "wore their usual farmer's clothing."

The decision facing Burgoyne was what his next move should be, and when he asked Phillips and Fraser for their opinions, the latter argued that while a siege might be the best way to keep the Americans inside a steadily shrinking box, the besiegers had too few troops to handle the job: the army would be spread too thin over too great an area. When Burgoyne said he wanted to throw a corps of Germans forward on the east side of the lake, to seize "the great road" the rebels had built from Fort No. 4 on the Connecticut to Mount Independence, Fraser disagreed. The Germans were "a helpless kind of troops in woods," he said, and the swampy land north of the Mount would require them to make a detour of at least sixteen miles, cutting them loose from their supply line and reinforcements.

The brigadier asked for permission to reconnoiter the west side in person, to see if the ground coincided with MacIntosh's description. But on this and his other suggestions, Phillips was adamantly negative. He intended to do this thing by the book: keep the army in its present position, husbanding its strength until roads capable of moving artillery could be constructed.

Burgoyne sided with Phillips, and Fraser recorded the commander's views in language that was vintage Burgoyne: if the rebels evacuated the forts, he feared, "the conquest would not have been sufficiently brilliant by [capturing] a great number of prisoners or a large quantity of stores."

Not enough glory, in other words, for the expedition's commander when the news reached London.

St. Clair wanted to get a jump on the redcoats who were disembarking. He sent orders to bring within the lines those provisions and stores that were piled at Lake George landing and instructed the bateaumen to stand by to move to Fort George at a moment's notice. At that, he was almost too late: before anyone realized what was happening, enemy soldiers reached the sawmills and bridge, drove in the pickets, and fired a volley at the breastworks (in the gap where MacIntosh had told General Fraser no cannon were in place) before retreating into the woods.

To keep the rebels busy, Fraser sent his nephew with the Canadians and Indians, supported by six hundred men of the advanced corps, around the American left. Shortly before nine o'clock on the morning of July 2, while these troops were on the move, hoping to reach the sawmills and cut off the rebels' escape route to Lake George, they saw smoke rising from Mount Hope. Seeing them approach, the defenders had set fire to the isolated, vulnerable outpost there, scrambled down the slope, and were hightailing it for the safety of the French Lines, about a mile and a quarter away. By one o'clock, Fraser's men were in possession of Mount Hope and the sawmills, which had also been burned by the rebels. The brigadier, thinking he might need support, sent word to Hamilton to move up the road from Crown Point, but just when he thought everything was going according to plan, all hell broke loose. Someone had disobeyed Burgoyne's orders against selling liquor to the savages, and now they were drunk and they smelled blood. Some two hundred yards from the French Lines, where thick brush made visibility poor, the Indians broke into a run, drove in the fifty-man American picket guard, and charged the defenses. Luckily for them, the defenders' fire was woefully inaccurate, but even so, two attackers were killed and three others wounded, and Lieutenant Richard Haughton, who ran up to recall the Indians, was wounded along with two rangers and one loyalist.

For more than an hour a rough little skirmish raged; the pickets were called in, and as the enemy advanced, the rebels opened fire with muskets and grapeshot, "which made them scamper," according to Henry Sewall, who was on guard duty at the fort, watching the whole affair. And there it ended, except that this time Americans were down, seven of them dead, including a lieutenant, plus eleven wounded. One of those killed was in Francis's Massachusetts regiment, as were four of the wounded; Moses Greenleaf knew three of these fellows and reported that David Downing was hit in the heel, Newport through both knees, and Oxford in the thigh. Seth Warner's Green Mountain Boys lost five killed and several wounded. Except for one British regular who was captured, no one knew the extent of enemy casualties.

The men inside the lines were proud of themselves, and deservedly so: their coolness under fire persuaded young Henry Sewall that they had "discover'd a fervent zeal for the cause by their alert behaviour on the first signal of the alarm." And from now on they were buoyed up by regular visits from St. Clair, who made a point of going out to the forward lines at the first sign of alarm, walking back and forth, patting men on the back, encouraging them, warning them to hold their fire until the enemy came within range so they could get off a good shot.

Fraser had just finished writing a note to Burgoyne, describing the action and informing him that his nephew Captain Alexander Fraser now held a strong position on the right. It was within fifteen hundred yards of the French Lines, and the brigadier proposed to join him there. At this moment Phillips appeared, "with his usual warmth," as Fraser tactfully described a choleric major general whose concept of discipline did not include Indians running amok. The savages had completely spoiled the element of surprise, the general fumed, and he wanted the troops to retire. Fraser disagreed and said he thought he could show Phillips why.

He suggested that the two of them inspect the ground on which the younger Fraser was now posted, and as soon as they did, Phillips agreed that it was critically important to hold. By now Phillips had his temper under control, and after ordering the 20th Regiment to move up and support the advanced corps' left, he told Fraser he planned to go aboard ship the next morning, leaving the brigadier on his own. At ten that night, Burgoyne came around and thanked Fraser "in the handsomest manner for the events of the day," and later still sent the brigadier a warning that the rebels were moving men and artillery to strengthen their defenses on his front.

After a hot, sultry night the British busied themselves setting up tents, bringing artillery ashore, and digging earthworks, while large numbers of their Indians moved about between the fort and Lake George landing. Adding to the impression of a very large and powerful force, forty-one more bateaus, each loaded with as many as thirty-five

German soldiers, landed on the east bank below Mount Independence, and it was not lost on the rebels that a pincer movement was in the making, increasing the possibility that they might be cut off from outside help. To give his men's spirits a boost, St. Clair ordered a *feu de joie** to hail the news that General Washington had defeated Howe's army, which was "fleeing precipitately," in Chaplain Hitchcock's words. (Alas, the report was a gross exaggeration: Howe was merely withdrawing from Brunswick, New Jersey, and despite Washington's hope of attacking his rear guard, the Americans never came close enough to do any real damage.)

Across the lake, the Germans were having a rough time of it. Before they came within range of Mount Independence they had to cross East Creek—a deceptively named body of water that was all but impossible for an army to negotiate on foot. The stream runs for some four miles from southeast to northwest, effectively blocking an approach to the Mount from the north, since it is less a creek than a bog, a half mile across in places. It took Breymann's corps a full day to move twelve hundred paces closer to the rebels, and the Brunswick brigades to their rear gloomily resigned themselves to bivouacking for the night in dense forest on marshy ground infested with insects.

Burgoyne still had his mind set on cutting off a rebel retreat into New England and ordered the Indians and Captain Fraser's marksmen and Canadians to the east side of the lake to break through to the Hubbardton road in case the Germans didn't reach it.

With no chance of defending Mount Hope and the mills, St. Clair's troops had pulled out of the works on the hill that commanded the only road between the fort and the north end of Lake George and set fire to the buildings. Burgoyne, who wanted at all costs to capture or destroy the American army, didn't want his quarry to get away and was thoroughly annoyed to see the "great smoke and other symptoms of confusion in the enemy's camp [as if] they were abandoning some part of their works, if not the whole." A blockhouse near the landing repelled one attack but was abandoned when St. Clair realized that its small guard

---

*This was the military's way of celebrating important news and was traditionally performed by the assembled troops firing their muskets into the air in sequence from one end of a line to the other. St. Clair, realizing that the British would count the number of shots and learn how small the garrison was, had thirteen cannon fire—one for each state.

detail could not hold out much longer. With that, all communication between Ticonderoga and Lake George was severed, ending the possibility of escape by that route. St. Clair had sent a work party to the landing to bring the accumulated stores back to the fort, but some of the oxen ran off, and between that and "the stupidity of the drivers" the salvage effort was a fiasco. Rather than lose the stores altogether, the general had them put aboard bateaus and ferried to Fort George.

During the day, three deserters came in from the British camp. Two were Germans, intelligent men by all accounts, and much of the information they offered came as news to the Americans. They confirmed earlier reports that Carleton had stayed behind as governor and had in his charge the relatively small number of troops remaining in Canada, that Burgoyne was in command of the large invasion army, and that General Riedesel, who reported to him, led seven Brunswick regiments, plus a light infantry battalion and four companies of dragoons. The latter were cavalrymen, but without horses; according to the deserters they were confident of finding mounts at Ticonderoga, which undoubtedly produced a laugh among the rebels, who knew how scarce animals of any description were in this vicinity.

The Germans also reported that Burgoyne's army was short of supplies, which the rebels took to mean they would not mount a siege but would try to overrun the works in a *coup de main*.

Further intelligence came unwittingly from the British regular captured in the skirmish. He refused to answer questions, but during the evening a roughly dressed Irishman, who was accused of being a spy, was brought to the room where he was confined. As the evening wore on, the Irishman produced a bottle, the two chatted amicably, and the regular told his cellmate everything he knew about Burgoyne's strength, the size of the British fleet, and the number of cannon. He had been out with scouts three days earlier, and he boasted that they had taken six prisoners and killed a number of others who were scalped by Indians. The British plan, he went on, was to surround the rebels, harass them continually with the Indians and light infantry, and cut off their communications with the outside world. The next morning the Irishman—who was in fact a disguised Lieutenant Andrew Hodges Tracy of Stevens's artillery battalion—was taken from the room and brought to St. Clair, to whom he delivered the information gleaned from the unsuspecting British soldier. At last St. Clair had the solid information he had lacked for the past three weeks, and it was anything but reassuring.

After a quiet night, daylight brought a warm breeze from the south. To judge from Moses Greenleaf's activities, anyone might have assumed that nothing much was happening: he came in from picket duty at sunrise, wrote a letter home—enclosing thirteen dollars for one Joseph Stanwood—and spent several hours as a member of a general court-martial, on which he had served for the past ten days. Henry Sewall described the enemy as "pretty calm," and he too wrote a letter to his family, accompanied by a thirty-dollar bill.

Another young man who took advantage of that quiet day to catch up on his correspondence was Henry Brockholst Livingston, just out of the hospital and recovered from a violent fever, who mentioned to his father that General St. Clair planned another *feu de joie* on "the anniversary of the ever memorable the 4th of July 1776 on which day we broke off all connection with Slavery & became the free & independent States of America." He had nothing but praise for St. Clair, who had slept no more than one hour in twenty-four on the average during the past week. Describing the man in charge of Ticonderoga as cool and determined, "ever vigilant & unruffled by every appearance of danger," he told his father he had "hopes of announcing to you in a few days the welcome News of the total defeat of the Enemy."

That day saw desultory firing of cannon by both sides with no visible effect, and the enemy began throwing up a battery in front of the French Lines, but good news for St. Clair in the form of reinforcements and food came with the arrival of Seth Warner and seven hundred militia from the Grants, bringing with them eighty head of cattle and some sheep. A source of fresh beef and lamb was especially welcome to the commissary officer, who was anticipating a long siege and didn't want to dip into the dwindling supplies of salt meat.

The ever memorable Fourth proved to be extremely hot and was deceptively uneventful, but the sharp-eyed Jeduthan Baldwin thought he saw activity on "the rising ground fronting French Lines" and noted that several cannon shots were fired in that direction, evidently without much result.

The next day rebel cannon fire kept both wings of the attackers at a distance as they continued to land more tents, baggage, and provisions. Balcarres was out walking with Brigadier Fraser, and they got to talking about the natural impulse of a soldier to duck when a cannon was fired. Balcarres commented that it was humiliating to be seen doing this by those who were not in the line of fire. Fraser began to argue with him when "*Whiz!*—down went the General's head and [he] lost the benefit of his argument." Yet Balcarres had noted an exception to the way most men flinched under artillery fire: some men with extremely sharp eyes were able to see the trajectory of a cannonball and calmly step aside to avoid it.

As Fraser surveyed his position, he saw at once the importance of occupying what his maps labeled Sugar Hill and the rebels called Mount Defiance, and in the afternoon he dispatched Captain Craig with forty light troops and a few Indians to reconnoiter. At midnight Craig was back. He had reached the top, he said, and found it "very commanding ground." Fraser would have gone to see it for himself next morning, but he had more pressing business: a cannonball had killed two men and a horse on his front, so he moved his right wing back two hundred yards, and by the time that was done it was about noon.

It was "abominably hot" when he and Lieutenant William Twiss, the engineering officer, hiked up the mountain, reaching the summit about two o'clock. From here they had a superb forty-mile view down Lake Champlain. Off to the left was the Chute, dead ahead the promontory on which Fort Ticonderoga and its outworks were situated, and across the water, connected by a bridge, Mount Independence.

As Craig had noted, the position commanded both Ticonderoga and Mount Independence, at a range of fourteen hundred and fifteen hundred yards respectively, which meant that the rebels could make no movement during daylight hours "without being discovered, and even having their numbers counted." Better yet, Twiss determined that it was entirely practicable to build a road to the top. Fraser was amused to hear "a sagacious Indian" say of the mountain that "the great father of the sun had created it," but when you considered all the battles fought for possession of Fort Ticonderoga, "he wondered it never occurred to any person to occupy it before we did." (Neither Fraser nor the sagacious Indian was aware of John Trumbull's recommendation.) When Fraser returned to camp, having ordered axemen to build an abatis on the summit, where he posted a detachment of troops, Burgoyne and Phillips heard his news and agreed "to use every possible expedition to get Cannon to the top."

It was tough going, even for experienced woodsmen, and it quickly became apparent that neither axemen nor soldiers pressed into duty shared the brigadier general's opinion of the ease with which a road sixteen feet wide and three leagues long could be built to the summit, a verdict confirmed when three English artillerymen had their heads blown off by enemy fire and another man suffered a badly broken leg. The uphill climb was "almost a perpendicular ascent," according to Lieutenant Digby, and required "most of the cattle belonging to the army" to haul two twelve-pounders from the *Thunderer* to the top, plus a work detail of four hundred men to clear the road and construct a battery, but somehow the thing was done, and as a reward the whole army received "a Refreshment of Rum."

It was a pity that no one had listened to the advice of Lieutenant Colonel John Trumbull when he warned a year earlier that it was possible to put artillery on top of Mount Defiance, from which vantage point guns could rake both Ticonderoga and Mount Independence, making those positions untenable.*

Sure enough, on July 5 at noon a plume of smoke and what were obviously scarlet coats could be glimpsed through the trees, moving about on the heights, and it was clear that the enemy was establishing a battery. Having a curious mind, Jeduthan Baldwin wondered why the British didn't open fire at once. It must have to do with the weather, he thought: a west wind had shifted into the north and was now blowing at gale force, convincing him that they were only waiting for the wind to abate.

As Brockholst Livingston described the American dilemma, the hill had "such an entire command of Ticonderoga that the enemy might have counted our very numbers, and enfiladed every part of our works. After possessing themselves of this commanding height, it would require but a few hours to invest us on all sides."

At that, it could have been worse. Lieutenant Twiss's remarkable engineering feat might have gone entirely undetected if some Indians had not lit a fire on the heights, revealing to the rebels what was going on.

---

*Belatedly, Gates had come around to Trumbull's point of view, and he wrote St. Clair in mid-June suggesting he consider occupying "The Sugar Loaf . . . which decides the fate of your campaign. . . ." No need to haul cannon up the hill, he added: howitzers would do the job just as well. But by the time the letter arrived the area was swarming with Indians, and with everything else St. Clair had on his mind the advice went unheeded.

Chapter 9

The Most Delicate and
Dangerous Undertaking

Time was paramount in the minds of the five officers who gathered in St. Clair's quarters in the early afternoon of July 5. Without preamble, the commandant looked into the eyes of Fermoy, Poor, Paterson, and Long and quietly laid his cards on the table. As all of them knew, the presence of the guns on top of Mount Defiance spelled disaster. They could open fire on Fort Ticonderoga at any time, and every sign pointed to the certainty that Mount Independence would be attacked simultaneously. If that should occur, neither post would be capable of supporting the other and both would be hard put to hold out alone.

As St. Clair saw it, they had two choices. One was to shift all the tents to lower ground, where they would be less exposed to enfilading cannon fire, and prepare for a British siege. The other was to move all the troops and artillery to Mount Independence, beefing up the defenses there so they could make a stand. On the off chance that anyone present was unaware of the pickle they were in, St. Clair called their attention to the latest returns, the stark, unbending records showing that the garrison consisted of 2,089* rank and file fit for duty, plus the corps of artillery, 124 unarmed artificers, and about 900 militia who had just arrived but

---

*St. Clair later amended the figure to 2,546, but the small increase would not have altered the decision.

could stay no more than a few days. It seems the newcomers "had not a second shirt to their backs," having been called out on short notice to drive a small party of the enemy away from Otter Creek. From the German deserters and the captured Briton the American command had a fairly accurate picture of the enemy's strength, and these collective tidings were not the sort to inspire confidence, not when the expected attack on the fort would be made by three or four times their own numbers. The generals were also aware that if the British laid siege to the two posts, they could expect no help from Schuyler: he not only lacked men, but had almost no meat to feed them and, what was almost as bad, no lead for cartridges except what might be stripped from the windows of Albany's houses.

The council's opinion was unanimous: given their weakness and that looming presence of the enemy battery on Mount Defiance, it would be impossible to defend the works with any hope of success, so troops, cannon, provisions, and stores should be transferred without delay—that very night—across the lake to Mount Independence.

That much was relatively easy, having been agreed upon at the meeting with Schuyler two weeks earlier. The next question was tougher to answer. Since both posts were nearly surrounded, and since it was improbable that Mount Independence could hold out for long, even with the addition of arms and men from Ticonderoga, what should the next move be?

Burgoyne had sprung the trap, but luckily it had not quite snapped shut. On the west bank of the lake the British, with their Indians and Canadians, had sealed off the escape route via Lake George. On the east side, opposite Three Mile Point, the Germans would soon be in position to outflank Mount Independence. But so far two small but vital areas remained unoccupied—the long peninsula between East Creek and Lake Champlain, and the narrows known as South Bay, which was the only means of reaching Skenesborough by water. If those were seized by the advancing enemy—and everything indicated that they would be before long—the game was surely up. Once in the land bordering East Creek, the Germans would be poised to cut off the road to Hubbardton and Castle Town. If the British also controlled the narrows, the trap would shut tight. Without a dissenting vote, the five officers resolved that a retreat into the open countryside east of the Mount "ought to be undertaken as soon as possible, and that we shall be very fortunate to effect it."

Omitted from the number of troops St. Clair had recited to the group were the few women and children remaining at the fort, plus sick and wounded soldiers, all of whom were bound to augment the difficulties of evacuating the fort under the eyes of the enemy, even though some of the invalids later picked up their muskets and swore they felt "well enough to stand one warm battle." Surgeons Brown and Townshend had shipped their medicines and hospital stores to Fort George, except for what was immediately needed, and the sick whose recovery was judged to be slow had also departed. Even so, about a hundred men, most of them wounded, were still in the hospital, and throughout the camp soldiers were recovering from an epidemic of measles that left them "languid with coughs," unfit for duty though not quite sick enough to be in bed.

St. Clair planned to have the main body of his army, more than two thousand men, march southeast from Mount Independence along the Hubbardton road, which had been hacked through the forest the year before at Gates's orders. Since this was little more than a rough cart track, laced with stumps, boulders, and ruts, it was impossible for artillery or heavily loaded wagons to negotiate, so the invalids, plus a regiment of healthy soldiers under Colonel Pierce Long to protect them, would be dispatched by boat to Skenesborough along with the guns and supplies. There they would be joined by the force that marched overland by way of Hubbardton and Castle Town, thence westerly to the little town at the southern tip of Lake Champlain.

If this risky movement was to succeed, a great deal was going to depend on the availability of boats to ferry their precious cargoes up the narrows to Skenesborough. Following the council meeting, St. Clair sent for Lieutenant Colonel Udney Hay, his acting deputy quartermaster general, and informed him that the fort was to be evacuated early the following morning. This piece of news came as a shock to Hay, and after apologizing for what he was about to say, he took the liberty of asking the general if he had received orders from Schuyler to make this move.

St. Clair knew what was behind the question and told Hay yes, he had considered very seriously the consequences of the extraordinary step he was taking. It was truly a Hobson's choice, which was to say, no choice at all. As Hay recalled the conversation, the general observed that if he defended the fort, "he would save his character and lose the army." On the other hand, if he retreated, "he would save the army and lose his character . . . which he was determined to sacrifice to the cause in which he was engaged." St. Clair had a premonition of how Congress would react to his abandoning the Gibraltar of the North without attempting to defend it and was keenly aware that such an action could destroy his reputation.

Enough of that; Hay must prepare to move the invalids and the stores by boat. This would not be easy, Hay replied, since a stiff wind was blowing out of the northeast and the bateaus were tied up at the south end of Mount Independence, at what was called the Skenesborough landing. It would be impossible for them to beat across the lake in the face of that wind, which was rising with every passing hour.

Having said that, Hay set about his business, but about sunset St. Clair caught sight of him and said that Generals Poor and Paterson opposed any attempt to bring the bateaus across the water from the Mount, on the grounds that it would delay the evacuation. So a number of vessels near the fort were designated for the artillery, and the most valuable stores were carried down to the wharf on that side. Hay was to cross the lake, ready the boats on the south shore of the Mount, and load them with the provisions that were being piled at the edge of a little cove below Jeduthan Baldwin's crane, saving room for medicine, ammunition, and other essentials.

The men in the ranks first got wind that something big was brewing when the word was passed about 6:00 P.M. to draw twenty-four extra rounds of ammunition plus provisions for five days. An hour later the pickets outside the lines were reinforced and the rest of the troops were ordered to move quietly to their alarm stations. Sentinels received strict instructions to challenge no one and to maintain silence at all costs. Meanwhile the soldiers were left to wonder why the eighteen-pounders at the Jersey battery were firing at regular intervals and if they were having any effect on the enemy.

The artillery officer, Major Ebenezer Stevens, was sick, so St. Clair went around to his quarters to break the news about the evacuation. Stevens had been in camp since early April, taking part in the urgent preparations that occupied the garrison for the next three months, and when he learned that a retreat was to take place that night he blew up. He was a feisty character, not one to mince words, and he told the general he had "reason to curse the day I ever put my feet into the country, there being so much retreating." Timidity was not Stevens's style: he was one of the seventy or eighty men who dumped the tea into Boston harbor, precipitating the infamous Port Bill; he had been confronting the British in one way or another ever since; and sick or no, he was determined to save his guns.

By now St. Clair had had almost no sleep since the enemy landed at Three Mile Point five days earlier, so he was functioning on sheer willpower and nervous energy, and if his temper was short there was reason for it. He bristled and replied that he had an even greater reason to curse the day, saying that he would catch more blame for what he was about to do than Stevens would if he lost the artillery. That seemed to mollify the major, and St. Clair then asked if they could hope to save all the guns. Impossible, Stevens responded; they didn't have enough boats to transport them. The upshot of this was that St. Clair assigned five hundred men to help Stevens load his cannon—all except the eighteen-pounders and larger guns, which were too heavy and cumbersome to carry off—but as the major had foreseen, boats were scarce, General Poor having already appropriated some of them for his troops' baggage and the sick, so the artilleryman had to make do with those that remained. Once they were full, he ordered his men to spike the guns that had to be left behind.

About nine that night the light in the western sky was fading when the rank and file and most officers received the incomprehensible order to strike their tents and stow them aboard boats bound for Skenesborough, after which they were to parade with their baggage. Colonel Francis's men were on picket duty when they received "the disagreeable News of Leaving the Ground," and Parson Hitchcock, "with great Reluctance," left his comfortable quarters in a newly completed building, headed for Mount Independence, and carried his belongings onto one of the boats. By the time everyone knew the fort was to be abandoned, the troops were not only stunned, they turned sullen and angry and frustrated, wondering what had caused the general to turn tail in the face of an enemy without putting up a fight.

The men in the ranks could only guess at the enemy's strength and the ramifications of Burgoyne's tactical advantage, but no matter—it was beyond all imagining that the post would not be defended to the last extremity. A New Hampshire soldier named Cogan spoke for a great many disillusioned rebels when he said, "Such a retreat was never heard of since the creation of the world."

So it had come to this: after enduring all the marching and drilling, the hunger and fatigue, the blackflies and mosquitoes, the measles and smallpox, the savagery of Indians, the backbreaking construction work— all of it came down to sneaking out the back door under cover of darkness, running away from their citadel in the wilderness just when they were ready and eager for action. The young men who had marched off to war with light hearts, anticipating the adventure that lay ahead, had boasted of how they couldn't wait for their chance at the lobsterbacks, and while some of that could be put down to bravado, something deeper was involved. Young and old alike, these individuals took the word "liberty" very seriously—seriously enough to fight and possibly die for it—and above everything they had wanted the opportunity to make that fight.

They may not have thought of it in such terms, but they had come to this remote outpost in pursuit of a vision—a concept of freedom that was something new in the entire world and had a variety of meanings depending on who was doing the talking. The goals they sought had been articulated in the unheard-of radicalism of the Declaration of Independence, in ideas and words that would bring nothing less than the reappraisal of all values, a process that might sweep away the rules by which society functioned. This new language possessed a singular significance for people who had become increasingly conscious of their status as subordinate, second-class citizens, dependent for respect and position on the whims of people in power and on a rigid class system that excluded all but the favored and the moneyed.

So while the men at Ticonderoga and Mount Independence had come there on what many regarded as an adventure, it was also a quest, as much so as the search for the Grail. At the end of their journey into the unknown they believed there would be liberty and a society in which ordinary people would hold power and have respect, with a voice in determining who their leaders would or would not be. These thoughts may have been inchoate, not spelled out, but they were there nonetheless, understood. And for these reasons it was simply unthinkable that they would give up without a battle.

Even if the retreat went smoothly, they were keenly aware of what would have to be left behind, all of it items in short supply—precious equipment, tents, ammunition, sheep and cattle badly needed for meat, and worst, four comrades too severely wounded to be moved.* For the young rookies who had come here spoiling for a fight, the romance of war and their dreams of glory came close to vanishing on the wind of a July night, when nature itself seemed to have turned against them.

Remarkably, considering the time and effort he had invested in the works here, Colonel Jeduthan Baldwin took the news in stride, as if a retreat was the only logical action. About nine o'clock, St. Clair informed him that the post was to be evacuated that night, so he should have his

---

*One of them may have been John Batty, the soldier who had been wounded and scalped while alive. He "was living the day before the retreat," the Reverend Thomas Allen stated, "and it was said was left behind."

artificers collect all their tools and deliver them to bateaus that were assigned specially to him. This was to be completed by 2:00 A.M. With characteristic efficiency and never a look back at the work on which he more than any individual had been involved these past months—the Great Bridge, the batteries, the numerous buildings and fortifications— Baldwin assembled his men and by midnight, two hours ahead of his deadline, had everything ready on the Ticonderoga side. He stopped at the stone magazine to see if he could help Captain Winslow move his guns and ammunition, but Winslow had already loaded them onto a flat-bottomed boat, so Baldwin checked in at headquarters, learned that St. Clair was over on Mount Independence, and located him there.

What could he do now? Baldwin asked. St. Clair replied with asperity that he had found all the men on this side, including General Fermoy, sound asleep, and that Baldwin could oblige him by waking the general. Although it can't have been easy, since the Frenchman had almost certainly had too much to drink, the engineer accomplished that mission and then went on to his next assignment, which was to extricate some hundred barrels of powder from a magazine and roll them down to the landing. He collected a group of men to manhandle the heavy casks downhill to the wharf, where he found the situation chaotic. A high wind was blowing, churning up the lake, and the big wooden boats were bobbing up and down, banging against the dock, making them extremely difficult to load. Baldwin could see that the men were "very cross," and he and the other officers on hand had all they could do to make them attend to duty.

Lieutenant Thomas Blake of the 1st New Hampshire Regiment arrived about this time and observed that everything was "in a moving posture, the boats and bateaus chiefly loaded, the provisions not all taken in, the clothing chests all broke open, the clothing thrown about and carried off by all that were disposed to take it, and everything in great confusion."

Without lanterns it was almost impossible to see whether all the readily portable articles had been collected on the Ticonderoga side— but by 1:00 A.M. General St. Clair returned once again to the mount and urged Hay to get the stores aboard the boats as quickly as possible, since this was one of the shortest nights of the year and anything that remained unloaded at daybreak would have to be left behind. Like Baldwin and Blake, Hay was caught up in the appalling disorder at the wharf, caused by Fermoy's unaccountable absence and failure to issue orders, and realized that some of the men were becoming panicky. He tried threats and promises to persuade them to unload the wagons used for hauling their gear down off the plateau and put the contents aboard the boats, but to no avail. Hay had known all along that there were not enough vessels to carry off the mountain of equipment and supplies littering the low land around the wharf, but now another shortage became evident—oxen were lacking to pull loaded wagons down to the landing. The garrison never had had enough draft animals, since this was heavily forested country with little grazing land to support them, and the handful of oxen on hand were poor specimens at best and no match for this job.

Although Brockholst Livingston was acting as an aide to St. Clair, secrecy was so tight that he had no idea what was behind the orders he carried to the sentinels, forbidding them to challenge anyone. He was perplexed, not understanding the reason for it, but he began to get the drift of things when he was sent off with another message—this to Captain Winslow, the officer in charge of the old redoubt protecting the footbridge across the lake, telling him not to spike the guns until he was told to do so. But as Livingston discovered, the vents had already been spiked, probably on orders from Stevens.

It was a busy evening for the young man, and he was beginning to sense that he would not see the fulfillment of his dream—"an Opportunity of being present at a Battle in which I promise myself the pleasure of seeing our arms flushed with victory." He had nursed that hope ever since he came here as Schuyler's aide-de-camp and had to remain behind on account of a severe fever. Now his health had improved but the anticipated battle, much less the victory he longed to see, looked to be very elusive indeed.

St. Clair's regular aide, Major Isaac Dunn, was also shuttling back and forth across the lake on urgent errands. Early in the evening, after watching cannon and ammunition being wrestled into the few boats below the fort, he had gone across the lake to get word to Fermoy to move everything possible to the foot of the hill and put it on board bateaus for transfer to Skenesborough. Then he crossed the floating bridge again, hustled to the Jersey redoubt, and instructed the officer in charge to continue firing his cannon at a battery the enemy were building nearby.

Around midnight, Dunn was back on Mount Independence, where he found Fermoy outside his house, surrounded by his personal baggage but seemingly unconcerned about what was going on. Walking down to the landing, Dunn saw Colonel Hay directing the loading of boats on this side, but it was a hopeless muddle: Fermoy's incompetence had resulted in three or four hundred men milling about without the vaguest idea of what to do next. Militiamen, artificers, Continentals—carrying whatever they had been able to bring to the wharf—now realized that the possibility of loading it on the boats was just about nil. As near as anyone could tell in the darkness, the bateaus were full. Hay was doing his level best to make order out of this chaos, but as more soldiers kept arriving he was having the devil's own time of it. Fermoy's men on the plateau were striking their tents, and they and the troops who had come over from Ticonderoga began to arrive at the wharf, adding to the confusion.

James Thacher didn't learn of the orders to leave until midnight, when someone woke him from a sound sleep and told him to hurry—he was to collect the hospital stores that still remained, gather the sick and wounded, and clear out. Thacher had been appointed surgeon's mate in the general hospital in April and was sufficiently removed from the mainstream of events that he had a hard time believing what was going on, but he got his charges together, and by 3:00 A.M. they were part of a flotilla he estimated to be five armed galleys, two hundred bateaus, and other craft crowded with cannon, tents, provisions, invalids, and women bound for Skenesborough.

By now what was supposed to be an army making an orderly withdrawal was little more than a pushing, shoving, undisciplined crowd of men who were angry or frightened or both. The thin crescent of a new moon threw just enough light on the scene to reveal grotesque figures moving through the darkness, bent under heavy loads, carrying barrels of salt pork and powder as well as bedding, tents, muskets, and their belongings. No fires were permitted, and fortunately the shuffling of hundreds of feet in a confined area was muffled by the regular boom of American cannon, firing to "amuse the enemy."

It was three o'clock, an hour before daylight streaked the sky, and exactly twelve hours after the council of officers decided to abandon the place, when Isaac Dunn finally located a boat with enough space to carry four men assigned to guard the pay chest, and he watched as it slid out onto the dark waters, bound for Skenesborough. Colonel Pierce Long, who was regarded by St. Clair as "an active, diligent, good officer," was charged with shepherding more than two hundred boats laden with cannon, gunpowder, stores, and baggage of all description, plus invalids and the men of his own regiment, to Skenesborough. There he was to assume command until St. Clair and the main body, marching overland, caught up with him; then they would proceed together as expeditiously as possible to join Schuyler at Fort Edward.

Meanwhile, responsibility for the most dangerous and crucial role in a military retreat, the rear guard, was assigned to the exceptionally capable Colonel Ebenezer Francis. The idea was that he would be in charge of the rearguard action during the march from Mount Independence to Hubbardton, where Colonel Seth Warner, who was more familiar with the ground there, would take over.

The job of Francis and his men was to protect the tail end of the retreating army, and it would be an operation requiring consummate skill. What made it especially tricky was that this was a night movement, difficult and prone to confusion even when executed by veterans, and it was likely to be a demanding challenge for men who were partly trained at best, lacking the discipline of an experienced outfit.

While delaying the advance of the enemy and avoiding close combat if possible, Francis and the rear guard would have to withdraw in such a way that they could take up successive advantageous positions, always one jump ahead of the pursuers. What was left unsaid but was implicit in the assignment was that the rear guard should expect to fight to the finish if that was what it took to keep the enemy away from the main body of troops.

No one knew better than St. Clair "that a retreat, with an inferior army, from before a superior one, is perhaps the most delicate and dangerous undertaking in the whole circle of military operations, and that it never will be effected without prudence, fortitude and secrecy." It had to be done, he knew, and as much as he despised the very idea of retreating, he could console himself with the thought that his motive was not to avoid a fight but to save his army.

The order of march put Poor's brigade in the van, followed by militia, Paterson's brigade, Fermoy's, and the rear guard of 450 men under Ebenezer Francis. By placing the militia companies between Continental troops, St. Clair hoped to keep the former from running off at the first opportunity. That very day two lieutenant colonels of Massachusetts militia regiments handed him a "certificate" stating that they had signed up for two months' service and "do consider the term expired." When pressed, one of the lieutenant colonels claimed to have urged his men to stay, hoping to shame them by saying that the enemy was at the very gates of the fort, but he had been rebuffed. The militiamen told him in no uncertain terms they didn't believe they would be paid, claimed that "they had not been invited to stay," and suggested that if they were to remain with the army, a bounty would not be amiss.

In spite of all the hitches and the bedlam at the landing, the retreat from the Ticonderoga side was nearly complete and by some miracle had lived up to St. Clair's prescription of "prudence, fortitude and secrecy." After satisfying himself that as much as possible had been removed, the general left the fort for the last time and arrived at Mount Independence to find the chaos resulting from Fermoy's ineptitude. A good many of the soldiers milling about were young, untrained, and ill equipped to boot, and the worst of it was that in the confusion of collecting their own belongings and the matériel that was to be sent off on the boats, units had fragmented and lost any resemblance to regimental organization. Veterans among them knew the feeling of being safe in the ranks and unsafe outside, and they stuck with their units insofar as it was feasible, but most militiamen did not, and it was all but impossible to handle or direct them because the men and their officers had completely lost touch with each other.

At the very moment St. Clair was doing his best to organize the troops for the march to Hubbardton, the unbelievable occurred. Suddenly, without warning, flames shot up from a building on the Mount, sending sparks and long tongues of fire aloft, illuminating the scene like some gigantic torch. For those who had considered it idiocy to put a man like Fermoy in a position of authority and responsibility, their worst fears were confirmed, for it turned out that the French officer had disobeyed the order to extinguish all lights of any kind—campfire, or even a candle—and had set his own quarters ablaze.

Some three hundred men, half from Poor's brigade and half from Paterson's, were still on picket duty out by the old French Lines, staring down the throat of the enemy, and Poor had gone to give them orders. They would make up the rear guard under Colonel Francis's command, he said, and as a means of keeping the British from learning of the retreat, were to form a chain of sentinels "from water to water," across the peninsula, to stop any Americans from deserting and alerting the enemy. Before Poor could call in the pickets he saw Fermoy's house burst into flames, exposing all of Mount Independence to view, throwing hundreds of figures into sharp relief so that he could make out every movement of Fermoy's men—striking their tents and loading and carrying off their baggage, sure signs that a retreat was in progress. If he could see what was going on, Burgoyne's lookouts certainly could.

In a classic of understatement, Major Dunn said that the firing of the house, which lit up the entire hillside, "damped the spirits of our own troops." The shock of knowing that the enemy, alerted to the retreat, might pounce on them at any moment from the rear and flank proved too much for the thoroughly bewildered, unorganized militiamen, who ran off on the road to Hubbardton, followed by a number of equally nervous Continentals. What had been simple confusion at the water's edge was now compounded by fear, turning soldiers into a mob of badly frightened and demoralized men, and the whole thing happened so fast there was no time to form up in organized units. St. Clair rode up from the rear to the front of the crowd and ordered them to halt, but the militiamen were having none of that and ignored him, pressing forward in the half-light that precedes the dawn. Most of those who did obey St. Clair's orders were Continentals, and he told them to form up in single file, which was the only way to negotiate the rough, narrow cart track. Then he returned to the Mount, where stragglers were still moving out, followed by the rear guard. Hay was there, and the general begged him to save his papers—the most valuable items in his baggage—and forget the rest of his possessions. Then he rode off after the marching men. It was almost 4:00 A.M. on July 6, 1777, and dawn was just breaking when the last Americans retired, having fired only a handful of shots from what had been considered an unconquerable stronghold.

Henry Brockholst Livingston had been raised in a privileged and immensely wealthy family that owned a 160,000-acre fiefdom on the east bank of the Hudson River below Albany; his father was the governor of New Jersey, and it was to the young man's credit that he had left a privileged position behind in order to serve a cause which he took very seriously indeed. But during what proved to be a grueling five-day forced march that began in the first light of July 6, taking the army "thro' pathless woods, and over mountains where no vestige of human foot remained," he may have had second thoughts about his decision to become a military man. He had neither bed nor blanket, only what food he could scrounge, and was deeply depressed at the thought of "the Misfortunes of my Country—all our Dependence & hopes on Tyonderoga are now blasted—Our Frontiers are open and a merciless, Savage Foe let loose on defenceless inhabitants." Writing later to his sister Susan, who was in New Jersey with their parents, he observed, "The Enemy with you"—by which he meant General William Howe's army—"had some glimmerings of humanity left—Those with us have none—Murder, Scalping, and plunder stain their steps everywhere."

He would have been unhappier still if he had known what occurred after he left Mount Independence. Colonel Francis's rear guard had been handpicked from several regiments, including his own, for their hazardous mission, and before leaving Ticonderoga they collected "every living thing" from the fort. Crossing the floating bridge and damaging it as much as they dared in the darkness to hinder pursuit, they formed up on the east shore in excellent order and brought up the rear behind their able commander.

A final precaution had been taken to safeguard the army's retreat. Four men, serving as a forlorn hope, remained behind. They were all that was left of the garrison, and their assignment was to man the cannon in the shore battery on Mount Independence and fire on the British while they were crossing the bridge and were most vulnerable, unable to respond. Then the four would disappear into the woods and make their way back to rejoin the rear guard. Only it did not come off quite as planned.

When the British crossed the bridge and cautiously approached the works on the Mount, alert for snipers, they came upon the battery. The four men were at their posts, all right, linstocks lighted and ready to fire, but beside them lay an empty cask of Madeira. They were all dead drunk.

Chapter 10

I Have Beat Them!

General Enoch Poor's brigade formed up about 150 yards from the Skenesborough landing on Mount Independence and stepped off on the road to Hubbardton and Castle Town. In the best of circumstances—which these most assuredly were not—this was hard going. Less than a year earlier the route they were to follow was only a footpath through the forest, compacted by the feet of men and horses winding this way and that to avoid the high ridges, deep valleys, and numerous ponds along the way. After General Gates ordered improvements to accommodate the growing traffic of wagons hauling supplies from Fort No. 1 on the east side of the Connecticut River, squads of soldiers hacked their way through the virgin timber with axes, but the result was little more than the promise of a road—a rough, narrow trace meandering through rolling, heavily wooded terrain and skirting the few scattered settlements, filled with potholes, ruts, and the raw stumps of enormous trees, with great piles of slash closing it in on either side.

Many of these men had traveled this route before, on their way from New England to Ticonderoga, and knew it led southeast from Mount Independence to Hubbardton, where it joined the Crown Point road. Seen on a map, it resembled the right half of a pear—narrow at the top, where its course lay between South Bay and East Creek, then swelling out to embrace Hubbardton, before tracing a gradual southwesterly curve through Castle Town to Skenesborough.

Clutching the pathetically few belongings they had managed to grab before setting off in the darkness the night before, the soldiers of St. Clair's main army stumbled along, fearful of being attacked from the rear and wanting desperately to hurry, yet unable to move faster than the man directly ahead because of the narrowness of the road.

Off to their left the rising sun promised another brutally hot day, making it plain that this forced march was going to be hell. Nor were St. Clair's the only men who would suffer: by six o'clock that morning, four separate bodies of troops were heading along the road as fast as they were capable of moving. In the van of St. Clair's main army were Poor's Continentals, with militia regiments theoretically tucked between those men and Fermoy's Continentals in the rear but in fact spread out across the landscape in a state of almost total disarray. In the wake of that large group, Colonel Ebenezer Francis's 450-man rear guard made its way. Francis had been ordered to "sweep every thing off the ground upon the Ticonderoga side, to bring every man and beast," and he had done that all right, but no one had reckoned with the number of stragglers he would have to pick up along the route. Most of these poor souls were suffering from shock and lack of sleep, they were plainly used up, and with each passing hour Francis's ranks swelled with exhausted individuals and groups, drenched with sweat, unable to keep pace with the main army because of the suffocating heat in the dense woods.

Some three or four miles behind the rebel rear guard came Brigadier General Simon Fraser, driving the grenadier and light infantry battalions, with two companies of his 24th Regiment, in pursuit of the fleeing Americans. And some distance behind him marched General Riedesel, who in his haste to get moving had collected a company of jägers and about eighty men from Breymann's corps, leaving orders for the rest of that outfit and the men of his own regiment to follow immediately. It had the elements of a classic chase—two bodies of Americans, followed by two groups of their enemies, each separated from the others, all pounding along the same narrow track.

Poor, who knew his business and did it well, kept riding back and forth along the lines of his marching troops, shouting encouragement, urging them to pick up the pace, and before they had gone many miles he had nearly all his command together as a unit. At the first halt the disciplined Continentals assembled by regiment, but the militiamen, according to the general, continued to behave "with the greatest disorder."

(Another officer described their conduct as "exceedingly insubordinate and seditious.") Yet despite the hazards and difficulties of the march, the Continental officers, St. Clair said later, were "diligent and attentive, and the men silent and obedient to a wonder." The militia, however, were something else. They created no end of trouble, grousing about the road, the difficulty of the march, and their lack of sleep and food, all the while clamoring to be dismissed and sent home. They wanted out of this army and made no bones about it, giving St. Clair one more worry he did not need just now.

The plan was to halt at a place called Lacey's Camp—about three acres of open land and what someone called "a Small indifferent Logg house"—above the swampy northern end of Lake Bomoseen, about sixteen miles from Mount Independence and ten from Castle Town, which was the first real clearing along the route. But about a mile before they reached Lacey's, Poor received the disturbing news from a local inhabitant that "a large number of the enemy and Indians" were up ahead at Hubbardton, two miles distant. Even so, St. Clair elected to push on, and the columns soon crossed Sargent Hill through a saddle southwest of the thirteen-hundred-foot summit, from which the road descended to Sucker Brook, a little stream flowing out of the wetlands. Here they climbed a hill, stepped over a stone wall, and found themselves on a flat plateau where Farmer Selleck's cows had grazed until the previous day.

Hubbardton, named for the grantee Thomas Hubbard, was settled in 1774 by two intrepid families, and a year later, when the Sellecks arrived, the community boasted nine widely separated farmsteads. On this hot, sultry afternoon it was a ghostly place. The Sellecks and some of the others had struck out for the safety of Massachusetts on the previous day, when the raiding party about which St. Clair had been warned suddenly appeared and captured several of their neighbors.

It was close to one o'clock when the footsore troops reached Hubbardton, and St. Clair was keenly aware of how desperately his men needed rest. They had been tramping for nearly nine hours in sweltering heat, covering more than twenty miles of rugged, tortuous terrain, and they had six more miles to go before reaching Castle Town. The more fortunate ones had drawn four days' provisions on July 5, before they evacuated the posts, but many had not, and were weak from hunger as well as fatigue. Fortunately, they had brought off some cattle from Ticonderoga and slaughtered them now to eat.

As the men fell out, St. Clair sent word to Francis, instructing him to have the rear guard follow the main body and take position a mile or two short of Castle Town, where the general intended to bivouac for the night. Although there was no sign of the Tories and Indians who had been through the hamlet, he was told that five hundred of them had gone down the road toward his destination. A force of that size was no threat to his army. What was worrisome was the fact that they had been here at all: they had to have come from the north, perhaps from Otter Creek, near the stream's mouth, where the presence of the enemy had been reported several days earlier. If more were approaching from that direction, it could mean trouble.

For several hours St. Clair delayed at Hubbardton, hoping the rear guard would catch up, but finally, when it failed to appear, he set out with the army for Castle Town after leaving orders for Seth Warner and his 150 Green Mountain Boys to remain here until Francis came up. Warner was to take charge of their combined units, plus Hale's 2nd New Hampshire Regiment, which would turn the rear guard into a respectable fighting force. He was instructed to follow the general and make camp within a mile and a half of Castle Town that night and, at four the next morning, march and join forces with St. Clair. As soon as all these elements were reunited, they would head for Skenesborough and join the people who had traveled by water from Mount Independence.

It was four o'clock in the afternoon by the time Francis and Colonel Nathan Hale, with something over a thousand men, finally arrived at Hubbardton, and the wonder was that they made it by then. As Captain Moses Greenleaf described their ordeal, it was "as fatigueing a March as ever known." Francis had been grievously burdened with stragglers, while Hale had been assigned the unenviable task of shepherding the walking wounded, the sick and disabled, and some whose only ailment was too much alcohol. Hale's accumulated halt, lame, and drunks amounted to several hundred men, and their progress had been painfully slow. At that, they had been forced to leave behind some of the feeblest individuals, because the British were so near that they could fire on the rebels at the tail end of the army. Ebenezer Fletcher, a sixteen-year-old fifer in Captain Carr's company in Hale's regiment, was acutely aware of the dilemma. He had just recovered from the measles and was having a terrible time keeping up, with the result that he was one of the last men in the retreating rebel columns.

St. Clair's troops were still at Hubbardton when the first of the rear guard, including Captain Woolcott, came on the scene. Woolcott immediately lay down and fell sound asleep; when he awakened he discovered that the main army had departed—to Castle Town, he was told, and the rear guard was to follow directly. The captain walked over to the Selleck house, where he found Colonels Warner, Francis, and Hale discussing the situation. Warner was now in charge, and Woolcott asked whether he and his men should prepare to resume the march. No, Warner replied, everyone was exhausted and deserved a night's sleep before moving on to join the main army.

These three colonels—all in their early thirties—were as good as they came. Nathan Hale was a New Hampshireman—a solid citizen who had served his community as first constable and moderator of town meetings before becoming captain of a militia company that marched to Cambridge at the time of the Lexington alarm. Like Warner and a good many others in this army, he had fought at Breed's Hill, and before being commissioned colonel of the 2nd New Hampshire Regiment, he had served under Washington in New York and New Jersey. He was an able fellow, much liked by the men in his command, but unfortunately he was about to run out of luck.

Ebenezer Francis, a Beverly, Massachusetts, resident, was commissioned a captain in 1775, became colonel of a regiment raised for the defense of Boston the following year, and was appointed by the Continental Congress to lead one of Massachusetts's fifteen battalions. Three of his brothers were officers during the Revolution, and Francis had left behind his wife and five children when he came to Ticonderoga. A tall, imposing man, he was greatly admired by the troops despite his practice of driving them hard and expecting a lot from them. His regiment was widely regarded as the best-trained, best-disciplined outfit in St. Clair's command, and Francis deserved the credit for that. Unhappily, he was to prove even unluckier than Hale.

Seth Warner was an old hand at protecting a retreating force, having fought till the end at Breed's Hill and covered the retreat from Canada, when he marched south with the pitiful remains of the army, bringing the wounded and disease-ridden victims to safety. Born in Connecticut about 1744, he moved to Bennington when he was twenty-nine and acquired a reputation as a skilled hunter. More than six feet tall, thin but very strong, he was a complete natural—unaffected, full of fun, an incurable adventurer—which made him extremely popular with the rough-and-ready folk of the New Hampshire Grants, whom he and Ethan Allen led in the violent prerevolutionary border disputes with New Yorkers. When both men were declared outlaws by the New York legislature, a reward was offered for their capture, but that was largely forgotten when Allen captured Fort Ticonderoga from the British (with

Warner in charge of his rear guard) and Warner went on to seize Crown Point.

When the Green Mountain Boys reorganized on July 27, 1775, they astonished just about everybody by ousting Ethan Allen, which they accomplished in a curious fashion—they left the colonelcy vacant and elected Seth Warner lieutenant colonel, thus making him *de facto* commander. One reason St. Clair put him in charge of this present operation was his experience; another was that Warner and his men were familiar with the countryside. But one facet of Warner's personality that St. Clair may not have reckoned with was a stubborn determination to be his own boss. He did not take kindly to playing a subordinate role (as one officer put it neatly, he was "a stranger to discipline"), and that trait—revealed in his decision to call a halt where his exhausted men lay instead of moving on according to orders and keeping within close range of the main army—was to cost the Americans dearly within a few short hours.

Warner would come in for a lot of criticism later for failing to comply with St. Clair's orders, but there is no telling what lay behind his decision. Certainly his men were dead tired, still suffering from the shock of abandoning their posts without a fight, plus the forced night march, and he probably believed them incapable of going farther until they had some rest. They were also in a strong position, well supplied with water, astride the junction of the road from Mount Independence and the one from the north, over which another British force might come. Along the perimeter of the cleared land around the Selleck farm were piles of felled trees and brush, forming a natural fortification on his western and northern flanks, and here he posted pickets against attack from the Mount Independence road.

Finally, Warner knew that two militia regiments were camped between him and the main body, two and a half miles down the road, at a place called Ransomvale. Presumably those men could come to his support (or St. Clair's) if the need arose.

Whatever his reasoning, Warner let his Green Mountain Boys hunker down where they were, in the area of the Selleck house. Below, in the valley along Sucker Brook, which any pursuers from Mount Independence would have to cross, the 2nd New Hampshire Regiment and most of the stragglers had bivouacked. To the north and right of Warner, Francis's men took position in the woods, where they could block an enemy advance from that direction.

As the spent rebels fell into a troubled sleep that night, they had no way of knowing that a determined Scot and his crack troops lay on their arms at Lacey's camp, just three miles away.

Brigadier General Simon Fraser had gotten off to a gallingly late start, which was one of the luckiest breaks the Americans had that day. Considering the hurried, even frantic, movements of several thousand rebels as they prepared to abandon the fortifications, along with the burning of Fermoy's house and the way it revealed what they were up to, it is almost impossible to comprehend the British failure to realize what was happening. Why Burgoyne's men weren't alerted is a mystery, for the fire set by Fermoy was only one of many reported by British and Germans that night. Surgeon Wasmus observed "many fires . . . as if houses and cottages were burning," and noted that the Americans "removed their flags before nightfall." Lieutenant Digby saw the rebels setting fire to several buildings, which, with the cannonade, produced clouds of smoke, and before midnight "perceived the great fires in the Fort. I never saw such great fires," he added. And Brigadier Specht also mentioned the blazes on Mount Independence, which he took to be brushfires or a hut that was burning. The besiegers knew something was afoot, but exactly what was not clear until daybreak on July 6, when three American deserters came into Fraser's lines with the news that St. Clair's army had withdrawn from the east side of Mount Independence, which was not visible to the British.

Fraser's immediate reaction was that this might be a trick to bring his men within range of grapeshot, but he was quick to act. He sent a message to Burgoyne and ordered his men to turn out immediately and be quiet about it. He ordered the colors of the 9th Regiment raised to serve as a guide for the men, rounded up Lieutenant Twiss and a few other officers, and hurried off into the darkness, ordering his pickets to follow. It did not take long to see that the enemy had vanished, but he was elated to find Jeduthan Baldwin's boom substantially intact. He sent for planks and as soon as they were laid had his men crossing. Even in single file they were soon on the other side, and Lieutenant Digby observed with professional scorn that the rebels' rear guard, incomprehensibly, had only partially destroyed the bridge by fire. Not only that, he said: if a single gun, loaded with grape and properly positioned, had been manned by two soldiers, they could have fired at the British and escaped, and "in all probability have destroyed all or most of us on the boom."

But of course the four rebels who had precisely that assignment had drunk themselves senseless. To make the farce complete, a curious Indian wandered up to the cannon, picked up a slow match that was still burning, and dropped a spark into the cannon, which was "loaded with all manner of combustibles" and exploded with a deafening blast. Fortunately for the oncoming light infantry and grenadiers, the gun was elevated too high and the shot passed over their heads.

Up onto the Mount the redcoats advanced, bayonets at the ready, but no one was there. While they were raising the king's colors over the picket fort they discovered one more instance of plans gone awry. The ground was strewn with gunpowder and several kegs of it sat nearby, ready to blow, but no one had troubled to put a match to the powder. The British could scarcely believe their eyes: the panic-stricken rebels had destroyed none of their ammunition, provisions, or barracks; clothing, cooking utensils, muskets, even money and personal belongings were strewn everywhere. Gleefully, the conquerors fanned out in all directions in search of souvenirs and loot—a breakdown of discipline that infuriated Fraser, who had all he could do to "prevent horrid irregularities." But by 5:00 A.M. he had the situation under control, with troops posted at Ticonderoga and Mount Independence, and since he believed the rebel rear guard must be within four miles of him, he was chafing to be on his way.

After assembling two companies of the 24th Regiment plus a detachment of the grenadier and light infantry battalions, he sent an officer to inform Burgoyne what had happened and to request that the rest of his own command, plus more troops, be sent to support him. He was "resolved to attack any body of the rebels that I could come up with," he added, and with that he was off.

The sun was up as they marched, promising another scorching day, but without allowing his men to pause long enough to take on provisions or even fill canteens, he led them on a punishing nine-mile march before finding any water. At this little oasis about twenty rebels were stretched out, "all very much in liquor," and here Fraser sent Captain Campbell back to Mount Independence with a message for Burgoyne. He judged that he was not far from the rebel rear now, and since he planned to attack, requested support, specifying *"British troops if possible."* As luck would have it, Campbell reached the Mount only to learn that the fleet had broken through the boom and bridge and was already under way to Skenesborough, with Burgoyne and Phillips on board. He did see reinforcements for Fraser, however—not the regulars the brigadier wanted, but Germans under General Riedesel, and they were already on the march.

Burgoyne had lost no time following up on the American retreat. Anticipating that Fraser might need help, before leaving for Skenesborough he ordered Riedesel to lead his own regiment and Breymann's command and follow Fraser along the road to Hubbardton. Meanwhile, the 62nd Regiment would take over Mount Independence while the Prinz Friedrich troops secured Ticonderoga.

The day was "very hot and sultry" and growing more so with each passing hour, the terrain "a continued succession of steep and woody hills," and about the time that Warner's command was establishing itself in and around Hubbardton, Fraser called a halt on the bank of a stream, where two bullocks rounded up along the way were slaughtered and devoured. The capture of the animals was of little solace to Lieutenant William Digby, who grumbled that the men were all that day without food "excepting one cow we happened to kill in the woods, which, without bread, was next to nothing among so many for two days." While the troops were eating, one of the rebel prisoners informed the brigadier that the man in charge of the American rear guard was Colonel Francis, who would likely "surrender to the King's troops, rather than fall into the hands of Savages." To confirm this story, Fraser sent the fellow off to talk with the rebel colonel, but the report he received was hardly what was expected: although Francis was not more than two miles from the British, he "paid no . . . attention to my message . . . except by doubling his diligence in getting away."

About 4:00 P.M. some German jägers overtook Fraser, and an hour later General Riedesel rode up, saying he had orders to support the brigadier. To the Scot's disgust, no provisions, no ammunition, no surgeons—let alone the rest of his corps—had been sent, on top of which he was annoyed and hurt to be superseded by a senior officer, and a German at that. (Riedesel, moreover, not only was his junior in age by ten years, but of course outranked him.) Burgoyne, Fraser confided to a friend, "is a liberal minded sensible gallant man, but there are persons secretly jealous of all my poor endeavors to forward the public service." Who those persons were he didn't say, but clearly he felt that other officers, possibly envious of his independent command and his close relationship with Burgoyne, were not eager for him to win any laurels on this operation.

Riedesel stated flatly that his own troops could move no farther that night; they were unused to such heat, encumbered by uniforms and weapons unsuited to a forced march through wooded, brushy terrain, and tormented by clouds of insects, and it was a wonder they had not succumbed to heat prostration. Although Fraser could take pride in the achievement of his own troops in overcoming the identical problems, it was irritating to have to request Riedesel's permission to proceed toward Hubbardton. Fortunately, the baron was sensitive to the situation and tactfully agreed that the brigadier should press on. Fraser said he would march about three more miles, or until he found a place that offered security and a source of water. He also informed Riedesel that he had been given discretion to attack the enemy wherever he found them, and to that end would have his men on the march at three the next morning. Riedesel replied that he too would get an early start, prepared to support Fraser if he encountered any opposition; meanwhile, his troops would bivouac here for the night.

Some hours later, when the rest of his Brunswickers came up, the baron had between a thousand and fifteen hundred men, but he seems to have had little confidence that all of them could keep up the demanding pace the pursuit required, so the next morning at three o'clock he led a select detachment of jägers and grenadiers out of camp, leaving the others to follow at their normal speed, which was anything but rapid. After proceeding about four miles they met Captain McKay, who had been sent back to inform Riedesel that Fraser was under way and would wait at Hubbardton for the Germans to join him. About fifteen minutes later, Riedesel heard the pop-pop of musket fire up ahead, and pushed forward as fast as he could after sending a message to Colonel Breymann to follow immediately. Then another of Fraser's aides appeared with an urgent message: the rebels were present in such numbers that the British would have difficulty holding out unless they were soon reinforced.

Fraser kept to his schedule and had his men ready to march at three o'clock on the morning of July 7. It was still dark, so their progress was slower and more arduous than what they had experienced the day before, but two hours later, as the sun was rising, they reached the end of a long climb and neared the saddle below Sargent Hill. Some Indian and Tory scouts were up ahead, reconnoitering, and suddenly shots rang out: rebel pickets had spotted them and fired before falling back toward the American camp. From Fraser's vantage point on the western slope of the notch through which the road passed before winding down to Sucker

Brook, he could not see the American position and had no real idea of the enemy's strength. Apparently he halted here while his scouts slipped into the woods to circle the rebels' flanks, and when they returned they undoubtedly brought word that the Americans were there in considerable force.

Now Fraser had to decide whether to await the arrival of the Germans or attack without them. The saddle at the top of the hill just ahead could be a death trap, since high ground on either side made it a perfect site from which to ambush a long column of marching men. Whatever made up his mind for him—and it is tempting to suppose that he had no doubts that his seasoned, disciplined troops could easily overpower the demoralized rebels—Fraser decided to move on without the Germans, crossed the saddle without incident, and headed down toward Sucker Brook.

In the van, Major Robert Grant led Fraser's proud 24th Regiment, with a century of tradition behind it, followed by Major Alexander Lindsay, Earl of Balcarres, with ten companies of elite light infantry, while Major John Acland's ten companies of big, husky grenadiers brought up the rear.

The brigadier's battle plan called for Grant's redcoats to lead the attack and deliver a knockout blow. Balcarres was to angle up along Grant's left flank in case enemy resistance proved stubborn, and the grenadiers would be held in reserve, ready to move in any direction if needed. Although it was daylight, the American camp was only now coming to life, with the men cooking, eating, packing up their gear, "all in a very unfit posture for battle," as the young fifer Ebenezer Fletcher observed.

According to Enos Stone, one reason the day began in such leisurely fashion was that Seth Warner had sent a two-hundred-man detachment to rescue two local families, and the order to march was delayed until they returned. So it was about seven o'clock when someone shouted, "The enemy are upon us!" Young Fletcher whirled around in the direction of the cry and saw pickets running for their lives with redcoats behind them, trotting up to deploy from column to line of battle. As the British began working their way almost blindly through the tangle of underbrush and trees, Fraser's good friend Major Grant—a "very gallant and brave officer," as Thomas Anburey described him—climbed up on a stump to see what he could make of the situation, gave his men orders to fire, and without another word toppled to the ground, killed instantly by a volley that cut down twenty of the redcoats.

The sixteen-year-old Fletcher saw at once that he and his buddies were in trouble: they were badly outnumbered, especially since a lot of them ran into the woods even before the first enemy volley. Captain Carr shouted to them to come back, and a few obeyed his orders and managed to form a ragged line, firing from behind the great number of huge girdled trees in the area, but Carr realized they could do no more than delay the British. That was really all that was asked of him, of course—his mission being to hold up the enemy long enough for the troops up ahead to make their escape.

For a lot of young men like Fletcher, this was their first battle, their first exposure to the whistle of flying lead or the dreaded bayonet charge, the first time they had seen a man's guts torn out or half of a face destroyed by a musket ball, and it was something they would carry with them as long as they lived. Nothing was worse than the waiting, watching the menacing red lines advance as their sergeant yelled at them, telling them to hold their fire and shoot low. That was when the terror gripped them, making the heart pound loud enough to be heard. Green troops, boys off the farm who had never seen a man killed in anger, lacked the discipline that comes with training, the confidence and esprit that hold an experienced unit together, and it was anyone's guess whether they would cut and run or keep firing in the face of those oncoming redcoats with their glistening bayonets. The end of boyhood for Ebenezer Fletcher and hundreds like him came on the 7th of July, 1777, on the banks of Sucker Brook.

Fletcher found what appeared to be good cover, discharged his musket once, and reloaded, only to have the piece misfire. He cocked the gun again, raised and sighted it, and was about to pull the trigger when he felt an excruciating pain in his back. His uncle, Daniel Foster, was nearby, and when Fletcher crawled toward him Foster saw that he had been hit and he and another soldier carried the boy away from the action and laid him behind a big tree, where another badly wounded rebel was crying out in agony. By this time the fifer had lost a lot of blood and felt faint, and he watched with mounting fear as his uncle and his comrades disappeared, falling back before the advancing redcoats.

He knew it was every man for himself now, and weak as he was, Fletcher had the presence of mind to seek a hiding place. He crawled on hands and knees for about thirty-five feet and hid behind a big log. The British were so close he could have touched them; they were running, heading up the steep hill, leaping over the log where the poor lad lay motionless, terrified that he would be discovered.

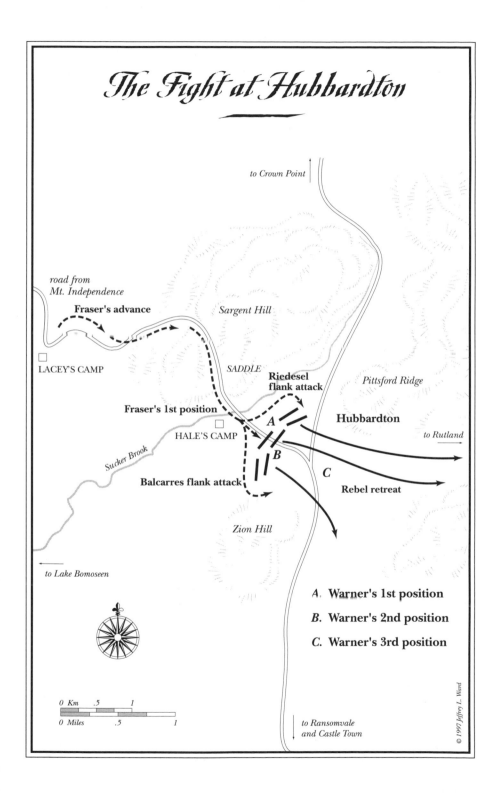

The Fight at Hubbardton

to Crown Point

road from
Mt. Independence

Fraser's advance

Sargent Hill

LACEY'S CAMP

SADDLE

**Riedesel
flank attack**

Pittsford Ridge

Fraser's 1st position

A

Hubbardton

HALE'S CAMP

to Rutland

Sucker Brook

B

Balcarres flank attack

C

Rebel retreat

Zion Hill

to Lake Bomoseen

A. **Warner's 1st position**

B. **Warner's 2nd position**

C. **Warner's 3rd position**

0 Km   .5   1

0 Miles   .5   1

© 1997 Jeffrey L. Ward

to Ransomvale
and Castle Town

At daybreak that morning, Colonel Francis enjoyed a cup of chocolate with his good friend Captain Moses Greenleaf, and at seven o'clock, before heading to the Selleck cabin, where he met Seth Warner, he directed Greenleaf to parade the regiment and prepare to march. Francis and Warner were discussing what to do next when a messenger from General St. Clair galloped up on a horse lathered from a hard ride. He told them that St. Clair's troops had driven the raiding party of Tories and Indians from Castle Town (they were led by Captain Alexander Fraser and an American, Captain Justus Sherwood; and there were only fifty of them, not five hundred as rumor had it). But he also brought the worst sort of news. British ships had broken through Jeduthan Baldwin's stout boom between Ti and the Mount—the barrier that was supposed to prevent the enemy from pursuing by water—and after sailing up the lake to Skenesborough, enemy troops had seized the army's baggage and presumably the invalids who were accompanying it.

St. Clair wanted Warner to march at once and follow him to Rutland. With the British at Skenesborough it was impossible to rendezvous there, so he planned to take a circuitous route toward the Hudson, where he would meet Schuyler. Francis hustled back to his regiment, met Greenleaf at seven-fifteen, told him the news, and ordered him to get under way. Five minutes later, Greenleaf had his companies lined up and they began moving south on the Crown Point–Castle Town road. At that moment someone yelled: a handful of redcoats could be seen emerging from the trees on the far side of Farmer Selleck's field, well within musket range, and without missing a beat, Francis's regiment faced right, swung from column into line, and headed for them on the double. These British regulars were the leading elements of Balcarres's light companies—the infantrymen who had leaped over the prone Ebenezer Fletcher's hiding place down by the brook—and by the time they picked their way over and through the piles of logs and brush, neared the crest of the hill, and came in sight of the Massachusetts men, they were winded and disorganized. These fellows were chosen for their athletic ability and strength, but this steamy July day was unmitigated torture for soldiers in heavy woolen uniforms and leather caps, and the steep climb was enough to wind any man, particularly one carrying a knapsack, full cartouche box, spare ammunition, canteen, hatchet, and a musket through thick brush and fallen trees.

One of them was William Digby, who had been in the army for seven-

teen years, serving with the 53rd Regiment of British Grenadiers that
came to America from Ireland in 1776, and this was his first "serious
engagement." As he struggled up the steep grade through the woods,
orders were passed to prime and load, which the troops barely had time
to do before they were hit by "showers of balls mixed with buck shot"
from the crest of the hill above them. At that moment it crossed Digby's
mind that he might soon meet his Creator, but he comforted himself
with the thought that "a proper resignation to the will of the Divine
Being is the certain foundation for true bravery." What was to be would
be, in other words, and he pushed on up the bank, making his way
through a tangle of tree trunks and branches. When he finally reached
the brow of the hill and caught sight of the rebels, he guessed that there
must be two thousand of them, "strongly posted . . . with breast works
before them, and great trees cut across to prevent our approach."

Francis's men had arrived here first and were lined up, waiting, muskets at the ready. Protected by the stone wall and the logs piled around
it, they were within thirty or forty yards of the British, and when they
opened fire it took the attackers by surprise, shattering their ragged line,
sending the redcoats plunging down the hill, where their officers halted
the flight. Behind them, scattered among the trees, were the broken
bodies of men writhing and calling out in pain; others were dead,
including Lieutenant Haggit, shot in both eyes, and young Lieutenant
Douglas, son of a colonel and "a very pretty lad," according to his commanding officer, Lord Balcarres. Soldiers were carrying the wounded
Douglas to the rear when he was shot through the heart.

At this point Fraser, who had run up the hill at the head of the light
infantry battalion, might well have wondered if he had bitten off more
than he could chew and should have waited for Riedesel to come up.
With the battle barely begun, his left flank was in danger of being
turned, while his advance party, the 24th Foot, with a score of men killed
or wounded, had been stopped in its tracks by the stiff resistance of
Warner's command, and was "depending on the arrival of the Germans,"
as he put it. But Fraser was nothing if not cool and composed, and as a
skilled tactician he decided to commit his reserves rather than lose the
momentum of his initial surprise attack. He detached some of Balcarres's light troops with Acland and his grenadiers, ordering them to
swing to the right to head off the Americans and prevent them from
reaching the Castle Town road. He was taking an enormous risk, and
he knew it—this maneuver seriously weakened the British left, where
Fraser remained in charge—but he was counting on the Brunswickers to

reinforce him before it was too late, and he dispatched a messenger to Riedesel urging him to come up at once.

Six miles down the road in Castle Town, St. Clair could make out the faint sound of distant gunfire and knew it meant trouble. Turning to his two aides—Lieutenant Colonel Henry Brockholst Livingston and Major Isaac Dunn—he told them to ride to Ransomvale and order the militia regiments there to reinforce Warner, and the two men kicked their horses into a gallop and disappeared around a bend in the road.

St. Clair had no clear idea of what was happening at Hubbardton, but neither did the people on the scene. Thomas Anburey described the fight as one in which "both parties engaged in separate detachments uncon-nected with each other." Captain Enos Stone, on the rebel side, called it "as hot a fire as was ever kept up. many fel on Both sides," and if those remarks make it sound like a free-for-all, that is exactly what it was turning out to be.

Combat wears many different faces, depending on where a man is during a battle, what he sees and experiences, and what occurs in the few square yards that constitute his own infinitely precarious universe. Because this battle was fought on a number of fronts simultaneously, few participants had a grasp of the whole—only of isolated fragments, bits and pieces of a much larger puzzle. Several soldiers said the fighting began at sunrise or a little later; others specified 5:00 A.M., which was close to the time of daylight at that season of the year; yet several state-ments indicated that the action started at 7:00 or as late as 7:20. One man was certain the fighting lasted no more than twenty-five minutes, but other estimates varied from an hour and ten minutes to three hours, and it is hard to deny the veracity of any of these facts since they were asserted by a number of soldiers in different parts of the field who knew only what they experienced or could remember. Interestingly enough, almost all the British and German troops who wrote of the battle in let-ters or journals believed that two thousand or more Americans opposed them (Balcarres guessed three thousand), when in fact the rebels had at most twelve hundred—many of them invalids.

The man how may have had the clearest perception of what was hap-pening at Hubbardton was Friedrich Adolph Riedesel. As his spent troops rested on the saddle below Sargent Hill shortly after eight that morning, the baron clambered up onto a rocky knob, from which he had a bird's-eye view of the scene below. Looking through his spyglass, he saw that the rebels had thrown back Fraser's light infantry and were angling to their right, where they would soon be in position to envelop the British left. Riedesel had no way of knowing that the tiny figures he saw far below him, obscured now and then by puffs of smoke from the battle lines, were the troops of Francis's 11th Massachusetts and Hale's 2nd New Hampshire under Benjamin Titcomb. What he did know was that reinforcements were urgently needed at that sector, and with a sure sense of what had to be done he ordered the jägers under Captain von Geyso to advance on the double and make a frontal attack on the rebels, while Breymann's grenadiers, led by a captain with the impressive name of Maximilian Christoph Ludwig von Schottelius, were to sweep around to their left, turn the American right, and fall on their rear. Just then the aide from Fraser rode up, with the message that the brigadier feared his left would be surrounded unless support came quickly, and the baron sent the man back to report that he was at that instant moving to attack the rebel right wing.

By the time Warner got his Green Mountain Boys into formation, four separate rebel units were either engaged or about to go into action. The American line of battle was in the shape of a half-moon about eight hundred yards, or nearly half a mile, long, snaking out from the west side of the road south of the Selleck house. Reading from left to right were the regiments of Warner and Francis and most of Hale's 2nd New Hampshire, led by his second-in-command, Titcomb. Nathan Hale himself was somewhere down near Sucker Brook with the scattered remnants of his regiment, including Captain Carr's company, plus those stragglers and invalids who had not caught up in time to accompany St. Clair when he pulled out of Hubbardton. Despite being taken completely by surprise, Hale's force, such as it was, had done its level best to delay the enemy's advance, but as a fighting unit it had all but ceased to exist, and the men, faced with overwhelming numbers, had slipped off into the woods.

On the British right, the detachment of grenadiers under Acland was heading toward a rocky precipice that commanded the road to Castle Town when Warner spotted them and sent part of his regiment to head them off. Two companies of grenadiers at the edge of the woods, where they had been stationed to prevent Warner's men from outflanking the 24th Regiment, saw about sixty rebels coming toward them across the field with their muskets clubbed. Since this was the conventional sign of surrender, the officer in charge ordered his men to hold their fire, but when the Americans were within ten yards of the British they suddenly turned their muskets around, fired at the grenadiers, taking them completely by surprise, and hightailed it into the woods. It was, Thomas Anburey wrote in disgust, "a breach of all military rules" that left men maimed or dying in its wake—and the grenadiers were not likely to forget it.

As eager as they were to get at the rebels, the grenadiers had their eyes fixed on that commanding hill. To Anburey, the summit appeared virtually inaccessible, with an ascent so precipitous the grenadiers had to sling their muskets and haul themselves up the rocky face, clinging to bushes and bracing their feet on the branches of trees, but there was no stopping them. As Anburey climbed, he thought to himself that the manual of arms so endlessly drilled into the regulars was "but an ornament"—its only virtue a certain proficiency in loading, firing, and charging with the bayonet and of no use whatever for fighting in the woods. Now, instead of putting the long hours on the parade ground into practice, the troops were improvising, and as they moved up the hill they found that they could prime their weapon, put a cartridge in the barrel, and rather than waste time ramming it home, slam the butt on the ground, raise the gun, and fire. But the method had its drawbacks: after the battle some of the men examined their muskets and found as many as half a dozen cartridges in the barrel, which meant that in the heat of the battle they hadn't fired at all.

When Warner saw grenadiers coming down the slope toward him he realized that his left flank was dangerously exposed and ordered his men, who were fighting stubbornly, to pull back to the east side of the Castle Town road and take a position behind a log fence that ran parallel to the road and then made a right-angle turn in the direction of Pittsford Mountain. It was a smart move: in order to attack Warner's troops at close range, where a bayonet charge would be devastating, the grenadiers would have to cross open fields under deadly American fire.

Whether Francis originally intended it that way or whether circumstances demanded improvisation, he directed his own men and Titcomb's to take up three successive positions. The first lay along the crest of the hill, behind the barricade created by the stone wall and logs, where they had pushed back the light infantry. The second, to which they withdrew when it became apparent that the initial position was at risk, was described by Brigadier Fraser as a "hill of less eminence." In reality this was less a hill than a gentle rise in the terrain, which afforded some protection (though not much) to troops lying behind it. The third position was the log fence on the east side of the Castle Town road, toward which Warner's men were falling back.

Francis must have noted that the log fence would have to be the final stop—the point at which his rear guard must disengage and somehow make its way to the main army in Castle Town. And it looked as though the only way that was likely to happen was if reinforcements arrived almost immediately, and in sufficient numbers to make the British back off.

At just about this time St. Clair's two aides, Livingston and Dunn, were galloping along the road for that very purpose, to rally reinforcements. They were to direct Colonel Bellows to march immediately to support the rear guard, assuring him that he could expect help if it was needed, since the main body was under arms and ready to march. But as the two messengers drew closer to the militiamen's camp they met those troops "marching with speed" toward Castle Town—running away from Hubbardton. They spotted Colonel Bellows and delivered St. Clair's orders, but in spite of what were apparently heroic efforts on the colonel's part, not a man made a move in the direction of the fighting. The troops simply refused to obey.

As Livingston described Bellows's predicament, "An unaccountable panic had seized his men, and no commands or intreaties had any effect on them." Seeing that the situation here was beyond anyone's capacity to control, Livingston and Dunn spurred their horses toward the sound of the action.

The British had heard that Colonel Francis was one of the rebels' best officers, and it was easy to see why he had earned his reputation. After turning back the initial attack by Balcarres's light infantry and sending them scrambling down the hill, Francis's men regrouped and fell back to the rise, behind which they took cover, primed and loaded their weapons, and waited for the redcoats to make another assault.

Lord Balcarres was in luck that morning: a musket ball that could have shattered the femur in his left leg glanced off a flint in his pocket and left him with only a slight flesh wound and contusion. After the battle he counted ten holes in his clothing made by gunfire, and he also had the barrel of his fusil and the lock shot off while it was in his hand. "You may observe," he wrote his sister Margaret, "on this occasion I am not born to be shot whatever may be my Fate." A friend of his, Sir John Harrington, had a similar experience. A rebel straggler emerged suddenly from behind some brush and leveled his musket at the British officer's head, but Harrington was too quick for the man and shot him. Approaching the fallen man, Harrington spoke to him and said he hoped he wasn't badly hurt, but there was no reply. Sir John had "the shock of knowing that he was stone dead."

Francis was a conspicuous figure—too conspicuous, as it turned out, moving up and down the line, talking to his captains, moving a company here and another there to shore up a weak spot, all the time rallying the troops and inspiring them with his own courage. Somewhere, probably during the withdrawal from the slight rise to the log fence, when the Americans were moving downhill across the open field, a musket ball hit Francis in his right arm, which now hung useless at his side. But he was not about to quit.

Sizing up the situation on his front, the colonel could see that the left flank of the oncoming British was dangling—their line was too short—and he at once sent troops out from behind the fence to enfilade that exposed section of the redcoats' formation. By this time the battle had been raging for about an hour and twenty-five minutes, according to the meticulous Moses Greenleaf, who said the firing lasted "without cessation" all that time. Yet despite fatigue and the demands of the long holding action, Francis's men began moving toward the British left flank, alerting Fraser that they were attacking, aiming to roll up his wing, and going about it "pretty briskly."

At that moment, over the noise of gunfire came the surprising and unmistakable notes of a military band—a small one, to judge from the sound—bugles blaring, fifes tootling, drums beating the grenadiers' march. Anburey mistook it for rebel reinforcements from the main army at Castle Town, "for they began singing psalms on their advance. . . ." But it was not American music: the Americans had run out of time and luck.

The Brunswickers had finally arrived, thanks no doubt to the baron's spirited cursing of them for their slowness, and they were making as much noise as possible on his orders "to proceed with resounding music," in order to give the rebels the impression of superior numbers. Their appearance was in the nick of time for Fraser. Out of nowhere, it seemed, came Captain von Geyso's jägers in green coats, with brown leather breeches and leggings, carrying German rifles and straight hunting swords, heading directly at the Americans with fixed bayonets "to the sound of music," while the blue-clad grenadiers under Captain Schottelius, their height accentuated by tall, mitered caps with brass facings, were driving in on the right. The hard-pressed New Hampshire regiment, which suffered more disabling wounds than Francis's and Warner's regiments combined, gave way and ran back to the protection of the fence, but the fire from the jägers' rifles was deadly and the rebels realized they were all but surrounded: the British grenadiers had pushed Warner's Green Mountain Boys before them and were sweeping in on the left. For a while the rebels held out (Joseph Bird had time to fire twenty cartridges from behind the fence), but it was a losing game. If they were to avoid the enemy's savage bayonet charge, the Americans had to reach the only fallback position that remained to them—a hedgerow on the far side of Hubbardton Brook. It was an obstacle that would not be easy to cross, but they had to get beyond it and reach the steep slope of Pittsford Mountain. These men were desperate now; unless they made it up and over the mountain, they were trapped.

They had had the protection of walls, trees, terrain, and a fence, but now their only hope of escape was to win a footrace across eighty yards of a wheat field under intense fire. The enemy was closing fast, and the Americans who made it to the hillside on the other side of the brook found the gunsmoke so thick they could not even see the enemy until the British and Germans fired. Henry Sewall, whose day had begun at sunrise and would not end until long after nightfall, noticed that he had two holes in his coat from musket balls, and he took off, retreating "precipitately thro' the Woods, over the Mountains."

Ebenezer Francis shouted to his troops not to shoot—they were hitting their own men. And that was his last command. It was followed by a volley from the enemy and Francis fell dead. As the colonel's friend Captain Greenleaf mourned, ". . . the Brave & ever to be Lamented Colo Francis, who fought bravely to the Last . . . rec'd the fatal wound thro' his Body Entering his right breast, he drop'd on his face. . . ."

It was the final, crushing blow. Without the leader who had inspired them, the rebels scattered and ran for their lives, scrambling up the cliffs behind Hubbardton Brook with the frantic speed of hunted men. Except for the occasional musket shot from the woods, the battle of Hubbardton was over.

Ebenezer Francis had been a notable figure in the action, and now that he was dead it was natural that a number of those who had faced him and admired his courage and coolness in battle should come to look at his body, as if to learn more about what manner of man he was. Lieutenant Digby was one of these, and as he gazed down at the tall, lifeless form, observed that "his figure . . . was fine" and even in death "made me regard him with attention."

Two hours after the firing ceased, a number of British officers gathered to read the papers taken from Francis's pocket. Captain John Shrimpton of the 62nd Regiment had the letters in his hand and was looking through them when he suddenly jumped in the air and then fell, crying out that he was badly wounded. The men standing next to him had heard the ball whiz to its target and, looking around, saw gunsmoke rising near a tree. Up into the woods the redcoats ran in search of the sniper, but no trace of him could they find. That isolated shot was the last act of retribution for a man who had fought against the odds and had never flinched from danger.

The Gibraltar of the North, the great bastion that watched over the Hudson-Champlain passage, was now firmly in the hands of General John Burgoyne. The routed American defenders were scattered to the winds, fleeing for their lives, and the British general was only a five- or six-day march from Albany and his rendezvous with Sir William Howe.

It was almost two months before the news reached Strawberry Hill, Horace Walpole's Gothic-style estate in the English countryside, prompting him to observe that Burgoyne's triumph had "given a new complexion to the aspect of affairs, which was very wan indeed." Even so, he understood from friends returning from America that "the alienation from this country is incredible and universal."

When His Majesty George III was informed of the victory he was so elated that he rushed into Queen Charlotte's chambers, ignoring the fact that she was clothed only in a chemise, and, waving the dispatch before her shocked courtiers, shouted, "I have beat them! I have beat all the Americans!"

Chapter 11

The Wolves Came Down
from the Mountains

When fate determined that Hubbardton was the place to have a battle, the first intimation its nine resident families had that their lives were going to be turned inside out was the sudden appearance on July 6 of a troop of loyalists and Indians. Swarming through the settlement, they made off with much loot and three captives—Uriah Hickok and two young men named Keeler and Kellogg—before moving on to Castle Town to see what damage they could do there. The man in charge of these raiders was Captain Alexander Fraser, the brigadier's nephew and fellow Scot, whose deputy, Captain Justus Sherwood, was an American loyalist fighting just as tenaciously for his beliefs as any American rebel. Sherwood was a real asset to Fraser, since he knew the territory, having farmed for a time in New Haven, about thirty miles north, before moving to Shaftsbury in the southwest corner of the Grants. In both places he had tried to make a home but ran into no end of trouble over his land claims and his politics.

Sherwood was a twenty-five-year-old, well-educated "man of culture," according to a British officer who knew him, and as a dedicated loyalist he elected to stand up for king and country. He was jailed by a local Committee of Safety for refusing to take an oath supporting the rebel cause and later was sentenced to life imprisonment in the mines of Simsbury, Connecticut. Somehow he succeeded in making a getaway and fled

to the mountains, where some forty other loyalists joined him and followed him to Canada to sign up with the Queen's Loyal Rangers under
John Peters. Like Peters, Sherwood had old scores to settle: both had it
in for the rebels in the worst way, and chances were they viewed them
with more unadulterated hatred than did any regular soldier in Burgoyne's command.

There is no telling exactly what Captain Fraser's instructions were
when his raiders came storming down the road from Crown Point on
that hot July morning, but since he had a number of Indians as well as
Tories with him it is probable that he had a license to raise as much hell
as possible along his route, giving the savages a free hand to loot and
burn while picking up all the horses and beef animals he could find.

Between Fraser's raid and the subsequent clash of the two little
armies here, the community that was only beginning to take root after
three years of incessant hardship and toil was decimated. Life was no different here from any other American frontier, after all—hard, infinitely
demanding, a battle by men, women, and children against everything
nature could throw at them, plus the constant threat of Indians, disease,
and death. Yet they had persevered and survived, and though they knew
the British were attacking Ticonderoga it probably did not occur to them
that they would be in the path of the marauders who swept through their
community and threatened to destroy in a few hours what they had
struggled for years to build. The soldiers who fought at Hubbardton were
by no means the only victims, in other words: civilians paid a heavy price,
as witness what happened to the Churchill household. Theirs was an
instance of how a family unlucky enough to be caught in the middle of
the venomous civil war between rebel and loyalist could be shattered.

Samuel Churchill, his wife, and their children lived far enough from
everyone else in Hubbardton that on the morning of the battle Seth
Warner was concerned for their safety, should Fraser's guerrillas return.
To get them to a secure area he dispatched about two hundred men—
enough, he guessed, to handle Fraser's force—but no sooner had his
troops reached the Churchill house than they heard firing down near
Sucker Brook. (They could not know it, but their absence on this errand
of mercy was responsible for Warner's delayed departure to join St.
Clair, the resulting surprise of his rear guard, and the battle that followed.) The detachment turned around at once and marched on the
double toward the sound of the guns, accompanied by two Churchill
boys, John and Silas, who wanted to join the fight. If the young men
thought their military experience would be brief and eventful, they were

right: Silas was taken prisoner but John escaped, returning home just in time to be captured by Captain Fraser's command, which came back after being roughed up and scattered by St. Clair's army in Castle Town, where some of them were taken prisoner. That experience had done nothing to improve Fraser's or Sherwood's disposition, and their irregulars now surrounded the Churchill house, seized the remaining young males, looted the place, and were about to burn it when one of the Churchill daughters is said to have screamed, "You have taken away our men and provisions—how can you be so cruel as to burn our house?" At which she fell into a faint, and Fraser relented, sparing their home. Even so, he was certain that Samuel Churchill had a supply of flour hidden somewhere, and he ordered the Indians to take him into the woods and make him talk.

The method chosen was to truss him up and prepare to burn him alive unless he revealed where the flour was concealed, but before that could happen Churchill's repeated denials were so convincing that Fraser had him untied. Then Churchill and his sons Silas and John, plus Uriah Hickok, Keeler, and Kellogg, were packed off under guard to Ticonderoga. Young William Churchill, who was lame, was left behind with his mother, three other women, and four small children, and with neither spare clothing nor food to take with them they somehow made their way across the Connecticut River to No. 4, on to Springfield, Massachusetts, and finally to Sheffield, Connecticut, which had been their home before they migrated to Hubbardton in 1775.

Several weeks later, when Samuel Churchill and Uriah Hickok escaped from Ticonderoga and returned to a deserted, desolate Hubbardton, they stopped long enough to look with horror inside Hickok's house, which held the putrefying carcasses of a number of American soldiers, with fragments of weapons and clothing; then they shut the door behind them and moved along in search of their families. Hickok was lucky: his wife and children had gone no farther than Castle Town. Churchill had to make the long journey to Sheffield before he found his people.

Following the instructions St. Clair left behind when he withdrew from Castle Town, what was left of Warner's rear guard retreated in the direction of Rutland on the night of the battle. Individually and in small, disorganized, mostly leaderless groups, those who fled across Hubbardton Brook before the bayonets of the oncoming Germans scrambled straight up and over Pittsford Mountain. Under any circumstances this was the most difficult route they could have picked, but for those frantic, desperate men no other choice existed, and the fact that so many of the beaten army made it at all was a considerable triumph.

As one disgusted rebel described their efforts to catch up with the main body after St. Clair left Rutland, heading south, they were harassed by Indians, who killed or captured several of them; they were "hurried at an unmerciful rate thro' the woods at the rate of thirty-five miles a day, oblidg'd to kill oxen belonging to the Inhabitants wherever we got them; before they were half-skinned every soldier was obliged to take a bit & half Roast it over the fire, then before half done was obliged to March. . . . never was soldiers in such a condition without cloaths, victuals or drink & constantly wet."

Hundreds of these bewildered rebels were now spread across the landscape, doing their best to follow in St. Clair's footsteps and rejoin their outfits. Captain Moses Greenleaf, sick at heart after the death of his friend Ebenezer Francis, retreated from Hubbardton Brook and struggled "over the Mountains such as I never saw before." At one o'clock in the morning he and six other men and a sergeant named Dormant, who was wounded in the hands and chest, reached Rutland and downed some grog, which Greenleaf called "the most refreshing drink ever Drank," and it says something about the toughness and stamina of these amateur soldiers that after the shock and fatigue they had undergone during the past twenty or more hours, they finished their grog, went outside, and strode off in the darkness to spend what was left of the night in the woods, with "no Blankets, nothing but the Heavens to Cover them." Understandably, Greenleaf thanked the Lord for fair weather.

Another survivor of the attack near Hubbardton Brook was Henry Sewall, who arrived in Rutland in the early evening with about ninety others from different regiments "promiscuously collected under the Command of Col. Warner." But unlike Greenleaf he and his friends had the devil's own time locating the main body. They camped in the rain near Otter Creek the night after the engagement and learned on the following day that they were only five miles behind St. Clair, who was then in Manchester and bound for Fort Edward, yet not until the 12th did they finally catch up with the army near Fort Miller. The general's troops, it appears, were marching "exceeding fast"—so fast that two men dropped dead from exhaustion along the way.

It must have seemed an eternity, yet only a week had passed since Jeduthan Baldwin watched great numbers of the enemy file ashore at

Three Mile Point while the British fleet formed in line across the lake and "made a formidable appearance." He accompanied St. Clair on the march from Mount Independence to Castle Town, and after they came into Rutland, the engineer attended to the gnawing feeling in his stomach by dining contentedly at Colonel Mead's house, where a number of men who had been in the action joined them during the evening. That night and for the next five days, Baldwin traveled through the woods for what he reckoned at 110 miles (another man thought it was closer to 150) and was dismayed to see men sickening, one after the other, from lying in the open with no fires or blankets.

Along the way he took stock of his personal belongings and was appalled to realize what he had lost. All his gear had been on the boats bound for Skenesborough, which meant that they were surely gone for good. With them was $6,491 of "Publick money" entrusted to him for paying his artificers, and what he had left was pretty much what he had on his person—a single shirt, stockings, and breeches. As he trudged along, silently bemoaning his own loss and the army's far more serious one of artillery, stores, provisions, and baggage, he was suddenly aware of how "Very dirty & uncomfortable" he was.

At that, he was a lot better off than the Americans taken prisoner during the battle, one of whom was Ebenezer Fletcher, the wounded fifer. While the British were scouring the thick woods and brush for their dead and wounded after the battle, Fletcher heard two men approaching and tried to play dead, lying flat on his stomach in a pool of blood, his head in his hands.

"Here is one of the rebels," one man said as he bent over and began to pull off Fletcher's shoes, thinking he was dead. That decided the fifer: better to be a prisoner than lose his shoes, and he looked up and told the redcoats he surrendered, begging them to use him well.

"Damn you!" replied the regular. "You deserve to be used well, don't you? What's a young rebel as you fighting for?"

The soldier's companion, an officer, said, "Give back the shoes and help the man into camp." When they got there, Fletcher found a number of Americans in the same fix, and he lay on the ground until afternoon, when two surgeons came and dressed his wound after pulling bits of clothing from it and telling him he was lucky to have survived. For several weeks he remained a prisoner, but when he had partially recovered he escaped and traveled alone and hungry across the mountains to the house of a friend, where he lodged for a few days. Then he returned home to Ipswich, New Hampshire, and as soon as he fully recovered rejoined his company and served out what remained of his time. After all, he figured, he had signed up for three years and three years it would be.

Captain Enos Stone came through the battle without a scratch, but was captured and held with Fletcher and others until the next night. It "Rained," he noted, "as hard as Ever it Rained, allmost. we lay in the water until 3 o'clock in the morning," when he and his fellow prisoners were ordered to get to their feet and march to Ticonderoga. That was the beginning of a long ordeal of poor and meager rations, sickness, death for some, and the detested "clost confinement under Duch Guard," as he called Lieutenant Colonel Christian Pratorius's Prinz Friedrich Regiment, which had been assigned to occupy the fort.

Toward the end of July several American officers were released, some of them paroled, which meant that they gave their word to return home and not serve again during the war; others were exchanged for captured British or German officers. With this flurry of activity, Stone's hopes rose, only to plummet when he and other prisoners were herded aboard vessels that sailed down the lake. Eventually they were taken to Quebec to be confined first on a British man-of-war, then a transport, and at last on October 1, "A very Squaley Day of Sno . . . and Very cold," he signed a parole and a month later sailed under a flag of truce for New York, arriving there about December 21. That was the end of the war for Enos Stone.

Colonel Nathan Hale, who remained near Sucker Brook during the battle with portions of his command and numerous stragglers he had picked up along the march, had seventy or more men in tow when a voice rang out from somewhere on the steep, wooded hill, telling them they were surrounded and ordering them to surrender. Hale's troops were still in an advanced state of shock from the fight that had raged about them on all sides, they were thoroughly disoriented, and had no idea what had become of the rest of the army, so prudence quickly won out. The colonel ordered them to lay down their arms.

When the enemy appeared from the woods he was stunned to see that the party which had "surrounded" him consisted of a single officer and only fifteen men. He had been taken in by a clever ruse that was, according to Lieutenant Hadden, "proof of what may be done against Beaten Battalions while their fears are strong upon them."

After the battle the British and Germans patched together huts of a sort, covered with the bark of trees, as shelter for the wounded until surgeons urgently summoned from Ticonderoga could arrive. (Often those who had been hurt had three or four wounds, all caused by the same shot, since it was common practice for the rebels to load their muskets with three small and three somewhat larger balls.) The doctors came before long to attend to the critically wounded, but for a day and a half those men were delayed at the battlefield because no stretchers had been prepared for the return journey. The road was a quagmire after all the rain, adding to the patients' suffering. Pitifully slow and painful, the march took more than thirty hours, including a night in the woods when an American died. As a German officer described the scene, "The 31 stretchers with the gravely wounded, each one of whom was carried by 4 soldiers on their shoulders, presented a far sadder sight as they passed by than the 5th act of the tragedy Romeo and Juliet." Unhappily for the convalescents who were left behind, not until July 27 was a twenty-man detachment of Germans dispatched to transport them to the hospital at Mount Independence.

The able-bodied spent the day after the battle dressing men's wounds, burying the dead, and rounding up cattle to feed the living, and it was a mark of their respect for Colonel Francis that the Brunswickers interred him with their own. But most Americans who had been killed—some forty or more—lay where they had fallen on the clay soil, and even as the burial details worked away with pick and shovel, one officer said, "the wolves came down in numbers from the mountains to devour the dead, and even some that were in a . . . manner buried, they tore out of the earth." Those the wolves did not get were pecked at by crows and slowly devoured by millions of flies and ants until nothing endured but a stench that "was enough to have caused a plague" and the bones bleaching in the sun and wind.*

Simon Fraser watched the gravediggers at their grisly task and reflected on the good men he had lost, particularly Major Grant ("no man was ever more attached to another than he was to me," he wrote to a friend). Adding to his sorrow were "the sufferings of twelve respectable Gentlemen"—by which he meant officers, of course—"who were languishing under their wounds in a very unpleasant situation." One of them was John Dyke Acland, who wrote his wife urging her to leave Montreal and join him while he recuperated. She set out on July 13, the same

---

*When the settlers who fled returned at last in 1780 they were too preoccupied with reconstructing their own lives to worry about battlefield debris. Three years later an influx of newcomers arrived, but it was not until 1784, a year after the Treaty of Paris—by which Great Britain recognized the independence of its former American colonies—was signed, that the residents turned out and finally laid to rest the crumbling remains.

day she received his letter, and despite a wild storm on the lake that almost drove her boat onto the rocks, the fair Lady Harriet, accompanied by her servant and the family dog, Jack, was at the major's side on Mount Independence by the 18th.

Corpses and maimed bodies were not the only reasons for Simon Fraser's troubled state of mind. He was dumbfounded and angry when the baron announced that he and the Brunswickers were leaving that very day to rejoin Burgoyne at Skenesborough, and sure enough, by noon Riedesel and his eleven hundred Germans departed and "made a march rather more rapid than when he moved to my support," the brigadier commented sourly.

Fraser had reason to complain. He was left with about six hundred effectives. Except for some cattle that had been shot in the woods and were devoured the moment they were cooked in the ashes of campfires, plus some gingerbread captured at Ticonderoga and sent as a joke to one of his officers, he had no provisions and saw no prospect of any until he reached Skenesborough. He now lacked support, he was running low on ammunition, and was "encumbered with 230 prisoners and 150 wounded, 200 stand of Rebel arms. . . ." Further cause for uneasiness was that he was adrift in an unfamiliar wilderness, in the heart of "the most disaffected part of America, every person a Spy," and in the evening he received intelligence that the rebels were nearby in force, gathering strength with each passing hour. He had no knowledge of St. Clair's strength or whereabouts, and he had just been given a severe lesson that the rebels were not the contemptible foe he had thought them.

Fraser put his prisoners to work constructing a fortification of logs in the event of attack, but then had second thoughts. He decided he should move quickly to catch up with Burgoyne. On July 9 the unhappy captives were rousted from sleep long before dawn to march to Ticonderoga, and the brigadier, knowing how few men he could spare as guards, told Colonel Hale that if they tried to escape no quarter would be shown them, and if they did manage to elude their escort, Indians would be sent in pursuit with orders to scalp them.

So some three hundred chastened, thoroughly spent rebels, including Hale and sixteen other officers, were delivered to proud Lieutenant Colonel Pratorius at Ticonderoga (where they joined seven Americans who never got the word about the retreat on July 6 and were captured before they could flee the post). After interrogating Hale, the Brunswick officer noted scornfully that the New Hampshireman, nattily turned out in green regimentals with black facings, had formerly been a mere sutler. The commander of the Prinz Friedrich Regiment had been nowhere near Hubbardton, but he thought he knew exactly what had gone wrong for the men who were now his prisoners. "The Provincials," he declared, "are not used to fighting as disciplined troops," and when they made contact with the king's forces, attacked "like rebels and arsonists hidden in the bushes who will only fight when they cannot find any other way out."

When Fraser pulled out of Hubbardton, he left behind his wounded and their attending surgeons, nurses, and a token guard to protect them against Indians, but with orders not to resist if a sizable rebel force approached. That done, his detachment headed down the road to Castle Town, where they found some fresh provisions and rum. They needed those refreshments. The march proved to be nearly thirty miles long through dense woods, uneven terrain, a downpour of rain, and marshland where water was nearly up to their knees, with the men expecting to be attacked by Indians every step of the way. Seven miles from Skenesborough the bridge across the Poultney River had been destroyed, so axemen dropped trees across the stream. After the crossing Fraser could breathe easier, and he finally brought his command into Skenesborough on the evening of July 9, weary beyond all imagining.

Tired as he was, the brigadier could count his blessings. It was his good luck that the American rear guard had done more than what was expected of it. During the retreat, Warner's men were supposed to close up, to keep in touch with the main body. Even if attacked, they were to fall back and rejoin St. Clair's army. Above all, they were not to fight a pitched battle and risk defeat. Had they followed this script, the story might have ended quite differently. The bulk of Riedesel's command, after all, was well to the rear and moving ponderously, and if Fraser and Riedesel had followed the Americans to Castle Town and found themselves confronted by the rear guard *and* St. Clair's rested soldiers, who together outnumbered them almost three to one, they would probably not have attacked, but if they had, would have been in serious—almost certainly fatal—trouble.

Anyone who thought Fraser should have chased the rebels after the battle sputtered out (and there were those who did) did not take into account the cruel terrain that was totally unfamiliar and forbidding ground for the redcoats, or the condition of those men, who were as worn out as their beaten foes. Indeed, Lord Balcarres and Lord Harrington felt that the brigadier had taken a considerable risk pursuing as far as he did, and both men praised the rebels for the gallantry and spirit that marked their resistance until that final deadly bayonet charge. Fraser knew better than anyone how close he had come to defeat and generously gave the Germans full credit for arriving in time to break the rebels.

The brigadier needn't have worried that St. Clair's men might attack after the battle: completely used up, they had neither strength nor will to do anything but head for safety. The first word the American general received about what had occurred at Hubbardton came from Brockholst Livingston and Isaac Dunn. When last seen these two aides were riding toward the sound of the guns with orders for Colonel Bellows to go to Warner's relief, but when they met Bellows's men haring off in a panic despite all the colonel's efforts to stop them, they galloped toward the battlefield to size up the situation there. They were too late: along the way they ran into Captain Chadwick and about thirty men hurrying down the road toward them. The action was over, Chadwick panted, Warner's command was completely dispersed, the enemy was in possession of the field, and communication with Hubbardton was cut off—a statement confirmed by the silence of the guns—so they headed back to Castle Town to report the bad news. Realizing he could do no more here, St. Clair ordered his men to fall in.

Before shoving off he paraded the two "eastern" regiments—the Massachusetts malcontents whose enlistments had expired just before the evacuation from Ticonderoga, and who had caused no end of grief on the retreat (General Poor threatened to fire on them if they refused to keep order)—and when he had their attention, St. Clair set them straight on a few matters. Regrettably, his appeal was not an unmitigated success: Livingston said St. Clair's emotional address made the regiments "ashamed of their conduct [and they] consented to remain with the army as long as there was any prospect of immediate danger from the enemy." But that resolve was short-lived: their continued looting and disorderly behavior "obliged the General a day or two afterwards to dismiss them from the army with disgrace."

Since the British were in Skenesborough, St. Clair aimed now for Rutland, leaving word behind that he would wait there for Warner and the stragglers to join him. But the general was thinking ahead and knew delay would be fatal. The next day found him twenty-five miles below Rutland, in Dorset, writing Schuyler to brief him on the affair at Hubbardton while reporting that he was "in great distress for provisions."

If he could be supplied in Manchester, he said, he would proceed directly from there to Fort Edward; but if provisions were not available, he would have to detour to Bennington, where he was more likely to find food and perhaps even reinforcements. He had already written the commander of militia in the Grants, ordering him to bring men by the shortest route to Bennington, and to direct any soldiers who came in from Fort No. 4 to the same destination, where they would be in easy reach of the Hudson and Schuyler's main army. Warner had not yet appeared, he added, but was reckoned to have no more than a hundred survivors of his badly mauled command with him; in the meantime, troops from all the other regiments but Hale's were joining St. Clair. Already sensitive to the criticism he knew was coming, he described himself as "very happy in effecting this retreat, as the loss of the army, small as it is, would have been a blow that this part of the country would have felt severely. . . ."

Exactly how large the army was that he had saved was a matter of almost pure conjecture. Thanks to the long, circuitous route he was forced to take, attrition inevitably took a toll through illness and desertion, but on the positive side, soldiers who escaped into the woods after the battle and were attempting to catch up were coming in every day, making it impossible to determine his losses or calculate his probable strength before he reached Schuyler.

He also wrote the president of the convention of Vermont, as the Grants had been renamed, confirming his orders to the militia and adding that his march would take him to the Hudson to "throw myself betwixt the enemy and the inhabitants and prevent Mr. Burgoyne from penetrating into the country." That looked to be a tall order, given the number and condition of troops presently available.

What worried St. Clair almost as much as the state of his army was the state of his reputation when news of Ticonderoga's fall became widely known. Already, he knew, the critics were sharpening their knives, and he was doing his level best to anticipate what they would say so that the public—and more especially, the commander in chief and members of Congress—would hear his version of events and his reasons for taking the actions he had. From Manchester on July 9 he wrote to Governor Bowdoin of Massachusetts. Bowdoin, after all, was the leader of a state that had contributed substantial numbers of men and resources to the general's army, and he was owed an explanation.

The garrison had consisted of 3,300 men, St. Clair said, of whom only

2,089 were fit for duty—many of them mere boys, not up to the rigorous demands of war. He mentioned the critical shortages of clothing and arms, the movements of the enemy, and the threat of immediate investiture that made it a certainty that his little army would soon be surrounded. Unless he retreated while escape was still possible and saved that army, he continued, there would have been no rallying point for the New England militia and no way of stopping Burgoyne. That was the most important consideration, and his decision was made to save the army, not to avoid the enemy. Then he described the night movement when the troops cleared out of the fort, the retreat to Castle Town, and the struggle with the British at Hubbardton, saying how happy he was to "make my retreat from under their nose." Now, he added, he was on his way to join General Schuyler at Fort Edward.

Either Governor Bowdoin was indiscreet or he wanted the letter made public, for it appeared in Worcester's *Massachusetts Spy* on July 24, with the author listed only as "an officer of distinction," as if that fooled anyone. Alongside it the paper published an unsigned editorial comment that shredded St. Clair's explanation piece by piece. The writer *knew* the garrison had more than four thousand effectives, he said, *knew* the enemy numbered at most six thousand, reminded readers that the very purpose of forts was to defend against superior force, yet "the place was given up before the enemy had . . . fir'd a single gun against it." Furthermore, if the post was not defensible, shouldn't the general officers who decided to abandon it have known this before and done something to remedy the deficiency? What had become of all those items furnished the army by the good people of Massachusetts—the provisions, the clothing, the baggage, the powder? And if the powder could not be saved, why wasn't it blown up to keep it out of enemy hands?

So it went, with a call for public inquiries and a popular uprising to stop Burgoyne's oncoming army. "Our people are well adapted to a partisan war," the correspondent boasted, and if they are well supplied and strongly led, "the enemy may soon sorely repent that they ever accepted the gift of Ticonderoga and came into our territories." Either St. Clair's account was inaccurate "or there is great unfaithfulness somewhere," he concluded darkly, thus implying that the general was at best a liar, and quite possibly a traitor.

St. Clair had had intimations that he would be pilloried for his action, and this was precisely the sort of uninformed comment he hoped to forestall. But the attacks in the press and in Congress would not be stilled; as he was to learn to his regret, his attempts to clear his name would be stalled for more than a year, during which time he was "hung up to be stung by the envenomed tongue of malice, and pointed at by the finger of folly," until the court-martial he steadfastly requested unanimously acquitted him of all charges against him.

A particularly vituperative critic was the Reverend Thomas Allen of Pittsfield, Massachusetts, who had arrived at Ticonderoga in mid-June and was a shocked and angry eyewitness to events at the post and the escape by boat to Skenesborough. Contrasting the army that was "blooming in health and courage . . . our men eager for the battle, our magazines filled, our camp crowded with provisions [and] flags flying" with the shameful abandonment of the place, the minister said the evacuation "has not been equaled [in] the history of the world"—which seemed something of an exaggeration—and had the most dire consequences: soldiers fleeing from the enemy with "their cloaths worn out and in tatters, their courage all gone, all confidence in their officers lost." (The parson had apparently not heard about the fight at Hubbardton.) Had the garrison defended the fort, he declared, even if half the men had been slain or captured, the spirit of resistance would have "burst forth like peals of thunder and flashes of lightning upon our enemies." Had that occurred, "O, how many tears, what infinite distress, how many precious lives had we saved" that would now be lost to the invaders.

If Allen's attack was a sample of the public outcry, somebody was going to pay for the shocking loss of America's most prestigious military post, and Congress had two particular scapegoats in mind—Arthur St. Clair and Philip Schuyler. The members of that body were groping their way through a red fog of confusion and uncertainty, brought about by the growing realization that this war might go on into the unfathomable future—assuming that the army survived, which was by no means certain. These civilians, a lot of them anyway, had it in for the likes of Schuyler, who represented a caste they couldn't quite understand or stomach. The general had come to epitomize what they thought was wrong about the war, and his opponents wanted to be rid of him once and for all. And now St. Clair, who suddenly appeared to be a loser and maybe even a coward, was being tarred with the same broad brush. The ugly mood of Congress after the fall of Ticonderoga was succinctly expressed by John Adams in a letter to his wife, Abigail: "We shall never be able to defend a post until we shoot a general."

While deliberating the rights and wrongs of the matter, John Jay wrote St. Clair with lawyerly caution, saying, "I hope the Expediency of the Measure may, contrary to the general Expectation, derive Proof from this Event; and that the Determination of the General officers on that road may on Inquiry be found undeserving the Censure it at present meets with."

Occasionally a voice of open support was heard: the *Pennsylvania Evening Post* printed a letter from a soldier in St. Clair's command, who argued that the general deserved the people's gratitude, "for had we stayed [at Ticonderoga] we very certainly should have been taken, and then no troops could have stood between the enemy and the country." Now, he went on, "we are gathering strength and re-collecting ourselves." That was Alexander Scammell's opinion, too. Ticonderoga was "a perfect Mouse Trap," he said, and "was evacuated for want of men [and] the untenableness of the post." St. Clair had been expecting reinforcements that never came and faced the threat of being "totally blockaded and every communication cut off, when Burgoyne would have had it in his Election to either kill, starve, or take us prisoners." If they hadn't run for it, Burgoyne would have soon been in Albany.

Re-collecting his army and gathering strength was exactly what St. Clair had in mind, but in the meantime more urgent business demanded his attention. On July 9 he was at Colonel Marsh's tavern in Manchester,* informing Jonas Fay, vice-president of the Vermont Council, that Schuyler wanted Warner's regiment (whatever remained of it) and the state militia to stay here "for the protection of the people." All wagons in the vicinity should be sent away or destroyed to keep them out of enemy hands, and all cattle in condition for slaughter taken by a secure route to Fort Edward. St. Clair still didn't know how much food he could scrounge near Manchester, although Moses Greenleaf—whose thoughts were seldom far from his stomach—managed to purchase some meal and milk for breakfast, fresh beef for dinner, and later some roast sheep, which he described as the "first meal of Substance" he had eaten since they left Ticonderoga. The Hudson River was St. Clair's destination, and five days after leaving Hubbardton, after marching in the steady rain, fording rivers, and slogging through swamps in water half a leg deep, with the army "almost without provisions, entirely without shelter," they arrived soaking wet, "beg'd a piece of bread & Laid down in our Duds." In a period of just over a week, the general's command had experienced its first taste of British power at

---

*This may not have been the ideal place for the commander and the staff of a retreating army to spend time discussing their plans, since Marsh was a Tory. In 1780, by which time his loyalties had probably been discovered, Marsh fled to Canada, leaving behind his wife and nine children.

Ticonderoga, evacuated the place by night, made a forced march to Hubbardton, fought a pitched battle, and come by a circuitous and enormously fatiguing route to the rendezvous where he expected to meet Philip Schuyler. No matter what Congress or anyone else might say, it was no mean accomplishment.

Chapter 12

Considerable Difficulties
May Be Expected

Colonel Pierce Long's armada had set off on July 6 from Mount Independence, bound for Skenesborough, and a spectacular night for a sail it was—balmy, with a light breeze out there on the water, the shadowy shapes of five armed galleys and their long convoy of bateaus reflected in the thin moon's shimmering light. The boats were loaded to the gunwales with women and invalids, cannon, tents, and provisions, plus their six-hundred-man escort made up of Long's New Hampshiremen and odd lots from other regiments that had been part of the Ticonderoga garrison. The new day dawned crystal clear, and Surgeon James Thacher's memory of the voyage made it sound like a pleasure cruise through the "enchantingly sublime" countryside. Navigating what was called the Drowned Lands, the procession of boats followed a channel that twisted and turned like a dark snake past seas of marsh grass on either side, framed by huge rocks and "thick impenetrable wilderness." With the coming of daylight the rhythmic splash of oars was accompanied by fife-and-drum music floating across the water and enlivened by wine liberated from the hospital stores. Men broke off the necks of the bottles, Thacher recalled, and "cheered our hearts with the nectareous contents."

By no means everyone was as content as the surgeon made out. The Reverend Thomas Allen, for one, was furious about what had happened.

"Once a few hours ago we were a terror to our enemies," he fumed. "Now we are the derision and scorn of the world!" Yet he could consider himself lucky: compared to what St. Clair's harried troops had had to face, this was an easy trip, so much so that none of the officers seem to have foreseen any trouble—convinced that Jeduthan Baldwin's boom and bridge would prevent the British from following, they made their way over the thirty miles to Skenesborough in as leisurely a manner as picnickers on an outing. For the last five or six miles of the trip the water became increasingly narrow and shallow, more like a river than a lake; then, at the southern extremity, where the channel broadens out into South Bay, they entered the outlet of Wood Creek, bearing almost ninety degrees to the southeast. Upstream from here lay Skenesborough, and to reach the settlement a vessel had to pass between two steep hills rising abruptly on either side of the confined waterway.

Unfortunately, Colonel Long made three egregious mistakes. Gates's deputy adjutant general, James Wilkinson, described Long as "a genteel, amiable man," and the temperament suggested by those words was his undoing this day. For one thing, he failed to drive his men to make better time on the voyage. For another, he neglected to move troops and guns up onto those high bluffs that commanded the narrows below, by which means he could at least have delayed, it not halted, the British. And he seriously underestimated his foe. It did not seem to occur to Long that he was up against a professional army that was resourceful, determined, and led by an officer who knew that victory belongs to the quick and the bold, to the leader who seizes the moment and makes it his own.

Burgoyne had spent the night of July 5 aboard the *Royal George,* and shortly after daybreak he read Fraser's report that the rebels had evacuated the post and a message that the brigadier was setting out in pursuit of those who had gone by land. The general immediately ordered Commodore Lutwidge to follow the Americans who had taken to the boats. This was no easy assignment for the naval officer, for as Burgoyne explained in a letter to Germain, he first had to break through the formidable network of barriers constituted by the bridge—those timber piers between which wooden floats were fastened by chains, and the timber boom secured by a chain of iron an inch and a half inches square. But Lutwidge and his seamen were more than equal to the challenge. He dispatched his gunboats, and with a few well-aimed shots they shattered the boom and floats. Within half an hour the frigates *Royal George* and *Inflexible* were sailing through the gap on a northerly wind, bound for Skenesborough.

That little settlement consisted of a cluster of buildings, including a palisaded fort that had been occupied for more than two weeks by Captain James Gray's company, from Scammell's regiment. They knew nothing about the fate of Ticonderoga; they were biding their time here, waiting for orders or something to happen, and the first indication they had that trouble was brewing was the sight of Long's bateaus heading up the Wood Creek outlet.

The fugitives' boats had been under way for twelve hours after leaving the Mount Independence landing, and the passengers disembarked on the east bank below the Skenesborough waterfall, where a portage of some three hundred feet wound uphill toward new Fort Anne and a blockhouse. (The old fort, built in Queen Anne's day, was destroyed before the Revolution.) Some of the troops moved into that modest structure, joining Gray's men, while the rest—"unsuspicious of danger," according to Thacher—unloaded the boats and began hauling them up the carrying place to Wood Creek.

Noonday dinner was served to Burgoyne and his staff aboard the *Royal George*, and it is not difficult to imagine them there in an informal wardroom atmosphere, snickering about rebel pretensions, predicting how quickly they would have this rabble in their clutches, joking and laughing with all the arrogant assurance of victors enjoying an easy triumph. The general was just finishing his first glass of wine after the meal when he was interrupted by the thunderous crash of cannons. That meant they had caught up with the rebels, and Burgoyne's secretary, Sir Francis Carr Clerke, immediately raised his glass "to the success of the evening" and the officers ran on deck to see the fun. Even a landlubber like Lieutenant Hadden could see that the passage to Skenesborough was so narrow in places "that the Ship's Yards almost touched the Precipices which over hung them; the Enemy might have done great execution by leaving a Detachment on the shore to harass [the British] and this Party cou'd have retired and concealed themselves from any force landed against them." Indeed they could have, but no one thought to do it.

Long had seen at once that the vulnerable blockhouse was no place for his soldiers when the redcoats reached Skenesborough, and he wisely sent invalids, women, and noncombatants like Parsons Allen and Hitchcock up Wood Creek with enough able-bodied men to row the bateaus. Before they pulled away, Hitchcock lugged his baggage to one of the boats while cannonballs whistled around him in "a brisk and mutual Canonade," and it was soon apparent that the gunners aboard the American galleys were no match for British firepower or skill; in short order three of the rebel craft—the *Enterprise, Liberty,* and *Gates*—were blown up or burned, while the *Trumbull* galley and the schooner *Revenge* struck their colors. The mountain of provisions that had been loaded on the boats at Mount Independence—hundreds of barrels of flour, pork and beef, salt, rum, and biscuits that would prove so useful to the British—were abandoned on the dock, while virtually all the baggage was burned, sunk, or seized.

Captain Gray and other rebel officers did their best to form the troops in line of battle, but with no success whatever; the frightened militiamen took off in all directions, some in boats on Wood Creek, which was shallow and clogged with logs, others through the forest along a wretched track that led to Fort Anne. Seeing the futility of remaining here, the officers retrieved as much of their baggage as possible and hurried after the men they were supposed to lead. James Thacher located his own medical chest, removed what few articles he could carry, and ran off with the others. They were pursued so closely, he said, that he kept hearing frequent shouts from the rear to "March on! The Indians are at our heels!"

Somewhere along the way, Gray took command of about 220 men, including those of his own company, and they spent the night in the woods. Like so many others, the captain lost everything but the clothes on his back—all his money and baggage—and to top it off, when they reached Fort Anne the next morning he found "everything in the utmost confusion [and] nothing to eat." Fortunately, 400 fresh New York militiamen under Colonel Henry Van Rensselaer came in from Fort George to join them.

Those rumors that the Indians and British were closing in on the retreating rebels during the night proved to be fantasy fed by fear, for it was evident almost from the beginning of the retreat that the British would be unable to close the gap. Burgoyne had landed the 9th, 20th, and 21st Regiments on the east bank of the lake about three miles from Skenesborough, hoping to cut off a rebel retreat, but the march was unexpectedly difficult and the Americans got away. On the morning of July 7 the 9th under Lieutenant Colonel John Hill set off by road with orders to march to Fort Anne, take post, and observe the enemy movements. Meanwhile, the other two regiments began dragging fifty bateaus over the carrying place to get men and guns to the fort by water. But almost nothing went according to plan.

Flames from the burning galleys had set fire to the American bateaus remaining at the dock. The rebels torched the blockhouse before they withdrew, and the blaze soon spread to a nearby sawmill, storehouses, barracks, and ironworks, and before long the spruce and pine covering the hillside became a roaring inferno. While they were still twenty miles north of Skenesborough, moving through the Drowned Lands, men of the 47th Regiment could see the smoke "like a Cloud in the sky," George Fox said, and he was stunned by the extent of the wreckage. Before the Americans "took to the woods," he remembered, "Their provision they had sunk and our men went down and see'd there was a deal sunk, then we got our grappling irons to hook up the barrels of pork and flour, but we had such quantities of pork that we were sick at the sight of it."

One British officer said he had never seen such a conflagration, and the thought crossed his mind that it threatened "universal destruction." While that unlikely calamity never came to pass, the 20th and 21st Regiments were delayed for hours. The harbor was awash with flotsam and jetsam—remains of provisions, a mortar here, a six-pounder there, barrels of ammunition, the masts and spars of a sunken schooner jutting out of the water, the incinerated residue of some two hundred bateaus, plus so many useful articles scattered about—tents, shirts, clothing of all descriptions—that the sailors and Indians put on a regular country fair the next day. Gleeful redcoats in the 9th Regiment displayed a trunk full of paper money and two regimental flags they had found—one a blue taffeta affair with a wreath of red and white stripes and the words "In Honor of Our Freedom" beneath "United States of America." The other was yellow with thirteen intertwining circles, each with the name of a state; in the center was a gold sun with the words "We Are One," surrounded by "American Congress."

Hill, slowed by abominable road conditions, shattered bridges, and a delay occasioned by seizing several rebel boats packed with invalids and baggage, made less than ten miles that day and was waiting in the woods on level ground between Wood Creek and a bony ridge when a party of rebels emerged from Fort Anne. Gray, out on a scouting mission at the head of a hundred and fifty men and seventeen rangers, headed into the trees and about half a mile from the fort ran headlong into Hill's pickets, who fell back as both sides opened up in a skirmish that lasted almost four hours and cost Gray one man killed and three wounded.

That evening Sir Francis Clerke dashed off on horseback from Skenesborough to find out what the situation was up ahead, and when he returned to report to Burgoyne after spending most of the night in the saddle he could vouch for the travel conditions that delayed all the British pursuers. Writing later to his friend Lord Polwarth, he said he had been directed "to pass what they call *the Great Road*, but I can assure your Lordship a Day's fox hunting about Gravenhurst Covers is a joke to it. No Whipper-in ever went *through* more difficult *Ground*, or [was] more draggled than I was on my return."

Shortly after dawn on July 8, Hill learned from an American deserter that Long now had about a thousand men, so he dispatched a messenger to headquarters requesting reinforcements, warning that he was too close to the rebels to withdraw safely and would hold his ground until support arrived. The American, who was no deserter but a spy, slipped away and ran back to Fort Anne with the welcome news that the British force numbered fewer than two hundred men.

In response to Hill's call for help the 20th and 21st Regiments were ordered to "quicken their march," but an all-day torrential thunderstorm slowed their movement to a crawl. So Hill was on his own when the rebels came at him again about ten-thirty in the morning. As at Hubbardton, anything resembling a battle formation was out of the question, and visibility was virtually nil because of the thick woods and craggy ground. The rebels, slanting through the trees, crossed Wood Creek, turned Hill's left, and worked their way behind him; he couldn't see them but could tell from their voices that he would soon be surrounded, so he ordered his men to withdraw up the precipitous slope to their rear—a critical move, as Burgoyne later described it (taking care that it should not sound like a retreat), that was executed "with the utmost steadiness and bravery." Steady and brave the British certainly were, but the rebels were even more so as they maintained a dogged advance in the face of enemy volleys.

Long had the support of Colonel Van Rensselaer and a party of militiamen, and they let loose with what a British officer described as "a heavy and well-directed fire." As they climbed the hill the Americans came across a British surgeon who was dressing an officer's leg, and those men, with two other wounded Englishmen Hill had abandoned in his retreat, were sent to the rear.

Up on the ridge the hard-pressed redcoats held out for two hours until their ammunition was exhausted, and were on the verge of having to surrender when an Indian war whoop was heard, signaling the approach of reinforcements. The British answered with three cheers. The frustrated rebels were forced to pull back, since their ammunition was also gone, and they retired to Fort Anne with their wounded, including Colonel Van Rensselaer, who had taken a shot in the hip that crippled him for the rest of his days. Accompanying them were the prisoners Hill had taken on Wood Creek, whom Long's men had liberated during the action.

The rebels could not know that the war whoops that brought on the battle's denouement had been delivered not by Indians but by a lone British officer, Captain John Money of the 9th Regiment, who was Burgoyne's deputy quartermaster and an old hand at soldiering. Money had been leading a party of Indians to relieve Hill, but the savages were too smart to get in the middle of the white men's free-for-all in the forest, so Money left them behind, ran toward Hill's position, and did his best to imitate the bloodcurdling savage yell. Luckily for the British, it worked.

At Fort Anne the American officers gathered to determine their next move. From a woman who was one of the freed prisoners they learned that a British relief party under the command of General Phillips, numbering two thousand regulars plus Indians, was coming up fast. Since the Americans were short of ammunition, they set fire to the fort and marched off toward Fort Edward, about sixteen miles away over what was no more than a patchwork road, crisscrossed with trails, creeks, and wide, deep swamps.

When it was over at last, each side claimed victory—the British since Hill and his men had neither been driven off the ridge nor forced to surrender, besides which, they added, the rebels retreated; the Americans because they had the enemy about to lay down their arms and were forced to fall back only because they ran out of powder.

But for James Gray the ordeal was far from ended. The next morning he awoke feeling miserable, still in his wet clothes with nothing to eat or drink, and he was walking about, trying to get warm, when he ran into a samaritan named Captain Peters ("a Dutchman & a Gentleman," Gray noted). Peters took pity on him, gave him a dram of rum and a hot breakfast, and then found a blanket for him and shelter for his company. Gray sent his wounded to Albany and requested kettles for his other men to cook with; when none were found the troops mixed flour in their hats and baked it on stones in front of fires, cooking salt beef on the coals.

Gray felt sicker now, and after trying unsuccessfully to locate a doctor, he sent a request to Schuyler to let him travel to Albany. Again, no luck. Not until five days after the battle, when Generals St. Clair, Poor, Paterson, and Fermoy came into camp from their roundabout march through southern Vermont, was he granted leave to depart for Saratoga.

On July 13 he mounted a horse and rode to Fort Miller, where he ran into his CO, Colonel Scammell; then he went on to Saratoga, only to find that all the inhabitants were moving out because Tory raiding parties were active in the vicinity. It was midnight before he found lodging and another full day before he reached Albany "in a weak state of health" and ate a decent meal. "This Fatigue has almost killed me," he wrote a friend. "If I can with Honour, I shall resign my Commission to some person who can undergo the Hardship of a Campaign better."

Back at the scene of battle, only a few survivors remained, among them a noncom from Hill's 9th Regiment, Sergeant Roger Lamb. If the affair had indeed been a British victory, he was in as good a position as anyone to know how dearly bought it was. He had been on the hill with Surgeon Shelly, helping to dress Captain William Montgomery's mangled knee,* when the rebels "came pouring down upon us like a mighty torrent. . . ." Lamb took to his heels, and as he glanced back over his shoulder saw that he was the last man to make it up the hill. At that he barely managed to escape: Montgomery and the surgeon were being led off by the rebels, and on one side of Lamb, Lieutenant Westropp fell, shot through the heart; on the other, a man dropped to the ground with a bullet through the forehead that removed the top of his skull.

Somewhere out there in the dense woods, with the flash and rattle of musket fire all around and above him, the sergeant collected the wounded and tried to make them comfortable, but it was truly "a distressing sight to see the men bleeding on the ground"—especially, Lamb said, with "the rain . . . pouring down like a deluge upon us." He had only the most rudimentary knowledge of how to treat these men he had taken under his wing; the medical chest had been captured with the surgeon, and Lamb had nothing with which to tie up wounds but strips torn from his shirt. Fortunately, he had help—a woman who had come along on the mission, whose husband was one of the sufferers—and the pair made bandages enough to staunch the bleeding and then supported and half-carried the halt and the lame to a small hut about two miles to the rear. Lamb's regiment had marched back to Skenesborough, and he and the woman remained in the crude shelter for seven days with the wounded, "expecting every moment to be taken prisoner."

---

*No one thought the twenty-three-year-old Montgomery's wound was mortal. Lord Balcarres wrote his sister Margaret that she could assure Montgomery's sister that "the wound is very slight, & we have learned he is exceedingly well treated." But despite that care he died soon afterward.

Not an American came near them, but throughout that long, suspenseful week they could hear the incessant thunk of axes and the crash of falling trees. It sounded as if the rebels were up to no good.

⬥

I have the honour to inform your Lordship that the enemy [were] dislodged from Ticonderoga and Mount Independant, on the 6th instant, and were driven, on the same day, beyond Skenesborough on the right, and to Humerton [Hubbardton] on the left, with the loss of 128 pieces of cannon, all their armed vessels and bateaux, the greatest part of their baggage and ammunition, provision, and military stores. . . .

So began General John Burgoyne's triumphant report to Lord George Germain, in which he detailed eleven days of campaigning and success that exceeded even his own buoyant expectations. He followed this up on the same day with another, briefer communiqué—separate, no doubt, because it was not for publication as the longer letter was obviously intended to be. In the latter he informed Germain that the loyalist battalions of Peters and Jessup were at last beginning to shape up, holding promise for future actions, though he intended to use them less for combat than as detached forces "for keeping the country in awe and procuring cattle." He felt sure that the presence of these Tories "acting vigorously in the cause of the King" would impress a good many doubters and be highly beneficial.

After roundly criticizing rebel committees that were imprisoning and hanging loyalists, compelling other people to arm, driving off cattle, and turning the countryside into a desert "by fire and massacre," he directed his attention to the Indians with his army. They were little more than unreasonable, spoiled children who, if left to their own devices, were capable of "enormities too horrid to think of," in which the guilty and innocent alike, along with women and children, would be their prey. The Indians he described so contemptuously were the "lower Canadians," but he was informed that "the Outawas and other remote nations"—Indians from the north and west under the direction of St. Luc and Langlade—were within two days' march of him and were "more brave and more tractable" and, more important, "profess war, not pillage."

Another reason this letter was not meant for the public eye was what the author described as a "lament" that his orders did not permit him "to make a real effort instead of a feint upon New England." He hadn't the slightest doubt that if only he had the latitude to march to his left instead of his right, he could subdue before the onset of winter those "provinces where the rebellion originated." Lacking that authority, however, he planned to propose something along these lines to Sir William Howe when they met in Albany.

The men of his army received his thanks in orders of the day, in which he also summarized the glorious events of the previous seventy-two hours, noting that Brigadier General Fraser—with only half his brigade and no artillery—had routed two thousand strongly entrenched rebels, inflicting casualties of two hundred killed and numerous wounded, plus three hundred prisoners.* Nor was Fraser the only officer singled out for praise: General von Riedesel, whose "judicious orders and the bravery with which they were executed, shared in the honor of the victory"—a victory to be celebrated on the coming Sunday at divine services, with the firing of cannon and small arms in a *feu de joie* at sunset at Ticonderoga, Crown Point, Skenesborough, Castle Town, and Lieutenant Colonel Breymann's camp.

Gentleman Johnny could be forgiven for crowing. After all, it had been so easy—the quick, bloodless surrender of Ticonderoga, the lightning strikes at Hubbardton, Skenesborough, and Fort Anne, the destruction of the American fleet on the lakes—as a result of which the countryside around him was now in a panic, with hundreds of loyalists joining him and more certain to do so. It was indeed a stunning achievement: he had recaptured for the crown the northern lakes that were the crucial link between Canada and upper New York, and now, thanks to his success, the British controlled the important posts between the St. Lawrence River and Fort Anne, plus the road from Mount Independence to Castle Town and Skenesborough.

Burgoyne knew as well as any man how this news would be received in London, where he would be the toast of the town, and he was right. Germain, taking credit for appointing him to command the expedition, informed the general that the wisdom of that decision "was immediately seen and universally applauded," especially after Burgoyne's account was published in the *Gazette*. Certainly he was in line for the Order of the Bath, an honor Burgoyne had in fact anticipated some months earlier,

---

*The British consistently overstated rebel strength and losses. The size of the Ticonderoga garrison was a case in point, as were accounts of Hubbardton, where as many as three thousand Americans were said to have been engaged, and Fort Anne, where Hill was said to have fought off six times his own numbers.

even before he reached Canada, when he asked his wife Charlotte's nephew, now the Earl of Derby, to inform the administration that he would not accept it if offered. The general was hardly a modest man, and considering his ego and his intense desire for fame and advancement, this refusal of a coveted honor was curious, to say the least. Although Burgoyne himself never revealed his motive, it seems likely that he thought his accomplishment of considerably more importance, and therefore worth more, than those of Carleton and Clinton and perhaps even Howe, all of whom received the Red Ribbon for victories against the provincials. He must have known that his decision would annoy both George III and Germain, so it is reasonable to assume that he intended his certain ultimate victory in this campaign to prove that he was entitled to something more—most likely a baronetcy.

Yet for all the army's celebration of triumphs won, there was more to the situation than met the eye and the reality of the matter was rather different from the appearance. True enough, the rebels had surrendered Ticonderoga without a fight, leaving behind countless guns, ammunition, and stores, but St. Clair had, after all, managed to extricate virtually his entire command from an untenable position by means of an extremely difficult night withdrawal. Hubbardton was a near-run thing, as Fraser was quick to admit, and a comparison of British and American casualties in that battle hardly warranted any boasting. There the British and Germans had lost sixty dead, the rebels forty-one; the attackers had 168 wounded, the defenders ninety-six. The chief difference in losses, of course, was that more than two hundred Americans were taken prisoner, yet as Lieutenant Hadden reflected, Fraser's troops discovered "that neither they were invincible, nor the Rebels all Poltroons. On the contrary, many of them acknowledged the Enemy behaved well and look'd upon General Riedesel's arrival as a matter absolutely necessary. . . ." And so it was at Fort Anne, of which Hadden noted that "the Enemy tho' not victorious were the real gainers by this affair." What was perhaps most significant about Burgoyne's attitude toward these battles was that he had witnessed neither one and did not now from firsthand observation how close his troops had come to defeat.

The Britons' predilection for overestimating American strength undoubtedly had something to do with their certainty that they had won substantial victories—that, and the obvious fact that the rebels were on the run. Yet it was worth noting that a beaten, demoralized army of amateur soldiers had stood up to the best troops in the world and given them a very close fight on two occasions. Anyone who stopped to consider the situation could see that a more cogent cause for alarm was that Burgoyne could not replace his losses, so that any diminution in his numbers was permanent unless Carleton could be persuaded to release some of his men. American reinforcements, on the other hand—provided the militia could be induced to turn out—could be raised relatively quickly and in substantial numbers.

On July 8, Burgoyne established his headquarters at Philip Skene's stone house in Skenesborough, and that act in itself said something about the way this campaign was going to be run. It was curious that the English general, who knew the rewards of hot pursuit, did not follow his own advice and send his men after the rebels following the affair at Fort Anne. After all, he had reminded his troops after the voyage from Ticonderoga to Skenesborough, "Every man must now perceive how essential it may be to the King's Service to continue vigorously the pursuit of a flying Enemy," adding that he depended on them "not to relax, whatever may be the fatigue, while there is a prospect of overtaking the Fugitives."

Yet here was the commanding officer, relaxing in his new headquarters, fretting about the troops' fatigue, and setting aside a full day of rejoicing while the army settled into a large new camp. Although Fraser's and Riedesel's men, who had had no food for four days, were understandably exhausted from their recent marches and the fight at Hubbardton, and while Hill's 9th Regiment was done in after the ordeal at Fort Anne, the 20th and 21st Regiments under Phillips had almost reached Fort Anne and could surely have run down the small body of Americans under Long. All things considered, Burgoyne's complacent attitude suggested nothing so much as overconfidence, an assurance that he was master of the situation and could move when and where he wanted, at his own pace.

From Skenesborough, where he had arrived about noon on the 9th, General Riedesel wrote to Duke Ferdinand and after confessing to be so tired he could scarcely move, proudly informed his liege that "a handful of German troops" had turned the tide of battle at Hubbardton. As indeed they had. Just now, the baron had heard that the rebels were trying to recruit another five thousand men, but even if they succeeded, Riedesel said, it would come to nothing, since all their artillery was in Burgoyne's hands. The German officer was as confident of victory as his commander, but he was given precious little time to recover from his recent exertions. On July 10 the Brunswick troops were ordered back to

Castle Town, where they were expected to patrol the neighboring countryside and encourage loyalists to take up arms (surely a strange mission for so many men who spoke no English), and on the 12th they marched on what looked to be a fool's errand. It was impossible to find horses to carry their gear, so the soldiers packed all their baggage on their backs and stumbled along over the "shockingly bad road." To make matters worse, the men in the Specht and Rhetz Regiments were suffering the agonies of dysentery and had to spend several rainy nights in the woods without tents.

Accompanying the Germans was Philip Skene, whose house was now Burgoyne's headquarters and whose community at the outlet of Wood Creek had been grievously damaged during the action there. Skene was an interesting character—a good example of how a shrewd, ambitious man, with foresight, zeal, and well-placed friends, could prosper handsomely by investing in land in the New World. A husky fifty-two-year-old with dark eyes and brows and an open, somewhat jowly face, he was born in London to Scottish parents, and at the age of eleven began a military career which lasted until he sold out of the army three decades later, having fought at Fontenoy and Culloden and in America during the Seven Years War. That war brought him into the north country, where he served under General Abercromby at the disastrous attack on Fort Ticonderoga and was wounded in the skirmish that cost Lord Howe his life. Later he was a brigade major under Amherst, and in 1759 he began planning a settlement at the head of Lake Champlain.

Skene had an eye for the main chance and was attracted to the place that bore his name by its strategic location near a lake that was already a busy avenue for trade and travel and by the value of its rich soil and forest. He persuaded General Amherst to present his application for land patents to the king and soon began acquiring what eventually amounted to 56,000 acres. On it a blockhouse and barracks already existed, and he added a sawmill, an iron forge, a coal house, a stone barn and stables, and the two-and-a-half-story limestone structure that became known as Skenesborough House. In addition to these main buildings he constructed dwellings for his overseer, workmen, slaves, and tenants, and more mills, wharves, numerous bridges, and productive farms that enabled his family and tenants to be largely self-sufficient. But for all his works, Skene was cordially disliked by many of his neighbors, and it was said if people were asked who they hated most, the answer would be the Devil, but if asked who, next to Satan, they most disliked, the reply would be either "the Pope" or "old Skene."

Then came 1775. Skene was in London and got word to Lord North that all it would take to squelch the rebellious colonists was the threat of force, backed by English veterans of the French and Indian Wars. North must have been suitably impressed: when Skene departed from England it was with the title of lieutenant governor of Ticonderoga and Crown Point, conveyed by George III. The man made no secret of where his sympathies and loyalty lay, or of his belief that he could raise enough troops to put down any uprising, and when he returned to Philadelphia from London he was naturally regarded by Congress as a dangerous man to have around, was placed under guard, and was sent off to prison in Connecticut, where he languished until he was exchanged late in 1776. Once again Skene sailed to England, where he learned that Burgoyne was on his way to America to lead an army that would reclaim the lakes and his Skenesborough property, which was now in rebel hands. Skene believed he could be useful and left for America, where he caught up with the army at Crown Point.

When at last he came home to Skenesborough he found that his schooner had been stolen* and his house ransacked by rebels, who also broke into the cellar where his wife was buried. Finding her coffin covered with lead, they stripped it off to be made into musket balls, and after stealing the jewelry from the body, interred her in the garden.

Skene's role in the expedition to Castle Town was to serve as commissary (since the Germans were expected to bring in cattle and other provisions) and to administer the oath of allegiance and grant certificates of protection to those who agreed to support the king, but he also had another assignment, outlined in a document he carried in his pocket. On the back of it was a brief message from General Burgoyne empowering Colonel Skene† "to assure Personal Protection and Payment for every species of Provisions &c to those who comply with the terms of his Manifesto." The paper, dated July 10, was signed in the name of Lieutenant General John Burgoyne, "commanding an Army and Fleet of Great Britain against the Revolted Provinces of America," who ordered inhabitants of Castle Town, Hubbardton, Rutland, Tinmouth, Pawlet, Wells, Granville, and neighboring districts to send a deputation of ten people

---

*Most of the ships commanded by Benedict Arnold in the battle off Valcour Island in 1776 were made of Skene's lumber, sawn in his mills.

†The rank of colonel dated from Skene's service with an American militia regiment, but it is interesting to note that in Burgoyne's Orderly Book he is referred to as *Major* Skene—his former rank in the British army. The "colonel" must have been to impress the local folk.

from each town to meet with Skene on July 13 at ten in the morning at Castle Town. At the appointed hour the colonel would have instructions for those who complied with the terms of Burgoyne's manifesto and would also communicate the conditions on which "the Persons and properties of the Disobedient may yet be spared."

When Skene wanted to curry favor with someone whose influence could be useful, he was not above putting a better face on the matter at hand than warranted. Writing to the Earl of Dartmouth at this time, he said, "The Inhabitants are free from Plunderers, every Degree of Humanity flows from the General's Breast and the Country people sound his praise with Gladness."

What this carrot-and-stick approach amounted to was a reiteration of the terms of Burgoyne's proclamation of June 20 in which he promised clemency to Americans who remained peaceably at home, made available cattle and fodder and food for his troops, and did nothing to impede the army's progress. But to those who remained recalcitrant he threatened to "give stretch to the Indian Forces under my direction," who would inflict "devastation, famine, and every concomitant horror."

That the Castle Town operation was not an unqualified success was suggested by a report in the *Virginia Gazette* that Skene was making "proclamations, threats, and flattering speeches to endeavour to persuade the weaker from their allegiance to the States," but "few of them have yet joined, and there is reason to expect few will, as Col. Warner is near him with a body of troops, to oppose him in his designs."

It was clear to everyone in the neighborhood that Warner had some muscle to apply where needed, and that he would be around long after Skene and his Germans departed, but the cool reception from many inhabitants of the area also had to do with who they were— strong-minded, independent folk in extremely modest circumstances, pioneering families who held no particular brief for Great Britain or its king, having received no special favors from either. A number of them had been given a hard time by the Yorkers over land claims, and since many of those rival claimants were loyalists, that was another reason to mistrust Skene, who was one of them. So despite Skene's proselytizing and Burgoyne's threats, few residents of Vermont took the oath of allegiance, while those who professed neutrality probably did so because they were wary of the Brunswick soldiers and fearful that taking a stand one way or the other might cost them their homes and possessions. Besides, it was a brave family in these parts that wanted a placard tacked to their house and barns stating that they were under Lieutenant General Burgoyne's protection.

Shortly after Riedesel reached Castle Town he got word that Seth Warner was between there and Manchester with four or five thousand men (an indication of how wild the rumors were), and he would have chased after them had it not been for Skene's pleas for help with the loyalists arriving to take the oath. As Skene might have known, a good many of those professed supporters of King George had come to town to see who the *real* loyalists were, and they reported the names to Warner, who immediately plundered the Tories' homes, stole their cattle, and made prisoners of some of them. Understandably, this upset the baron, who had promised to protect these folk, and he sent a message to headquarters requesting permission to attack Warner at once, but Burgoyne stalled, saying he wanted his entire army to move forward as soon as possible, so Riedesel had to content himself with sending detachments to Tinmouth and Wells, where they learned that Warner, who had only a fraction of the numbers he was rumored to have, had fallen back on Manchester and that all the suspected rebel sympathizers in that neighborhood had departed with him, taking their livestock out of harm's way. One of the general's patrols brought in a few cattle and carts, another showed up the next day with a better haul—four prisoners, sixty head of cattle, and information that Warner had gone on to Arlington. Even so, it was not much to show for a week's work; the only really good news for the Germans was that some 250 recruits had arrived in Canada and would be parceled out among the Brunswick regiments.

Yet from this operation Riedesel learned something extremely useful. The people in the former Grants might not be willing to take the oath of allegiance, but neither, he believed, would they take up arms against Burgoyne. He found them "frightened and submissive," unlikely to put up much resistance. More important, his scouts informed him that the road through Manchester and Arlington to Bennington was the route used to drive cattle from all over Vermont to Washington's army. And more interesting yet, at Bennington was "a large deposit of horses and of wheel carriages," guarded only by militia. The baron stored this intelligence away: he had an idea how those treasures could be taken, and he planned to mention it to Burgoyne when he returned to Skenesborough.

One of Riedesel's Brunswickers conducted a private opinion poll that was at odds with the baron's conclusions. This officer observed that Poultney was entirely rebel territory, since all its houses were empty. Castle Town, he figured, was about one-third loyalist and

two-thirds rebel; Clarendon was neutral ground. On average, he estimated, a maximum of one-sixth of the local population were loyal
to the crown, another sixth were neutral, and four-sixths were rebel
sympathizers.

The Germans discovered that Poultney was not the only town where
houses were deserted: everywhere they went they saw desolate farmsteads whose owners had fled with their goods and chattels, leaving
behind their cattle to shift for themselves. (Naturally enough, the
Brunswickers regarded those animals as lawful prizes.) The brave folk
who did remain were described by the inquisitive visitors as "large,
sinewy, well-built, strong and healthy men," and the women were fair,
"well-formed and plump, and give promise of a numerous and healthy
progeny."

Quite apart from politics, this foray into hostile territory gave the
curious German visitors a rare glimpse of a raw frontier about which
they knew almost nothing, and they discovered that each of the arbitrary
squares drawn on a map by a London cartographer bore the name of a
township even though nothing resembling a real settlement might exist
there. That was certainly true of Castle Town, which consisted of "seventeen miserable houses," and other townships, including Hubbardton,
boasted even fewer dwellings. Someone asked why the houses had been
built in a certain style—if it could be called that—and learned that they
were initially intended only to provide shelter of a sort from the beginning of spring until the end of autumn—the temperate season when
trees could be girdled or cut and arable land, meadows, and gardens
worked up, after which most homesteaders headed back to Massachusetts or Connecticut for the winter.

A majority of the dwellings were simple blockhouses with no parti-
tions, glass windows, or stoves, and as soon as one was built the head of
the family would send his offspring there to clear the land and return
home in the fall. When they married, the house made a welcome wedding gift: a couple could set up housekeeping while converting it to a liv-
able home.

This seemed a land of milk and honey to the Brunswickers—superb
pastures, beautiful fields of grain, and big, fat-horned cattle that were
far superior to those they had seen in Canada (though the horses were
not as good). The oxen pulling a plow or cart compared favorably with
those in Friesland, and the gardens were better and more sensibly laid
out than those in Canada. But above all, one of them wrote to a friend at
home, "a lover of real, *genuine* trout ought to come to Castle Town."

The end of the campaign's first phase was a moment to savor, and Gentleman Johnny was no man to hold back when it came to the pleasures of a victory, the good company of jolly, convivial officers and a woman, some splendid wine and brandy, and the excitement of the gaming table. Comfortably established in Skene's house, with an abundance of food and drink (some thirty wagons were devoted to hauling his own baggage and that of his staff, enabling him to travel in the comfort that was one of the perks of eighteenth-century generals), he was buoyed by the arrival of several hundred loyalists who came into camp as a result of his proclamation and the proximity of His Majesty's armed forces. For the next eighteen days he tarried in Skenesborough—waiting, to be sure, for his baggage train and provisions to come up, but waiting nonetheless for two and a half weeks while his enemies got away, licked their wounds, and began to regroup and take steps to halt his progress.

The major decision confronting him was which route he would take to the Hudson. He knew from intelligence reports that the Americans were falling back toward Albany, and at some point he would catch up with them, but in the meantime the route to be traveled would determine the direction and organization of his supply line, on which everything depended. Progress to date had been so rapid that the army had outrun provisions and artillery. Suddenly, logistics topped the list of priorities.

Already, as his orders for July 12 indicated, he was concerned about the volume of baggage to be moved, and he ordered his officers to send all unnecessary gear back to Ticonderoga, reminding them tartly that officers who served in the French and Indian Wars often got along for months at a time on the contents of their knapsacks. Lieutenant Digby, who had found himself a good mare after the fight at Hubbardton, was more grateful than ever to have her now: he left his bedding behind, figuring that he would sleep under a buffalo skin and his cloak. By day the horse could carry his belongings and he would walk.

It had all seemed so simple back in January, when Gentleman Johnny composed his "Thoughts for Conducting the War from the Side of Canada," but that was while he was taking the waters at Bath—not slogging through the steaming wilderness of New York. Burgoyne had no doubt then which route he preferred: from Lake Champlain to the Hudson the army would move by water over the length of Lake George, as "the most expeditious and most commodious route to Albany," which would leave an easy march to the river. "Any operation," he had said in a note to Germain, "should be advisable by that route." Only if he encountered serious opposition would he consider moving overland from Skenesborough, since "considerable difficulties may be expected" in that direction—-Americans could easily block the passage from South Bay along Wood Creek, and there would be "a necessity for a great deal of land carriage for the artillery, provision, etc. which can only be supplied from Canada." Besides, if the rebels continued to hold Lake George it would be essential to establish a chain of posts to prevent any breakdown in communications.

But for some reason he changed his mind, and here he was, doing exactly what he had advised against. The head of Lake George was ten miles as the crow flies from the Hudson and about twelve miles from Fort Edward, where a waterfall interrupted river traffic, but now that Burgoyne was on the scene, consulting knowledgeable local people instead of plotting a course on a chart in London, he decided that the army would continue along its present path and march overland the sixteen miles to Fort Edward. Fraser's advance corps would lead the way, taking ten small fieldpieces that had been brought to Skenesborough. However, provisions, baggage, ammunition, thirty-three cannon, horses, and everything else would be carried by water from Ticonderoga to the head of Lake George and then carted overland to Fort Edward. It was almost as though Burgoyne had forgotten the steep incline of the portage between the lakes, over which all the boats and hundreds of tons of cargo would have to be hauled.

Two years after the fact he maintained that his reason for not choosing the water route via Lake George was his concern for the negative impact it would have on the army's morale. Since the men would be obliged to retrace their movement to Ticonderoga before embarking on Lake George, such a "retrograde motion" would give them a sense of heading backward, sacrificing the momentum developed during the previous month of campaigning and even encouraging the enemy. Nor were his soldiers the only ones who had to be considered: there was the psychological effect of this move on the loyalists, whose well-being and safety depended on the army and its promise of protection.

Although no evidence exists that it happened this way (and none suggesting it did not), another factor in the equation was surely the presence of Philip Skene, who was regularly at Burgoyne's side after completing his missionary work at Castle Town. It is hard to believe that he remained silent when the discussions turned to the subject of a road that could have a profound impact on his settlement and the 56,000 acres of which it was a part. Skene was a promoter and a developer, after all, and the future prosperity of the enormous fiefdom in which he had a huge investment of time and money would ultimately depend on its accessibility to land-seekers from more settled areas. If settlers came by way of the Hudson, accessibility meant a road, and a road between Skenesborough and Fort Edward was what Burgoyne's army must have before it could reach the river. It is unlikely that Skene's personal interests prompted the general's decision, but it stretches credibility that the former British major did not point out that the shortest route from Skenesborough to the Hudson was overland—and not a return to Ticonderoga for a trip up Lake George.

Whatever lay behind his reasoning, Burgoyne opted to go by foot, not by water. As might be expected, some of his officers took a dim view of the Fort Anne–Fort Edward plan. Lieutenant Digby claimed that many "were of opinion the general had not the least business in bringing the army to Skenesborough," that he should have followed through with his original scheme and moved south by Lake George; and according to Thomas Hughes, an eighteen-year-old ensign in the 53rd Regiment, the long halt at Skenesborough was the worst mistake Burgoyne could have made.

In support of the general's decision, his deputy quartermaster general, Captain John Money, argued that three or four hundred bateaus were needed to ferry the troops over Lake George and it would take at least a fortnight to haul that number of boats over the Lake Champlain–Lake George portage. This was true enough, but because of the shortage of horses and harness it took longer than that to get those bateaus and supplies over the carrying place, and Money's premise took no account of factors beyond Burgoyne's power to control—namely, that his supply line was tenuous at best and there were hints that it was beginning to unravel; besides which, it was a safe bet that the Americans would do what they could to impede the army's progress.

A German officer who appreciated Burgoyne's difficulties wrote a perceptive letter to a friend at home explaining some fundamentals of logistics. The best way to supply the army on the march, he pointed out, was to collect cattle from abandoned homesteads, as his fellows had been doing around Castle Town, and to buy beef animals from friendly farmers, at the same time acquiring draft animals by the same methods. Then he put a finger on the nub of the dilemma confronting the British in America, wherever their armies might be. You must realize, he said, that the soldiers "eat bread composed of flour which has been prepared in England, also meat which has been salted in the same country, and that, before it

can be put into pots and thence into our mouths, it has to be transported
... over oceans, wide streams, large tracts of land, waterfalls, etc." More
often than not, since horses and carts were scarce, provisions had to be
carried by the soldiers to compensate for Schuyler's scorched-earth policy,
which was destroying crops along the path of the invaders.

The linchpin of the army's supply line was Ticonderoga and its dependencies, and Burgoyne considered it so important that he detached two
regiments to garrison the place. He wrote twice to Carleton urging him
to send reinforcements for that purpose, reminding him of Germain's
orders that Sir Guy was to assist the army in every way possible. What
worried Burgoyne, of course, was not only the present drain on his
manpower (some nine hundred men now composed the garrison at
Ticonderoga alone) but the awesome risk that the loss of Ticonderoga or
Fort George would cut his communications and his supply line, forcing
him to retire and costing him the campaign. To his bitter disappointment, Carleton turned him down.

At the moment, Brigadier General James Hamilton was in charge at
Ticonderoga, with the Prinz Friedrich Regiment of Germans under Lieutenant Colonel Pratorius and the 62nd British under Lieutenant Colonel
Anstruther. But as St. Clair had discovered to his sorrow, it required a
great many soldiers to man these works properly, and in addition to carrying on the normal day-to-day operations of the base, Hamilton was continually obliged to send troops hither and yon to handle other assignments.

Simply to escort a number of horses to Fort George, lest the rebels
take them, he had to dispatch three officers, eight noncoms, two drummers, and a hundred privates, with three days' provisions. Each bateau
loaded with provisions for the army had to be accompanied by five armed
men in addition to the oarsmen. A detachment of two hundred men and
officers was sent to remove the wounded and the women nursing them
from Hubbardton and escort them to Mount Independence (only one-
third of those troops could bring weapons—the others had to carry the
wounded on biers). This rescue operation entailed those troops plus fifty
horses loaded with four days' food for the soldiers and two for the convalescents at Hubbardton, since the patients would have to spend a night
in the woods on the trip to Mount Independence.

Nor was Ticonderoga a happy post: from the beginning, friction
existed between British and Germans. One night too much liquor led to
an exchange of words in which each side criticized the other's equipment, lack of discipline, and, ultimately, courage, which led to an ugly
brawl. The Germans were still complaining about the lack of tobacco

and whiskey and the British commissary's practice of supplying flour, not bread; they were homesick; and occasionally they took out their anger and frustration on anyone who spoke English.

Possibly the sharpest thorns in Hamilton's side were the rebel prisoners, who had to be fed, housed, and continuously watched. He had them working through all the daylight hours, but they lost no opportunity to slip away into the woods. Samuel Churchill, Uriah Hickok, and Ebenezer Fletcher all managed to escape; so did others—seven of them in one two-day period. Hamilton became aware of nasty incidents in which the German troops abused the prisoners, forcing him to issue orders that they were "by no means to be struck or ill treated." Some of this obviously resulted from the language barrier, so finally the prisoners were taken to the large barn near Lake George landing, "where being under the charge of the British they will be able to explain themselves and are to be humanely used" (but where in fact they were treated even worse at the hands of a brutal British major).

Provisioning was another problem: a shortage of cattle prompted Hamilton to reduce the quantity of fresh meat issued to the hospital on Mount Independence, reserving what was on hand for those most in need. At the same time, certain other foodstuffs were so plentiful that they were spoiling and had to be buried or burned. And the abundance of liquor brought into camp by sutlers was a continuing curse: the brigadier saw enough convalescents with serious wounds falling-down drunk that he forbade vendors from selling it on Mount Independence.

Eventually he had most of the garrison and all his able-bodied prisoners working to get the immense stockpiles of food and ammunition to the army, because Ticonderoga had become the bottleneck in the army's supply line. These exhausted men spent day after day manhandling boats, supplies, equipment, and thirty-three artillery pieces up the portage and across Lake George, but still something had to be done to speed things up, and Burgoyne figured that the tough artilleryman William Phillips was the man to do it. Phillips was sent back to look at the situation and very quickly discovered what a daunting task it was. Even with the rebel prisoners working from daybreak to sunset, he reported, "the many departments which require assistance here are so pressing that I am almost distracted with the various confusion which cannot be avoided and which nothing but time and more men will get forward into order."

The result of this foul-up, Burgoyne observed, was "a system of embarrassments and disappointments hardly to be conceived by those who have not experienced them."

In a letter to Lord George Germain written on July 11, Burgoyne concluded a summary of recent operations with a brief note that seemed
to contradict all the objections he had made in his "Thoughts" to the
land route from Skenesborough to Fort Edward. As he had foreseen, the
enemy was now blocking the roads and damming streams, and he was
forced to do exactly what he had determined to avoid: open the road and
clear Wood Creek of felled trees, boulders, and other objects put there
by the retreating rebels. These were "laborious works," he admitted, but
still, nothing his men couldn't handle relatively easily. Besides, it would
take some little time for provisions to overtake the army, mainly because
of the difficulty of dragging gunboats, rafts, and bateaus over the portage
between Ticonderoga and Lake George.

As Burgoyne pondered what shape the next stage of the campaign
would take, his peace of mind was not improved by the troubling reports
from Ticonderoga and the realization of what remained to be accomplished before he could make his move. The general had not the slightest
doubt that his army would overrun the rebels and reach Albany, but his
decision to sit tight at Skenesborough was based on a number of considerations. Now was the time the realities of a wilderness campaign conducted far from a base hit home like a blow to the stomach, and what had
seemed simple when he studied his options on a map in London began to
take on a daunting complexity. The army's real base of operations was
Canada, and although depots, or magazines as they were called, had been
established along the way—notably at St. Johns—the round trip for ships
sailing back and forth was painfully slow, even with no enemy vessels to
oppose them. The business of furnishing food, ammunition, and other
necessities for a force of some seven thousand men plus women, camp followers, and heaven only knew how many animals was beginning to
assume awesome proportions if for no reason other than the length of the
supply line and the time it took for any essential item to travel from Montreal or Quebec to Skenesborough or beyond. The general dared not
order his entire army to march until he was satisfied that he had an adequate store of everything on hand and a fully operative, reliable system
for supplying the army's needs on a regular basis.

John Burgoyne could not know it, but the days of rapid forward movement and lightning successes were over.

Chapter 13

The Rebels Will Chicane You

If ever a man had a full plate, laden with ingredients for indigestion, it was Major General Philip Schuyler. On that early July day when Burgoyne's men set up a battery on Mount Defiance, forcing St. Clair and his generals into a decision to abandon their post, Schuyler was in Albany, anxiously awaiting the arrival of reinforcements from Peekskill. From western New York he received word that a captain and corporal of militia had been scalped at Fort Schuyler. The British under St. Leger were in Oswego, poised for an eastward march to join Burgoyne's army. Tryon County was calling for help, the frontier was in a "weak and defenceless state," and the garrisons at Fort Schuyler and Oneida were low on men, provisions, and ammunition. The Six Nations of the Iroquois were still observing a shaky policy of neutrality, but they had been listening attentively to British propaganda about how the Americans could no longer supply them with trade goods, since all ports were blockaded, so Schuyler—worrying lest they decide to side with the enemy—sent $10,000 to the governor of Massachusetts via Major General Heath with an urgent request for blankets and the coarse linen cloth called stroud. But what hung heaviest on his mind was what might occur at Ticonderoga, for if the troops there should be lost, he would be left with a relative handful of militia, no artillery, and not even a single artilleryman. This was precisely the dilemma he had foreseen when he wrote George

Washington on June 28, saying that in such an event no obstacle would remain in Burgoyne's path since "I have not a man to oppose him."

At five o'clock on the morning of July 7—just about the time the battle at Hubbardton began, and the same day the British pursued Long and attacked at Skenesborough—an express rider from Fort Anne clattered up to Schuyler's headquarters with the staggering news that confirmed Schuyler's worst fears: Ticonderoga and Mount Independence were taken and no one had any idea what had become of St. Clair's army.

Writing at once to George Washington, the general speculated that the troops at those two posts might well have fallen into British hands, that every cannon must surely have been lost, and that "all this part of the country will soon be in [Burgoyne's] power unless we are speedily and largely reinforced." Later that day he received both bad news and good: Ticonderoga and Mount Independence had indeed been lost to the enemy, but to his relief at least some of St. Clair's troops (it was not known how many) had reached Skenesborough.

Schuyler left Albany at once, riding toward Fort Edward, where he hoped to find St. Clair, and at each halt along the way he sent off letters in every direction appealing for militia. Not until July 10 was he able to inform the commander in chief that he had heard from St. Clair for the first time since the fall of the posts; that officer was about fifty miles to the east of him, but to Schuyler's regret was probably marching to Bennington, which would put him even farther away and in "the inhabited part of the country" where desertions would be ever more frequent. His gloomy prediction was that St. Clair would have no more than a thousand troops when he joined him. That number, plus the men he hoped he would find in Brigadier General Nixon's brigade, which was expected from Peekskill any day now, would give him about three thousand Continentals and fewer than a thousand militia, with which "I am to face a powerful enemy from the north, flushed with success, and pressed at the same time from the west" by the British force at Oswego.

In the meantime he would do everything possible to make life unpleasant for that enemy. Schuyler's plan, unlike Burgoyne's, was simple: it was to keep his army out of harm's way, husband his slim resources, and prevent the British from doing whatever it was they had in mind to do. He began by dispatching Brigadier General John Fellows with a Massachusetts militia detachment to obstruct the route between Fort Edward and Fort Anne, felling trees, destroying bridges over Wood Creek—anything to delay the redcoats.

Schuyler may not have been the best field commander around, but he was a superb and energetic organizer with a no-nonsense way of calling a spade a spade, informing people what they had to do, bucking up the ones who needed some iron in their spine, reminding them what was at stake in this fight. He told the authorities in Tryon County that he was disgusted with the "pusillanimous spirit" prevailing there and fed up with the Committee of Safety's continually badgering him for soldiers; he was sorry, very sorry, he said, that they should ask him again for Continental troops when he had already spared every man he could and "when the militia of every county in the State, except yours, is called out. For God's sake," he went on, "do not forget that you are an over-match for any force the enemy can bring against you, if you can act with spirit." If they took heart, showed no signs of fear, and acted vigorously, they would surely save the country and "gain immortal honour."

He informed a nervous Committee of Safety in Cambridge, New York, that rumors of four or five hundred Indians in their vicinity were absolutely groundless and urged them to ignore the promises of clemency made by Burgoyne. Responding to Seth Warner, who had requested clothing and money to pay his men, he sent word that he was supplying both, and in the meantime Warner should round up cattle and wagons to keep them out of enemy hands, stick as close to Burgoyne's army as possible, seize the Tories, and send them away; above all, "Be vigilant; a surprise is inexcusable. . . . If we act vigorously, we save the country. Why should we despond? Greater misfortunes have happened, and have been retrieved. Cheer up the spirits of the people in your quarter."

As ever, along with the words of encouragement his letters revealed a man who knew only too well the dearth of all essential items and the dreadful conditions under which the troops must labor. From his headquarters at Fort Edward a steady stream of dispatches were handed to express riders. Major Yates at Fort George was told to forward all his powder, entrenching tools, cannon, salt, musket balls, and bullet molds before they fell into enemy hands and was ordered to quit his post if the British drew near. Messages to Philip Van Rensselaer in Albany pleaded for immediate delivery of musket balls and cartridge paper. He was beating the bushes hoping to replace all the carpenters' tools lost at Ticonderoga, for want of which he lacked gun carriages and a much-needed bridge across the Hudson. "We may be utterly ruined for lack of wagons," he wrote another. "Axes are greatly wanted." "The army is in danger of starving." "The army have not a mouthful of fresh provisions." And still the requests went out.

To George Washington he confided on July 14: "Desertion prevails and disease gains ground . . . for we have neither tents, houses, barns, boards, or any shelter except a little brush. Every rain that falls, and we have it in great abundance almost every day, wets the men to the skin. We are . . . in great want of every kind of necessary, provision excepted. Camp kettles we have so few, that we cannot afford one to twenty men." A day later he begged Major General William Heath to send anything he could spare—adding the piteous note that "our whole train of artillery consists of two iron field pieces."

Fortunately, Nixon's brigade joined Schuyler on July 12, and though it amounted to a disappointing 581 effectives he knew exactly how they could best be put to use and sent them without a moment's rest to join Fellows's road-destruction crew. The wooded trail Burgoyne would take from Fort Anne followed for some miles the course of Wood Creek, and it was possible, even though the stream was narrow and shallow, to transport some supplies by bateau, so Schuyler wanted that stream plugged. But most of the impedimenta and the army itself would travel by road—and the general was determined to turn that route into a nightmarish jungle. It happened that his troops were superbly suited to that type of work. A man who has cleared acres of forest to create a farmstead, who has built his own home out of timbers he cut and hewed, and whose sole source of heat in winter comes from his stack of firewood gets to be uncommonly handy with an axe. And when hundreds of such fellows are put to work at what they do best, the results are likely to be prodigious, as the British and Germans were about to learn.

It is hard to figure why Burgoyne, with his cavalry background and familiarity with sudden, surprise strikes, did not send Fraser with a flying corps and several light fieldpieces in pursuit of the retreating Americans, who were so few in numbers. By electing to pull his troops back from Fort Anne to Skenesborough and wait for supplies until the entire army could advance, he presented the Americans with a magnificent gift of time, during which Nixon's and Fellows's soldiers-turned-axemen made great progress felling trees, damming streams, and dismantling bridges, in which they were aided by a providentially rainy July that flooded scores of acres and created vast new bogs. Every ten or twelve yards the men dropped enormous trees across the road in such a way that their branches formed an impenetrable tangle that had to be hacked apart, after which the weary British artificers had to construct forty bridges and rebuild others. Adding to the difficulty was the sheer size of Burgoyne's train of baggage and artillery, and the army was further encumbered with camp followers that included 297 women, plus some children, as well as officers' wives and orderlies.

One obstacle nature had provided along the eighteen-mile stretch between Fort Anne and Fort Edward was three miles of swamp that could be negotiated only over a log causeway intended for a man on horseback or a single cart, but definitely not for an army. Schuyler ordered Nixon to destroy that "in the most effectual manner," while reminding him that two roads existed in the area and that he was to block both—one that ran past the home of a settler named Jones, the other by Huffnagel's place. With luck, Schuyler calculated, as soon as thousands of marching feet and draft animals hauling heavy guns and wagons floundered through it the road would not only be blocked, it would be turned into a viscous mass like quicksand. Finally, after the demolition crew finished its job the men were to drive off all the cattle, leaving only milk cows for families unable to move, and bring off iron from the mills operated by Jones and Huffnagel. While all this was going on, Nixon had his scouts out "at almost every point of the compass," and the news they brought back was very disturbing—the woods were alive with Indian parties, one of which surrounded Captain Lane of Alden's regiment, killed one man, and captured the captain and twenty others.

Poor Surgeon Wasmus was still seeing snakes wherever he went. In the lines outside Skenesborough he was introduced to his first copperhead, whose bite was said to be lethal, and two days later he saw a four-foot rattlesnake with seven rattles that a soldier had killed. "Its head and eyes were terrible," he said of the reptile he found so mesmerizing, and went on to cite the camp rumor that a man bitten by a rattler would sink into a coma within an hour, "never to wake up again. Within a period of 24 hours, his dead body will have taken on the color of the snake." Wasmus was by no means the only soldier to mention that the country "teems with rattlesnakes"; many of these Britons and Germans never knew such creatures existed and were understandably terrified of being bitten.

Snakes were not high on Thomas Anburey's list of what made the march out of Skenesborough so tortured. It was almost impossible to imagine the havoc the rebels had created at the same time they were retreating, he admitted with something like admiration, and when you added to that the normal difficulties of moving an army through densely wooded country riddled with streams and "deep morasses . . . watery grounds and marshes," you had some first-class problems.

This was mean, unforgiving country, no place for an army to travel—gloomy, forbidding, the swamps throbbing with the sounds of insects, the air stifling, dark little streams and meanders that seemed to go nowhere. If you were a city lad from Liverpool or Cork, it was the last place you wanted to be.

The road between Skenesborough and Fort Anne was so treacherous that packhorses and oxcarts had to travel without loads; otherwise the animals would have been up to their bellies in mud. Not until the empty wagons arrived at Fort Anne could the men pack them—lightly, according to orders—with muskets, tents, and other necessities, but the orders against overloading were issued repeatedly—and futilely. Meantime the flimsy carts, made of green lumber, creaked and groaned over the forest track, inching through muck to the crack of whips and sutlers' curses.

Now and then the marchers emerged into small clearings where the elderberry was in bloom, white clusters against the dark woods beyond, where the men saw patches of ripe, red strawberries and blackberries beginning to form on the prickly branches. In the morning, woodsmoke from the campfires hung low in the air, still and oppressive on these hot, airless days.

July was excessively rainy, hot, and humid, and the weather brought forth swarms of blackflies, horseflies, deerflies, mosquitoes, no-see-ums, gnats, ants, ticks, and chiggers—to torment these poor devils stumbling through thickets in their woolen uniforms. When the rain was not falling—which was seldom—the forest was like a dank tropical jungle, alive with organisms that flew into the eyes and nostrils of the soldiers and crawled inside their clothing to feast. The suffocating heat of the day was followed at night and in the early morning by "such a heavy fall of dew and mist that it penetrates through our tents into our blankets even, causing them to become soaking wet," one soldier wrote.

Every man toted a knapsack, blanket, haversack with provisions, canteen, hatchet, his share of the gear that belonged to a shared tent, clothes, and arms and ammunition—a dead weight of at least sixty pounds. The German grenadiers on this purportedly rapid march carried the same load, further burdened with a cap with heavy brass facing, an enormous sword, a canteen filled with a gallon of water, and a long-skirted coat.

Normally, provisions for more than bare sustenance would accompany the troops, but even when it was possible to load wagons with food they were unable to keep pace with the marching men, because the road was so badly obstructed or damaged the men had to rely on what they packed on their backs. You could forget about the artillery, Anburey declared; "not the smallest ammunition tumbril could be carried with the army." And he found that regrettable, since the rebels had a particular genius for throwing up earthworks in a matter of hours that were capable of stopping "ten times their number of the bravest troops in the world, who had not artillery to assist them."

From July 14 to 25, General Phillips's artillery corps—which Lieutenant William Digby described as a brass train that was "perhaps the finest and probably the most excellently supplied as to officers and men that had ever been allotted to . . . an army"—was having difficulties of its own, hauling gunboats, bateaus, and cannon over the portage between Ticonderoga and Lake George, soldiers and prisoners working until they were gray-faced and stupid with fatigue. When they finally arrived at the southern end of the lake and had to move guns, ammunition, boats, and provisions from the landing to Fort Edward, it was "a d——d hard task," according to a German officer, "in the hottest part of the year, and one could hardly breathe when sitting still in the tents; dysentery raged among us, but we had to work to maintain life."

No wonder Burgoyne later wrote that for every hour he could devote to planning "how he shall fight his army, he must allot twenty to contrive how to feed it."

With the British advancing on Fort Edward, Schuyler led his men to Moses Kill, some four miles to the south. With him went fewer than three thousand Continentals and about fifteen hundred militia, many of whom were deserting with each passing day, as he informed Congress. He was forced to play this retreat by ear, maneuvering one step at a time without a real plan, because he had no alternative. He hadn't time or manpower or much of anything else to work with and could do no more than improvise, dancing to Burgoyne's tune. His only option was to stay in one place long enough to delay the enemy by means of those busy axes, skirmishing now and then, and pulling back at the last moment, before he was lured into a clash in which he might lose all.

But somewhere between here and Albany a knockdown battle would surely have to be fought, and how Schuyler might handle his army in combat was anyone's guess. More to the point, perhaps, was how effectively the troops would respond to his leadership. In most wars a lion's share of a soldier's time is spent doing little or nothing, passing the time in boredom, waiting for something to happen. But this was different: for nearly a month the men who had manned the lines at Ticonderoga, watching for the British to appear, had been continuously in motion—running, always running. It was as though a curse had been put on them, as if some star had come loose in the firmament to ensure that these bone-tired amateur soldiers would be tested again and again.

To date, their experience with the New York general was largely the experience of defeat, of falling back before the redcoats and their German allies, moving from one miserable campground to another, almost never with an opportunity to rest, never quite daring to look over their shoulders because the enemy might be gaining on them. During their retreat the army had been savaged by desertion and disease; insubordination among militiamen was rampant. In the rear were a growing number of stragglers, some too lame or too old and tired to keep up, others who were faint-hearted, ne'er-do-wells, and skulkers—essentially worthless men. Yet the Continentals, in particular, were sick of running for their lives. They had signed up to fight and believed if only they could stop and face the enemy they would give a good account of themselves even though they were outnumbered.

Among the militia not a semblance of a uniform existed—only what they had had on their backs when they left home, now badly torn or worn through. They carried muskets of every age, description, and condition, not many of them with bayonets, and their shoes—if they had them—were relics of endless marching through water and broiling sun over rugged, unfriendly terrain. Few had blankets, fewer still had tents, and as the columns kept moving south, passing Fort Anne, Fort Edward, and Fort Miller and finally reaching the Hudson, it was a wonder that no more of them were too sick to go on.

In his public utterances, in letters to George Washington and the Congress, it sometimes seemed that Schuyler had lost his nerve, which was certainly not the case. From the way he talked, you would have thought he saw a bottomless chasm opening beneath his feet, yet his actions were those of a man who knew exactly what to do and how to go about it in the most effective way. What he had accomplished was absolutely essential if the army was to be saved, but a retreat with no end in sight was not the kind of leadership to inspire confidence among the troops or the civilians who were running this war.

The legislators in Philadelphia had no real idea what the general was doing, or why, and there is some question if certain New Englanders really cared. All they knew was that Ticonderoga was gone and that every soldier in Schuyler's department appeared to be running from the enemy. As Samuel Adams put it in no uncertain terms, "The surrender of Tyconderoga has deeply wounded our cause. The grounds of it must be thoroughly inquired into. The people at large have a right to demand it. They do demand it, and Congress have ordered an inquiry to be made." In a letter to Roger Sherman he came directly to the point: "Schuyler has written a series of weak and contemptible *things* in a style of despondency which alone, I think, is sufficient for the removal of him . . . for if his pen expresses the true feelings of his heart, it cannot be expected that the bravest veterans would fight under such a general. . . ."

Sam's cousin John was getting an earful from a host of angry constituents. The loss of the post "will lay open our Country to the Enemy," wrote Joseph Warren. "I much fear there has been rascally conduct," commented Joseph Ward. "No event since the Commencement of the War has excited such Indignation and Astonishment as the Evacuation of Tyconderoga in so disgraceful a manner!" said Samuel Cooper. Worse, an ugly, preposterous rumor was making the rounds: Schuyler and St. Clair, the story went, had been "bought up by Burgoyne, who had actually fired silver balls into their camp" as a reward for surrender.

No matter who had been in charge there would have been an uproar, with calls for an investigation and perhaps dismissal, but this unavoidable spasm of recriminations was particularly nasty because Schuyler was seen as the villain—Schuyler the rich, haughty patrician, who had taken the side of Yorkers against the people of the Grants and thus, in a sense, against all New England. The New England congressmen didn't like the way he looked down his long aristocratic nose at them. They were galled by his description of the troops their states had sent as "old men, Boys, & negroes . . . unfit for garrison duty and their Armes very bad & but one baginet [bayonet] to ten men," and they had had enough of his bellyaching.

A year earlier, representatives of thirteen states had assembled in Philadelphia and declared their intention to form a more perfect union, but what had come of their declaration was a long way from being a union, let alone a perfect one, and Schuyler, along with all his other problems, was caught up in one of the regional rivalries that would surface as long as the republic endured. Describing the colonies, Benjamin Franklin once noted that each had "peculiar expressions, familiar to its own people, but strange and unintelligible to others." An early traveler observed, "Fire and Water are not more heterogeneous than the different colonies," and it was said before the Revolution that the disjointed collection of settlements would come to no good, that they would soon engage in civil war.

So Schuyler, and to a lesser extent St. Clair, were to be sacrificial lambs. In time of war it is easy to see things as white or black, with very little gray between, and in the case of Schuyler—who was, after all, responsible for the Northern Department and thus for the reprehensible loss of Ticonderoga—a great many of his foes in Congress (and they were numerous) looked on the dark side, condemning him before the man was given a chance to prove otherwise. The military took a more charitable view of St. Clair: Henry Knox probably reflected Washington's views when he said that "we suspend our Judgements untill we hear St. Clair's report. This is but fair—for however dreadful the consequences . . . if he was not able to stand an attack he is not answerable for it."

No one knew better than Schuyler what he was up against, as a letter of his to the delegates in Philadelphia made clear. Admitting his predicament, he said, "If an accident should happen to us, it would probably be said by the people in the country that we had ten or twelve thousand men, and that we are traitors or cowards, as it is with great industry propagated that I and the general officers who were at Ticonderoga are." But criticism from Congress and the public was hardly his only concern, nor could he afford the time to combat it. Writing to General Heath on July 28 to share his woes about the paucity of provisions, he attacked the venality that characterized his dealings with suppliers. "America cannot be subdued by a foreign force," he stated firmly, "but her own corruption may bring on the final catastrophe." That same day, having learned that a number of Albany citizens had abandoned their homes upon hearing of a skirmish near Fort Edward, he did his best to reassure the town's Committee of Safety that if General Burgoyne succeeded in getting down the Hudson as far as Half Moon "he will run himself into the greatest danger and . . . in all probability his whole army will be destroyed." Given the general's tribulations and the extremely unlikely possibility that his army was capable of destroying an enemy, that was either whistling in the dark or the mark of a very determined man who was not about to give in to adversity.

On July 10 an express rider had pulled up before General Washington's headquarters in the elegant Ford mansion at Morristown, New Jersey, a location that made possible a rapid move toward the Hudson or Philadelphia, depending on what Howe did. The letter in the messenger's saddlebag was from Schuyler, written three days earlier, bearing the incredible news that St. Clair had evacuated Ticonderoga and that most of the garrison might have been captured. Understandably, the commander in chief couldn't believe his eyes: not only was this incomprehensible but for a man already set upon by monumental problems, it opened a whole new range of menacing possibilities. If the report was true, it could mean that Burgoyne's army would soon be sailing down the Hudson to join forces with Howe. Or it could be that Britain's Northern Army would head east to ravage New England.

On the 11th came another communiqué from the commander of the Northern Department, confirming the loss of Ticonderoga, which Washington called "among the most unfortunate that could have befallen us"—though perhaps no more unfortunate than the word that Schuyler still had no idea what had happened to St. Clair's army. Along with this dreadful news, Schuyler was making demands Washington was incapable of meeting, and each day brought conflicting reports about what Howe would or would not do. Despite all the question marks, the commanding general was absolutely certain about one matter: he must have a larger army that was better fed and better clothed than the ragged force he had. And he was also sure of his goal: if possible, he had to avoid minor fights and husband his limited resources in such a way that he could ultimately do battle with the enemy on his own terms, where he would have them at a disadvantage.

Still awaiting Howe's next move, still lacking hard information about his opponent's destination, Washington did know that some fourteen thousand rank and file of the British army had started to board ship and were presumably waiting for favorable winds to sail, and now he had to factor in the possibility that the main British army might move up the Hudson and attack—and probably take—the vital Highland defenses before linking up with Burgoyne, after which their combined armies could destroy at leisure Washington's badly outnumbered force. So convinced was the commander in chief that this was Howe's destination that he marched from Morristown to Smith's Clove, a wild, rugged gorge on the west bank of the Hudson, to await further developments.

At last, one piece of the puzzle fell into place: on July 23 the huge British fleet, carrying Howe's army—"one hundred and seventy topsail vessels and about fifty or sixty smaller ones"—was seen off Sandy Hook, heading for the open ocean, and after digesting that news, and with the outcome of the war quite possibly hinging on his decision, Washington gambled that Howe would head for Philadelphia. Although he was tortured by the possibility that the British general might be making an elaborate feint to draw his attention away from the Hudson, he left a garrison in the Highlands and set off with the rest of his army on a rapid march across New Jersey, where he would be closer to Philadelphia.

While this was going on, Washington had to cope with the disaffection among his senior lieutenants occasioned by yet one more Frenchman— Philippe Charles Tronson de Coudray, who had arrived in America with eighteen officers and ten sergeants in his retinue and an agreement from Silas Deane, one of Congress's representatives in France, guaranteeing him the rank of major general in charge of artillery and the power to direct "whatever relates to the Artillery and the Corps of Engineers." Understandably, this came as a stunner to Henry Knox, Washington's faithful friend and reliable chief of artillery, who was strongly supported by Nathanael Greene, John Sullivan, and other officers. The commander in chief was obliged to deal with this flap along with numerous other matters, one of which was that his army might soon have to disperse for lack of food, thanks to Congressional meddling with the commissary department and its purchase system.

As he considered what could be done to aid Schuyler, Washington recognized that the New England states must be prevailed upon to send militia, and he knew just as certainly that those men would only serve under leaders they trusted and admired. The name of Benedict Arnold came immediately to mind, but Arnold at that moment was threatening to resign because Congress had promoted several junior officers, who now outranked him. (Happily for all concerned, Arnold set aside his quarrel with Congress and for the good of the service agreed to hurry north.) At the same time, Washington also loaned Schuyler Major General Benjamin Lincoln—a forty-four-year-old Massachusetts farmer who had "proved himself on all occasions an active, spirited, and sensible man," according to the commander in chief.

Given all the problems, it was fortunate for the Americans that the man who was calling the shots for Washington was having difficulties of his own.

Before the British fleet sailed, trouble arrived at General William Howe's headquarters in the shape of vain, balding, quarrelsome Major General Sir Henry Clinton, just off the ship from England. Clinton was as waspish as ever, and on the long voyage across the Atlantic he had given much thought to the coming campaign and his own immediate future, and he did not like the look of what lay ahead. Howe's letter of April 2, informing Germain of his plan to move against Philadelphia, had arrived before Clinton left London, so he knew in general what was afoot, and he came ashore on July 5 convinced that nothing could possibly warrant an advance on Philadelphia unless there was a chance to lure Washington's army into a general action. And the chances of that happening, he believed, were just about nil. Therefore "all attention should be given to Hudsons River, & Philadelphia left to the last." As for the rebels, "they will chicane you & annoy you all they can but will not risk a general action, tho chicane on your part may force them to it or oblige them to disperse."

Howe's army might be aboard the ships, but because of fickle winds did not sail for eighteen days, and while the July sun turned the crowded vessels into ovens and men and horses stifled belowdecks, Howe and his new second-in-command talked—and talked. In fact, it would be hard to say which Howe found more disagreeable and unsettling—the inability to launch his campaign or the hours he had to spend bickering with Clinton.

It was not just that Clinton disapproved of Howe's determination to make Philadelphia, not the Hudson, his objective. When he landed in New York he was dumbfounded to learn that the army was still in winter quarters, that the campaign had not even begun because Howe had been playing cat and mouse with George Washington in New Jersey, going nowhere. Even more galling was the news that Sir William intended to take his entire army by sea, save only a token force of three thousand loyalists, three thousand Hessians, and one thousand regulars, who would be left behind with Clinton to defend Manhattan and nearby posts.*

Clinton had recently been at Whitehall and knew, as Howe could not, how much the administration counted on ending the war in 1777. King and cabinet alike were relying on the armies of Howe and Burgoyne to deliver the knockout blows that would bring victory, and in Sir Henry's opinion this could never come about by capturing a Pennsylvania city and ignoring the opportunity to link up with Burgoyne. Control of the Hudson, on the other hand, would sever New England once and for all

---

*As of August 1, 1777, the British army with Howe numbered 18,998, 7,418 others were in New York and outlying posts, 5,261 in Rhode Island, 1,352 in Nova Scotia, and 1,355 in the Floridas—for a total of 34,384, not including Burgoyne's Northern Army.

from the other states, and if Washington wanted to do something about it he would have to confront the combined might of British arms.

Sir William and Sir Henry devoted those sweltering July days to a running argument about Howe's plan, accompanied by petty quibbling and sparring that made them sound like petulant six-year-olds. After each conversation Clinton returned to his quarters and, while still smarting over insults real or imagined, recorded his recollection of all that had been said. His notes reveal that the generals had never "agreed in any one thing" for two years—from the time they first landed in Boston through the Long Island, Westchester, and Rhode Island campaigns, during which time Howe had done everything possible to humiliate him and had even questioned his zeal. When Clinton sulked, Howe apologized; he had said no such thing or had meant no harm in saying what he did say. On the other hand, Sir William stated, gearing up for battle, *he* had been offended on several occasions to learn what Sir Henry had said about *him*. Not so, said Clinton, saying that he admired him as an officer and a man (which was patent nonsense, since he did neither) and had only "modestly differed with him." Upon which both agreed that they had a favorable opinion of each other, "but by some cursed fatality we could never draw together."

Typical of the level of conversation was Clinton's claim to have written two letters to Howe before leaving England and Howe's retort that he had received only one, after which he admitted that he might have mislaid the second. Perhaps he had been wrong, Howe said, but declared "he had not meant the least insinuation." When Clinton requested permission to return to England after the present campaign, Howe replied that that decision was not his to make. Clinton persisted: he asked permission to *write* for leave, and Howe consented, saying he feared "it would be impossible for us to live together in that harmony so necessary for Chiefs composing this Army. . . ." And when Clinton said he deferred to Howe's rank, the latter replied that "the very word 'deference' hurt him." And so it went, day after tedious day.

One matter of substance they discussed was Clinton's role as Howe's second-in-command, and that, for a peevish man looking for any excuse to take offense, was the ultimate ignominy. Howe claimed to be extremely sorry that he had to leave Sir Henry high and dry and on the defensive, but if Clinton saw an opportunity to go on the offensive, he should take it, with one caveat—he had permission to do so only if he could get to his destination and back in forty-eight hours: "if the object lay too far off, it could not be risked." In other words, stay close to

Benjamin Franklin, by John Trumbull
YALE UNIVERSITY ART GALLERY

Philip Schuyler, by John Trumbull
NEW-YORK HISTORICAL SOCIETY

Sir Guy Carleton
NATIONAL ARCHIVES OF
CANADA

Sir Henry Clinton, by John Smart

NATIONAL ARMY MUSEUM

Barry St. Leger

AUTHOR'S COLLECTION

Lord George Germain, after George Romney

BRITISH MUSEUM

Simon Fraser

John Burgoyne, by Sir Joshua Reynolds

Lady Harriet Acland,
by Sir Joshua Reynolds
BY PERMISSION OF
SIR JOHN ACLAND

John Dyke Acland,
by Sir Joshua Reynolds
BY PERMISSION OF
SIR JOHN ACLAND

Arthur St. Clair, by John Trumbull

George Washington at Trenton, by John Trumbull

Friedrich Adolph,
Baron von Riedesel (c. 1762)

Frederika Charlotte Louise,
Baroness von Riedesel (c. 1762)

Benedict Arnold, engraving by
I. Fielding from a drawing by Pierre
Eugène du Simitière, c. 1777
NEW-YORK HISTORICAL SOCIETY

GENERAL ARNOLD.

John Stark (c. 1817), by Samuel F. B. Morse
COURTESY THE WHITE HOUSE

Burgoyne's Surrender at Saratoga, by John Trumbull YALE UNIVERSITY ART GALLERY

Horatio Gates, by Charles Willson Peale
INDEPENDENCE NATIONAL HISTORICAL PARK

Manhattan, thus enabling Howe, as Clinton perceived it, to "make further Conquests" and reap the honors.

A more significant and abrasive topic was how the main army should be employed. Howe clearly regarded the conquest of Philadelphia as the sole task for his army that summer, making the point that by the time the fleet finally got under way it would be too late to contemplate another operation even if he wanted to undertake one. (This from the Howe who had once proposed a two-pronged attack, along the Hudson-Champlain route and against Boston; the Howe who said control of the Hudson would be his primary object.) His current opinion was that the rebels would not defend Philadelphia (Clinton thought they might); and he raised again the old will-o'-the-wisp of a loyalist uprising, saying he hoped to attract great numbers of Tories by the capture of Philadelphia—an achievement that would also deliver New Jersey into British hands. Once again Clinton disagreed, reminding his superior unkindly of last year's boast that he would stir up loyalist opposition in New Jersey and look what came of *that* in the unfortunate affair at Trenton. Indeed, contrary to Howe's opinion about the value of taking Philadelphia, Clinton informed him haughtily that "government did not seem to hold that language"—which came as a surprise to Sir William.

In this, Clinton was not altogether correct, if a statement by His Majesty's prime minister, Lord North, represented official thinking. Putting Howe's and Burgoyne's campaigns into perspective and suggesting the logical outcome, North indicated that Clinton and Burgoyne would "make themselves masters of the North River"—the Hudson—and when Howe (in or around Philadelphia) cut off Washington from the southern states, the American general must either fight or disband his army.

Writing the Duke of Newcastle on July 11, Clinton unburdened himself in a manner unbecoming a second-in-command: "I totally disapprove of the present plan of Operations, I have taken the liberty of saying so: I see no chance of finishing the War this Campaign. . . ." In a message to his friend Lord Percy, written just before word of Burgoyne's triumph at Ticonderoga reached New York, he admitted what had undoubtedly been gnawing at him all along: "I am a little mortified I confess by Burgoyne's having the command of the Northern Army." And to General Edward Harvey he confided, "The only thing therefore in my opinion left for us now in the middle of July is to cooperate in force with the northern army, not by a junction with it (for that I can never advise) but [by] that sort of communication which will give us possession of Hudson's River;

As it is, I almost doubt whether the northern army will penetrate as far as Albany."

No matter what his motives were, Clinton was addressing the central question that should have been decided unequivocally by Germain before the campaign was launched. If the government truly wanted to end the war this year, a leisurely advance on Philadelphia was no way to do it. And for all Clinton's small-minded, oversensitive quibbling with Howe and his obsession with imagined slights and insults, he was right, and Howe might have seen it if only he had been less pigheaded, more willing to strain every nerve to win.

Clinton got nowhere, of course. He and his chief had too many festering wounds, too many basic differences of opinion, so the friction between them was irremediable and—as it proved—ruled out any possibility that Howe might change his mind. When that general saw that his arguments failed to sway Clinton, he fell back on a rationale often used to defend or explain an action that might not achieve the desired result: his plan had been approved in London, therefore he must proceed with it. So on July 23 the sails of the great fleet disappeared over the horizon.

Not even the naval officers knew what their destination was, according to Francis Kinloch, who quoted from a letter he had received from one of them: "Our General says he has embarked us with a view no doubt of conquering some new country, but whether it lies to the north or to the south he alone knows. I suspect that he has Philadelphia in view, & that we shall enter Chesapeake-bay—wherever we go I make no doubt of our succeeding, as we are 14000 as fine troops as can be in the World—the strictest orders have been issued to respect the Property of individuals." (To which Kinloch added, "I wish he would go to Boston.")

The winds that had prevented the ships from leaving New York remained contrary or nonexistent, making progress down the coast painfully slow, and it was July 29 before the fleet reached the Delaware capes and entered the bay with the apparent intention of heading upriver. After proceeding for some distance they mysteriously reversed course, slipped out to sea, headed south again, and took three more weeks to reach Head of Elk on the northernmost reach of Chesapeake Bay. On August 25, Howe's army at last went ashore and prepared to follow the valley of the Schuylkill to Philadelphia.

On the long, uneventful voyage one of the few messages Howe received was Germain's letter of May 18, approving his plan to move on Philadelphia but reiterating the hope that the general would cooperate with Burgoyne when his own campaign was at an end. On August 30, Howe replied, saying it was already too late to do anything about that.

Whatever else it may have accomplished, the general's foolishness had certainly confused Washington, who still believed he might go up the Hudson or perhaps even to the Carolinas and remained in the dark as to where the enemy was until July 31, when he ordered his army "to cross the Delaware with all possible dispatch and proceed for Philadelphia." Howe's decision to bring his troops by water had consumed thirty-three days of the best campaigning season to reach a destination only 120 land miles from New York. He was as far from Philadelphia now as when he set sail. Had they gone by land, that city was only ninety miles from New York—at most a nine-day march.

So the chain of events set in motion eight months earlier, at the time John Burgoyne returned to London, was picking up an irreversible momentum with two separate campaigns under way. It was generally agreed that the two campaigns were separate but complementary, and that was where practice parted company from theory. Like most military operations, this one had many fathers, but whether anyone would have claimed the present manifestation of the plan as his own is doubtful. Among other problems, some very important considerations had gone begging. For instance, while Burgoyne was expected to come to Howe's assistance if needed, no provision was made should Burgoyne require help. Compounding that omission, Howe had neither instructions nor inclination to go up the Hudson and bail out Burgoyne: Britain's commander in chief subscribed to the thesis outlined in a memorandum from Germain's office that the northern operation was merely a diversion which would draw rebel reinforcements away from Washington's army to facilitate Howe's own operation.

Nowhere did Burgoyne hint that his army would depend for its safety on a junction with Howe's force at Albany, yet it is hard to believe that he did not have in the back of his mind that the two armies would actually meet. Even before heading south from Canada he informed Simon Fraser, "The military operations, all directed to make a junction with Howe, are committed to me." He had total confidence that he could reach Albany unassisted, and, having taken Ticonderoga, he was fairly bursting with assurance, making no secret even of his wish to march east to Connecticut. Once he reached Albany, he expected to be free to consider other movements, subject only to Howe's approval. (In Paris the Comte de Vergennes was speculating that Burgoyne's capture of Ticonderoga made a move by Howe to join him in Albany an absolute certainty.)

Despite George III's firm statement that the army from Canada "must join [Howe] at Albany," Germain and Howe obviously subscribed to Clinton's view that a "junction" did not imply a merger of the two forces but merely control of the Hudson by means of a string of strongpoints bolstered by ships of the Royal Navy. This vague, amorphous concept was hardly adequate as the basis of strategy. As for the possibility that Clinton would assist Burgoyne in securing the Hudson, as Lord North evidently expected him to do, Howe's only concession to this was mentioned as an aside in a letter to Germain. There might be "a corps to act defensively upon the lower part of Hudson's river," he said, which could "facilitate, in some degree, the approach of the Army from Canada." But more recently, in one of his arguments with Clinton, Howe retreated even from that lukewarm premise, scotching any idea that Clinton's force would travel more than a day's march beyond Manhattan.

Only one man, who had not been involved in any phase of the planning, had a clear vision of where the scheme was flawed. In attacking Howe's move to take Philadelphia, Henry Clinton's criticism went directly to the heart of the matter, but his prickly manner guaranteed that no one would listen.

As soon as his troops were under way toward Fort Edward, Burgoyne began to suffer from the army's lack of a functioning service corps. The premise behind the system of that day was that all procurement and the transport of food, ammunition, and other supplies were in the hands of civilians answerable to the Treasury. And while a commissary general and his staff traveled with the army and supposedly arranged for its many needs to be met, in a strange, hostile country out in a junglelike wilderness such arrangements were more often than not on a catch-as-catch-can basis.

Burgoyne could have profited from the services of a man like Francis Rush Clark, a civilian employee of the Treasury who was in charge of General Howe's provision train. What Clark did not know about wagons was not worth knowing; among other things, he discovered that the English wagons that had been sent across the Atlantic were too heavy by far for the crude American road system, so in an effort to improve matters, he modified several of those conveyances, reduced their weight by five hundred pounds, and fitted them out with covers to protect food-stuffs and shelter the sick and wounded. And this got him exactly nowhere. Howe was bored by Clark and his tedious talk of carts and simply dismissed his ideas. In addition, Clark's proposals were ignored by the commissary staff, which quickly spotted the opportunity to make money by supplying wagons to the army. The method was to threaten local farmers with military reprisals if they did not lease or sell their "country wagons" at outrageously low prices. Then, having cheated the farmers, the commissaries proceeded to cheat the government by selling the vehicles to the crown at huge fees and pocketing the profits. Clark figured he could easily save the Treasury £100,000 a year by converting English carts but discovered sadly that "private emolument has been more attended to than publick good."

At the mercy of a commissary department that was riddled with con men, the army was obliged to contend with sutlers who were extremely reluctant to expose themselves or their teams to risk. While in Canada, Burgoyne first requested seven or eight hundred horses and later upped that number to accommodate his train of artillery. Then he asked the commissary general at Montreal to estimate how many animals he would need to haul thirty days' provisions and a thousand gallons of rum for ten thousand men, and on the basis of that estimate informed Carleton that at a minimum he required enough horses for the artillery plus two horses for each of five hundred carts—a number that would "barely carry fourteen days' provisions at a time."

In practice, less than half of his five hundred wagons were operational at any one time—the rest had broken down completely or were being repaired. In fact, less than a third of the horses he needed were rafted up Lake Champlain from Canada, and after they arrived they were worked mercilessly dragging bateaus and wagonloads of provisions over the portage from Ticonderoga to Lake George, after which the poor weakened animals had to make an endless number of round trips between Fort George and Fort Edward. Sometimes it was necessary to hitch ten or twelve oxen to pull a single bateau, and they and the horses hauled between eighty and one hundred heavy boats over that route, to be used ferrying provisions down the Hudson. Each round trip, Burgoyne stated, "made a hard day's work for six or more horses."

At Fort George an American garrison retreated once again without putting up a fight, and while that made a splendid supply depot for the British army, by the time the various brigades reached Fort Edward, sixteen miles to the south, it became apparent that the insufficiency of horses and carts was still such that the army could barely be fed from day to day. It was then that the intelligence Riedesel brought back from Vermont, with the promise of all the grain, cattle, and horses in the Bennington area, became irresistibly appealing. Burgoyne and the baron began discussing the idea of dispatching a strike force to that area at the earliest possible moment.

Until now this campaign had gone according to the book, with the rebels retreating and putting up resistance that slowed, but could not halt, the relentless progress of Burgoyne's troops. Except for obvious differences in terrain and the relative professionalism of the rival armies, the British and German advance had proceeded along lines that might have been followed in Europe. Then an entirely new element was added. Initially suggested by Burgoyne in his "Thoughts," it was adopted at the insistence of George III and Germain. It provided the invading army with a weapon that would spread terror through the northeast and have a profound impact on Burgoyne's plans.

Chapter 14

Giving Stretch to the Indians

Burgoyne's secret weapon was unveiled near Skenesborough on July 17. Shortly after eight in the morning the soldiers in camp were startled to hear three volleys of small arms from the direction of the portage, followed even more surprisingly by four cannon shots near the general's headquarters. Obviously this was some kind of signal, and as the army turned out on the double, word was passed that the musket fire was a salute from the general's new allies—five hundred or more Indians, many of whom had traveled great distances from the *pays d'en haut*—the upper Great Lakes—to come here. No sooner had Burgoyne's troops appeared than the newcomers announced their arrival with the chilling war whoop that usually preceded an attack.

These Indians were unlike any the English or Germans had seen. That keen observer Surgeon Wasmus noted that the nations represented were Ortoguais (by which he may have meant Ottawa), Fox, and Mississauga and Chippewa, both known also as Ojibwa, as well as Mohawk, Onondaga, Cayuga, Seneca, and Tuscarora—members of the famous Iroquois League of Six Nations. The warriors who were present in the largest numbers (four hundred or more), and who most impressed Brigadier General Johann Specht, were the Ottawa, or Ouatois. Theirs is "a very formidable and belligerent nation, but also harsh and mean," Specht said, noting that these people had been "sworn enemies of the English up to this time and had frequently caused them grievous damage during the last war," notoriously at the massacre at Fort William Henry in 1757, when wounded British soldiers, plus women and children, were slaughtered and scalped or led off as captives. Another direct link to that calamity was the man who now led these Indians into camp to "take up arms for the Crown of England for the first time"— St. Luc de la Corne.* Specht understood that St. Luc had spent many of his sixty-six years among the Indians, leading them in various campaigns for the French against the British, but he may not have realized that the Quebecois had stood by twenty years earlier, watching and doing nothing to stop the savagery, as members of this same nation dragged wounded English troops from huts inside the fort and killed and scalped them before the eyes of the appalled surgeon and provincial militia. Nor were whites the only victims then: before that occurred, the Ottawa captured three of Captain Israel Putnam's rangers—two Mohicans and a mortally wounded American—tore one Indian apart and ate him, and burned the other.

Each of these warriors was daubed with his distinctive version of war paint, many wore beautiful garments, others were stark naked, all were impressive—bigger than the Indians who accompanied the army from Canada. Wasmus was especially fascinated by the Mohawks, who had a well-deserved reputation of being "the most dangerous of all the Savage nations," and he noticed that the Canadian Indians, when confronted by them, stepped aside and averted their eyes.

The very word "Mohawk" came from the Algonquian root meaning man-eater or cannibal, and these people specialized in exquisitely cruel tortures, in which by custom the victim was expected to demonstrate his own valor by singing his song of death while women and children burned him with torches and hacked at his flesh with knives or pieces of shell in a ghastly ordeal contrived to delay death as long as possible. Most of the other Iroquois tribes and those from the northwest could be as ferocious as the Mohawks—the difference being that the latter lived at the edge of the white settlers' ever-advancing frontier and were better known to the Dutch and English.

For most warriors the weapon of choice was the club known as a tomahawk, for they preferred close-in combat, which improved their chances of killing or taking captives, and as Americans living on the fron-

---

*Lieutenant Hadden, no admirer of St. Luc or his Indians, observed caustically that the French-Canadian was "famous for his cruelties to the English Prisoners during the last War."

tier could testify, they stole up on their prey as silently as foxes, fought like lions, and vanished into the forest like birds. Every Indian was a hunter and could throw his tomahawk with deadly accuracy at a retreating animal or enemy: as an awed Thomas Anburey observed, if they could not catch their quarry they threw "with the utmost dexterity . . . this terrible implement of warfare" and "seldom fail striking it into the skull or back of those they pursue."

While warfare was central to their way of life, the six nations that composed the famous League of the Iroquois—Mohawk, Oneida, Onondaga, Cayuga, Seneca, and Tuscarora (an Iroquoisan people who were given land and a place at the council fire by the others after they were driven from North Carolina)—were known also for superb farms with endless rows of corn, squash, and beans, within a village situated alongside a lake or stream and enclosed by an elaborate palisaded stockade. Each of their famous communal "longhouses," built of poles and bark, housed the extended family of the female line, for theirs was a thoroughly matriarchal society: women owned the longhouses, the gardens, and the tools used for cultivating. Women appointed the sachems, who dealt with intertribal relations, and removed them when they failed to fill the office satisfactorily. To the women's line belonged the children; women oversaw law and order in the longhouses. Contrary to reputation, they were more often at peace than at war, their crowning achievement being the confederacy that held them together for two centuries and, although they numbered fewer than twenty thousand souls, won them power and influence exceeding that of any other native American nation north of Mexico. In the beginning they were hostile to just about everybody, including their next-door neighbors, but sometime in the second half of the sixteenth century a mystic from the Huron nation inspired them to form a brotherhood based on law and order, as a result of which they got along with each other while cowing or conquering tribes from present-day Maine to Michigan, from the Ottawa River to the Cumberland in Tennessee. To the continued consternation of the French and the English, they mastered the art of playing off one against the other, which meant that they controlled the balance of power in the region, forcing whites to deal with them by means of treaties.

Until now, Burgoyne's experience with his Canadian Indians had been a major disappointment. He found them useless in pursuit of the rebels, for "when plunder is in their way, which was the case at Ticonderoga, it is impossible to drag them from it." (Had he read the letters of General Ludwig Dieskau, a German fighting with the French a generation earlier, he would have been forewarned. "They drive us crazy from morning till night," Dieskau wrote. "There is no end to their demands. . . . One needs the patience of an angel to get on with these devils; and yet one must always force himself to seem pleased with them.") One of the Brunswick officers remarked that they "behaved like hogs. When it comes to plundering they are on hand every time. . . ."

Yet it was the lure of plunder—along with scalps and prisoners who could be exchanged for worldly goods—that St. Luc and his mixed-blood colleague the Canadian-Ottawa Charles-Michel Mouet de Langlade held out as a carrot to induce these warriors to travel hundreds of miles from home. Burgoyne was pleased to note that the western Indians, unlike the Canadian tribes, "profess war, not pillage," and hoped they would prove "more brave and tractable" than the others, which suggests that he had not inquired too carefully into St. Luc's recruiting methods.

Braves who joined Burgoyne came as volunteers, individual soldiers of fortune, or sometimes with other members of their clans, and the very nature of their participation ensured that most were young and powerful, eager to prove their manhood and skill as warriors by returning home with a clutch of scalps and other booty. They were not going to fight as a unit of the British army, but outside it—scouting, watching the movement of enemy troops, and above all, prowling beyond the periphery of Burgoyne's advance, moving silently through the dark forest to pounce on unsuspecting troops and isolated farmsteads, spilling blood and spreading terror in their wake.

The Indian technique of fighting was entirely different from that of Europe's armies. Each war party had a leader who took them into combat, but he neither commanded them nor compelled obedience, and warriors were free to leave the war party if they lost confidence in him. All of which is to say that Burgoyne's Indians were not subject to discipline in the British or German sense of the word, and might well prove fickle allies if his army suffered real reverses.

A German officer observed that the Ottawa "were uncivilized, large-framed and enterprising, but as fierce as Satan [and] accused of being cannibals." He had heard rumors that they tore enemies to pieces with their teeth, but whatever else they might be accused of, it was certain that they were here to take scalps.

The American James Thacher, who had treated several survivors of a scalping, took a surgeon's interest in the techniques of the procedure: "with a knife [the Indians] make a circular cut from the forehead, quite round, just above the ears, then taking hold of the skin with their teeth, they tear off the whole hairy scalp in an instant, with wonderful dexterity. This they carefully dry and preserve as a trophy, showing the number of their victims. And they have a method of painting on the dried scalp, different figures and colors, to designate the sex and age of the victim, and also the manner and circumstances of the murder." The practice of scalping did not originate with the American Indian but was known in Scythian times, some four to eight centuries before Christ. No matter. It was the principal element behind the dread of Indians that was a constant of frontier life, and behind the charge leveled against George III in the Declaration of Independence that he unloosed "the merciless Indian Savages, whose known rule of warfare is an undistinguished destruction of all ages, sexes, and conditions." (Close inspection of the scalping knives in warriors' hands revealed that they were made in England.)

Until the Revolution began, it had been a decade and more since a farmer living in the area now traveled by Burgoyne's army had thought it necessary to carry his musket across the plow handles as he tilled his fields. Now that had changed, and every settler here had to wonder if the rustle of leaves meant the approach of an Indian, if he and his wife and children were being stalked by savage men waiting for an opportunity to attack. The woods were tailor-made for ambushes, the clearings within them isolated, and when you turned loose hundreds of skilled killers who had no use for whites and promised them booty and a bonus for every scalp they brought in, the inevitable result was a horror story.

Yet it must be remembered that while warfare may have been the norm for many Indian nations, so was it for Europeans, who had been at each other's throats for most of the century. And while British and Americans alike were dismayed by Indian tortures and scalping, they had grown accustomed to the white man's mores in which those guilty of even minor infractions were put in stocks, to be jeered and spit at by women and stoned by men and boys. There were, in London, some 166 offenses, including stealing food, for which human beings could be hanged, and the spectacle of the condemned being taken to Tyburn and strung up on the gallows was a form of popular entertainment. In the eighteenth century men were still being drawn and quartered and burned at the stake. And at the same time Burgoyne's Indians were being unleashed to the outrage of Americans, a woman in London had her eyes put out for performing abortions, and two of the general's own soldiers were sentenced to a thousand lashes. It was a brutal age, and the brutality was by no means limited to native Americans.

Burgoyne was clearly uncomfortable with the devil's bargain he had struck. Then and later he defended his actions, saying he did everything possible to prevent the killing of innocents (while having to tolerate the Indian custom of scalping men they had killed in battle), but as anyone might have foreseen, his gentlemanly rules were simply not going to be followed by these allies. Surely it was the height of naiveté to imagine that he could call upon the Indians to spread terror, at the same time expecting that they would change their customs or their temperament—especially when the latter was fed by the liquor he supplied them (despite his punishment of troops and sutlers who did so).

Since no Indian cared about the white men's loyalties, and in any case could not distinguish Tory from rebel, inherent in Burgoyne's threat to "give stretch to the Indian Forces" under his direction was the strong probability that enemy soldiers were not the only ones who were going to be hurt. The terrible swift blows of these hunter-warriors were almost certain to fall on the helpless as well. A white male, after all, was a white, and unless he was in the uniform of an English or German regiment (and in some cases even if he was) the Indians were going to attack him if the conditions were right, while women and children, who wore no symbols of their allegiance, were almost certain to be fair game. To make matters worse, Burgoyne was severely handicapped in dealing with the Indians by the fact that neither Captain Alexander Fraser nor other officers in his command could converse with them. That forced him to rely heavily on St. Luc—a man he came to dislike intensely.

Although Burgoyne was the perpetrator, the employment of Indians could not be laid exclusively at the general's door. The king himself had insisted on it, and so had his prime minister and his secretary of state for the colonies, who was running the war. Carleton endorsed the plan, and William Tryon, former royal governor of North Carolina and New York, who had recently led a force of loyalists in a raid on Danbury, Connecticut, urged Germain to impose terror on the frontier communities by unleashing Indians. St. Luc, as might be expected, was all for it: his phrase was that the war must be brutalized. (The Americans had a small number of Stockbridge Indians, serving principally as scouts, and both they and some rebel soldiers scalped enemy troops, though on nothing like the scale of Burgoyne's Indians.)

So it was pretty much a foregone conclusion that the war *would* be brutalized, but first Burgoyne had an intricate and elaborate diplomatic ritual to perform, and the big moment came two days after the western tribesmen first appeared. A detachment from the 9th Regiment escorted the commander in chief to the Indian camp to welcome them into the service of the king, and when he and his generals arrived he found his new allies waiting in two facing rows. After a *feu de joie*, St. Luc led Burgoyne between the lines of warriors to a large arbor in which a chair was set. On either side of it the Indians had felled great trees so the British and German officers could sit on the trunks. While those honored guests looked on and the tribesmen smoked, the oldest chief solemnly shook hands with Burgoyne. Perhaps neither man recognized it or gave it much thought, but theirs was a brief encounter between leaders representing cultures so different they might have come from two separate planets. The only thing they had in common was that both were warrior chieftains whose business was killing and winning; there all similarities ended. Each lived by his own customs and rules, and while elaborate courtesy was involved in their dealings, whether they could ever arrive at a real meeting of the minds was extremely doubtful.

The chief delivered a flowery welcome, translated into French by St. Luc, the burden of which was that these warriors had set out in response to Carleton's call as soon as the winter snows melted, leaving homes, wives, and children behind. Some had left on March 11 and claimed to have traveled three thousand miles* to get here, and while many different nations were represented, they were "all friends and allies and are of one mind, one mouth and one language," which was to serve their king. "You see us all here in front of you. Say what is your will. Speak, and we shall obey."

Whereupon the general replied in French, with St. Luc translating again, thanking the Indians in the name of King George III for coming so far so quickly, telling them it would be their task to "chastise, not destroy" the king's "disloyal and unfaithful subjects . . . and lead these monsters back to obedience." It would be permissible to scalp those they killed in battle, but in the name of the king, he forbade them to do so with prisoners, wounded men, and, most particularly, old people, women, and children. To discourage scalping, he promised them a bonus for every prisoner they brought into camp, and privately to St. Luc said he would "rather lose every Indian than connive at their enormities. . . ."

At this the old chief began singing a war song, and as he danced past the assembled Indians they showed their approval of the proceedings "by emitting a sound with all their strength from their chests that is as indescribable as it is inimitable," Wasmus reported. Then St. Luc took

---

*The maximum distance was probably closer to one thousand miles, but no matter—it was a long and difficult journey.

center stage; attired in a green dress with silver fringe, the sixty-six-year-old danced before Burgoyne singing a war song in an Indian tongue, followed by all the warriors, in order of rank, all dancing in time to the steady beat of drums, their bodies bent so that they faced the ground, singing in what an eyewitness described as "partly harmonious and rhythmical," though at times it sounded eerily like "the howling of wolves or dogs." Since the occasion was regarded as a feast, the English commander in chief had arranged for a barrel of rum to be opened, after which the singing and dancing became ever more frenzied and the warriors drank without stopping until they could no longer stand, let alone dance. Two days later they had sobered up sufficiently to take to the warpath, and it was immediately evident that they meant business, and their method of "chastising" rebels would be virtually impossible to control.

Within hours they captured a rebel captain with nineteen of his men and scalped three others, but somewhere along the way they lost two braves to rebel gunfire and requested that Burgoyne permit them to keep three of the men. In revenge for their own loss, they intended to roast and eat two of the captives while the third looked on; then they would release him and send him back into the enemy lines to warn the rebels what to expect. The general refused them, but Surgeon Wasmus predicted the worst: "I pity the first Americans that fall into their power; it will be a horrible feast for them. . . . The Savage resembles a tiger that is only moved by blood and prey." As he suspected, ahead lay terror sufficient to satisfy even a king bent on vengeance. And an immediate American reaction to the growing presence of Indians was noted by Benjamin Farnum, who observed that "halfe the molishey" deserted.

When the invading army broke camp at Skenesborough on July 24 for the march to the Hudson, the high spirits that characterized the trip up Lake Champlain were not much in evidence. It was not lost on the troops that a provost had been appointed, in charge of a twenty-two-man guard, half British, half German, to serve as a military police force, patroling the rear of the army to guard prisoners, deal with stragglers, and—the bad news—search all tents or other shelters of the sutlers and camp followers to prevent the sale of liquor "to Soldiers, Women, or Savages, or . . . Servants of Officers." This march through wilderness was not like any these men had known: although the country is little more than rolling in most places, to Wasmus the road seemed to lead over "terrible cliffs and rocky mountains," and the long columns had to stop again and again and wait while work crews cleared debris that Fraser's advance corps and the Canadian loyalists had been unable to deal with. On Wood Creek the boats carrying the Germans' gear were being pulled by "sick and weary dragoons," so the others slept without tents and wished themselves back on the lake in their beloved bateaus. During the two maddeningly long days it took to reach Fort Anne the only cheering sight for the struggling troops was a glimpse of Burgoyne himself, trotting along with his staff, jaunty and full of smiles for the men in the ranks.

They arrived at a campsite that proved as unsavory a location as could be imagined. What had once been Fort Anne was now little but charred ruins where the rebels, fearing that Indians would attack their burial details, had left their dead on the battleground (some of them scalped). It was bad enough to put up with what Lieutenant Digby called the "violent stench"; worse psychologically was finding the decomposed remains of Lieutenant Richard Westropp, who had been killed when Sergeant Lamb was running up the hill. Because of the odor the detail simply covered his corpse with leaves and turned away.

That evening Burgoyne and his staff presented quite a different picture: they sat around a table set with linen, silver, and crystal under a big tree near the general's sleeping tent, and anyone overhearing the civilized chit-chat and the tinkle of wineglasses as toasts were raised to King George and the Duke of Brunswick would never have suspected that the horror unleashed by the man at the head of the table had already begun, a few miles away.

During the day a party of Indians and provincials—some four or five hundred strong—attacked American pickets a mile from Fort Edward and seized a log breastwork after killing a lieutenant and nine privates. Rebel reinforcements came up, the enemy retreated, and when the Americans entered the defenses to collect their dead they found them lying naked, scalped, with hands and noses cut off, and "their bodies hewn almost in pieces with tomahawks."

John Allen was harvesting his wheat crop that same Friday morning, and his father-in-law, George Kilmore, who lived about a mile away, had lent him three slaves to help out. Kilmore's youngest daughter had gone along for a visit with her sister, taking with her a black girl to look after the three Allen children. The men came in from the fields for noonday dinner and were eating with the family when Indians led by a man named Le Loup (also called Wyandot Panther), smeared with paint, sweating, shouting, waving hatchets and knives, suddenly burst through the door, and as the terrified whites and blacks screamed and begged for mercy, shot Allen, knifed and tomahawked the others, scalped them all, and looted the house. On Sunday, July 27, a slave who had been sent to find out why the others had not returned came galloping into Kilmore's dooryard with the sickening news.

About the time the terrified black man delivered his gruesome message, a picket guard of nervous Albany County militiamen waited anxiously at Fort Edward for a patrol led by their lieutenant, Tobias Van Vechten, to return. Schuyler had pulled his troops out of the fort on July 23, leaving only a token force to keep an eye on British movements and protect stragglers, but the rear guard kept dwindling with desertions, and a few days later not many men were left. In certain respects, this was a good spot for a fort, since it was the head of navigation for the Hudson and the river here was shallow enough to be fordable, but unfortunately it was dominated by higher ground within point-blank range of cannon fire, and it had been allowed to deteriorate and now was no more than a mound of dirt surrounded by rotting palisades, a lonely, isolated pocket of no-man's-land, which the departing army or the pickets had done nothing to enhance by destroying doors and windows in all the outbuildings and making a shambles of two solid houses nearby.

The lieutenant's scouting party was approaching the crest of a hill overlooking the fort, unaware that Le Loup's warriors, having massacred the Allen household, were lying in ambush for them. An unexpected Indian volley caught them completely by surprise, and the result was recorded in the terse words of a letter written from Albany: "We have just had a brush with the Enemy at Fort Edward in which Lt. Van Vechten was most inhumanly butcher'd and Scalped, two Serjeants and two privates were likewise killed and Scalped—one of the latter had both his hands cut off."

Then came a murder so shrouded in hearsay, wild tales, and propaganda that it was the stuff of legend for a century and more, retold in lurid prints, etchings, and paintings, in novels and plays, making it virtually impossible to determine the truth of what occurred on that Sunday in July.

Jane McCrea was one of seven children born to a Presbyterian minister in New Jersey by his first wife, and after both parents died she moved to the Fort Edward area to live with her oldest brother, John, a colonel in the New York militia. She was in her early twenties and by almost all accounts was uncommonly attractive—tall and well-formed, with reddish hair said to be so long it touched the floor.* During her stay with her brother she and a local man named David Jones fell in love, but his loyalist sympathies were so strong that he went to Canada and joined Peters's American Volunteer Corps. With the approach of Burgoyne's army, Jane's brother John decided to move his family to Albany, and he urged her to accompany them, but she had hopes of meeting and perhaps marrying her fiancé and elected to remain near Fort Edward with an elderly woman, a Mrs. McNeil, who was a cousin of Brigadier General Simon Fraser. There they were presumably warned by a militiaman fleeing Fort Edward after the ambush of Van Vechten's party that the Indians were coming.

The two women sought cover inside the log cabin and evidently were climbing through a trapdoor into the cellar when they were discovered by the war party. Both were seized and taken off as prisoners toward Fraser's advance camp, but somewhere along the way the women became separated, and near the spot where Van Vechten had been killed two Indians began arguing about whose prisoner Jane McCrea was. One brave, in a fit of rage, shot and scalped her, stripped off her clothes, and mutilated her body; then her corpse and that of the lieutenant were rolled down an embankment and covered with leaves.

Both raw scalps were taken to Burgoyne's camp at Fort Anne that evening, and a shocked David Jones was said to have seen and recognized Jane's hair as the Indians danced about their trophies in triumph. Then the Widow Jones was brought to Fraser's camp. She was huge, the warriors had stripped off her clothes, she had a tongue that could blister paint off a wall, and the embarrassed brigadier discovered that none of the women with his corps had clothing large enough to fit his cousin, so he finally draped her in his own greatcoat until something more suitable could be found. But nothing he could do or say could make up for the loss of her young companion.

When Burgoyne learned of the tragedy he was as shocked as anyone else. That night he sent a note to Fraser: "The news I have just received of the savages having scalped a young lady, their prisoner, fills me with horror." He went on to say he planned to visit the Indian camp the next morning and asked Fraser to have the warriors assembled. "I would

---

*Her hair was featured in everything written about her. It was not only unusually long but silken or glorious or luxuriant, and the color also varied according to the teller—black or blond or somewhere in between. One woman claimed to have seen a lock of her hair, and a justice of the peace who examined Jane's remains in the 1840s concurred with the woman's verdict: it was red or reddish.

rather put my commission in the fire than serve a day if I could suppose Government would blame me for discountenancing by some strong acts such unheard of barbarities." What that meant is somewhat obscure, but obviously he was thunderstruck by what had happened.

The following day the general met with the Indians and demanded that the murderer be executed. Fraser and other officers were leery of such drastic action and urged caution; so did St. Luc, who warned that it would cause mass defections by the Indians, who might go over to the enemy or, if they headed for home, would surely attack white settlements in Canada. Between that advice and the pleading of the assembled tribesmen to spare the killer's life—he was young and a promising warrior, they said—Burgoyne relented and had to content himself with an agreement that all future raids would be supervised by a British officer—as unlikely a scenario as could be imagined.

All things considered, Thomas Anburey concluded, while the unfortunate young lady's death must be "universally lamented," in the context of all the other violence related to the war this "is but of little moment."

In theory he may have been right, but in fact he was not. Something about Jane McCrea's murder differed from all the other lurid stories so that it fired the imagination of a thoroughly alarmed public. Her demise was one of the first and in some respects the most dramatic of the atrocities now being committed almost daily by Burgoyne's Indians, and coming on the heels of his earlier threats, it made for extremely effective propaganda. Mentioned again and again in soldiers' journals and in letters home, it soon became the chief item of conversation across New England and New York State, especially in communities close to the frontier where the fear of Indian attack was palpable.

Schuyler's aide Brockholst Livingston was certain the murder of Jane McCrea—"a young Lady of Beauty & Family"—had "proved of service to the Country. Many of the Inhabitants who had resolved to stay in consequence of Burgoyne's Proclamation & submit to the terms of the Victor, are now determined to a Man to disregard his promises (which he has already repeatedly broke). . . ." Captain Rufus Lincoln— an original speller if ever there was one—noted in his diary that "it was about this time Mrs.[sic] McCrea and many other peasable inhabitance were Crualy murdred by the Indianes. And indeed the Ravages they Commtted aded much to the number of the American Army as the Inhabitance Rather Chused to turn out and oppose them than to be Cruely Murdered With their famelys and all that was dear to them."

One reason the story struck home was the almost universal description of the woman as young and beautiful, with a pleasing disposition, intelligent, and possessed, of course, of those lovely long tresses.* Another was that she was engaged to marry a loyalist officer, was staying with a woman related to a British general who was Burgoyne's most trusted friend, and—since the rebel army had withdrawn from the area—was in a house considered to be a safe haven. In other words, if Burgoyne could not even protect his own from his hirelings, how could any American family in the vicinity, regardless of political affiliation, age, or sex, expect to be spared?

News, especially sensational news of this sort, traveled like heat lightning, with gory details ballooning as it made the rounds by word of mouth and letters and before long in newspapers—on August 11 in Rivington's *New York Gazette and Weekly Mercury*; the next day in the *Pennsylvania Evening Post*; on the 14th in the *Massachusetts Spy* and the *Maryland Gazette*; on the 16th in the *New Hampshire Gazette*; on the 22nd and 29th in the *Virginia Gazette*. Without exception these accounts of savagery, which were not limited to the McCrea murder, were based on letters written during the week following the murder. The *Massachusetts Spy* quoted a report from Saratoga saying Indians were everywhere—very bold—killing and scalping sentries in sight of the army and murdering and scalping about sixty women and children, "making no distinction between whigs or tories." The *New Hampshire Gazette* noted that terrified Albany residents were moving down-country after two little girls who were picking berries were scalped.

It was this sort of thing that gave Schuyler new reasons to worry. The panic in the area was such that he felt obliged to write Albany's Committee of Safety deploring that "a little skirmish we had near Ft. Edward should have struck such a panic as to induce my fellow-citizens to leave their habitations." It was all very well for the general to make reassuring noises, but the fact was that while Indians had represented a threat from the time Burgoyne's army left Canada, that threat had now escalated to the point where men in the ranks and civilians alike were just plain scared. The government in London and the commander in chief of the expedition had meant to terrorize the rebels, and to a considerable extent they were succeeding; as a paymaster in Schuyler's army observed,

---

*The only sour note was sounded by James Wilkinson, who may have seen her and described her as "a country girl of honest family in circumstances of mediocrity, without either beauty or accomplishments."

"One Hundred Indians in the Woods do us more harm [than] 1,000 British troops. They have been the Death of many brave Fellows."

The worst of it was that Schuyler's army seemed incapable of countering the Indian attacks, which continued to mount in fury. It is hard to imagine any outfit having a worse time of it during these weeks of terror than the 7th Massachusetts Regiment. On July 21 a thirty-four-man scout was surrounded by Indians and only twelve escaped. The next afternoon one sentry was killed and another scalped, whereupon the brigade turned out and had what Captain Benjamin Warren described as "a smart engagement" lasting half an hour with heavy fire on both sides. That cost the Massachusetts lads eight killed and fifteen wounded. Two days later a lieutenant and a sergeant were shot dead. On the same day that Lieutenant Van Vechten and Jane McCrea were killed, Major Daniel Whiting's detachment came under hostile fire near the hill where Van Vechten's men were posted. Some five hundred soldiers under Ebenezer Learned were sent out to rescue them, but a downpour delayed them long enough for the Indians to escape.

On July 28 a man trying to move his family away from their home near Fort Miller was shot and scalped. The 7th Massachusetts was moving away from Fort Edward, but the men still found themselves within range of the largely unseen savages, and on July 29 a sentry and a sergeant with a fatigue party felling trees near a campsite were killed. Hearing that four hundred Indians were closing in on his rear, Schuyler ordered a withdrawal to Fort Miller and in a hot little rearguard action lost three killed and three captured.

Burgoyne's oncoming army found one of the dead men, an officer, scalped, with the soles of his feet sliced off; seeing him, Surgeon Wasmus wondered if this horror had been performed before he died, and suspected that it had. Two days later a lieutenant was found drawn and quartered and hanging from a tree; another picket was killed and scalped; and a Dr. Leonard, presumably frightened and depressed by what was going on, committed suicide. The next day a terrified woman named Mrs. Rankin cut her throat with a pair of shears but survived to confront her private demons anew. And so it went, day after frightful day—more killings near Fort Miller, twenty soldiers attacked three-quarters of a mile from the post, fifteen scalps taken on August 3, and always more men captured or deserting because of the savagery they dreaded. Word of these atrocities spread like grassfire fanned by the wind, heightening the anxiety of farmers in isolated pockets beyond the fringe of military operations.

As Schuyler's weary army moved steadily south, parties of Indians and loyalists followed on their flanks and rear, nipping at their heels, waiting for any chance to waylay them. Along the retreat they had hopscotched from one position to the next, slowly falling back toward Burgoyne's destination of Albany, but Schuyler was running out of moves. After a council of war on July 30 the general issued the order to withdraw to Saratoga, and the men struck their tents and worked through the night carrying stores and loading them on rafts along with huts they had constructed, while the enemy came closer hour by hour.

Whether under attack or the threat of attack, Schuyler's army continued to retreat—always with too little food and a maximum of discomfort. When the 7th Massachusetts arrived at Fort Miller it was nightfall and they had had no food for twenty-four hours. Next morning, before they could finish cooking breakfast, they were ordered to move on, and after a twelve-hour march during which they forded two rivers, they reached Saratoga "dirty, hungry, weary, and wet," according to Benjamin Warren. Yet he lay down in his wet clothes and "slept pretty well."

Then two men were killed and scalped; their scout was ambushed with some twenty or thirty dead or wounded; a rescue party by Hugh Gray was beaten off by Indians and loyalists, with one man taken prisoner and the lieutenant mortally wounded. And so it went, on and on. Samuel Smith's outfit reached Stillwater during the first week of August, and it had been a long piece of work getting there, he complained—halt one day and march the next, and the troops constantly being killed. "Our men has got such a Notion of running that fifty Indians will Drive three hundred of them"—the militia, he added quickly, not the Continentals. "Where we Shall Stop I don't no," he wrote his wife: "I am tired of marching with my Back to the Enemy but I hope it will be our turn next to Drive them." He reckoned that Schuyler's army was outnumbered about five to one, but if only more Americans would turn out like bold Sons of Liberty they could "drive the enemy from Whence they Came." It was the last letter Smith's family received—five weeks later he was dead.

At Saratoga, Schuyler welcomed the experienced Brigadier General John Glover and his regiment, described by Captain Benjamin Warren as "1,200 men clean and tidy." That was the Continental brigade Washington had ordered up from Peekskill to reinforce the Northern Army, and the new arrivals quickly learned what kind of war they were in for. During their brief stay in Saratoga they were constantly in a state of alarm, day and night, Glover said—"scouting parties a great part of the time cut off, killed, scalped and taken prisoners." And the worst of it was the invisibility of the enemy: Glover detached four hundred men to scour the woods and the only trace of Indians they found was three blankets. By the time he reached Stillwater he had had twenty-five or thirty men killed and scalped, with an equal number captured, all within four days. "This strikes a panic on our men," he wrote, "which is not to be wondered at, when we consider the hazard they run as scouts, by being fired at from all quarters (and the woods so thick they can't see three yards before them) and then to hear the cursed war hoop which makes the woods ring for miles. Our army at this Post is weak and shattered, much confused, and the numbers by no means equal to the enemy."

Glover was a Marblehead fisherman who had been further schooled in adversity by the war. He and his 21st Massachusetts Regiment of sailors—men ruined by the British Fisheries Act, who understood that a crew has to work together and obey commands immediately—had joined George Washington's army at Cambridge in '75 and the next year rescued it from disaster after the battle of Long Island by rowing the troops from Brooklyn to Manhattan under cover of darkness. Washington called on them again on Christmas night of 1776, when with freezing hands they shuttled forty-foot Durham boats back and forth across the flooded, ice-choked Delaware River, carrying the remnants of the army to attack the Hessian garrison at Trenton.

The way Glover saw it now, the odds against Schuyler were getting longer all the time. Colonel Long left camp with his New Hampshire regiment—their time was up and "nothing will induce them to stay one day longer"; Poor's brigade of New Hampshire militia was due to leave in a few days; and with the departure of Nixon's six hundred Massachusetts men, the army's strength would be reduced to three thousand at best— by no means all of them fit for duty. As Schuyler described his predicament to Washington, the number of Continental troops was steadily declining and "not a man of the militia . . . will remain above one week longer." In the meantime, Tories were joining Burgoyne—not in great numbers, but still enough to widen the disparity between the two armies.

The road from Fort Anne to Fort Edward led south and slightly west, turning away from Wood Creek, so Burgoyne's troops could no longer use bateaus for carrying supplies. Between the two forts the army camped in the gloom of the Pitch Pine Plains, where, exactly as Schuyler had predicted, the overloaded two-wheeled carts churned the primitive roadbed into a rutted mess as gummy as molasses, and the redcoats' spirits soared when Fort Edward finally came in view.

In their camps near the fort, the troops relaxed and rested, waiting for supplies and the heavy guns to arrive from Ticonderoga, thrilled that they had finally put the hated wilderness behind them and were out in the open, soaking up sunlight on the east bank of the Hudson, with Albany within easy striking range. Around Fort Edward the forest had been cleared for about two miles, and the farmhouses, fields of grain, and ripening raspberries and blueberries gave them a feeling that they were back in civilization again. Their buoyant spirits were contagious: Burgoyne was so confident that nothing could stop him that he wrote Germain requesting permission to return to England before winter, with Phillips to succeed him in command.

For its part, the American Congress was despondent enough that the Foreign Affairs Committee felt obliged to inform an influential Frenchman that "General Burgoyne's advances over the Lakes are disadvantages to us . . . and General Howe will probably gain some ground . . . but be assured, Sir, we have firm hopes of final success. . . ."

During those early days of August, growing numbers of loyalists arrived at Burgoyne's camp, but as elated as he was when some four hundred came in, he had misgivings about the new recruits. Fewer than half were armed, and those were the only ones he could really count on—the rest were "trimmers," motivated by self-interest. Nor could he rely on the Canadians with his army—they were all homesick and miserable. His provincials, moreover, all "professed loyalists," taxed his time and patience: this man was in it for the money he would receive when his corps was complete; that one was interested only in protecting his home district; another wanted revenge against personal enemies; and not a one of them had the foggiest idea of discipline. They wrangled constantly about who was to be an officer or in what corps they would serve, while they were fit only for bringing in cattle, clearing roads, or guiding troops on the march. As Lieutenant Colonel Kingston remarked of the Canadians, provincials, and Indians, "I never considered them as regulars, because they were not disciplined."

Of all the elements in his command, the Indians were the worst, and Burgoyne was sick of them. He finally concluded that the western tribes' "only preeminence consisted in ferocity," and he realized what a grave mistake he had made indulging "their most capricious fancies" at the insistence of St. Luc. When he confronted them in the council at Fort Edward after Jane McCrea's death he tried again to lay down the law, stating that he would not tolerate the killing and scalping of women and children, nor would he put up with thievery* and the plunder of noncombatants and their homes.

But by now most of the Indians had also had enough of Burgoyne and his absurd notions of combat, and they announced they were leaving for home. This was not only embarrassing to the general, since they had been procured at considerable expense to the government; it also meant the loss of his eyes and ears. If they departed, he would have to rely on his light infantry for scouting, and those men had been "trained to higher purposes," by which he meant their skill at leading the army in battle. He couldn't afford to have them scattered hither and yon, prowling through alien woods where they would be at the mercy of rebel snipers, yet to give in to the Indians was to renounce his principles, to lose face, and to settle for "blood and rapine."

Later that day, at St. Luc's urging, he held another "congress" with his ungovernable allies and with counterarguments made more palatable by liberal doses of rum told them he would stick by his conditions. Oddly, they seemed to accept the rebuff and asked only if those warriors who were closest to home might leave to help with the harvest; those from remote areas pledged to remain with the army. He agreed, but it did not work out that way: the next day scores vanished, laden with loot, and the exit continued until hardly an Indian remained who had joined his army at Skenesborough.

On Sunday, August 3, the British and German camps buzzed with excitement. Three mounted men—a British officer and two soldiers—emerged from the nearby woods and were directed to the general's headquarters. The fact that they had made it through or around the rebel lines was remarkable enough (Burgoyne already knew that two messengers he had dispatched to Howe had been hanged, and since he had not heard that any others arrived safely, had to assume that none of Howe's expresses were reaching him, either). The soldiers were itching to know what news these men brought concerning the main army, but nothing was forth-

---

*One of the Indians' favorite tricks was to steal a horse that had been brought from Canada to haul baggage and then sell it to one of Burgoyne's officers.

coming. Whatever he learned, Burgoyne kept to himself, saying only that "everything had gone well to the Southward," and that Howe's army was posted in and around New York.

Not even to his second-in-command, Riedesel, did Burgoyne disclose the contents of Howe's letter, which had been enclosed in a small, hollow silver bullet in case it had to be swallowed by the messenger, and that only made the army more curious, since the general's silence was so uncharacteristic. Normally Burgoyne was gregarious, talkative, open with his staff and other trusted officers, and his unwillingness to reveal more than the most superficial information was unsettling.

Howe had written the letter on July 17 while his troops were sweltering belowdecks on the transports, waiting to sail for Chesapeake Bay, so his news was now seventeen days old. He began by congratulating Burgoyne on taking Ticonderoga—"a great event," he called it—and went on to lament the difficulty of communicating with a man in the northern wilds. Washington, he said, was waiting to see what Howe would do and in the meantime had detached Sullivan with about 2,500 men for Albany. Then he turned to his own plans and dropped the bombshell. With sinking heart, Burgoyne read, "My intention is for Pensylvania, where I expect to meet Washington, but if he goes to the northward contrary to my expectations, and you can keep him at bay, be assured that I shall soon be after him to relieve you.

"After your arrival at Albany, the movements of the enemy will guide yours; but my wishes are, that the enemy be drove out of this province before any operation takes place in Connecticut. Sir Henry Clinton remains in the command here [in New York], and will act as occurences may direct. Putnam is in the highlands with about 4000 men. Success be ever with you."

On the day Burgoyne received that letter, Howe and his army were south of the Delaware capes, but no matter where they might be, Burgoyne now knew that something had gone very wrong with the plans he had drawn up so carefully. There would be no meeting in Albany, no opportunity to mount a real expedition instead of a feint into the heart of New England. While Howe headed in the opposite direction, his own movements were to depend on what the rebels did, and only now was he told that Putnam had 4,000 troops in the Highlands and had sent two brigades to join Schuyler's army, while Sullivan was coming north with 2,500 more. St. Leger was on the way to meet Burgoyne in Albany, of course, but with only a small force, and who could possibly say whether Howe would detach Clinton to "act as occurences may direct"?

So now he was on his own with no help in sight, his only instructions to force his way to Albany. In fact, unbeknownst to Burgoyne, Sir Henry was suddenly overcome by doubts and fears for the safety of his little army should Washington attack him. While that was the unlikeliest of possibilities, Clinton decided not to hazard his defenses by sending men north, and although he knew Burgoyne was marching toward Albany, he waited almost three weeks before informing him that he could offer no assistance. Meanwhile, Burgoyne's shaky supply line was barely able to keep up with the army's needs from day to day, and desertions were on the rise (though held somewhat in check by word that a number of men who left the ranks had been scalped). For a man who had been on the crest of the wave two weeks earlier, Howe's letter was a cruel blow. It was John Burgoyne's first intimation that serious trouble lay ahead.

Chapter 15

The Dismal Place of
Bennington

On July 18, the day after Burgoyne's western Indians arrived in Skenes-borough to much fanfare, the General Court of New Hampshire met in special session in the town of Exeter. The business at hand was an urgent request for help from Ira Allen of the newly independent state of Vermont. The members were only too familiar with the threat to "the defenceless inhabitants on the frontier" to their west and were keenly aware, as the Vermonter was so careful to point out, that "when we cease to be a frontier your state must take it." They also knew that after the battle of Hubbardton Seth Warner probably had no more than 150 men, and those troops were all that stood between New Hampshire and Burgoyne's invading army, which might head east any day now.

It was clear that while delegates were sympathetic to Vermont's distressing situation and eager to provide assistance, in practical terms they had no way of doing much, since New Hampshire was a poor state, only recently settled, and without accumulated capital with which to pay and equip an ambitious expedition across the Connecticut River. Happily, an angel was at hand in the person of the speaker of the General Court, John Langdon, one of the few wealthy men in the area who was not a loyalist. He rose to his feet and offered to contribute $3,000 in hard cash, his household plate to be used as security for a loan of $3,000 more, and seventy hogsheads of Tobago rum to be sold. Langdon figured he would be reimbursed if the Revolution succeeded; if it did not, he would have no use for money, since he would be bound for prison or the scaffold, and now, having made this extraordinarily generous offer, he proposed how to turn it into reality.

"We can raise a brigade," he said, "and our friend Stark, who so nobly sustained the honor of our arms at Bunker Hill, may safely be entrusted with the command, and we will check Burgoyne." On the heels of his speech, the members voted to make John Stark a brigadier general, adding that he was to be "always amenable . . . to the General Court or Committee of Safety" of New Hampshire—not, in other words, answerable to Congress or officers of the Continental Army. This rather curious instruction was based on a realistic assessment of the situation. As a member of the General Court put it, the New Hampshire militia "had lost all confidence in the General officers who had the command at Tyconderoga . . . they would not turn out nor be commanded by such officers." On the other hand, lives were at stake, and if the New Hampshire contingent was subject to the orders of Congress, those soldiers might be ordered south to join General Washington. So it was imperative that a capable, highly respected New England officer be selected to command the force they dispatched, and they had seen enough of John Stark to know he was their man, and the only way to get him was to let him operate outside Congressional authority.

Stark was proud, touchy, difficult, cantankerous, contrary, ornery, determined, and as independent as a hog on ice. A portrait made some years after the war shows the spare, sinewy figure, a lean face with prominent nose and high cheekbones, peering from the corners of piercing blue eyes with a suspicious, vinegary look, as if daring the painter to alter his appearance in any way. But never mind his disposition: he was a superb soldier and leader of men and knew as much about frontier warfare as anyone you could find. He had been raised in the woods, and although he was still in his late forties, was famed as an old Indian fighter who had served as Major Robert Rogers's right-hand man in the Seven Years War, fought the French under Abercromby at Ticonderoga, and the British starting in 1775. Stark had a particular knack— call it luck or instinct—for being in the right place at exactly the right time, a characteristic that was to serve him well in the coming weeks.

Two years earlier, when news of Lexington and Concord reached him he mounted a horse without pausing to put on a coat, asked his wife, Elizabeth (known, apparently, as Molly), to forward his clothing to Medford, Massachusetts, and rode off toward the fighting, summoning his neighbors to follow. Two months later, as a colonel in the new Continental Army, he went into action in the battle for Bunker Hill and demonstrated what kind of leader John Stark was.

He marched his regiment to Charlestown Neck just before the fighting began and was leading his men along a road that was being hammered by broadsides from British ships in the harbor. When a nervous officer suggested they speed up the march, Stark snapped, "Dearborn, one fresh man in action is worth ten fatigued ones," and walked on at the same deliberate pace. Off to the left, on the beach, he spotted a gap in the rebel lines; pushing his troops quickly toward it, he arrived in time to give them a "short but animated address" just before the British attack began. Throughout the battle he was under fire continuously, but strolled coolly back and forth along his lines, praising and encouraging the men, and when the Americans in the redoubt on Breed's Hill were finally overrun, he led his soldiers toward the rear, putting up a running fight as they fell back in good order and brought off their wounded. It was a retreat witnessed and admired by John Burgoyne, who said it was "no flight, it was even covered with bravery and military skill."

After serving with distinction at the battle of Trenton, Stark figured he was entitled to a promotion. But when new brigadiers were appointed by Congress in February of 1777, John Stark's name was not on the list, and to make matters worse, that of Enoch Poor, another New Hampshire colonel, was. Stark did not take a slap in the face lightly and in any case had had a bellyful of an army run by politicians who played favorites. In March he resigned, announcing that "I am bound on Honour to leave the service, Congress having tho't fit to promote Junr. officers over my head." And there matters stood when New Hampshire's General Court summoned him.

Stark agreed immediately to take the independent command, and the effect was startling. Within six days, twenty-five companies—almost fifteen hundred men—signed up to follow him, some of them walking out of a church service to enlist when they heard of his appointment. That number was more than 10 percent of the males over sixteen in New Hampshire; in one town some 36 percent of the eligible men volunteered. Part of the enthusiasm reflected Stark's enormous popularity; some undoubtedly was due to Burgoyne's rapid advance and the threat it posed; and some, it must be said, was the result of being paid in advance, thanks to Speaker Langdon's generosity.

Thomas Mellen was typical of the men who signed up. As soon as he learned that Stark would accept the command, he said, he got his gun and with half a dozen others from Francestown enlisted in Colonel Stickney's regiment. They marched to Fort No. 4 and spent a week preparing, waiting for other outfits to join them, and in Mellen's case, making more than two hundred bullets for what lay ahead.

Stark's first order of business was collecting soldiers; the next was to outfit them—locate camp kettles, ammunition, bullet molds, cannon, wagons, and a host of necessities, including rum, "as there is none of that article in them parts where we are a going," Stark reminded the Committee of Safety. Once he assembled the men his orders were to head for Vermont and cooperate with the troops of that or any other state or those of the Continental Army—which gave him the leeway to do just about anything he pleased. He was in a hurry and by August 2 had sent seven hundred men to join Colonel Seth Warner in Manchester, Vermont, promising to dispatch three hundred more the following day. By August 6 he was at Bromley, near Peru, Vermont, writing to the Committee of Safety in Charlestown: get some guns from Walpole, he advised, "fix them cannon for your defence [and] forward, with all convenient speed, all the rum and sugar."

Captain Peter Clark, a farmer and justice of the peace from Lyndeboro, brought his company into Manchester on Sunday, August 3, and they were having a thoroughly unpleasant time of it—"all of us something disordered with the Quick step, occasioned by change of climate and diet"—but they were recovering from the diarrhea and had made tents out of boards, as shelter from the rain that fell almost every day. Clark wrote his family to say that he was bound for Albany to join the Continental Army and stop Burgoyne, adding that he hoped to live to see home again. Mellen had a better time of it than Clark: he and a hundred others were sent down Otter Creek, where they "lived like lords on pigs and chickens in the houses of tories who had fled" and came back to Manchester with two hogsheads of West Indian rum.

George Washington had sent Benjamin Lincoln and Benedict Arnold to strengthen Schuyler's northern command, assuming that these two New England officers—Lincoln from Massachusetts, Arnold from Connecticut—would be more palatable to the Yankees than the New York general. Stark himself was not on the best of terms with Schuyler, with whom he had quarreled when the latter decided to abandon Crown Point a year earlier, and now he had another reason to mistrust him when he rode into Manchester and saw his brigade paraded, ready to move out. He asked what was going on and was told that General Lincoln had ordered them to march to the Sprouts, where the Mohawk River empties into the Hudson.

Stark found Lincoln, inquired what was meant by this, and learned that Schuyler had called for the troops to join him. In no uncertain terms Stark told Lincoln to inform Schuyler that he, John Stark, "considered himself adequate to the command of his own men," handed Lincoln copies of his commission and his orders, and stalked off to join his men.

Now Lincoln was in a ticklish position. He was a fat 240-pound farmer who was competent enough, but he was five years younger than Stark and hadn't a fraction of that officer's experience in battle, having served without seeing action in his father's regiment before being commissioned a major general in the Continental Army. It helped not at all that Congress had awarded him that rank at the same time Stark was passed over. But Lincoln was a sensible fellow, as Washington observed, and fortunately he was equal to the diplomatic challenge described by Captain Clark in a letter to his wife. After Stark's brigade formed up to march to Bennington, en route to join Schuyler's army, Clark reported, "there was a considerable turn in affairs, by reason of General Stark arriving in town. The orders we had for marching were given by General Lincoln— what passed between Lincoln and Stark is not known, but by what we can gather . . . Stark chooses to command himself. I expect we shall march for Bennington next Sabbath, and where we shall go to from there I cannot tell."

What passed between Stark and Lincoln made it clear to the latter that Stark did indeed choose to command his own men and was furious that his volunteers had been given orders without his knowledge, and Lincoln realized that unless he took steps to calm Stark down he might turn around and take his men back home. Lincoln informed Schuyler that the New Hampshire officer was "exceedingly soured and thinks he hath been neglected and hath not had Justice done him by Congress—he is determined not to join the Continental Armey untill the Congress give him his Rank therein. . . . Whether he will march his Troops to Stillwater or not I am quite at a loss to know." It was clear that Stark was going to operate independently and had no intention of taking orders from any officer in the Northern Department but Schuyler, since all the others had either been commanded by him or joined the army after him. And that was that—a "very unhappy" business, Lincoln added, "especially at a time when Every exertion for our Common Safety is so absolutely Necessary."

Schuyler, knowing it was vital to hang on to Stark and his men, told

Lincoln to smooth the waters by assuring the New Hampshire officer that Congress had been informed of his situation. Then he should try to persuade him to put aside his quarrel with the legislators in Philadelphia and realize that "the greater the sacrifice he makes to his feelings, the greater will be the honor due him." Before the storm passed, Lincoln warned Stark that he was pushing his luck by refusing to obey Schuyler's orders, to which Stark replied that he was used to taking responsibility and would continue to do so when necessary for the good of the cause. He had come here expecting to attack Burgoyne's left flank and rear, he said, and that's what he was going to do; and Lincoln wisely fell in with this plan. It was, in fact, the strategy Schuyler had devised in July: by keeping a force in Manchester or Bennington, he hoped to blunt any move Burgoyne might make in that direction and harass him with flank attacks whenever possible. Washington had concurred, saying it would "keep [Burgoyne] in continual anxiety for his rear." When Schuyler got cold feet in the face of Burgoyne's steady approach to Albany and ordered all the men in Vermont to join him, the commander in chief called that "a very ineligible plan," saying, "An enemy can always act with more vigor and effect when they have nothing to apprehend on their flanks and rear."

As it happened, Stark's intransigence was an important factor in determining what followed. He marched his brigade to Bennington—a village consisting of a meetinghouse and twelve or fourteen dwellings, which a British officer called "the metropolis of the state of Vermont." There he met with an anxious Council of Safety, whose members strenuously opposed his taking men to join Schuyler. That was fine with Stark: no one needed to tell him that he had been sent here in response to the Vermonters' plea for help, and he reassured the council that he had no idea of "leaving that part of the country almost naked to the ravage of the enemy." It was fortunate that he did not.

Lincoln had gone to Stillwater, and probably it was he who persuaded Schuyler to revert to the original plan and make use of Stark's brigade to snap at Burgoyne's heels. From Half Moon, below Stillwater, he wrote Stark to say he was glad the troops had not left Bennington, since "our plan is adopted," and he was returning with badly needed camp kettles, axes, ammunition, and flints. The scheme now was for Lincoln—who had five hundred men with him—to join Stark, Warner, and their troops in Cambridge, New York, and go on to Skenesborough, where they would create a diversion by attacking the enemy's rear. In a letter to the Massachusetts Council, Schuyler described the movement and concluded by saying, "Happily I have assurances from General Stark that he will not hesitate to do what is required." But as it turned out, there would be no rendezvous of rebel forces in Cambridge. Generals Burgoyne and Riedesel had plans for a diversion of their own, which completely altered American intentions.

The Germans were camped at Fort Edward, with the Hudson River on their right and, on a hill to the left, what Wasmus described as a beautiful building "which could be called a small castle," causing him to wonder what it was doing here in the wilderness. Another Brunswicker said it was "the first house built in good taste that we had seen for a long time"—a two-story building with a pavilion on each side that belonged to William Duer, a friend of Schuyler's and a New York delegate to Congress. At the moment it was occupied by Simon Fraser and would soon be taken over by Burgoyne for his headquarters.

A more modest building known as the Red House was outside Fort Edward on the road to Fort George, and it too had new occupants. On August 14, Baroness Riedesel, her three little girls, two maids, and a cook (who was an expert at scrounging food) arrived by calèche, to the delight of her husband, who spent the following day with them before more pressing business took him away. The baroness looked as fragile as a china doll, but she was tough, resourceful, and remarkably cheerful in accepting the hardships of wilderness campaigning. She adored her husband and learned that Lady Harriet Acland was responsible for her presence near him. One evening while Burgoyne was dining with his officers he heard that Acland's wife was on her way to join the major at Fort Edward. "General," he said to Riedesel, "you ought to let your wife come too." So here she was with her family, all of them sleeping in one room, eating meals outdoors whenever possible (including rattlesnake soup and bear meat, which she found quite tasty), enjoying a lovely time — "happy and satisfied, for I was with my children and beloved by all about me." She was less content to discover that "Burgoyne liked having a jolly time and spending half the night singing and drinking and amusing himself in the company of the wife of a commissary, who was his mistress and, like him, loved champagne."

A week before her arrival every man in the ranks knew that something was up when the Brunswick dragoon regiment was told to prepare for a march and bring its standards to Riedesel's headquarters at midnight on August 8. The next morning at five, leaving tents and baggage behind, a corps under the command of Lieutenant Colonel Friedrich Baum stepped off along the east bank of the Hudson, heading south past fields of overripe, withered wheat and rye abandoned by farmers unwilling to risk their lives harvesting it. When Baum left Fort Miller he had something like 650 men in tow, including artillery, to which Riedesel added another 100 Brunswickers. Along the way to his destination Baum picked up what may have amounted to 500 or more Tories, giving him a total strength of nearly 1,200 men, and a curious lot they were. The solid core of the detachment was the regiment of dragoons. A small number of Brunswick light infantry and jägers were present, plus several loyalist outfits under Colonel John Peters and Captain Justus Sherwood. Along the route Captain Simeon Covel of Cambridge and Francis Pfister, a retired British officer, joined the march with about 150 men, and Baum's little army was augmented by other Tories from neighboring communities who had been tipped off about the movement, though their usefulness was highly questionable since many lacked training or arms.

More than a hundred Mohawk Indians, led by Captain Charles-Louis Tarieu de Lanaudière, St. Luc's son-in-law, and Captain Colin Campbell, accompanied the force. Fifty British marksmen, commanded by Captain Alexander Fraser, and a handful of Hesse-Hanau artillerymen, who brought a pair of three-pounders, made up the balance of the detachment. Captain Samuel McKay was there in an unofficial capacity, and three British advisers had been assigned to Baum—Captain Laurentius O'Connell, Riedesel's aide-de-camp; an engineer named Desmaretz Durnford; and the ubiquitous Colonel Philip Skene.

The impetus for this operation came from Burgoyne, who had been flirting with the idea of some such move for months, and his deputy commander, Baron Riedesel. Uncomfortable and restive in his subordinate position under Howe (a feeling that was not improved by that general's recent letter to him), Burgoyne had never really abandoned hope of having a command of his own, independent of Howe, and still envisioned an expedition toward the Connecticut River, where he could link up with a British force from Rhode Island and seal off New England. Though nothing came of this, as he doggedly followed orders to march to Albany he could hardly ignore the threat to his exposed left flank posed by rebels in those same New England states. One way to blunt a potential attack was to send a detachment eastward, which would make the Yankees "very cautious of leaving their frontiers and much facilitate my progress to Albany."

While Riedesel agreed in principle with this idea, he had an entirely different concept of the expedition's goals. He had concluded that once the army moved any great distance from lakes and rivers, the best way to handle the transport problem in this "vast country" of wretched roads was to abandon wagons altogether and use packhorses for carrying the army's provisions and equipment. While he was on detached duty near Castle Town, watching in frustration as his men struggled along carrying tents and provisions on their backs, he heard that horses abounded throughout the Connecticut Valley. That was rich farm country, untouched by war, its barns full of grain, and known to be a horse-breeding area. Since the only concentration of armed rebels in the region just then was Warner's command, which had been badly chewed up at Hubbardton, he reasoned that a hit-and-run raid could be made to carry off the horses and be gone before the Americans knew what had happened. But now, of course, the situation had changed. The rebels were known to be assembling in Vermont in what Burgoyne called a "gathering storm upon my left," and Riedesel didn't like the idea that the odds might favor them, especially if they were given time to throw up a strong defensive position. Still, the need for horses was desperate: the continuing shortage of teams prevented the army from advancing more than a few miles at a time before waiting eight or ten days for supplies to catch up. The baron's idea was that the fifteen hundred or so horses brought from Canada could be used for drawing artillery and provisions, while animals confiscated or purchased in the Connecticut Valley would serve as cavalry mounts, haul baggage, and enable the army to march wherever it pleased. When Riedesel first discussed this with Burgoyne on July 22, his chief liked the idea, said it coincided with his own views, and promised the Brunswick general that his dragoons would have their horses at last.

On the afternoon of August 4, to Riedesel's astonishment, Burgoyne came to his tent and handed him a set of instructions he intended to give Lieutenant Colonel Friedrich Baum for a foray into Vermont. Burgoyne said the plan—which he claimed later was the one Riedesel had given him—was to be executed immediately, and the baron saw at once that it differed entirely from what he had in mind. This was no hit-and-run strike but a major operation, and the German was stunned to learn what the commander in chief expected Baum to accomplish. The lieutenant colonel was to proceed to Manchester, where he was to test the "affections of the country, to disconcert the councils of the enemy, to mount Riedesel's dragoons, to complete Peters's corps, and to obtain large supplies of cattle, horses and carriages."

Nor was that the end of it. His ultimate destination was Rockingham, near the Connecticut River, where he should take post while waiting for his Indians and light troops to return from a scouting mission to the north, after which he was to head south to Brattleboro and then march posthaste to Albany to rejoin the main army. On top of that, he was to collect wagons and oxen plus some two hundred horses, saddles, and bridles for the dragoons, and another thirteen hundred that were to be roped together in strings of ten—each string to be led by an unarmed man from Peters's corps and conducted to Burgoyne's force.

This awesome assignment entailed a formidable round trip of more than two hundred miles across the Green Mountains to Rockingham and back to Albany, and Burgoyne cannot have comprehended the difficulties Baum would encounter when he announced that it was to be achieved within a fortnight. On one point, Baum was given leeway to make his own decision: while it was expected that Seth Warner, in Manchester, would retreat before Baum could engage him, if he should by chance decide to make a stand, Baum was to use his discretion about attacking, since "your corps is too valuable to let any considerable loss be hazarded on this occasion."

Riedesel objected: either Baum should go foraging for supplies and horses or he should go prepared to fight, but not both. The detachment was not strong enough to engage in serious combat, it was made up of a mixed bag of troops, many without experience, and it couldn't possibly achieve all the goals Burgoyne had set. Besides which, Rockingham was too far away, and so, for that matter, was Manchester. But Burgoyne was adamant. He tapped Riedesel on the epaulette and said, "My friend, I intend to kill two flies with one blow," explaining that since he was about to advance on Saratoga, General Benedict Arnold (who the British believed to be in command of the rebel army now) wouldn't dare detach troops to support the rebels in Vermont, and since Lieutenant Colonel St. Leger was now besieging Fort Stanwix on the Mohawk River, Arnold would *have* to send reinforcements there.

In the back of Burgoyne's mind was the further idea that a success by Baum would enable him to cut loose from his long, tenuous supply line and send Brigadier Fraser, whose corps was on the west bank of the Hudson near Saratoga, south to take possession of the heights near Stillwater. There Fraser would dig in to wait for the main army and provisions to reach him. That done, Burgoyne reasoned, "the whole country on the west side of the river, to the banks of the Mohawk, would have been our own." The pieces of the puzzle were falling into place nicely. Or so he believed.

Under protest, the German general wrote out Baum's instructions "in the same way as an adjutant writes the order of his general," and Burgoyne took them back to headquarters to study that evening. Several days later, just before Baum was scheduled to march, Burgoyne learned from Justus Sherwood, who had it from Philip Skene, that the rebels had a substantial supply depot in Bennington which was only lightly guarded. The general mounted his horse, rode to Baum's camp, and verbally ordered him to go not to Rockingham or Manchester but to Bennington. This may have been an impromtu, spur-of-the-moment decision, as Riedesel believed, or it may have been in Burgoyne's mind for some time, as he claimed later. "Surely," he explained, "there is nothing new or improbable in the idea that a general should disguise his real intentions at the outset of an expedition, even from the officer whom he appointed to execute them, provided a communication with that officer was certain and not remote." This was hostile territory, after all, infested with spies and informers, and it made no sense to take unnecessary security risks.

Despite the baron's misgivings, he was in a jubilant frame of mind, as well he might be considering the army's success to date. Writing to the Duke of Brunswick from Fort Edward on August 8, he boasted that "we are masters of the Hudson." The rebels had abandoned all the advantageous military positions available to them, and it was now possible to put boats on the river and have clear sailing to Albany. Not only that: Washington was said to be retreating before Howe, the rebels in the north were falling back toward Albany, Burgoyne's army was in high spirits, and he expected they would soon surround the enemy and win a decisive victory. Within the week a bridge of rafts would be thrown across the Hudson, enabling the army to be supplied with all those provisions and horses Baum was to bring back. Then the final march on Albany was to begin.

Burgoyne seems not to have examined very carefully the qualifications of the man recommended by Riedesel for this ambitious mission. Friedrich Baum was a capable, conscientious, fifty-year-old professional soldier who began army life as a corporal, saw action in a number of minor engagements in Europe during the Seven Years War, and was given command of this dragoon regiment in 1776. But he had never led more than a few score men into battle, had no experience whatever waging war in the wild lands of America, and, what should have been of great concern, spoke not a word of English. The last shortcoming was to be remedied by the three

Englishmen who went along on his "secret expedition" (a secrecy some-what compromised by the presence of a band of musicians): Captain O'Connell, Lieutenant Durnford, and Philip Skene. Yet with the best of intentions, communications were likely to be cumbersome, since Skene was to talk to the local folk and pass along what they were saying to a German-speaking officer, who would then translate for Baum's benefit. The former British major, who had been an enthusiastic promoter of an expedition such as this, was also to help Baum "distinguish the good sub-jects from the bad," recruit loyalists with whom the countryside was sup-posedly swarming,* and gather intelligence about the enemy.

Baum got off to a slow start. After leaving Fort Edward on the 9th of August and marching to Fort Miller, he was stalled for a day because the Indians assigned to the strike force were reluctant to accompany him and the complement expected from Captain Alexander Fraser's outfit was busy in the vicinity of Stillwater, keeping watch on Schuyler's army. On Burgoyne's orders, Riedesel reluctantly gave Baum a hundred more men from Breymann's corps, and with that the strike force got under way—but not without notice. An indication that security had already been compromised was the entry in Johann Bense's journal noting, "The Dragoons marched off to the dismal place of Bennington today."

After receiving his new instructions, Baum broke camp the following morning at four o'clock, and as usual it was tedious going through the hilly, densely forested land that kept his Indians and Fraser's sharp-shooters alert for an ambush, and it took twelve hours to march the six-teen miles to Cambridge. Like so many roads these men had traveled during the summer, the route that led through Cambridge to Ben-nington was little more than a rough track, honeycombed with roots, ruts, seeps, and soft spots, blocked here and there by giant fallen trees or branches. These roads were almost never wide enough for two-way traffic, let alone marching men and artillery, having been cleared to a width that barely permitted passage of a single farm cart, and the over-arching limbs of pine and spruce kept out the sunlight, leaving them shaded and dank. The dragoons were further hampered by having to struggle along with broadswords described by Lieutenant Hadden as weighing at least ten or twelve pounds.

Along the way Baum's advanced guard ran into forty or fifty rebels

*Skene informed Burgoyne that the ratio of loyalists to rebels was five to one, and the former were only waiting for the appearance of a protective force to come forward.

guarding cattle and took five prisoners before the others escaped. They had a second brush with about fifteen Americans who fired on them, wounded one of Sherwood's men, and then vanished into the woods. From the prisoners and from loyalists fleeing from Bennington Baum learned that the troops there numbered between fifteen hundred and eighteen hundred. That was unsettling news; so was the fact that his Indians brought in some horses, demanded to be paid for them, and when he was unable to give them cash destroyed the animals or drove them away. This was especially galling to Baum and the dragoons, who viewed this expedition as a rare opportunity to acquire mounts.

John Stark and his New Hampshiremen headed down the road from Manchester to Bennington at just about the same time Baum's task force was leaving for the same destination. When Stark arrived he found a growing number of militiamen who had drifted into town from several directions, men wearing clothes of every conceivable description—loose coats "with colors as various as the barks of oak, sumac, and other trees of our hills and swamps could make them," homespun shirts and vests, with smallclothes that fastened below the knee or long linen trousers that reached down to a pair of calfskin shoes ornamented with buckles. Almost all wore a broad-brimmed hat with a round crown. Each man carried a powder horn, a bullet bag, a flask with rum, and a gun, and those weapons were as varied as the colors of their clothing; most were antique English, French, or Spanish firearms. A few of the soldiers carried swords hammered out by a local blacksmith; even fewer had bayonets.

In early August, responding to appeals from Schuyler, the Massachusetts General Court had ordered one-sixth of the state's able-bodied men between the ages of sixteen and fifty, plus what was called the alarm list (all other eligible men up to age sixty-five), to reinforce the Northern Army, and many of these volunteers—especially from Berkshire and Hampshire counties, which were most at risk from Burgoyne's invasion force—had already mustered and marched toward Bennington. Jonas Fay of the Vermont Council of Safety had written on August 13 to colonels of that state's militia requiring them "without a moment's Loss of Time to march one half of the Regiment under your Command" to Bennington. In addition to the local militia companies, troops had come in from nearby Salem, New York, and Pownal, south of Bennington, sent a company,* so

---

*Suggesting how sharply many communities were divided, Pownal also furnished Baum's force with sixty-four men under Samuel Anderson.

that by August 13 Stark could count on about a thousand men, plus Warner's much-reduced Continental regiment stationed at Manchester.*

By this time, Stark was the soul of amiability and cooperation. Writing to Schuyler on August 13, he said, "I join with you in sentiment and shall throw away all private resentment, when put in Ballance with the Good of my Country." His first intimation that the enemy was approaching was word that fifty Indians had come into Cambridge, twelve miles away, and at four that afternoon he sent an express to Schuyler informing him that "a large party are on their march to Cambridge in order to join the above." These, of course, were part of Baum's advanced troops, and Stark sent a reconnaissance force of some two hundred men under Lieutenant Colonel William Gregg to intercept them. Late in the afternoon of August 13, Gregg reached a grist mill at St. Croix—known locally as Sancoick†—about nine miles from Bennington, where he decided to hole up until the enemy appeared.

There they were posted when Baum's force marched into the hamlet at eight o'clock the following morning. Gregg's men cleared out immediately, slipping away in the woods, firing as they withdrew toward Bennington and wounding one Indian, who was patched up by Surgeon Wasmus. It was already hot with the promise of worse to come (one man said they "ran the risk of being suffocated while on the march") when Baum sat down and hurriedly wrote a letter to Burgoyne on the head of a barrel. Repairing the bridge at Sancoick, which had been broken down by the rebels, delayed him for an hour or so, he reported, but the mill had yielded a welcome seventy-eight barrels of excellent flour, twenty barrels of salt, and large quantities of pearl ash and potash, and Skene soon ordered his deputy to put a good miller to work, grinding "as fast as possible without heating the flour," while a cooper made casks in which to carry it. Leaving thirty loyalists and an officer to guard these provisions, Baum said he was proceeding toward Bennington along the course of the Walloomsac River, and he planned to attack at first light on the morning of the 15th. Meantime, he added, "People are flocking in hourly, but want to be armed; the savages cannot be controuled, they

---

*As an indication of how difficult it was for general officers to know how many men they could count on at a given moment, on August 3, Warner's command, so badly mauled at Hubbardton, mustered 23 officers, 5 staff members, 20 noncoms, 10 "Drum and Fife," and 79 rank and file present and fit for duty; 7 men were sick and present, 4 sick and absent, 8 on command, and 1 on furlough. Since that return, 10 had deserted, 1 was discharged, 5 men had joined, and 56 were missing.
†Now North Hoosick, New York.

ruin and take every thing they please." With Skene vouching for those Americans who were "flocking in" to take the oath of allegiance to George III, Baum had no reason to doubt their loyalty, and they were allowed to mingle freely with the soldiers, picking up whatever information they chanced to overhear.

After crossing the bridge by the mill at Sancoick, the Germans rustled some horses from neighboring farms and had another minor skirmish in which a Mohawk chief, bent on looting, got too far ahead of the detachment and was killed. The troops rested here in the gardens behind two houses whose owners were caught loading their furniture on wagons drawn by six oxen. The cattle were appropriated, and a guard was placed on each house to prevent looting, but Wasmus could not help worrying: "it was the habit of the Savages to scalp and demolish everything," he observed. The Indians were so "very grieved and sad" about the loss of the oldest chief, whom they "venerated as their king," that an elaborate impromptu funeral service was arranged during which sixteen dragoons followed a makeshift coffin to the gravesite and fired three volleys, which seemed to mollify the Indians and alarmed the rebels, who thought an attack had begun.

When Gregg's outnumbered force was chased out of the mill he sent word to Stark that he was withdrawing. Stark had already learned by express during the night that a large body of troops was following in the wake of the Indians, so he had his militiamen on the march when he got Gregg's message and sent a call for assistance to Seth Warner and nearby militia companies. But at that it was a near-run thing. About five miles from Bennington they caught sight of Gregg's men with the enemy trotting along less than half a mile behind them, and when Baum spotted the Americans coming at him in force he halted his troops and posted them in what Stark immediately sized up as a strong defensive position.

Understandably, there was a good deal of confusion here. These two little armies had met almost accidentally, neither knowing much about the other's strength or whether more troops were on the way to join them, and they were like two dogs sniffing around, taking the other's measure, and until that was accomplished the sensible thing seemed to be to hang back and see what developed. Both sides were a curious mix of soldiers and skills. On the surface, Baum's corps appeared to have an edge in experience and training, yet although Stark's men were militia a good many were veterans of some rough combat duty—in the French wars, around Boston in '75, and at Trenton and Princeton. On the other hand, both forces also included a number of men and officers who had probably never before heard a shot fired in anger.

Stark was spoiling for a fight but still had no real idea of what he was up against and didn't like the lay of the land where he was, so he pulled back about a mile and encamped. There he called a council of war and determined how they would attack the next morning. Meantime Baum had his patrols out, and it was quickly apparent that the rebels were not going to let them get too close. A sharp exchange of musket fire near the brow of the hill sent the German skirmishers pelting back out of range.

Colonel Baum ordered his three-pounders up to the bridge where the road from Sancoick crossed the Walloomsac, and the Hesse-Hanau gunners quickly scattered a group of rebels who had taken cover in the cluster of houses on the east bank. On the other side of the river Baum seized a steep hill that rose about three hundred feet above the stream and had the cannon dragged partway up the slope so as to command the bridge and the Bennington road. Through the afternoon of the 14th the valley echoed to the sound of scattered gunfire, and Wasmus noted the rebels' technique of fighting: each man stood behind a tree, loaded his musket, shot, and made a dash for another tree, where the process was repeated. The surgeon found himself tending several Indians who had been wounded (another Mohawk was killed), and since they were the only ones hit it seemed as if the Americans, having heard so much about Indian atrocities, were concentrating their fire on them. "The Savages were so enraged about this loss that they wanted to depart for Canada tonight," Wasmus remarked, supposing the Indians probably had acquired enough loot to keep them happy: almost every one had a horse laden with stolen goods.

After the skirmish at the bridge the surgeon stopped to chat with Captain Samuel McKay, who was obviously angry, disgusted by the commanding officer's failure to follow up on this initial scrape with the rebels. "Now they will become bold," McKay predicted; "we leave them too much time, for they will gather by the thousands during the night. I cannot understand how one can entrust a detachment to such a man as Lieutenant Colonel Baum, who has no military expertise at all, cannot take proper measures, particularly here in the wilderness, and who has no knowledge at all of foreign languages."

That was not the end of it. "How is it possible," he growled, "that General Riedesel could entrust such a —— man with such an important expedition, who is so coarse and rude and also despises the counsel of those who had been sent along for guidance, assistance and advice?"

Whether or not McKay realized it, Baum was worried, and worry had made him cautious. The report of those fifteen hundred to eighteen hundred rebels was unnerving, and he decided to hold his ground and ask for reinforcements. That night Wasmus had reason to remember McKay's remarks. Everything was quiet in the camp, the men lay secure behind trees, but incomprehensibly not a sentinel was posted and no pickets were out beyond the lines.

August 15 began with a downpour that continued all day, preventing any general action because of the difficulty of keeping powder dry, but Stark's patrols managed to harass the Germans by sniping at the troops on Baum's right wing. On top of the hill Captain Alexander Fraser, with a fatigue party of loyalists and some of his own British regulars, constructed a three-sided redoubt of logs, shaped like a broad arrowhead, aimed north and west to guard Baum's rear. Here fifty-four of the dragoons were posted. Near the foot of the slope a group of light infantrymen covered a ravine where a small stream flowed into the Walloomsac. About fifteen hundred feet south of them, at the apex of the triangular-shaped hill, about sixty grenadiers and infantrymen kept watch over the two three-pounders, sited in an elevated spot overlooking the bridge and a cluster of houses on the other side of the stream, which were now occupied by some Canadians and Indians. The strongest position, astride the road at the center, was where Baum stationed his best troops, consisting of most of the dragoon regiment, British marksmen, and Brunswick jägers.

Farther south, on the east bank of the stream and about a thousand feet from the bridge, loyalists had constructed another redoubt of fence rails, large enough to hold several hundred of them. More loyalists, backed up by Brunswick grenadiers, took post on the west of Baum's position, where they could protect what little baggage the detachment had brought, plus a growing collection of booty picked up along the route (which now included, among other items, quantities of flour, more than 180 oxen, and a growing number of horses). Wasmus noted with disgust, "The Savages are all lying behind the baggage, dispirited; they do not want to go forward." Nor was that all that troubled the surgeon: throughout the day, he observed, "the inhabitants living around here come and go through our camp; they will surely give the enemy information of our weakness."

While Baum waited for reinforcements and dug in, as if for a siege, he got word from Burgoyne warning that if the rebels appeared in such strength as to make it impossible to attack them, Baum was to take a defensible post and sit tight until the general supported him or ordered him to withdraw. That left it to the colonel to decide whether he should proceed as planned or await further orders, and he elected to stay where he was. But it was questionable whether the lieutenant colonel had chosen the right place to make a stand in case he had to do so. His men were scattered about, widely separated, making it possible for attackers to deal piecemeal with each unit. He had not even visited the dragoon redoubt and had no firsthand knowledge of how difficult it might be to communicate with the men there, let alone come to their aid if need be.

It is entirely possible that Baum elected to occupy this hill temporarily—not as an ideal defensive position, but as a reasonably safe place to spend the night—on the assumption that reinforcements would soon come up and the combined forces would then march on Bennington.

Burgoyne reacted quickly to Baum's request for support and sent his aide Sir Francis Clerke to Riedesel that night requesting him to order Lieutenant Colonel Heinrich Breymann to reinforce Baum immediately. Riedesel didn't like the smell of what was going on here: he sensed that Baum's position was precarious and he wanted him withdrawn so that Baum and Breymann could join forces and act together as circumstances dictated. The baron said as much to Clerke, adding that if Burgoyne insisted on carrying out his plan, he washed his hands of the matter, and then, rather than issue the orders to Breymann himself, he sent Captain Gerlach to obtain them from Burgoyne.

Why Burgoyne chose Breymann for this assignment was as puzzling as his choice of Baum. The Brunswickers—especially Breymann's heavily equipped grenadiers—were notoriously slow marchers, besides which Breymann was widely known as a bully and there was reputedly bad blood between him and Baum. Perhaps Burgoyne was not aware of that or perhaps, as he admitted later, he was unwilling to commit his best British troops to a secondary movement. Whatever the case, he dispatched Captain Gerlach to Breymann's tent with orders that had no sense of urgency and left the colonel free to attack or not after he joined forces with Baum. To the latter he sent word that help was on the way.

Breymann's corps consisted of a company of riflemen, a battalion of light infantry and grenadiers, and two six-pound cannon, and at 9:00 A.M. on the 15th they were under way. But as with Baum, nothing about the march was easy: soaked to the skin, they slogged through torrential rain and waded the Batten Kill, dragging the cannon up one hill after another. The ammunition wagons turned turtle and "the bottomless roads . . . made the march so tedious that I could scarcely make one-half of an English mile an hour," Breymann explained. To make matters worse, his guide lost the way and couldn't find the road again, so instead of reaching Cambridge, from which it was a fairly easy march to Baum's position, he encamped seven miles short of that community and sent a message to Baum giving his whereabouts. Baum received the letter at eleven that night and told Skene to send horses and wagons to expedite Breymann's movement.

Rain continued to fall through the night, and dawn brought an eerie silence to the hills and valley. Baum took advantage of the respite to dispatch a hundred oxen to Burgoyne and sent out patrols, but there was no sign of a rebel anywhere—not even an hour's march away, according to his scouts (who must have been looking in the wrong direction). Meanwhile, more horses had been collected—almost enough to mount the regiment of dragoons—and the news that Breymann's relief force was on the way was a tonic for the Brunswickers. They needed a lift: Stark's skirmishers—mostly veterans of the French and Indian War—had done deadly work the previous day in spite of the inclement weather. "Every 40 paces a man is standing behind a tree," Wasmus wrote in amazement, and during the day thirty Canadians and Indians were shot, including two chiefs whose silver ornaments were taken from their bodies and displayed as trophies in the rebel camp.

By now Stark had a lot more information about the enemy—intelligence brought in by his patrols and by those local inhabitants rightly suspected by Wasmus of providing the rebel command with details about Baum's defenses. He also had more men—mostly militia companies from Vermont and Berkshire County, including a Pittsfield contingent led by the fire-eating pastor Thomas Allen, who had been so critical of St. Clair's evacuation of Ticonderoga. The clergyman had come into camp during the night complaining to the general that if the Massachusetts militia didn't get to fight they would never answer another call to arms. Stark told him to get some rest: if the Lord sent sunshine the following day and they did not get fighting enough to suit them, he would never call on them again.

That same evening a steady procession of men passed Sally Kellogg's house near Bennington. It was dusk, and she noticed that they were hurrying—moving at a dog trot, pausing only long enough to drink from pails of water her mother had drawn for them. Sally's family had seen its share of war this past year. Before moving to Bennington they had lived north of Crown Point on the Vermont side of Lake Champlain, and when they saw Benedict Arnold's shattered fleet trying to escape the enemy's guns they knew they had better clear out. They threw their belongings into a bateau and headed south, only to be caught between Arnold's ships and the British. By some miracle they narrowly escaped, fleeing to Mount Independence and then to Bennington, where they reckoned they would be safe. Then her father volunteered to serve with Stark, and now he and the others were trailing through town, heading where the fighting was sure to take place.

When the sun broke through the clouds on the morning of August 16, Stark began putting his plan into action by dividing the army into three divisions. The New Hampshireman had served under Abercromby in 1758 when the British general sent rank after rank of redcoats in a frontal assault on the French, who were solidly entrenched outside Fort Ticonderoga, and he had no intention of repeating that ghastly mistake, where almost 15 percent of the attackers were mowed down. He knew that Baum's men had made the most of the rainy day to lay up logs and dig trenches, and Stark's idea was to take advantage of his own superior numbers by hitting the enemy on all sides at once.

He suspected that the isolated dragoon redoubt, held by a relative handful of men, was vulnerable, and he planned to take it with a pincer movement. Lieutenant Colonel Moses Nichols of New Hampshire was to lead 250 men around to the rear of the enemy's left wing, while Colonel Samuel Herrick, a Vermonter, and 300 soldiers would wade the Walloomsac, cross the Bennington road, and fan out in a wide arc to the south, screened by a long, wooded ridge, and after recrossing the river, steal up the protected valley of Little White Creek to a position within earshot of Nichols's destination. At the same time another detachment under Colonels Thomas Stickney and David Hobart, both New Hampshiremen, had the job of assaulting the loyalist redoubt, while the remainder of Stark's force—some 300 men—were to storm the enemy center in a frontal attack.

This encircling maneuver required three divisions to go into action simultaneously, and while it was a good plan it was tricky to execute, even by units accustomed to working together—which these men were not. Everything would hinge on timing, discipline, and the element of surprise.

As John Stark knew, something besides tactics accounts for military success, and chances are he gave his officers a "short but animated address" as he had done at Bunker Hill. Whatever else he may have said, the remark men attributed to him long afterward was "There are the redcoats and they are ours, or Molly Stark sleeps a widow tonight."

Chapter 16

A Continual Clap of Thunder

Seventeen-year-old David Holbrook was one of the Berkshire County men who signed up "to serve until duly discharged." Early in June he and about thirty others followed Lieutenant William White to Bennington, and after serving guard duty on the storehouses there they hiked to Manchester and on to Pawlet to protect arms stored at Willard's Tavern.

A month later they hit out to join St. Clair. But as they approached Skenesborough they discovered that Burgoyne's army was between them and their destination, so after a skirmish with British troops and a wild chase through the forest around Wood Creek, they made their way back to Pawlet. That's when Holbrook gave out: he was sick, was granted a furlough, and went home, where he received word on August 14 that troops were urgently needed in Bennington. He took off at once with Captain Enos Parker's company.

Thomas Mellen's outfit had been ordered south from Manchester when the Brunswickers were approaching, and they marched that Friday, August 15, through the rain, mud, and darkness, camping outside Bennington. Mellen and a friend bedded down in a haymow, slept until the chickens woke them, and found some bread and milk before hurrying west to join Stark's main body.

After a day spent patrolling enemy lines, David Holbrook's company was part of the three-hundred-man force under Colonel Herrick that took a circuitous route of six miles across country on Saturday morning, circling around Baum's right flank to come up in a wooded area at the rear of the enemy, where they waited silently, undetected, for the firing of two muskets that signaled an attack.

Inside the dragoon redoubt, just beyond Herrick's hidden men, Major von Meibom was uneasy. He was isolated up there on the crest of the hill and had to depend on messages from a variety of sources, none of them close at hand, all of them delayed by the steep hill and thick underbrush. That morning, when his patrols brought back reports of numerous rebels moving through the trees, he requested that a cannon be brought to the redoubt. Baum knew that his Indians were out there in the woods keeping an eye on the rebels, and he had been assured that the men Meibom took for rebels were actually loyalists, so he had very little sympathy with the major's case of nerves. But he sent the fieldpiece anyway, with the starchy comment that a few rebels did not mean that a regiment was approaching.

Julius Wasmus was at the redoubt and had spotted the Indians nearby, but word reached the dragoons that they refused to attack the rebels. (The traditional European battle formations and reliance on defensive works had absolutely no appeal for these warriors, who preferred to conceal themselves and rely on stealth and surprise, not head-on confrontation.) Fortunately for the dragoons' peace of mind, news reached them that Breymann's corps was nearby and would soon join them, although Wasmus commented wistfully, "Everyone wished they were here already."

Stark's plan called for Lieutenant Colonel Nichols to launch the assault on the dragoon redoubts when everyone was in position, triggering an advance on all three fronts, but Nichols wasn't sure he had enough men and requested reinforcements. Stark sent him one hundred more troops, bringing the combined strength of Nichols and Herrick to more then six hundred, and at precisely three o'clock they moved forward. As soon as Meibom's scouts saw them coming they raced for the redoubt, shouting that the rebels were attacking from two directions, and suddenly "a violent volley of fire erupted against the entrenchment." Herrick's men burst out of the woods and were within ten or twelve rods of the Brunswickers before opening fire from behind trees and fallen logs; then they reloaded, advanced, and let loose again. John Stark, who was no stranger to the sounds of battle, described the furious salvos of muskets and cannon as "the hottest engagement I have ever witnessed, resembling a continual clap of thunder."

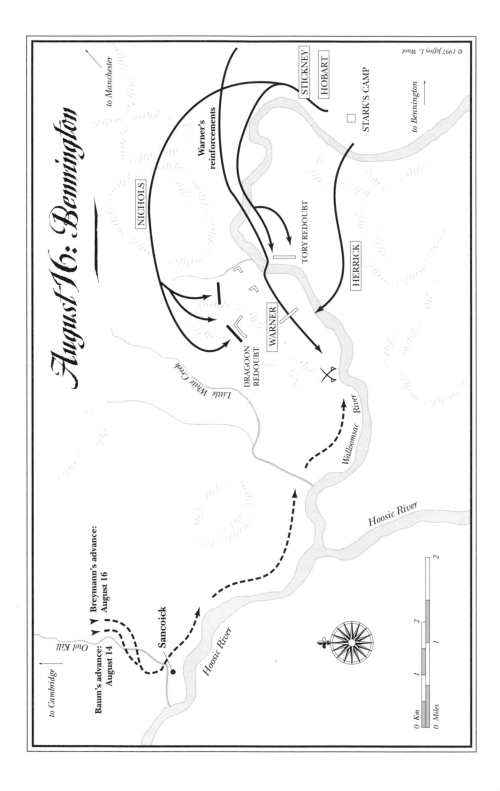

August 16: Bennington

© 1997 Jeffry L. Ward

to Manchester

to Bennington

STICKNEY

HOBART

STARK'S CAMP

Warner's reinforcements

NICHOLS

TORY REDOUBT

HERRICK

WARNER

DRAGOON REDOUBT

Little White Creek

Walloomsac River

Hoosic River

Breymann's advance: August 16

Baum's advance: August 14

Sancoick

Owl Kill

to Cambridge

Hoosic River

0 Km   1   2

0 Miles   1   2

The dragoon redoubt was sited on a large knob at the top of the hill, and even though Herrick and Nichols were coming at it from two directions and vastly outnumbered the defenders, they found it very tough going indeed. One rebel said the dragoons "fired by platoons and were soon covered with smoke," and those volleys tore holes in the lines of advancing men. Yet each time the Brunswickers reloaded and took aim they were blasted by rebel musket fire, and in short order the "tallest and best dragoons were sent into eternity." German gunners were firing balls and grapeshot to left and right, the Indians "made terrible faces and ran from one tree to the next," and within a matter of minutes Americans were inside the redoubt, using their guns as clubs and lunging with bayonets. It was bedlam with the deafening slam of muskets at close quarters, men screaming, shouting, and cursing, and suddenly the Germans were struggling desperately to get out before they were slaughtered. Down the steep hill they plunged with the rebels only a few yards behind, and on this hot day the footrace was no contest between the dragoons in their thick wool uniforms and the Americans, most of whom wore light shirts and trousers.

A number of dragoons were shot in the redoubt, others as they raced downhill, and once they started running, a rebel said, "there was no regular battle—all was confusion—a party of our men would attack and kill or take prisoners. . . . Every man seemed to manage for himself" in a free-for-all that resembled mob violence more than any organized attack. It did not take long. Captain Peter Clark said the battle lasted half an hour "and was equal to Bunker Hill excepting there was not so many cannon." He remarked of the Germans, "The Lord of Hosts sent them off in such haste they left their all and run. . . ."

Julius Wasmus found shelter of a sort behind a huge oak tree at the rear of the redoubt, where he did his best to dress wounds. Four or five Indians crowded around him, but when the American fire intensified one of them made an indescribably strange cry and they all raced downhill toward the baggage park.

From David Holbrook's vantage point it was impossible to tell what was going on in the rest of the field; he only knew that it was bedlam inside the redoubt as the fight that began with some intricate maneuvering turned into desperate hand-to-hand combat. When his line reached the enemy barricade he put his right hand on top of the breastwork, but as he vaulted up and over a bayonet pinned his right leg and he pitched headfirst into the dirt, where a German soldier clubbed him in the head. The American behind Holbrook shot the dragoon, and in the violence of battle Holbrook completely forgot that he was wounded.

The cannon in the dragoon redoubt fell silent: the sergeant in charge ˘ was shot dead, eight other men serving the piece were killed or wounded, and time ran out for Wasmus and the other survivors. With their ammunition exhausted, the small garrison was simply overwhelmed, so Wasmus finally quit trying to bind wounds and scampered for safety with the others. He stumbled over a fallen oak and as he picked himself up, rebels fired at him, and he dropped to the ground with bullets whistling around him.

Two Americans approached, and as one pulled him to his feet the other stuck the point of his bayonet against the Brunswicker's chest and said he would kill him. "Are you Britisher or Hessian?" the man asked, to which Wasmus replied in German that he was a surgeon and then made the disarming gesture of holding out his hand and saying he was a *Freund und Bruder*, which the rebels fortunately comprehended. One of them took his watch and put it in his pocket, then offered him a drink of rum from the wooden flask around his neck. Several other soldiers came up, searched his pockets, and made off with his purse, which contained only a few coins, his knife, and writing paper. Then they made him sit on the ground, where he listened to the firing that continued down near the bridge and worried that he might be the only prisoner.

A middle-aged American, hearing that Wasmus was a surgeon, asked him to come and treat his son, who was wounded in the thigh, and when the German reached the young man and looked around he could see the terrible damage inflicted by the dragoons before they were overpowered. General Stark came up while the doctor was bandaging his patient and told him to treat the other Americans as well, but Wasmus soon hurried off to tend his own wounded, who were crying for help. Before he could reach them he was seized and dragged back to deal with the American casualties. He was overjoyed to find his surgical implements and bandages beside the great oak tree, but an American took those from him and urged him to drink some rum. All the rebels, he noticed, were well provided with strong drink, which they swigged from wooden flasks, and by now almost all those around him were drunk. He also noticed how healthy and husky they were—much more so than the Canadians he had seen—but he couldn't get his mind off those Brunswickers up at the redoubt bleeding to death with no one to answer their cries of agony.

Down on the flats along the river the prisoners were herded together and sent off under guard to Bennington while the victorious militiamen scattered across the area, "some resting and refreshing themselves, some looking up the dead and wounded, and others in pursuit of plunder," according to Jesse Field, who had been with Colonel Herrick in the surprise attack on the redoubt.

On other fronts the rebels were also closing in. Captain Dommes and his men, who were covering the ravine where the small brook joined the river, were driven back and captured, and Seth Warner directed a captain named Stafford, from western Massachusetts, to attack the loyalist redoubt. Within the raw earthworks, perched behind such a high bank that they felt perfectly safe, as many as 250 men were dug in, including Lieutenant Colonel John Peters's Queen's Loyal Rangers and the men Francis Pfister had collected around Cambridge. Peters had managed to raise 600 men before and during Burgoyne's advance from Canada, and they had seen a lot of rough duty. Not only had they fought in every skirmish except Hubbardton, but because they were attached to Alexander Fraser's advance party, Peters said, they were killed off almost as fast as he could muster new recruits, and now only about 150 remained. But the worst test was yet to come, and while Peters was prepared psychologically for what was ahead, his physical condition was far from good. For some time he had suffered from fever and chills and was lame from a wound he had taken in the skirmish the previous day.

When Stafford's collection of militia companies stepped off toward the loyalist redoubt, the captain noticed that an old man was present—a slender fellow, "stooping a little with advanced age and hard work, with a wrinkled face, and well known as one of the oldest persons in our town." There was no telling what lay ahead when they reached that redoubt, but Stafford knew it was no place for an aged man, and he told him to stay where he was and keep watch over the baggage. At that the old-timer came forward, smiling, pulled off his hat exposing "loose hair [that] shone as white as silver," and replied, "Not till I've had a shot at them first, captain, if you please." A cheer went up from the others, and off they went with the old man marching along.

Stafford noticed that a ravine running along the bottom of the hill would screen him from the enemy almost all the way to their position. The loyalists hadn't realized that the gully was long and deep enough to conceal attackers, nor was Stafford aware that instead of terminating at a distance from the loyalists, the ravine ended directly below their redoubt, so both parties were surprised when the rebels emerged to find the startled Tories peering down at them. Stafford was in the lead when the first shots were fired, and as he turned to order the charge he fell, not knowing quite why. Then he saw that a musket ball had gone through one foot, and as a man ran to help him he jumped up, saw a red-coated figure racing across a distant field, and shouted, "Come on, boys! They run! They run!" And suddenly the hotheaded preacher Thomas Allen appeared at the breastworks demanding that the enemy surrender in the name of the Congress, which was greeted by another volley, and with that the men scrambled up to the earthworks and leaped over before the loyalists could reload.

A former neighbor and friend of Stafford's was one of those who shot at him, and the man said later that he took as careful aim "as I ever did at a bird in my life." When he saw Stafford fall he was dumbfounded to see him get up and figured he missed because he was forced to fire straight down at men climbing up the hill and they made very small targets.

When Peters saw the rebels approach he caught a glimpse of a man taking aim at him. Reacting immediately, he fired, but the rebel reloaded, ran closer, and discharged his musket again, shouting as he rushed forward, "Peters, you damned Tory. I have got you!" and bayoneted Peters just below the left breast as he finished reloading his weapon. By this time the loyalist commander had recognized his foe as "a rebel Captain, Jeremiah Post by name, an old schoolmate and playfellow, and a cousin of my wife." Those relationships might have counted for something at one time, but not now, and when Peters fired, "though his bayonet was in my body I felt regret at being obliged to destroy him."

These violent encounters between neighbors were common on this day, when so many local men of opposite persuasions, despising the other's political sympathies, came up against one another in what was really an accidental battle. Despite the cacophony of cannon fired every half-minute and the shouts and chaos of the fight, Joseph Rudd somehow recognized four or five fellow townsmen fighting on the other side—"the bigger part of Dutch Hosack was in the battle against us," he felt certain. Those men had joined the task force a day or so before the engagement, as had one Samuel Anderson, another man he knew.

Routed and pursued by the rebels, the loyalists ran for their lives toward the river, where a number of them were shot in the water and others were captured. Francis Pfister was one of the casualties, along with 120 of his men who were killed, wounded, or taken prisoner. Peters escaped—Post's bayonet had been deflected by his ribs, so his wound was not serious—but his corps lost 75 percent of the men he had mustered before the engagement.

John Stark was calling the tune for this battle, and his tactics worked spectacularly well, with his men deployed in such a way that Baum's outnumbered soldiers had almost no way to escape once the trap had been sprung. But the action was far from over.

Unfortunately for the Brunswickers, after the dragoon and loyalist redoubts fell, probably five or six hundred Americans were freed to join the assault on Baum. So again the Germans were outnumbered, by about two and a half to one in this case. Baum had withdrawn his remaining cannon in order to protect his left flank, which meant that it no longer covered the bridge across which rebels were advancing.

They were coming on fast now and in great numbers, swarming forward to within eight paces of the Brunswickers to fire at almost point-blank range, but twice the defenders held them off with their disciplined volleys, forcing them to withdraw. Then the Germans' ammunition was gone, there was no more powder for the cannon, and the rebels came pouring over the defenses. For a brief moment Baum and his dragoons stopped them; the colonel shouted to his men to sling their muskets, and they slashed at the rebels with swords or stabbed frantically with bayonets, trying futilely to hack their way through the crowd of shouting rebels pressing in on them, but the disparity in numbers was too great, and the Brunswickers who were not killed or wounded took to their heels.

South of the bridge the Walloomsac makes a sharp turn to the west, and between the river and the hill that anchored Baum's defenses was a large, rectangular field. Some of the dragoons, including Baum himself, made it to the meadow, but before they could reach the stream they were surrounded and Lieutenant Colonel Baum fell, badly wounded in the abdomen.

When Wasmus's captor took the surgeon to the foot of the hill where Baum had stood, the colonel was nowhere to be seen—nothing but dead bodies floating in the river and a long line of loyalists who, "like cattle, were tied to each other with cords and ropes and led away," presumably to be hanged. Then he and the man he called his "guide" headed down the road toward Bennington and about two miles from the bridge came upon Baum, lying in a wagon, "crying and begging that the cart should go slow," but his captors understood no German, they were in a hurry, and they took him to a nearby house and laid him on a dirt floor. Wasmus and another surgeon followed them inside and Baum directed that one of them should stay with him, but the guard refused, permitting them only to shake Baum's hand in farewell and listen to his last messages for Riedesel and someone in Brunswick before the rebel shoved the doctors out the door and sent them reluctantly on their way.

Breymann had set out early on the morning of August 16 after receiving a message from Baum urging him to come up, but he was a stickler for discipline and halted every now and then to have his soldiers dress ranks. His progress was also delayed because the horses pulling his artillery were weak from hunger, so he sent Major von Barner ahead with the advance guard to find fresh horses and wagons. These didn't show up until just before noon, when the Germans resumed their march. For two miles below Cambridge the valley is wide and flat; then the road climbs one hill after another, making for difficult marching and even more difficult hauling of wagons and heavy guns, with the result that Breymann's troops were strung out all over the landscape and he had to call yet another halt to reassemble his columns. It was close to two in the afternoon when two men rode up with a message from Skene, urging Breymann to detach an officer and twenty men to occupy the mill at Sancoick to prevent the rebels from taking it. The colonel took no chances: he sent Captain von Gleisenberg with an advanced guard of sixty grenadiers and chasseurs plus a score of jägers, saying he would follow as quickly as possible. But once again some of the ammunition wagons broke down, and his men plodded along at a snail's pace.

Whatever lay behind Breymann's laggardly march—whether his troops were congenitally incapable of rapid movement, whether he had no desire to hasten to the rescue of a man he disliked, whether a poor road was to blame—what happened was a classic example of a junior officer fearful that caution might be mistaken for timidity, with a resulting failure to communicate in simple, direct, and exact terms. Nothing in Baum's confident message of August 14 to Burgoyne had suggested the need—urgent or otherwise—for reinforcements. The sole hint of what might lie ahead was a reference to the presence of fifteen to eighteen hundred rebels in Bennington, but any threat they might pose was passed off with the prediction that they "are supposed to leave it on our approach," followed by Baum's statement that he intended to attack the Americans early the following morning. That resulted in a letter from Burgoyne's aide-de-camp, Sir Francis Carr Clerke, to Breymann that lacked any sense of foreboding or the need for speed. On the contrary, ". . . in consequence of the good news [Burgoyne] has this moment received from Lieutenant Colonel Baum," he wrote, "he would be very glad—providing there be not too much risk—if his design in regard to the expedition could be carried out." And whether or not Breymann was to implement that vague "design" was left to the colonel and his "talents to do that which you consider best."

Major von Barner joined Gleisenberg at the mill in Sancoick, and he was about to push on with the little detachment when Skene came up and begged him "to be cool and wait" for Breymann. As the colonel rode into the little crossroads community at the head of his troops and met Skene and the others it was four-thirty in the afternoon, which meant that he had marched less than one mile an hour—the same rate as the day before—on this relief mission, and nothing he saw now altered his earlier sense that all was well. No rebels were in sight, and the Brunswicker reported later that he heard nothing to indicate that a battle was being waged in the vicinity (a statement that seems improbable, to say the least, since the scene of action was only two miles away and the fighting had reached a peak of intensity at that moment).

Just then a loyalist refugee from the battle appeared with news that Baum was cut off, but Skene refused to believe him because of what happened next. Captain Campbell and some Indians showed up—they had been circling around toward the rebel rear, hoping to take the Americans by surprise, when they were caught between two fires and barely managed to escape. But despite this close call, Skene said, Campbell told the assembled officers that "things were not so bad." (It may be that Breymann and Skene were covering for themselves: the former was justifying his actions in a later report to General Riedesel, the latter in a letter to Lord Dartmouth, Germain's predecessor as secretary for the colonies. Yet Campbell insisted he had informed Breymann—"in as good French as I was master of"—that Baum had been attacked and told him the hour and minute it had occurred.)

Whatever the case, Breymann—not realizing that the battle up ahead was now over—decided to join Baum at once and asked Skene to take six chasseurs and lead the way. Before this little advance party had gone a thousand yards, Skene spotted a small body of Americans at the end of a post-and-rail fence up ahead. Some wore shirts, others jackets, and he couldn't tell if they were loyalists or rebels, but since they had white feathers or bits of white paper in their hats he decided they were friendly and kicked his horse into a gallop. About a hundred yards from them he shouted, "Are you for King George?" and received a ragged volley from their muskets—one shot hitting his horse, but missing him. The chasseurs charged ahead far enough to return the rebels' fire, and von Barner led some two hundred light troops to a hill on the left and drove the rebels back. Meanwhile Breymann ordered his two cannon to a post on the right flank near a log house, from which they opened on the Americans. As they did so, the grenadiers ran up and took position in the center, completing Breymann's line.

At about the time the Germans were forming their line of battle, Colonel Herrick caught sight of David Holbrook and another man and ordered them to follow him toward Sancoick. When they sighted Breymann's approaching troops the colonel wheeled around and galloped off to alert Stark while Holbrook and his buddy hid behind a haystack until the enemy came closer, when they took one shot at them and ran.

Stark's troops were pretty well used up by now, having fought Baum's detachment for two hours or more. These men were drained emotionally and physically, many of them had been drinking heavily, as Wasmus noted, others were scattered over the battleground hunting for loot— German muskets and swords, dragoon helmets, boots, gorgets, whatever came to hand. So it was surprising that enough militia remained even to form a skirmish line along the edge of a wood adjacent to the meadow in which the Germans were posted. Musketry was heavy now on both sides, the cannon were firing grapeshot, and Breymann was out in front of his men, leading them forward as the outnumbered rebels fell back, dodging from tree to tree.

Seth Warner's Green Mountain Boys, under the command of Major Samuel Safford, had tramped down the road from Manchester in the driving rain on August 15, camped near Bennington village near midnight, and spent most of the next morning drying out their clothes and equipment. They were also short of ammunition, and by the time they were prepared to march it was noon or a little later. Two miles from Bennington they could hear scattered musket fire up ahead; then they halted at Stark's campground, where they left their coats and knapsacks and each man received four ounces of rum with water. By now the heat of the day was intense, and shortly after they reached the river and paused for a drink the gunfire ahead suddenly became much heavier. As they hurried forward they began to meet wounded men heading for the rear. Farther on they could see Baum's Germans pelting down the hill with the rebels in hot pursuit. By the time they reached the bridge the battle here was over, but just then Warner rode up, saying the militia were in trouble and his men were to come on at the double.

Returning to the front Warner found that the militia were indeed in a bad way. Pleading with them to hold their ground, he promised that reinforcements would arrive in ten minutes, though where that support was to come from he didn't know, since his own troops probably couldn't arrive in less than an hour. Haring off on a shortcut to the rear, he ran into a detachment of mounted militia led by an elderly major named Rand. Warner told the major to have his men dismount and leave their horses behind, out of gunshot range, adding—disingenuously, since he had just seen the reverse to be true—that the enemy would be beaten by the time Rand reached the scene and that he should hang on their rear. "Your men are fresh," he went on, "and [the Germans] are tired by a long march and we will have a fine parcel of them." With that he kicked his horse into a gallop and returned to his regiment.

Unaccountably, Breymann's grenadiers failed to advance on the rebels but continued to shoot at them with no effect whatever, since they were beyond musket range. Even so, Stark's men were in serious trouble: the two German six-pounders were in action, firing round after round of grapeshot, driving the Americans back to a log fence near a ravine. The Brunswick infantrymen were about a hundred yards away, closing in, and were on the verge of outflanking the militiamen. Luckily, soldiers from all over the battlefield where Baum had been defeated heard the firing and started to run in that direction. One of them was Silas Walbridge, a Bennington man who had walked back up the hill with Captain John Warner to look for wounded after the battle. While the two of them were there they heard gunfire off toward Sancoick, and as they ran toward the sound of the fighting found themselves with scores of men as confused as they were, all from different units coming from different directions. This was no orderly advance: some officers were ordering men forward, shouting, "Give it to 'em," others were calling them to retreat, and it was clear that the officers knew no more about what was happening than anyone else did.

David Holbrook looked up to see "an old man with an old Queen Anne's sword ... mounted upon an old black mare," wearing a hat cocked up as sharp as if he were going to Sunday meeting, leading what looked to be ninety "robust men following him in files two deep." The old-timer was Major John Rand, who had brought his command all the way from Worcester County, Massachusetts, just in time to be ordered forward by Seth Warner. Rand's men quickly began to fill in the gaps between the hard-pressed men of Captain Parker's company, where they found themselves in the middle of the roughest fight they could have wanted. Warner soon reappeared and found Rand "as calm as if he was about his work on his farm," and heard the major shout, "Why, colonel, you told me to hang on the rear; but I can't find any rear—it's all front here: why, I never see such hot work in my life!"

Warner saw that the major's old mare was shot through the nose, with blood spurting out both sides, and a moment later a musket ball hit her in the rump. "Why, major," he yelled, "they give it to you bow and stern, do they?"

About then Holbrook heard a tremendous crash in the woods at the right wing, followed by the most terrible yell he had ever heard and Warner's voice like thunder: "Fix bayonets! *Charge!*" Rand's wounded mare fell to the ground, and the old major jumped up on a stump and yelled, "Charge, boys!" His men and Warner's, some with and some without bayonets, rushed at the Germans, who suddenly turned and ran. The rebels pounded after them, overrunning one of the Brunswickers' fieldpieces just as it was about to be fired; a sergeant knocked down the gunner, caught hold of the limber, whirled it around, and opened up on the retreating enemy, mowing down a number of them before they were ten rods away.

When Warner's Vermonters materialized, plunging into the melee at the crucial moment, the Brunswickers had all but exhausted their ammunition, and their drummers beat a parley. But as Thomas Mellen recalled, the rebels did not understand it and pursued the frantic grenadiers, who were in full flight down the road and thrashing about in the woods, where many caught their scabbards in the thick brush and were soon captured.

One man who was in the thick of things was the Pittsfield parson Thomas Allen, who had come into Stark's camp demanding action. Clearly he got it, since Allen regarded the victory as "equal to any that has happened during the present controversy." When he returned home someone asked the minister if he had killed anyone at Bennington, and his reply was uncharacteristically oblique. He said he had observed the flash of a musket that was fired repeatedly from behind a certain bush, and noticed that one of Stark's men fell after most of those shots. No, he couldn't say whether he had killed anyone, but he did know "he fired that way and put the flash out."

John Stark described the battle as "very warm and desperate," and while saying that had his men "been Alexanders or Charleses of Sweden, they could not have behaved better," he also credited the victory to the capture of the enemy guns: "We used their cannon against them," he reported, "which proved of great service to us . . . [and] pursued them till dark, when I was obliged to halt for fear of killing our men." All four Brunswick brass cannon were prizes, as were quantities of baggage, and a number of horses and wagons. Twenty of Breymann's men were dead, 140 of them prisoners, and "had daylight lasted one hour longer," Stark wrote, "we should have taken the whole body of them." As it was, "we have returned the enemy a proper compliment for their Hubbardton engagement."

Thomas Mellen was helping to drag one of the captured guns when Seth Warner rode up and someone told him his brother was dead by the side of the road.

"Is it Jesse?" Warner asked, and when a voice replied, "Yes," he leaped from his horse, "gazed in the dead man's face and then rode away without saying a word."

Philip Skene laid the blame for the debacle on Breymann's grenadiers, who never closed with the Americans "but continued flinging away their Ammunition at too great a distance," adding that victory was in their grasp had the grenadiers been quicker to march and keep up with the left and right wings. Skene claimed he did what he could to remedy the situation: as the sun was setting he galloped to the ammunition wagon and had it brought forward, but he was too late—there was no halting the flight of Breymann's men by then. The Brunswick colonel was not with them, Skene realized, so he "took the Liberty of halting them at the Mills of Sancoick."

The reason Breymann did not appear was that he had lagged behind, trying desperately to organize a detail to bring off his two cannon, but the artillery horses were all dead or wounded and so many of the troops were severely cut up in the attempted rescue that he was forced to abandon the guns. It was a painful loss (more so than that of his men, to judge from the way he spoke of it); he told Riedesel he would have given his life to avoid it,* but there was no recapturing them under the withering fire from the mob of rebels, and there was nothing more he could do but head for Sancoick as darkness enveloped the valley. He was the last man to come in. Skene supervised the destruction of the bridge,

*He very nearly did: his coat had five bullet holes in it and he was wounded in one leg.

all the wounded who could be found were rounded up, and after he and Breymann conferred for half an hour or so, the beaten, thoroughly demoralized detachment headed off on the road to Cambridge, where they arrived near midnight.

Somehow in his letter to Lord Dartmouth, Philip Skene managed to cast the engagement in a light that was favorable to Philip Skene. He had been "Commissioner of Supplies," he said, charged with providing wagons, and had brought off the wounded and baggage—"even to all the knapsacks"—in the retreat to Cambridge. The rebels, he gloated, had "retreated during the night to Bennington"; they had lost a great many men and some officers and failed to pursue Breymann. Baum's loss, he went on, had occurred while he, Skene, was behind on some business, and although the dragoon commander had taken a strong position and covered the ground advantageously, he made the mistake of dividing his force in such a way that his defenses were weakened.

"I had no military command," Skene continued in a martyred tone, "but shall have my share of censure for what should be as well as what was not." Yet he knew, as did others who were there, that it was he who had failed to recognize the locals as rebels and spies, not as loyalists coming to join the Brunswickers, but he laid this misunderstanding to Burgoyne's manifesto inviting "Inhabitants to return to their duty and take the Oath of Allegiance. . . ."

What Skene did not admit in his letter was the extent of the disaster. Between nine hundred and a thousand men had been lost—killed, wounded, captured, missing—and it might have been worse had darkness not prevented further American pursuit. For Burgoyne, whose only means of augmenting his army was to hope more loyalists would join him, to lose nearly 15 percent of the professional soldiers he had brought from Canada was calamitous, and while his private secretary described the result of the battle as a "check," the commander knew better. Only seven dragoons returned to the army, and that regiment was left with a mere eighty men—a camp guard, a few sick, and others who had remained behind.

While Baum was skirmishing with the rebels at Sancoick on August 14, Brigadier Simon Fraser's advanced guard began building a bridge of rafts across the Hudson to enable Burgoyne's army (and the horses and provisions Baum was expected to bring from Bennington) to cross to the west bank. Work was completed on the 16th, the day of the battle, and

Fraser established a post on the far side from which he could thrust south toward Albany ahead of the main body. Burgoyne had made some other changes in the disposition of his troops. Major Hille noted that "the dignified Brigadier Hamilton" had exchanged places with "the not very refined Brigadier Powell," with the latter taking over the command at Ticonderoga while Hamilton would march with the army.

Meanwhile, stores at Skenesborough were moved forward to Fort Edward and at 9:00 that evening orders were passed instructing the troops to move out at 6:00 A.M., cross the Hudson, and go into camp near Saratoga. In the morning, however, with the entire army standing under arms ready to march, word of Baum's defeat arrived. Skene had sent a letter to Burgoyne sometime during the night, and Lanaudière, who had escaped unharmed, confirmed the news orally. It was, Lieutenant Colonel Specht observed unhappily, "one of those sad events often caused by the changing fortunes of war." Lanaudière had few details to offer except that Baum and Lieutenants Bach and Durnford had been wounded and captured, and a large number of soldiers remained on the field of battle, lost somewhere in the thicket of woods and underbrush, dead or dying of their wounds. (Two weeks after the fight, Peter Clark said, scouts were still finding bodies in the forest— twenty-six of them on one day.) The Canadian also reported that Breymann's relief column had had a heated exchange with the enemy, but beyond that nothing was known.

Until he obtained further intelligence, Burgoyne had no choice but to go to Breymann's support, so the army, instead of crossing the Hudson, headed toward the Batten Kill. They had gone only a few miles when further information was received, indicating that Breymann was safe and on his way to rejoin the main body, so Burgoyne ordered the troops back to camp except for the 47th Regiment, which he led off to meet Breymann. At four in the afternoon Breymann's corps returned, "extremely weak and exhausted," according to Specht, and as the details of the engagement emerged, it was clear that the battle had been devastating for the Brunswickers. That evening and through the night, stragglers found their way back to camp—many of them wounded, all of them worn out—and they added bits and pieces of information to the catalogue of disaster: Captain von Schieck left on the battlefield, as were Lieutenants Muhlenfeld, Meyer, Gebhard, and d'Annieres; von Barner shot in the arm and chest; von Geyso with a leg wound; Gleisenberg with a bullet in his abdomen; Captain von Bartling missing. As is so often the case, lieutenants had had a bad day: Hannemann shot in the neck, Spangenberg in the shoulder, Breva severely wounded and taken prisoner. Many cornets and color-bearers had been killed or wounded or were captives. The chasseur battalion, which had set out with 317 men, had twenty-eight wounded and 101 missing, and the grenadiers reported ninety-seven privates unaccounted for. And so it went, on and on, friends, relatives, and comrades dead or missing, many of the wounded almost certain to die.

Johann Bense was an enlisted man with the grenadiers who had marched with Breymann, and he told how they "ran into the fire at full speed," throwing back the rebels. But the Americans outnumbered them, they knew the lay of the land, and quickly outflanked the grenadiers, forcing the Germans to withdraw. As they fell back, Bense was shot in the belly, but he was lucky enough to escape with a number of others who struggled back to the main army one by one and were sent to a house that had been converted to a hospital, where Bense remained for a month.

Captain Alexander Fraser returned to camp a few days after the battle, one of the few Britons to escape. As Burgoyne observed afterward, young Fraser's men constituted "the select corps of the army, composed of chosen men from all the regiments," and their loss was a tough one to take.

The Indians, Canadians, and loyalists who made their way through dense woods and all but impassable roads to get back to the army brought word that although the rebels were said to be treating the German prisoners well enough, the captured Tories were being handled "with all imaginable cruelty." The remaining Indians had had enough of the white man's war by this time and declared their intention to return home. Led by St. Luc and Langlade, they informed Burgoyne that when they first joined his army "the sun arose bright and in its full glory . . . the sky was clear and serene, foreboding conquest and victory," but then the "great Luminary was surrounded and almost obscured from the sight by dark and gloomy clouds . . . which threatened by their bursting to involve all nature in a general wreck and confusion." The general was unmoved by the imagery: he made no objection to their departure, having already concluded that they were hopelessly unreliable.

There was plenty of blame to go around, Lieutenant Hadden concluded, since "almost every person concerned seems to have had a principal share in the disaster." He was no admirer of Philip Skene and called him "a famous marplot . . . showing his powers to every man who pretended to be friendly." Hadden was convinced that Skene was completely taken in by the rebels who took the oath of allegiance and then stuck white paper in their hats to disguise themselves as loyalists. Then "to crown the folly of this farce they were permitted immediately to return [and] join their respective Corps in the Rebel Army." Hadden also bitterly criticized Riedesel for insisting that his Germans carry out the enterprise; the dragoons for failing to hold off the rebels; the "Indians to a Man, and most of the Canadians" for running away; and Breymann for his unpardonable delay (he "did not march a Mile an hour") in going to Baum's relief. The lieutenant had more harsh words for Breymann: when the colonel heard the firing up ahead, he was heard to say of Baum's command, "We will let them get warm before we reach them," an attitude Hadden attributed to the "old picque" between the men.

With the skepticism of a Scot, Simon Fraser had suspected things would turn out this way: he had opposed sending the Germans on such an important mission, he told Burgoyne's aide, Lieutenant Colonel Kingston; he regarded them as "not a very active people"—too slow for the job.

For his part, General Riedesel took little comfort from the confirmation of his concern that Baum's force was too weak to accomplish what was expected of it, but he also faulted Baum for advancing too far before he knew how strong the rebels were, and for failing to convey the urgency of his need for reinforcements. Burgoyne assured the baron that "nothing can be said against the troops in regard to bravery," but he had some sharp words about Breymann, whose march had been painfully slow, and he was furious about the lack of loyalist support—not one of whom "was found earnest enough to convey me intelligence."

By now it was clear that the British command's hope of obtaining fresh provisions and horses was forlorn, ensuring that the army would have to depend on its supply dumps and shipments from Canada until further notice. Given the increasingly difficult logistics involved as the army moved ever farther from its source of supplies, this was not a comforting thought. Most of the time the German regiments were bringing up provisions by boat, carrying them around rapids because horses and wagons were so scarce—all this in heat so stifling they could hardly draw breath in their tents, and with dysentery raging throughout the stinking camps.

Accompanying this flood of bad news was a deterioration in morale and a rising number of desertions. Burgoyne knew he had to clamp down hard on that problem: he ordered the execution of several captured deserters and saw to it that pickets from every regiment were present to witness the firing squad's work.

Julius Wasmus was one of the hundreds of men taken prisoner near Bennington. As he was led away from the battlefield he noticed a pile of round stones beside a silent German fieldpiece—mute evidence of how desperate the German gunners were when they ran out of cannonballs. Then he was taken to a house where he spent the night with eight dragoons and several Americans, all of whose wounds he dressed. He learned there that his nephew had been shot in the abdomen and was now missing.* All that night frightening rumors and even more shocking facts trickled in: a report that Breymann's corps was defeated and driven back with half its men fatally wounded or captured; a long list of officers badly hurt or taken prisoner—among them Lieutenant Colonel Baum, Major von Barner, Captain O'Connell, Lieutenant Durnford, even Pastor Melzheimer. A handsome rebel major was in charge of the group of prisoners that included Wasmus, and the surgeon was outraged to see him cavorting around, showing off, wearing a grenadier's cap, a gorget that belonged to Ensign Andrée, and a long straight sword that had once been carried by a dragoon. "One can well get an idea of the simplemindedness of these creatures," was Wasmus's waspish comment. Captain O'Connell spoke to the major on behalf of Wasmus, told him how the surgeon had been robbed of his belongings by his captor, and to everyone's surprise the guide appeared fifteen minutes later and returned many of them politely and without the least embarrassment. Like most Brunswickers in Baum's detachment, who had been told when they set out that they would return shortly, Wasmus brought worn clothes and few of them; now he worried about what the future held for a man with no money and not even a change of shirt.

In the fading light, Sally Kellogg watched prisoners and wounded pass by her house after the battle, and it was "a sight to behold—some men with broken legs, some with balls shot through their bodies, some with heads done up, some men on litters . . . others on horseback. . . . Those on horseback had their heads bound up and look'd sorrowfully," she said. "There was not a house but what was stowed full of wounded," and these unfortunates were "distributed through the town, the British and Hessians among the tories, the Americans among Whigs."

---

*On September 13, Wasmus found that the young man had died of his wound and "embraced eternity."

Throughout that long day, nearby families had suffered the agonies of worry and uncertainty. In Williamstown, Massachusetts, a group of women spent the long hours at the meetinghouse with the minister, praying for their men and suffering the anguish of not knowing what was happening until late that night, when a courier arrived with news from the front.

After Nathaniel Lawrence left home to march with the militia, his wife remained at their farmhouse with the six children, and all that day she fed hungry, frightened people moving along the road—families from the outskirts of Bennington, leaving home with all they could carry. Five times during the day she baked bread for the refugees, and she and her two oldest children—one twelve, the other ten—loaded an oxcart with food, clothing, and bedding, yoked the oxen, and saddled her horse in case they had to move out in a hurry. Late that night Nathaniel returned, covered with dust and blood, blackened with gunsmoke. A bullet had grazed his scalp and taken off a lock of hair over his ear.

John Wallace, one of Stark's men, described what it was like on the road leading in and out of Bennington: "Women and Children flying before the enemy with there Effects, women crying, sum walking, sum Rideing, the men Joyn our army, the women left to shift for themselves, sum Rideing on horses with there Children at there Brests, Sum before, sum behind tyed to there mothers, People Packing there Goods Loading there teams." According to Wallace, the savage contest between neighbors did not end with Breymann's retreat: ten men were found dead in a nearby meadow, victims of the loyalists; and a party sent to drive cattle to Stillwater was returning home when they were fired on by eighty Tories, who killed two and wounded one of the rebels.

When the firing finally sputtered out and died, many rebels—Thomas Mellen among them—dropped exhausted to the ground where they had fought and slept with their heads on a hill of corn. Next morning he was "so beaten out" he had trouble getting to his feet, and as he looked around the battlefield he saw wounded men who had lain on the battlefield all night. No more than twenty feet from him was the body of Major McClary, stripped of his clothing, which meant that scavengers had arrived along with the burial details, and in a single mass grave he found thirteen Tories, most of them shot in the head.

The spirits of the prisoners with Julius Wasmus lifted when they were given a meal of pork, potatoes, and punch and were joined at the table by an American who turned out to be Colonel Seth Warner. After dinner Warner took from his pocket a metal box that belonged to Wasmus, containing his lancets. Six of these the colonel returned, along with the surgeon's journal, but for some curious reason he kept the other six.

In the morning General Stark visited the prisoners and assured them that as many of their possessions as possible would be returned, after which they were marched to Bennington, where the other prisoners were lodged—officers at the Catamount Tavern, 480 privates crowded into the meetinghouse. At one point the captives in the church pushed toward the front to make room for some Canadians and the guards outside, hearing shouting and thinking the captives were trying to escape, shot at the door, killing two men and wounding one. That indefatigable Good Samaritan Mrs. Lawrence carried food to the wounded here and remembered how small groups of Germans would gather around a dying man, kneel by his side, clasp hands, and, bowing low, sway up and down, repeating prayers in their native tongue. When death came at last they moved on to another and went through the ritual again.

Wasmus and another Brunswick doctor were invited to share a meal with an American physician, but as they sat down a great hue and cry went up outside the house, everyone rushed out, and the two Germans, concerned about their safety, headed for their quarters, only to be accosted by the Reverend Thomas Allen, with drawn sword in hand. As he struck at the two surgeons, the militiamen with him cocked their muskets and were preparing to fire when someone came up behind Wasmus and ordered the rebels to put down their weapons. It was the major who had guarded them the night before, and he was nearly too late: Wasmus's companion had been hit forty or fifty times "by the barbaric pastor . . . with his naked sword."

At noon on the 19th of August, after two days in Bennington, and after signing a parole that they would not desert or talk about the war with inhabitants of the countryside, Surgeon Wasmus and the other prisoners learned that they were going to Boston. On the long march they found themselves inspected with "the same curiosity as the people in Germany when the first rhinoceros arrived there," and no wonder, since a woman who served as Wasmus's landlady one night hid her nine offspring because she had heard the Germans were cannibals and slaughtered children. In the little communities through which they passed on their march to the east the prisoners admired "the beauty of the fair sex" and their English-style dress and were astonished to learn that they were merely "farmers' servants." They also noticed that few men were to be seen—so many had gone to war—and that most houses had "black slaves and many children."

For Julius Wasmus and the hundreds of Brunswickers captured by the militia under John Stark, the war was over, but Wasmus was something of a special case. Neither soldier nor civilian, he received special treatment because he was a doctor, but unfortunately that did not include the right to be exchanged. So he lived in Massachusetts for four long years, eternally hopeful that he would be exchanged, treating patients and making new friends wherever he lived, observing with keen insight the new land in which he was obliged to remain in his rather ambiguous role. Then he was sent to Canada to languish for two more years before finally returning to Brunswick in 1783 with General Riedesel, with whom he had set out for America in 1776.

Not long after the battle the General Assembly of New Hampshire went out of its way to pay suitable tribute to John Stark, and after acknowledging receipt of the spoils of victory taken at "the Memorable Battle of Bennington," advised the general that they were presenting him with "a compleat suit of Clothes becoming his Rank, together with a piece of Linnen."*

The general may have been pleased, but clearly he had a more important matter on his mind, as indicated by the advertisement he placed in the *Connecticut Courant*:

Twenty Dollars Reward

Stole from me, the subscriber, from Wallumscoik, in the time of action, the 16th of August last, a Brown Mare, five years old, had a star in her forehead. Also, a doe skin–seated saddle, blue housing trimmed with white, and a curbed bridle. It is earnestly requested of all Committees of Safety, and others in authority, to exert themselves to recover said thief and Mare, so that he may be brought to justice, and the Mare brought to me; and the person, whoever he be, shall have the above reward for both,

---

*On October 5, John Hancock, president of the Congress, wrote Stark enclosing a message of thanks from the body and, of more interest to the New Hampshireman, a commission as "brigadier in the army of the United States."

and for the Mare alone, one half of that sum—How scandalous, how disgraceful and ignominious, must it appear to all friendly and generous souls, to have such sly, artful, designing villains enter into the field of action, in order to pillage, pilfer, and plunder from their brethren when engaged in battle!

JOHN STARK, B.G.
Bennington, 11th Sept., 1777

Chapter 17

The Moment Is Decisive

Bennington was "the compleatest Victory gain'd this War," Matthew Clarkson boasted to his cousin Susan Livingston. James Wilkinson informed St. Clair that it had "relaxed Mr. Burgoyne's ardor." And Gates observed to John Hancock that the triumph had reduced Burgoyne's boasting manner so much "that he begins in some Degree to think and talk like other Men."

Not surprisingly, Baron Riedesel saw the affair quite differently. Doing his best to soften the blow for his masters in Brunswick, he reminded Duke Charles, perhaps unnecessarily, that "Fortune is often fickle, but especially in war," and to the hereditary prince sounded the same note: "Fortune not being on one side every day . . ." Although the army was much weakened by sending out detachments as at Bennington, he was confident that they would attack the main body of the rebels soon, and then "fourteen days will decide the result."

Whatever anyone else might say, Bennington brought home to John Burgoyne the realities of his situation as nothing else had, as a private letter to Lord George Germain revealed. The loyalists on whom he had counted to join in large numbers had failed him. The Indians had proved almost totally undependable: they were out of control at Bennington and fewer than a hundred of the original five hundred now remained. (Some of the braves who quit the army carried news of the defeat to the British garrison at Lake George landing, which had been completely cut off from communication with Burgoyne when rebels moved into the vacuum in his rear as he advanced. Learning of the Indians' defection, Ensign Thomas Hughes accurately diagnosed their departure as a bad omen. "They seldom leave a victorious army," he observed; they stayed "only for the sake of plunder.")

Burgoyne knew there was no replacing his losses at Hubbardton and Bennington, Carleton had refused to send him any troops, forcing him to leave behind the Prinz Friedrich Regiment and the 53rd Foot to garrison Ticonderoga and Fort George, plus two companies of the 47th on Diamond Island, and he was threatened by an enemy force that was evidently growing every day. He informed Germain that "the great bulk of the country" supported the Congress and wherever the king's troops went three or four thousand militia assembled in a day's time, bringing their provisions with them. Then, as soon as the alarm was over, they returned to their farms. Another cause for concern was that Vermont— until so recently an unpopulated wilderness—now "abounds in the most active and most rebellious race of the continent and hangs like a gathering storm on my left."

In the path of Burgoyne's army Schuyler's forces had burned the bridges, driven off the cattle, and turned their horses loose into fields of grain or burned standing crops, forcing him to rely entirely on his shaky supply line for provisioning the troops, severely restricting his mobility and his capacity to maneuver. As if that were not bad enough, the British commander had had no word from General Howe since August 3 and assumed that messengers coming from New York had met the same fate as several men he had sent in that direction, who had been captured and executed.

He could never have imagined that he would be left entirely on his own this way, he told Germain, hung out to dry, unsupported by an operation from New York, and with no latitude in the orders requiring him to push on to Albany. Were it not for those insistent demands upon him to "force a junction with Sir William Howe," he would wait where he was until support arrived, or possibly retire to Fort Edward, where he would be in closer communication with Ticonderoga. (He was not about to say so to Germain, but his pride would not permit that; as Viscount Petersham observed, if he had halted at Fort Edward his reputation "would not have stood very high either with the army, this country, or the enemy.")

His instructions, the general added, permitted no such leeway—or so he now chose to believe—and he decided his only option was to accumulate at least twenty-five days' provisions and then forge ahead. Major risks were involved in that course, including the probability that the rebels would close in on his rear, yet by moving soon he would at least have time to fight his way back to Ticonderoga before the onset of winter and before he was completely surrounded.

The only faintly positive note in this gloomy recital was that Barry St. Leger had laid siege to Fort Stanwix and would join Burgoyne as soon as that garrison surrendered. Meanwhile other reinforcements were on the way—not seasoned British regulars, unfortunately, but a few Germans and fresh recruits.

Written on August 20, that letter was the cry of a discouraged, apprehensive general who had lost control of his operation and was no longer confident of success. This was not the old, self-assured Burgoyne, cocksure of himself and his army and contemptuous of the enemy he faced, but a man whose anguished state of mind was implicit in a sentence that began "Whatever may be my fate . . ." and concluded with the hope that "whatever decision may be passed upon my conduct, my good intent will not be questioned."

In another letter to Germain on the same day, written with an eye to its publication in Britain's press, he seemed to be laying the groundwork for a future defense of his actions. Listing the reasons that had necessitated the expedition to Bennington, he put the best possible face on that affair, praising the courage (though not the performance) of the Germans and laying the blame for the "misfortune" on Philip Skene (unnamed, but readily identifiable by anyone familiar with the expedition as the "provincial gentleman of confidence who . . . was so incautious as to leave at liberty such as took the oath of allegiance"). With little regard for the facts, Burgoyne cited his own loss at "about 400 men" killed and captured, with rebel casualties at more than double that.* Then, after assuring the administration and the public that nothing would prevent him from executing His Majesty's orders to the best of his abilities, he intimated where blame should fall in the event of an unforeseen reversal: "I hope circumstances will be such that my endeavours may be in some degree assisted by a co-operation of the army under Sir William Howe."

In his orders of the day on August 26 Burgoyne once more laid the

---

*Once again the British vastly overestimated the number of rebels facing them: some reckoned the size of Stark's force at four thousand to five thousand and assumed that American casualties must be proportionate.

responsibility for the Bennington defeat on "the Credulity of those who managed the Department of Intelligence" (Skene, again) plus the slow movement of Breymann's relief column. Both failures gave him an opportunity to deliver a homely lesson to the troops. Let the treachery of those Americans who swore allegiance to the king and then fought against His Majesty's army be remembered well. And let the slowness of the relief force remind them how essential it was for soldiers on the march to be alert and exert every effort, since "the loss of two hours may decide the turn of the enterprize, and . . . in some cases, the fate of a Campaign."

As Burgoyne was painfully aware, the grand design that was to bring him fame and honors was unraveling, for eight weeks after his triumph at Ticonderoga the army he believed invincible was actually facing the possibility of starvation and possible defeat. The only hope of salvaging the campaign was that Henry Clinton would decide to lead a relief force up the Hudson and that St. Leger would soon reach him from the west.

Suddenly one of those hopes was dashed, giving the general yet another reason to worry. In the night of August 28, Indians coming into camp brought word that Lieutenant Colonel Barry St. Leger had been forced to lift the siege of Fort Stanwix and was retreating. Although St. Leger's expedition had always been considered something of a sideshow, his withdrawal and the resulting loss of those troops must have seemed to Burgoyne another nail in the coffin.

Over the years many a well-laid plan of the European powers had come to grief in the immense wilderness of America because of a completely unforeseen turn of fate, and St. Leger's failure was one more example of how things could easily turn sour. Like other relics of the French and Indian Wars, Fort Stanwix was an abandoned wreck when rebel troops set about restoring it in 1776 and renamed it Fort Schuyler. At the head of navigation on the Mohawk River, it was 110 miles west of the Hudson and in early August was manned by 550 of Colonel Peter Gansevoort's New York Continentals, nervously awaiting the approach of Barry St. Leger's 200 British regulars, some 100 Hesse-Hanau jägers, a contingent of loyalists and Canadians, and between 800 and 1,000 Indians—something like 2,000 troops all told. St. Leger's command, of course, constituted the other strike force of Burgoyne's original invasion plan—the army that was to advance down the Mohawk Valley to join Burgoyne in Albany.

Warned by a friendly Oneida Indian that St. Leger was nearing Fort Stanwix, a tough, hard-drinking brigadier general of Tryon County militia named Nicholas Herkimer quickly assembled an eight-hundred-man army and set out on August 3 to reinforce the garrison at the fort. Unhappily for the rebels, St. Leger got wind of this and sent Thayendanagea, a remarkable Mohawk chief also known as Joseph Brant, with his Indians to ambush Herkimer between Oriskany and Stanwix. After a murderous fight lasting six hours—during which the American commander was badly wounded in the leg and directed his men while coolly leaning back against a tree, smoking his pipe—the Indians finally withdrew into the woods, leaving behind about seventy dead, including several chiefs, while the Tryon County men were too badly cut up to pursue them.

When the Indians returned to St. Leger's camp they discovered that their blankets, deerskins, packs, ammunition, and provisions were gone—stolen during their absence by a party of rebels led from the fort by Marinus Willett, Gansevoort's second-in-command. This loss and the casualties they had suffered at Oriskany convinced the red men that St. Leger was not the man to keep the promise he made when they joined him: that they would have to do very little fighting and would collect a lot of loot. Now, it appeared, they would bear the brunt of the action and spend their nights with nothing between them and the ground but a breechclout.

On August 6, Philip Schuyler got word that Herkimer's force had been attacked and "cut to pieces." As yet he had no idea as to the size of St. Leger's army, but he did know that Gansevoort had sufficient food to hold out until relief arrived, including five hundred barrels of flour, sixty barrels of salted provisions, and something on the order of seventy head of cattle. So with any luck, and if he could possibly spare enough troops to rescue the garrison, the fort might survive until St. Leger could be driven off. Otherwise, the general knew, a flood of Tories in Tryon County, the Iroquois, and St. Leger's men would pour down the Mohawk Valley, closing the jaws of a trap between themselves and Burgoyne's army, forcing the rebels to defend the Mohawk and Hudson simultaneously.

The fort *had* to be held, and Schuyler took the extreme step of sending off a detachment of Massachusetts Continentals toward Fort Dayton, about forty miles east of Stanwix, while agonizing over committing more troops to the effort. A number of his officers objected to detaching more units to Fort Stanwix, and their opinion had a lot going for it. Among the numerous deficiencies was an almost total lack of cannon. Ebenezer Stevens, writing to Washington's artillerist Henry Knox on August 7, bemoaned the loss of his beloved guns at Skenesborough and told Knox about the piteous state of the artillery. He had been obliged to send all his gunners back to their regiments, he said, because he had no guns and therefore nothing to command. Burgoyne's powerful army was now within a day's forced march of the main rebel force, and any reduction in American numbers would jeopardize whatever chances remained of holding back the British, yet Schuyler's hunch that Burgoyne was having enormous difficulties maintaining his supply lines and was unlikely to attack soon proved correct.

Schuyler elected to dispatch General Ebenezer Learned's Continental brigade to Stanwix, and when Benedict Arnold characteristically volunteered his services for the expedition, ordered him to proceed to Tryon County as quickly as possible and take command of all Continental soldiers in that area and "such of the militia as you can prevail upon to join your troops" to relieve the fort. Given Schuyler's dwindling manpower, nothing more could be done.

Arnold reached Fort Dayton on August 21, where he learned that St. Leger's men were within 150 yards of Stanwix, and he pushed on immediately after approving a ruse that was to prove wildly successful. Who deserves credit for the scheme is unclear, but someone suggested that Arnold make a deal with a mentally defective man named Hon Yost Schuyler, a nephew of General Herkimer and a distant cousin to Philip Schuyler. Hon Yost and a group of Tryon County loyalists had been captured by Arnold, and when his relatives appealed for his release Arnold struck a bargain: the young man would be set free (though his brother was kept as a hostage) provided he would travel to the British lines outside Fort Stanwix and do his best to convince the Indians there that a large rebel army was approaching. What lent credibility to this unlikely-seeming plan was that Hon Yost, who was given to raving in unknown tongues, was looked upon by the Indians as one who was in touch with supernatural powers—a prophet who spoke for the Great Spirit.

Hon Yost slipped into his new role enthusiastically, shot some bullet holes through his coat to suggest that he had narrowly escaped from the rebels, recruited a number of Oneida Indians to corroborate his story, and journeyed to St. Leger's camp, where he informed the already restive, disaffected Indians that Arnold was nearing the fort with overwhelming numbers. Asked by a British officer to be more specific, he stared at the treetops, rolled his eyes, and managed to convey the idea that Arnold had a force as numerous as the leaves overhead. That was all it took for St. Leger's Indians to decamp, but before doing so they "grew furious," the British commander wrote, "seized upon the officers' liquor and clothes, and became more formidable than the enemy...." Deserted by their allies, St. Leger's troops withdrew from their siege lines and as they retreated toward Oswego were pursued by Indians, who killed and scalped the stragglers.

On August 23, Hon Yost met Arnold advancing toward Fort Stanwix and reported his mission a success. The next day the rebel commander sent a detachment in pursuit of St. Leger, but they arrived just in time to see the enemy boats pulling away from the shore. After leaving two militia regiments to support the garrison, Arnold marched eastward to rejoin the army on the Hudson, where he learned that he had a new commanding officer.

For Philip Schuyler the day of reckoning was Sunday, August 10, the same day Colonel Baum's detachment marched off toward Bennington. The general was leaving his Albany home to rejoin the army at Stillwater and was just mounting his horse when a courier handed him a message from John Hancock, president of Congress. With it were copies of two resolutions passed by that body—one calling for an inquiry into the evacuation of Ticonderoga and the conduct of general officers in the Northern Department, the other directing Schuyler and St. Clair to report to General Washington's headquarters, almost certainly to face courts-martial.

Schuyler had been agitating for an impartial investigation into his conduct for some time, convinced that he could not be held accountable for loss of the fort and wishing to clear his name, but this summary dismissal from his post was something he had not reckoned on. Now that his scorched-earth policy was at last paying off, a definite change in the momentum of Burgoyne's advance could be felt. The British general had stayed fourteen days at Fort Edward waiting for supplies to come up and since August 14 had headquartered at William Duer's house, where he would remain for twenty-eight more days for the same reason.

But Schuyler's luck had run out. If only the victories at Bennington and Fort Stanwix had occurred several weeks earlier, he would have been the beneficiary of the good news, but he was not destined to reap the rewards of his planning and hard work. Congress's action was all but inevitable, as he surely knew in his heart. He was caught in the middle of a fight between regional factions and for some time had been up against a determined opposition in Philadelphia—those who questioned his ability and capacity for the job, those who wanted him thrown out because they said he did not command the respect of the New England militia, those who were partisans of Horatio Gates, and those who simply had a visceral dislike for the New Yorker, among them the Adamses and John Hancock. Nathaniel Folsom of the New Hampshire delegation summarized the decision in a letter to Josiah Bartlett: "The Loss of Ticonderoga hes given grate unEasyness: Generall Schuyler and Sant Caire aire orderd to head Qurters in order for an inquirey into thaire Conduckt . . . General Gates is ordered to take Comemand in the northern Department." And as Schuyler's friend and neighbor William Duer wrote him, the general's enemies in Philadelphia had done so much "to blast your character" and blame him for the loss of Ticonderoga that nothing his supporters might say could "stem the torrent of calumny."

Before settling on Gates, however, the delegates requested George Washington to name a replacement, but the embarrassed Virginian declined, reminding Congress that the Northern Department had always been considered a separate command "peculiarly" under Congressional direction. When John Hancock broke the humiliating news to Schuyler he did not even have the courtesy to inform him who his replacement would be, and to make the pill more bitter still, Schuyler learned several days later that he would be superseded by his old rival and enemy Horatio Gates, and that Congress had instructed the states of New Hampshire, Massachusetts, Connecticut, New Jersey, New York, and Pennsylvania to dispatch as many of their militia as General Gates thought necessary for the defense of the region.

Poor Schuyler: if only he had been given that level of support things might have gone very differently indeed. Understandably crushed, he was unable to speak to anyone for several days, yet despite what he called "the Indignity of being relieved of the command of the army at a time when an Engagement must soon take place," he was too proud and too responsible to quit his post or follow orders to travel south until his successor was on the scene. Until August 19—the day Gates finally turned up at headquarters to assume command after taking a leisurely two weeks to journey from Philadelphia to Albany—it was business as usual in the Northern Department. Morale was terrible. The soggy first half of the month had been a hard one from the standpoint of the men's health: some had smallpox, some the familiar "camp disorder," and many were still down with fever and ague, which was hardly surprising, one soldier observed, considering that they were sleeping on "the bare

Ground cover'd with Dew without Blanketts having a few boards for Cover." Brigadier General John Nixon had a bad enough case that he was sent to the hospital at Albany; Alexander Scammell was another officer reported "very poorly of the same Disorder but getting better."

Schuyler ordered the army to fall back from Stillwater to the Sprouts, as the little islands at the mouth of the Mohawk River were called, while entreating Massachusetts and New York to send him more militia. Unlike some earlier withdrawals this one was relatively unhurried and orderly, with Paterson's brigade (which included the weary, sore-pressed 7th Massachusetts) and Gamaliel Bradford's regiment leading the way, followed by the troops under John Glover and Enoch Poor, with Nixon's brigade (minus its leader) bringing up the rear.

Detachments were posted along the south bank of the Mohawk to prevent a British crossing there, and Schuyler spent his last days with the army writing to Committees of Safety, giving them the glorious news from Bennington and Fort Schuyler, as he liked to call the western outpost.

What Gates inherited when Schuyler turned over the command on Van Schaick's Island on August 19 was a blessed gift of time won by a strategy that had by now stretched the enemy's lines to the breaking point, plus an adequate supply of provisions without which no growing army could survive. Many of Schuyler's fellow officers understood very well what he had achieved: Nathanael Greene stated flatly that "the foundation of all the Northern success was laid long before [Gates's] arrival there" and that Gates appeared "just in time to reap the laurels and rewards."

To Schuyler's immense disappointment, his successor seemed to have no use for him or his plans and did not even deign to take advantage of the New Yorker's intimate knowledge of the countryside—the hidden roads and fords, the locations from which it would be possible to stage a defense or mount an attack. Crueler yet, when the new commanding general held his first council of war, to which all Continental officers and a brigadier general of Albany County militia were invited, he pointedly left out Schuyler. Clearly, Gates wanted to be rid of him, and Schuyler reluctantly returned to his home in Albany before leaving for Philadelphia, where Arthur St. Clair had gone on August 12.

To no one's surprise, Jeduthan Baldwin was as industrious as ever, destroying now rather than building. On the day of the Bennington battle he led 280 men, including those of the 7th Massachusetts, to

Stillwater and set fire to all the wooden planks left there by the army, except those they could carry off on rafts, while they burned bridges and tore up roads. As the men were heading back to camp with forty thousand planks and the stores they retrieved, someone spotted two civilians with packs on their backs crossing the river, and Baldwin sent a party to see what was going on. It turned out that a group of Tories—four men, seven women, and seventeen children described by Baldwin as "persons of welth, Inhabitants of Stillwater"—had fled from their homes, taking their belongings to a desolate wooded island in the river where they hoped to remain undiscovered until they could return home under the protection of Burgoyne's approaching army. Three days later, Baldwin, pleased with himself for having captured those loyalists, was dining with General Poor when the exhilarating news of the victory at Bennington came in, followed closely by the arrival of Major General Horatio Gates.

August droned on, hot and sulky. Of the last twenty-one days of the month, thirteen were unbearably warm, excessively wet, or both, making a soupy mess of campsites and roads. Hardly a day passed without deserters—especially Tories and Germans—coming into camp. A troop of rebel cavalry from Connecticut clattered in on August 28, another on September 1. Daniel Morgan's riflemen marched in on August 30, Arnold and Learned returned from Stanwix on August 31, and militia companies seemed to be arriving all the time.

An uneasy quiet settled over the front, broken sporadically by more hit-and-run attacks by Burgoyne's Indians and loyalists. But most of the time it was the old army story of hurry up and wait, as Ebenezer Wild could testify. He was a sergeant in Colonel Joseph Vose's regiment from Massachusetts, and his outfit began marching and countermarching at the end of July, traveling back and forth between Half Moon and Stillwater. A few days later they marched to Saratoga in the rain and slogged back to Stillwater; on August 12 "had orders to get ready to march, but did not march." Again the next day and the day following, their marching orders were countermanded, but not until they had struck their tents, stowed baggage, and cooked food for the next twenty-four hours. On August 18, when Wild was suffering from fever and ague contracted during a dark rainy spell, they struck their tents again and returned to Half Moon.

Yet something different was in the air after Bennington and Fort Stanwix, bringing new heart to rebels within and beyond the battle lines. George Washington was elated by what he called "the great stroke struck by Stark near Bennington," and a member of his official family wrote a friend to say, "I give you joy from the Bottom of my Heart on Account of the fortunate and Signal stroke given by *Old Stark*, and also the threshing the Enemy got at Fort Schuyler. There was a cloud in the North, but I really think matters in that Quarter look well just now. I trust Burgoyne will be severely mauled."

That gentleman was forced to face just such a possibility as he confronted a rising tide of the same old difficulties—abominable roads, broken wagons, used-up horses, the relentless attrition of foodstuffs and provender, a plague of dysentery, the increasing incidence of straggling and desertion. Outwardly he managed to keep up a good front most of the time, exuding confidence and good spirits, but he was understandably on edge, and there were moments when one could almost smell approaching doom.

Suddenly discipline became notably harsher. One morning Riedesel's entire regiment and the army's picket guard were paraded to witness the execution of a German musketeer named Fasselabend. The unlucky fellow had gone over to the rebels and was aboard an American vessel when the British captured it near Skenesborough. Now, instead of being a free man, he stood before a firing squad to serve as an example of what would happen to anyone else foolish enough to desert. Two men convicted of robbery received a thousand lashes each. All sentinels and patrols were ordered to tighten security. Sabotage was very much on Burgoyne's mind: orders were issued for guarding both ends of the bridge Fraser's men had constructed across the Hudson lest "ill-designing people" might "injure it." Indians were offered rewards for bringing in deserters and told to scalp any turncoats they killed. A soldier from the 9th Regiment was executed for abandoning his post; a man in the 47th was given a thousand lashes for desertion; at the same time the troops were cautioned against the dual perils represented by strong drink and "Emissaries of the Enemy," those being named as the only agents that could conceivably break down the "general zeal" of the army; and a reward was offered for the apprehension of any person who induced men to desert.

Nor was there any end to the problems. "Great abuses" continued in the trade in horses stolen from loyal local residents and sold to officers. Sutlers, provincials, and camp followers were warned that they were subject to military law, and as if anyone needed to be reminded of the dwindling foodstocks, orders included a warning that the "fate of the Campaign" might depend on provisions, as indeed it might.

Yet despite mounting evidence that all was far from well, some of

Burgoyne's officers seemed blissfully unaware of the army's predicament—either that, or they were whistling in the dark. Take Sir Francis Carr Clerke, the general's private secretary, who was surely aware of the situation and must have shared at least some of the commander's doubts and concerns. Writing to a friend in England, he observed that the rebels had driven off all the livestock that might have provided the army with fresh meat, forcing them to rely on salt rations, but he dismissed this as not worth worrying about. They were experiencing some difficulties because the rapids on the Hudson forced them to rely on ground transport, yet this would not interfere with their determination to "try the Countenance of Mr. Gates." The rebels, he went on, "pretend to be in spirits and threaten us a drubbing, but on the approach of the red Coats I rather believe it will be as usual. They will find out that they can take up better ground in their rear."

It was true that the Germans had met with a "check" at Bennington, he went on, but even that loss had its bright side: because of it and the increasing distance from their supply depots on the lakes, "we set our faces forward, and mean to bite hard if any thing dares to show itself." Clerke had heard that the American army was steadily growing, "*mais n'importe,* what are we not equal to?" As evidence of the army's spirit, he mentioned that the ladies were in good spirits and had no intention of leaving: Lady Harriet Acland "graces the advanced Corps" and Baroness Riedesel was with the Brunswick troops. Morale was excellent and they had "frequent dinées and constantly musick." All in all, it would be difficult to imagine a more exciting and pleasurable adventure—"a lively Camp, good Weather, good Claret, good musick and the Enemy near." How could one ask for anything better—especially when "a little fusillade during dinner does not discompose the Nerves of even our Ladies."

That jaunty letter was vintage Gentleman Johnny and suggested the conviviality of the general's mess, but it contained no adequate reflection of the worries pressing on Burgoyne's mind. He had learned that a party of rebels was moving toward Fort Anne, a grim reminder that the army could no longer maintain communications with that place, so he told Riedesel to have his men bring off as many supplies as could be removed before the enemy closed in. Swearing the baron to secrecy, he also expressed his readiness to be of service to the baroness, whose safety was obviously a concern—yet another indication of his nervousness about the expedition. "I foresee great fatigues for a lady," he said.

He recognized the futility of maintaining a cordon between the northern forts and his army—he simply lacked the manpower to do it. In another secret communiqué he informed Riedesel that nothing was to be left at Fort George, that wagons laden with stores from that post could be expected to pass Fort Edward the next day, after which the Brunswick troops serving as the army's rear guard were to move forward. Meanwhile, Riedesel was to have two bateaus with oars buried as quietly as possible inside Fort Edward, covered with dirt and marked with crosses as if they were graves. These were for use by Lieutenant Colonel St. Leger, who had left Oswego and was expected to come up the lakes and join Burgoyne with reinforcements, though how on earth the general could have believed St. Leger's small force could be of use to him at this juncture is difficult to comprehend. After falling back from Fort Stanwix the colonel had marched to Oswego, rid himself of his fractious Indians, and sent word to Burgoyne that he planned to descend the St. Lawrence and retrace Burgoyne's own route up the lakes and down the Hudson—a journey of more than four hundred miles.* Yet even if he should succeed in this daunting venture, his failure on the Mohawk had already cost the British all hope of attracting the hundreds of loyalists he was supposed to enlist along the way to Albany.

Burgoyne had one last observation for Riedesel. He had ordered Brigadier General Powell at Ticonderoga to dispatch to Riedesel the Brunswick troops who were still held in reserve at that fort. This made it clear that General John Burgoyne had no intention of falling back. He was set on reaching Albany come what might. As he observed to the German, "The moment is a decisive one."

Once again Burgoyne was forced to choose between two routes leading to his destination. Albany lay about forty-five miles below Fort Edward, and either he could continue down the east bank of the Hudson and cross the river opposite the town, or he could cross in the vicinity of Fort Miller and march south along the west bank. Each had its disadvantages. On the east bank he was unlikely to encounter serious opposition but would have to make a crossing below the Hudson's junction with the Mohawk, where the river was wider and deeper and where the enemy would certainly be waiting. His troops would be sitting ducks out on the water and at a terrible disadvantage when they tried to climb the riverbank in the face of enemy fire. On the other hand, while taking the road along the west bank made for an easier crossing, he would have to fight his way

---

*Some of St. Leger's force—four companies of the 34th Regiment and a battalion of New York loyalists—arrived at Ticonderoga on September 27, and a German officer who was there commented that "L. Col. St. Leger is a very thirsty soul."

through the rebel army, which was bound to be drawn up in a strong defensive position, and Burgoyne—because he had lost so many of his Indians—did not know where that might be. What he did know was that once he marched down that road there could be no turning back.

His officers were acutely aware of the hazards involved in crossing the Hudson and Burgoyne may have heard objections from them or at least sensed their apprehension, because he decided entirely on his own to make the move. As he explained later to Germain, "I did not think myself authorized to call any men into council, when the peremptory tenor of my orders and the season of the year admitted no alternative."

On September 10 the British army broke camp at Duer's house and spent the next two days at an ideal campsite near the mouth of the Batten Kill, a big chunk of land as flat as a table, where they prepared to cross the river and move south. Thanks to herculean efforts by men and beasts, Burgoyne now had enough provisions for four weeks (rationing having been instituted), which would have to suffice until the army reached Albany, and on September 13—a glorious day with sunlight shimmering on the ripples of the Hudson—the redcoats on the right wing walked over the bridge of boats to the west bank and set off for Saratoga, followed two days later by the Brunswickers. After the bridge was dismantled and floated downriver, which meant that "all communication with Canada [was] voluntarily cut off," as one nervous officer put it, the army stepped off in three columns, drums beating, regimental flags flying, as if this were a parade-ground drill, except that the uniforms were torn and patched, faded and sweat-stained. This was not the picture-book army that had left St. Johns bursting with confidence and the cockiness that comes with the certainty that your enemy hasn't the ghost of a chance. These men were dead tired, they had a gnawing hunger in their bellies, and they had no real idea what lay ahead.

Before long the artillery, flanked on the right by the British and on the left by the Germans, was barely crawling down the road that had been all but destroyed by the rebels, trailed by the Baroness Riedesel's entourage in her calèche and some three hundred other women and assorted camp followers. Paralleling the army's route, supplies were floated downstream in bateaus to a large sheltered bay shaped like a giant fishhook known as Van Vechten's Cove, or Dovegat.* But all this took time, and the army's advance was slower than it had ever been.

---

*Dovegat or Dovecote—present-day Coveville—was so called because of the thousands of migrating birds it attracted. It was the home of a militia colonel named Van Vechten, who was serving on Gates's staff.

That this was no ordinary movement was evident from orders stating that no officer was to leave camp and that the several corps were to proceed "in such a state as to be fit for *instant Action*." When it became evident that it was impossible to continue in three columns because the road was so badly torn up, the entire body of infantry shifted to the left, marching in single column along the riverbank and halting at last at Dovegat, where they remained for two days while work crews went out to repair bridges up ahead. A large detachment sent out to locate the American army returned that evening and reported that they had seen nothing, but heard the rebel evening guns distinctly.

During the night some excitement was caused by a burning tent occupied by Major John Acland and Lady Harriet. As she wrote in her journal, their trusty Newfoundland dog, Jack Catch, overturned a candle that started the fire and "we were in great danger of being burnt to death." Her hard-luck husband very nearly was: he leaped into the flames to rescue his pregnant wife, not realizing that she had escaped by crawling under the rear of the tent. By the time his orderly saved him, his face and body were badly burned.

The following day the army set up camp near Sword's house, about fifty yards from the Hudson at Saratoga, with orders to be in full battle gear and to make no moves until the fog cleared. But despite the strict instructions and warnings they had received, a number of hungry men and women slipped away on a foraging expedition, and fourteen were killed, wounded, or missing—a certain indication that Gates's army was nearby, though where no one knew, since the British advance corps had not yet located the enemy's position. Once again general orders reproached the surviving offenders, saying they had sustained a loss during a ten-day period that, had it occurred in battle, could have resulted in the death of hundreds of rebels. The lieutenant general would no longer put up with the loss of men for "the pitiful consideration of potatoes or forage." He had repeatedly tried admonitions and corporal punishment, but with no results, and now he reminded them that "the life of the Soldier is the property of the King." Henceforth a man caught beyond the advanced sentries would be instantly hanged.

Hints of autumn were everywhere—nights growing colder despite the heat of the days, heavy dews or even frost in the morning, ground fog hanging in the valleys and hovering over the rivers, here and there the leaves of swamp maples beginning to turn from green to scarlet—one more reminder to Burgoyne of the urgency of reaching Albany, for he could not survive the winter where he was.

As the seasons changed, so did life in the American camp. It was as if the army, having been an unwanted stepchild for so long, had suddenly acquired respectability through its unexpected affluence of numbers. Not only that: some of the soldiers were beginning to look on what had happened at Ticonderoga as not so bad after all, since they had neither been defeated nor captured and had lived to fight the enemy on far better terms. In a letter to his brother, Alexander Scammell said he thought the loss of the post would "prove of infinite advantage to America [since] It has led Burgoyne into a Hobble." Now, if heaven smiled on the rebels, they might destroy his army. His communication with Canada was cut off and the provisions remaining to him were all he was going to have. He had no line of retreat and "his Army is drove to desperation and a most bloody Battle must ensue."

The Reverend Enos Hitchcock had a premonition that a fight was brewing, and on Sunday, September 1, he took his text for the morning sermon from Exodus—"The Lord is a man of war." That afternoon he reminded his flock of Jeremiah's warning, "Thine own wickedness shall correct thee, and thy backslidings shall reprove thee," and added a prayer suitable to the occasion: "Do thou, great Liberty, inspire our Souls & make our Lives in thy possession happy or our Deaths glorious in thy just Defence."

Jeduthan Baldwin sensed a different mood and high spirits in camp that he attributed to Gates's arrival, and with some unaccustomed leisure time on his hands he rode to Albany, left his watch to be cleaned, and ordered a new suit of clothes. (At the same time he bought lottery tickets and gave two of them to Udney Hay's wife, probably hoping she would have good luck and perhaps repay him the $650 he had lent her husband.) Those high spirits Baldwin detected were born of a newfound optimism and assurance—emotions this army had not experienced since before the fall of Ticonderoga. The soldiers seemed to realize the pickle Burgoyne had got himself into and what this would mean for the rebel cause. As General John Glover put it, "I think matters look fair on our side & I have not the least doubt of beating or compelling Mr. Burgoyne to return back at least to Ticonderoga, if not to Canada. His situation is dangerous, which he must see & know if he is not blind, and if he is not strong enough to move down to fight us, he cannot remain where he is without giving us a great advantage."

Before leaving Philadelphia, Horatio Gates had taken advantage of

Congress's willingness to give him all the troops he wanted by requesting 7,750 men—nearly half of them from Massachusetts, with the balance about equally divided among Connecticut, New York, Pennsylvania, and New Jersey. When he finally reached Northern Army headquarters on the evening of August 19 he found most of his new command billeted on Van Schaick's Island, with a brigade under Enoch Poor posted five miles up the Mohawk to fend off a possible attack by St. Leger (who had not at that time withdrawn from Fort Stanwix). Between these two locations were as many as 6,000 men, plus another 2,000 under Lincoln in Vermont, and before long other units began to appear—a contingent of New York militia, Arnold's 1,200 returning from Fort Stanwix, and, possibly the most valuable addition of all, Colonel Daniel Morgan's Pennsylvania, Maryland, and Virginia riflemen.

Several factors were involved in the presence of Morgan's men. One was General William Howe's decision to move his army to Philadelphia by sea. While Washington waited to learn where Howe would land he decided he could spare some troops to reinforce Gates and selected two of the Continental regiments at Peekskill and Morgan's riflemen. Washington was reluctant to part with the latter outfit, but he was under pressure from Congress to do something about the continuing Indian attacks that terrorized soldiers and civilians alike up north. Congress in turn was reacting to the claims of local Committees of Safety that soldiers in the Northern Army "shudder at the very appearance of Indians and hardly dare Stir out of their camp." Washington informed Gates on August 20 that he had dispatched Colonel Morgan and his corps of riflemen to assist him. "This corps I have great dependence on," he said, "and have no doubt but they will be exceedingly useful." They would check the savages and keep them "within proper bounds," prevent Burgoyne from getting intelligence, and boost the morale of the army by ridding it of the menace represented by the Indians. (In fact, despite the presence of Morgan's men, Indian attacks did not immediately disappear. On September 4, five days after the "shirt men" arrived, a scouting party from Scammell's 3rd New Hampshire Regiment was surprised by some three hundred Indians and loyalists and lost nine men killed or captured.)

Daniel Morgan himself was big—huge, some described him—an impressive man with a remarkable physique and a quick, fiery temper. Having run away from home at the age of seventeen, he matured in the wilderness of Pennsylvania and Virginia, working as a teamster hauling freight between remote frontier outposts. That experience left him scarred by Indian fighting and the consequences of his innate distaste for authority: an Indian bullet had gone through his neck, taking the teeth on one side of his mouth with it, and his back was crisscrossed with the marks of a whip laid on after he knocked down a British officer who had reprimanded him. Sentenced to 500 lashes, he liked to say that he owed the British one stripe because the fellow who flogged him had quit at 499.

He was an alumnus of General Edward Braddock's disastrous defeat in 1755, which laid open the colonial frontiers to attack by French, Indians, and Canadians. Morgan was with Braddock's army as an independent wagoner and was part of a distinguished group of survivors that included George Washington, Thomas Gage, Charles Lee, Horatio Gates, Daniel Boone, Christopher Gist, George Croghan, and others. He also served as a lieutenant in Pontiac's War before fighting Indians in the Ohio Valley in 1774, and the following year led a company of frontiersmen north from Virginia to Cambridge, Massachusetts, traveling at the unheard-of rate of twenty-eight miles a day to join Washington's army besieging Boston. Certainly no one in the vicinity of Cambridge had seen the likes of those boisterous, cocky men clad in fringed buckskin shirts and leggings, who could put one ball after another into a seven-inch target at 250 yards with their remarkably accurate long rifles. They followed Morgan to Quebec as part of Benedict Arnold's heroic march, and after Arnold was wounded Morgan took command in the fight for the city and surrendered only after being backed against a wall and surrounded by the enemy. After he was exchanged late in 1776 he raised the corps of sharpshooters that he now brought north to join Gates.

For the moment, Morgan's command had so many men on the sick list that he could count on no more than 374 effectives (Morgan himself was suffering from the severe sciatica and rheumatism that would eventually cause him to retire from the army), but by the end of the first week in September, Gates had more than 10,000 troops, including artillery, engineers, and cavalry. How many of these men came in as a result of the call to governors for troops is hard to say, but certainly many were influenced by the Jane McCrea incident and Gates's popularity with New Englanders. Indeed, much of the changed mood that Jeduthan Baldwin noticed was directly attributable to Gates.

The general had a genuine concern for the men's welfare and well-being and immediately concentrated on restoring discipline. He held regular drills and inspections, improved the quality of their food, obtained better clothing and equipment for them, and saw to it that the camp and hospital were cleaned up. Major Henry Dearborn, who led five light infantry companies from New Hampshire, observed that Gates's arrival put "a New face upon our affairs," and so it seemed. Yet the credit was not entirely Gates's: as Brockholst Livingston observed, the growing number of troops and the recent successes had a lot to do with it, as did the knowledge that Burgoyne "has got himself into such a situation that he can neither retire or advance without fighting." Whatever the cause of the new optimism, it produced the healthiest atmosphere this army had seen. When Timothy Bigelow arrived on the first Saturday in October he found "a perfect union among the different corps of officers, it is the happiest camp I ever was in: the officers & soldiers put the greatest confidence in the General." Gates's treatment of his troops, he went on, "is quite opposit to that of Schuyler's."

"Granny" Gates was far more popular with the men in the ranks, and nothing could have cemented that relationship more than his orders of September 7. The army would march the next day, he said, not south, as these soldiers had been accustomed to doing for the past two months, but north—*toward* Burgoyne's oncoming force.

On September 9 the Americans reached Stillwater and began digging some partially completed trenches Kosciuszko had begun during a previous stop at the place, while Baldwin's engineers constructed a bridge of rafts more than nine hundred feet long and sixteen feet wide across the Hudson, establishing communications with the 11th Massachusetts Continental Regiment, posted on the east bank, making it possible to drive a large number of sheep and cattle to the camp that evening.

Scouts who had watched the enemy cross the river reported "too large a number to pick a wrangle with," and Stillwater was definitely not the place to make a stand against them. The fertile alluvial bottomland west of the river here was too wide to defend, and when John Neilson and other local residents pointed out that Bemis Heights, about three miles to the north, was a better site, Gates sent an aide, twenty-year-old Colonel James Wilkinson, and Colonel Udney Hay to check it out. When they returned and reported that the local folk were right, Gates went off to see for himself. That settled it: the army would move at once to Bemis Heights.

Named for Jotham Bemis, a farmer who kept a tavern nearby, the broad, thickly wooded plateau was higher than others in the immediate vicinity and afforded an unobstructed view for miles in almost every direction. Below it, the bottomland, cleared of trees, narrowed down into a defile no more than five or six hundred feet wide between the string of bluffs and the Hudson. Through this defile passed the only road to Albany on the west bank of the river, and this was the road along which Burgoyne's heavy train of artillery and baggage would have to travel.

Command of Bemis Heights left the enemy with two choices: one was to march headlong down the road, which would be swept by American cannon fire; the other was to climb the bluffs and hope to circumvent the rebels. As Gates knew, the British and German soldiers were at their best in open terrain, where their disciplined formations and experienced artillery operated most effectively. They would find themselves at a considerable disadvantage making their way through the heavily timbered bluffs, laced with ravines and streams, with only a few relatively small clearings hacked out of the forest by farmers.

By the time the British army reached Sword's house on the 16th, the rebels had had nearly a week to prepare their defenses in the vicinity of Bemis Heights, and Burgoyne—who had seen the earthworks raised overnight at Bunker Hill—knew enough about the skill and vigor with which these American soldiers threw up defenses to be aware of what was likely to confront him as he moved forward. As yet he had no accurate assessment of where the rebels were or how many of them he would encounter. He did know that in order to get to Albany he must attack— and soon.

That much Horatio Gates also knew. He fired off an urgent letter to various Committees of Safety in the region telling them that the enemy had evacuated the posts at Skenesborough, Fort Anne, Fort George, Fort Edward, and another south of Lake George, while moving artillery and all the stores forward to a position seven miles north of Gates's army. On the basis of this intelligence, he said, "it is Evident the General's Design is to Risque all upon one Rash Stroke." Gates realized that a battle was at most a matter of hours, or a few days, off, and he wanted every last militiaman the committees could send him.

While the British, short of Indian scouts, were moving blind through unfamiliar terrain and knew next to nothing about rebel strength or even the exact position of Gates's force, the Americans were short of intelligence for some of the same reasons. Gates was relying on Morgan's men to serve as his eyes, but those troops were not yet familiar with their surroundings and were further hampered by forests that were all but impenetrable in places, and dense early-morning fogs that often did not lift until midday. In the American camp, each day brought new rumors that the enemy was on the march. On September 13, Benedict Arnold led a detachment and "took a view of the enemy's encampment," capturing eight prisoners in the process, and Morgan's riflemen skirmished with the British about two miles from camp, but the next day when a party of two hundred riflemen and light infantry under Henry Dearborn and Richard Butler took off toward Saratoga their guide lost his way and they "made no great Discoveries." The following day they reconnoitered with no better luck, and while other scouts brought word that the enemy was advancing, no one could say exactly where.

At this critical moment, when everyone was aware that the decisive battle of the campaign was imminent, with the foot soldiers waiting behind earthworks for the crackle of musket fire out on the picket lines that would signal the enemy attack, the American command was engaged in a destructive internal power struggle that had split it into two hostile camps.

Chapter 18

We Had Something More at Stake

The American officer was not tall—about five feet nine inches—but stocky, with a look of restless animal energy about him. A portrait drawing made that year shows a high, sloping forehead, a sharp prow of a nose, an almost feminine mouth, and a jowliness about the chin. But his most notable features were cold, pale gray eyes, whose contrast with his black hair and swarthy skin gave him an almost sinister look.

Benedict Arnold was now thirty-six years old, a major general, and the kind of field commander generals dream about—utterly fearless and daring, a natural leader, with stamina and determination that allowed nothing to stand in his way. He also had more action under his belt in this war than most other officers, beginning with the capture of Fort Ticonderoga with Ethan Allen, his remarkable wilderness march to Quebec, and the attack on that city, where his leg was badly wounded, leaving him with a limp. He had fought with conspicuous gallantry at Valcour Island and Danbury, and was just back from the successful expedition to Fort Stanwix. On the strength of his record there was no question about Arnold's remarkable ability as a battlefield leader, but behind the record and beneath the surface was a man driven by terrible self-doubts and a hunger for fame, social acceptance, money, and rank that had, thus far, been denied him. He was a man whose pride was easily wounded, one who could accept neither opposition to his ideas nor criticism while at the same time being totally insensitive to the feelings of others. Like John Stark, he had been passed over in February of '77 in favor of more junior officers, including Lincoln and St. Clair, and although he was promoted to major general in May, it was infuriating to be outranked by a number of men he regarded as second-raters.

Through no fault of his own he landed in the middle of the festering feud between Philip Schuyler and Horatio Gates. Actually, Arnold liked both men: Gates had befriended and supported him, and they were two of a kind—men on the make, striving to rise above modest beginnings. Schuyler was a different cup of tea: from the time Arnold first met him, he was attracted to him personally and admired hugely the urbane atmosphere and the trappings of wealth abundantly evident in the elegant Albany mansion.

By the time Arnold returned from Stanwix, Schuyler had left the army and was at his Albany home preparing for what an aide called his "tryal," but the animosity between his supporters and those of Gates threatened to tear the top levels of the army apart. Schuyler kept in daily touch with affairs at headquarters through correspondence with his former secretary, Richard Varick, who was now deputy commissioner general of musters, and Varick's venomous innuendos and sneers at Gates were understandably resented by members of that general's staff. Gates was aware of all this, of course, and when he perceived that Arnold and Varick appeared to be on extremely good terms (Varick had done a first-rate job of supplying Arnold's little fleet on Lake Champlain the previous year), his suspicions were aroused.

But Varick was not the only burr under the general's saddle. Arnold had invited Henry Brockholst Livingston, who was temporarily at liberty while waiting to accompany Schuyler to Philadelphia, to spend a few weeks on his staff, and on September 9, Livingston joined him. Another of Arnold's aides was nineteen-year-old Matthew Clarkson, Livingston's cousin. Clarkson had been wounded at the end of July near Moses Creek as he was trying to rally troops to repel an Indian attack. A ball hit him in the neck and went through his windpipe and out the other side, but he recovered soon enough to accompany Arnold's expedition to the west. Back in Stillwater by September 11, he wrote Susan Livingston, mentioning that he was seated next to the general, who was writing his will. "I shou'd do the same," he went on, "but God knows I have nothing to leave."

In the normal course of events, the presence of these two young men on Arnold's staff should have created no problem. But given the time and place and the players involved, trouble was inevitable. Gates's gossipy aide James Wilkinson, who seemed to delight in pitting individuals against each other, was stirring the pot by reporting comments made by Schuyler's partisans to the commanding officer. (Letters written from both camps were rife with petty remarks—from Varick to Schuyler: "I wish to God we had a Commander who could see a little Distance before him without Spectacles"; and from Wilkinson to St. Clair: "General Gates despises a certain pompous little fellow [i.e., Arnold] as much as you can.") Gates detested Schuyler, and as far as he was concerned Livingston and Clarkson were cut from the same aristocratic bolt of cloth, and when Arnold took those two into his official family, it was a clear signal to Gates that Schuyler's spies were stirring up trouble in camp. After all, Gates had made clear to Arnold his feelings about Livingston, but Arnold, with his usual disregard for the feelings of others, chose to ignore the problem until it was beyond curing. All of which led Gates to believe that Arnold was Schuyler's man and not to be trusted.

Until now Gates had gone out of his way to do the right thing by Arnold. He gave him command of what was to be the left wing of the army, with a division that included several crack outfits—including Morgan's riflemen and Major Henry Dearborn's light infantry,* plus two regular New Hampshire brigades under Ebenezer Learned and Enoch Poor, composed of veterans in the regiments of Joseph Cilley, Alexander Scammell, and Nathan Hale (who was not with his men, having been captured at Hubbardton). To these he later added the New York and Connecticut militia, all of which added up to a strong corps that should have delighted the major general. But loyalty and gratitude were never Benedict Arnold's strong suits, and he ignored the honor Gates had done him when the ugly and totally unnecessary dispute came to a head. General orders issued by Wilkinson† assigned three New York militia regiments to John Glover, whose brigade was a component of the right wing. Arnold exploded. When those soldiers were "anexed" to Glover's brigade, he fumed, it placed him "in the ridiculous light of presuming to give Orders I had no right to do, and having them publickly Contradicted." Surely this was a mistake on Wilkinson's part.

---

*These outfits complemented each other well: the frontiersmen's long rifles could not accommodate bayonets, so the sharpshooters were particularly vulnerable to enemy attack after they had fired a round. Dearborn's men carried muskets with bayonets, which made them ideal support for Morgan's troops.

†Wilkinson, like Dearborn, was a veteran of Arnold's march to Quebec.

No, Gates replied tartly, the responsibility for the order was his. He passed it off as an oversight and said the order would be countermanded. But it was not, and Arnold assumed correctly that he was being punished for retaining Livingston. (These were tense hours in camp for the Livingstons: in the 4th New York Regiment of Henry Brockholst's cousin Henry Beekman Livingston, a quarrel broke out and one Samuel Hemenway plunged a knife into the neck of Dudley Broadstreet, cutting his jugular vein. And the hot-tempered Brockholst fought an inconclusive and bloodless duel with a militia major by whom he thought himself insulted.)

Benedict Arnold was not the only American general to give Gates fits at this critical moment. In the evening of September 15, John Stark, hero of Bennington, came into camp, following six hundred of his New Hampshiremen, who had arrived four days earlier. For almost a month they had been inactive, remaining near the scene of their triumph in Vermont, only now joining the army that awaited Burgoyne's attack. Whether their tardiness was the doing of their prickly and totally unpredictable commanding officer is hard to say, but the fact is that three days after Stark appeared they suddenly marched off. Like so many other militia outfits in this war they were able to argue that they had signed up for two months, they were not about to serve an hour longer than their terms of enlistment required, and if that meant they left camp today, well, that's how it had to be. They were going home. So in spite of anything Gates might do (including offering ten dollars to each man who stayed), and despite the crying need for every able-bodied soldier, they shouldered their muskets and with scrupulous attention to punctuality tramped off toward the east at midnight on the day their enlistments expired.

In fairness, it should be added that the New Hampshire Committee of Safety was keenly aware of the shortcomings inherent in the enlistment process and, knowing that these men would be returning home almost momentarily, had already raised one-sixth of the "lower regiments" to take their places. In fact, the new men were on the way to Bennington, but it seemed extremely unlikely that they would arrive in time to be of service to Gates unless the battle that appeared so imminent was somehow delayed.

Bemis Heights was one of a number of bluffs rising above the Hudson here, and these irregularly shaped masses were separated by a network of ravines down which small streams coursed to the river. It was ideal ground for an army that was expected to stand pat and wait to be attacked, and Kosciuszko—who was in his element as Gates's engineer—planned and supervised the building of a defensive network that was complete by September 15. To block an enemy advance down the river road, a trench was dug from the foot of Bemis Heights, near the tavern, to the river. Behind it was a strong battery that could sweep the road, protect the nearby floating bridge, and command the plain on the opposite shore. About a mile north of this barrier, where the road crossed a stream known as Mill Creek, a short line of breastworks and another battery were established.

From the summit of Bemis Heights, about three-quarters of a mile northwest of the tavern, a magnificent panorama of forested hills unfolded—the distant ranges flanking Lake George, the Taconics and Green Mountains, and the heights around Bennington about thirty miles due east. (It was said that smoke from the battle there had been visible from this vantage point.) This vast timberland was broken only by a few clearings, and on Bemis Heights a farmer named John Neilson, newly arrived from New Jersey in 1772, had erected a log cabin, followed by a proper house and a log barn, while he began opening up the level land around him. Now he was soldiering in Gates's army protecting his homestead.

On the brow of the hill, Kosciuszko laid out a three-sided or U-shaped breastworks, about three-quarters of a mile in extent, with a battery at each corner and in the center. The open side was safeguarded by a steep ravine behind it, and at the northwest corner of the redoubt the works incorporated the log barn, which was strengthened and named Fort Neilson.

A wagon track connecting Bemis's tavern to the bluff forked inside the redoubt—the left branch leading west, the right skirting a ravine formed by the south branch of Mill Creek and heading off in a northwesterly direction alongside the Quaker spring past what was called Freeman's farm, presently owned by Isaac Leggett, a Quaker and a loyalist. (John Freeman had traveled north to join Burgoyne's invasion army; Leggett had had the good sense to clear out before the two forces moved into the area and began shooting at each other, but as far as the local folk were concerned it was still Freeman's farm.) Less a farm than another opening in the forest, it was essentially a roughly cleared space of twelve acres or more, about 350 yards long, running east-west and, like other fields in the area, "in very imperfect cultivation, the surface broken and obstructed with stumps and fallen timber," as one American recalled it.

Gates was satisfied with his defensive position, and it could be said that the naturally strong site, strengthened by Kosciuzko's planning and some prodigious labor with axes and shovels, was a good indicator of his personality. The American general was cautious, unimaginative, at his best as an administrator and organizer rather than a field commander, and these characteristics combined to produce a defensive mentality. As a former British officer he had great respect for the terrible carnage those disciplined redcoated ranks could inflict with a bayonet charge, and he had no wish to risk his men's lives needlessly. As he saw it, he had only to wait in his rugged stronghold—wait for Burgoyne to come this way and watch his army destroy itself storming the barricades. Unless the British turned around and withdrew, they had no choice but to attack, and Gates believed he was ready for them.

At what passed for daybreak on Friday, September 19, it was cold and damp, with the two camps blanketed beneath a dense low-lying fog, but the hostile armies were close enough that each side's drums could be heard by the other. When the fog finally lifted, American pickets patrolling the east bank of the Hudson spotted the sort of activity in the British camp that could mean only one thing: the enemy was preparing to advance. Through the foliage that partially screened their view, they could make out enough movement of scarlet and blue uniforms and the glint of sunlight on weapons to tell that the artillery and the Germans were forming up to march down the river road, while British regiments were preparing to move up the slope west of Sword's house.

Even with this intelligence in hand, Gates did nothing. He was content to sit behind his defenses and wait for Burgoyne to come at him, and he had deployed his troops in two wings. The right, technically under Benjamin Lincoln, but in his absence directed by Gates himself, consisted of Glover's, Nixon's, and Paterson's Continentals. Arnold, on the left, had Learned's and Poor's Continental troops, Morgan's men, and Dearborn's light infantry. Supplementing these units were a number of militia regiments (in which Gates had little confidence), bringing the total number of American effectives to more than nine thousand.

And that would have been that, but for the impetuous major general in command of the army's left wing, who had an entirely different view of how this thing should be handled. Benedict Arnold argued that the enemy should not be allowed to seize the initiative: if the British moved onto the heights instead of making a frontal assault along the river road, they would be in a good position to outflank Gates's army and would certainly take advantage of those cleared fields, using their cannon to blast holes in the American earthworks before following through with a bayonet charge. He wanted to attack them in the woods, where the redcoats would be at a disadvantage and the rebels would be at their best. This was mean, rough country, and if you could get those regulars off in the thick woods, moving up and down hill between ravines, and climbing over clumps of brush, roots, rocks, and fallen limbs, it wouldn't be long before the parade-ground formations would break apart and scatter and the redcoats' ability to mount a bayonet charge would be greatly reduced. What was more, even if Gates's men were beaten at this game, they could fall back to their entrenchments and fight on. Finally Gates acquiesced, but only to the extent of permitting Morgan, supported by Dearborn's light troops, to move out on the left to investigate what was going on and, if necessary, blunt any enemy attack from that direction.

From the time Burgoyne's army left Canada, the order of march had consisted of three divisions—Germans on the left, the British line in the center, and Brigadier Fraser's advanced corps on the right. That was also to be the order of battle as soon as the fog lifted, permitting the advance to begin.

Burgoyne had the option of taking his entire army down the river road, massing his artillery, and making a frontal assault on the rebels but had decided against that—probably wisely, considering Gates's defensive preparations. Scouts brought back word that the heights about two miles west of Gates's lines were unoccupied and unfortified. From American deserters he learned that his enemy now consisted of ten or twelve thousand men, and while he had no way of knowing how accurate this number was, it indicated that Gates's strength was growing all the time as militiamen continued to arrive in his camp. (A man passing through Bennington was astounded to hear how many militia had been seen there en route to join Gates, and the local folk were saying that "the lion is caught in the net" and Burgoyne's capture only a matter of time.)

As yet Burgoyne was unaware of the disposition of those forces, but he had good reason to believe that possession of the ridge was the key to a successful attack, just as Benedict Arnold had foreseen. So the die was cast. The idea was that Fraser would swing west onto the ridge, far to the right of the main body in order to cover its advance, then turn the rebels' exposed left flank and drive the defenders toward the river, where they could be surrounded and mopped up by British and German forces in the center and on the left sweeping forward. The tactic was risky, since it meant separating the several divisions of Burgoyne's numerically inferior army, but under the circumstances it was probably the best that could be devised.

Simon Fraser, the officer in whom Burgoyne had the greatest confidence, had the elite corps—Acland's grenadier and Balcarres's light infantry battalions, and Fraser's own 24th Regiment, supported by two German regiments under Lieutenant Colonel Breymann. Some Indians and Canadians, plus loyalists under Peters and Jessup, were out in front and on the flanks. Fraser's role in the attack was expected to prove crucial.

The center, commanded by Brigadier Hamilton, consisted of four battalions of the British line—the 9th, 20th, 21st, and 62nd Regiments, plus four fieldpieces. Burgoyne and his staff rode with these men, and he instructed Hamilton to follow Fraser up the hill from Sword's house and at a certain point turn due south, marching parallel to Fraser's column and feeling his way toward the American center.

General Riedesel's command comprised the left wing: the Specht, Riedesel, and Rhetz Regiments, flanking four British six-pounders under Captain Pausch, and the train of heavy artillery. This contingent was to head south along the road and the meadows bordering the river, leaving the British 47th Regiment behind to guard the bateaus and hospital, with the Hesse-Hanau troops forming the rear guard. All three divisions had some artillery—Riedesel's the most, of course—and in all the army included about 7,700 men—the left and right wings with about 3,000 each, and some 1,700 under Hamilton in the center.

When the sun finally broke through the fog, the troops began trotting into position—the movement observed by rebel scouts on the opposite shore. It was after ten when several cannon shots signaled that the advance was to begin, but because of the terrain the three columns soon found the going extremely difficult and communications more so. Fraser was the first to reach the formidable Great Ravine (which young Charles Stanhope, Viscount Petersham, described as "one of the deepest I ever saw") and was forced to travel farther west before he located a suitable place to cross the stream. By then he was nearly two miles from the center column, traversing a circuitous route along the high ground, where he was able to cover the march of the main army against attack from that direction and could drive in any troops he found on the rebel left.

Hamilton's corps arrived at the north bank of the ravine at a point approximately midway along this natural obstacle that extended to the river—and headed down the dark, densely wooded slope. His troops were carrying sixty rounds of ammunition per man, and this, with their other gear, meant that they were lugging a dead weight of about fifty or sixty pounds, stumbling and sliding awkwardly downhill until they finally reached the stream (a watercourse sufficiently large to power a mill near the river road). Crossing that, they struggled up the opposite bank, climbing through a tangle of brush and trees that made rapid movement impossible, especially for the fieldpieces they brought with them. At the top they found themselves in the woods bordering Freeman's farm, and on the edge of the clearing where cows had grazed until recently they waited—tired, sweating profusely, ill at ease in woods that offered little opportunity for their accustomed volley firing—waited to give Fraser time to come abreast of them. Hamilton sent out Major Gordon Forbes with one hundred pickets to investigate the buildings standing in the center of the clearing, in which some rebels appeared to be posted. As an old hand, Forbes could be trusted with this sort of business. Almost forty, he had spent more than half his life in the army, including nine years in Louisiana after it was ceded to Britain by Spain. Arriving in Canada in 1776, he was made a major in the 9th Foot and had fought at Hubbardton, so he had an idea what to expect from these rebels.

As slowly as the British center column moved, the left was slower, its leisurely pace dictated by obstructions the rebels had placed in the road the heavy artillery had to take. The Brunswick regiments found their route effectively blocked at each stream crossing, where bridges were destroyed and had to be rebuilt by felling trees and removing debris the Americans had stacked there. It was maddeningly tedious work: one hundred paces beyond the first bridge (which they had reconstructed the previous day) was another that had been burned. Replacing that cost them an hour, and they found a like situation at a third crossing, four hundred paces farther on, from which the rebel lines on the hill were clearly visible.

Yet with all the delays it says a lot about this army's professionalism and the caliber of its officers that despite having to tramp through woods and ravines, uphill and down, over completely unfamiliar, forbidding terrain, the three columns managed by some miracle to arrive just where they were supposed to be and at approximately the same time. Thus far they had executed Burgoyne's plan perfectly. About two o'clock—almost four hours after leaving camp near Sword's house—the Brunswickers heard the signal guns fired, which meant that a general advance was to begin, and this was followed almost immediately by the distant rattle of small arms that continued "in a lively fashion" for a good half hour.

Riedesel's troops were near a rough wagon trace that wound uphill from the river, and hearing the sounds of fighting that came from somewhere up there on the forested bluffs the baron immediately dispatched Pausch with two guns along this route, his idea being that this would achieve the dual purpose of establishing communications with Burgoyne (since the British regiments were now about two miles, or more than half an hour's march, from the Germans) while enabling him to support Hamilton and even Fraser's left wing if need be.

September 19's ghostly, seemingly impenetrable fog smothered the American camp that morning, shrouding any movement the enemy might be making, but sometime past sunrise the haze began to lift, scouting parties were sent out, and about ten o'clock word reached headquarters that the British were three miles away, moving toward the rebel works. Sergeants shouted orders, drums rolled, the troops struck their tents and ran out to man the lines.

This American army was not much to look at. A great many of the soldiers had literally marched out of their shoes and whatever clothing or uniforms they wore. It was a motley crew, but just now, as if to prove that appearances might be deceiving, they were itching for the real fight that had been so long in coming—a knock-down-drag-out slugfest that would decide the campaign in the north, determining whether George Washington's army outside Philadelphia would be trapped between Howe and Burgoyne, or whether Burgoyne's force would be knocked out of the war, permitting Gates's men to head south and join the commander in chief. For the first time since the British invasion army had moved south from Canada, the rebels had an advantage in numbers, with more militia companies arriving all the time. In fact, they were drifting into camp as late as two o'clock this very day. Burgoyne, on the other hand, had no reinforcements he could count on and was in a position where if he did not win an absolute victory he would very likely suffer total defeat. He was a gambler who might risk everything on one throw of the dice, as Horatio Gates said, but the odds against him were mounting with each passing hour.

According to the agreement extracted from the reluctant Gates, Arnold dispatched Morgan and Dearborn with instructions to keep a sharp eye on the army's left flank and harass any enemy troops that came in sight. Not long before one o'clock about three hundred of these riflemen and light infantry, led by a Pennsylvania captain named Van Swearingin, advanced through the trees and reached the southern edge of Freeman's clearing. Some of the men moved into the field and took possession of a log hut, others stationed themselves behind a rail fence; still others waited behind trees or perched up in the branches. The area was forested with virgin timber—enormous maples, oak, and white pine that afforded blessed relief from the sun and provided cover for soldiers who knew how to make the most of it, as Morgan's back-country people most assuredly did. Before long the frontiersmen caught sight of Major Forbes's skirmishers emerging from the tree line at the opposite end of the field and moving cautiously toward the farm buildings. By all logic Burgoyne's attack should have caught the rebels off-guard, and that it did not had a lot to do with Benedict Arnold's insistence on going out to meet the enemy rather than waiting to be attacked. Because of that, when Burgoyne's troops were poised for battle he was unaware that Dan Morgan's men had reached the field just ahead of him—but only just.

Almost invisible in the woods and in back of the rail fence, the riflemen took careful aim, especially at the officers, and along with the Americans waiting inside the log cabin fired with devastating effect, routing Forbes's astonished redcoats. Running forward for the kill, Morgan's men burst into the open and dashed after the fleeing British, not realizing until too late that they were headed straight for the massed British line. That charge was very nearly fatal, for just then Captain Fraser's light infantry companies brought up a cannon, rushed into the clearing to support Hamilton's men, and hit the unsuspecting Americans squarely on their left flank.

Hamilton's men were formed along the tree line, ready for action, and it was almost more than they could stand to wait there as onlookers of the chaotic scene out in the clearing—a cacophony of musket fire and men shouting or screaming in pain, bewildered soldiers running every which way, the air full of bullets, and off in the forest somewhere, an eerie, high-pitched "gobble-gobble-gobble," Morgan's imitation of a turkey call, by which he collected his scattered command, signaling them to fall back to the woods. Wilkinson, who was at his side, said the old wagoner was so upset he was in tears, thinking his corps was ruined. Captain Van Swearingin was wounded and, along with twelve others,

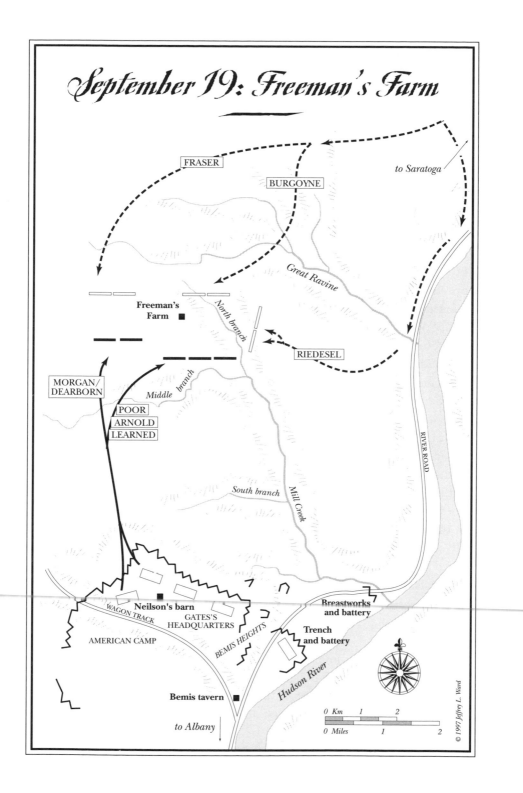

September 19: Freeman's Farm

FRASER

BURGOYNE

to Saratoga

Great Ravine

Freeman's
Farm

North branch

RIEDESEL

MORGAN/
DEARBORN

Middle branch

POOR
ARNOLD
LEARNED

South branch

Mill Creek

RIVER ROAD

Neilson's barn

GATES'S
HEADQUARTERS

Breastworks
and battery

WAGON TRACK

BEMIS HEIGHTS

Trench
and battery

AMERICAN CAMP

Bemis tavern

Hudson River

to Albany

0 Km   1   2

0 Miles   1   2

© 1997 Jeffrey L. Ward

taken by Fraser's Indians, who began to strip him and steal the pocket-book containing his commission, papers, and money. Fortunately, Simon Fraser's batman rescued him from the Indians and took him to the brigadier for interrogation, but to Fraser's annoyance, all the prisoner would say was that the Americans were led by Gates and Arnold. Fraser threatened him: if he didn't reveal the exact disposition of Gates's force he would hang him. "You may, if you please," was the captain's cool reply, and the general rode away, so impressed by this sangfroid that he left him in the custody of an artillery lieutenant with orders that he was not to be ill-treated.*

With rebels scrambling pell-mell toward safety, British skirmishers retreating, both sides trying to carry off their wounded at the same time Fraser's light troops came booming in from the right, the strain finally proved too much for Hamilton's waiting men to remain idle, and they opened fire without orders, killing a number of their own soldiers who were falling back toward the main line. Lieutenant Colonel Robert Kingston, Burgoyne's deputy adjutant general, had the presence of mind to stop this unnecessary slaughter by ordering Lieutenant Hadden to fire a cannon. The crash of the fieldpiece silenced the British muskets; "By that accident," Hadden recalled proudly, "I fired the first Shot from the main body of this Army."

But the damage was done. Every officer with the pickets was either killed or wounded, giving rise to the suspicion—quite accurate as it turned out—that Morgan's sharpshooters were singling out the men with silver gorgets at their throats that identified them as officers. Major Forbes was hurt, but continued to rally his men despite the injury. One of the dead was the Canadian Captain David Monin, whose eleven-year-old son was fighting at his side when he fell.

At his headquarters in "a small hovel" behind the American lines, Gates learned from captured enemy soldiers that "the whole British Force and a Division of Foreigners" were about to attack, and he ordered Poor to dispatch more men in support of Morgan. Some nine hundred troops, including two New Hampshire regiments—Joseph Cilley's 1st and Alexander Scammell's 3rd—took off at once, Cilley in the lead, angling off to the left in hopes of flanking the enemy, followed by Scammell, who went straight ahead through the woods toward the clearing. As usual, Arnold found it impossible to remain aloof from the fighting,

---

*He was not. He resigned from the army in 1779, signed up a dozen years later as a captain of Kentucky militia, and was killed fighting Indians.

and one of Dearborn's men saw him "riding in front of the lines, his eyes flashing, pointing with his sword to the advancing foe, with a voice that rang clear as a trumpet and electrified the line." He cantered up to a picket guard of men from the 8th Massachusetts under Major William Hull, called for volunteers, and sent about three hundred of them off in the direction of the fighting to join Poor. With rebel reinforcements moving into position the British line was also filling out with more men, and as this maneuvering was going on the gunfire sputtered out. The skirmish, as intense as any full-scale battle, had lasted between half and three-quarters of an hour, and Farmer Freeman's clearing was now piled with the bodies of rebels and redcoats, some dead, some terribly wounded, for whom there was precious little help, since anyone moving out into that field to aid a wounded mate was likely to be shot.*

Except for the pitiful cries of the wounded calling for water or begging someone to put an end to their suffering, the battlefield was silent for about two hours, baking in the hot midday sun, but the rustle of leaves and the continuous movement of shadowy figures in the woods were sure signs that the quiet would not last.

At three-forty by Parson Hitchcock's watch the front exploded again. As General Glover described it, "Both armies seemed determined to conquer or die." In that airless clearing hemmed in by trees and darkened by black powder smoke, the deafening slam of cannons was almost more than the eardrum could bear. Alexander Scammell was in the thick of the fighting and called it "the hottest Fire of Canon and Musquetry that ever I heard in my life," and his commanding officer, Enoch Poor, later told a friend that "the blaze from the artillery and small arms was incessant, and sounded like the roll of the drum. By turns the British and Americans drove each other, taking and retaking the fieldpieces . . . often mingling in a hand to hand wrestle and fight. Scammell fought like a hero," he added, "leading his regiment where the fire was the hottest. . . ." Scammell's lieutenant colonel, Andrew Colburn, was killed—an invaluable man who would be greatly missed; one of his second lieutenants was also dead, and he had two more subalterns injured, plus twenty-six other soldiers killed, wounded, or missing. More of his men would have fallen, he felt certain, had the hand of heaven not been on them: a ball went

---

*According to Henry Hallowell of the 5th Massachusetts, some men in his regiment broke ranks and "went to plundering the dead," for which Colonel Rufus Putnam gave them unshirted hell.

through the breech of his fusil, another through his overalls, just missing both legs, and a sergeant major standing at his side had both of his hamstrings cut by a musket ball.

The colonel's 3rd New Hampshire Regiment was facing five fieldpieces and some of the best troops in the British line, and they were in trouble from the moment they attacked. Once, when they were almost surrounded, they were rescued by Colonel Cook's Connecticut militia regiment; again, by Cilley, who altered the deployment of his troops in order to help out. For two hellish hours Scammell and his men fought on alongside Morgan and Dearborn, and Scammell was proud to see that none of his men stopped to plunder fallen British soldiers—only "when their guns and ammunition fail'd," he said, "then they would stoop down and pick up the enemy's, [which] lay thickly scatter'd upon the Ground which we had drove them from." Then Poor arrived with the rest of his brigade, followed by part of Learned's command and Hull's Massachusetts men, and somewhere in the melee Arnold was said to have rushed "into the thickest of the fight with his usual recklessness, and at times acted like a madman." Whatever Arnold's role, the primary objective of these rebel units was the British artillery, whose commander was picked off by one of Morgan's sharpshooters. The horses that had pulled the guns into battle were all dead, and after "several smart struggles" the Americans captured the cannon, only to find it impossible to haul them away across the thick brush and rough ground, since they had no horses. But the British were not about to let those guns go, in any event; Hamilton sent fresh troops into action, drove the rebels back, and began firing grapeshot and canister at them at a range no more than a good musket shot. In the midst of all this, Scammell caught sight of General John Burgoyne on horseback, resplendent in uniform, directing his troops, and the rumor spread later that the general had been shot from his horse and carried off, badly wounded—perhaps dead. Like another report that Simon Fraser was killed, this one proved false: it was not Burgoyne who was shot but Captain Charles Green, an aide-de-camp of General Phillips, who was delivering a message to the commanding general and was especially conspicuous because of a beautiful lace saddlecloth with which his horse was equipped.*

Hull had formed his men on a little rise near the south end of the field, and when he saw redcoats coming at him from a distance of about five

---

*Burgoyne learned later that the bullet that hit Green had indeed been intended for him, so he owed his escape from injury to a fancy saddle blanket.

hundred feet he told them to hold their fire until he gave the command and warned them not to shoot too high—to aim at the enemies' knees. The British were about fifty yards away when the major shouted, *"Fire!"* and suddenly gaping holes opened up in those even lines and behind them men could be seen writhing on the ground. Still they came on, until Hull ordered a bayonet charge that finally drove them off. He only had time to send his wounded off to the rear before another crisis developed, this time on the right flank, so he shifted his command to a position where they had the cover of woods, where they fought until dusk. When they finally left the field, exhausted, their ammunition gone, half of the three hundred men who went into action had been killed or wounded.

Throughout the fight, each of the opposing generals was sufficiently worried about what the other might do that he didn't dare commit his entire army to the battle. Gates's concern was the possibility of attack by the German foot soldiers and British artillery along the river, which made him withhold badly needed support from Poor's brigade. In Burgoyne's case, he kept most of Fraser's force in reserve up on the heights because he feared a flank attack on Hamilton's corps and was late in calling on Riedesel for assistance. The result was that the battle was concentrated in the center, exactly where Lieutenant James Hadden was stationed with two cannon.

Hadden, the son of a captain in the Royal Marines, had commanded one of the gunboats on Lake Champlain that destroyed Benedict Arnold's little navy off Valcour Island in the fall of 1776. In July of the next year he and his detachment of thirty men and three noncoms were ordered to join Captain Thomas Jones's company, and here he was, up against Arnold again, serving two guns on the left of the 62nd Regiment. The 62nd was under intense fire from the rebels, as were Hadden's fieldpieces, and it was bloody work. Of twenty-two artillerists with him, nineteen were either killed or wounded in the firefight, and Hadden ran to ask Hamilton for infantrymen to replace his gunners. But the general's vantage point was no place to be just then: as Hamilton was telling him to request reinforcements from General Phillips, a bullet knocked off the lieutenant's cap. Phillips was in one of the log huts with Burgoyne just then, and he acted at once, ordering Captain Jones to take another lieutenant's gun crew and assist Hadden.

By the time they reached his battery, rebel support troops under Major William Hull had driven back the 62nd Regiment, which lost 187 men killed or wounded, plus twenty-five captured, and was exhausted, thoroughly confused, and in a state of near-panic. The artillerists quickly opened fire on the rebels, but they were no match for the overwhelming numbers and almost immediately Jones and all the men he brought with him were casualties, many of them victims of those long Pennsylvania rifles.

Hadden lifted the captain and carried him to a log hut that was so full of wounded that the lieutenant had to wait some time for a place to lay him. But Jones's wound was mortal, and Hadden barely made it back to the British lines, narrowly escaping capture when the rebels overran his guns, swept the men of the 62nd off the hill where they had stood, and threatened to roll up the regiment's left flank. At this critical juncture, with the 62nd very nearly routed, the Americans came close to mopping up the British center and might have done so had the 20th Regiment not suddenly appeared at the eastern edge of Freeman's cornfield, just a hundred yards away. These fresh troops were led by that tough artilleryman Major General William Phillips, who ignored the enormous personal risk involved in riding at the head of the infantrymen and kept the rebels at bay long enough for Major Griffith Williams to bring up four heavy cannon and start blasting away at them. Like Phillips, Burgoyne seemed to have a charmed life, for he was in the thick of the fighting, paying no attention whatever to the dangers to which he was exposed. Sergeant Lamb observed that his presence and coolness under fire "animated the troops (for they greatly loved the general)," and Lieutenant Digby noted that "General Burgoyne was every where and did every thing [that] could be expected from a brave officer." Unlike these British generals, Gates never left his headquarters.

Because of their orders to hold on to the ridge, only a fraction of Fraser's advanced corps saw any action—some men from the 24th Regiment, the grenadiers, and light infantry—but the fighting was near enough to them for Lieutenant Anburey to witness much of what went on. Off to the left the gunfire was incessant, and he saw something he would never forget: to his horror, Lieutenant Don of the 21st Regiment was struck in the heart by a musket ball and leaped into the air almost as high as a man is tall before falling like a stone to the ground. The battle raged with no letup for three hours, four, some thought an eternity—certainly until nightfall—"such an explosion of fire I never had any idea of before," Digby wrote. The deafening peals of thunder from the heavy artillery were amplified by echoes reverberating through the woods as the fighting seesawed back and forth, with regiments constantly on the move, now relieving a hard-pressed unit, now driven off by rebel reinforcements. Men lost touch with each other in the dim, tangled wilderness beyond the clearing, where it was all but impossible for officers to see more than a fraction of their troops; they had to send aides out to deliver orders. And still the muskets fired interminably, soldiers shooting as fast as they could load until the air throbbed with the concussions. As Benjamin Warren described the action, "We beat them back three times and they reinforced and recovered their ground again, till after sunset without any intermission when both parties retired and left the field."

By contrast, the Brunswickers posted along the river were having an easy time of it, having fired no more than a few shots. Then, shortly after three o'clock when the pace of the unseen battle on the hill picked up, the eager Riedesel grew increasingly anxious and wondered what Burgoyne wanted him to do, since he had received neither information nor orders from the commander in chief. He dispatched Captain Willoe for instructions, and Willoe returned two hours later with word that Burgoyne wanted him to see to the safety of the artillery, the baggage, and the bateaus, but at the same time to bring as many troops as could be spared to assist the hard-pressed British center and, if possible, to attack the rebel right wing. It was a tall order, but it was all Riedesel needed: he told Brigadier Specht to take command of the men guarding the stores and left at once for the scene of action, leading about five hundred infantrymen—his own regiment and two companies from von Rhetz's brigade—and picking up Captain Pausch and two of his six-pounders along the way. For Burgoyne this move was a calculated risk, exposing his army to starvation, for if the Americans attacked now along the river road he stood to lose all his precious provisions.

Riedesel's detachment marched up the wagon track just south of the Great Ravine, and when they reached the plateau the general rode off with the two Rhetz companies he had sent ahead and soon came in sight of the bloody clearing on Freeman's farm where rebel troops were hammering away at Hamilton's left, which was very near collapse. These redcoats, standing among piles of their dead and wounded, had been compelled to retreat several times, but regrouped on each occasion to fight back, only to be hit by fresh American forces. Now they were thoroughly fought out and on the verge of disaster. But as at Hubbardton the Brunswickers arrived at the right place and the right moment to tip the scales in favor of the British. Riedesel sent the two infantry companies ahead on the double, with orders to make as much noise as possible with the beating of drums and shouts by the men. These fresh troops slammed into the startled Americans, closed ranks, and delivered a murderous fire at their flank. Pausch's cannon arrived and began raking the rebels with grapeshot, and when the Riedesel regiment ran up the battered redcoats came to life, and "with great shouts of joy, made a furious attack on the enemy."

It was too much for the New Hampshire Continentals and Hull's detachment, who had been fighting desperately for three hours and whose lack of major support revealed how difficult it was to carry out any maneuvers in the dense forest in the confusion of this battle. Arnold had ridden back to headquarters to request reinforcements, and Gates ordered Learned's brigade to support the troops under attack by Riedesel. But no officer familiar with the terrain or the deployment of American units accompanied Learned's men, with the result that they wandered off in the wrong direction, stumbled into Fraser's skirmishers, and never did locate the troops they were supposed to rescue. Fortunately for the latter, dusk was falling and they were able to fall back in good order, carrying off their wounded.

The coming of darkness finally put an end to it—darkness that stopped the shooting and hid the horrifying sights of the battlefield but could not put an end to the sounds of agony. In the eighteenth-century perception of things, the British were the victors because, as Lieutenant Anburey said, the enemy "left us masters of the field." But those Britons who thought they had won had not totted up the cost. British losses were severe: 160 dead, 364 wounded, and 42 missing.

With a bravado that is difficult to comprehend, on September 20 Burgoyne put a bold face on matters when he wrote to Brigadier Powell at Ticonderoga, telling him of "a smart and very honorable action," after which possession of the battlefield "must demonstrate our victory beyond the power of even an American newswriter to explain away." Yet surely Powell could read between the lines, and certainly some of Burgoyne's junior officers knew better. Notwithstanding that "the glory of the day remains on our side," Anburey observed, "I am fearful the real advantages resulting from this hard-fought battle will rest on that of the Americans, our army being so much weakened by this engagement as not to be of sufficient strength to venture forth and improve the victory, which may, in the end, put a stop to our intended expedition; the only apparent benefit gained is that we keep possession of the ground where the engagement began."

Because the battle had raged in the woods and underbrush as well as the clearing, without maps it was virtually impossible for Burgoyne's people to get a handle on where and how things had happened, except in the most general terms. Brigadier Specht knew, for example, that

Fraser's and Breymann's corps had taken part, but under what circumstances remained obscure. He did know that Breymann, through some "fortunate maneuvering," had saved Fraser from being cut off from the rest of the army, but he became aware of this only because Burgoyne publicly commended the Brunswick colonel for his action. The British were largely in the dark about rebel losses but assumed that American casualties greatly exceeded their own, believing the rebels had carried off most of their dead and wounded when they retired from the field.

Whatever else Burgoyne's army had learned from this experience, most of them now had a better sense of their opponents' fighting skill. (An exception was Joshua Pell, Jr., a captain in a New York regiment of loyalists, who commented that "the Rebels fought bravely in the woods, but durst not advance one Inch toward the Open field," and went on to say that the Americans in general were drunk, which was the only way Gates could get them to fight.) But Burgoyne was more of a realist. After praising the valor of his own men, he acknowledged the same quality in the Americans and remarked that the behavior of the three British regiments that suffered the heaviest losses (the 62nd Regiment was left with less than sixty men and four or five officers, the equivalent of a single company at full strength, while only twelve of forty-eight artillerymen who accompanied the center column were not killed or wounded), after being under continuous fire for four hours, was no less honorable because their opponents were "irregulars and militia." It was a "dear bought victory," Lieutenant Digby admitted, and Anburey had only praise for "the courage and obstinacy with which the Americans fought." Those characteristics, he said, "were the astonishment of everyone, and we now become fully convinced they are not that contemptible enemy we had hitherto imagined them, incapable of standing a regular engagement, and that they would only fight behind strong earthworks."

In fact, both sides had battled to the limit of endurance and ability, and John Glover put it well when he said Burgoyne's men were "bold, intrepid, and fought like heroes [while] our men were equally bold and courageous & fought like men, fighting for their all." But no American expressed it better than Henry Dearborn, who said that "we ... had Something more at Stake than fighting for six Pence Pr Day."

Baroness Riedesel had observed that quality in the Americans and put her finger on what gave them something of an edge. Noting that every inhabitant of the region "is a born soldier and a good marksman," she added, "The thought of fighting for their country and for freedom made them braver than ever." She had been an eyewitness to the fighting, she said (though how she could have seen much of what took place in the woods and beyond is a mystery), and, knowing that her husband and his troops were engaged in the action, "was filled with fear and anguish and shivered whenever a shot was fired, as nothing escaped my ear." Inevitably, she saw the casualties come in, three of whom were brought to the small, deserted house she was sharing with Lady Harriet Acland and the wives of Major Harnage and Lieutenant Reynell. As the battle continued the place was commandeered by the surgeons, and orderlies began carrying in the wounded. To the dismay of Mrs. Harnage her husband was one of them, badly hurt with a shot in the abdomen, and soon afterward the distraught Mrs. Reynell was told that her lieutenant was dead, leaving her with three small children in the middle of a war in the American wilderness.

All this understandably heightened the apprehension of Madame Riedesel and Lady Harriet, whose husband and brother were both in the action. Through the night the baroness was kept awake by the groans of Harnage, who was being nursed by his wife in the next room, and cries of agony from a young English lieutenant lying on a bed of straw in the room on the other side. He was suffering from a leg wound that had caused him to lose a great amount of blood. The doctors wanted to amputate, but he would have none of it, and although the baroness did what she could to make him comfortable, gangrene set in, the operation was performed too late, and in a few days he died.

Nighttime on the field of battle was one of sheer horror for the wounded left behind, while those who had come through unscathed slept on their arms and suffered the torture of listening to the groans of the wounded and dying, knowing they could do nothing to help them for fear of being shot by the rebels. To make matters worse the wolves were out there tearing at the flesh of dying men, and their blood-chilling howls were heard all night. "Sleep was a stranger to us," Digby wrote, as it was for Anburey, whose outfit camped on the trampled weeds of the clearing where the three British regiments had been engaged. Since there were "only a few wretched houses and 3 barns" in the vicinity, Anburey's unit was surrounded by corpses and badly wounded men who lay all night in below-freezing temperatures, "perishing with cold and weltering in their blood." In the morning Anburey had the grisly task of going out with a burial detail, interring as many as twenty men in a single grave (scrupulously putting officers in a hole by themselves), and he liked to think that his detail had done a better job than others, who left heads, legs, and arms uncovered, above ground. As a young officer himself he was shaken when he was obliged to lay away three subalterns of the 20th Regiment, the oldest of whom was seventeen.

Total American casualties were somewhere between 273 and 313—approximately half the British loss—and the rebels killed numbered almost a hundred fewer than Burgoyne's forces. But there was no lack of suffering by Gates's men, as John Glover knew after seeing scores of amputees and hearing the cries of the wounded and the moaning of the dying. These unfortunate fellows were treated by men whose knowledge probably came from apprenticeship to a doctor, in whose medical library they read; from their mentor they learned to mix prescriptions and with him made the rounds of the sick to get some hands-on experience, and if this suggests a modicum of education, that was certainly true in most cases. But whatever their skills, army surgeons could do little about the appallingly primitive conditions under which they had to function. Usually the field hospitals were tents or an abandoned barn, but whatever form they took they were likely to be death traps. Even if a man sent there recovered from his wound he stood an excellent chance of contracting one of the many epidemic diseases medical science was then incapable of preventing or curing.

James Thacher, one of thirty surgeons in the overcrowded makeshift hospitals in Albany, observed that the mutilated bodies, mangled limbs, and incurable wounds were bad enough, but equally depressing were men "languishing under afflicting diseases of every description." A military hospital, he decided, "is a fine field for professional improvement."

The men lying in the field hospitals that night were the accidental victims of a battle that was almost totally unplanned. Before it began, neither general had a very clear idea of where his enemy was or what he was likely to do, nor did either have more than the most general knowledge of what his own tactics would be. Horatio Gates was never even close to the fighting and could only imagine, on the basis of reports, what was occurring out there where the billowing smoke clouded the sky. John Burgoyne was in the thick of it, but his army was separated in such a way that none of its three units were in touch with the others or knew what they were doing, and, except at the very end, never really fought as a team. It was, in other words, a battle in which the men who fought it so gallantly—not the generals—deserved all the credit.

With the coming of night it was not even clear who had won. As the Reverend Enos Hitchcock said, "tis impossible to determine what

Success as we can*t* find either their or our loss. it must be considerable on both." But victory and defeat are not always clear cut, and something beyond numbers went into the accounting. All afternoon the momentum had shifted back and forth and it was a tribute to the rebels' courage and determination that Burgoyne's veterans never found an opportunity to mount a bayonet charge except at the end, when Riedesel's men burst on the scene. In four hours of hand-to-hand combat the Americans had held their own against some of the best troops in the world. Those four hours marked a turning point in the morale of both armies.

Lieutenant General John Burgoyne could not know it, but the gallant charge by Riedesel on the night of September 19 marked the high-water mark of his campaign.

Chapter 19

I Will Make a Push
in About Ten Days

Alexander Scammell sat in his tent with blurred images of battle crowding his mind as he prepared to tackle one of the hardest jobs a soldier faces—how to break the news to a woman that her husband is dead. It was best to be straightforward about it, he knew, and he informed the newly widowed Mrs. Andrew Colburn that the man she loved had been killed near Saratoga on the 19th of September "after being in battle 3 hours, perhaps the hottest ever fought in America." To these melancholy tidings he added that before losing his life, Colburn "unluckily lost his baggage in the retreat from Ticonderoga but [I] have got an account of his loss." When and if the army was reimbursed he would see to it that she received compensation. But there was more: to make matters worse, her husband's body had been robbed on the battlefield. "An advance party of the enemy plundered his watch and shoe buckles on the 19th" but the men of his regiment "made them pay dearly" for that. Concluding the letter, Scammell said he was enclosing the buttons from Colburn's uniform coat and his commissions, "to keep in your mind what a brave and noble husband you once had."

John Francis, brother of the intrepid Ebenezer, who was killed at Hubbardton, took advantage of a rainy morning to write his widowed sister-in-law, who was worrying about her debts. John wanted her to know that he had succeeded in selling some of Ebenezer's clothes and that he would buy several additional items from her if she would send them. Clothing was in short supply in Gates's camp and he had not been paid for a while, but if he lived until winter he would also buy a saddle from her. Meanwhile she could rest easy about her indebtedness: Ebenezer's friends had agreed to settle them for her as soon as they drew their pay. Then, as an afterthought—could she send him a pair of gloves or mittens? The weather had turned cold.

On the night after the battle, before Gates's exhausted soldiers drifted off to sleep, it seemed a good bet that they could expect more fighting the next day. But the events of the previous eight hours had given these farmers and artisans, so recently come to the practice of war, an enormous satisfaction and a new confidence, knowing that they had met the best the British army had to offer and inflicted far greater loss than they suffered. In fact, they had come within a whisker of giving the enemy a thorough beating, and although they had finally been forced to withdraw they had done so in an orderly manner and without pursuit. For that, they were lucky. One German officer was convinced that if darkness had not put an end to the fighting the Brunswick troops could have kept on going, right into the rebel camp. And perhaps he was right, for the Americans were worn out, physically and emotionally, the Brunswickers were fresh, and although the American soldiers were not aware of it, only about forty rounds of ammunition per man remained in their magazine.

The early morning of September 20 was a reprise of the previous day—camp buried under a thick, wet fog that soaked every article of clothing, cold enough that the tents and the ground around them were white, covered with hoarfrost. Before the sun burned off the mist a British deserter who came into the lines said the grenadiers would attack soon, and the rebel troops turned out immediately to man the breastworks, wondering when the big men in mitered caps would materialize out of the gloom. For several hours they waited, but nothing happened. And when the sun finally illuminated the field not a redcoat was to be seen.

Lieutenant Digby, who seems to have had an acute ear for camp scuttlebutt, heard that Generals Fraser and Phillips wanted to capitalize on the last-minute momentum of the previous evening and attack on the morning of the 20th but Burgoyne, after first favoring the idea, had second thoughts and decided against it—probably, Digby figured, because the hospitals were so full and the army's provisions inadequately protected. Perhaps. But it is worth remembering that Fraser had seen little action and Phillips was a latecomer to the battle, and neither had been exposed to the fighting for as long as Burgoyne, who had been with the center column and knew that it had been nearly cut to pieces. Very likely that vivid knowledge had something to do with his decision to delay an attack until Sunday the 21st. But before dawn on that day he received a message from Sir Henry Clinton that reinforced his opinion, changed his plan, and completely altered the nature of the campaign.

The two British generals had agreed in advance that when Clinton wrote to Burgoyne the latter would use a decoding mask to get at the actual message. This was a cutout in the shape of an hourglass that when laid over what appeared to be an innocuous letter would reveal the operative words of the message. Burgoyne had lost the pattern but made another from memory and was able to read what Sir Henry had written from New York on September 12:

> You know my good will and are not ignorant of my poverty [of troops]. If you think 2000 men can assist you effectually, I will make a push at [Fort] Montgomery in about ten days. But ever jealous of my flanks if they make a move in force on either of them I must return to save this important post. I expect reenforcement every day. Let me know what you would wish.

This was hardly an unqualified promise of support, but since it was the first word Burgoyne had received from the south since Howe's letter of July 17, it revived the hope that had inspired and sustained this expedition from the outset—that an army from New York would link up with his own at Albany. For some time Burgoyne had known that reinforcements from Europe were expected in New York during the summer, though he could hardly have imagined that the slow-moving Dutch transports carrying them would take an agonizing three months for the Atlantic passage, not arriving off Manhattan until the fourth week of September. Clinton's hint that they might appear any day now was the best possible news, yet Burgoyne's rash assumption that a force of two thousand men could extricate him from the jam he was in is a measure of his desperation. Nevertheless, he decided at once to dig in, remain where he was, and wait for Clinton, which was quite possibly the worst move he could have made.

In the first place, Clinton had indicated his intention to start toward Fort Montgomery "in about ten days." In other words, he would leave New York on September 22 at the earliest, and even if he was blessed with favorable winds and was not held up by rebel-held fortifications on the Hudson above Peekskill, the trip to Albany would take at least five or six days, after which his army would have a forty-mile march to Stillwater. At best, then, he would be in position to take some of the pressure off Burgoyne in another week or, more likely, two. It was not a prospect on which to pin the hopes of an army that was almost out of food.

While he waited, Burgoyne decided to beef up his defenses. His left would continue to be anchored on the river to guard the bateaus and stores, but with his right wing on the heights his front was more than two miles long, and the rebels were so close that their morning gun and drums sounded to the British as loud as their own and they could hear the crash of falling trees that meant the Americans were adding to their defensive works. "I suppose seldom two armies remained looking at each other so long without coming to action," Lieutenant Digby observed, and this uneasy half-truce was to last for two and a half weeks.

Each side was building a bridge across the river—the British lashing bateaus together for theirs, the Americans using fresh-sawn lumber from Schuyler's mill, which came as a gift from the general, and on the same day that Clinton's message arrived the British heard the sound of wild cheering, followed by a thirteen-gun salute. A few days later an escaped prisoner returned and informed them that the celebration followed news of a successful rebel attack on Ticonderoga.

This sideshow to the main event was the brainchild of Major General Benjamin Lincoln, who was by this time camped in Pawlet, Vermont, about fifteen miles north of Manchester, with some 2,000 or 2,500 men. At the time Gates took over the army in mid-September he wrote John Stark requesting suggestions for future operations. Stark and Lincoln, who were in Bennington, put their heads together and came up with the idea of assembling a militia force to harass the posts in Burgoyne's rear. As the two saw it, the surest way to prevent the British general from concentrating the full weight of his army against Gates was to threaten his flank and rear, forcing him to leave sizable detachments at the outposts between his army and Ticonderoga while employing still more troops as escorts for his supply wagons. In addition, Lincoln pointed out, such a campaign would "restrain the unfriendly"—the loyalists. John Stark was bound on just such a mission when he chanced to run into Baum's force outside Bennington.

By September 7, Lincoln had collected enough flour to fill his men's bellies for a while, and he marched to Manchester, then north to Pawlet, where he found a strong position, protected by an outcrop of bony mountains—some of them impassable, according to the fat general, reminding him of where the Greeks made their stand at Thermopylae. When scouts brought word that the garrison at Ticonderoga under Brigadier Powell was widely dispersed and almost surely off guard, Lincoln decided to make a surprise attack. He detached three colonels, Brown, Woodbridge, and Johnson, each with five hundred men, to "annoy, divide, and distract the enemy," while he remained behind in Pawlet with the balance of the command.

Brown had the toughest job: he was to cross the narrows, attack the landing at the north end of Lake George, release any American prisoners he found there, destroy the enemy's boats and supplies, and, if he could do so "without risking too much," attack Fort Ticonderoga. Woodbridge was to head to Skenesborough, which the British had evacuated, where he could cover Brown's line of retreat, while Johnson would threaten Mount Independence in support of Brown and make a genuine attack if the situation warranted.

Brown was an interesting character. A 1771 graduate of Yale, he settled in Pittsfield, Massachusetts, and was sent on a mission to Canada in 1775 by the Massachusetts Committee of Correspondence and returned with a scheme to capture Ticonderoga. Nor was that all: he had even arranged for Ethan Allen and his Green Mountain Boys to carry out the attack as soon as the committee approved the plan. It happened that this bit of audacity put him immediately at loggerheads with Benedict Arnold, who had the same idea himself (though somewhat later than Brown) and naturally wanted to be in charge of the operation. That got the two off on the wrong foot, and they became real enemies when Brown later brought charges against Arnold for alleged misdemeanors in Canada. Brown had seen enough of Arnold by 1777 to conclude with remarkable prescience, "Money is this man's God, and to get enough of it he would sacrifice his country."

Now it was September, with Arnold and Gates feuding and Arnold's ego suffering from slights real and imagined, when word arrived from the north that some of Lincoln's men had surprised the British near Ticonderoga and liberated a number of American prisoners. To Arnold's chagrin the leader of this coup was none other than his old nemesis John Brown.

The raid on Ticonderoga required considerable skill and coordination, and that militiamen succeeded in bringing it off was cause for wonder.

As Brown described his feat, after an all-night march he reached the heights above Lake George landing on September 17, reconnoitered to assess the situation, and the following morning before dawn's light attacked the enemy posts at the landing and Mount Defiance. "In a few minutes," he said, we "carried the place." One reason the operation went so smoothly, according to a British naval officer who was nearby, was that Brown and his men, concealed in the woods, had plenty of time to observe "every transaction at the Portage and in the Camp, even the punishment of a soldier the preceding evening. . . ."

A more immediate cause of success was that the British sentinels, a corporal and three privates, carelessly let a party of rebels approach, assuming they were Canadians in a work detail hauling provisions between the lakes. After the inattentive guards were seized, the Americans surrounded the encampment and sneaked up to the enemy's tents before they were discovered. The experience of a young British officer in the 53rd Regiment was typical: he awoke to the sound of musket fire, saw that the guards had been overpowered, and realized that resistance was futile. In the meantime a company of rangers under Captain Ebenezer Allen stormed the British position atop Mount Defiance—ascending "a craggy Precipice under the Fire of the Enemy" and overrunning the sergeant's guard there in six minutes. Allen's men suffered no casualties, while killing or wounding a number of the enemy and taking twenty prisoners.

By this time Brown's men had fanned out in all directions: after liberating American captives and rounding up a number of British troops in a barn between the camp and the landing place, they seized a group of naval officers and men at the end of the quay, boarded a vessel carrying three six-pounders, and then ran toward a barn about a mile from the fort, where they took more prisoners. The noise of the waterfall had prevented the defenders at the French Lines from hearing the gunfire at the landing, enabling the attackers to surprise a company of British troops there and free more rebels.

It was an amazing performance. At the cost of three or four killed and five wounded, Brown's raiders released 118 Americans who had been "confined, fatigued and dejected to such a degree that one could scarcely conjecture what they were. They come out of their Holes and Cells with Wonder and Amazement," Brown said, "indeed the Transition was almost too much for them." In addition, the colonel's men captured twelve British officers, 143 noncoms and privates, 119 Canadians, several hundred stands of arms, and a large quantity of baggage.

There was more to come: after some 150 bateaus in Lake Champlain and another fifty vessels in Lake George fell into his hands, Brown, in the flush of victory, sent a message under a flag of truce to the British commandant, demanding a surrender of Ticonderoga and Mount Independence in what he called "the strongest and most peremptory terms." The response was about what one might expect from a testy brigadier like Powell: "The garrison intrusted to my charge I shall defend to the last. I am, Sir, your humble servant. H. Watson Powell, Brig. Genl."

John Brown then bit off too big a mouthful. He bombarded Fort Ticonderoga for quite a while ineffectually with his captured cannon, but was realist enough to recognize that he had no chance of storming the place, so he turned his attention elsewhere. After destroying the wagons and all but twenty boats in Lake George, he burned the stores near Ticonderoga, sent off the cattle and horses, and with some four hundred men boarded a small schooner and several gunboats armed with five cannon and embarked for the enemy posts at the other end of that lake. En route up the lake, Brown said, "an unluky Circumstance happened." That night a violent storm came up and a prisoner Brown had taken escaped, made his way to the Americans' destination—British-held Diamond Island, to which all the supplies from the various enemy posts had been removed—and alerted the garrison to the coming attack.

The two companies of the 47th Regiment under Captain Thomas Aubrey and some dozen German soldiers were ready: their cannon hulled the sloop, forcing Brown to tow her away; one gunboat was damaged and "many other Boats shattered to pieces," at which the colonel "thought Proper to retreat," burned what was left of his boats, and headed for Skenesborough.

Despite the disappointing denouement, Brown's achievement (made possible in part by Brigadier H. Watson Powell's appalling negligence in allowing his men to be caught off guard) gave a boost to American morale, revealed the fragility of Burgoyne's line of retreat, and came as one more sober notice to his soldiers that the only way out of their dilemma was to break through Gates's lines.

At this late date, there was no way the British engineers could create a continuous line of works along a two-mile front. North of the Great Ravine they established a so-called Great Redoubt. This was not so much a fortification as three gun batteries on adjacent hilltops directly overlooking the ravine and the river road below, designed to protect the artillery park, bateaus, baggage, the bridge of boats, and the hospital, which consisted of one large barn, two or three small ones, and a number of tents.

Between the river and Freeman's farm the lines fronted on a series of ravines, making fortifications there unnecessary, so the problem facing the engineers was how to secure the right flank. They resolved this by building a huge enclosed fort in the gap between two ravines, known as the Balcarres redoubt—five hundred yards long, with logs and earth mounded twelve to fourteen feet high. Beyond this impressive bulwark a large flat area afforded easy access to the British camp, and to cover this opening they constructed a palisaded breastwork two hundred yards long and seven or eight feet high. Named for Lieutenant Colonel Heinrich Breymann, the redoubt not only covered the British right flank but the road to Quaker Springs as well, which was the probable line of attack from the rebel camp.

Between these redoubts were several log cabins, one facing the road to Wilbur's Basin on the Hudson, manned by a group of dispirited Canadians. Burgoyne's headquarters was located on high ground south of the Great Ravine, between the British and German troops.* To make life easier for the artillerymen, a thousand men were cutting trees to open up three-hundred-yard fields of fire, and when the formidable job was completed a satisfied Brunswick officer described the camp as "almost like a fortress."

Burgoyne's defenses may have been in good order, but not his food supplies: salt pork and flour, which constituted the entire British ration, were running out, and little was to be obtained from the sutlers, except at exorbitant prices. Worse, one German said, "No vegetables, no tobacco, no brandy."

Gates, who was keenly aware of Burgoyne's dwindling food stocks, had a shortage problem of his own—he was still short of ammunition for cannon and small arms and as a result was content to sit tight and wait for the enemy to make the first move. All the while, more men drifted into camp, including a number who had been in the hospital in Albany and were now fit for duty. Meanwhile his troops were giving the British and Germans fits—skirmishers made nightly forays toward the enemy's lines, picking off sentries and capturing foragers who strayed too far. Lady Har-

---

*Here, years later, a farmer who owned the land on which the headquarters had stood was accustomed to finding great quantities of gin and wine bottles each spring when he plowed, confirming Baroness von Riedesel's comment about Burgoyne's habit of carousing with his staff officers.

riet Acland's journal includes the observation that "our advanced picquets & patroles were perpetually engaged with the enemies so that neither night or day were we free from skirmish's near some part of the
camp or other," and according to her the rebels took particular delight in
harassing one set of German sentinels whom they took care "to keep very
alert from the time of their mounting to their being relieved."

Organized foraging was essential for Burgoyne's army, of course—as
one officer wrote, "all our grass was ate up and many horses dying from
want"—and details were sent out more and more often to collect food for
man and beast, but these made extra demands on the army. On one such
venture a staff officer with two hundred men covered the foragers and
Brigadier Specht stood by with three hundred more soldiers and two six-
pounders to come to the rescue if necessary.

The rebels smelled victory. Gates told them, in the event they
were unaware of it, that the enemy's only hope was to make "one rash
Stroke"; when that failed, as it surely would, Burgoyne was ruined, and
the jubilant men became so noisy that they were ordered to keep quiet
after eight o'clock at night. But there was no rest for the enemy. Their
defenses were stretched so thin and vigilance was so critical that no
"officer or soldier ever slept during that interval without his cloaths,"
Burgoyne said, while no general or regimental commander "passed a
single night without being upon his legs occasionally at different hours,
and constantly an hour before daylight." Because of nocturnal attacks on
pickets, Riedesel ordered his advance posts pulled back one hundred
paces after dark, and at points where concealment was impossible, fires
were lit every evening one hundred yards in front of the lines so pickets
could detect any hint of rebel incursions.

The most worrisome problem was the constant attrition in the army's
strength caused by capture or desertion. Oliver Boardman, whose company had marched from Middletown, Connecticut, on September 2 and
arrived at Bemis Heights ten days later, was astonished to see a regular
procession of British and German soldiers—mostly the latter—coming
into the American camp, six prisoners one day, seven captives and four
deserters the next, an entire company of Brunswickers on another. And
so it went. One afternoon a party of Stockbridge Indians brought in a
Tory and General Arnold let the red men have him for a time. They
buried him up to his neck and held a powwow in a circle around him,
then built a huge fire, pulled him out of the ground, and alternately held
his feet and head to the flames, "hooting and hollowing round him" until
Arnold put a stop to it and sent him off to jail in Albany.

Along with the mounting tension, Burgoyne's men were becoming increasingly fatigued. The entire army had to be on the lines an hour before dawn and stand to arms until the fog lifted, which rarely happened before nine in the morning. The days remained uncomfortably hot, the nights cold, and this made for more illness, increasing the number of sick and wounded to more than seven hundred—almost all of them in tents—and hardly a day passed without at least a few deaths. On October 3, in an effort to boost morale, Burgoyne announced that "other powerful Armies of the King" were cooperating with them, but that same day the daily bread allowance was cut. "At no time did the Jews await the coming of their Messiah with greater expectancy than we awaited the coming of General Clinton," one German officer remarked, and in the knowledge that he was on the way, "the Army submitted with the greatest cheerfulness" to the reduction in rations.

Soldiers aware of the predicament they were in could only wonder what sort of quarters they might expect to occupy during the coming winter if they could neither advance to Albany nor fall back to Ticonderoga or Canada, and for all these reasons the inducements that came in regularly from the rebel camp, with promises of lenient treatment, looked increasingly attractive. The news that John Brown's raiders had seized Fort George and successfully stormed the outworks at Ticonderoga did nothing to alleviate the general uneasiness.

On October 3, Captain Fraser led a detachment north on a scout to determine whether the army's rear was threatened, and although they saw no sign of rebels within four miles, a report came in with the disconcerting news that a courier from Carleton in Quebec had been apprehended at Jones's Mill, suggesting that the rebels were privy to Burgoyne's correspondence and knew the routes taken by British couriers.

Surprisingly, more Indians from Canada showed up in camp, and Burgoyne sent them on several scouting missions; then, capricious and independent as ever, they vanished just as suddenly, leaving only about thirty behind. On October 6 another major foraging effort was made, covered by Simon Fraser's corps, and about noon the rebels attacked von Rhetz's pickets at the left of the British line. Hearing the firing, about sixty Indians who had left camp the previous day ran to the scene, and the firefight continued for about an hour and a half, during which two Indians were wounded and the Americans suffered several casualties. That evening the rebels made another attack on the Brunswick pickets—almost certainly a probe to determine if this was a vulnerable spot, since several generals were seen reconnoitering—but were thrown back by Indians who crept in from the brush along the riverbank and opened fire on them.

At midnight a single shot from a British twelve-pounder shattered the stillness, followed immediately by three rockets sizzling into the dark sky. No one in Burgoyne's army seemed to have any idea what this meant, but Brigadier Specht couldn't help wondering if Clinton was close enough to see these signals or whether Burgoyne "wished to have our army believe it—we never found out."

Whatever else Henry Clinton might be planning, it did not include traveling to Saratoga to rescue his friend John Burgoyne. It was unthinkable that a man as cautious as Clinton would risk exposing Manhattan, Staten Island, and Long Island to attack by rebel raiders by removing too many of his troops for a protracted period of time. So, instead of heading north within ten days as Burgoyne had been led to believe, he dillydallied in Manhattan for yet another week, sent a detachment to New Jersey whose only accomplishment was to bring back some beef on the hoof, and finally, on October 3—four days after seventeen hundred reinforcements arrived at long last from Britain—set out with three thousand men aboard transports, bound not for Albany but for the rebel forts in the Highlands.

As his men were disembarking at Verplanck's Point, below Forts Clinton and Montgomery, a messenger from Burgoyne caught up with him. Captain Alexander Campbell of the 62nd Regiment had left Saratoga on September 20 and brought shocking news: Burgoyne's entire army did not exceed five thousand men and he had lost between five hundred and six hundred on September 19. The rebels—some twelve or fourteen thousand strong—were within a mile and a half of his lines, and another considerable force was threatening his rear. He estimated that his provisions might hold out until October 20 but said the only reason he had given up his supply line to Ticonderoga was his belief that an army from the south would join him at Albany. That was the first stunner for Clinton. Then came the second.

Burgoyne, who had certainly never considered himself under the command of Sir Henry Clinton, was now requesting that general to give him orders—either to attack or retreat to the lakes. He requested a "positive answer" as soon as possible, advising how soon Clinton expected to be in Albany. If no such reply arrived by October 12, he would retreat.

Although Clinton realized by now that the failure of Burgoyne's army to reach Albany was more than a temporary delay—that it could in fact spell disaster—he was the last man to play along with a scheme that might lay him open to blame or censure, nor was he about to risk his command or his reputation on some harebrained venture. Burgoyne knew him well enough to realize this, but Burgoyne was grasping at straws, and if he had seen the letter Clinton wrote Howe on September 27 he would have known what to expect.

At that time Clinton informed his commander in chief that he would "probably" take three thousand men on a short expedition to the Highlands. It might prove "a little desperate," he added, ever on the lookout for an admiring word, "but the times may possibly require such an exertion." The purpose of this was not to meet Burgoyne in Albany but to create a diversion. He informed his superior that he would remain in the Highlands only long enough to destroy the cannon at Forts Clinton and Montgomery, which would be an irreparable loss for the rebels, and would then return to New York. Only recently Burgoyne himself had written, "An attack or even the Menace of an Attack upon [Fort] Montgomery must be of great Use," by drawing away some of Gates's army. "Do it, my dear Friend, directly," he pleaded. So Clinton could argue—as he did later—that he was undertaking just what Burgoyne had urged on him.

As soon as he digested Campbell's message, Clinton sent the captain back to Burgoyne with a cold, formal reply that could leave no doubt where he stood. He had no instructions from Howe for the Northern Army, he said, and knew only that it was supposed to march on Albany. More—and one can almost hear the tone of voice—"Sir Henry Clinton cannot presume to give any Orders to General Burgoyne." Surely Burgoyne could not suppose that Sir Henry had any idea of coming to Albany with the meager force available to him. He had offered to make a diversion. Burgoyne had said it would be of great use. And that would be that.

Perhaps it was fortunate for Gentleman Johnny's state of mind that neither this letter nor two duplicates carried by other couriers reached him. (Captain Campbell and Captain Thomas Scott, whom Burgoyne had also dispatched to Clinton, were unable to make their return through enemy-held territory, and a third man who carried a message concealed in a silver ball swallowed it when he was captured, was forced to drink an emetic, and when he coughed up the ball and the note was read, was tried and hanged.)

Whatever his shortcomings, Clinton was a thoroughly capable soldier. Several beautifully executed feints totally confused the American general Israel Putnam, who figured the British were going to attack the passes on the east side of the river and hurriedly withdrew his troops to the hills, taking a number of men from the forts' garrisons with him. After Clinton and the commander of the naval squadron, Sir James Wallace, carried out an impressive land and water assault on the thinly manned forts (only thirty militiamen were at Fort Montgomery), Sir Henry was able to write Burgoyne from Montgomery: "*Nous y voici*, and nothing between us but Gates. I sincerely hope this little Success of ours may facilitate your Operation. . . ."

On October 11 a puffed-up Clinton was back in New York, but two days later had a change of heart and sent Major General Vaughan with seventeen hundred men upriver to Esopus.* Exactly what he intended them to do is not clear—another diversion, perhaps—but within a few days he received orders from Howe that quite possibly changed the course of the Revolution.

Sir William wanted reinforcements for his own army and he wanted them immediately, and despite his knowledge that Burgoyne was in mortal peril he ordered Clinton to abandon the Highlands and recall Vaughan. Years later, Clinton wrote that if Howe had only done everything possible to keep the Hudson open "it would most probably have finished the war."

While this was going on, what had begun as a petty quarrel between Horatio Gates and Benedict Arnold erupted into a terrible open sore that troubled the whole officer corps. What set it off was the letter Gates wrote to Congress with an account of the battle of September 19, in which he pointedly avoided any mention of Arnold's name, much less his contributions to victory that day, and did not even list the units that went into action as Arnold's division.

This was the sort of backhanded insult guaranteed to drive the vain, ambitious Arnold into a fury, and it was coupled with an action by Gates that proved the final straw. Orders of the day on September 22 announced that Morgan's corps would no longer be under Arnold's direction, but would report directly to the commanding general. That evening the enraged Arnold stalked over to Gates's quarters, burst in on him, and the two had a flaming row, shouting and cursing at each other, with Gates needling Arnold unmercifully, saying he didn't know that he was a

*Present-day Kingston.

major general (a reference to Arnold's threat to resign when he had been passed over for promotion), nor was he aware that he held a command of any sort in the army. Adding more fuel to the flames, he said he had ordered Lincoln to return to the army as a division commander, whereupon he would have no further use for Arnold. At this, Arnold stormed back to his own quarters and wrote a long letter to Gates, enumerating the slights he had suffered. Whether he went about it in the right way is open to question, but in most particulars his grievances were justified. He reminded Gates that the New York and Connecticut militia had been added to his corps, only to be reassigned to Glover. On the 19th, Arnold's troops had been the only units engaged in action, except for one other regiment, yet Gates in his letter to Congress had described them merely as a "detachment" from the army, suggesting that they were insufficiently important to deserve a major general's direction. Since then, every proposal Arnold made was either denied or, if accepted, countermanded later; he had been treated with a studied coolness at headquarters "in such a manner as must mortify a Person with less Pride than I have." And now he was informed that the army could get along just fine without him. Concluding the letter, he requested permission to return to Washington's army with his aides, where he might serve his country, since he was unable to do so here.

What was behind this, of course, was the intense jealousy each man felt because of the other—Gates because of Arnold's courage and exploits in battle, which were the talk of the camp; Arnold because the credit, glory, and prestige he so desperately wanted were being denied him. In many respects the dispute revealed Gates at his worst, taking advantage of what he knew to be Arnold's most sensitive trigger points, deviling the man until he could take it no longer and giving the screw an extra twist for good measure. Gates was being more than petty: his behavior could only be described as vindictive and nasty, for as he well knew, he had the command and therefore the last word.

Arnold's pride was further wounded when Gates, instead of replying directly to his letter, sent him unsealed a brief note he had written to John Hancock, saying Arnold had his permission to leave. Protesting that he was being treated "with Affront & indignity in a publick manner," Arnold again requested permission to depart. To this Gates replied that Arnold's letter contained nothing but what had been "altercated" between them on the evening of the 22nd, said he couldn't imagine what was meant by "Insult or Indignity," and enclosed what he called a "common pass" permitting him to go to Philadelphia.

For almost ten days this increasingly ugly fight went on until every general officer except Gates and Lincoln signed a petition asking Arnold to remain with the army, which he did, even though Gates never did let him know what, if anything, he was to command.

Writing to his wife, Betsy, Gates told her that one more week would decide the campaign; by that time the enemy would either retire or by "one Violent push endeavour to recover the almost ruined State of their affairs." He was dead tired, he said, and "the Fatigue of Body & Mind which I continually undergo is too much for my Age & Constitution. A General of an American Army must be every thing & that is being more than one Man can long Sustain." This campaign would be the last of his military career, he assured her.

That final violent push, the "rash stroke" gambler Burgoyne would surely make, according to Gates, was coming closer every day. It was the height of autumn now, that spectacular interlude in the northern hardwood forest when the hills resemble a lush Persian carpet, woven with every hue of red and orange, yellow and green. Flaming-red swamp maples, sumac leaves the scarlet of the British officers' coats, the fiery yellows of sugar maple and white birch, the deep mulberry of beech and elm, accented by the rich green of softwoods, created a magical sight many of the European soldiers had never seen or imagined. For all the beauty of these glorious days, some as warm as summer, and the crisp, starry nights that grew steadily colder, with a frosting of white covering the ground most mornings, and mist so dense, a German said, that you could "grasp it with your outstretched hands," there was an ineffable sadness about the season. Whether they came from Europe or America, these soldiers knew that the harvest was in and the barns full. The dead, bitter months of winter lay ahead.

For the first time in the campaign, Burgoyne called Phillips, Fraser, and Riedesel to a council of war on the evening of October 4. This was the day after the army went on short rations, and these officers knew better than anyone that something had to be done, and quickly. Two weeks had passed since Burgoyne received Clinton's qualified promise of assistance, two weeks during which he had hourly expected to be informed that help was on the way, but no such word had come and now the next move must be determined.

The American right was so strongly posted it would be suicidal to attack there, so he proposed to leave eight hundred men by the river to guard the stores, the hospital, and the floating bridge, while the rest of the effective troops—something like four thousand of them—would make their way through the woods and overwhelm Gates's left. He had probably sounded out Phillips and Fraser on this scheme, but it was new to Riedesel, who was not one of Burgoyne's confidants, and the German general saw immediately the risks involved in making an all-or-nothing thrust with what was nearly the entire army. The baron objected, saying it would take several days for the troops, impeded by cannon, to march on unfamiliar roads through the forest tangle, while all their provisions and the bridges that held the promise of escape might be taken if the rebels learned what was going on and overran those eight hundred men.

Next morning the generals inspected the entrenchments to be held by the men Burgoyne intended to leave behind and agreed that the works were too extensive for the number of defenders and open to attack from nearby ravines. That evening, at another council, General Riedesel argued that the army's situation was so critical that unless they could reach the enemy's rear in a single day's march they should retreat—falling back to the mouth of the Batten Kill on the east bank of the Hudson, where they had camped in mid-September. Here they could open up communications with their forces on the lakes while waiting to see if Clinton appeared. If he did not, as Riedesel suspected, they could move to Ticonderoga and head for Canada before winter set in.

Burgoyne would have none of it. He had not come this far to suffer the disgrace of retreat, nor would he leave Gates's army to join Washington against Howe—a junction "that might possibly decide the fate of the war." By now it seemed to have dawned on Burgoyne that his expedition, from the beginning, had been viewed by London as little more than a calculated risk—a mere diversion that would draw strength away from Washington and ensure Howe's triumph. If that was indeed the case, he reasoned, "the failure of my junction with Sir Harry Clinton, or the loss of my retreat to Canada could only be a partial misfortune." This was said in hindsight, and whether it was in his mind at the time he met with his generals no one knows. But other statements, coupled with his actions, suggest that he had made up his mind to go on to Albany at all costs. Perhaps the most important consideration was that his reputation was at stake, and to save it he had every intention of making one last roll of the dice.

Enough doubts had been raised by his three lieutenants to persuade Burgoyne to modify his initial proposal. Instead of leaving only eight hundred men in camp and attacking with the rest of the troops, he would make a reconnaissance in force with 1,500 regulars, supplemented by the auxiliaries—some 100 Canadians, about 50 Indians, and 450 loyalists. The idea, as the general explained it, was to reconnoiter the enemy's right wing and determine its strength. If an attack there appeared feasible, they would march on the following day—October 8. If not, the army would retreat to the Batten Kill on the 11th.

He lacked intelligence about the exact location of the American position, but even apart from that his plan was highly questionable if not downright foolhardy. Taking two thousand men on a reconnaissance mission meant exposing them to destruction by superior rebel forces, while leaving the rest of his weakened army to man the extensive lines (Specht said they were so thinly spread out that most regiments could form no more than a single line behind the entrenchments). To confuse the matter further, Burgoyne spoke of "dislodging" the enemy left in order to facilitate his own retreat, and said the movement was also intended to secure critically needed forage for the army's animals.

Desperation and prudence are unlikely companions, and Burgoyne was a desperate man. On October 6, to raise the men's spirits and compensate for reduced rations, he distributed twelve barrels of scarce rum to the troops.

The movement would be made on October 7.

Chapter 20

They Poured Down Like a Torrent from the Hill

It was a golden autumn morning, clear and crisp, without much going on as far as the Americans could tell. Morgan's corps, including Dearborn's light troops, had been out on an early scout without detecting any signs of trouble, but as the day wore on a British deserter alerted the American camp to an impending move by Burgoyne.

A number of Americans used the quiet time to catch up on correspondence, and James Wilkinson, in a letter to General Arthur St. Clair, confided gleefully that "Generals Gates and Arnold have differed beyond reconciliation"—an opinion that was to be borne out convincingly within a few hours. He went on to take a swipe at "the celebrated General Stark, the Bennington hero, [who] by way of gilding his reputation and finishing his character, left the camp at a time when we hourly expected an engagement, and on the day before the action" of September 19.

In his quarters on the heights above the river, General Riedesel was worried. Ever since Baum's task force had been overwhelmed near Bennington he had been increasingly concerned about the way things were going. The Bennington operation had not been to his liking, and he was strongly opposed to this present plan. He had a good deal more experience with large armies in the field than his commanding officer, yet he was in an awkward position, in charge of a contingent of hired soldiers who were looked down upon by the British and who didn't want to be here in the first place. Not only that: from the outset of the expedition he too had been treated like a second-class citizen, never fully taken into the confidence or the councils of the lieutenant general, always made to feel the outsider.

But this reconnaissance in force had the smell of doom about it. Outnumbered two, three, maybe four times to one, Burgoyne was sending the best troops in his army on what the baron considered a reckless mission that had little chance of success. The danger of taking so many men on the operation was that the enemy would overreact. There was no disguising an operation of this size—the sounds of horses heaving in their traces as they hauled the guns, the pained squawks of heavily loaded ammunition wagons, the beating of drums, the shuffling of what now amounted to seventeen hundred men through woods cluttered with dry, fallen leaves. If only Burgoyne were content to send out a small scouting party—maybe a hundred men—they could acquire the information needed without alarming and bringing out the entire rebel force, and the risk would be minimal. But if this movement failed, what then?

For the past week, ever since it became obvious that Clinton was not coming soon enough to rescue them, Riedesel felt that the only sensible course was retreat—to withdraw while the army was still intact and had the strength to carry it off, while they stood a chance of making it through to Fort Edward and Lake George. But now, in his judgment, the odds were heavily stacked against them, and the British general whose object seemed to have more to do with salvaging his reputation than saving his army was leading them down a road to almost certain ruin.

Baroness von Riedesel, with her three small daughters and two maids, was staying in a small two-story house with two rooms on each floor that had belonged to a family named Taylor, and one of the enjoyable moments in her daily routine was to join the baron for breakfast at his quarters. As the weather grew colder, Major Griffith Williams of the artillery offered to have a proper house built for her for five or six guineas, and she leaped at the opportunity. It was a snug log cabin about twenty feet square with a good fireplace, near enough to the baron's camp that he could move in with her, and on October 8 it would be ready for occupancy.

On the morning of the 7th the two of them were having breakfast when she became aware of commotion outside—soldiers moving on the double, shouted orders, the tattoo of drums—and the baron told her the men were going out on a reconnaissance, which was reassuring, since that was a frequent occurrence. She walked outside with him before he left with his staff, and on her way back to the house, where she planned to give a dinner for Generals Burgoyne, Phillips, and Fraser that evening, she met a number of Indians in war paint, carrying guns. Where were they going? she asked, and the reply was "War! War!" Stunned at the thought that a battle was imminent, she hurried to her children. "This moment," she wrote, "was the beginning of our unhappiness!"

What was afoot now may have been a reconnaissance in force, but a sign of the importance Burgoyne attached to it was that he was leading the troops personally, accompanied by Phillips, Riedesel, and Fraser, plus several members of his headquarters staff, including Sir Francis Carr Clerke and Lord Petersham. It was enough of a mission, in fact, that some hefty artillery was to be brought along—six six-pounders, two twelves, and two squat howitzers. Major Williams, who was in charge of the guns, was grousing about taking the twelves: his view was that once a twelve-pounder was removed from the artillery park and taken into the woods in America it was as good as gone. These were the veteran's "thunderers," and a German officer commented that "Old Major Williams . . . can only be likened to an old 12-pounder himself . . . [he] adores no creature on earth more than a twelve-pounder—and none, by the way, can handle one better than him."

The men forming up that morning were not fresh troops by any stretch of the imagination. Between getting to their posts an hour before dawn every day and their constant harassment by rebel skirmishers at night, a real night's rest was a thing of the past. Tired and exasperated, they waited for Burgoyne to emerge from his headquarters, while Riedesel and Phillips walked about, chatting, watching the regiments dress their lines, and very likely wondering how long it had been since this ragged lot had looked like a proper army. Simon Fraser had eaten a big breakfast that morning, figuring that he might have no more food until he returned to the baroness's house for supper, and he was now at the Balcarres redoubt, where his nephew's rangers and Indians—some one hundred strong— were preparing to move out westward, well in advance of the main body. They had orders from Burgoyne to "go by secret paths in the woods to gain the enemy's rear, and by showing themselves there" to keep the enemy occupied. Those three generals, with Burgoyne, were the only ones who knew the object of the mission—not even the other brigadiers were in on the secret.

Although the troops were ready to march at ten, it was one o'clock before they were finally under way, leaving behind Brigadiers Specht,

Hamilton, and von Gall to see that the entrenchments were manned until the reconnaissance force returned. If the enemy should attack them, they had orders to defend the works to the last man, and Johann Friedrich Specht had an uneasy hunch they might have to do exactly that.

As he had done on September 19, Burgoyne divided his seventeen hundred regulars into three elements. The right was commanded by Fraser, who had his nephew's advance party, Balcarres's light infantry, plus the 24th Regiment. The center belonged to Riedesel, and was something of a mixed bag led by Lieutenant Colonel Ernst von Speth, who had soldiers collected from all the Brunswick units plus von Barner's jägers. The left consisted of British grenadiers commanded by Acland. Breymann had some five hundred German grenadiers in his redoubt, and he was ordered to detach three hundred of them to join Speth, leaving the other two hundred to man the works.

The march was neither quick nor easy: the terrain made for hard going, and the long column was forced to make numerous halts along the way while bridges were thrown across the streams for the artillery. It was between one and two o'clock before the soldiers emerged into the sunlight in Farmer Barber's wheat field, where the wagon track from the Neilson house crossed the middle branch of Mill Creek; they were about three-quarters of a mile from the rebel lines, as near as anyone could tell, and here many of them sat down and awaited further orders. While waiting to hear what his nephew's scouts had learned about the rebel position, General Fraser found two buildings filled with hay and sent to the camp for men to come get it. And still the troops waited—in what General Riedesel called "a miserable position."

It was. The clearing was about three hundred yards from east to west, with one small building on it, which the Germans inexplicably referred to as the "Weisser" or "Weiser" house. What troubled the baron was that the detachment's left and right flanks were up against woods—just the kind of cover relished by the Americans—and beyond the right was a hill, densely wooded, from which it would be possible to enfilade Burgoyne's position. The field sloped down from the north and then rose at the opposite end, about 250 yards away.

Climbing to the roof of the abandoned cabin, Burgoyne, Riedesel, and Phillips looked through spyglasses to see the American defenses. They saw exactly nothing—nothing but the deep, silent forest, which meant that Burgoyne's elaborate mission to discover Gates's position had failed.

The British did not know it, but their movements had been closely observed. The advanced guard in the American center sounded the warning, and when a picket brought word to Gates that Burgoyne's troops were on the move he dispatched James Wilkinson to investigate. About the time the enemy was drawing up in the Barber wheat field, Wilkinson reached a point in the woods where he could safely observe them from a distance of a thousand feet or so. He watched the men in faded red and blue coats sit down in double ranks in the standing grain, holding their firearms between their legs. He took note of foragers cutting the wheat and loading it on horses. And he saw the generals clamber up on the roof with their spyglasses. For fifteen minutes he stayed there, quietly watching the enemy, before returning to headquarters on Bemis Heights, where he related all this to Gates. "Well then," said the general, "order on Morgan to begin the game."

While Gates and his officers were still at their mess, dining on ox heart, the scattered firing of muskets was heard, unmistakable sounds that the pickets were under attack, and Benedict Arnold immediately requested permission to go out to the lines and see what was happening. Gates was dubious, fearing that the impetuous officer might start something the army wasn't prepared to handle, and after a moment's hesitation he said, "I am afraid to trust you, Arnold." The major general replied with a promise to be cautious and, if it turned out that the three hundred men on the picket line did not need support, not to commit the commander in chief to action. Reluctantly, Gates agreed, but took the precaution of sending Lincoln with him. Drums were beating to arms as the two generals mounted and cantered off to see what they could make of the enemy's intentions.

Half an hour later they were back and informed Gates that a sizable body of the enemy was moving in a direction that threatened the army's left flank. Lincoln added that unless reinforcements were sent promptly the army's lines were in real danger of being rolled up. Gates said he would order Morgan and Dearborn to make a wide swing beyond the left in hopes of outflanking the British, whereupon Arnold looked at him with those cold expressionless eyes and said sharply, "That is nothing; you must send a strong force."

This was enough for Gates, who had run out of patience with this man. "General Arnold," he retorted, "I have nothing for you to do. You have no business here." And with that Major General Benedict Arnold appeared to have lost his last chance to participate in what was surely the climactic battle of this campaign. Lincoln, more restrained and persuasive, urged Gates to commit a stronger force to support Morgan—three regiments, at least—with the result that Poor's brigade was ordered to attack the left of the British line while Morgan circled around their right, the idea being that the two detachments would move through the woods as quietly as possible and hit the enemy from two sides at the same moment. Learned's brigade was to be held in reserve, ready to attack the British center when the two flanking parties had reached their objectives.

Ephraim Squier, a veteran of Bunker Hill, Arnold's march to Quebec, and several campaigns in Connecticut and New York, had recently signed up for another two-month hitch and was now with Poor's outfit. He hadn't had much sleep lately: the previous day he was a member of a "covering party" or scout that got lost, stayed out all night in a cold rain without provisions, and were so close to the enemy they had to observe complete silence. They hadn't returned to camp until ten this morning, and now, four hours later, they were headed for battle.

While Morgan and Poor were under way, Captain Fraser's skirmishers succeeded in driving in the rebel pickets, and the firing slowly sputtered out. The disparity in numbers between the two forces was huge. By now Gates had about twelve thousand effectives, including more than six thousand Continentals, to throw against the enemy's seventeen-hundred-man detachment, while Burgoyne's entire army had been reduced to slightly more than seven thousand, including several hundred wounded. Yet even now, Burgoyne had no accurate information on how many troops Gates had or how they were deployed, and in the ominous quiet that descended over the wheat field a British officer figured the rebels had decided to stay behind their defenses and wait to be attacked. "But we were soon undeceived on that Point," he said.

Small parties of rebels were seen off to the right, slipping through the trees, others on the left, as if intending to surround them. Suddenly, about three o'clock, a large body of Americans appeared in the woods opposite the British left, and Major Griffith Williams's heavy cannon opened up, slamming six- and twelve-pound balls toward them. But the forest was so thick that the cannonballs had little effect, and the rebels formed up and began to move forward. These were Poor's men—the battle-hardened 1st, 2nd, and 3rd New Hampshire Continentals led by Joseph Cilley, George Reid (now leading Hale's regiment), and Alexander Scammell, and as they headed directly for the British left—

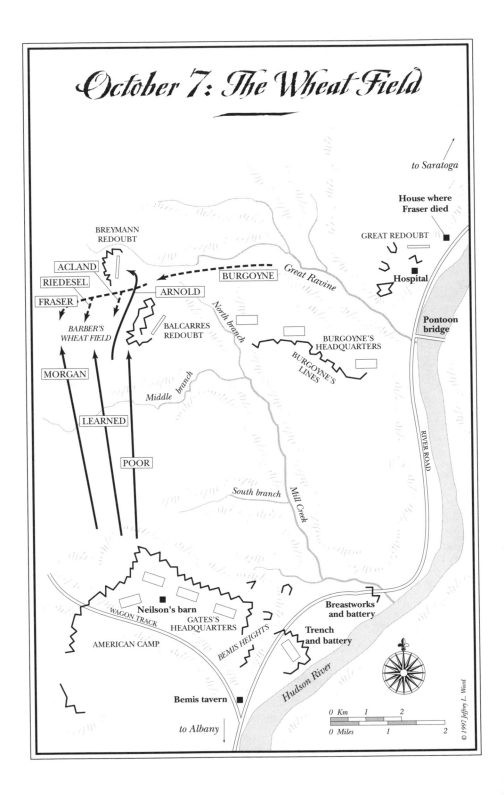

October 7: The Wheat Field

to Saratoga

House where
Fraser died

GREAT REDOUBT

BREYMANN
REDOUBT

Hospital

ACLAND

RIEDESEL

BURGOYNE

Great Ravine

FRASER

ARNOLD

Pontoon
bridge

BARBER'S
WHEAT FIELD

BALCARRES
REDOUBT

North branch

BURGOYNE'S
HEADQUARTERS

MORGAN

BURGOYNE'S
LINES

branch

LEARNED

Middle

POOR

South branch

Mill Creek

RIVER ROAD

Neilson's barn

GATES'S
HEADQUARTERS

Breastworks
and battery

WAGON TRACK

BEMIS HEIGHTS

Trench
and battery

AMERICAN CAMP

Bemis tavern

Hudson River

to Albany

0 Km   1   2

0 Miles   1   2

© 1997 Jeffrey L. Ward

Scammell and his men out in front—Acland's grenadiers, who held a position on a rise above them, opened up, firing muskets and grapeshot. But as so often happens when the target is below the gunner, their aim was high. Acland, believing he saw the rebel lines falter, shouted orders for a bayonet charge, but before the grenadiers could make a move the rebels exploded from the woods beyond the enemy line, rushing the flank and front of the British, running "madly and blindly," a German artilleryman said, firing at the big men in bearskin hats with white belts crossed over their faded red coats, firing, reloading, and firing again, literally mowing down the shocked grenadiers, who were swept away by the ferocious charge. Major Acland was down, wounded in both legs, and was carried off on Captain John Shrimpton's broad back.

James Wilkinson had been sent to the rear to order up Abraham Ten Broeck's New York militia, some eighteen hundred strong (almost exactly the number of Burgoyne's regular troops engaged here), and he returned to find "a scene of . . . horror and exultation" where the grenadiers had stood. In a space twelve or fifteen yards square he saw eighteen redcoats dying, and three officers propped against trees, two of them mortally wounded, while the exultant Colonel Cilley sat astride a captured twelve-pounder waving his arms and yelling. An American surgeon with hands blood-smeared from dressing an officer's wounds shouted to him, "Wilkinson, I have dipt my hands in British blood!"— which brought a sharp rebuke from his commanding officer. Cilley helped his men load the cannon and turned it on the retreating enemy, but if the Americans thought they could make off with the British guns they were mistaken—all the horses were dead.

Wilkinson joined the rebels who were pursuing the enemy, jumping over or around the dead and wounded lying on the ground, and heard a voice call out from the corner of a rail fence, "Protect me, sir, against this boy." A youngster thirteen or fourteen years old stood over a wounded British officer and was about to pull the trigger when Wilkinson stopped him and asked the officer for his rank. "I had the honor to command the grenadiers," came the reply, and Wilkinson realized it was Major Acland. Shrimpton, who had been carrying him, was a large fat fellow, winded from exertion, and Acland had told the captain to leave him here and save himself. When Wilkinson inquired if Acland was badly wounded, he said, "Not badly, but very inconveniently. I am shot through both legs," and then asked for help getting to the American camp. Wilkinson and his orderly hoisted him onto the orderly's horse and he was led away to Gates's headquarters.

Morgan's riflemen had taken longer to reach the field because of their wide swing around the enemy right, but now, while Poor's men were charging the grenadiers' position, they brushed aside Captain Fraser's scouts and "poured down like a torrent from the hill," hitting Balcarres's command on the front and right flank. As the major tried to change front behind a rail fence, Dearborn's light infantry swept in from the rear.

These men had left Bemis Heights on the double and climbed the wooded hill 150 yards behind the British right, from which they could see below that the firing was intense, with Poor's men in action. Dearborn got the impression that some of the Americans were about to give way, and he conferred quickly with his officers. They decided to rush the enemy's rear and take them by surprise if possible. Down the hill they ran, leaping over a fence, shouting at the top of their voices, and suddenly Balcarres's startled troops, seeing scores of fresh rebel troops dashing in on them from another direction, broke and ran. Dearborn's men had not fired a shot.

The British light infantry abandoned their guns and "all Retreated with great Precepitation & Confusion," as Dearborn put it, hotly pursued by the Americans for about three-quarters of a mile. The 24th Regiment had not been heavily engaged yet, and with these men bolstering the light troops Balcarres tried his best to form another line behind a fence, but Morgan's and Dearborn's men had the momentum, they were out for blood, and there was no holding them off. The desperate redcoats turned again and headed for the Balcarres redoubt in disorder. From the time the first shot was fired that afternoon until the British left and right wings were in full retreat exactly fifty-two minutes had elapsed.

When Burgoyne saw the light infantry fall back on the right, he realized how critical his position was and sent Sir Francis Carr Clerke with an order to bring off the guns, but before the aide could deliver the message he was shot and taken prisoner. The capture of Major Acland and the cannon left that side of the British line without leader or artillery, and the headlong retreat of the grenadiers exposed the adjacent wing of the center under von Speth. As they waited for Learned's brigade to come within range, the Brunswickers saw a man in the blue uniform of an American general, riding a bay horse hell-for-leather, racing alongside the rebels to the front line of marching men, shouting for them to follow him. It was Benedict Arnold.

He had been in his quarters, humiliated and shocked by his loss of command, when he heard the pounding of cannons and musket fire. From a courier he learned that the British had advanced into a wheat field not far from the Freeman farm, and after pacing angrily about, cursing his luck (and almost certainly Granny Gates) and, his enemies said later, drinking heavily, his emotions finally got the best of him. He stormed out of the cabin, downed a dipper full of rum from a nearby keg, and leaped on a small brown horse he had borrowed from a Connecticut friend. Galloping toward the sound of the guns, he came up on the rear of Learned's command, where he encountered several Connecticut militia regiments. Shouting to the nearest group, he asked whose outfit it was. "Colonel Lattimer's, sir," came the reply, and Arnold grinned. "My old Norwich and New London friends," he cried. "God bless you!" they cheered as he spurred his horse on toward the head of the brigade.

Hearing that Arnold had bolted toward the action, Gates assumed he was drunk and sent Major Armstrong to order him back to camp, but Arnold saw the messenger and outran him, and Armstrong hung on the rear of the troops, having no desire to follow someone who "behaved more like a madman than a cool and discreet officer" into the teeth of those Brunswick defenses.

Arnold yelled to the three leading regiments to follow him—an outrageous breach of military propriety—but fortunately Learned was a mild soul and raised no objection to the usurping of his command. A cheer went up from the men; they broke into a run and charged up the slope toward Speth's Brunswickers, who were ready for them and had no intention of giving way. The Americans had brought up some small field-pieces that were slamming away with canisters as fast as they could be reloaded, without even swabbing out the barrels; the whole line of battle seemed to be enveloped in flame, and in the smoke it was almost impossible to see the direction of the fighting or tell what any one outfit was doing. The rebels made no progress against the determined stand of the Brunswickers and began to withdraw in the face of the intense fire, and at just that moment Balcarres's troops were driven back by Morgan and Dearborn, exposing Speth's other flank. But these Brunswickers were tough and they kept on fighting until Speth saw that he was nearly surrounded and ordered his men to fall back.

Burgoyne was big, he was mounted on a horse, and he was wearing a scarlet coat with gold epaulets—about as conspicuous as a man could be—but amazingly he was untouched, although one horse was shot from under him, a bullet pierced his hat, and another tore his waistcoat. Off on the right, Simon Fraser was equally visible on his handsome gray mount, riding back and forth, calmly reassuring the men of the light infantry and the 24th—his own regiment—while he tried to form a second line. It was clear to the oncoming Americans that this man who was rallying a whole detachment of troops by the force of his personality had to be reckoned with. Whether Arnold suggested it to Morgan or Morgan decided it on his own is unclear, but the old wagoner called one of his riflemen, Tim Murphy, an experienced Indian fighter whose skill with his double-barreled rifle was legendary, and told him to get rid of the man on the gray horse. With that, Murphy climbed a tree and took aim. His first shot cut the horse's crupper, the strap looped under its tail; his second went through the mane, just behind the horse's ears, and an aide pleaded with Fraser to draw back out of range. No, the brigadier said, his duty was here. Murphy's third shot hit him squarely in the stomach, wounding him badly, and two junior officers—one on each side—helped him to sit the horse while he was led back to the British lines.

The heart seemed to go out of Burgoyne when he saw Fraser double up and fall forward on his horse's neck. Of all his officers, the Scot was the one on whom he relied most, his close friend and confidant, and Lieutenant Digby sensed that the general knew at that moment that it was all over. The loss of Fraser "helped to turn the fate of the day," he said, adding that he was the only wounded officer they were able to take back to camp. Burgoyne knew he had to get what was left of his reconnaissance force to safety inside their lines and sent word to Phillips and Riedesel to cover the retreat.

The batmen, who had gone foraging near Fraser's position on the right, suddenly galloped into the camp, having thrown away their fodder in order to save their lives and their horses. It was an indication of how things were going on the battlefield and "no very favorable omen of success," observed Lieutenant Anburey, who saw the frantic men arrive, followed shortly afterward by Fraser, looking like death, as anxious soldiers and women crowded around to ask about his wound. The only answer he gave was a shake of the head, indicating "that it was over with him." He had seen the fellow who shot him, Fraser said later—the man was a rifleman, perched in a tree. Outside Baroness Riedesel's house, the brigadier was carefully lifted from his horse and carried inside on a stretcher, where they laid him gently on a bed that replaced the table where he was to have dined that evening.

Captain George Pausch, the crusty commander of the Hesse-Hanau regiment's artillery, noted caustically that Speth's men "left their position without informing me," abandoning him and his guns some seventy-five paces out in front to face the rebels while the foot soldiers headed for the rear. "Each man for himself, they made for the bushes," he said in disgust. He and his gunners alone held off Learned for a while, but when he realized he could not keep it up any longer he looked around to summon the infantrymen who were supposed to cover his retreat and saw not a man. They had disappeared across the road into a field, some taking cover in the woods, others holed up in a house from which they were shooting at oncoming rebels, still others in the Balcarres redoubt.

Confusion was just about total, British and Germans running in whatever direction seemed to offer safety. The thick woods that had abutted the right flank were now at the men's rear. The road they had followed from their camp to Barbour's wheat field was probably in rebel hands, cutting off a retreat by that rough track. And Pausch found himself "alone, isolated, and almost surrounded by the enemy," his only escape route toward a house to which an abandoned twelve-pounder had been hauled. On his way there he happened onto a small earthwork eighteen feet long and five feet high and posted the two six-pounders he had brought off—one at each end of the berm—and opened fire in the face of savage rebel charges.

An English artillery lieutenant came up, saying that he and a sergeant and two privates were willing to serve the twelve-pounder, but he needed ten of Pausch's men and two junior officers to do so. The German was impressed by the lieutenant's courage and determination but decided not to lend him the men—he had only four or five privates plus a subaltern for each of his six-pounders, having lost two men killed, three or four wounded, plus a number who had deserted. Besides, he reasoned, a six-pounder could fire three times as many shots as a twelve. Why should he silence his own cannon "and thereby contribute to raise the honors of another corps"? But time was running out for Pausch and his gun crews: he had scared off the attackers in front and on both flanks, but he could hear gunfire coming closer in his rear, where the 24th Regiment and Balcarres's light troops were now engaged in a more orderly but inevitable retreat.

Pausch was nothing if not stubborn. Somehow he and his men got the guns on limbers and headed for the road to camp, hoping to meet some infantrymen who would help them make a stand. But no one was in sight, and by the time he reached the woods he found them full of rebels, firing at him. "Seeing that all was irretrievably lost," he told his men to save themselves while he made off with the last ammunition wagon, drawn by a couple of horses.

"All the different nationalities of our division [were] running pell-mell," he realized as panicked fugitives passed him, heading for the British lines. From the sound of gunfire back on the hill he realized that the Balcarres and Breymann redoubts were being "furiously assailed." What he could not know was that the dynamic leadership of a single American was behind this attack.

Those two redoubts anchored the right of the British entrenched camp. Before the battle, Balcarres, with his light infantry and the 24th Regiment, was posted behind the newly constructed works at Freeman's farm. North and somewhat west of them, Breymann and his Brunswick troops held the other strongpoint on a knoll. Between these two redoubts a group of Canadian irregulars occupied several cabins near the road to the river.

At the moment Simon Fraser was shot and led from the field, General Abraham Ten Broeck with his eighteen-hundred-man brigade marched into view—too late to be of real service, but an awesome sight to those badly battered, demoralized British and Germans who still held out. Burgoyne's entire battle line had collapsed, vanishing except for the bodies of the dead and the writhing wounded, surrounded with a litter of guns, personal belongings, and the equipment of what had once been an army. A large number of the retreating soldiers had fled to the Balcarres redoubt, and given the strength of that position the battle might well have ended in stalemate had it not been for Benedict Arnold.

Most generals would have been satisfied to drive a defeated enemy from the field of battle, but Arnold had the killer instinct, and as long as those two redoubts stood and the British had a chance of escaping, there was no stopping him. Somehow in the terrible confusion of the fight he had picked up elements of Paterson's and Glover's commands, and with these men he now assaulted the stronghold manned by Balcarres's light infantry and the 24th Regiment, augmented by refugees from other parts of the field. Charging in the face of heavy musket fire and grapeshot, his troops stormed through the abatis while Arnold, raging like one of the Furies, urged them on, shouting and waving his sword (with which he managed to wound an officer from Morgan's corps in the head without even knowing it). But the defense was too tough; the redoubt had been carefully sited to offer a clear field of fire; and the rebels were forced to fall back, continuing to shoot from behind trees or depressions in the ground that offered protection.

Arnold looked off to the left, saw that Learned's brigade was moving toward the extreme right of the British lines where Breymann commanded, put spurs to his horse, and without a moment's hesitation galloped between the American and British lines, exposed to gunfire from both, and emerged untouched near the cabins where the Canadians were holed up. With Learned's men he quickly cleared them out, and after picking up additional soldiers headed for the unprotected rear of the Breymann redoubt. Morgan's riflemen were already attacking the works from the front, and Arnold's charge took the outnumbered Brunswickers completely by surprise. Riding around behind the redoubt, Arnold's luck ran out. He was shot in his bad leg, his borrowed horse was killed, and the leg was broken when he was pinned to the ground beneath the animal.

The battle was over. Breymann was shot dead (some said by one of his own men—supposedly he had sabered several of them to keep them at their posts), and the defenders were overwhelmed by superior numbers, but not before fighting ferociously for better than half an hour defending what Captain Benjamin Warren called their "strange fort." When the Brunswickers finally gave way, Warren and others of the 7th Massachusetts took possession of their cannon and great quantities of baggage and burned the tents, and as he looked around, Warren realized that "the fields are strowed with the dead," including seventeen killed or wounded from his own outfit. By the following morning most of those dead would be stripped naked by scavengers and camp followers.

An American was about to bayonet the German who had shot Arnold when the fallen general called out, "Don't hurt him! He only did his duty." By this time Major Armstrong had caught up with Arnold, but there was no need to order him back to camp. Several soldiers from Asa Bray's Connecticut militia company helped pull him from beneath the little brown horse, carried him off on a litter made of blankets slung between two poles, and took him to a field hospital, where he refused to have his bloody, smashed leg amputated.*

By ten o'clock on that frosty night about two hundred other wounded

---

*For three months, Arnold remained in an Albany hospital in agony, not certain he would ever walk again. In January he sat up for the first time, but his wounds reopened and he was back where he began. Not until late May did he rejoin the Continental Army, in which his seniority had been restored.

men had been brought by wagon from the battlefield, but there were no tents, sheds, or other buildings to shelter them, so they were laid out in a circle on the ground. Several surgeons were frantically busy extracting bullets, amputating limbs, and performing other operations. Samuel Woodruff of Bray's company, tired as he was, had no desire to sleep and spent the long hours of darkness hauling water and comforting suffering men as best he could, but about seventy of them died of their wounds before morning.

Even though darkness was falling over the battlefield when Arnold was carried off, there is no saying what might have happened had he not been hurt. The British right and rear were now dangerously exposed to attack, and it is entirely possible that the American major general might have tried to sweep down on Burgoyne's broken, discouraged army. It is also possible, of course, that such an attempt would have ended disastrously, coming apart in the failing light and losing all coherence as men lost touch with their outfits and turned to looting.

Unlike Burgoyne, who chose in both battles to be out on the front lines with his troops—ever at center stage but often only vaguely aware of the location of some of his divisions—Gates never moved from his headquarters, two miles from the battlefield, too far removed even to see what was happening. The American general, to repeat, was no tactician, yet while his remoteness was perceived by critics as excessive caution or even timidity, the commander of an army has to be part strategist, part master puppeteer with his hands on the strings, cognizant of the movement of his own units and those of the enemy, prepared to capitalize on every twist and turn in the flow of battle. As it happened, his only contributions to the battle on this day were the order to Morgan to circle around the British right, and sending out additional detachments while the fighting went on.

Benedict Arnold had many faults, as the future was to make even more clear, yet it is not too much to say that this climactic battle was won in part because of his extraordinary bravery, magnetism, and energy. Somehow he managed to be everywhere when needed, flourishing his sword, leading men by example, and while the odds were against Burgoyne's force from the outset because he was so badly outnumbered, the victory clearly belonged to Arnold, to Morgan and Dearborn and the New Hampshire Continentals, to those hardy survivors of Ticonderoga, Hubbardton, and the long, humiliating retreat, and to the thousands of militiamen who turned out in the hour of greatest need.

When Burgoyne arrived back in camp he wore the look of a man whose worst fears had been realized: it was "impossible to describe the anxiousness" in his face, Lieutenant Anburey said. His casualties were horrendous. While he was not yet aware how extensive they were, in the day's action the British had lost 184 killed, 264 wounded, and 183 taken prisoner—631 men, of whom 31 were officers. The Germans had 94 dead, 67 wounded, and 102 captured, which meant that of slightly more than 1,700 in the reconnaissance force, 894—more than half—had been lost. (By comparison, the Americans had an estimated thirty killed and one hundred wounded.) Riding up to the camp guards, the general gave them orders to defend the post to the very last man, and when Anburey heard that he realized how desperate their situation was. The attack on the Balcarres redoubt continued unabated, sheets of flame from the exchanges of cannon and muskets silhouetting the men and cannon up there on the battlements, while balls from the rebel guns hurtled into the British camp before nightfall at last put an end to the fighting. The day that had begun in dense fog ended in darkness, but despite the hour, Burgoyne was keenly aware that his right flank or rear might be overrun, so at one in the morning he ordered his exhausted troops to strike their tents and move in total silence to the heights overlooking the river in the fastness of the Great Redoubt.

There would be no rest for Frederika Charlotte Louise von Riedesel that night. The surgeon had broken the news to Simon Fraser as gently as possible that his wound was fatal; unfortunately the heavy breakfast he had eaten had distended his intestines so that the bullet, which might have passed between them, had ripped open his bowels. All through the darkness the baroness listened to his moans and his apologies for the trouble he was causing her, heard him call out in grief for his wife and for Burgoyne. She worried lest her children wake up and cry, disturbing the dying Fraser and the other wounded in her house, and about three in the morning, when she was told that the Scot was nearing the end, she bundled her daughters in blankets and took them into the hall for what remained of the night.

She had also taken Lady Harriet under her wing. Acland's wife slept in a tent not far from the Taylor house, and someone brought word that her husband was critically wounded and had been taken prisoner. The baroness did her best to comfort the distraught Englishwoman, saying the major's wound was surely slight, and that she should make arrangements to go and nurse him. (Lady Harriet must have grown accustomed to tending her hard-luck husband: she took care of him when he was sick in Canada, then after he was wounded at Hubbardton, and now he was hurt again—perhaps dangerously so, for all she knew.) It was evident to Mme. Riedesel that Harriet loved her major, although from the baroness's perspective Acland "was a rough fellow who was drunk almost every day, but, nevertheless, a brave officer."

At eight o'clock the next morning, an hour after a large number of rebels were seen advancing along the river toward the British fortifications, Simon Fraser breathed his last. His body was washed, wrapped in a sheet, and put back on the bed, where it lay throughout the day. Meantime, more wounded officers kept arriving at the baroness's makeshift hospital, the dueling cannons boomed steadily, Balcarres's position was continuously under rifle fire, and there was talk of retreat, though nothing immediate came of it. At four that afternoon, Madame Riedesel saw smoke and flames shoot into the air from what was to have been her new house, and knew the rebels were closing in. Each passing hour, Burgoyne recalled, was "measured by a succession of immediate cares, increasing doubts, and melancholy objects"—among them wounded men struggling on crutches to defend the lines or being carried to their posts. Yet Lieutenant Anburey sensed that the rebels—after appearing in force that morning and evincing every sign of assaulting the wounded army—had a disinclination to resume the action, which was curious considering their overwhelming numbers and the conditions within Burgoyne's lines. But Gates was apparently playing his customary waiting game, certain that "there were other and less expensive means of reducing his foe than by blood and carnage," as one American put it.

It was a beautiful evening, and at six o'clock the lowering sun illuminated a strange pageant. The last request Simon Fraser made of Burgoyne was that he be buried in the Great Redoubt, with no one but the officers on his personal staff in attendance, and while the general honored his friend's request concerning the interment, he was present himself, as were Phillips, Riedesel, and their aides. The procession of mourners filed up the hill to the gravesite, where the Reverend Edward Brunell read the Anglican burial service—his voice never faltering, Burgoyne said proudly of him, even though cannonballs from rebel guns fell close enough to shower dust on the chaplain. The British were outraged that their enemies—"with an inhumanity peculiar to Americans"—fired on the procession and the group of graveside mourners, but it seems likely that the rebels had no idea what was going on, that they merely saw a large group of men—all officers—and shot at them.

As yet Burgoyne was unaware that he was also losing the man he called a "useful assistant, an amiable companion, an attached friend"— Sir Francis Carr Clerke. Seriously wounded, Clerke had been taken to Gates's quarters, where he asked the surgeon who treated him, "Doctor, why do you pause? Do you think I am afraid to die?" and was then told that his wound was fatal. When Wilkinson returned he found Gates arguing with the young man, trying to convert him to the ideals of the Revolution. Despite his suffering, Clerke held his own, and when the angry Gates left the room he asked Wilkinson if he had ever heard "so impudent a son of a bitch."

Madame Riedesel complained that Fraser's funeral "caused an unnecessary delay and served to increase the army's misfortune," but in fact Burgoyne had no wish to retreat during the hours of daylight. The exchanges of gunfire had done little damage beyond killing one artilleryman and a horse (while wounding Major General Benjamin Lincoln, whose leg was shattered by a musket ball, leaving Gates with no officer over the rank of brigadier to assist him). The British position was extremely strong, and a retreat by day would have invited attack when the army was most vulnerable. Burgoyne knew the Americans would be pursuing him, he was sure more of them were up ahead, and he was keenly aware that his "defeated army was to retreat from an enemy flushed with success, much superior in front, and occupying strong posts in the country behind." The retreat must be made at night. It was either that or surrender, and since he still hoped that Clinton might appear on the scene, he decided once again to gamble.

Chapter 21

All Remains Still Like Sunday

The baroness and her little family were among the first to leave. It was clear to Burgoyne that he would have to abandon his hospital, which consisted of a large barn, several huts, and a number of big tents, leaving more than four hundred sick and wounded to the mercy of General Gates and trusting the rebels to treat them compassionately, but Major Harnage, for one, had no intention of remaining behind, and shortly after Fraser's funeral he hobbled over to Madame Riedesel's quarters and ordered her—despite her pleas—to depart in the calèche immediately. He warned her to be as quiet as possible once they were under way, which she did so conscientiously that every time little Frederika started to cry with fright she held a handkerchief over her mouth.

At eight that evening the army received orders to march, but it was midnight before the train of artillery and the wagons laden with baggage were ready to move, at which time Riedesel set off in the van, with the Earl of Balcarres, now commanding Fraser's brigade, bringing up the rear. This withdrawal was a tricky, highly dangerous business. The worst worry was that an overturned wagon, a broken wheel, or the stupidity of a drunken driver could halt the baggage or artillery train, which was restricted to a single column on the narrow road, slowing the army to a crawl, so the infantry marched alongside, through the fields. Somehow the procession of disheartened, bone-weary men and women made it through the night without incident, and at three in the morning Specht's brigade and most of the Brunswickers reached what Burgoyne called "very advantageous ground" on the heights above Dovegat. Yet they had covered little more than four miles and were dismayed to find General Riedesel and the advance corps waiting for orders to move on when everyone expected that they would have continued north without delay. It was a cold, raw morning, and at about six Balcarres came up to report that the baggage and artillery train were safe, but it was eight o'clock before the army resumed its march.

The halt astounded Baroness von Riedesel, especially when "General Burgoyne ordered the cannons to be lined up and counted"—a particularly useless exercise, she believed, when a few good marches would take them to safety. The lieutenant general obviously thought otherwise: he had ordered the troops to fall out because they were spent, ready to drop from fatigue, and because time was needed for the bateaus with their precious cargoes of food to be rowed upstream and come abreast of the army. Even at that, he worried that this delivery of food might be the last one, since the river narrowed enough in places to permit rebels on the east bank to attack the boats.

Yet the petite Brunswick noblewoman's point was well taken. If Burgoyne really believed he had a chance of breaking away from the pursuing Americans and reaching Ticonderoga, sixty miles to the north, the first thing to do was abandon his cannon. Then he could remove the supplies from the bateaus, whose slow progress against the current would continue to delay the army, use his remaining artillery horses to carry food, and proceed by forced marches to his destination. Whether this was feasible, given the increasing strength of the rebels, is open to question, yet it was almost certainly his sole remaining option.

How keen Burgoyne's judgment was at this point is difficult to say, but certainly he was as bone-tired as his men were—tired mentally as well as physically, considering the stress he was under and the decisions he had to make. Once again, he had almost no intelligence concerning the Americans who were ahead of his army's line of march. What knowledge he had, he said later, was "generally contradictory, always imperfect . . . I never saw any instance of service where it was so difficult to obtain information." Loyalists who might have been expected to supply it were too frightened to do so.

The 9th was a day of short marches and repeated, incomprehensible delays. General Riedesel, fatigued beyond endurance, joined his wife in her calèche, put his head on her shoulder, and slept for three hours. She could see Indians leaving the army and vanishing into the woods. "The slightest setback makes cowards of them," was her acid comment, not imagining that they must have felt, as any sensible man would, that this army had suffered more than a slight setback. One of the baroness's maids finally snapped under the tension, tearing her hair and wailing about her plight. Madame Riedesel urged her to be quiet, "as otherwise she would be taken for a savage," at which the woman exploded: "It is easy for you to talk! You have your husband, but we have nothing except the prospect of being killed or of losing all we have." The baroness got her quieted down by reassuring her she would be compensated for any loss, but this was one of many instances revealing how individuals were beginning to crack under the terrible pressure, while the army itself seemed to be disintegrating.

During the day word reached them that a rebel detachment had been sent ahead to cut them off from the Batten Kill crossing, and the men in the ranks grumbled that they had better move faster, even if they had to abandon all the baggage, including personal belongings. At ten that morning the sky turned black and heavy and an all-day rain began—a cold, driving rain that made the troops increasingly apprehensive as they contemplated the impassable roads that lay ahead. Four hours later, word was passed that each man would receive six days' provisions, which he was to carry, but not until four in the afternoon did the march resume. The retreat was a nightmare. Continuously harassed from the rear by American riflemen, the exhausted footsoldiers had all they could do to make their way through the mud, while horses foundered and tents as well as personal gear were dropped and abandoned. It was nine that night, in a violent storm of wind-driven rain, when they forded Fish Creek* in water up to their waists and moved onto the heights above Saratoga,† which they had fortified on their way south. In twenty-four hours they had come only eight miles from the battlefield.

On one of the numerous halts, Lady Harriet Acland had her tent pitched and the baroness joined her, urging her again to go to her husband to nurse him. Finally she agreed and asked Captain Stanhope, Viscount Petersham (who, it was said, had in his veins "noble blood enough to have inoculated half the kingdom"), to carry her request to Burgoyne. The commanding general was astounded: in his florid recollection of the event, "After so long an agitation of the spirits, not only exhausted by

*Also known as Fish Kill.
†Present-day Schuylerville, New York.

want of rest but absolutely want of food, and drenched in rains for twelve hours together, that a woman should be capable of such an undertaking as delivering herself to the enemy, probably in the night, and uncertain of what hands she might first fall into, appeared an effort above human nature." Yet go she did, never wavering, setting off on the dark waters of the Hudson in an open boat with the Reverend Edward Brudenell, her maidservant, and her husband's wounded valet, braced for the ordeal with a cup of rum mixed with dirty water, given her by an understanding soldier's wife.

Henry Dearborn, who was a good distance ahead of Gates's army and unsupported, had doubled his sentinels after sunset and between midnight and 1:00 A.M. was alerted that two boats were coming downriver. It was nearly impossible to see them in the pouring rain, but at intervals a drum was heard beating a parley, and when the boats drew near, Dearborn hailed them to ask who they were. "A flag of truce from General Burgoyne" was the reply, and Dearborn told them to come ashore.

A soldier handed the American an unsealed note from General Burgoyne to General Gates stating that "Lady Harriet Ackland, a lady of the first distinction by family rank, and by personal virtue" was so concerned about her husband that he was entrusting her to Gates's care so that she might join the major. Dearborn read the note and asked the very determined, very pregnant Lady Harriet to go to his house and stay till morning, since it was impracticable for her to proceed farther that night, and to reassure her added that her husband's wounds were not serious. Dearborn had a fire laid for her, her baggage was brought in, and she remained in bed until morning, when one of Gates's aides and a Dr. Brown arrived to escort her to headquarters.

Gates, who was easily taken in by a title, was suitably impressed. Writing to his wife, Betsy, he described his visitor as "the most amiable, delicate piece of Quality you ever beheld." He guaranteed the Aclands safe passage to Albany and New York, but they were delayed for more than eleven weeks while Acland recuperated, and arrived in New York on January 2, 1778.

According to Lieutenant Anburey, Burgoyne's troops were so exhausted when they reached Saratoga that they lacked the strength to cut wood and make fires, and lay down in their soaked clothes on the wet ground while the rain continued to fall. At some time during the night, welcome news swept the camp that the bateaus had arrived safely, and this was followed by a rumor that St. Leger with nine hundred fresh troops would probably join them the next day. Once again it was noised about that Clinton was advancing toward them. But there would be no St. Leger* or Clinton, nothing but this miserable, dispirited body of men, who learned a little later that a considerable number of Americans had moved up the east bank of the Hudson as far as the Batten Kill, closing off that escape route. And rebel guns on the other bank of the river were now firing on the bateaus. Until midnight the rain fell; "afterwards," Brigadier Specht observed, "a cold wind arose; it started to freeze hard. Our men, who had to camp in the open, spent a very bad night."

Baroness Riedesel—doubtless reflecting her husband's views—was bitterly opposed to the way Burgoyne was handling the retreat: despite the appalling conditions she wanted to push on. She was soaked to the skin and lying on some straw with her children when General Phillips came up. "Why don't we retreat while there is still time?" she asked, saying her husband was prepared to cover the retreat and see the army through safely. Phillips was the sort of man who admired fortitude like this, and he told her so. But Burgoyne is too tired, he added, and wants to spend the night here and give the generals supper. Although it is hard to imagine Burgoyne carousing on this particular occasion, as the baroness suggested in her journal, he was certainly in no mood to proceed—certainly not until he knew what the rebels were up to near Fort Edward.

At the time the Massachusetts militia received the call to join Gates it was obvious they were needed in a hurry, and many of them rode their horses to Bemis Heights. On October 9, Gates issued orders for all the army's horses except those needed by the artillery to be rounded up for use by a detachment of thirteen hundred militiamen under Brigadier John Fellows. Since there were not enough animals by half, the men who assembled that evening at sunset were instructed to ride two to a mount, with one soldier on each horse that pulled their two cannon. In a heroic performance the detachment made twenty-six miles by eight the following morning—enough to pass the British and take position on the east side of the Hudson opposite Saratoga, where they could block any attempt by the British to cross the river at the mouth of the Batten Kill.

Gates was painfully slow getting started, but fortunately for him, Burgoyne's army had moved at a snail's pace. The rebel troops drew rations and cooked enough food for four days. The delay gave a much-needed

*He never did leave Ticonderoga.

rest to the Continental troops, who had borne the brunt of the fighting, and the army's ammunition was replenished. Meanwhile, rain turned the road into a bog, and it was made worse by the retreating British, who "burnt most of the buildings as they went, and cut away the bridges," according to Lieutenant Thomas Blake of Cilley's New Hampshire regiment. "Whenever their waggons or tents or baggage broke down," he went on, "they knocked the horses on the head and burnt the baggage."

The next morning dawned cold and clear, and when Burgoyne dispatched Lieutenant Colonel Nicholas Sutherland with two regiments up the west bank to assess the situation north of them, it began to look as though he had come to agree with Riedesel's proposal that they make a rapid retreat to Fort Edward. Apparently the idea was that the army would move north, ford the Hudson near the rapids above Saratoga, and retreat toward Fort George on the only practicable route, on the east bank of the river. Sutherland was another old-timer in the new world, having served in the Forbes expedition that took Fort Duquesne, fought the Cherokees, and served in Martinique and Havana before coming out in 1776 to join Carleton, when he became lieutenant colonel of the 47th Foot. With him went a detachment of artificers under Lieutenant Twiss with orders to open the road to Fort Edward and repair bridges, but no such luck. About 2:00 P.M. the rebels appeared in force on the heights above Fish Creek, giving every appearance of making an attack, and although it proved a false alarm, Twiss's escort troops were recalled, and the loyalists left behind to protect the artificers fled when a few Americans attacked, leaving the workmen to escape as best they could. An exchange of cannon fire between the two armies followed but did little damage to either side. In the meantime, Philip Schuyler's elegant house and outbuildings were torched on instructions from Burgoyne, to prevent them being used as cover by Gates's advancing troops. One hapless Brunswicker, too sick to move, burned to death in the blaze.

Gates's force continued to increase as units from Bemis Heights that had been delayed by weather came up, followed by incoming militia. Advancing with the 7th Massachusetts, Benjamin Warren met fifty or sixty prisoners taken from Burgoyne's retreating army and found twenty large tents filled with wounded—some of them dying. The road, he said, was "strowed with waggons, baggage, dead carcases, Amunition, tents &c ... much of it damaged ... houses and buildings mostly burnt as they retreated and the bridges [burned] as our people got there."

Burgoyne's men had orders to dig in, but the Germans on the right found it impossible in the stony soil to scratch out foxholes more than eighteen inches deep. Out on the perimeter of the army, not far from where Saratoga Lake empties into Fish Creek, the British had thrown up a small redoubt made of logs piled three or four feet high, to serve as an observation post. It was manned by three companies under orders not to start a fight, but unfortunately for the redcoats crowded into the enclosure, Morgan's riflemen were posted nearby and every morning at daybreak climbed into the highest trees, from which they could fire into the redoubt. Several soldiers careless enough to look over the wall had already been killed, and from then on, to see if the riflemen were still watching, someone would put a grenadier's cap on a pole and raise it just high enough to simulate a man peering over the logs. Almost every time this trick was pulled the cap was pierced by a bullet; on one occasion three hit it.

Finally they could take no more of this, and on October 14 an ensign was sent to headquarters to say if they couldn't be allowed to fire back at the rebels they wanted to be relieved. Arriving at headquarters, the young officer was astonished to find three generals—Burgoyne, Phillips, and Hamilton—sound asleep on mattresses, with only an oilcloth to cover them, and their aides hunched in front of a large fire. He delivered the message to William Noble, another ensign, who took it to General Phillips, and the noise roused the commander in chief. The ensign said, "I shall never forget the anxiety . . . upon the face of General Burgoyne and his emotion when, starting up out of sleep and hearing Mr. Noble speak, he asked the subject of our conversation. General Phillips answered that it was of little importance." Reassured, the exhausted Burgoyne covered himself again, rolled over, and went back to sleep.

On October 11, when everything seemed to be going his way, Gates made what was very nearly a fatal mistake. Camped on the bank of Fish Creek, the general received reports that most of Burgoyne's army had retreated to Fort Edward. Assuming that what now faced him was the enemy rear guard, he ordered Nixon's brigade to cross the creek at daylight, with other Continental units to follow. Under cover of a dense fog, Nixon's men waded ashore on the north bank, advancing blind toward where they reckoned the British position to be. After they crossed, Brigadier John Glover's troops began to ford the stream, and the general had just stepped into the water when he saw a British soldier in the river, headed for the American lines. The man claimed to be a deserter, and in reply to Glover's question about the deployment of Burgoyne's army said, "It is encamped the same as days past."

Glover was skeptical. "If you are found to be deceiving me," he said, "you shall be hung in half an hour." If he was telling the truth, however, he was promised safety and good treatment, and Glover asked if a large number of troops had not already marched to Fort Edward. No, the redcoat replied; "A small detachment [meaning Sutherland's party] was sent off . . . but are returned on finding the passes occupied by the Americans, and the whole army is now in camp."

Glover was horrified. The American army was headed for a death trap, crossing the creek at the strongest point in the British line, where Hamilton's and Balcarres's troops were dug in. He sent the deserter and an aide galloping off to Gates's headquarters, and a message came back immediately countermanding the orders to attack. Glover sent word at once to Nixon and Morgan's riflemen, who had also crossed the stream, and they returned as the fog was lifting—just in time to avoid an ambush.

As the deserter informed Glover, Sutherland had come back from Fort Edward, but not for the reasons described. In fact, Sutherland was infuriated by his recall and made no bones about it—when he received orders to return to camp immediately he was within an hour of the fort and had five hundred men to the rebels' one hundred. In Brigadier Specht's words, he "not only express[ed] surprise but also the greatest annoyance that the army had not followed him" and that he was required to turn back.

Burgoyne seemed to have lost his grasp of the situation; he was indecisive, discipline was deteriorating, and the army's infrastructure, like its personnel, was collapsing. As Baroness von Riedesel informed the general, his troops were starving because the commissary had neglected to distribute food. Some thirty hungry officers had come to her quarters, asking for something to eat, but her own meager stocks were soon exhausted, and she appealed to Petersham, who brought Burgoyne to see her. The general said he would do something about it immediately, but he was obviously embarrassed and nettled that his orders had not been carried out, and Madame Riedesel believed "in his heart he never forgave me for this interference."

The artillery barrages were increasing in intensity, the bateaus were under constant attack, and every day brought more skirmishes. On the night of the 11th an entire picket guard of Germans, except for their officer, a sergeant, and the drummer, left their posts and went over to the rebels. By October 13 the Americans had taken 120 prisoners and received 160 deserters, and all the while "numerous parties of American militia . . . swarmed around . . . like birds of prey," Sergeant Lamb said.

"Roaring of cannon and whistling of bullets from their rifle pieces were heard constantly by day and night."

It was bad enough, one British officer remarked, that their supply of liquor was gone, but they had no water. No one dared go to the stream by day for fear of being shot, and at night they worried about being captured. As a result their only sources of water were a muddy spring or "the holes made by the horses' feet," where moisture collected. The only good thing about the constant downpours was that the men caught the water in their hats and mixed it with flour to make bread cakes.

About two o'clock one afternoon, General Riedesel told his wife to go immediately to a nearby house, but as they approached it she could see Americans on the far shore aiming at them. She threw the little girls to the floor of the calèche and lay on top of them at the same time a wounded English soldier behind her had his arm shattered by gunfire. They arrived at the house and a cannonade began, so they went to the cellar to spend the night, the children sleeping on the floor with their heads in her lap. In the morning the barrage began again, but since it was not directed at them the baroness suggested that everyone clear out of the cellar, which reeked of urine and excrement from those who had taken shelter there. She assembled a volunteer crew, had them sweep the place and fumigate it with vinegar, and then assigned the wounded to one of the vaulted stone chambers, women and children to another, and all others to the third. Then the guns across the river opened on them again; eleven cannonballs hit the house, and one poor devil who was about to have a leg amputated had his other leg blown off by a shot.

For six days the indomitable woman and her little family remained underground in the house, she worrying constantly about her husband's safety but unable to get to him. Equally alarming was what she heard from their faithful servant Rockel, who told her the baron was drinking heavily "because he is afraid of being taken prisoner and he is tired of living." Meantime, they had food, but no water, and the solution to that finally proved to be a soldier's wife brave enough to go to the river with a bucket; the rebels would not fire at her. Captain Thomas Blomfield was brought into the house to be treated for a wound. A bullet had passed through both cheeks, smashing his teeth and cutting his tongue, with the result that he could take no nourishment except bouillon until the baroness gave him a bottle of Rhine wine to cleanse his wounds, which promptly healed. But not all her companions were wounded: some were "cowards who had no reason whatever for staying in the cellar," and on at least one occasion she had to stand in the doorway of the house to keep skulkers from crowding into the place. At last word reached them that the army was surrounded, that no hope of retreat remained, and there was talk of surrender.

By then the Americans had captured or destroyed most of the bateaus; Morgan, Learned, and some Pennsylvania troops had moved into position west of the British; and with the rebels on three sides of them, the only escape route was to the north, along the west bank of the Hudson. Riedesel continued to push for abandoning baggage and the artillery and retreating by night, with each soldier carrying his own provisions. And finally it was agreed. At ten o'clock on the night of the 12th, Riedesel sent a message to Burgoyne informing him that the rations were distributed and requesting marching orders. To the baron's dismay the reply came back that the retreat was postponed. By the following morning the army was completely surrounded.

The northern escape corridor had been sealed off during the night by the mercurial hero of Bennington, John Stark, who had suddenly appeared with more than a thousand New Hampshire militia, led them across the Hudson near the mouth of the Batten Kill, and erected a battery on the west side.

By now the plight of Burgoyne's army was truly appalling, and no one described it more vividly than General Riedesel, who wrote:

> There was no place of safety for the baggage; and the ground was covered with dead horses that had either been killed by the enemy's bullets or by exhaustion, as there had been no forage for several days. . . . Even for the wounded, no spot could be found which could afford them a safe shelter—not even, indeed, for so long a time as might suffice for a surgeon to bind up their ghastly wounds. The whole camp was now a scene of constant fighting. The soldier could not lay down his arms day or night, except to exchange his gun for the spade when new entrenchments were thrown up. The sick and wounded would drag themselves along into a quiet corner of the woods and lie down to die on the damp ground. Nor even here were they longer safe, since every little while a ball would come crashing down among the trees.

A heartbroken British ensign wrote that he was forced to have his newborn foal destroyed. His groom told him the nursing colt was exhausting the dam, and if they had to leave camp the mare would be unable to carry their luggage. As it was, she had had nothing to eat but dried leaves.

On October 13 at three in the afternoon all the generals and regimental commanders were summoned to "a solemn council of war," at which Burgoyne gave his opinion that it was impossible to attack the rebels or sweep around them to Albany. Even if by some miracle they could defeat the Americans, they hadn't enough food even to reach Fort Edward. The only possibility for escape was for each man to make his way alone to Ticonderoga.

General Phillips bridled at that. It was all very well for a few Indians or frontiersmen, he said, but it was absurd to think that four or five thousand men could accomplish it on their own. Hunger, misery, attack by rebel forces, the onset of rainy weather—there were a dozen reasons why it could not be contemplated. Not least was that the army would fall apart in the resulting chaos. Even now the army's right and center were untenable should the enemy attack. They had supplies on hand for only five days, and once those were gone they would be in an even worse predicament.

At that Burgoyne put three questions to the officers: in the history of war had any armies in their situation surrendered (yes); was it dishonorable to capitulate in their situation (no); and was this army in such a fix that surrender was necessary? The first two questions were answered immediately and unanimously. The third was not so easy, but the long and short of it was that if the general believed it possible to attack the enemy with any chance of success, they would willingly risk their lives in the attempt. If not, a surrender on honorable terms would keep the army intact and avoid the further suffering that was inevitable when their food ran out or if they were routed by an enemy attack.

Having heard them out, Burgoyne then produced a draft of a surrender document, saying if his terms proved acceptable to Gates, a capitulation would "save the army for the King, who could then use it for other purposes." That seemed a rather dubious outcome, but no matter. What was clear from the existence of the draft was that the general was coming around to the officers' view that surrender was the only way out.

A drummer, Major Griffith Williams's fifteen-year-old nephew,* was sent to Gates's lines with a message that General Burgoyne wished to have one of his field officers discuss "a matter of high moment" the next

---

*That nephew, George Williams, was reputedly the last survivor of the battle. He died in 1850 at the age of eighty-eight.

day; if acceptable, a truce would be in effect meanwhile. Back came word that Gates was agreeable to the proposal and would expect the officer to be at his army's advanced post at 10:00 A.M. on October 14.

The American camp had been rife with rumors for days, all suggesting that the fighting was over. A rebel called to a German picket who threw down his gun and ran into the lines, saying the enemy had just drawn the last of their provisions—seven days' worth. It was said that forty major generals (there were only two) were conferring with Burgoyne about terms of the treaty. Another man heard that the Canadians had mutinied and Burgoyne had promised they could go home in a few days. The truce was on, it was off. Burgoyne had gone back on his word and distributed sixty rounds to the redcoats, but the "Hessians . . . refused to take them." It was noised about that Morgan's riflemen had orders to scale the enemy works and "spare no man."

Horatio Gates spent the morning of October 12 writing a letter to John Hancock, president of Congress, reporting on "the great Success of the Arms of the United States in this Department" on October 7. After detailing the cannon, arms and ammunition, and baggage taken in the "very warm and bloody" battle, he listed the principal enemy officers captured—the artillerist Major Williams, Major Acland, and Burgoyne's aide Clerke. Simon Fraser, leading the "Flying Army" of the enemy, had been killed. In the meantime, he continued, desertion "has taken a deep Root in the Royal army, particularly among the Germans who come to us in Shoals." His own wounded included "the Gallant Major General Arnold," and he went on to cite the performance of Morgan's riflemen and Dearborn's light infantry as key factors in the victory.

Perhaps the glowing mention of Arnold was to atone for the deliberate omission of his name in his summary of the September 19 battle, or perhaps now that Arnold was badly wounded and might never walk again he was no longer a threat to Gates. In any case, Gates now had another fish to fry and once again was indulging in personal infighting, as he had done earlier with Arnold. Unbelievably, he did not communicate news of the victory to George Washington, going out of his way to insult the commander in chief, possibly hoping to make personal capital out of his own triumph when it was contrasted with Washington's two recent defeats at the Brandywine and Germantown. It was the beginning of a serious rift between the two senior generals in the Continental Army and a prelude to a series of attempts by Gates to undermine Washington.

To serve as his intermediary in dealing with Gates, Burgoyne chose his deputy adjutant general, Major Robert Kingston, a proud, ruddy-faced cavalryman who had served with him in Portugal. From the moment he crossed over into the rebel lines, Kingston knew he was in for a nasty time. There he was greeted by Wilkinson, who told him he would have to be blindfolded, to which Kingston took indignant exception, but he finally consented provided he could use his own handkerchief. Then he was led over the long mile that took him to Gates's headquarters.

Inside the tent the blindfold was removed and Kingston said, "General Gates, your servant."

"Ah, Kingston, how do you do?" was Gates's chummy reply.

Kingston then read from a paper the proposals he carried from Burgoyne, beginning with the suggestion that having fought Gates twice, he was quite prepared to do so a third time, but now—aware of the rebels' superiority in numbers and the disposition of those troops—he felt justified "to spare the lives of brave men upon honourable terms." If Gates concurred, he proposed a cessation of the fighting while they discussed preliminary terms.

Then, to the amazement of Kingston and Wilkinson, Gates reached in a pocket and produced a paper listing the conditions to which Burgoyne must agree. It was essentially a demand for unconditional surrender, prefaced with a humiliating statement of fact: "General Burgoyne's army, being exceedingly reduced by repeated defeats, by desertions, sickness, etc., their provisions exhausted, their military stores, tents and baggage taken or destroyed, their retreat cut off and their camp invested, they can only be allowed to surrender prisoners of war." He required British and German troops to ground arms in their camp and march out as prisoners, and the truce was to last until sunset, before which time Burgoyne must reply.

Neither Kingston nor Wilkinson knew it, but Gates was bluffing, and in doing so he made a serious and costly misjudgment. Customarily, the defeated general proposed terms the conqueror could either accept, modify, or refuse, but in ignoring Burgoyne's proposals and responding with demands of his own, Gates opened the door for the British commander to negotiate and call his bluff—which meant that Gates would be in the position of having to accept Burgoyne's terms or reject them outright.

It was all Kingston could do to deliver these mortifying stipulations to his chief, and on the way back to Fish Creek, blindfolded again, he boasted of the proud record of an army that had six regiments in action at Minden. When he read Gates's shocking terms, Burgoyne reconvened the officers who had met the day before and they "declared unanimously that they would rather die than accept such dishonorable conditions." Their objection was principally to two particulars in Gates's demands: that they would ground arms inside their camp and surrender as prisoners of war. Burgoyne's reply to the American general minced no words: "If General Gates does not mean to recede from the first and sixth articles of his proposal, the treaty [is] to end and hostilities immediately to commence."

Even now the bad blood between British and Germans persisted, though it did not come out in the open until later, when Riedesel wrote that the troops of his command were willing to fight to the last man. Burgoyne, however, claimed that the Brunswickers were dispirited, ready to lay down their arms at any moment. That view was put more colloquially by the loyalist captain Joshua Pell, who said when the German officers tried to see how their men stood, the answer was "nix the money, nix the rum, nix the fighten."

At sunset Burgoyne sent Kingston back with his own proposals, saying he would accept no changes. To Gates's statement that the British retreat was cut off, he replied dramatically that his army, "however reduced, will never admit that their retreat is cut off while they have arms in their hands." His troops were to march out of camp with the honors of war and ground arms at the bank of the Hudson at the command of their own officers. All officers would retain their swords and equipment, the soldiers their knapsacks; and the army was to march to Boston, where they would be properly fed and sheltered before embarking for England. The only condition imposed was that they were not to serve in North America again during the present war (which came as a great relief to some of his own officers and must of the Germans). The Canadians were to be given *laissez-passer* to return home, and noncombatants were to be treated as British citizens. A host of other provisos followed, relatively minor, all generous to the defeated force. Once again Gates astonished everybody by accepting all the British proposals with only a single provision: "This capitulation to be finished by two o'clock this day and the troops march from their encampments at five. . . ."

Burgoyne's suspicions were immediately aroused. Why should Gates agree so readily to what were extraordinary terms, and what was behind his demand for concluding the surrender so precipitately? Surely this meant that Clinton was coming closer every day and Gates was in a rush to conclude the business so he could defend himself against the attack from the south. The Briton requested a postponement of the surrender, and once again Gates agreed.

The British general was right. Gates had received word that a British fleet of twenty sail was heading upstream carrying Vaughan's troops to Esopus, and since he had no information on the size of that force, he wanted to waste no more time on negotiations. Unfortunately his motives were all too apparent, and Burgoyne now sent a message to him that although they both saw eye to eye on most matters, others required "explanation and precision," and more time would be needed for discussion. He would name two officers who could speak for him and asked that Gates do the same.

On October 15, Benjamin Warren wrote in his journal, "All remains still like Sunday," and in the stillness a marquee was raised between the advanced guard of both armies for the meeting of the four officers— James Wilkinson and militia brigadier William Whipple for Gates, Lieutenant Colonel Nicholas Sutherland and Captain James Craig for Burgoyne—and by early evening they had signed articles of capitulation and taken them to their respective commanders.

After Wilkinson turned in for the night, an unexpected message from Captain Craig, dated October 15 at 10:30 P.M., was delivered to his tent. Apologizing for bothering him at the late hour, Craig said that the terms had been accepted by Burgoyne and his principal officers but for one word, to which all took exception and which Sutherland and Craig in their zeal to complete the treaty as quickly as possible had overlooked. They had "unguardedly called [it] a treaty of *capitulation* which the army means only as treaty of *convention*." Craig and Sutherland would meet Wilkinson and Whipple in the morning with a signed copy of the agreement containing this single change.

Back came a reply to Craig stating that "Major General Gates will admit the alteration required."

But the game was not finished.

During the night a loyalist from Albany came into the British camp with news that rebel troops had been seen moving away from Gates's army and that Clinton had reached Esopus and by now was probably in Albany. Once again Burgoyne's hopes soared. He summoned his officers to yet another council, told them what he had learned (even though it came from a stranger and was based on hearsay), and asked if they considered it honorable to break an agreement he had promised to sign. A vote was taken. A majority of fourteen to eight (the latter group including Phillips, Hamilton, and Balcarres) said he could not honorably withdraw from an agreement he had promised to accept, which had already been signed by his chosen proxies.

Yet even now Burgoyne adamantly opposed surrender despite all the arguments that favored it. Clinging to the will-o'-the-wisp that Clinton would rescue him, he believed (with some reason) that his army, much reduced as it was, could not only withstand an attack by the rebels but win enough of a victory to gain time for reinforcements to arrive. Several factors favored this argument: possessing the interior lines, he could counterattack at almost any point on the perimeter; he could rely on the disciplined volley firing by the veteran British and German troops, plus their skill with the bayonet; and his artillery would be an important factor, for he still had a number of the thirty-six cannon he had brought from Ticonderoga.

Ignored entirely was the desperate condition of his army. Most of the officers present recognized his suggestion for the futile, wishful thinking it was. Even if Clinton was on the way (which, of course, he was not), he was too far away to reach them before they were starved into submission. And the carnage Burgoyne had told Gates he wished to avoid was all too probable, given the army's weakened state and the huge numerical superiority of the rebels.

It was too late for forlorn hopes, but Burgoyne could not bring himself to give up: he decided to stall for more time. Early in the morning of October 16 he dictated another letter to Gates stating that he had "received intelligence that a considerable force has been detached" from the American army, and since a paramount reason for the surrender was that army's superiority in numbers he insisted that two of his officers be permitted to determine Gates's strength and verify that no substantial changes had been made.

That tore it. Gates was furious—above all at the questioning of his word and at Burgoyne's impudence to "require" him to submit to a count of his army. The fact was that a few hundred militiamen, whose hitches were up, had left the army for home, but this in no way diminished Gates's force, since more were arriving daily. Gates replied icily that he "condescends to assure your excellency that no violation of the treaty has taken place," that the request was inadmissible, that it was up to General Burgoyne "to ratify or dissolve the treaty," and that he expected an immediate response. Word quickly spread through camp that Gates believed "there is treachery" afoot, and the men were ordered to lay on their arms and parade at three in the morning, according to Ephraim Squier.

Wilkinson carried Gates's peremptory note to British headquarters, with an ultimatum that Burgoyne had exactly one hour in which to answer. Years later Wilkinson recalled vividly the occasion of their meeting and wondered what the British general's thoughts must have been. Here was the famous leader of a British army; a familiar of His Majesty George III, ruler of the world's mightiest empire; he had hobnobbed with dukes and earls; married the daughter of a nobleman; and now to be confronted by this nobody—"a youth in a plain blue frock, without other military insignia than a cockade and a sword." It must have seemed like waking to find that the nightmare was all true—his hopes shattered, his name disgraced, his career at an end.

Whatever he may have felt inwardly, Burgoyne was as stubborn and determined as ever. "I do not recede from my purpose," he said loftily, "the truce must end."

The two men synchronized their watches, and Wilkinson turned on his heel and left.

Long afterward Wilkinson claimed that he showed Captain Craig's letter of the previous night to Burgoyne, who, seeing Craig's statement that the agreement was acceptable except for the substitution of the word "convention" for "capitulation," changed his mind and accepted the inevitable. What seems more likely, given Burgoyne's anguish and desperate determination to put off the evil moment as long as possible, is that he requested two hours instead of one in order to confer with his officers, and that the young American agreed.

One last council was held. Was the treaty in its present form binding? And was the general obliged to sign? The eight officers who had voted with Burgoyne the previous day now joined the fourteen who had not. Despite the unanimous opposition, the obstinate commander in chief argued on: he was not bound by what had taken place, he said; his army might yet be relieved.

On the other hand, he continued, the treaty was most advantageous, and Clinton—even if he was in Albany—could not arrive in time to save them. Hearing that admission, his officers decided to talk turkey, and the comments were devastating. One declared his post untenable and predicted widespread desertion if the convention was not signed. Two others said the 47th Regiment could not be relied upon; another cited the condition of the 62nd, which had been decimated on September 19 and could no longer be considered an effective fighting unit. The army was worn out and some of the best officers were sick or wounded. A defeat would be fatal and a victory would avail them nothing, since they had no food, and more rebels would surely rise to attack them. As a final consideration, someone reminded him that the life and property of every loyalist, Canadian, and noncombatant depended on execution of the treaty.

When the two-hour deadline passed without word from Burgoyne, Gates dispatched Colonel John Greaton on horseback to demand compliance within ten minutes or he would launch an attack. The colonel returned at once with the signed convention.

It was over.

Chapter 22

The King Fell into Agonies

In one respect nothing had changed: the morning dawned "very dark and foggy." But in all others this was a day like none that had gone before, and no one who was there would ever forget it.

Within the British and German lines the men who were about to surrender had spent much of the night preparing for their long march to Boston—some two hundred miles, they were told—and with the rains and cold coming on soon the business of transporting their gear was bound to prove difficult. The few surviving horses "exhibited a most wretched picture of poverty and want, made up of nothing but skin and bone," according to Lieutenant Digby.

Early that morning, John Burgoyne removed the uniform he had worn for sixteen days and nights and dressed with particular care, putting on the gorgeous scarlet coat with the gleaming gold braid and a hat fitted with plumes—the spotless regimentals he had planned to wear for his triumphant entry into Albany. The first order of business was a final meeting with all his officers. It was an anguished moment for the general, who wanted them to understand the reasons behind his actions from the time he took command of the army, but recounting the story was too much for him and he broke down, too upset to go on. Then, getting himself under control, he continued, speaking now of his enormous chagrin that the meeting with Clinton had not come to pass. He read aloud the articles of the convention as a way of reassuring the officers that the terms were much easier than they could have expected, adding that he never would have talked peace with Gates if they hadn't run out of provisions or had had any hope of extricating themselves from the predicament they were in.

Meanwhile Baron Riedesel was assuring his own men that it was no fault of theirs or lack of courage that had brought this about. He had all the regimental flags brought to him and later gave them to his wife, who sewed them inside a pillow to be taken secretly back to Brunswick.

Then it was ten o'clock, time to go. After the soldiers left their dying campfires, some of them had a good deal of reshuffling to do: since a need no longer existed for an advanced corps, the flank companies that had been assigned to it now returned to their own regiments. Sergeants shouted orders, ranks were closed and opened, and after the lines were dressed the troops stood at attention as company and regimental officers walked back and forth, slowly inspecting them. It was their final parade as soldiers of General John Burgoyne's army, and in spite of all that had occurred they remained remarkably fond of him. Sergeant Lamb observed, "He possessed the confidence and affection of his army in an extraordinary degree, that no loss or misfortune could shake . . . not a voice was heard throughout the army to upbraid, to censure or blame their general."

One after another, the proud regiments of the British line—9th, 20th, 21st, 24th, and 62nd, colors flying, fifes and drums playing—along with the Royal Artillery and assorted surgeons, chaplains, adjustants, quarter-masters, and engineers, all in tattered uniforms or whatever clothing they could piece together, marched out of the lines with their heads high and headed toward the river. The Americans who had camped on the north side of Fish Creek had all withdrawn at Gates's orders so as not to be witnesses to the enemy's ultimate humiliation.

William Digby of the 53rd, the Shropshire Regiment of Foot, who had served throughout the campaign with Balcarres's light infantry, was sick at heart, but he knew what this occasion must mean to the rebels, and he had enough respect for the opponents who had beaten his army that his journal entry for the day had an extra-large heading: "A day famous in the annals of America." Yet as he stood at attention waiting for the order to march, he realized that the regimental drums had lost their magic to excite him, while the grenadiers' march "seemed . . . as if almost ashamed to be heard on such an occasion." He couldn't express his own feelings: tears filled his eyes and he knew if he had been alone he would have burst out crying.

Behind the redcoats came a steady procession of blue-uniformed Germans—dragoons and grenadiers, the Rhetz, Riedesel, and Specht regiments, some green-clad Hesse-Hanau infantrymen and artillery—moving in precise formation toward the flats by the river, just north of Fish Creek's junction with the Hudson, where a few low mounds were all that remained of the walls of Fort Hardy, a redoubt covering fifteen acres, built during the French and Indian War. Here scores of horses lay dead, and the intolerable stench of decaying bodies, added to the mortifying task that engaged the troops, forced them to finish the business as quickly as possible. Even so, it took time. The artillerymen parked their cannon while infantrymen emptied cartridge boxes and stacked their muskets, but the experience was too much for a few drummers, who stomped holes in the skins of their drums, while some angry foot soldiers smashed the butts of their muskets and threw them on the piles.

Burgoyne had already checked out the site where his army's bitter rendezvous with reality was taking place. Before the troops marched there, James Wilkinson came to escort him to Gates's headquarters and before doing so showed him the big field flanking the Hudson. When the general asked whether the river was fordable here, Wilkinson wondered if he still had hopes of escaping and said it was, "but do you observe the people on the opposite shore?"

"Yes," said Burgoyne, "I have seen them too long."

The main body of Gates's army was now spread out along the south bank of Fish Creek, and while Burgoyne's soldiers were stacking their arms the first rebel units marched to the Saratoga church (the meetinghouse, as New Englanders called it) and began to line up on either side of the river road that led to Dovegat and beyond. As they paraded, Fellows's troops on the other side of the river were drawn up to see what they could of the enemy.

By now the sun was up, the fog lifted, and the autumn colors of the hills, softened by the lingering mist, appeared to be floating on the river's swiftly moving current. For the first time in weeks the valley was quiet, without the thunder of gunfire. Only the rattle of drums and shouted commands broke the silence, and in the American camp a chaplain delivered a sermon of Thanksgiving, taking as his text words from the prophet Joel: "But I will remove far off from you the northern army, and will drive him into a land barren and desolate with his face toward the east sea. . . ."

Sometime around noon, Burgoyne and his staff, accompanied by

Wilkinson and followed by Phillips and Riedesel, forded the swollen Fish Creek and rode past the blackened remains of Philip Schuyler's house and outbuildings toward Gates's headquarters, almost half a mile distant. Suddenly, eyewitnesses were given an unforgettable image of the campaign to which this meeting was the climax. Here was John Burgoyne, tall, imposing, still with some of the good looks that had made him such a dashing figure in England and on the Continent, resplendent in the shocking-scarlet uniform that looked as if it had just been delivered by his tailor. Behind him rode his aides and his two major generals, one a nobleman from Brunswick, with their respective staffs. And there was Gates, alone, smaller than the English general, riding to meet them, having just emerged from what someone called the "small hovel" that served as his lodging, looking seedy and old in a simple blue coat, his thin gray hair lank, squinting at his visitors through spectacles that only partially corrected his nearsightedness.

Protocol called for young Wilkinson to introduce the two principals, but that was hardly necessary. They had known each other since 1745 when they served together as lieutenants and when their names, almost unbelievably in view of this confrontation three decades later, appeared as numbers 15 and 16 on the roster of the regiment they were joining. After that their paths diverged, as might be expected when one was the offspring of a boatman on the Thames, the other said to be the bastard son of Lord Bingley. In a world where family and connections were everything, it was hardly surprising that Horatio Gates became disillusioned about the possibility of advancement in the army and sailed to America to begin a new life.

Now, some three decades later, the two men who rode up to greet each other were the very symbols of entrenched British power and the America that was challenging it.

"I am glad to see you," said Gates with a smile as Burgoyne reined in his horse.

The Englishman removed his hat, bowed slightly from the waist, and is said to have replied, "I am not glad to see you. It is my fortune, sir, and not my fault that I am here."* The two commanders dismounted. Burgoyne drew his sword and handed it to Gates, who held it for a few moments as they exchanged words and then returned it.

Now the men in the ranks were to meet, in a manner of speaking.

---

*Several versions of the conversation exist, and whether these were the exact words spoken cannot be said for sure, but certainly this was the substance.

The prisoners were approaching with fifes and drums playing, and the waiting Americans lined both sides of the road, standing with muskets at their sides, eyes looking straight ahead or lowered in deference to the defeated men, though it was "a very agreeable sight," according to Ephraim Squier. Brigade by brigade, regiment by regiment, the British and Brunswickers paraded through this gauntlet, their jaws tight with anger and pride, arms swinging freely now that they had no weapons to carry, seeing for the first time the face of destiny.

The road ahead sliced through the rich bottomland along the Hudson, and it was a gumbo of pockmarks and ruts, the scars left by more than fifteen thousand pairs of feet, horses, wagons, and gun carriages sloshing through rain and mud during the past two weeks. Along the road, stretching out as far as the eye could see, were those rows of rebels, and American fifers suddenly struck up the shrill notes of "Yankee Doodle," the impudent little tune that was introduced during the French and Indian War by a British doctor who composed verses mocking the rustic Yankee recruits.*

All Gates's regiments and his artillery were standing at arms and "not a one of them was regularly equipped," a German officer wrote. "Each one had on the clothes which he was accustomed to wear in the field, in the tavern, the church, and in everyday life." But he was quick to see that "they stood in an erect and a soldierly attitude. All their muskets had bayonets attached to them, and their riflemen had rifles."

Several other things impressed the seasoned European soldiers. "There was absolute silence in those regts. as can only be demanded from the best disciplined troops," said one officer. "We were utterly astounded," said another; "not one of them made any attempt to speak to the man at his side." Equally remarkable was the appearance of the men in the long lines: they were "so slender, fine-looking, and sinewy, that it was a pleasure to look at them" a German thought, awed "that Dame Nature had created such a handsome race!" In Europe the Prussian army set the standards, and there a man had to be at least five feet tall to be accepted in the military, with the average probably between that and five feet five. A majority of these Americans, on the other hand, were five-eight to five-ten, and a number were taller still—"far ahead of those in the greater portion of Europe."

---

*An English officer said the Yankees "love [it] the best of all their songs; they sing it in camp & consider it as warlike as the grenadiers march: it is the *a b c* of lovers & the song which lulls to sleep their children. After our rapid successes we had accustomed ourselves to regard the *Yanks* with contempt, & it was not a little mortifying to us to hear them play that air when their army assembled to be witnesses of our surrender."

Those militia officers who did have uniforms wore every color imaginable—many of them brown coats with sea-green facings, white linings, and silver dragons, others gray coats with yellow buttons and straw facings. Brigadiers and staff officers generally wore blue coats with white facings and had colored sashes around the waist indicating rank, but more often than not, colonels and junior officers wore everyday clothes. Almost all carried pouches and powder horns slung over their shoulders and stood, right hand on their musket, the left hanging by their side, with their right foot placed slightly forward.

By no means all were handsome specimens, of course, and the marchers couldn't help being amused by fifty- and sixty-year-olds wearing wigs the likes of which few Europeans had seen. Here were men with white wigs beneath which shocks of long dark hair and ponytails hung down; there "the glistening black wig of an abbé surmounting some red and copper-colored face"; others wore "white and gray clerical-looking wigs made of horse and goat hair, and piled up in successive rolls. In looking at a man thus adorned one would imagine that he had an entire sheep under his hat, with its tail dangling around his neck." The wigs, one Brunswicker supposed, were calculated to give the wearer—particularly a selectman or committee member—a learned appearance, and while they appeared comical, the look on their faces and the determination with which they grasped a musket made it clear that they were not to be tangled with, "especially in skirmishes in the woods."

What most impressed and gratified the tired, defeated soldiers in Burgoyne's ranks was that "not a single man gave any evidence or the slightest impression of feeling hatred, mockery, malicious pleasure or pride for our miserable fate." On the contrary, "it seemed rather as though they desired to do us honor." As Lord Francis Napier put it, "They behaved with the greatest decency and propriety, not even a Smile appearing in any of their Countenances, which circumstance I really believe would not have happened had the case been reversed."

Gates invited all of Burgoyne's brigadiers and regimental commanders to join him and his own officers in his marquee, where planks laid on barrels held food—a ham, a goose, some beef, and boiled mutton, four separate dishes of "ordinary viands," according to one of Gates's officers, who thought it necessary to explain that the Americans were "accustomed to plain and frugal meals." Liquor was offered, but there were glasses only for the two commanders; the others drank from basins. And the drinks were hardly up to Burgoyne's standards—cider or New England rum mixed with water. Remarkably, though, Burgoyne was in excellent form, the hearty Gentleman Johnny of old, laughing and joking with the Americans, still the actor on center stage, behaving almost as if he were the victor and Gates the vanquished. He admired the dress and discipline of Gates's army, he said, and above all the extraordinary courtesy and decorum they demonstrated on this most difficult of days. He also told the rebel general he envied him his inexhaustible supply of men; "like the Hydra's head, when cut off, seven more spring up in its stead."

The atmosphere in the marquee was cordial and congenial—quite astonishing considering the ferocity with which the two armies had gone at each other. The Germans were elated to find among Gates's officers a Frenchman and a Prussian with whom they could converse, and the Americans showed the losers "all possible niceties," according to Brigadier Specht. Then it was time for toasts, an uncomfortable moment for Burgoyne, who resolved his dilemma by raising a glass to George Washington. After Gates responded tactfully with a toast to the king's health, the officers left the tables and went outside to observe King George's bedraggled soldiers as they continued to file through the double lines of Americans. The first contingents crossed Fish Creek at 2:00 P.M., Parson Hitchcock said, and even though one eyewitness noted that "they marched brisk," they were still passing by at sunset, trailed by almost 300 women (215 of them British, and 82 Germans), plus a ragtag collection of camp followers, and accompanied by a number of bewildered deer, raccoons, and other wild animals that had been turned into pets by the lonely, homesick Brunswickers.

While Baroness von Riedesel waited to learn what lay in store for her family she was delighted to see that the woman who had carried water from the river for so many noncombatants and wounded was receiving her just reward: everyone threw a handful of money into her apron and she went away richer by more than twenty guineas. A messenger came from the baron: she was to join him in the American camp with the children, and off in the calèche they went, fearful of what might await them. But she was thankful to find—in contrast with her experience in London—that "nobody glanced at us insultingly, that they all bowed to me, and some of them even looked with pity to see a woman with small children there."

When they reached the officers' tents a handsome man approached the carriage, lifted out her three daughters and kissed them, then helped her step down, saying, "You are trembling. Don't be afraid," and led her to Gates's marquee. There she found her husband and saw Burgoyne and Phillips chatting genially with Gates. Burgoyne came over and reassured her, saying that her sufferings had now come to an end.

She had an awkward moment when she realized the generals were about to have dinner: this was no place for a woman and little children. Just then the man who had welcomed her so thoughtfully came up and said, "It would embarrass you to take dinner with all these gentlemen; come to my tent with your children and although I can only give you a frugal meal, it will be given gladly." The frugal meal was a lot better than what Gates had to offer: delicious smoked tongue, beefsteaks, potatoes, and good bread and butter, and she said nothing had ever tasted better. It turned out that her host was Major General Philip Schuyler, who couldn't resist coming to witness the surrender he had tried so hard to bring about.

After they had eaten he invited her to stay with his family at Albany, and when the baron told her to accept the invitation she and the little girls departed. Burgoyne also encountered Schuyler and expressed regret at the destruction of his property (worth some £10,000, he later told the House of Commons), but Schuyler, with his customary noblesse oblige, told him to think no more about it: that was "the fate of war." The sun was setting when Generals Burgoyne, Phillips, and Riedesel rode off toward Stillwater, escorted by a detachment of nattily dressed Connecticut dragoons and accompanied by Schuyler's aide, Richard Varick, who had orders to procure for Burgoyne "better quarters than a stranger might be able to find." As indeed he did: the general's lodgings proved to be "a very elegant house" where he was astonished to be greeted by Mrs. Schuyler and her family.*

October 20 proved to be an excruciatingly painful day for the Schuylers' principal guest. Here was John Burgoyne, a captive in an American general's home, having to write what must have been the most difficult letter of his career—summarizing for Lord George Germain the tumultuous events from early September, when he last wrote, until the black day of surrender. What made it even more difficult was that Germain would almost certainly use this letter in such a way as to save his own skin and throw the entire blame for the disaster on Burgoyne. So it was imperative for the general to cast his experience in such a light that the king, Parliament, and the public realize that the fault lay in London, not on the banks of the Hudson River; that the planning, not the execution, was defective.

---

*Burgoyne was not eager to leave the Schuyler house. Instead of going at once to Boston he stayed with his hosts for five days—a difficult time for Catherine Schuyler, since his presence created "a great deal of trouble with her servants."

He began by reciting the causes of his misfortune: the rigors of the march, the defection of the Indians, the desertion or timidity of the Canadians, the failure of "other armies" to cooperate. At the last his own force was reduced to 3,500, of whom less than 2,000 were British; they were surrounded by 16,000 rebels; they had provisions for only three days. This catalog of woes was followed by a summary of events after September 13 and 14—when the army crossed the Hudson because "the peremptory tenor of my orders and the season of the year admitted no alternative." Thus having laid the blame for defeat on Howe, Germain, and his allies, he concluded by mentioning the one faintly positive note—the defense of Ticonderoga by Hamilton and the repulse of the rebels near Diamond Island. It was precious little to show for the heavy cost in lives and treasure for an expedition that was expected to put an end to the rebellion, and he closed by saying that it was now up to His Majesty George III, his fellow officers, and the public (especially, as he phrased it, the "respectable parts of my country") to decide whether he was to be praised or condemned.

Knowing that his numerous enemies were itching for an opportunity to disgrace him, he sent off another letter to a friend and ally in London, Colonel Phillipson, who could be relied on to get Burgoyne's side of the story to Lord Derby, grandson of his former father-in-law and patron. Conveniently forgetting his own role in planning and promoting the expedition, Burgoyne said it had been a "forlorn hope" from the beginning, "totally unsupported by Sir Wm Howe." What would his critics have had him do after the triumphs at Ticonderoga, Hubbardton, Skenesborough, and Fort Anne? What if he had "remained supine" in his camp at Fort Edward instead of pursuing Schuyler's retreating army? Surely, failure to do so would have brought "the contempt of my own army, the condemnation of Government and the world. . . ."

Still, there was one more letter to write—this to his nieces, to explain what had happened and why, to give them some ammunition with which to blunt the taunts and humiliating laughter that were sure to come their way—and it was the most revealing of all. To Germain he had spelled out the facts as seen by an angry, injured man who felt abandoned by those in authority who had given him the assignment. But to his nieces he spoke of his exhaustion in mind and body and hinted that he might not survive an American winter, "should that be my fate," if Howe did not order him back to London. It was an emotional, mawkish letter, filled with self-pity and self-justification, yet he spoke from the heart, explaining that he had been "under perpetual

Fire and exhausted with laborious days and sixteen almost sleepless nights without Change of Cloaths or any other Covering than the Sky. I have been with my Army within the Jaws of Famine, shot [through] my hat and waistcoat, my nearest Friends killed around me," and now, having survived these misfortunes, must endure "a War with Ministry, who will always lay the blame on the employd who miscarries." This was not the bold, fearless cavalryman, but a Burgoyne broken in spirit by circumstance and his own mistakes. Otherwise it is difficult to explain the extraordinary statement that he had been "surrounded by Enemies, ill treated by pretended Friends, and abandoned by a considerable part of my own Army. . . ." Granted that this was written by a man who had been under terrible stress for more than a month, his accusation that much of his army had forsaken him was unconscionable and unworthy. That army had gone through hell for him, and not even in the depths of self-pity should he have questioned his men's extraordinary loyalty.

The defeated soldiers who were to march to Boston, as stipulated in the convention, were doomed not only to disappointment but to a march that finally took them from Saratoga to Charlottesville, Virginia. As Sergeant Lamb described it, the painful, humiliating journey "was universally considered by the privates as a very great hardship, and by the officers as a shameful violation of the articles of capitulation." Under terms of the treaty they were to go back to Britain on condition that they serve no more in America during the Revolution. George Washington was not happy with the arrangement to which Gates had agreed: the arrival of those men in England, he argued, would trigger the release of a like number of troops for service in this country. Congress took the same view and for this and other reasons came up with a series of petty arguments with which they justified delay in ratifying the convention. Unhappily for the prisoners, Burgoyne added to the dispute by complaining that his officers had not received the housing in Boston to which they were entitled, which meant "the public faith is broke."

Congress did not take kindly to aspersions on its integrity and suspected Burgoyne was trying to build a case for disavowing the convention. And so it went until the prisoners were marched in 1779 to Charlottesville, leading Thomas Jefferson to write, "I cannot help feeling a most thorough mortification that our Congress should have permitted an infraction of our public honour. . . ." Burgoyne with two staff officers had returned to London nine months earlier, where he remained technically a prisoner of war on parole until he was exchanged for more than a thousand American prisoners in British hands. He devoted the next two years to an effort to vindicate his decisions and actions during the campaign, hoping to prove that the fault for his failure lay with Lord George Germain. Finally he succeeded in arranging an inquiry by the House of Commons (of which he was now a member of the opposition), after which he considered himself exonerated.

Americans were understandably jubilant about what had happened at Saratoga. On the same day that Burgoyne was explaining the defeat to Germain, Horatio Gates wrote his wife and son from Albany, telling them that the British had "surrendered themselves to me and my Yankees. Thanks to the Giver of all victory for this triumphant success." As he went on to describe the great occasion it almost seemed as though the high point for the former British commoner was not the capture of an entire enemy army but having in his possession "Major-General Phillips . . . Lord Petersham, Major Ackland, son of Sir Thomas, and his lady, daughter of Lord Ilchester, sister to the famous Lady Susan, and about a dozen members of Parliament, Scotch lords, &c." Another sentence was equally revealing: "If Old England is not by this lesson taught humility, then she is an obstinate old slut, bent upon her ruin."

Taking time out on the day of the surrender to write a thoughtful letter to Arthur St. Clair, Jeduthan Baldwin cast the affair in a different light. "A more compleat victory you could not wish for," he said, and went on to tell the brigadier that most people in the army had changed their opinion about the evacuation of Ticonderoga. All the officers had come around to the view that "a better plan could not have been adopted & nothing but your leaving that place could have given us this success." In other words, had it not been for St. Clair's courageous decision to abandon Ticonderoga, there would have been no Saratoga.

Oliver Boardman had a vivid recollection: "It was a glorious sight to see the haughty Brittons March out & Surrender their arms to an Army which but a little before they despised & called paltroons. . . ." Surely, he thought, "the Hand of Providence work'd wonderfully in Favour of America," and he hoped that every heart would be affected by "the wonderful goodness of God in delivering So many of our cruel unnatural Enemies into our hands, & with so little loss on our Side. . . ." Many if not most of the American soldiers had an abiding faith in the Almighty and His influence on the affairs of men, and Boardman's thoughts were echoed in letters throughout the army by soldiers who considered the victory as something of a miracle, wrought by the Lord. After describing the events to his wife, Joseph Hodgkins expressed the hope that we "may . . . all rejoice and give the glory to whom it is due."

Ralph Cross, who had been part of John Brown's raid on Ticonderoga in late September, had joined Gates just in time to participate in the October 7 fight and now reported that when "the Grand Army of Gen. Burgoin Capittelated & agreed to bee all Prisoners of Warr" it was "a Grand Sight as ever was beheld by Eye of man in America."

Henry Sewall of York, Maine, understood what a triumph it was militarily: "Perhaps an unprecedented Instance that near 6,000 British & foreign Troops, under the command of an accomplish'd General, should surrender themselves Prisoners of War *in the field* to an Army of raw Continental Troops & Militia!" In fact, 5,895 British and Germans lay down their arms on October 17. That was two-thirds of the force that had approached Fort Ticonderoga on July 1, since which time 1,728 others had been killed or captured in various actions. Burgoyne had been forced to detach almost 1,300 men to garrison Ticonderoga and Diamond Island—996 at the former place and 301 at the latter—and those troops were all that were salvaged of the original army that left Canada. Burgoyne had lost 86 percent of his expeditionary force—almost nine men out of every ten.

It was a stupendous victory for the Americans, but Gates gave his soldiers no time to sit around congratulating themselves. On the morning of October 18 an express brought word that the British had come up the Hudson with a large army, and before the morning fog lifted the troops struck their tents and were on the road, heading south. Between eleven and noon they reached Stillwater, where they passed the German prisoners, who had bivouacked while waiting for the British to be ferried by bateau across the Hudson. Brigadier Specht, who had a keen eye for discipline, watched the Americans march by in the stifling heat and was impressed: "The whole day as well as the whole night, very many American regts. filed past us from Saratoga in the strictest order with considerable trains of artillery and continued their march toward Albany."

Gates's first units reached their destination at nine the following morning and after a brief halt "pushed on with great dispatch," according to Parson Hitchcock, who lingered in Albany long enough to purchase four gallons of West India rum, linen for shirts, and buckram and hooks and eyes for a new suit that cost him £2 16s. South of them the task force under Major General John Vaughan was waiting for Burgoyne—or at least for news of him. The British naval vessels convoying Vaughan's troop transports had sailed upriver from the Highland forts abandoned by the Americans, pausing long enough to shell a shipyard at Poughkeepsie. Then Vaughan turned his eyes toward the opposite shore and Esopus, where the New York legislature was in session and where Gouverneur Morris was writing to a friend: "We are hellishly frightened but don't say a Word of that for we shall get our spirits again and then perhaps be so full of valor as to smite the air for blowing in our faces."

On the theory that Esopus was "a Nursery for almost every Villain in the Country," Vaughan set the town ablaze, but before the flames died out received the incredible news that Burgoyne's army had fallen to the Americans. Clearly, Esopus was no place to linger with his seventeen hundred troops, but while there was still time Vaughan paid a visit to the east bank of the river at Rhinebeck, where he landed his men with orders to march north, destroying and looting rebel property before they rejoined him at Clermont. Clermont was Robert Livingston's gracious Georgian mansion, with a magnificent view of the Hudson and the Catskills beyond, and it was a tempting target for a man who despised rebels as Vaughan did, so he torched the brick house as well as Chancellor Livingston's Belvedere, a few miles to the south. As the Livingstons mourned the loss of their lovely homes they could take some comfort from the knowledge that eight men from their distinguished family had fought Burgoyne at Freeman's farm.

Burgoyne's defeat put an entirely different complexion on the situation in the north. Carleton's entire front was suddenly at risk, and as short-handed as he was he could no longer spare the troops isolated at Ticonderoga and Diamond Island, so they were ordered north. In addition to the soldiers, the convention provided that volunteer sailors, bateaumen, and artificers could return to Montreal and they left Saratoga on October 17 and arrived three weeks later. It was an entirely different story for the Tories with Burgoyne's army—men regarded as "enemies to America" by the rebels, to be hunted down mercilessly. John Peters, who commanded the Queen's Loyal Rangers and had fought in every action but Hubbardton, spoke to General Phillips prior to the surrender and was asked why he was still there; why hadn't he gone north? Peters replied sensibly that he wasn't leaving without orders to do so, for fear of being accused of desertion by the British. With orders in hand at last, he and some thirty-five men made a hair-raising escape through rebel-infested woods beyond the British lines and made their way cross-country to Lake George and then by boat to Montreal and Quebec. On November 8, General Powell evacuated Ticonderoga and Mount Independence, and by December the entire inland waterway from New York to Canada was clear of enemy troops.

News traveled from one place to another only as fast as a man on foot or horseback could move, and often enough it was a soldier stopping at a farmhouse for a dipper full of spring water, repaying his host with an account of what he had just seen, along with rumors picked up along the way. In the case of the man entrusted to deliver the momentous news to Congress, it was a remarkably slow journey. James Wilkinson had the honor of bearing Gates's report to the members of that body, but he evidently stopped off en route to his destination to do some courting. When he arrived fifteen days after leaving Saratoga, a member of Congress suggested that he be rewarded with a pair of spurs. As for George Washington, he did not receive word of the surrender until October 25, in a letter from Israel Putnam—not from Gates, who did not deign to write him until November 2.

October 22 found Brigadier General John Glover in Albany, preparing to leave for Boston. He had the honor and the responsibility of guarding the prisoners on their march to Cambridge and had sent on that day some 2,400 British troops by way of Northampton, and almost 2,200 Germans via Springfield. He planned to leave the next day with Burgoyne and figured they would be in Worcester in ten days, so he was writing ahead to request that provisions be waiting for them there.

Glover's messenger was not the first to bring the news. The Reverend Manasseh Cutler recorded in his journal that word of the surrender was received on the East Coast on October 23, prompting "a general discharge of cannon at Boston, Marblehead, Salem, Beverly, Cape Ann, Newbury, and Portsmouth, and all the ships and vessels of force in all those harbors."

When the news reached Washington's army in Pennsylvania, Colonel Josiah Parker of a Virginia regiment wrote to John Page, lieutenant governor of his state, to tell him that Burgoyne, with his army and generals, and "a number of young noblemen, have surrendered themselves prisoners of war to the High and Mighty States of America." Shortly thereafter, Governor Patrick Henry set aside the 13th of November for "a solemn Thanksgiving . . . to celebrate the victory."

Militiamen like Ephraim Squier were being discharged and heading for home and considered themselves lucky, for it was already spitting snow; but the Continentals in Gates's army were fated to get little rest and a lot more discomfort. After camping on the heights near Albany and drawing some badly needed clothing, Morgan's riflemen and Poor's brigade shouldered their weapons and tramped south through a three-day downpour, about which one man observed that "it is Said so heavy a Rain was Never known here Before." These and other units were bound for the south to join George Washington's army in winter quarters outside Philadelphia, where they learned they would build their own log huts, chinked with mud, in an encampment on a series of hills eighteen miles from the city. The place was called Valley Forge.

Congress's Foreign Affairs Committee had heard nothing that autumn from its three agents in France—Benjamin Franklin, Silas Deane, and Arthur Lee—save a letter dated April 19. Since the commissioners were expected to send a monthly packet of information, their silence was disturbing, yet it was assumed (correctly) to be the result of the increased vigilance and activity of the British fleet, which drastically reduced the flow of information and cargoes between France and America. Beyond a doubt, the blockade was working.

Writing on October 6 from York, Pennsylvania, where Congress took refuge when Howe occupied Philadelphia, the committee summarized events of the past several months for the envoys, saying they finally had some good news to report along with the bad. In the latter category were the defeat suffered by General Washington at the Brandywine in September, the botched attack on the British at Germantown on October 4, and the loss of Philadelphia. But in the north the situation was considerably brighter: St. Leger had been turned back from Fort Schuyler, while Stark had soundly defeated Baum "at a place called Benington." Meanwhile, Burgoyne's loss on September 19 at Bemis Heights, coupled with John Brown's attacks in the rear of the enemy army, gave the committee members reason to hope that they would soon "give you information of definitive success over the British army in that quarter."

Since this letter was intended to provide the commissioners with ammunition for their ongoing negotiations for an alliance with the

French government, the loss of Philadelphia was played down as something that had been expected all along, and the agents were cautioned not to let this news create "ill impressions." Then, after complimenting the trio in Paris for obtaining additional clothing and military matériel, the committee urged them to strain every nerve to foil British efforts to obtain Russian or German soldiers for the next campaign, to do everything possible to win the support of Prussia for American independence, and above all to solicit a source of "marine strength," even to the extent of purchasing warships (on credit, of course, to be paid for with tobacco and other commodities wanted in Europe).

On October 18 the Foreign Affairs Committee sent off a copy of General Gates's letter describing his victory of October 7 over Burgoyne—a message that spoke for itself—and two weeks later it transmitted the joyous news of Burgoyne's capitulation and the surrender of his entire army, adding, "We rely on your wisdom and care to make the best and most immediate use of this intelligence to depress our enemies and produce essential aid to our cause in Europe"—most important, "public acknowledgment of the Independence of these United States."

All that fall England anxiously awaited the war news. On September 18, Horace Walpole wrote that they had been in the dark for more than three weeks. "It is so inconvenient to have all letters come by the post of the ocean," he grumbled. "People should never go to war above ten miles off, as the Grecian States used to do." October 26 found him complaining that nothing certain was known about the situation, with the result that "impatience is very high and uneasiness increases with every day." To make matters worse, the government consistently circulated false or erroneous reports, and there was something ominous about France's failure to act. Surely that was coming, he thought, and when it did the war would end in Britain's ruin.

Not until November 7 did he finally hear about "the check" Burgoyne had received in the action of September 19, plus "the distress of his army [which is] in danger of being starved." When and how this news arrived he did not say, but he lamented the wounding of twenty-six of Burgoyne's officers, and since no names were given out, the resulting uncertainty that would create anxiety in ten times that many families: "The distance of the war augments its horrors almost as much as its expense."

December 2 brought official news from Carleton, reporting "the total annihilation . . . of Burgoyne's army," and according to Walpole the king "fell into agonies on hearing this account, but the next morning, at his levee to disguise his concern, affected to laugh and be so indecently merry that Lord North endeavoured to stop him." Many, like Francis Rush Clark, saw Howe as the culprit: his measures *"have cost Great Britain America."* One disgusted New York loyalist observed that his delay in New York harbor, "his voyage to the mouth of the Delaware, where he played at bopeep with the rebels, and in his circumbendibus to Chesapeak Bay, expended nearly three months of the finest time of the campaign; and all this to go out of his way to desert his real business, and to leave Burgoyne with 6,000 regulars to fall a sacrifice." Howe, who had never had the least intention of moving up the Hudson to join Burgoyne, was thoroughly sick of a war for which he had never had much enthusiasm. Frustrated by the government's unwillingness to provide adequate support, on October 22 he wrote Germain asking to be relieved "from this very painful Service," making clear that since he did not enjoy the confidence of his superiors he wanted out.

Burgoyne's friend Charles James Fox, who was after bigger game than Howe, rose in the House of Commons to attack Lord George Germain, calling him "an ill-omened and inauspicious character . . . unfit to serve the Crown." The secretary was incapable of conducting a war, Fox declared, reminding members of the Minden affair by saying he hoped Germain would be tried again.

"We are . . . very near the end of the American war," Walpole concluded, and when he learned that Ticonderoga was back in rebel hands, said, "I must rejoice that the Americans are to be free, as they had a right to be." When he heard that Lord North had put peace proposals before the House (ignoring the likelihood that the terms would be unacceptable to the rebels, since they were not to be granted the independence for which they had been fighting for more than two years), Walpole suggested that Benjamin Franklin should order the cabinet to come to Paris with ropes around their necks and then "kick them back to St. James's."

That gentleman was hardly in a position to carry out Walpole's wish. Now that autumn had come to France he was thoroughly enjoying the creature comforts of living there, but he was continually frustrated by the unwillingness of Louis XVI and his ministers to act on the proposed treaty of alliance. Writing to his sister, Jane Mecom, Franklin reported that his health was excellent and his situation ideal. He had a grand-nephew and two grandsons with him, one of whom acted as his secretary; he lived in a splendid, airy house on a hill in Passy, only half an hour's drive from Paris; he was surrounded by lovely gardens, inviting walks, and congenial neighbors; and French cooking agreed with him better than English. He enjoyed frequent trips to the capital to attend meetings of the Academy of Sciences or the opera, and every time he appeared he was acclaimed by a warm, respectful crowd—"an honor seldom paid to the first princes of the blood," according to Silas Deane. And another American wrote that "the curiosity of the people is so great, that he may be said to be followed by a genteel mob. A friend of mine paid something for a place at a [third-floor] window to see him pass by in his coach. . . ." All things considered, it was a perfect life—or would have been had it not been for the exasperation of thwarted diplomacy.

A succession of crises had plagued the American commissioners. Although France had begun in July to explore with Spain the advantages of declaring war on England, she was by no means prepared to fight, the Spanish were even less so, and the discouraging news from America, which put the outcome of the Revolution so much in doubt, was not conducive to an alliance or worth risking a major conflict. From a Swiss friend Franklin heard that "your adversaries are now crowing on Burgoin's Success [at Ticonderoga]. Another mischief . . . is the Impression it makes on the French Cabinet in your Disfavor."

By now the three envoys were so disheartened that Silas Deane wanted to warn France and Spain that if effective support was not forthcoming immediately, America would seek terms from Britain. Franklin and Lee vetoed that proposal, fearing that France might turn against them, but the commissioners were up against some harsh realities. Unfortunately the dream of financing the war with the sale of tobacco in Europe had all but vanished, thanks to the efficiency of the British fleet; America's credit was exhausted; and American privateers were causing no end of trouble by using French ports to outfit themselves and sell captured British merchant ships, which violated France's pretense of neutrality.

Despite being blocked at every turn, Franklin was unusually philosophical about the lack of progress. In fact, he believed that much good would come of the delay, for the longer France and Spain waited to make an alliance with the United States, the less chance they had of getting favorable terms. In a conversation with Arthur Lee, the old man outlined his reasons for optimism. What had occurred in America, he said, was "a miracle in human affairs," and if he had not been in the middle of events and seen them with his own eyes he could not have believed it. For months the people who made the Revolution had had no government, no laws. They had to create a civil government, raise an army and a navy from scratch, make alliances where none existed, and do all this "not at leisure nor in a time of tranquillity and communication with other nations, but in the face of a most formidable invasion by the most powerful nation." They lacked money, arms, artillery, ammunition; their coast was blockaded; they faced internal opposition—brother against brother in the divisive tug of contrary opinions, old loyalties to the crown, personal animosities, and just plain fear of "so dreadful and dubious an undertaking." Yet despite all the odds against them, the Americans had brought the thing off "with an expedition, energy, wisdom, and success of which . . . the whole history of human affairs has not, hitherto, given an example."

Few men in America had given so much thought to the question of separation from England as Dr. Franklin, and few understood the reasons for its success better than he. The Revolution was grounded in "the opinion and voice of the majority of the people" on certain principles, he said, and as a result each believer did his best for what Thomas Paine called "the cause of all mankind." Elected officials at all levels gave their whole thought to the public interest (Franklin said he devoted an average of twelve hours a day to the public business); those who fought did so with whatever weapons, ammunition, and clothing they could bring with them or procure. The people, in other words, were "ready to sacrifice every thing to the common cause, a thousand fold."

Their government and codes of law, "for wisdom and justice, are the admiration of all the wise and thinking men of Europe." Lee should remember, he went on, that "the greatest revolution the world ever saw is likely to be effected in a few years," and a power that had made Europe tremble for centuries would be "humbled by those whom she insulted and injured, because she conceived they had neither spirit nor power to resist or revenge it."

Maybe the old man wanted to boost his younger colleague's morale; perhaps his musing was also to reassure himself. Whatever his reasons, few men saw so clearly the achievement of those Americans who made the Revolution.

Franklin would have rested easier if he had known that a young man named Jonathan Loring Austin, a prominent merchant and the owner of one of those privateers that were creating such difficulties for France, had boarded a packet in Boston harbor on October 31, carrying dispatches that included the official word of Burgoyne's surrender. (Austin could not have been reassured by the prayer offered by a local minister for the success of his mission. The parson made it clear that whatever the Lord chose to do with the messenger, He might at least see that those important papers reached their destination.)

Austin came ashore at Nantes with his dispatches and galloped off in the direction of Paris. On the morning of December 4, 1777—a year and a day after Benjamin Franklin landed in France—he reached Versailles, where he lingered for an hour to do a bit of sightseeing, then just before noon rode into Franklin's court at Passy. Rumors of his arrival had preceded him, and the commissioners were waiting anxiously. Before he could dismount, Franklin asked, "*Is* Philadelphia taken?" and received the reply, "Yes, sir."

The old man clasped his hands as if he had heard of a death in the family and turned to go inside, at which Austin said quickly, "But sir, I have greater news than that. GENERAL BURGOYNE *and his whole army are prisoners of war!*" The effect, Austin said later, was "electrical."

That it certainly was. As the commissioners reported to the Continental Congress, the news "occasioned as much general Joy in France as if it had been a Victory of their own troops over their own Enemies." Caron de Beaumarchais, the agent who had been channeling French arms and money to the rebels through the dummy corporation of Hortalez & Cie., was so excited that he rushed off to Paris, driving so recklessly that his carriage overturned, injuring his arm. (Beaumarchais was almost certainly in a hurry to use this inside knowledge for his own speculative purposes; in Paris an important British spy with knowledge of the news dashed off to London to do the same thing.)

Now the question confronting the commissioners was how to get the news immediately to those in the best position to influence the course of events. Printing Austin's report would take too long, so they composed a brief, twenty-two-line announcement, made copies by hand, and dispatched them to friends in Paris and Versailles. Lee also wrote to the Spanish ambassador. But by far their most important task was to notify the Comte de Vergennes, and they sent him all the information they had, listing 9,203 British, German, Canadian, and loyalist troops killed, wounded, and captured, plus known deserters. Then they itemized the various types of cannon seized during the campaign, and concluded this impressive document with the triumphant note that the prisoners included "4 members of Parliament."

Once the news reached Versailles, everyone from Louis XVI on down openly rejoiced that England's despised rebels had forced the surrender of an entire army of George III, and two days after receiving the news, Vergennes obtained permission from the court to open negotiations with the American envoys. At a meeting on December 12, discussions began in earnest, after which Vergennes sent a courier to Madrid urging Spain's concurrence with the proposed treaty. The messenger could travel there and back in three weeks, Vergennes said, so the commissioners resigned themselves to yet another period of waiting and wondering. But to their huge surprise they received word five days later that the king's council had approved the alliance; out of consideration for Spain, it would not be made public until the courier returned.*

At the same time Ralph Izard, a wealthy South Carolinian in Paris, reported to the Congressional Foreign Affairs Committee that the Grand Duke of Tuscany would shortly declare in favor of America. Not only that: the duke had persuaded the king of Prussia to permit no more German troops bound for America to cross his dominions. Behind this happy turn of events, Izard observed, was that "one successful battle will gain us more friends & do our business more effectually than all the skill of the ablest Negotiators."

As Franklin had predicted, the patient waiting game paid off. One surprise was a letter from London asking if the American commissioners would accept terms "a little short of independence," and when Franklin showed this to Vergennes the foreign minister used it to influence the king. Whether or not Spain agreed to the alliance, it was now squarely up to France to decide on its own, and fortunately for the United States the risk that Britain would somehow entice the revolted colonies back into the empire was now dominating French policy. As Franklin had foreseen, France wanted the alliance as badly as America did.

On December 17 the first assistant secretary of the foreign ministry appeared in Passy and informed the commissioners that His Majesty Louis XVI "was determined to acknowledge our Independence and make a Treaty with us of Amity and Commerce." The king, moreover, promised to support America's insurrection and its independence "by

---

*When Spain did reply, it was to say she would not join the alliance, but by then it did not matter. The Spanish furnished secret subsidies to the Americans via Hortalez & Cie., but did not declare war on Britain until 1779.

every means in his Power," which clearly meant war against England. Now the oldest royal house in Europe and the first power on the Continent would be fighting on the side of the rebels.

During the evening of February 6 the treaty for which the commissioners had labored so long and so hard was signed at the foreign ministry, but the real day of triumph was put off until March 20—one week after Britain and France were officially at war. Louis XVI was to receive the three commissioners, and when they arrived by coach and went first to Vergennes's apartments, a large crowd had gathered. Arthur Lee and Silas Deane were dressed formally, as prescribed by protocol, but Benjamin Franklin was by far the most conspicuous figure present. Knowing exactly the effect it would have in this glittering setting, he wore neither wig nor sword, only a plain brown velvet suit with white stockings. His hair hung loose, his spectacles were perched on his nose, and he carried a white hat under one arm. Versailles was renowned for its lavish displays, but the courtiers agreed that nothing they had seen was so dramatic as the republican simplicity they witnessed that day.

Louis XVI greeted them cordially and, as one eyewitness noticed, spoke with unusual care and grace. "Firmly assure Congress of my friendship," he said. "I hope that this will be for the good of the two countries." Franklin, who deserved most of the credit for the diplomatic triumph that was as important as the victory at Saratoga, replied, "Your Majesty may count on the gratitude of Congress and its faithful observance of the pledges it now makes."

War between France and Great Britain had been declared, but not until June 13, 1778, were the first shots fired. On that day a French frigate and two English ships exchanged gunfire near Ushant, a tiny island off the Brittany coast, in the first action of what became a world war. Ever since the humiliating defeat in the Seven Years War the French had been modernizing their navy, preparing to attack the British West Indies, and now they were ready. For George III and his ministers, the rebel alliance with France that was their worst fear meant that the likelihood of reconquering the former colonies was remote at best. The fleet was needed in European waters, in the West Indies, and in the Channel, to repel an invasion from France, and from now on the government's military goals in America would be greatly reduced. Operations would be moved to the south, where, it was believed, loyalists would flock to the royal banner and where the army would remain close enough to the coast to be supported by the fleet. The brutal logistical lesson of the northern campaign had been learned.

The diplomatic maneuvering and the clash of armies and navies often obscured what the Americans were fighting for. It was, to be sure, independence from England, but it went deeper than that, and an example of what it was all about occurred on the shore of Lake Champlain, near the site of Burgoyne's "Congress of Indians" five months earlier, when he had threatened to "give stretch" to his savage allies.

On November 20, Horatio Gates wrote New York's Governor Clinton to say that Ticonderoga and Mount Independence had been evacuated by Brigadier Powell on the 8th of the month. The forts were stripped of everything that could be carried away, all the buildings were burned, and some efforts to destroy the remainder of the works were made before the British and German troops began the long journey to Canada. Powell was not leaving to chance the possibility that the rebels might reoccupy the two lonely posts for future use. But neither were the Americans going to rest until Powell and his troops were gone.

Ebenezer Allen, a captain of Herrick's Vermont rangers, had his scouts follow the British to make certain they were really withdrawing, and on November 12 those men got into a skirmish with Powell's men near Gilliland's farm on the Bouquet River and took a few prisoners, including a black woman named Dinah Mattis. The scouts brought her back to headquarters at Pawlet, and on November 28, 1777, Captain Allen gave the woman a highly unusual letter that suggested what some of these young men had in mind when they turned out to fight Burgoyne's army of invasion:

> To whom it may concern. Know ye that whereas Dinah Mattis a negro woman with nancey her Child of two months old was taken Prissnor on Lake Champlain ... by a scout under my command, and according to a Resolve passed by the Honorable Continental Congress that all [prisoners] belong to the Captivators thereof I being conscientious that it is not right in the sight of god to keep Slaves ... I do therefore give the said Dinah mattis and Nancey her child [their] freedom to pass and repass any where through the United States of America ... as though she was born free, without being Mollested by any Person or Persons. . . .
>
> (signed) Ebenezer Allen *Capt.*"

Bibliography

Note: Where place-names occur in diaries, letters, and journals, original spelling has been used. *The Bulletin of the Fort Ticonderoga Museum* is abbreviated in the Bibliography and Notes as FTB.

1. PRIMARY SOURCES

American Antiquarian Society, Worcester, Mass.

Major General Horatio Gates to Committee of Berkshire County and Several Committees west of Connecticut River, Sept. 17, 1777.

American Philosophical Society, Philadelphia, Pa.

Sir John Dalrymple, "Reflections upon the military preparations which are making at present in Scotland," c. 1777.

General Le Begue de Presle Duportail to Claude Louis St. Germain, Nov. 12, 1778.

Benjamin Franklin *et al.*: Committee of Secret Correspondence to William Bingham, June 3, Oct. 1, and Oct. 21, 1776.

Benjamin Franklin to John Emery, March 23, 1778.

Francis Kinloch to Johannes von Muller, Aug. 30 and Dec. 18–19, 1777.

Arthur Lee to Richard Price, Apr. 20, 1777.

Robert McPherson to David Grier, June 20, 1777.

Charles Rockingham to [——], July 31, 1775.

Anthony Wayne to Abraham Robinson, April 1, 1777.
Anthony Wayne to Thomas Robinson, Nov. 5, 1776.
Benjamin Franklin announcement, Dec. 4, 1777.
Benjamin Franklin to Genet, April 28, 1778.
Benjamin Franklin to Benjamin Vaughan, Nov. 22, 1781.

Bennington Museum, Bennington, Vt.

Hall Park McCullough Papers
The Rev. Thomas Allen, "Account of the Battle of Bennington," *Connecticut Courant*, Aug. 25, 1777.
Peter Clark to his family, Aug. 6, 7, 18, and 29, 1777.
Jonas Fay to colonels of the State Militia, Aug. 13, 1777.
Herrick Genealogy.
Philip Schuyler to Benjamin Lincoln, Aug. 19, 1777.
John Stark to Philip Schuyler, Aug. 13, 1777.
Statements by Jesse Field, Jacob Safford, Solomon Safford, Isaac Tichenor, Silas Walbridge, John Wallace.
Return of Seth Warner regiment, Aug. 3, 1777.
Joseph Rudd to his father, Aug. 26, 1777.
Philip Skene to John Skimmings, Aug. 16, 1777.
"Smith Family of Addison Co., Vt."

Beverly Historical Society, Beverly, Mass.
John Francis to his sister-in-law Judy, widow of Ebenezer Francis, Oct. 1, 1777.

Boston Public Library, Boston, Mass.
Horatio Gates to Benjamin Lincoln, Sept. 5, 1777.
Henry Knox to Henry Jackson, May 4, July 2, 13, 21, and 30, and Aug. 3 and 25, 1777.
Alexander Scammell to Abigail Bishop, March 22, 1777.
Philip Schuyler to Benjamin Lincoln, Aug. 8 and 9, 1777.
Captain Thomas Stanley to ——, July 15, 1777.
General George Washington to General William Howe, April 9, 1777.

William L. Clements Library, Ann Arbor, Mich.
General Horatio Gates to General Benjamin Lincoln, Sept. 15, 1777.
Gates to Committee of Safety of Bennington, Sept. 17, 1777.
Gates to Matthew Vishter, Oct. 4, 1777.
Thomas Dundas to Edward Bird, Jr., Aug. 10, 1777.
Tobias Fernald to Andrew P. Fernald, Aug. 31, 1777.
Josiah Parker to Lieutenant Governor John Page of Virginia, Aug. 5, 1777.
Alexander Scammell to Jonathan Chadbourn, Sept. 26, 1777.
Alexander Scammel to —— [no date].

Sir Henry Clinton Papers

June, July, Aug. 1777; Sept. 1 to Oct. 24, 1777; Oct. 25 to Nov. 15, 1777;
Nov. 16 to Dec. 31, 1777.

Germain Papers

Vols. 6, 7, and 8.

MacKenzie Papers

Return of Lieutenant General Burgoyne's troops killed, wounded, prisoners,
and missing in the actions of Sept. 19 and Oct. 7, 1777.
Return of German troops killed, wounded, prisoners, and missing in the
actions of Sept. 19 and Oct. 7, 1777.

Simcoe Papers

State and condition of His Majesty's armed vessels on the lake service, under
General Sir Guy Carleton, May 30, 1777.

David Library of the American Revolution, Washington Crossing, Pa.

Auckland Papers

John Banister to Theodorick Bland, Nov. 1777.
General John Burgoyne to General Horatio Gates, Oct. 9, 1777.
General John Burgoyne to Lord George Germain, Oct. 20, 1777.

Francis Rush Clark Papers

General Horatio Gates Papers

Sir Robert Pigot to Mrs. Wagner, Jan. 17, 1778.

General Arthur St. Clair Papers

General George Washington to George Baylor, Aug. 25, 1777.
John Jay to Arthur St. Clair, July 28, 1777.

House of Lords, London, England

Proposals for furnishing Horses, Carriages and Drivers for the Service of the
Army under the Command of Lieut. Genl. Burgoyne.
Proposals for furnishing Horses & Drivers for the Service of the Artillery on
the Expedition under Lieut. Genl. Burgoyne.
Account of an Affair which happened near Walloon Creek, August 16th, 1777.
Relation of the Expedition to Bennington.

Library of Congress, Washington, D.C.

John Adams to Foreign Affairs Committee, Dec. 24, 1777.

John Burgoyne–Horatio Gates correspondence, Sept. 27 and Oct. 8, 9, 12, 13, 14, 15, and 16.
John Burgoyne parole statement, April 2, 1778.
James Craig–James Wilkinson correspondence, Oct. 15 and 17, 1777.
Foreign Affairs Committee–Commissioners in France correspondence, June 18, Oct. 6–9, 18, and 31, and Dec. 18, 1777; Jan. 21, 1778.
Foreign Affairs Committee to Mr. Dumas, Aug. 8, 1777.
Simon Fraser–Horatio Gates correspondence, Sept. 1 and 2, 1777.
Horatio Gates to John Hancock, Aug. 20, Sept. 3, 10, and 22, and Oct. 12, 1777.
Horatio Gates memorandum re Saratoga convention [no date].
John Hancock to Certain States, June 25, 1776.
Robert Honyman diary.
Ralph Izard to Foreign Affairs Committee, Dec. 18, 1777.
John Paul Jones to Marine Committee, Oct. 29, 1777.
Arthur Lee to Secret Committee, Jan. 5, 1778.
Benjamin Lincoln to Philip Schuyler, Aug. 19, 1777.
Philip Schuyler to George Washington, June 15, 16, 1777.
Michael Kirkman—pass to William Amsbury, June 4, 1777.
Examination of Charles Stomp and Leonard Maybuss, July 2, 1777.
Statement by Andrew Hodges Tracy, July 3, 1777.

Maryland Historical Society, Baltimore, Md.
Charles Carroll to his father, March 25 to June 11, 1776.

Massachusetts Historical Society, Boston, Mass.
Benjamin Farnum diary, 1775 to 1778; also quoted in Bailey.
Henry Sewall diary, July 5 to December 31, 1777.
James Gray to Theodore Parsons, July 14, 1777.

Gray Family Papers
James Gray Journal, May 8–17, 1777.
James Gray to his wife, Susan, May 18, 1777.
James Gray to the Rev. Moses Parsons, June 26, 1777.
James Gray Journal, July 6–14, 1777 [obverse of Scammell's return of June 28, 1777].

Moses Greenleaf Papers
Moses Greenleaf diary, April 23, 1777, to Nov. 7, 1777.

C. P. Greenough Papers
Matthias Ogden to Aaron Burr, from Ticonderoga, July 19, 1776.

William Heath Papers
Memorandum of Agreement between Colonel Jedu[tha]n Baldwin, Jedih Thayer, and Nathaniel Emerson, Dec. 16, 1776.

Timothy Danielson to Jeremiah Powell, May 14, 1777.

Colonel Thomas Marshall to Major General William Heath, from "Mount Independance," May 19, 1777.

Brigadier General Enoch Poor to General John Fellows, from "Tyconderoga," May 28, 1777.

Major General Arthur St. Clair to ——, from "Tionderoga," June 26, 1777.

General Heath to George Washington, June 30 and July 13, 1777.

Major General Arthur St. Clair to General Heath, July 1, 1777.

Major General Philip Schuyler to General Heath, July 1, 1777.

Colonel Anthony Wayne to the Council of the State of Massachusetts Bay, March 25, 1777.

Colonel Anthony Wayne to General Heath, April 18, 1777.

Samuel Adams to General Heath, August 13, 1777.

Livingston Family Papers

Matthew Clarkson to his cousin Susan Livingston, Aug. 5, 10, and 22, Sept. 11 and 21, and Oct. 5, 1777.

Henry Brockholst Livingston to Governor William Livingston, June 20, 25, and 30, July 3, 12, 17, 21, 24, and 28, and Aug. 6 and 11, 1777.

Henry Brockholst Livingston to his sister Susan Livingston, July 17 and Aug. 4, 1777.

S. P. Savage Papers

Major Ebenezer Stevens to Samuel Philip Savage, June 24, 1777.

Lemuel Shaw Papers

Alexander Scammell to Mrs. Andrew Colburn, September 22, 1777.

New England Historic Genealogical Society, Boston, Mass.

Letters of a British army officer under General John Burgoyne, Nov. 1777–Dec. 10, 1778.

Joseph Eliot correspondence with Joanna Eliot, Aug. 26, 1776–Oct. 19, 1777.

Edmund Quincy to Katherine Quincy, Oct. 16, 1777.

Samuel Smith to Rachel H. Smith, Aug. 5, 1777.

New-York Historical Society, New York, N.Y.

Horatio Gates Papers

Jeduthan Baldwin to Gates, May 15, 1777.

Thaddeus Kosciuszko to Gates, May [?] and May 18, 1777.

Major General Philip Schuyler to Gates, July 13, 1776.

Gates to Major General Benjamin Lincoln, Sept. 15, 17, 19(2), and 22, 1777.

Gates to Governors Clinton, Trumbull, and the several Committees of Albany, Bennington, and Berkshire, Sept. 17, 1777.

Jonas Fay to Gates, Sept. 20, 1777.

Gates to his wife, Betsy, Sept. 22, 1777.

Gates to Brigadier General Benedict Arnold, Sept. 20 and 23(2), 1777.

Gates to John Hancock, Sept. 15, 22(2), and 23 and Oct. 5(2), 12, and 18, 1777.

Gates to —— Powell, Sept. 29, 1777.

Gates to Governor Trumbull, Oct. 5, 1777.

Gates to General George Washington, Oct. 5, 1777.

Brigadier General Powell to Colonel Herrick, Oct. 30, 1777.

Peabody Essex Museum, Salem, Mass.

Joseph Hodgkins to his brother James, Oct. 17, 1777.

Colonel Samuel Johnson to his wife, Oct. 2, 1777.

Historical Society of Pennsylvania, Philadelphia, Pa.

Jonathan Potts Papers

Rhode Island Historical Society, Providence, R.I.

Enos Hitchcock, accounts and receipts.

Thompson-Pell Research Center, Fort Ticonderoga, Ticonderoga, N.Y.

Jabez Colton to the Reverend Dr. Stephen Williams, June 19, 1777.

Mrs. Sally Markham [née Kellogg]. Draft ms. of pension application, 1846.

Vermont Historical Society, Montpelier, Vt.

Records of the Council of Safety and Governor and Council of the State of Vermont: Records of the General Conventions from July 1775 to December 1777; Vol. 1, 1775–1779. Montpelier, Vt: 1873.

Virginia Historical Society, Richmond, Va.

John Burgoyne to Phillipson, Oct. 20, 1777.

Sir Andrew Snape Hamond Papers

H. Sloane to "My Dear Hammond," April 26, 1776.

Robert Honyman diary.

2. SECONDARY WORKS CONTAINING PRIMARY MATERIALS

ACLAND, LADY HARRIET. *The Acland Journal: Lady Harriet Acland and the American War.* Ed. Jennifer D. Thorp. Winchester, England: Hampshire County Council, 1994.

ALLEN, REV. THOMAS. Manuscript Journal in *Connecticut Courant*, Sept. 1, 1777.

ADAMS, JOHN. *Papers of John Adams*. Ed. Robert J. Taylor. Cambridge, Mass.: The Belknap Press of Harvard University Press, 1983.

ANBUREY, THOMAS. "The Taking of Ticonderoga—1777." Letters dated June 30, July 5, and July 12, 1777. FTB 2(1).

ATKINSON, C. T., ed. "Some Evidence for Burgoyne's Expedition." *Journal of the Society for Army Historical Research*. 26 (108) (Winter 1948).

BALDWIN, COLONEL JEDUTHAN. *The Revolutionary Journal of Col. Jeduthan Baldwin, 1775–1778*. Thomas Williams Baldwin, ed. Bangor, Me.: Printed for the DeBurians, 1906.

———. "Extracts from the Diary of Colonel Jeduthan Baldwin, Chief Engineer of the Northern Army, July 6th, 1776, to July 5th, 1777." FTB 4(6).

BARKER, G. F. RUSSELL, ed. *Horace Walpole: Memoirs of the Reign of King George the Third*. New York: G.P. Putnam's Sons, 1894.

BARTLETT, JOSIAH. *The Papers of Josiah Bartlett*. Ed. Frank C. Mevers. Hanover, N.H.: Published for the New England Historical Society by University Press of New England, 1979.

BENSE. See DOBLIN.

BLACK, JEANNETTE D., and WILLIAM GREENE ROELKER. *A Rhode Island Chaplain in the Revolution: Letters of Ebenezer David to Nicholas Brown, 1775–1778*. Providence: Rhode Island Society of the Cincinnati, 1949.

BLAKE. See KIDDER.

[BLOODGOOD, SIMEON DEWITT, ed.] *The Sexagenary or Reminiscences of the Revolution*. Albany, N.Y.: W. C. Little and O. Steele, 1833. Author's name does not appear in the book, but Fort Ticonderoga bibliography, "Mount Independence . . . " gives it as Bloodgood or John P. Becker.

BOARDMAN, OLIVER. "Journal of Oliver Boardman of Middletown 1777. Burgoyne's Surrender." *Collections of the Connecticut Historical Society*. 7. Hartford, Conn.: Connecticut Historical Society, 1899.

BROWN, LLOYD A., and HOWARD H. PECKHAM. *Revolutionary War Journals of Henry Dearborn, 1775–1783*. New York: DaCapo, 1971.

BURGOYNE, GEN. JOHN. Letter to Lord George Germain, July 11, 1777 from Skenesborough House. Letter to Lord George Germain, July 30, 1777, from headquarters upon Hudson's River, near Fort Edward. London: *Gentleman's Magazine and Historical Chronicle*, Vol. 47 (1777).

———. "A Broadside, by John Burgoyne, Esq." [Proclamation to Americans, July 2, 1777.] FTB 2(3).

———. "Women at War." Excerpt from *State of the Expedition*. FTB 3(4).

———. *A State of the Expedition from Canada as Laid before the House of Commons by Lieutenant-General Burgoyne. . . .* London: printed for J. Almon, 1780. Facsimile from microfilm copy and published by University Microfilms International, Ann Arbor, Mich.

———. *Orderly Book of Lieut. Gen. John Burgoyne, from his Entry into the State of*

New York until his Surrender at Saratoga, 16th Oct. 1777. Ed. E. B. O'Callaghan. Albany, N.Y.: J. Munsell, 1860. [Facsimile from microfilm copy and published by University Microfilms International, Ann Arbor, Mich.]

CAMPBELL, MARIA HULL. *Revolutionary Services and Civil Life of General William Hull, Prepared from His Manuscript.* New York: E. F. Campbell, 1848.

[CARLETON, GENERAL GUY] "Instructions to Captain Samuel Greaves Appointed to Command All His Majesty's Vessels upon Lakes Champlain and George." FTB 7(2).

CARROLL, CHARLES. *The Journal of Charles Carroll of Carrollton as One of the Congressional Commissioners to Canada in 1776.* Ed. Allan S. Everest. Fort Ticonderoga, N.Y.: Champlain-Upper Hudson Bicentennial Committee, 1976.

CARROLL, JOHN. *The John Carroll Papers.* Ed. Thomas O'Brien Hanley. Notre Dame, Ind.: University of Notre Dame Press.

CHAMPLAIN, SAMUEL DE. *Voyages and Discoveries.* Excerpt in FTB 3(1).

CHASE, JONATHAN. *General Jonathan Chase (1732–1800) of Cornish, New Hampshire: His Papers.* Cornish, N.H.: Cornish Bicentennial Commission, 1978.

CHASTELLUX, MARQUIS DE. Travels in North America in the Years 1780, 1781, and 1782. Trans. and ed. Howard C. Rice, Jr. 2 vols. Chapel Hill: University of North Carolina Press, 1963.

CLARKE, CAPT. WILLIAM BUTLER. "Col. John Brown's Expedition Against Ticonderoga and Diamond Island, 1777." *The New England Historical and Genealogical Register.* 74 (October 1920).

CLINTON, GENERAL GEORGE. "General George Clinton at Fort Montgomery." Draft letter of March 5, 1778, to George Washington giving his account of the loss of Fort Montgomery. *Quarterly Journal of the New York State Historical Association* 12(2) (April 1931).

COFFIN, CHARLES CARLETON, ed. "Captain Peter Kimball's Diary," in *The History of Boscawen and Webster from 1733 to 1878.* Concord, N.H.: 1878.

CROSS, RALPH. "The Journal of Ralph Cross, of Newburyport, Who Commanded the Essex Regiment, at the Surrender of Burgoyne, in 1777." *Historical Magazine* 7(1) (Jan. 1870).

CUNNINGHAM, PETER, ed. *The Letters of Horace Walpole.* 8 vols. Edinburgh: John Grant, 1906.

CUTLER, WILLIAM PARKER, and JULIA PERKINS CUTLER. *Life, Journals and Correspondence of Rev. Manasseh Cutler, LL.D.* Athens, Ohio: Ohio University Press.

DAVID. See BLACK.

DAWSON, HENRY B., ed. *New York City During the American Revolution.* A collection of original papers. New York: Mercantile Library Association, 1861.

DE ANGELIS. See SNYDER.

DEARBORN, HENRY. "A Narrative of the Saratoga Campaign." Letter to General James Wilkinson, Dec. 20, 1815, from Boston. FTB 1(5).

————. See also BROWN.

DIGBY, LIEUTENANT WILLIAM. *Journal, 1776–1777*. In *The British Invasion from the North, the Campaigns of Generals Carleton and Burgoyne from Canada, 1776–1777*. Introductory chapter and notes by James Phinney Baxter. Albany: Joel Munsell's Sons, 1887.

DOBLIN, HELGA, trans., and MARY C. LYNN, ed. *An Eyewitness Account of the American Revolution and New England Life: The Journal of J. F. Wasmus, German Company Surgeon, 1776–1783*. Westport, Connnecticut: Greenwood Press, 1990.

————. *The American Revolution, Garrison Life in French Canada and New York: Journal of an Officer* [Ensign Hille], *in the Prinz Friedrich Regiment, 1776–1783*. Westport, Conn.: Greenwood Press, 1993.

————. "A Brunswick General with Burgoyne: The Journal of Johann Bense, 1776–1783." *New York History* 66(4) (Oct. 1985).

————. "Journal of Lt. Colonel Christian Julius Pratorius, 2 June 1777–17 July 1777." FTB 15(3).

————. "Journal of Ensign Carl Wilhelm Reinerding, Braunschweig Regiment Prinz Friedrich." *Journal of the Johannes Schwalm Historical Association* 5(3) (1995).

————. *The Specht Journal: A Military Journal of the Burgoyne Campaign*. Westport, Conn.: Greenwood Press, 1995.

FITCH, ASA. *Their Own Voices: Oral Accounts of Early Settlers in Washington County, New York*. Collected by Dr. Asa Fitch. Ed. Winston Adler. Interlaken, N.Y.: Heart of the Lakes Publishing, 1983.

FITZPATRICK, JOHN C., ed. *The Writings of George Washington from the Original Manuscript Sources, 1745–1799*. 39 vols. Washington, D.C.: U.S. Government Printing Office, 1932.

FITZPATRICK, CAPTAIN RICHARD. Letters to his brother, the Second Earl of Ossory, 1777–1778. 84th Congress, 2nd Session; Senate Document No. 104. Washington: U.S. Government Printing Office, 1956.

FLETCHER, EBENEZER. Narrative, in *Crumbs for Antiquarians*. Charles Bushnell, ed. New York: privately printed, 1866. From Saratoga file of E. A. Hoyt, Vermont Historical Society.

FORD, WORTHINGTON CHAUNCEY, ed. *The Writings of George Washington*. 14 vols. New York: 1889–93.

FRANKLIN, BENJAMIN. *The Papers of Benjamin Franklin*. Ed. William B. Willcox. Vols. 22–24. New Haven, Conn.: Yale University Press, 1982.

FRASER, BRIGADIER-GENERAL SIMON. "Inquisition of a Spy." FTB 10(3).

————. Letter to John Robinson, July 13, 1777. In *Proceedings of the Vermont Historical Society* 4(1898): 139–147.

Journal of the Society for Army Historical Research 26(108) (Winter 1948). Letters to Fraser.

FREEMAN, CONSTANT. "Record of the Services of Constant Freeman,

Captain of Artillery in the Continental Army." Ed. William Lee. *Magazine of American History* 2 (1878).

GATES, GENERAL HORATIO. Letter to Governor Clinton, Sept. 17, 1777. FTB 6(4).

GLOVER, GENERAL JOHN. "A Memoir of Gen. John Glover of Marblehead." Ed. William P. Upham. *Historical Collections of the Essex Institute* 5(2) (April 1863); 5(3) (June 1863).

———. Glover to Major General William Heath, Oct. 9, 1777.

GORDON, REVEREND WILLIAM. "The Reverend William Gordon's Autumn 1776 Tour of the Northeast." Ed. Malcolm Freiberg. *New England Quarterly* 45(3) (Sept. 1992).

[GRANT, MRS.] *Memoirs of an American Lady, with Sketches of Manners and Scenery in America as They Existed Previous to the Revolution.* 2 vols. London: A. K. Newman, 1817.

HADDEN, JAMES M. *Hadden's Journal and Orderly Books: A Journal Kept in Canada and upon Burgoyne's Campaign in 1776 and 1777 by Lieut. James M. Hadden, Roy. Art.* Also Orders kept by him and issued by Sir Guy Carleton, Lieut. General John Burgoyne, and Major General William Phillips, in 1776, 1777, and 1778. With an explanatory chapter and notes by Horatio Rogers. Albany, N.Y.: Joel Munsell's Sons, 1884. With a new introduction and preface by George Athan Billias. Boston: Gregg Press, 1972.

HAMILTON, BRIGADIER-GENERAL JAMES. "Orders, July 10, 1777 to August 11, 1777." Transcribed and annotated by Willard M. Wallace. FTB 8(7).

HEATH, WILLIAM. *Memoirs of Major-General Heath.* Boston: I. Thomas and E. T. Andrews, 1798. Reprinted New York: A. Wessels, 1904.

HERRICK, SAMUEL.

———. Letter to Brigadier General Henry Watson Powell, Nov. 1, 1777.

———. Letter to President of Council, Nov. 14, 1777.

———. Letter to Major General Horatio Gates, Nov. 27, 1777.

HILLE. See DOBLIN.

HITCHCOCK, ENOS. "Diary of Enos Hitchcock, D.D., a Chaplain in the Revolutionary Army." Ed. William B. Weeden. *Publications of the Rhode Island Historical Society* 28(1900).

HUGHES, MAJOR J. M. "Campaign of 1777 Against General Burgoyne." *Proceedings of the Massachusetts Historical Society*, Feb. 1858.

HUGHES, THOS. *A Journal by Thos. Hughes—For His Amusement, & Designed Only for His Perusal by the Time He Attains the Age of 50 If He Lives So Long (1778–1789).* Introduction by E. A. Benians. Cambridge: Cambridge University Press, 1947.

HULTON, ANN. *Letters of a Loyalist Lady.* Cambridge: Harvard University Press, 1927. Appendix contains the Canadian journal of her brother, Henry Hulton. No editor is listed, but Introduction is signed "H. M., C. M. T."

JEFFERSON, THOMAS. *The Papers of Thomas Jefferson.* Ed. Julian P. Boyd. Vols. 1–2. Princeton, N.J.: Princeton University Press, 1950.

KIDDER, FREDERIC. *History of the First New Hampshire Regiment in the War of the Revolution.* Hampton, N.H.: Peter E. Randall, 1973. Includes Lieutenant Thomas Blake's journal. Reprint of 1868 edition.

LAMB, R. *An Original and Authentic Journal of Occurrences During the Late American War, from Its Commencement to the Year 1783.* Dublin: Wilkinson & Courtney, 1809.

LINCOLN, JAMES MINOR. *The Papers of Captain Rufus Lincoln of Wareham, Mass.* Privately printed, 1904.

MURRAY, SIR JAMES. *Letters from America, 1773 to 1780.* Ed. Eric Robson. New York: Barnes & Noble, 1950.

NAPIER, LORD FRANCIS. "Lord Francis Napier's Journal of the Burgoyne Campaign." *Maryland Historical Magazine* 57(4) (Dec. 1962).

PAUSCH, GEORG. *Journal of Captain Pausch, Chief of the Hanau Artillery During the Burgoyne Campaign.* Trans. William L. Stone. Albany, N.Y.: Joel Munsell's Sons, 1886.

PELL, JOSHUA JR. "An Officer of the British Army in America 1776–1777." Diary. FTB 1(6).

PILLSBURY, JOSHUA. "To Saratoga and Back, 1777." Ed. Ray W. Pettengill. *New England Quarterly* 10(Dec. 1937).

POWELL, BRIGADIER-GENERAL H. WATSON. Letters to Sir Guy Carleton, Sept. 18–30, 1777. FTB 7(2).

PUTNAM, ISRAEL. *General Orders Issued by Major-General Israel Putnam, when in Command of the Highlands, in the Summer and Fall of 1777.* Ed. Worthington Chauncey Ford. Brooklyn, N.Y.: Historical Printing Club, 1893. With a new introduction and preface by George Athan Billias. Boston: Gregg Press, 1972.

RIEDESEL, BARONESS. Excerpt from *Life and Letters.* FTB 3(4).

———. *Baroness von Riedesel and the American Revolution; Journal and Correspondence of a Tour of Duty, 1776–1783.* Trans. Marvin L. Brown, Jr. Chapel Hill, N.C: University of North Carolina Press, 1965.

RIEDESEL, MAJOR GENERAL FRIEDRICH A. VON. *Memoirs and Letters and Journals of Major General Riedesel During His Residence in America.* Ed. Max von Eelking. Trans. William L. Stone. Albany, New York: 1868.

ROMAINE, LAWRENCE B. "From Cambridge to Champlain, March 18 to May 5, 1776: A Manuscript Diary." Author unknown. Middleboro, Mass.: Lawrence B. Romaine, 1957.

ST. CLAIR, GEN. ARTHUR. Letter from General St. Clair to Congress, July 14, 1777, from Fort Edward. FTB 1(2).

———. *Proceedings of a General Court Martial Held at White Plains, in the State of New-York by Order of his Excellency General Washington, Commander in Chief of the Army of the United States of America, for the Trial of Major General St. Clair, August 25, 1778. Major General Lincoln, President.* New-York Historical Society Collections, Publication Fund Series, vol. 13, 1880.

————. *The Life and Public Services of Arthur St. Clair, with His Correspondence and Other Papers.* Ed. William Henry Smith. Cincinnati, Ohio: Robert Clarke, 1882.

SCAMMELL, ALEXANDER. "A Love Letter." Letter to Naby, June 8, 1777, from Fort Ticonderoga. FTB 2(3).

SCHUYLER, GENERAL PHILIP. Letter to Congressional Committee, Nov. 6, 1776, from Albany. FTB 3(6).

————. "Original Documents." Letters to and from General Schuyler, July 7 to Aug. 10, 1777. *Magazine of American History.* 3, Pt. 2.

————. *Proceedings of a General Court Martial Held at Major General Lincoln's Quarters near Quaker-Hill, in the State of New-York, by order of his Excellency General Washington, Commander in Chief of the Army of the United States of America, for the Trial of Major General Schuyler, October 1, 1778. Major General Lincoln, President.* New-York Historical Society Collections, Publication Fund Series, vol. 2, 1879.

SKENE, PHILIP. Letter to the Earl of Dartmuth, July 15, 1777. Stevens's Facsimile.

————. "Philip Skene of Skenesboro." FTB 6(5).

————. See also MORTON.

SNYDER, CHARLES M. "With Benedict Arnold at Valcour Island: The Diary of Pascal De Angelis." *Vermont History* 42(3) (Summer 1974).

SPARKS, JARED. *Correspondence of the American Revolution; Being Letters of Eminent Men to George Washington from the Time of His Taking Command of the Army to the End of His Presidency.* Vol. 2. Boston: Little, Brown, 1853.

SPECHT: See DOBLIN.

SQUIER, EPHRAIM. "Diary of Ephraim Squier." *Magazine of American History* 2(11) (Nov. 1878).

STANLEY, LT. COL. GEORGE F. G., ed. *For Want of a Horse: Being a Journal of the Campaigns Against the Americans in 1776 and 1777 Conducted from Canada, by an Officer Who Served with Lt. Gen. Burgoyne.* Sackville, New Brunswick: Tribune Press, 1961.

STARKE, JN. "Remarks on Affairs at the Portage Between Ticonderoga and Lake George, and at Mount Independence, in September 1777." FTB 1(1).

————. "An Open Letter to Captain Pringle." June 8, 1777, from St. Johns. Includes map of Valcour Island engagement. FTB 1(4).

STONE, ENOS. "Captain Enos Stone's Journal." *New England Historical and Genealogical Register* 15 (1861):299–304.

STONE, WILLIAM L., trans. *Letters of Brunswick and Hessian Officers During the American Revolution.* Albany, N.Y.: Joel Munsell's Sons, 1891.

THACHER, JAMES, M.D. *Military Journal, During the American Revolutionary War, from 1775 to 1783.* Hartford, Conn.: Silas Andrus & Son, 1854.

TRUMBULL, JOHN. *The Autobiography of John Trumbull, Patriot-Artist,*

1756–1843. Ed. Theodore Sizer. New Haven, Conn.: Yale University Press, 1953.

UHLENDORF, BERNHARD A., trans. *Revolution in America: Confidential Letters and Journals 1776–1784 of Adjutant General Major Baurmeister of the Hessian Forces.* New Brunswick, N.J.: Rutgers University Press, 1957.

VERMONT HISTORICAL SOCIETY. "Documents in Relation to the Part Taken by Vermont in Resisting the Invasion of Burgoyne in 1777." *Collections.* vol. 1. Montpelier, Vt.: 1870.

WARREN, CAPTAIN BENJAMIN. "Diary of Captain Benjamin Warren on Battlefield of Saratoga." Ed. David E. Alexander. *Journal of American History* 3(2) (1909).

WASMUS: See DOBLIN.

WAYNE, GENERAL ANTHONY. Letter to Major General Schuyler, Feb. 4, 1777, from Fort Ticonderoga. FTB 4(1).

WEEKS, WILLIAM. Letter to his brother[?], from Stillwater, Aug. 6, 1777. Letter to his father, from Fishkill, Nov. 3, 1777. In Hiram Bingham, Jr., *Five Straws Gathered from Revolutionary Fields.* Cambridge, Mass.: 1901.

WHEELER, RUFUS. "Journal of Lieut. Rufus Wheeler of Rowley." *Essex Institute Historical Collections Quarterly* 68(Oct. 1932).

WILD, EBENEZER. "Journal of Ebenezer Wild." *Proceedings of the Massachusetts Historical Society* (1890, 1891).

WILKINSON, JAMES. *Memoirs of My Own Times.* Vol. 1. Philadelphia: Abraham Small, 1816.

3. GENERAL WORKS

ACLAND, ANNE. *A Devon Family: The Story of the Aclands.* Phillimore, 1981.

ALBERTS, ROBERT C. "Braddock's Alumni." *American Heritage,* Feb. 1961.

ALDEN, JOHN R. *A History of the American Revolution.* New York: Knopf, 1969.

ALLEN, FREEMAN H. "St. Leger's Invasion and the Battle of Oriskany." *Proceedings of the New York State Historical Association* 12 (1913).

ANDERSON, TROYER STEELE. *The Command of the Howe Brothers During the American Revolution.* New York: Oxford, 1936.

ATKINSON, C. T. *The South Wales Borderers: 24th Regiment of Foot.* 1937.

BAILEY, SARAH LORING. *Historical Sketches of Andover* [Mass.]. Boston: Houghton Mifflin, 1880.

BARBER, JOHN W., and HENRY HOWE. *Historical Collections of the State of New York.* New York: S. Tuttle, 1842.

BARROW, WILLIAM J. "Black Writing Ink of the Colonial Period." American Archivist 11(4) (Oct. 1948).

BENSON, ADOLPH B., ed. *Peter Kalm's Travels in America.* New York: Dover, 1987.

BILL, ALFRED HOYT. *New Jersey and the Revolutionary War.* Princeton, N.J.: D. Van Nostrand, 1964.

BILLIAS, GEORGE ATHAN, ed. *George Washington's Generals.* New York: William Morrow, 1964.

———. *George Washington's Opponents.* New York: William Morrow, 1969.

BIRD, HARRISON. *March to Saratoga: General Burgoyne and the American Campaign, 1777.* New York: Oxford University Press, 1963.

BOARDMAN, D. S. "Reminiscences of Colonel Seth Warner." *Historical Magazine,* July 1860.

BOATNER, MARK MAYO, III. *Encyclopedia of the American Revolution.* New York: David McKay, 1966.

BOLTON, CHARLES KNOWLES. *The Private Soldier Under Washington.* London: George Newnes, 1902.

BOTTUM, ROSWELL. *History of the Town of Orwell, Vt., from 1763 to 1851.* Rutland, Vt.: Tuttle, 1881.

BOWLER, R. ARTHUR. *Logistics and the Failure of the British Army in America, 1775–1783.* Princeton, N.J.: Princeton University Press, 1975.

BRANDOW, JOHN H. "General Daniel Morgan's Part in the Burgoyne Campaign." *Proceedings of the New York State Historical Association* 12(1913).

BRANDT, CLARE. *The Man in the Mirror: A Life of Benedict Arnold.* New York: Random House, 1994.

———. *An American Aristocracy: The Livingstons.* New York: Doubleday, 1986.

BURNHAM, KOERT DUBOIS, and DAVID KENDALL MARTIN. *LaCorne St. Luc—His Flame.* Keeseville, N.Y.: Highlands, 1991.

BURNS, BRIAN. "Bloody Burgoyne and the Patriot Martyr, or, a Most Regrettable Fortune of War: British Policy During the Northern Campaign of 1777." Master's thesis, University of Vermont, 1973.

BUTLER, J. D., and GEORGE F. HOUGHTON. "Address on the Battle of Bennington and the Life and Services of Colonel Seth Warner." Burlington, Vt.: Vermont Legislature, 1849.

CLARK, JANE. "Responsibility for the Failure of the Burgoyne Campaign." American Historical Review 35(3) (April 1930).

CLINTON, GEORGE. "General George Clinton at Fort Montgomery." *Quarterly Journal of the New York State Historical Association* 12(2) (April 1931).

COHN, ARTHUR. *The Great Bridge: "From Ticonderoga to Independant Point."* Lake Champlain Basin Program. 1995.

COMMAGER, HENRY STEELE, and RICHARD B. MORRIS. *The Spirit of 'Seventy-Six.* New York: Bobbs-Merrill, 1958.

———, ed. *Documents of American History.* New York: Appleton-Century-Crofts, 1968.

CRARY, CATHERINE S. *The Price of Loyalty: Tory Writings from the Revolutionary Era.* New York: McGraw-Hill, 1973.

CROWN POINT ROAD ASSOCIATION. *Historical Markers on the Crown Point Road.* 1992.

DANN, JOHN C. *The Revolution Remembered: Eyewitness Accounts of the War for Independence.* Chicago: University of Chicago Press, 1980.

DAVIDSON, MARSHALL B. *Life in America.* 2 vols. Boston: Houghton Mifflin, 1951.

DE COSTA, BENJAMIN FRANKLIN. *Notes on the History of Colonial and Revolutionary Periods, with Contemporaneous Documents and an Appendix.* New York: J. Sabin & Sons, 1871.

DEMOS, JOHN. *The Unredeemed Captive: A Family Story from Early America.* New York: Knopf, 1994.

DOBLIN, HELGA. "German-American Postal Service During the Revolution." *Battlements* 4(2) (Summer 1992).

DRAPER, ANDREW S. "The Place of Saratoga in the Revolutionary War." *Proceedings of the New York State Historical Association* 12 (1913).

FARB, PETER. *Man's Rise to Civilization as Shown by the Indians of North America from Primeval Times to the Coming of the Industrial State.* New York: Dutton, 1968.

FISCHER, DAVID HACKETT. *Paul Revere's Ride.* New York: Oxford University Press, 1994.

FLEMING, THOMAS. *The Man Who Dared the Lightning.* New York: Macmillan, 1971.

FLEXNER, JAMES THOMAS. *George Washington in the American Revolution (1775–1783).* Boston: Little, Brown, 1968.

———. "How a Madman Helped Save the Colonies." *American Heritage*, Feb. 1956.

FONBLANQUE, EDWARD HARRINGTON DE. *Political and Military Episodes in the Latter Half of the Eighteenth Century, Derived from the Life and Correspondence of the Right Hon. John Burgoyne, General, Statesman, Dramatist.* London: Macmillan, 1876.

FORCE, PETER. *American Archives.* Fourth Series [March 7, 1774, to July 4, 1776]. 6 vols. Washington: 1837–46.

———. *American Archives.* Fifth Series [July 4, 1776, to Sept. 3, 1783]. 3 vols. Washington: 1848–53.

FORTESCUE, SIR JOHN, ed. *The Correspondence of King George the Third from 1760 to December 1783.* Vol. 3, July 1773–Dec. 1777. London: MacMillan, 1927–28.

FOSTER, HERBERT D., with THOMAS W. STREETER. "Stark's Independent Command at Bennington." With appendices. *Proceedings of the New York State Historical Association* 5 (1904).

FREEMAN, DOUGLAS SOUTHALL. *George Washington: Leader of the Revolution.* 6 vols. Vol. 4. New York: Charles Scribner's Sons, 1951.

FRENCH, ALLEN. *The First Year of the American Revolution.* Boston: Houghton Mifflin, 1934.

FRESE, JOSEPH R. "A Trumbull Map of Fort Ticonderoga Rediscovered." FTB 13(2).

FURNEAUX, RUPERT. *Saratoga: The Decisive Battle.* London: George Allen & Unwin, 1971.

GERLACH, DON R. *Proud Patriot: Philip Schuyler and the War of Independence, 1775–1783.* Syracuse, N.Y.: Syracuse University Press, 1987.

GOODWIN, MARY R. M. "Clothing and Accoutrements of the Officers and Soldiers of the Virginia Forces." From Records of the Public Store at Williamsburg [Va.] Unpublished paper, Colonial Williamsburg Historical Research Department.

GUTTMACHER, MANFRED S. *America's Last King: An Interpretation of the Madness of George III.* New York: Charles Scribner's Sons, 1941.

GUTTRIDGE, GEORGE H. "Lord George Germain in Office, 1775–1782." *American Historical Review* 33(1) (Oct. 1927).

HALL, HENRY D. "The Battle of Bennington." *Proceedings of the Vermont Historical Society*, Oct. 20 and Nov. 5, 1896.

HALSEY, FRANCIS WHITING. "General Schuyler's Part in the Burgoyne Campaign." *Proceedings of the New York State Historical Association* 12 (1913).

HAMILTON, EDWARD PIERCE. "Was Washington to Blame for the Loss of Ticonderoga in 1777?" FTB 11(2).

HARGREAVES, REGINALD. *The Bloodybacks: The British Serviceman in North America and the Caribbean 1655–1783.* New York: Walker, 1968.

———. "Burgoyne and America's Destiny." *American Heritage*, June 1956.

HARGROVE, RICHARD J., JR. *General John Burgoyne.* East Brunswick, N.J.: Associated University Presses, 1983.

HAVILAND, WILLIAM A., and MARJORY W. POWER. *The Original Vermonters.* Hanover, N.H.: University Press of New England, 1981.

HAW, JAMES, FRANCIS F. BEIRNE, ROSAMOND R. BEIRNE, and R. SAMUEL JETT. *Stormy Patriot: The Life of Samuel Chase.* Baltimore, Md.: Maryland Historical Society, 1980.

HEITMAN, FRANCIS B. *Historical Register of Officers of the Continental Army During the War of the Revolution.* Washington, D.C.: Rare Book Shop Publishing Co., 1914.

HILL, ELLEN C. *Revolutionary War Soldiers of East Montpelier.* East Montpelier, Vt.: Bicentennial Committee, 1975.

HOFFMAN, ELLIOTT W. "The Germans Against Ticonderoga." FTB 14(4).

HOLDEN, JAMES AUSTIN. "Influence of Death of Jane McCrea on Burgoyne Campaign." *Proceedings of the New York State Historical Association* 12 (1913).

HOLLISTER, HIEL. *Pawlet for One Hundred Years.* Bicentennial Edition. Pawlet, Vt.: Pawlet Historical Society, 1976.

HOULDING, J. A., AND G. KENNETH YATES. "Corporal [George] Fox's Memoir of Service, 1766–1783; Quebec, Saratoga, and the Convention Army." Unpublished paper.

HOYT, EDWARD A. "The Origin and Function of the Expedition to Pawlet, September, 1777." Unpublished ms. at Vermont Historical Society. Montpelier, Vt.

JENNINGS, ISAAC. "Relation of the Battle of Bennington to the Battle of Saratoga." *Proceedings of the New York State Historical Association* 12 (1913).

———. *Memorials of a Century.* Boston: Gould and Lincoln, 1868.

JOHNSON, CHARLES W. *The Nature of Vermont.* Hanover, N.H.: University Press of New England, 1980.

JONES, THOMAS. *History of New York During the Revolutionary War.* 2 vols. New York: New-York Historical Society, 1879.

JOSEPHY, ALVIN M., JR., ed. *The American Heritage Book of Indians.* New York: American Heritage, 1961.

KAMMEN, MICHAEL. *A Season of Youth.* New York: Knopf, 1978.

KETCHUM, RICHARD M. *Decisive Day: The Battle for Bunker Hill.* New York: Anchor Books, 1991.

———. *The Winter Soldiers: The Battles for Trenton and Princeton.* Anchor Books, 1991.

———. *The World of George Washington.* New York: American Heritage, 1974.

———. "England's Vietnam: The American Revolution." *American Heritage,* June 1971.

———. "Men of the Revolution." Series of articles. *American Heritage,* Aug. 1971–June 1976.

———, ed. *The American Heritage Book of the Revolution.* Narrative by Bruce Lancaster, with a chapter by J. H. Plumb. New York: American Heritage, 1958.

———, with Irwin Glusker, eds. *American Testament: Fifty Great Documents of American History.* New York: American Heritage, 1971.

KINGSLEY, RONALD F. "The German Auxiliary Forces in the Burgoyne Campaign; The Crown Point Road; Settlers of the Hampshire Grants, West Bridgport; Sir Francis Carr Clerke." Vermont Division for Historic Preservation, April 1996. A bibliography.

KIPPING, ERNEST. *The Hessian View of America, 1776–1783.* Monmouth Beach, N.J.: Philip Freneau Press, 1971.

KOEPPEL, GERARD. "A Struggle for Water." *Invention and Technology,* Winter 1994.

LANCTOT, GUSTAVE. *Canada and the American Revolution, 1774–1783.* Trans. Margaret M. Cameron. London: George G. Harrap, 1967.

LARTER, COLONEL HARRY C., JR. "German Troops with Burgoyne." FTB 9(1).

LEFFERTS, CHARLES M. *Uniforms of the American, British, French, and German Armies in the War of the American Revolution, 1775–1783.* Old Greenwich, Conn.: WE, Inc., no date.

LORD, PHILIP, JR. *War over Walloomscoick: Land Use and Settlement Pattern on the Bennington Battlefield—1777.* New York State Museum Bulletin No. 473. Albany: State Education Department, 1989.

LOSSING, BENSON J. *The Pictorial Field-Book of the Revolution.* 2 vols. New York: Harper & Brothers, 1860.

LUNT, JAMES. *John Burgoyne of Saratoga.* New York: Harcourt Brace Jovanovich, 1975.

LUTNICK, SOLOMON. "The American Victory at Saratoga: A View from the British Press." *New York History* 44(2) (April 1963).

LUZADER, JOHN. *Decision on the Hudson: The Saratoga Campaign of 1777.* Washington, D.C.: National Park Service, Department of the Interior, 1975.

———. "Preliminary Documentary Report on Benedict Arnold at Saratoga." Stillwater, N.Y.: Saratoga National Park, 1958.

MACKESY, PIERS. *The War for America, 1775–1783.* Lincoln, Neb.: University of Nebraska Press, 1993.

———. *The Coward of Minden: The Affair of Lord George Sackville.* New York: St. Martin's Press, 1979.

MAIN, JACKSON TURNER. *The Social Structure of Revolutionary America.* Princeton, N.J.: Princeton University Press, 1965.

MALONE, DUMAS. *The Story of the Declaration of Independence.* New York: Oxford University Press, 1954.

MARLOW, LOUIS. *Sackville of Drayton.* London: Home & Van Thal, 1948.

MASON, BERNARD. *The Road to Independence: The Revolutionary Movement in New York, 1773–1777.* Louisville, Ky.: University of Kentucky Press, 1966.

MILES, LION. "The Battle of Bennington, 1777: An Event Happy and Important." Graduate seminar paper, University of Massachusetts, May 1987.

MILLER, JOHN C. *Origins of the American Revolution.* Boston: Little, Brown, 1943.

MILLS, BORDEN H. "Albany County's Part in the Battle of Saratoga." *Proceedings of the New York State Historical Association* 15 (1915).

———. "Troop Units at the Battle of Saratoga." *Quarterly Journal of the New York State Historical Association* 9(2) (April 1928).

MINTZ, MAX M. *The Generals of Saratoga: John Burgoyne & Horatio Gates.* New Haven, Conn.: Yale University Press, 1990.

MOORE, FRANK. *Diary of the American Revolution from Newspapers and Original Documents.* 2 vols. New York: Charles Scribner, 1860.

MOORE, HOWARD PARKER. *A Life of General John Stark of New Hampshire.* Privately printed, 1949.

MORRIS, RICHARD B. *The American Revolution Reconsidered.* New York: Harper & Row, 1967.

MORTON, DORIS BEGOR. *Philip Skene of Skenesborough.* Granville, N.Y.: Grastorf Press, 1959.

NASH, CHARLES ELVENTON. *The History of Augusta.* Augusta, Me.: Charles E. Nash & Son, 1904.

NEILSON, CHARLES. *Burgoyne's Campaign, and the Memorable Battles of Bemis's Heights, Sept. 19 and Oct. 7, 1777.* Albany, N.Y.: J. Munsell, 1844.

NELSON, PAUL DAVID. "The Gates-Arnold Quarrel, September 1777." *New-York Historical Society Quarterly* 55(3) (July 1971).

NELSON, PETER. "Learned's Expedition to the Relief of Fort Stanwix." *Quarterly Journal of the New York State Historical Association* 9(4) (Oct. 1928).

NICKERSON, HOFFMAN. *The Turning Point of the Revolution, or Burgoyne in America.* Boston: Houghton Mifflin, 1928.

OFFENDSEN, DOROTHY. "History of the September 1777 Encampment of General Benjamin Lincoln in Pawlet." 1977 commemoration program.

PARKER, AMELIA CAMPBELL. "Baroness Riedesel and Other Women in Burgoyne's Army: Heroines on the Wrong Side." *Quarterly Journal of the New York State Historical Association* 9(2) (April 1928).

PARKMAN, FRANCIS. *Montcalm and Wolfe.* 2 vols. Boston: Little, Brown, 1884.

PELL, ROBERT T. "John Brown and the Dash for Ticonderoga." FTB 2(1).

PELL, S. H. P. *Fort Ticonderoga: A Short History.* Ticonderoga, N.Y.: Fort Ticonderoga Museum, 1954.

———. "Lady Harriet Acland." FTB 3(4).

———. "Jane McCrea." FTB 2(6).

PLUMB, J. H. *England in the Eighteenth Century.* Harmondsworth, England: Penguin, 1966.

QUINLAN, MAURICE J. "George Knox, a Black Soldier in the American Revolution." Hanover, N.H.: *Dartmouth College Library Bulletin* 20(2) (April 1980).

ROBERTS, KENNETH. *The Battle of Cowpens.* Garden City, N.Y.: Doubleday, 1958.

ROBERTS, ROBERT B. *Encyclopedia of Historic Forts.* New York: Macmillan, 1988.

ROSSIE, JONATHAN GREGORY. *The Politics of Command in the American Revolution.* Syracuse, N.Y.: Syracuse University Press, 1975.

SABINE, LORENZO. *The American Loyalists.* Boston: Charles C. Little and James Brown, 1847.

SCHEER, GEORGE F., and HUGH F. RANKIN. *Rebels and Redcoats.* Cleveland, Ohio: World, 1957.

SEWALL, HENRY. "Diary of Henry Sewall." June 1776 to July 7, 1777. FTB 11(2).

SMYTHE, BEN. *History of the Lancashire Fusiliers [XX Regiment].* Bury, Lancashire, England: 1903.

SNELL, CHARLES W. *A Report on the Organization and Numbers of Gates' Army, September 19, October 7, and October 17, 1777, Including an Appendix with Regimental Data and Notes.* Stillwater, N.Y.: Saratoga National Historical Park, Feb. 1, 1951.

———. "A Report on the Strength of the British Army Under Lieutenant General John Burgoyne, July 1 to October 17, 1777, and on the Organization of the British Army on September 19 and October 7, 1777." Stillwater, N.Y.: Saratoga National Historical Park, Feb. 28, 1951.

————. "A Report on the Left Wing of the British Fortified Camp at Freeman's Farm, September 20 to October 8, 1777." Stillwater, N.Y.: Saratoga National Historical Park, Feb. 28, 1950.

————. "A Report on the Balcarres and Breymann Redoubts." Stillwater, N.Y.: Saratoga National Historical Park, no date.

STARBUCK, DAVID R. *Mount Independence and the American Revolution, 1776–1777.* Montpelier, Vt.: Vermont Division for Historic Preservation, 1991.

STARK, CALEB. *Memoir and Official Correspondence of Gen. John Stark.* Concord, N.H.: G. Parker Lyon, 1860.

STEELE, IAN K. *Betrayals: Fort William Henry and the "Massacre."* New York: Oxford University Press, 1990.

STEVENS, JOHN AUSTIN. "Ebenezer Stevens, Lieut.-Col. of Artillery in the Continental Army." *Magazine of American History* 1(1877).

STILLMAN, WILLIAM O. "The Memorable Battle Fought on the 16th Day of August, 1777, at Walloomsac." *Proceedings of the New York State Historical Association* 5 (1904).

STITT, EDWARD W., JR. "Horatio Gates." FTB 9(2).

STONE, WILLIAM L. *The Campaigns of Lieut. General John Burgoyne and the Expedition of Lieut. Col. Barry St. Leger.* Albany: Joel Munsell, 1877.

————. *Visits to the Saratoga Battle-Grounds, 1780–1880.* Albany: Joel Munsell's Sons, 1895.

THOMPSON, ZADOCK. *History of Vermont, Natural, Civil, and Statistical.* Burlington, Vt.: Chauncey Goodrich, 1842.

TORRES, LOUIS. "Historic Resource Study, Barber Wheat Field, October 7, 1777." Denver, Colo.: National Park Service, U.S. Department of Interior, Dec. 1974.

TUCHMAN, BARBARA W. *The First Salute.* New York: Knopf, 1988.

VAN DOREN, CARL. *Benjamin Franklin.* New York: Viking, 1938.

————. *Secret History of the American Revolution.* New York: Viking, 1951.

WARD, CHRISTOPHER. *The War of the Revolution.* 2 vols. New York: Macmillan, 1952.

WHEELER, JOSEPH L., and MABEL A. WHEELER. *The Mount Independence–Hubbardton 1776 Military Road.* Benson, Vt.: J. L. Wheeler, 1968.

WHITNEY, DAVID C. *Founders of Freedom in America.* Chicago: J. G. Ferguson, 1964.

WICKMAN, DONALD H. "Built with Spirit, Deserted in Darkness: the American Occupation of Mount Independence, 1776–1777." Master's thesis, University of Vermont, Oct. 1993.

————."The Diary of Timothy Tuttle." *New Jersey History* 113(3–4) (Fall/Winter 1995).

WILLCOX, WILLIAM B. "Too Many Cooks: British Planning Before Saratoga." *Journal of British Studies* 2(1) (Nov. 1962).

WILLIAMS, JOHN. *The Battle of Hubbardton.* Montpelier, Vt. Vermont Division for Historic Preservation, 1988.

WOOD, GORDON S. *The Radicalization of the American Revolution.* New York: Knopf, 1992.

YOUNG, PHILIP. *Revolutionary Ladies.* New York: Knopf, 1977.

Notes on Sources

Insofar as possible, this account is based on the testimony of eye-witnesses—the men and women who participated in the stirring events that took place more than two centuries ago. Every writer of history is the beneficiary of his sources but is at their mercy as well, for the truth lies in what they (and sometimes only they) can reveal. So the conclusions you find here are drawn from the words of individuals who were either present at or somehow related to the occurrences, and I have tried to see events as they saw them, in the context of their time. Where later material has been used—especially an excerpt from memoirs or reminiscences of the war—I have chosen what could be confirmed by other sources or what met the test of plausibility.

In many respects the historian of the campaign that culminated in General John Burgoyne's surrender at Saratoga is fortunate indeed. First, two of the American generals intimately involved—Philip Schuyler and Arthur St. Clair—were called before a court-martial to testify concerning their actions, and the records of those proceedings, with testimony from the generals themselves, their supporters, and their detractors, provide a wealth of information.

Much the same thing may be said of Burgoyne. Though he was not tried by a military court—largely because neither George III nor Lord George Germain wanted him interrogated by military men understandably vexed by civilian conduct of the war—he was so eager to salvage his reputation that he finally contrived to appear before the House of Commons, to make his case. This resulted in a publication with the unwieldy title *A State of the Expedition from Canada, as laid before the House of Commons, by Lieutenant-General Burgoyne, and verified by evidence, with a collection of authentic documents, and an addition of many circumstances which were prevented from appearing before the House by the prorogation of Parliament. Written and collected by himself, and dedicated to the officers of the Army he commanded.*

The document reveals Burgoyne's skill as a phrasemaker and man of letters, and in his long and often dramatic defense he was abetted by the testimony of officers who served with him in the campaign (most of them questioned by Burgoyne himself). Yet while it throws considerable light on most aspects of the expedition (and in certain instances is the sole source of information), it must be remembered that it is sometimes—as in the cases of the Schuyler and St. Clair court-martial documents—evasive and self-serving.

Certain other British and German sources are valuable, but few are without flaws. Baron von Riedesel's *Memoirs* are understandably weighted in favor of his own command and his desire to protect *his* reputation, and I am told that Stone's translation of the work leaves much to be desired. The *Journal* kept by the baroness is a chatty, extremely personal account written from the unusual point of view of a plucky general's lady who endured many of the hazards and hardships of a private soldier.

For my purposes the two most valuable German sources were the *Journals* of Colonel Johann Friedrich Specht and company surgeon Julius Friedrich Wasmus, both translated by Helga Doblin and edited by Mary C. Lynn. Specht covers the entire Burgoyne campaign, ending at Saratoga. Wasmus carries the military story only through the Bennington battle, since the author was captured there; but his story continues to 1783, reporting the sad story of the Convention Army and its wanderings in captivity. Another excellent journal by a Brunswick officer is that attributed to Ensign Julius Friedrich von Hille, translated and edited by Doblin and Lynn. This was less useful to me, since the author was part of the garrison left behind at Ticonderoga when Burgoyne's army marched farther south.

Among British records of the campaign, Lieutenant Thomas Anburey's *Travels* was published in 1789 and is unfortunately marred by numerous instances of plagiarism—many sections taken verbatim from Burgoyne's *State of the Expedition*. Sergeant Roger Lamb published an account of his service in America in 1809, and he too drew on other sources, though in a more scholarly manner than Anburey.

The Canadian military historian George Stanley came across the journal of an unknown British officer with Burgoyne's army which is, as Stanley says, "a straightforward, unembellished record that carries conviction." It is notably factual, with rare instances of editorial comment. Another particularly valuable source is Lieutenant James Hadden's *Journal*, and my favorite of the British accounts is that of Lieutenant William Digby—an observant, sometimes prejudiced eyewitness whose spontaneous comments are often highly revealing.

Thanks to Major A. J. Maher, assistant regimental secretary of the Queen's Lancashire Regiment in Preston, I obtained the interesting memoir of George Fox's service from 1766 to 1783, edited by J. A. Houlding and G. Kenneth Yates. Fox probably spent his early years in the potteries in north Staffordshire before enlisting. His active American service, which began in 1773, ended with his capture at Saratoga, when he became one of the Convention Army prisoners, and in 1783 he returned to England. Fox may have been illiterate, which could account for his dictating the memoir to a nephew about 1786. While based on his recollection of events, the document is filled with useful details that have the ring of truth. It leaves no doubt that George Fox was an observant participant in the events he describes, and it is one of the few accounts by a private soldier.

General Sir Henry Clinton's papers and those of Sir Guy Carleton are useful for certain aspects of this story, but neither was intimately involved in the campaign. The papers of Lord George Germain, on the other hand, are essential.

Regrettably, almost no original letters or memoranda from Burgoyne survive. His biographer Edward de Fonblanque, writing in 1876, claimed to have access to the general's papers, but since they have disappeared one must conclude, as his recent biographer James Lunt believes, that Burgoyne's "immediate descendants, conscious of their illegitimacy, destroyed their father's personal correspondence." Another tragic gap is the lack of any papers of General Sir William Howe. The family documents were destroyed by fire, besides which, as Troyer Anderson— biographer of the general and his brother—notes, "never did two men keep their own counsel more carefully."

The great majority of rebel accounts are in the form of letters, diaries, and journals, and it is something of a minor miracle that so many of them survive. It is curious that few American participants wrote books about their experiences—almost as though they had no time for such matters. Letters and journals have, of course, been assembled and published, and correspondence and records exist in dozens of historical societies and libraries, but they are widely dispersed, as my bibliography suggests. Fortunately, several fine published collections of such materials exist. *The Spirit of 'Seventy-Six* by Henry Steele Commager and Richard B. Morris includes a wealth of lively, intensely interesting excerpts, selected with great skill and strung together with a commentary that is in itself a short history of the War for Independence. Another excellent source of letters and journals is Scheer and Rankin's *Rebels and Redcoats*, also accompanied by an unfailingly informative narrative. For the much-neglected story of the loyalists, or Tories, as they were also called, Catherine S. Crary's *The Price of Loyalty* is very useful, especially since it contains much biographical information about the correspondents she quotes.

Other sources of information, whose usefulness must be assessed case by case, are the many pension applications filed by veterans or members of their families. Since these were recorded long after the events and frequently reflect what a man had read or imagined rather than what he had seen or done, they are not generally to be relied upon.

A notable example of material that must be approached gingerly is James Wilkinson's *Memoirs*. As the historian Stephen Ambrose writes, Wilkinson was "notorious for swimming with the tide," and "until his death in 1825 he never met a conspiracy he didn't embrace." He was a thoroughly amoral character, and how much his recollection of events is to be trusted is open to question. However, since Wilkinson was the only American present on several occasions at the time of the surrender, I have used his testimony (cautiously) in describing those events.

Among the most rewarding American journals dealing with the campaign are those of Jeduthan Baldwin, Thomas Blake, Ralph Cross, Henry Dearborn, Ebenezer Fletcher, Enos Hitchcock, James Thacher, Benjamin Warren, and Ebenezer Wild. They are characterized by a wonderful freshness and authenticity and make you feel that you are talking with a man who is telling you what he experienced the previous day.

The following notes indicate the chief sources of quotations or assertions, so that the general reader interested in further inquiry will know which I found most helpful. I have not provided citations for all the sources consulted for background information—only those whose contents deal specifically with the occurrences described here. Works cited are usually identified as briefly as possible; they are listed fully in the Bibliography. For example, *The Bulletin of the Fort Ticonderoga Museum* is abbreviated as FTB; *Force Fourth Series,* Volume 5, 381–384 is abbreviated as Force IV 5:381–384; a scholarly journal, Volume LXVI No. 4, October 1985, is denoted as 66(4) (Oct. 1985). Unless otherwise indicated, dates may be assumed to be 1777.

Chapter 1
The Secret Mission

Dr. Franklin's comments on this phase of the difficult journey to Canada and various aspects of the Revolution appear in his endlessly interesting and entertaining letters in *The Benjamin Franklin Papers*. These quotations are from 22:379–93.

Christopher Ward's two-volume *The War of the Revolution* is a reliable, thorough, highly readable account of the war, and I have used it frequently as a general reference on military engagements and for assessments of personalities on both sides.

Marshall Davidson's *Life in America* is an excellent brief source on colonial cities during this period. For specifics on Manhattan, Dawson's introduction to *New York City During the American Revolution* contains a wealth of material, which is supplemented by Thomas Jones's *History of New York During the Revolutionary War*—an account by a loyalist justice whose tongue was as sharp as his pen. Lieutenant Bernard Ratzer's contemporary map, reproduced in Jones 1:389 and in Dawson, is most illuminating.

Information on the little-known topic of smuggling—particularly in the context of the Tea Act—is in Miller.

Franklin's call on Mrs. Barrow is described in Fleming 324. Carl Van Doren's biography of Franklin has the story of his unhappy relationship with his bastard son William.

Sabine's classic *The American Loyalists* 222 mentions New York's Stamp Act riots. The Liberty Boys' activities are noted in Dawson 12. Jackson Turner Main's *Social Structure of the American Revolution* is informative on New York's merchant population and the class differences in the city.

Benson Lossing's noteworthy *Pictorial Field Book of the Revolution*, 2:587–88 has an account of the Sons of Liberty seizing arms and ammunition intended for Boston.

My book *Decisive Day* 214–17 discusses Henry Knox and the remarkable feat of bringing cannon from Fort Ticonderoga to Boston in the dead of winter to relieve the siege of Boston.

The letter on the subject of separation and independence appears in the monumental series of volumes by Peter Force, IV 5:40.

John Adams's letter to William Cushing is in Freeman 4:111.

Stirling's activities are described in Ward 1:202–6, and Force IV 5:381–84, which also has the plaintive note saying "I have no cash," IV 5:448–49.

Charles Carroll, in a letter to his father dated March 29, 1776, described the gentlemen shoveling for earthworks, the soldiers led by Heath, and New York as a "centrical place." The assessment of the city as "almost a desert" is from John Carroll, and the disappearance of the houses of ill repute is in Wickman's "The Diary of Timothy Tuttle" April 26, 1776.

The commissioners' journey is covered in detail by the two Carrolls in their graphic letters, which fortunately survived. Franklin's letters, as noted, are also valuable. Those from Samuel Chase tend to be official communications and rather brief.

Figures on the number of evacuees from New York are in Mason 78.

Koeppel 20–21 gives "Manahata" as the Indian name and has much to say about the Hudson and the port of New York. Mrs. Grant, on the other hand, has the name as "Manhattoes," 1:9.

Most details about New York City in 1776 are drawn from the James DeLancey map of his Bowery farm in Jones 1:558; the Ratzer map in Jones and Dawson; and Dawson 14–30 and 61.

Charles Carroll's letter of March 29, 1776, gives his first impressions of Benjamin Franklin. His letter to a member of Parliament, from his *Journal* 8–9, is eerily reminiscent of Winston Churchill's famous defiance of Adolf Hitler: ". . . we shall fight on the beaches, we shall fight on the landing grounds . . . we shall never surrender. . . ." Useful information about Chase is in Malone 196–98 and Whitney 63–67. The biography of him by Haw *et al.* is helpful, and collections of Chase papers are held by the historical societies of Pennsylvania and Virginia, as well as the New-York Historical Society. The Maryland Historical Society MS 1234— "The Samuel Chase Letters"—contains originals and copies of most of his known correspondence. Charles Carroll is described in Malone 191–92 and Whitney 58–62. All the commissioners are discussed in the introduction to Charles Carroll's *Journal*. The Maryland Historical Society has the Carroll family papers, including twenty-one letters from Charles to his father about the trip up the Hudson and beyond, which are lively, descriptive, and essential to a study of the commissioners' expedition, as is his excellent *Journal.* John Carroll's *Papers* is also important.

My characterization of Franklin in this chapter and elsewhere is based on letters from, to, and about him, and I have also consulted Fleming 83–84, Tourtellot xvi, and Van Doren 90–91, 529–41, and 631.

John Carroll 11 and Haw *et al.* 59 discuss Congressional intentions and the problems confronting the commissioners.

Brandt 44–85 and Ward 1:163–80 have excellent depictions of Arnold's heroic march and attack on Quebec. Boatner 177–78 and 906–7 is also very useful.

Relations between the American colonies and Canada and especially the background and consequences of the Quebec Act are in Lanctot 4–46; Allen French's lucid discussion in chap. 26 is especially good. Lanctot 24–25 has the Jay quotation.

Father Carroll's description of de Woedtke is in his *Papers*, 47.

Brandt's book on the Livingston family is a rich source of information on the baronial landholdings in the Hudson Valley.

Hoffman Nickerson's splendid volume *The Turning Point of the Revolution, or Burgoyne in America*, published in 1928, has been since that time the classic work on the Burgoyne expedition, well researched, thoughtful, and eminently readable. Some of his conclusions have been superseded by more recent research, but the book's major flaw for the scholar is the frustrating lack of notes on his sources. (He justifies this amusingly, if maddeningly, by saying, "Everything that interferes with vivid presentation must go." Appendices explain certain of his conclusions.) His chap. 2 contains a good discussion of the Hudson-Champlain waterway and how it influenced British planning.

The quotation from Burgoyne is in Nickerson 39.

Charles Carroll's *Journal* 22–25 covers the arrival in Albany and reception by Schuyler and his family.

Chapter 2
They Wish to See Our Throats Cut

Ward 1:141 provides a good summary of Schuyler's responsibilities at this time.

The Connecticut chaplain, Cotton Mather Smith, is quoted in Scheer and Rankin 251.

The background and depth of Yankee antipathy to Schuyler are discussed in Billias, *George Washington's Generals* 54–62, Ward 1:140, French 378–79, and Boatner 991–93. New York's penchant for approving deeds in the Grants and handing them out to prominent loyalists is discussed by Mason 48. Ethan Allen's threat to the Yorkers was quoted in *Liber*, the newsletter for Friends of Special Collections at the University of Vermont, 8(23):3.

John Carroll's thoughts about Schuyler are in his Papers 47–48. Charles Carroll's *Journal* 23–28 is full of interesting comments about the physical difficulties encountered by the travelers and the condition of forts along the way.

Mrs. Grant 1:12–13 is my source for the terms of leases.

Franklin's despair about the rigors of the expedition and his deteriorating health are chronicled in his *Papers* 22:400.

Charles Johnson's *The Nature of Vermont* 19–21 deals with the geology of Lake Champlain and environs.

Descriptions of Fort Edward appear in Carroll's *Journal* 26, Steele 4–6, Roberts, and Lossing 1:95–96, which also contains valuable information on the features of contemporary forts.

The history, location, and condition of Fort Anne are in Roberts, Hadden 107, French 143, and a map "sketched on the spot" in August 1830 by Jared Sparks. The Fort Ticonderoga Research File paper "Champlain–Hudson Corridor Place Names" is helpful.

Much of this chapter's coverage of the trip down the lake is based on Charles Carroll's *Journal* 30–49, his letters to his father of April 13 through 21, John Carroll's *Papers* 48, and Franklin's *Papers* 22:399 and fn.

The origin of Fort Carillon's name is discussed in the Fort Ticonderoga Research File paper "The Meaning of Carillon," where it is convincingly argued that the name was not inspired by the musical sound of the nearby waterfall, as was supposed for some time, but came from the name of the French trader based here. The same paper gives "between the great waters" as the meaning of the Mohawk word "Ticonderoga."

I have relied on John Trumbull's beautifully drawn 1776 map of the fort and environs for some of my descriptions.

Ward 1:418 describes the attack on the fort by Ethan Allen and Benedict Arnold.

Franklin's recognition of the need to pay for goods with hard currency is in his *Papers* 22:413.

Peter Kalm 402–12 has perceptive comments on Montreal.

Both Carrolls—John in his *Papers* 47 and Charles in letters of April 30 and May 6, 1776—describe the elegant and exhausting reception given them in Montreal.

Stanley 69fn quotes the British officer on raising the siege of Quebec. Accounts of the American retreat appear in Houlding and Yates ("George Fox's Memoir") 8, Force IV 6:450–51, and Brandt's biography of Arnold 84–86.

Franklin's poor health and decision to head south are in John Carroll 49, and Charles Carroll's *Journal* 50. Chase's correspondence of May 6–27, 1776, includes his letters to Thomas. The rebel retreat and Thomas's death are reported in Ward 1:197, Freeman 4:108fn, and Charles Carroll's *Journal* 54. My footnote on the subject of smallpox comes in part from Wickman's "Diary of Timothy Tuttle" note 46 and Manasseh Cutler's diary 43, 56. The British pursuit is noted in Stanley 72–73 and Digby 117fn.

John Adams's description of the rebel army's plight is quoted in a letter from Dr. Jonathan Potts. Other quotations on the disastrous scene are from Trumbull's *Autobiography* 27, Gates in Wickman thesis 2, and Digby 117fn.

The commissioners' report to John Hancock comes from Charles Carroll's *Journal* 59–61, and the material on Hazen is from the same source 5–6. Carroll's optimistic assessment was written in a letter of June 4, 1776, and his *Journal* 57–58 records the visit to Washington's headquarters in New York.

Franklin's letter to Carroll and Chase is printed in his *Papers* 22:439, and his concerns and those of his sister appear in 22:442 and fn. and in Van Doren 547.

The material on the Declaration of Independence comes from Van Doren 549, Whitney 19, Malone 71–72, and Samuel Chase's letter of June 29, 1776, to Richard Henry Lee.

Chapter 3
The Enemy's Plans Are Dark and Mysterious

". . . nothing will come of the expedition this year" is a notation in the journal of Julius Friedrich Wasmus, a Brunswick surgeon. One of several journals translated by Helga Doblin and edited by Mary C. Lynn which have been indispensable in the writing of this book, it is especially rich in details about the campaign (up to the battle of Bennington, where he was captured) and his subsequent experiences as a prisoner. Perhaps the most appealing aspect of the record he kept is his sense of wonder at the new land he was seeing for the first time, coupled with his insatiable curiosity.

Nickerson 170 describes the work of Lieutenant Shank.

Lieutenant William Digby of the 53rd Regiment of Grenadiers arrived in Canada in 1776 at the time the siege of Quebec was lifted, and kept a careful, extremely readable account of his experiences during the next year and a half, ending with the surrender at Saratoga. His is an invaluable resource, and in this chapter I have relied on his descriptions of the Canadian winter.

Fox's descriptions of the naval construction are from Houlding and Yates 13.

The quotation from General Phillips is from Lunt 111.

Schuyler's letter of November 6, 1776, is quoted in FTB 3(6):243.

Josiah Bartlett's impassioned appeal for enlistments, dated May 3, 1777, appears in his *Papers* 161.

Donald Wickman's excellent master's thesis, the best study of Mount Independence during this period, describes the terrible conditions at Ticonderoga. Wayne's comments are in a letter to Schuyler, February 4, 1777, in FTB 4(1):23, and his remarks on the imminent threat of attack appear in the Heath Papers. Wayne's letters to Hancock are dated April 2, that to his wife April 1, 1777.

The engaging Mrs. Bland is quoted in Scheer and Rankin 224, and Flexner's *George Washington in the American Revolution* (hereafter Flexner *Revolution*) 202–3. Discussions of Washington's army at this time appear in Fitzpatrick 7:270, 413, and Bill 45, and excellent descriptions of the New Jersey terrain may be found in Lossing 1:331–35.

Portrayals of George Washington are in Flexner *Revolution* 12 and 401, Freeman 3.6, and Bill 51, and his frontier experience is also detailed in my *World of George Washington* 30–41.

Allen French, in his superb *First Year of the American Revolution* 503, marvels at Washington's remarkable achievement of holding an army together. The quotation revealing the general's self-doubts appears in Flexner *Revolution* 9.

I have drawn on my book *Decisive Day* 215–16 for material on the liberation of Boston.

The size of Howe's army at New York is given by Boatner 798 as 31,000; Ward 1:322 puts it at 27,000. I believe the first figure is more accurate.

Washington's awareness of the animosity of Lee and Gates is in Flexner *Revolution* 100.

Quotations from the British officer and the English traveler appear in Scheer and Rankin 221, 228.

George Washington's efforts to obtain troops, the evils of the bounty system, desertions, the relative size of his own and Howe's armies, and his comment on the British fleet are drawn from Freeman 4:382fn, 404–5, and 420–27, Flexner *Revolution* 193–94, and Fitzpatrick 8:17, 331.

Congress's decision to refuse commissions to certain foreign officers is in the *Journals of Congress*, March 14, 1777.

A perceptive and generally favorable picture of Gates appears in Max Mintz, *The Generals of Saratoga*. Rossie's study, *The Politics of Command*, is exactly that, and his depiction of the Gates-Schuyler feud 135–53 is very good.

Willcox 63–64 discusses Howe's decision to move against Philadelphia.

Material on Howe comes from a number of sources, including Parkman 2:89–97, French 195, Ketchum *Decisive Day* 4–6, Mintz 110, Hargreaves 246, Mackesy *The War for America* (hereafter Mackesy *War*) 75–76, 151–52, Anderson 47–50, Jones 1:171, 351, and Billias *George Washington's Opponents* (hereafter Billias *Opponents*) 64. For a different view of Howe's purported dalliance, see Alden's *History of the American Revolution*, which argues that Mrs. Loring may not have been his inamorata.

Washington's uncertainty and his trials in New Jersey are covered by Freeman 4:398–416. His correspondence with Schuyler and intelligence concerning Howe's movements and rumors thereof are in Fitzpatrick 7:272–462 *passim*. The letters to Heath and McDougall are in Fitzpatrick 8:2–9, as are letters from Gates 8:17, 190, and 198 and activities at Middle Brook 8:268–69.

Chapter 4
To Effect a Junction with Howe's Force

Van Doren 565–70 relates the story of Franklin's arrival in France.

George III's statement "I wish nothing but good . . ." is quoted in my article "England's Vietnam."

Burgoyne wrote touching letters about his wife's death on Jan. 19, 1777, to Lord and Lady Dacres, who were apparently her close friends, and on Jan. 23 to an unknown woman, addressed to "Dear Madam."

Much of the material on Germain is drawn from two works by Piers Mackesy—*The Coward of Minden* and *The War for America, 1775–1783*—in both of which he recounts Lord George's actions in the battle and his subsequent disgrace.

The statement by George III about the good fortune of the "revolted Provinces" to live under a mild government is from his Oct. 31, 1776, speech to Parliament, in Force V 3:962. His remark that "Blows must decide" is quoted in my "England's Vietnam," as is the British major's comment after Lexington. Germain's call for using "the utmost force" to subdue the rebellion is in Mackesy *War* 55, where Generals Murray and Wolfe are also quoted, 30.

Sandwich's remark is in my *Decisive Day* 10.

Harvey's opinion, cited here in a footnote, comes from Nickerson 43–44.

Germain's criticism of the Howes' peace effort is related in Mackesy *War* 105; the secretary's insistence on compliance with Parliamentary intentions is in Guttridge 28, as is the excerpt from Carleton's letter, 33.

Nickerson's opening chapter is excellent on the policy of the French crown and its implementation by Vergennes and Beaumarchais.

Burke's eloquent appeal and his statement about the futility of opposition are mentioned in my "England's Vietnam."

The quotation from Germain on town meetings is in Morris 33.

James Lunt's fine study of the Burgoyne expedition emphasizes the general's driving ambition and devotes five pages to his subject's legitimacy, concluding that he was not the natural son of Lord Bingley, though his mother was probably Bingley's mistress at one time or another. Nickerson, in an appendix, deals with the same topic and cites his reasons for believing that Bingley *was* Burgoyne's father.

Gambling by rich and poor is discussed by Lunt 5. *The American Heritage Book of the Revolution*, which includes a splendid portrayal of eighteenth-century England by J. H. Plumb, describes the evils of gambling, 13.

Although it was written nearly fifteen years after the Burgoynes' return from their European exile, a letter from H. Sloane to Sir Andrew Snape Hamond on April 26, 1776, sheds new light on the relationship between Burgoyne and his father-in-law. Reporting an extraordinary "melancholy story," Sloane states: "Old Earl Derby dies, Lady Derby was so struck that she dies in two days after the Peer, one of the Daughters who had been sometimes indisposed was so shocked at hearing both their deaths, that she died likewise. The Old Peer never forgiving G[enera]l Burgoyne for making away with his Daughter, leaves Lady Charlotte nothing, but leaves all the rest of the Old Maids his Daughters

25,000 a Piece; as one of them died so suddenly after the Peers death as not to have time to make a will, Burgoyne comes in for a fifth, as an Heir general, and will by this odd circumstance get 5,000£."

Lunt 31 quotes Burgoyne's lively poster and has the comments on discipline 33–34. Hargreaves's article is also useful.

I based my description of Reynolds's portrait of Burgoyne on a reproduction on the cover of *American Heritage*, June 1956.

Both Lunt 46 and Hargreaves 233–34 speak of Burgoyne's reputation in the House, and the latter 235 cites Keppel's rejection of command and remarks concerning the three generals posted to Boston.

Walpole's *Last Journals* 1:433 is the source of his comment.

Billias *Opponents* has a perceptive chapter on Burgoyne, describing his feelings about holding a secondary command and his criticism of Carleton. Burgoyne's "Reflections" is quoted in Lunt 101; Lunt discusses the exchanges between the king and Germain 112–14.

Burgoyne's letter of Jan. 1, 1777, to Germain is printed as Appendix I in his *State of the Expedition . . .* (hereafter *State*). The general's jockeying for the command is treated in Mackesy *War* 107–9.

Howe's letters to Germain appear in Force V 3:926–27, 1317–18, and are the subjects of comment in Nickerson 78–82, Clark, and Willcox. Two excellent articles—Jane Clark's "Responsibility for the Failure of the Burgoyne Campaign" and William B. Willcox's "Too Many Cooks: British Planning Before Saratoga"—are essential to an understanding of the plan that went awry. Reference should also be made to the Clinton Papers (during early July 1777, when he tried to dissuade Howe from going to Philadelphia), Nickerson 76–78, and Fonblanque 486–87.

Horace Walpole's remarks about Howe, in a letter of Aug. 11, 1777, to Sir Horace Mann, are in his *Letters* 6:466.

The touchy relations between Clinton and Germain are treated by Boatner 238, and Jones 2:132 has interesting insights into what occurred when the general returned to England, as does Lunt 118–20.

George III's thoughts on the campaign appear in Nickerson 89–90.

Nickerson 97–98 and Clark 548–49 cover the business of the missing dispatch, as does Anderson 255–57. The latter also makes a case for the inconsequence of such an order, saying that the administration never intended more than that Howe would "stretch out his posts to meet Burgoyne" before the end of the year. An excerpt of Germain's March 26 letter to Carleton is in Nickerson 91–94.

Digby 187 and Hadden 43 note Burgoyne's arrival on May 6, 1777. James Hadden of the Royal Artillery kept a journal from the time he sailed for Canada on March 4, 1776, until the end of the battle of Freeman's farm on Sept. 19, 1777, and like Digby's account, it is absolutely essential to a study of the campaign. Hadden tends to quote orders of the day and officers' letters, while Digby offers more personal observations and lively commentary throughout.

Chapter 5
A Matter of Personal Interest and Fame

George III's uncharitable remark about Fox is in Fortescue 3: introduction.

The Acland material is drawn from Lady Harriet's *Journal* xvii–xviii, and from Anne Acland 29–31.

Digby 83 and 87–88fn states that forty-three ships made up the convoy; the Acland *Journal* puts it at forty-two. Digby adds that thirty sail joined, making the convoy seventy-three ships, plus escorts.

The quotation from the German officer comes from the *Journal* of Johann Friedrich Specht, colonel of the Specht brigade, who held the local rank of brigadier general during the campaign. This is another of the Brunswick journals so ably translated by Helga Doblin and edited by Mary Lynn which have proved invaluable in the course of writing this book. Probably Specht did not keep the journal himself but checked the daily entries which were most likely made by his adjutant. It is a superb record of the entire Burgoyne campaign and contains comments on logistical problems, military actions, the names of British and German officers in each engagement, troop strength, casualties, and a wealth of other details. Specht's rank also meant that he was aware of why certain command decisions were made.

Surgeon Wasmus's *Journal* is eloquent on the horrors of a North Atlantic crossing.

The introductions to the documents translated by Helga Doblin all contain valuable information on the Brunswick troops, and further data are in Larter and Nickerson 107. The most complete bibliography of this subject I have seen is the one prepared by Ronald Kingsley.

Nickerson 45–46 quotes George III's disappointment over Empress Catherine's failure to provide Russian troops.

Helga Doblin has chronicled the difficulties German soldiers suffered in receiving letters from home in "German-American Postal Service During the Revolution."

The bitter statement about the isolation and loneliness of the Brunswickers is from Hoffman 34. Doblin and Lynn, in a translation of another officer's journal presumed to be Ensign Hille's (hereafter Doblin Hille), provide the financial details of the hiring of German soldiers, xvii. Descriptions of the troops' departure from Wolfenbüttel are in Doblin Hille xv–xvii and Wasmus 2–4.

Wasmus's perceptive observations of Canadian wildlife, mores, fashions, and the native Americans he encountered are in his *Journal* 45–62 *passim*. Digby's *Journal* 122 has the comment on Canadians as happy people, and Lady Harriet's view of them is in her *Journal* 18–19; her comments on the hatchet ceremony are on page 21. Hadden 15 describes the Congress of Savages; the Indians' skills are noted in William L. Stone's *Letters of Brunswick and Hessian Officers During the American Revolution* (hereafter Stone *Revolutionary Letters*) 63–64.

Specht's *Journal* 48–49 notes where Germans were billeted.

The Briton's comment on the Canadian winter is in Stanley 94—a most informative journal kept by an unknown British officer.

Digby 180–83, Specht 48–49, and Hadden all speak at some length about social activities during the long winter. A footnote in Digby 180 states that "carrioling"—not "cabrioling," as Hadden has it—is the proper term. The carriole was a vehicle peculiar to Canada.

The queen's birthday festivities are noted in Doblin Hille 65, and Specht's remark about "fly news" is in his *Journal* 51.

Captain McKay's attack is mentioned in Hadden lxxx and 39–42.

Fraser was no admirer of Carleton, as his remark suggests. The passage is in his extremely important letter of July 13, 1777, to John Robinson. Burgoyne's respectful comment about Carleton was written to General Harvey and is quoted in Stanley 21.

Hadden 45–50 discusses the makeup of the Northern Army.

Both Nickerson 102 and Lunt 134 discuss Carleton's reaction to Germain's insulting letter. Specht 42 quotes the official reason for the choice of Burgoyne over Carleton, and Anburey 1:203 is the source of the remark about Burgoyne's popularity with the troops.

Digby's *Journal* 187 defends Carleton's decision to return to Canada in the fall of 1776.

Stanley 95 mentions Burgoyne's intention to join Howe, and Lunt 133 has the excerpt from Germain's letter urging Sir William to cooperate with Burgoyne after taking Philadelphia—a letter revealing Germain's abysmal ignorance of distances and the difficulties of travel in America.

Willcox 67 comments on the consequences of Germain's failure to order Howe to follow the original plan.

Stanley 15 quotes Burgoyne's "Thoughts" in which he mentions his concern for "personal interest and fame."

Burgoyne's complaint about inadequate supplies is in *State* Appendix X. Britain's long, tenuous supply line is discussed in my "England's Vietnam" and Mackesy *War* 66. The latter book 64 is my source for Admiral Palliser's comment and is valuable for the Sandwich-Germain relationship 53–54 and Britain's daunting logistical dilemma 61–65.

Specht 41, Nickerson 103, and Stanley 22 touch on the shortcomings of carts and the understandable worries of hostlers. Two documents in the House of Lords Records Office—Manuscripts No. 6.24/21 and 6.24/22—are devoted to wagons ordered for the army and artillery, respectively. Contractors were to receive seven shillings per day "Halifax currency" for each cart, with driver and two horses. In the event of loss, the contractor would be reimbursed £10 for a horse, £5 for a cart, and £3 for harness.

Auxiliary troops are discussed in *State* Appendix V, Hadden lxxx, Specht 54–55, and Stanley 24. Clearly these units were a matter of great concern to the army's officers.

Wasmus 48–49 tells how disgruntled the Canadians were that they were to serve as porters, and Stanley 24–26 mentions opposition to the corvée and the disappointment at how few loyalists turned out. Doris Morton's book is the authority on Skene, and Hadden Appendix 16 is helpful.

Crary 69 describes the woes John Peters's loyalty caused him, and Peters's own narrative in the Toronto *Globe & Mail* is most informative on his activities throughout the campaign.

According to Steele 144, the massacre at Fort William Henry cost the lives of anywhere between 69 and 185 victims.

The best study of St. Luc is Burnham and Martin; his early career is chronicled 55–62. Hadden Appendix 17 is also informative.

Chapter 6
A Theatre of Glory

According to Nicholas Westbrook, director of Fort Ticonderoga, it is possible to see approximately three miles down the lake from the fort, or to the present site of the St. Regis paper plant. USGS maps place the height of Mount Independence at 306 feet, Mount Defiance at 853 feet, and Fort Ticonderoga at 193 feet.

Stone's *Revolutionary Letters* 130 quotes a Brunswick officer's description of American generals wearing uniforms and "a band around the waist to designate their respective rank."

Hancock's assurance that all would be quiet on the northern front is in St. Clair's *Court Martial* 149, and Gates's prediction is in the same document 84–85. The two chief architects of the American defenses were Arthur St. Clair and Philip Schuyler, and the fact that both were court-martialed (and both acquitted) and that full records of those proceedings, including their own and witnesses' testimonies, were later printed is a godsend to scholars, for the two documents reveal the thoughts and reasons behind the decisions of both commanders during this critical period and are filled with immensely useful details about the goings-on. Hereafter I will refer to these court-martial reports as St. C CM and S CM, for St. Clair and Schuyler respectively.

Dr. Jonathan Potts, in a letter of May 25, 1777, speaks of the "Great uneasiness" of British and Canadian soldiers over slow recruiting and scanty supplies.

St. C CM 149 records the general's decision to bring his young son.

Wilson's Feb. 20, 1777, letter to St. Clair is in the latter's *Papers*.

Information about St. Clair is in Boatner, Nickerson 132–33, and the St. Clair *Papers* 5–6. A splendid sketch of him by Trumbull is reproduced in this book.

The visit of Baldwin and Trumbull to Rattlesnake Hill is recorded in the *Bulletin of the Fort Ticonderoga Museum* (hereafter FTB) 4(6):11 and Wickman thesis 3.

Trumbull's map is in the 1841 edition of his *Autobiography* 33. His unheeded warning about the threat represented by Sugar Hill is recounted in Furneaux 54–55.

Roswell Bottum's *History of Orwell* notes the arrival of a copy of the Declaration of Independence. Digby 208fn and Wickman thesis 14 record the celebration and renaming of Rattlesnake Hill and Sugar Hill.

The description of the flag is in Thacher 87.

Nicholas Westbrook informed me that both shorelines of the lake had been cleared of trees for miles.

Thomas Marshall's letter of May 19, 1777, to Heath is in the Heath papers.

St. Clair's letter of June 13, 1777, to Schuyler (St. C CM 16–17) has an eloquent if grim picture of the fort's condition.

Black and Roelker 42 and 42fn mentions the letter that took thirty-six days from Peekskill to Providence.

The footnote on iron gall ink is based on papers by Goodwin 149 and Barrow 292–306.

Baldwin's early career is traced in the introduction to his *Journal*, a document that records his activities during 1776 and his return to Ticonderoga the next year. It is an extraordinary account, rich in details, and particularly noteworthy as representing the viewpoint of an engineer.

The quotation from John Adams is from Morris 14.

Both Thacher and Digby were impressed by the remarkable Great Bridge and describe it in their journals; Thacher 80, Digby 215. Wickman thesis also provides many details. An excellent study is Cohn's Lake Champlain Basin Project report.

Kosciuszko's letter to Gates was dated May 18, 1777.

Baldwin noted in his *Journal* 38 that St. Clair "came in" [to Ticonderoga] on June 12. St. C CM 7 states that the general assumed command the next day.

Michael Kirkman's pass, dated June 14, 1777, to Amsbury and Schuyler's June 15 letter to Washington are from the Library of Congress. Further information about Amsbury may be found in S CM 103–6 and 110, St. C CM 14–17, Van Doren's *Secret History* 44–49, and (on Livius) Boatner 644–45.

Much information on this period of watchful waiting appears in St. C CM, especially 18 and 29, and in the Greenleaf diary and Baldwin May 28, 1777.

Donald Wickman points out in his thesis that what was thought to be the enemy's morning gun was undoubtedly the report of a cannon aboard a ship.

Schuyler's June 16, 1777, letter to Washington is in S CM 110.

Ford 3:398 and 4:392 has George Washington's thoughts on the efficacy of earthworks for amateur soldiers.

Chapter 7
The Scalping Knife and the Gospel

Riedesel's thoughts about the coming campaign are in his *Memoirs*, translated by Max von Eelking and edited by William L. Stone (hereafter Riedesel), 97–98, 236–38.

Anburey 1:300 tells how difficult it was to handle bateaus in a high wind. Mrs. Theresa C. Lonergan, during four decades of research, compiled what is certainly the most authoritative study of eighteenth-century naval activity on Lake Champlain. Her detailed notebooks, with transcripts of primary sources and her own comments, compose the Theresa C. Lonergan Research Collection on the First American Navy at Fort Ticonderoga's Thompson-Pell Research Center. I have benefited from her work for this section on the British fleet. Hadden 15 observed the larger vessels being disassembled and taken to St. Johns. Specht 61 and Pratorius 58–59 describe the arduous task of moving the bateaus, and Wasmus 51 and Doblin Hille 69 offer a picture of St. Johns at the time, with the British fleet anchored in the harbor.

Personal details about Riedesel are in Riedesel xv–xvi and xxxii; Nickerson 117–18 is helpful.

Mackesy *Coward* 112–14 describes the action at Minden.

Phillips's banquet and news that Baroness von Riedesel had arrived is described in Riedesel 35–38 and 196–97 and Wasmus 51 and 53.

Capture of a British transport by an American privateer is in Force V 3:1212. Anburey 1:197 discusses the modifications in the regulars' uniforms, as does Nickerson 109. Changes in the Brunswick dragoons' uniforms and weapons is one of the many discoveries made by Lion Miles and reported in his paper, 15.

Specht 61 has an account of Carleton's final review. Hadden 51–54 chronicles the army's departure and a footnote on 52 describes the significance of the royal standard.

Carleton's distribution of rum is in Doblin Hille 69–70, and Specht 19 mentions the fifteen-gun salute for Burgoyne.

Fraser's assignment is discussed in Atkinson 139–41. Napier 294 notes the review by Burgoyne, and Fraser's movements are in his letter to John Robinson. Pell lists ships in the fleet and some components of Fraser's advanced corps, which are all named in Lunt 142.

General Phillips's remarks about Captain Fraser are in Atkinson 136.

Letters from Alexander Lindsay, 6th Earl of Balcarres, to Carleton (Feb. 1777) and his mother, the Countess of Balcarres (May 15, 1777), have his thoughts on the possibilities of advancement in the army.

Hadden lxx–lxxx is excellent on the composition of the British and German forces, and my *Decisive Day* 122–23 discusses the function of various categories of troops.

Burgoyne's letter and that of a London friend to Fraser are in Atkinson 138–39.

Hargreaves 297fn notes that Fraser and Riedesel were old comrades-in-arms. Fraser's innovations are mentioned in Atkinson 136.

For this section on Phillips I have consulted Nickerson 108, 116, Digby 174fn, Atkinson 136, and Hadden xlvi, l–li, lxxiv, and 343 *et seq.*

The *Annual Register* is quoted in Stanley 27.

The organization of the army is covered in a number of journals, among them Doblin Hille 97 notes 16 and 17, Digby 196, and Stanley 95. Burgoyne's Orderly Book for June 20 specifies the positioning of boats.

Anburey's favorable opinion of Burgoyne is in his *Travels* 1:203.

Information concerning the strength of the British and Germans can be found in Wasmus 48, 74, and *State* xxvii–xxviii. Tactics in battle are mentioned in my *Decisive Day* 125, and Mackesy *War* 77–78. The directive concerning the importance of the bayonet is in Burgoyne's Orderly Book 3.

Atkinson 141 tells of plans for the Indian council.

Descriptions of landmarks along the lake shore are in Hadden 16, 134–35, Specht 46–47, and Digby 134fn.

Anburey 1:274–75 and Wasmus 52–53 express the men's delight in the wildlife they saw. Hoffman 36 describes the battles with voracious insects.

Burgoyne's pleasure that his men had mastered baking without ovens is in his Orderly Book for June 24, 1777.

The arrival at Cumberland Head is depicted by Specht 64, Hadden 17, and Wasmus 52. Wasmus 53 reports on the growing seriousness of the situation.

Burgoyne's Orderly Book July 3 and Pratorius 61–62 note what was to happen if the army had to move in a hurry.

Digby 123–25 has a vivid portrayal of the Indians' canoes and their skill in handling them; the procession of boats is eloquently described in Anburey 1:304–6.

Digby's comment on Burgoyne is in his *Journal* 157.

Hadden 59–62 quotes Burgoyne's proclamation, and Fraser's letter to John Robinson tells how it was distributed. Walpole's derisive reaction is in his *Letters*, Cunningham 6:467.

Wickman thesis 105–6 notes the capture of MacIntosh, and the extent of the information the Scot provided is in St. C CM 17 and in Fraser's letter to John Robinson.

Napier 295fn lists the Indians present at the congress and Anburey 1:281–90 and Specht 48–49 have accounts.

Burke's ridicule of Burgoyne is quoted in Nickerson 126.

Captain Fraser's report to his uncle is mentioned in General Fraser's letter to John Robinson.

Chapter 8
The Scene Thickens Fast

Moses Greenleaf noted the Reverend Enos Hitchcock's text in his diary, May 25.

Marshall's plea for shoe leather is in letters of June 3 and 17 to S. P. Savage.

The Pennsylvania captain's complaint about New England troops is in a letter from Persifer Frazer, Aug. 6, 1776, in FTB 10(5).

Brockholst Livingston's prediction that an attack on Fort Schuyler (Stanwix) would be vigorously contested is set forth in a letter of June 20, 1777, to his father—one of many such epistles quoted in this work. He was a conscientious correspondent, a young man keenly interested in personal glory, and almost always more optimistic than the situation warranted, but the chatty letters are valuable for their newsy character and his observations of events.

Thomas Blake's May 15 letter in Kidder 25 and Alexander Scammell's of June 18 (completed on June 23) leave no doubt about the condition of the roads.

Bartlett's plea for troops is in his *Papers* 160–61.

Kidder 11–21 discusses Stark and his fight with Congress.

The comment about the comical appearance of the American citizen soldiers is from Fischer 154, a splendid book that has much to say about the origin of minute companies and militia. In this section I have also drawn on my *Decisive Day* 59–62 and *The Winter Soldiers* 140–49, St. C CM 45ff, French 33ff, and Freeman 4:*passim.*

The quotation from Glover is in a letter of June 17, 1777, in his memoir.

Fischer records the remark about the rapid assembling of militia at Lexington and Concord. The two statements about the Americans' reluctance to enlist for long periods are in Mackesy *War* 32, and the example of Cornish, N.H., men appears in Chase 40. Brimfield's experience is described in a letter from Timothy Danielson to Jeremiah Powell, May 14, 1777. Alden 251–52 has a good discussion of the relative qualities of American, British, and German soldiers.

Activities at Ticonderoga in June are discussed in St. C CM 109, Dunn's testimony.

Lotteries are mentioned in a number of contemporary journals—this one in Hitchcock 107.

Gordon's anecdote appears in the account of his tour of New England 473.

The excerpt from Hitchcock's journal is on 109. Both he (June 7, 11) and Greenleaf (May 26) cite examples of harsh punishment.

Scammell's letters to Nabby Bishop are dated March 22 and June 8, 1777—the latter in FTB 2(3):106–7. Information about the colonel's career may be found in Ward 888–89, Freeman 4:581, 5:351, 492, and Kidder 102–4.

The Reverend Thomas Allen's letter of June 26, 1777, contains an account of the attack on Whiting and Batty, and this and the subsequent episode are mentioned in Hitchcock June 17, Colton June 19, James Gray's letter of June 26, and St. C CM 18.

The record of St. Clair's court-martial (St. C CM), which includes his own testimony and that of others, is the richest source of information about his army's dilemma, the opinions of other officers on the number of men required for a proper defense, his plans, the pitiful condition of men and the fort, scouting missions, and the frantic efforts to prepare for the imminent British attack.

Hadden 4–7 and 236–37 relates the story of Gordon's shooting; the footnotes on 4–5 are illuminating. Whitcomb's own story of the event is in Force V 1:828. St. Clair, in a letter to Schuyler, in St. C CM 122–23, mentions his reluctance to risk sending Whitcomb on a scout. The German's surprise at Whitcomb's enterprise is in Riedesel 1:244. Stevens's letter to Savage on June 24, 1777, tells of Whitcomb's grim trophies.

St. Clair's despair over his army's predicament is in St. C CM 22, and the same source 35 and 102 has details on incoming men and supplies and the concurrent increase in Indian activity.

Some disagreement exists as to the distance of the British camp from Ticonderoga: Nickerson 127 states eight miles; Bird gives it as twenty; my figure of 11 is from St. C CM 114.

Burgoyne's general order is in Hadden 81.

Wickman 14 has the story of the unfortunate cow.

St. Clair's decision to send his son to safety is in St. C CM 64–65 and 149. From the same source 16, 22, and 24 come estimates of the number of troops at Ticonderoga.

Napier 298 describes Burgoyne's deployment of his forces.

Numerous sources record the approach of the British fleet: Baldwin June 30; Greenleaf June 30 (who says two twenty-gun frigates and about fifty boats and troops landed two miles away); Sewall June 30 (who says the enemy appeared at eight o'clock with five or six floating batteries, and the line of boats was about two miles from the Jersey redoubt); Wickman thesis 107; Digby 201; Specht July 1; Hadden 82.

Livingston and Baldwin—both June 30—speak of efforts to save the stores at Lake George landing and the attack on the sawmills.

Young Fraser's action is detailed in Pell 8, Hadden 83, Napier 298, and Simon Fraser's letter to John Robinson 142.

Henry Sewall July 2 has a good description of the skirmish, as do Greenleaf and Baldwin on the same date.

Livingston July 3, Sewall June 30, and St. C CM 68 and 111 discuss rebel morale and St. Clair's active encouragement.

Hitchcock June 30 and Sewall July 1 tell of the British forward movement; Livingston July 3 notes the German landing.

The Brunswickers' difficulties negotiating East Creek are observed by Specht July 2.

St. C CM 115–16 covers the loss of the blockhouse.

Greenleaf July 2 and Livingston July 3 report the information provided by the German deserters.

Andrew Tracy's statement about his interrogation of the British soldier is in the Library of Congress and is dated July 3, 1777. The episode is mentioned in Wickman thesis 117.

The Greenleaf and Sewall letters are dated July 3.

Baldwin's *Journal* July 3 and 4 mentions reinforcements and food (as do Hitchcock and Sewall, July 3) and the increased Indian activity.

Balcarres describes the psychological effect of cannon fire in one of his "Anecdotes."

Lossing 1:131 has an excellent description and drawing of the view from Mount Defiance; Twiss's survey of the terrain is noted in *State* Appendix XVI. Pratorius in FTB 15(3):64 tells the fate of the English artillerymen.

Baldwin July 5 records his surprise at the British failure to cannonade the fort.

Livingston's observations on the dilemma are in St. C CM 116. Digby 205 mentions the fire started by Indians.

Chapter 9
The Most Delicate and Dangerous Undertaking

This chapter relies substantially on testimony in Arthur St. Clair's court-martial, which is the best American source of what quickly became a *cause célèbre*. The general's gloomy picture of what confronted the defenders is on 55, Schuyler's inability to aid them 107–8, and the council of war's decision 33–34.

The material on invalids is from Wickman 112 and St. C CM 50–53.

Nickerson 146 and Williams 8 discuss the plan of retreat.

Weather conditions appear in Hitchcock July 5.

Hay's misgivings and his conversations with St. Clair are in St. C CM 54–56. I have used Trumbull's 1776 map for orientation purposes.

Greenleaf, Hitchcock, and Sewall, all July 5, discuss the troops' reaction to news of the retreat.

The exchange between the outraged Stevens and his commanding officer is in Stevens 588–600 and St. C CM 111.

Cogan's disgust is reported in Williams 7.

Baldwin chronicled his own actions in his testimony at the trial, St. C CM 88–91.

Kidder 28 has the quotation from Blake.

Hay's summary of events is in St. C CM 53–57.

Livingston's thoughts are recorded in a June 30 letter.

Surgeon Thacher 82–83 has a vivid account of the retreat.

Major Dunn's testimony St. C CM 109–20 covers in great detail the entire operation on the night of July 5.

Williams 5–6 discusses the role of Colonel Francis.

St. Clair's comment on the difficulty and the necessity of retreat is in St. C CM 154–55, and his difficulties with the Massachusetts militia are from the same source 46, 97. The burning of Fermoy's house is on 81.

The final moments of the evacuation are related in St. C CM 65–66, 77, and 112–13 and Williams 8.

Livingston's July 17 letter to his sister Susan describes the horrendous march toward Hubbardton.

The failure of the forlorn hope is treated by Anburey 1:323–24 and Nickerson 146–47.

Chapter 10
I Have Beat Them!

For a minor (though significant) engagement, Hubbardton is extremely well documented, and John Williams's booklet is an excellent source, with many of the important accounts and a perceptive interpretation. The battlefield itself is virtually unchanged since 1777.

For distances and the route between Mount Independence and Hubbardton I have relied on the Wheelers' exhaustive study of the old military road, which has disappeared in many places. The maps 94–95, 202, and 208–9 are helpful, and the Trumbull map of "Ticonderoga & its Dependencies" is reproduced in that book following 97.

The order of rebel troops on the march is in St. C CM 77.

The most important British account of the pursuit and ensuing battle is Simon Fraser's literate, detailed letter to John Robinson (hereafter Fraser). In it 144 the brigadier mentions that he had everything "tolerably well secured" by 5:00 A.M., and I have assumed that he was on the march within the hour and that Riedesel was also moving with his advance party by 6:00. Riedesel 1:114ff has his own account of the event.

Francis's assignment is in St. C CM 85 and Poor's testimony is on 80–86. The description of the militia in "the greatest disorder" is from Wilkinson *Memoirs* 1:187, and the trouble they caused is documented in St. C CM 152. The latter source 85 mentions Poor's receipt of news concerning the party of loyalists and Indians, and Ralph Cross's journal entry Sept. 15, 1777, describes Lacey's camp. The altitude of Signal Hill is from the Bomoseen quadrangle topographic map.

Information on Hubbardton and the Selleck place is in the WPA *Guide to Vermont* and Lossing 1:144. I benefited greatly from visits to the battlefield, where I was briefed by Carl Fuller, Len Lumsden, and Donald Wickman. The automated display at the Hubbardton Battlefield Historic Site is extremely helpful.

Greenleaf July 5 and St. Clair's *Papers* 435 speak of the men's hunger and the slaughter of cattle.

St. Clair's orders and the report on Tories and Indians are in St. C CM 118 and 85.

Warner's assignment is discussed in St. C CM 85–86, Poor's testimony and that of Dunn in St. C CM 113. Williams 9 states that St. Clair waited two or three hours. (Poor states three or four hours; Dunn says "for nearly two hours.")

The size of the force under Hale and Francis is in Moore 1:472.

Williams 32, 9, and Appendix D tells of the drunks and the delays suffered by Hale.

Fletcher's story is in his brief, poignant Narrative.

St. C CM 87 has Woolcott's testimony.

Information about Warner, Francis, and Hale is in Williams 10. Boardman 200–2 and Nickerson 150 discuss Seth Warner in some detail, and French 390 has the story of his election as lieutenant colonel. Wilkinson, quoted in St. Clair *Papers* 423, called him "a stranger to discipline," and Ward 412 and Williams 10–13 mention his decision to call a halt. Additional material on the terrain is in an unpublished monograph by Colonel R. Ernest Dupuy at the Vermont Historical Society.

Curiously, American accounts mention only the blaze from Fermoy's house, not the many fires noted by British and Germans (Wasmus 59, Digby 204–8, Specht 52). Digby 208 reports rebel deserters providing news of the evacuation and mentions his scorn at the American failure to man a cannon at the bridge. Anburey 1:351 tells of the Indian setting off the weapon and describes the weather and the terrain traveled by pursuers 325–26.

Fraser 144–45 is the source of his comments on Francis, his own detractors, the frustration of having to request Riedesel's permission to press on, and his movements on the morning of July 7. Riedesel 1:114–15 records his own actions. Williams 17 discusses Fraser's last-minute decision to attack.

Carl Fuller at the Hubbardton Battlefield Historic Site argues convincingly that it was not a single shot from a sniper that killed Major Grant, as many historians have supposed, but a volley that also felled a score of his men.

Greenleaf July 7 discusses his meeting with Francis.

St. Clair mentioned Fraser's raiding party to Schuyler in a letter of July 8, St. Clair *Papers*.

Digby's thoughts on going into battle are preserved in his *Journal* 1, 83, and 209–10.

Dupuy's monograph 16–17, Pell 9, and Balcarres's letter of July 11 to his sister Margaret depict the reception Francis's men gave the attackers. Anburey 1:339 tells how Douglas was killed.

Fraser 145 admits to his doubts and mentions the risk he took in detaching Acland, and Hadden 85 notes the danger to the British left. The action is also discussed in Dupuy 15–16, Williams 25–28, and Greenleaf July 7. The contemporary map by the German Gerlach in Williams, Appendix K, 69–71, is very useful.

Anburey's remark appears 1:337, and Enos Stone characterizes the battle in his diary July 7.

As for the time and duration of the battle, a number of opinions exist: Balcarres, to his sister Margaret, says two hours; Moore, *Diary of the Revolution*, states twenty-five minutes; Greenleaf specifies 7:20 to 8:45, or one hour and twenty-five minutes; Sewall recalls that it began a little after sunrise; Fletcher also puts it at sunrise; Stone has it beginning at 7:00 A.M. and the duration one hour and ten minutes; Napier says it started at 5:00 A.M.; Digby says it lasted "near three hours"; Anburey states it was two hours until the Germans appeared; Burgoyne *State* xvii says it began about 5:00 A.M.; Pell says it began about 6:00 A.M. and lasted one and a half hours.

Riedesel 1:115 has the account of his actions in moving to attack the rebel right. More information is in Riedesel Order Book Sign, 237N Nr. 95, at the Niedersächsisches Staatsarchiv in Wolfenbüttel, Germany.

The Gerlach map in Williams shows the rebel battle line.

Hale's plight is noted in St. C CM 113.

Anburey 1:328–34 recalls the rebels' mock surrender and the difficult ascent made by the grenadiers.

Successive rebel positions are depicted by Williams 29–31.

The refusal of Bellows's men to come to the rescue is in St. C CM 113, 118. The same pages include Dunn's and Livingston's testimonies.

Balcarres reported his narrow escape in his letter of July 11 to his sister and the experience of Sir John Harrington in his "Anecdotes."

The arrival of the Germans with singing and a band playing is mentioned in a number of sources and piqued my interest. Fraser 146 says only that they "entered into action in the handsomest manner possible" but mentions no music; however, Riedesel 1:115 and Order Book Sign. 237N Nr. 95 says he ordered the band to play, and Anburey 1:329 says the noise of men "singing psalms" persuaded the British that rebel reinforcements were on the way. In a letter of October 10, 1994, from Niedersächsisches Staatsarchiv to Helga Doblin, the point is made that hymn-singing was most unlikely. Mrs. Doblin suggests that any singing in this particular instance must have been a spontaneous outburst, and of course it is true that Riedesel had ordered them to make as much noise as possible to give the rebels the impression that they were being attacked by a large body of troops. A letter of March 8, 1995, from Niedersächsisches Staatsarchiv to me is more specific: "To put still more fear in the enemy, the entire advance-guard had to proceed with resounding music." But they have no evidence pro or con of singing of any kind at this time, and it must be remembered that Anburey is frequently inaccurate. Even so, I prefer to say that they sang.

German uniforms are depicted by Larter, FTB 9(1):13–25.

Williams 34 states that the New Hampshire regiment suffered the most casualties and quotes Joseph Bird 30.

Sewall's account is in his journal July 6.

Bird, quoted in Williams 30 and Greenleaf July 7, describes Francis's death. Where and when the colonel was killed is difficult to determine, but the following sources are useful:

Riedesel 1:116 states that he "fell while leading the third attack on the [British] left wing, and was buried by the German troops."

Greenleaf July 7: He was "at the head of our Troops" until he was shot, and that was when "our people being overpowered by Numbers was oblidg'd to retreat. . . ." This would suggest that it happened at or near the log fence or in the withdrawal to Hubbardton Brook.

Bird, quoted in Williams 30, confuses the issue, saying that the retreating rebels had "got over" the brook and brush fence. He climbed a tree and waited for the enemy to come within range. "We fought through the woods, all the way to the ridge of Pittsford mountain, popping away from behind trees."

Doblin Hille 75: when the Germans arrived, the Americans retreated "in a short time."

Anburey 1:337, 328–29: The arrival of the Germans dispersed "the enemy in all quarters." Following the Germans' arrival, "the Americans fled on all sides."

Fraser 146: This to me is the most convincing. He states that the German light troops came up, "entered into action in the handsomest manner possible, the *firing slackened immediately & ceased entirely in about six minutes after the arrival of any part of the Germans*" (my emphasis). In a way, this reflects badly on Fraser, since the Germans were able to accomplish in six minutes what his men could not. So there was no reason to include this in his letter. But Fraser was not a man for hyperbole, and this suggests that the event made an indelible impression on him. It also suggests that Francis was killed sometime during that six minutes, meaning that it almost had to be while he and the rest of his command were behind the log fence.

While Fraser gives six minutes as the duration of the battle after the Germans arrived, the Niedersächsisches Staatsarchiv letter of March 8, 1995, quotes an orderly book as saying, "The enemy was overthrown in less than 12 minutes." Six or twelve, it still seems likely that Francis fell during that interval.

Digby 212 has the description of the dead Francis.

Anburey 1:331–32 reports the shooting of Captain Shrimpton.

Walpole's comment on the alienation of Americans is in a Sept. 1, 1777, letter to Sir Horace Mann, Cunningham *Walpole Letters* vol. 6. His report of the royal jubilation is quoted in Hargrove 141.

Chapter 11
The Wolves Came Down from the Mountains

Sherwood's background appears in Crary 374.

Thompson Part III 91–92 contains a good discussion of Hubbardton, its first settlers, and the trials of the Churchill family and Uriah Hickok.

A thoroughly disgruntled New Hampshire soldier named Cogan wrote to General John Stark on July 17 describing the retreat. The letter is in Hadden Appendix 15, 486–487.

Greenleaf July 7 and 8 has his comments, and Sewall's remarks are in his diary July 7–12.

Baldwin July 7–12 records his unhappy experience following the evacuation.

Fletcher's narrative includes the story of his capture and escape. Stone's journal has a cryptic account of his imprisonment. Hadden 88, 483, and 213 describes Hale's surrender and shelter for the wounded.

The rebel custom of loading muskets with six balls is noted in Stone *Revolutionary Letters* 90.

Doblin Hille July 30 portrays the sad procession of wounded; Fraser 146 covers the burial details; and Williams Appendix I:65 has figures on casualties. Digby 246 provides the graphic description of wolves devouring corpses.

Lady Harriet Acland's efforts to reach her wounded husband are in her *Journal* xxxi and 28.

Anburey 1:340–42 notes the shortage of food for Fraser's men and the brigadier's stern warning to Hale.

Accounts of rebel prisoners at Ticonderoga are in Doblin Hille 75 and Pratorius 66–67.

Fraser 146–47 and Anburey 1:344 describe the arrival at Skenesborough.

The opinions of Balcarres and Harrington are in their testimony in *State* 29, 48.

St. Clair's decision to leave Castle Town and his disgust with the "eastern" regiments are in St. C CM 119, as is his confidence that he had done the right thing to evacuate Ticonderoga 153ff.

The slow return of soldiers to the army is mentioned in Moore 1:473.

St. Clair's letter to the president of the Vermont convention is in his *Papers* 422–24, as is his letter to Bowdoin on July 9.

The outburst of indignation over the evacuation of Ticonderoga was widespread and immediate. The unsigned attack on St. Clair appeared in the *Massachusetts Spy* July 24, and his determination to clear his name is found in St. C CM 145–46. Thomas Allen's diatribe was printed in the *Connecticut Courant* September 1. John Adams's *Familiar Letters* 292–93 has his starchy comment to his wife, and Jay's cautious letter to St. Clair was written on July 28. Support for St. Clair is in Moore 1:474, and Alexander Scammell defended the general's actions in a letter to his brother Samuel on September 21.

St. Clair's *Papers* has his letter of July 9 to Jonas Fay.

The Greenleaf diary July 9–11 and Kidder 29 depict the men's suffering from hunger and exposure.

Chapter 12
Considerable Difficulties May Be Expected

Both Hitchcock July 6 and Thacher 83 have accounts of the fugitives who traveled by boat. Allen's outrage was printed in the *Connecticut Courant* Sept. 1.

Charles Carroll 56, Morton 28, and Lossing 1:137fn describe Skenesborough and the approach from the north.

Wilkinson's *Memoirs* 1:163 has his characterization of Long.

Commodore Lutwidge's work is noted in *State* xvi–xvii.

Captain Gray's June 26 letter relates his activities.

An 1830 map by Jared Sparks locates the site of the pre–Revolutionary War fort.

Clerke regaled his friend Lord Polwarth with details of the pursuit in a letter of July 17, and Hadden's observation is in his *Journal* 89.

Hitchcock July 6 and *State* xvii cover the retreat and the chaotic scene at the dock.

Thacher 83–84 relates his experience; Gray's letter of July 14 and Ward 415 offer further details of the flight.

The burning of Skene's buildings is mentioned in Anburey 1:318, Morton 53, and *State* xvii–xviii. Wasmus 60–61, Houlting and Yates 15, and Specht 73–75 list the booty found by the Germans and British.

One of the best accounts of the fight at Fort Anne is Captain James Gray's, dated June 28 and written on the verso of the June 20 return of the 3rd New Hampshire Regiment. More information is in *State* 61 (Forbes testimony) and xix. Details on the engagement are also in Hadden 90fn, Anburey 1:349, and Ward 415–16.

Thacher 84 explains that lack of powder was why the American attack sputtered out.

Gray's story is from his account (June 28) and a letter of July 14.

Sergeant Lamb's experience is recounted in his *Journal* 143.

Burgoyne's low opinion of the Indians is from a letter to Germain, printed in *State* xx–xxi; his thanks to the army are in his Orderly Book 32–36.

Hargrove discusses Burgoyne's decision to decline the Order of the Bath 142–43. On 158 he suggests that Burgoyne turned down the knighthood because he wanted to be certain the campaign would conclude successfully, and he was then still some distance from Albany. However, the request to Lord Derby was made long before the campaign got under way and antedates the letter to Germain (July 30) cited by Hargrove.

As is so often the case, it is extremely difficult to pin down casualties with certainty. I have used figures in Williams Appendix I:65. Williams examined twenty sources and concluded that the number of killed was British-German 60, American 41; the wounded, British-German 148, American 96. Specht, who was not there, lists on 74 the British-German losses at 32 killed and 140 wounded. Mintz 152 has substantially the same numbers of wounded on both sides, but puts the British force's dead at 49 vs. the Americans' 30.

Hadden's grudging admission of the rebels' edge in the battle at Fort Anne is in his *Journal* 95.

Burgoyne's Orderly Book 29 has his admonition to the troops, telling them not to relax.

Riedesel 1:119–20 records his letter to the duke.

The neighbors' dislike of Skene is in Hadden 517. For years the story was told that Skene kept his wife's coffin in the basement, since she was, through inheritance from an uncle, to receive an annuity as long as she "remained above ground." While there is a certain morbid humor to it, Doris Morton 47 makes a convincing argument that it was not true. There was no annuity.

Burgoyne's orders to Skene are in the H. P. McCullough collection at the University of Vermont library; his letter to Dartmouth is dated July 15.

Riedesel's experience in Vermont and the germ of the plan to seize horses there appear in Riedesel 1:118–21 and *State* 105, xxii.

Excellent letters from the Germans with Riedesel in Vermont are in Stone's *Revolutionary Letters* 84–95; Specht July 14 gives a detailed summary of what they saw there.

Convincing evidence of Burgoyne's protracted stay in Skenesborough is in his Orderly Book, entries beginning July 7 and ending July 23. His tart—and hypocritical—criticism of the officers' excess baggage may be found on July 12.

Digby 212 and 227 records his pleasure over the captured mare.

Burgoyne's "Thoughts" on the coming campaign are quoted in Nickerson 83–89. The general's explanation of his decision to travel overland is in *State* 12; Digby 226–27 notes the army's opposition to the plan. Thomas Hughes 11 concurs; but Captain Money testified (*State* 40) that it would have taken as long or longer to take the Lake George route.

The German's explanation of how an army lives off the country is in Stone's *Revolutionary Letters* 97–98.

State 74 records the size of the Ticonderoga garrison, and a chart on xli reveals how many carts were needed to carry provisions for different numbers of troops, ranging from 3,375 carts to haul ninety days' supplies for an army of ten thousand down to two carts for two days' supplies for five hundred men.

"The British Occupation of Fort Ticonderoga, 1777" in FTB 8(7) discusses deteriorating morale at the post, and Doblin Hille July 14–30, is also informative.

Phillips's July 16 letter to Fraser in Atkinson 141 discusses problems at the fort. Burgoyne's comments on the "system of embarrassments" is in *State* 98, and his letter of July 11 to Germain, from the same source xix, gives his rationale for taking the overland route.

Chapter 13
The Rebels Will Chicane You

Much of the early portion of this chapter is drawn from the testimony in the court-martial of General Philip Schuyler (hereafter S CM)—a proceeding that resulted in his exoneration on all charges

The request for blankets and Schuyler's concern about the dwindling number of troops are in S CM 118, 136–39; the news of St. Clair's army, reinforcements from Peekskill, and his letters to officials in Tryon County, Cambridge, and Albany and to Seth Warner, in 150–180. His letter to Washington about desertion is on 167, his letter to Heath on 169.

Burgoyne's July 30 dispatch to Germain contains his comments on the difficulties of the march, and Schuyler's instructions to Nixon are noted in S CM 170–71. Nixon wrote to Heath on Aug. 1 telling him what was afoot. Hadden lxxxxi and 314–15 has Major General Phillips's stern comments on the use of provision carts by officers and men for their baggage, and a note that Burgoyne's personal belongings required thirty wagons.

Wasmus's encounters with snakes are in his *Journal* July 13–15.

Specht July 28–29 and Hadden Aug. 7, 18, and 19 comment on logistical problems. Stone's *Revolutionary Letters* 96 has the soldier's thoughts about weather.

Anburey's remarks are from his *Travels* 1:358–59, 364, 377–87. These statements, like many others, are identical—almost word for word—with testimony Burgoyne gave, which was printed in his *State of the Expedition from Canada*. Anburey's work was published in 1789, long after Burgoyne's defense appeared in print, and one has to wonder how much more of his book was borrowed generously from other sources.

Numerous journals deal with the rigors of the march and the suffering of the troops—among them Wasmus July 29, Digby 226, Hadden July 25–31, and a German officer's letter of Nov. 15, quoted in Mintz. Burgoyne's comment is quoted in Stanley 35.

As for the Continentals' eagerness to fight, see Thacher, writing sometime after July 17, as an example.

Samuel Adams's demand for an inquiry is in a letter to Heath on Aug. 13, in Heath *Papers*, and his attack on Schuyler is from a letter of Aug. 11 to Roger Sherman, quoted in Scheer and Rankin 257.

John Adams *Papers* 5:246–50, has letters from various critics of Schuyler and St. Clair; the ugly rumor about betrayal is in Bloodgood 65.

George Frost, writing to Josiah Bartlett and citing the opposition of New England congressmen to Schuyler, is in Bartlett's *Correspondence* 169.

The early traveler's observation on colonial differences is from Davidson 1:59.

Knox's letter (to Harry Jackson) is dated July 13.

Schuyler's realization of what he was up against is in S CM 177; his reassurance to Albany's Committee of Safety is on 181.

The size of the British fleet is noted in Flexner 2:211, and Freeman 4:436–47 *passim* traces Howe's movements. Speculation on the senior British general's destination was rampant, but as one of Josiah Bartlett's correspondents informed him, "it is soposed he dont know what to do himselfe at present," Bartlett *Correspondence* 168.

Flexner 2:210 and Brandt 124 discuss Arnold's quarrel with Congress.

Washington's assessment of Lincoln is in Scheer and Rankin 260.

The running dispute between Howe and Clinton forms a fascinating section in the latter's papers. After each discussion Clinton returned to his quarters and wrote down a comprehensive account of their talk while it was still fresh in his mind. These illuminating documents reveal the pettiness of the antagonism between the two men as well as Clinton's continuing (and justified) disagreement with his superior officer over strategy. They begin with his memorandum of July 1, written at sea, and continue in further memoranda and letters—especially to Newcastle, Percy, and Harvey—through July 13.

The statement by Lord North is in Anderson 254–55.

Francis Kinloch's letter to Johannes von Muller is dated Aug. 30.

Freeman 4:461 recounts the movements of the British fleet and Howe's landing on Aug. 25.

Mackesy *War* 126 mentions the Germain-Howe exchange.

Washington's orders to his army to proceed toward Philadelphia are in Flexner 2:212. Further information on Howe's actions and their effect on Washington's plans may be found in Anderson 274–82 *passim*, Willcox's "Too Many Cooks," Clark's "Responsibility for the Failure of the Burgoyne Campaign," and Clinton's memoranda of July 1, 6, 8, 9, and 11. Willcox says planning for the campaign of 1777 in London and New York was the worst of the war and completely indefensible. He and Jane Clark discuss the blunders and misunderstandings that led to Burgoyne's surrender at Saratoga and are essential to a study of the campaign.

Burgoyne's assumption that his goal was to "make a junction with Howe" is in a May 6 letter to Fraser, in Atkinson 139.

Vergennes's hunch that the capture of Ticonderoga guaranteed a junction of the two British armies is in a letter to the Duc de Noailles.

Howe's letter to Germain, stating his reluctance to send troops from New York to join Burgoyne, was written on Dec. 20, 1776.

Anderson 246–73 has a number of insights into the proposed relationship and the link between the armies of Howe and Burgoyne. Anderson cites in particular the lack of instructions to Howe and Howe's understanding of what he would and would not do, and refutes the argument that the general was supposed to move up the Hudson. He also describes Howe's decision to go by water 274–83. As noted, Clark and Willcox also explore this complex matter in detail.

Francis Rush Clark's encyclopedic knowledge of transport is amply evident in his *Papers* at the David Library. His fruitless effort to persuade Howe to his innovative thinking is related in a letter to John Robinson, Treasury secretary, on Sept. 14, 1778.

Burgoyne's estimate of his need for horses and carts is in Stanley 22. *State* 13–14 and xxii has more on logistics.

Chapter 14
Giving Stretch to the Indians

It is almost impossible to get an accurate count of the Indians who joined Burgoyne at Skenesborough. Wasmus states eighteen hundred; Specht gives "almost" a thousand; a German officer estimates five hundred. It was almost certainly more than five hundred, but how many more is difficult to say.

In the case of distances traveled, accurate figures are missing, and claims range from three hundred to three thousand miles. The latter is obviously much too high. I believe few, if any, Indians traveled more than a thousand miles.

Wasmus and Specht both mention the Indians in entries for July 17. Steele 115–17 has the full story of the notorious "massacre" at Fort William Henry and the capture of Putnam's rangers on 84.

Farb is an excellent source on Indian customs and fighting techniques; see especially 104. Anburey 1:169 has his description of their skill with the tomahawk.

The Burns thesis 24 and 30 discusses trade with white settlers and the Iroquois dependence on the British.

My discussion of the Iroquois nations owes much to American Heritage *Indians*, introduction and 176–93; see also Wasmus July 17 and Van Doren 209. Benjamin Franklin's 1754 Plan of Union for the colonies was patterned on the Iroquois confederation. As Peter Farb notes 109–10, Karl Marx read about the Iroquois League with keen interest while writing *Das Kapital*, and Friederich Engels, believing it the ideal society, adopted its concepts in a book that subsequently became an important source of theory in communist countries.

That portion of Burgoyne's letter of July 11 in which he criticized his Indian allies appears in Stanley 119fn. Dieskau is quoted in Parkman 1:297. Stone's *Revolutionary Letters* 91–93 has the Brunswick officer's complaint and his mention of supposed cannibalism. Burgoyne's low opinion of the Indians he brought from Canada and his high hopes for the western tribes are in *State* xxi and Stanley 26.

The nature of Indian participation in the campaign is discussed in Burns's thesis 19–23 and 34–35.

Thacher 115 and Digby 121fn describe scalping.

George III's insistence on the use of Indians is in Lunt 123, and St. Luc's advocacy of brutalization is in Burnham and Martin 94–99. Burgoyne's statement to St. Luc is in *State* 49.

Wasmus July 19–20 and 24 describes the Indian dance and the ominous consequences. Farnum's journal July 21 notes the departure of militia.

In a letter of July 28 to his father, Brockholst Livingston reported the slaughter near Fort Edward.

The Allen farm was about three-quarters of a mile northeast of the present town of South Argyle. According to the road map, this would be approximately twenty miles from Fort Anne. Re its location see Bird 75 and Holden 276. The deaths of John Allen and his family and the letter from Albany about Van Vechten are recorded in Holden 276–77.

My discussion of the murder of Jane McCrea is based on a study of the many sources—many of them contradictory or apocryphal—and on the basis of acceptable evidence I believe this account is close to the truth.

Atkinson 142 has Burgoyne's note of July 26 to Fraser. Although it is assumed by most historians that Jane McCrea's murder took place on Sunday, July 27, two pieces of evidence suggest otherwise. For one, Burgoyne's letter to Fraser was written at eight o'clock on the night of July 26. For another, Captain Benjamin Warren's diary entry for July 26 states: "They [the Indians] took two wemen out of a house, killed and scalpt them. . . ." He also notes that Van Vechten and others of his party were killed on the same date. On the 27th he states that the bodies of the lieutenant and Miss McCrea were brought into his camp ("mount Pleasant though wrongly named") and buried. Of course both men could have been mistaken about the date, but considering the sources, it is tempting to think that this is just one more mystery in what is a thoroughly baffling story.

To complicate matters, Lieutenant Digby writes 235–39 that the army left Skenesborough on July 24 and reached Fort Anne two days later—i.e., on the 26th. "In the evening," he goes on, "our Indians brought in two scalps, one of them an officer's which they danced about in their usual manner." That would seem to confirm the July 26 date, but he does not mention that the other was a woman's scalp, and it seems likely that he would have remarked on hair as long as Miss McCrea's. Elsewhere he notes "the melancholy catastrophe" of the young woman.

Finally, Napier states that Burgoyne "held a private Congress with the Indian chiefs and reprimanded them in very severe terms for their late behaviour, one of the Ottawas having the Evening before scalped a young Girl." This is Napier's journal entry for July 27, which would seem to confirm Burgoyne's July 26 letter to Fraser saying he would meet with the Indians the following day.

Stanley July 27 and *State* 49 record Burgoyne's unsatisfactory meeting with the Indians, and Anburey's thoughts on the matter are in his journal 1:371.

Brockholst Livingston's July 28 letter and Lincoln 15 mention the effect Miss McCrea's death had on recruiting. How much influence is a matter of some disagreement among historians, owing to the scarcity of evidence; my own opinion is that there is every reason to believe (as Livingston and Lincoln did) that it had a very considerable effect.

Schuyler's concern about public panic is in a letter of July 28, S CM 181, and Scheer and Rankin 260 quotes the paymaster on the effectiveness of Indians.

Warren's note about the "smart engagement" is in his journal July 29, and the butchery by Indians is reported in Wasmus July 30, Hitchcock July 29 and Aug. 1–2, Farnum 1–2, and Napier 307–8.

Yet another account of an Indian raid and its aftermath is in Bloodgood 65–84.

Hitchcock and Farnum July 30, Warren July 21–Aug. 16, Pell 10, and Napier 3–7 provide numerous details on the retreat.

Samuel Smith's letter to his wife is dated Aug. 5.

Schuyler's complaint about militia is in a dispatch to Washington on Aug. 4, and Glover's letters of July 28 and Aug. 6 convey his misgivings.

Hadden 29 and Specht Aug. 5 reflect the elation of the king's troops at emerging from the woods and reaching the Hudson. Burgoyne's confident letter to Germain was written July 30.

The Foreign Affairs Committee's letter of Aug. 8 to M. Dumas reflects Congressional concern.

Burgoyne's annoyance with his auxiliary forces—loyalists and Canadians alike—is in *State* 101–2 and xxv; the same source 74 has Kingston's disgusted comment.

The Indians' disapproval of Burgoyne and their decision to leave is in Specht Aug. 5 and *State* 99–101. On xxv–xxvii of the latter source is Howe's letter to Burgoyne.

The strain on the British supply line and growing desertions are noted in Burgoyne's Orderly Book for Aug. 5–6.

Chapter 15
The Dismal Place of Bennington

An especially useful study on the battle of Bennington, emphasizing the role of John Stark, is that by Herbert D. Foster and Thomas W.

Streeter. The authors relied on contemporary sources available in 1905, and their appendices are very helpful. One is a calendar of documents, chiefly relating to Stark; this is followed by a select bibliography of the battle and campaign, listing contemporary and more recent sources, maps, and a table showing daily positions and movements of the various forces involved.

One account to be avoided is the narrative by one "Glich, a German officer who was in the Engagement, under Col. Baum." Printed in *Collections of the Vermont Historical Society* 1:211, in 1870, this is a spurious document—a work of fiction by George Robert Gleig published in *Tales of Military Life*, 2nd series, Philadelphia 1833.

Two outstanding modern studies are a graduate seminar paper by Lion Miles, which contains much new material, and Philip Lord's richly illustrated *War over Walloomscoick*.

Preliminaries to John Stark's assumption of command of the New Hampshire troops, Speaker Langdon's role, Stark's correspondence during this period, the march to Manchester, and the contretemps with Lincoln and Schuyler are in Foster and Streeter 24–59.

Nickerson 225–26 describes Stark and his service in the French and Indian War.

My *Decisive Day* 143–81 *passim* has details on Stark's performance at the battle of Bunker Hill.

Thomas Mellen's account is in Butler and Houghton.

Peter Clark's Aug. 6 letter has an addendum of Aug. 7.

In Thomas Hughes's journal Sept. 25, he calls Bennington "the metropolis of . . . Vermont."

Wasmus's account of the Bennington campaign, which is one of the best, begins on Aug. 9–10 at Fort Edward, in the shadow of the Duer house.

The Acland Journal 28–29 accounts for Lady Harriet's presence at Fort Edward. Baroness Riedesel's *Journal* 42–45 has more of the same, and 55–56 register her disgust with Burgoyne's carousing.

Specht Aug. 14 describes Baum's departure.

A good, brief narrative of Baum's fateful expedition appears in Manuscript No. 6.16/22c in the House of Lords Record Office, bearing the note "In Baron de Reidesel's [*sic*—dispatch?] of 28th August 1777." Baum had orders to take 506 troops on the mission, including 150 dragoons and 50 of Fraser's men, plus Peters's corps, provincials, Canadian volunteers, and Indians. But some of these men were on other duty, he was given 100 additional Germans, and he picked up loyalists on his march to Bennington, so the total number is difficult to judge. Riedesel 1:262–63 has a figure of 656 for Baum's force, to which must be added 14 Hesse-Hanau artillery. Miles 12–14 gives 775, including artillery. Both figures also include 150 loyalists with Peters, but Miles lists also the following: Sherwood, 75; Covel, 25; Anderson, 64; Cameron, 30–40; Ruiter, 45–60; and Pfister, 150. This makes some 389 to 414 Tories, which I have rounded off at 400, making the total 1,175 or more—rounded to 1,200.

Wasmus Aug. 9–14, Specht Aug. 9, and Miles 12–14 discuss the composition of Baum's force.

In *State* xxxi, Burgoyne speaks of his hope to send a detachment eastward, and Riedesel 1:247 gives his reasons for recommending a strike into Vermont.

Riedesel 2:260–64 and "Instructions for Lieut. Col. Baum" contain that officer's orders.

State 105 explains what was in Burgoyne's mind, and Riedesel 1:248–49, elaborates on that. The latter source 263–64 covers Burgoyne's decision to have Baum go to Bennington, and *State* 107 gives his justification for it.

Riedesel 1:238 has his letter of Aug. 8 to the duke.

Information about Baum and his three English aides is in Wasmus 38fn and Riedesel 1:262–63.

Bense's journal Aug. 9 records the dragoons' destination; Hadden 132–33 describes those men's encumbrances.

Baum's letter of Aug. 13 to Burgoyne is in *State* xxxviii.

The description of Stark's command is drawn from Moore's *Stark* 41, Wasmus Aug. 16, and Commager and Morris 568–69.

Miles 9–13 accounts for Stark's reinforcements. Stark's Aug. 13 letters to Schuyler are in the Hall Parke McCullough papers, as is the muster roll of Warner's command 134.

Wasmus records the Indians' action on Aug. 14. Baum's letter to Burgoyne on the same date is in *State* xxxix.

Moore's *Stark* 126–27 and Stark's Aug. 22 letter to Gates, in Commager and Morris 572, depict the initial contact between Stark and Baum.

Baum's request for reinforcements is mentioned in *State* 50 and Miles 17.

Wasmus's observations on rebel sniping against their dispirited Indians are in his *Journal* Aug. 15. Lord 9 and Miles 18–19 describe the defenses and posting of Baum's men.

Burgoyne's Aug. 14 dispatch to Baum is in *State* xliii, and Riedesel 1:264 mentions the baron's concerns about the coming operation.

Burgoyne's selection of Breymann is discussed in *State* 50, Cleve's journal 84 (quoted in Miles 17), Riedesel 1:264, and Nickerson 118 and 144.

Riedesel 1:256–57 has Breymann's apologia; Skene mentions his message from Breymann in an Aug. 30 letter to Dartmouth.

Wasmus Aug. 15–16 is informative on the calm before the battle and the technique of the concealed rebel snipers.

Moore's *Stark* 58 quotes the general's reply to Pastor Allen.

Sally Kellogg told her story in 1850 when, as Mrs. Sally Markham, she applied for a pension based on the Revolutionary War service of her father and husband.

Miles 20–21 discusses Stark's plan of attack.

Chapter 16
A Continual Clap of Thunder

Several accounts used in this chapter—those of Jesse Field, Jacob Safford, Solomon Safford, Isaac Tichenor, Silas Walbridge, and John Wallace—are in the Hall Park McCullough papers and bear a note written by Governor Hiland Hall: "Statement of Men who were in the Battle of Bennington, taken & written from their lips in 1833 & prior to that by Hiland Hall." Although they were recorded long after the events, I have used those portions that could be checked against other sources or that rang true in a particular context.

David Holbrook's narrative appears in Dann 87–91; Mellen's story is in Butler and Houghton.

Beginning with the picture of Meiborn's scouts hotfooting it for the redoubt, Surgeon Wasmus once again is an invaluable eyewitness and recorder of the facts. All but one of the references from his journal are from Aug. 16.

Simon Walbridge describes Herrick's sudden attack from the woods. Stark's comment comes from an Aug. 23 letter to Gates, in Moore's *Stark*, 129–32. The statement that the dragoons fired by platoons is from Mellen, in Butler and Houghton 27.

Wasmus depicts the German flight from the redoubt and Jesse Field tells of the rebel pursuit.

Peter Clark, writing to his wife, Aug. 18, 1777, says this phase of the battle lasted a half hour, and I am inclined to take his word for it. He was writing the day after the battle, whereas most other statements concerning the time were made long afterward and ranged from two to five minutes to thirty minutes. (See Jesse Field, Solomon Safford, and Simon Walbridge statements.) Whatever the truth, the fight was a brief one.

Mellen and Wasmus speak of the Indians' exodus.

Riedesel 1:302 mentions Captain Dommes's position.

Peters's lengthy story of his experiences with Burgoyne's army—including the engagement near Bennington—appeared in the Toronto *Daily Globe*, July 16, 1877.

Stafford told his story to his son, who reported it to Theodore Dwight, who sent it to William L. Stone, a dedicated early historian of the Burgoyne campaign. It appears in Riedesel 1:299ff. That account is followed 302ff by that of "one who was in the Tory Fort," the erstwhile friend of Stafford.

Moore 1:482 has the story of Thomas Allen.

Casualties are reported by Wasmus and Miles 23.

The final moments of Baum's defense are detailed in Stone's *Revolutionary Letters* 100–1, by a fellow Brunswick officer.

Wasmus and Miles 25 mention Baum's wound and capture, and the former speaks of the loyalist prisoners and Baum's farewell.

Baum's letter of Aug. 14 to Burgoyne is in *State* xxxix.

Clerke to Breymann, undated, is in Riedesel 1:259.

Breymann's own account is available in Manuscript No. 6.16/22b from the House of Lords Record Office, and although brief, it provides an admirable summary of the engagement from the vantage of the Brunswick officer. According to Breymann, he was camped seven miles the other side of Cambridge; from Cambridge to Sancoick is seven miles. Thus it took him eleven and a half hours to march fourteen miles.

Campbell's insistence that he informed Breymann of the situation is noted in Miles 28.

Skene wrote of his experiences to Dartmouth on Aug. 30; Breymann's actions are in Riedesel 1:257–58 and Miles 28–29.

The condition of Stark's militia is noted in Dann 89–90.

Boardman 200–1 records Warner's encounter with Rand. Simon Walbridge speaks of the confusion on the battlefield, while Holbrook in Dann 91, Miles 30, and Boardman describe Rand's actions.

Parson Allen's story of his exploits appeared in the *Connecticut Courant* Aug. 25.

Stark's reports are in a letter of Aug. 18 to the Council of New Hampshire and his Aug. 22 dispatch to Gates.

Skene tells his story in the letter of Aug. 30 to Dartmouth; Breymann in his report to Riedesel 1:258.

I have estimated Burgoyne's entire force at 7,000. Casualty figures for both sides at Bennington are anything but consistent. Stark put enemy losses as 960 killed and captured, then as 991. Lincoln states them as 890, and several American journals say 936, and this seems to have been the figure circulated among the troops. The closest one can come to American losses is twenty to thirty dead and forty wounded.

Hille's *Journal* Aug. 12 notes the change of commanders at Ticonderoga.

Peter Clark's Aug. 29 letter mentions the unburied dead.

Specht Aug. 14–19 and Stone's *Revolutionary Letters* 109 have details on the wounded Germans.

Bense Aug. 15–21 relates his story; and Hadden 474 indicates the gravity of the loss of Fraser's men.

Burgoyne's final, unhappy meeting with the Indians is related in Digby 254–55 and Specht Aug. 19–20.

Hadden 132 and 136 has his comments on Skene and Breymann.

Kingston in *State* 76 repeats Fraser's remark about Germans.

Riedesel 1:249 and 272 and *State* provide insights into the two generals' post-battle thoughts.

The scarcity of wagons and the intense heat are subjects of a letter in Stone's *Revolutionary Letters* 110.

Sally Kellogg's memory of that night are in her account.

Butler and Houghton 23 tell of the Williamstown families, and of Thomas Mellen 29.

The Lawrence family's experiences are in "Smith Family of Addison County, Vt.," folder in Bennington Museum. Mrs. Lawrence's first husband was a Smith, and her story was handed down from one generation to the next. Excerpts from Wallace's diary were published in the Bennington *Banner* on Aug. 20, 1930.

Wasmus's descriptive journal for Aug. 16–19 is excellent on the aftermath of the engagement, and the introduction to this volume xi–xx has an account of his captivity and final release.

Hadden's *Journal* 130–31 records Stark's reward; Butler and Houghton 23 quotes his advertisement.

Chapter 17
The Moment Is Decisive

American comments on Bennington are from Clarkson's letter to Susan Livingston Sept. 11, Wilkinson to St. Clair Sept. 7, and Gates to Hancock Sept. 3.

Riedesel's remarks are in an Aug. 28 letter to the hereditary prince of Brunswick and another, undated, but of approximately the same time, to the Duke of Brunswick.

Hughes's observation is in his *Journal* 12.

Burgoyne's worries are evident in his Aug. 20 dispatch to Germain in *State* xxi–xxiv, as is his clear intention to implicate Howe.

Petersham's statement is in *State* 51.

In his Orderly Book Aug. 26, Burgoyne urges speed.

Napier Aug. 29 reports on intelligence from the Indians.

Figures on the garrison at Stanwix are from Ward 482, and Herkimer's action is described in the same source 482–88 and in Nickerson 269. The latter 269–70 and Boatner 962 discuss Willett's raid.

Schuyler's knowledge of what was happening in the west is in his letter of Aug. 8 to Congress, S CM 185.

James Flexner's "How a Madman Helped Save the Colonies" is a good account of Hon Yost's role in St. Leger's withdrawal.

St. Leger's report to Burgoyne is quoted in Brandt 128.

The locations of Burgoyne's headquarters can be followed in his Orderly Book July 30–Sept. 10.

Folsom's letter is in Bartlett *Papers* 168–69.

Gerlach 286–87 and 296 has Duer's notes to Schuyler.

Freeman 4:465 discusses Gates's appointment.

Schuyler's withdrawal to the Sprouts is recounted in Gerlach 300, and the same source has Greene's candid remark about Gates.

Scheer and Rankin 272 notes Gates's snubs of Schuyler.

Baldwin Aug. 16–19 and Warren Aug. 16 discuss the expedition to Stillwater.

Weather is a frequent topic in journals, and those of Hitchcock and Wild are useful examples for this period.

Fitzpatrick's *Writings* 131 contains the Aug. 25 letter to Colonel George Baylor, to which Robert Hanson Harrison appended a postscript.

Discipline in Burgoyne's army is mentioned in Stone *Revolutionary Letters* 98 and 195, Specht Aug. 11, and the general's Orderly Book Aug. 1–Sept. 12.

Clerke's jaunty message to Lord Polwarth is dated Sept. 10.

Communiqués from Burgoyne to the baron were written on Aug. 25, 26, and 31 and Sept. 10 and are printed in Riedesel 1:272–76.

State xlvii has Burgoyne's Oct. 20 dispatch to Germain.

Stanley Sept. 13 notes that communication with Canada was severed.

Baroness Riedesel's *Journal* 47 and Hadden lxxxi mention the entourage accompanying the army, and the transport of supplies to Dovegat appears in Burgoyne's Orderly Book Sept. 12–17, Stone's *Burgoyne's Campaign* 37fn, Neilson 132, and Lossing 1:71.

Stanley Sept. 14 reports the failure to locate the rebel army.

Lady Harriet's *Journal* Sept. 15 speaks of the fire in their tent.

Orders to the army to be ready for action are in Burgoyne's Orderly Book Sept. 14–16.

The illicit foraging expedition is mentioned in Stanley 144 and Burgoyne's Orderly Book Sept. 18.

Scammell's letter to his brother was written on Sept. 21.

Baldwin's account of his trip to Albany and the purchase of lottery tickets is in his *Journal* Aug. 14 and 27 and Sept. 2, 7, and 17.

Glover's observations are in a letter to Jonathan Glover and Azor Orne on Sept. 5.

Mintz 180–82 notes Gates's request for troops and what he found on his arrival.

Holden 288 cites Washington's comments on Morgan.

The Indian attack on the 3rd New Hampshire is reported by Dearborn Sept. 4.

Material on Morgan is drawn from my "Men of the Revolution" series, no.16, in *American Heritage*, Feb. 1976; Robert Alberts's "Braddock's Alumni," in *American Heritage*, Feb. 1961; and Kenneth Roberts's *The Battle of Cowpens* 101.

Praise for Gates's impact on morale is in Mintz 181, quoting a letter from Nixon; Dearborn Aug. 19; and Henry Brockholst Livingston to his sister Sept. 14. Timothy Bigelow's comments are in a letter to Stephen Salisbury Oct. 7.

Benjamin Warren Sept. 10 and 14 mentions the activities in and around Stillwater. Neilson 114 notes the advice given by local people to move to Bemis Heights.

Lossing 1:45 describes Bemis Heights, as do Neilson 116 and Nickerson 300–1.

Gates's letter to the chairman of the Committee of Safety in Berkshire County (and others) was dated Sept. 17.

Chapter 18
We Had Something More at Stake

The most authentic portrait of Arnold is the drawing by Simitière, reproduced in this volume. His career is described in Clare Brandt's splendid biography, *Man in the Mirror*. Further information is in Scheer and Rankin 47–48 and 114, Boatner 23–27, and Nickerson 182.

Livingston reported developments to his sister on Sept. 14, as did Clarkson on Aug. 5, 10, and 22 and Sept. 11.

Varick is quoted in Mintz 184, Wilkinson in Scheer and Rankin 279.

On relations between Gates and Arnold, see Brandt 129–31, Scheer and Rankin 279, and Mintz 183–84. The series of letters between the two men tell the story supremely well.

Hitchcock Sept. 17 mentions Hemenway's assault.

Nickerson 302 and Mintz 190 discuss the affair of Stark's command. Baldwin Sept. 12 and 14 speaks of New Hampshire troops arriving in camp; also in Kidder 33, Blake says 700 or 800 militia came in from Bennington on Sept. 11. The new men are mentioned in Josiah Barlett's *Correspondence*—letter of Sept. 22 to William Whipple.

Neilson's homestead is described in a brochure from the Saratoga National Historical Park. American defenses and the environs are also depicted in Wilkinson *Memoirs* 1:235–36, Lossing 45–49 and 52fn, Neilson 116–17 and 282–85, Stone's *Burgoyne's Campaign* 323–24, and Stone *Saratoga Battle-Grounds* 192ff.

Lossing 51 and Nickerson 306–7 note the early-morning sighting of British troops on the move.

Stanley Sept. 18 mentions rebel deserters providing Burgoyne with information. Thomas Hughes, who was one of those captured in a raid by John Brown, was passing through Bennington on Sept. 25 with his fellow prisoners when he heard that "the lion is caught in the net."

The Acland Journal and Specht, both Sept. 19, list troop deployments. See also Anburey 1:410 and Mintz 189–90.

Stanley Sept. 19 has an excellent description of the battle on that date.

A footnote in Hadden 162 describes Major Forbes.

State xlvii and xlviii has Burgoyne's dispatch to Germain summarizing his plan of attack. Specht Sept. 19 is also good.

The American situation is depicted in the Hitchcock, Wild, and Warren journals Sept. 19, Glover's letter to Jonathan Glover and Azor Orne Sept. 21, and Clarkson to Susan Livingston Sept. 21. The clash between Morgan's men and the British line is in Brandow 126.

Wilkinson's vivid picture of Morgan is quoted in Scheer and Rankin 275. Pell 10 notes the capture of Van Swearingin and his men.

Hadden's first shot is recorded in his *Journal* 163; a brief sketch of Kingston is in Digby 305fn.

Captain Monin's death and the presence of his son are mentioned in Stone's *Revolutionary Letters* 116.

Scammell told about his part in the action in a letter of Sept. 21 to his brother, and in another to Jonathan Chadbourn, Sept. 26.

As for the time of the battle, American letters and journals generally indicate that it began about 1:00 or 1:30 P.M. and that the fight lasted anywhere between fifteen to forty-five minutes. Baldwin states that it began at 1:00 and lasted forty-five minutes. Hitchcock says it started at 1:30 and lasted for thirty minutes. I am inclined to take their word for it, since Baldwin, an engineer, was a bystander in the battle and Hitchcock, a minister, was certainly not engaged. In addition, both men had watches.

Glover's assessment of the ferocity of the fighting is in his letter to Jonathan Glover and Azor Orne Sept. 21.

Poor's letter is quoted in Moore 1:497–98. Poor stated that Scammell was wounded and helped off the field, but this is questionable. Scammell himself mentioned in letters to his brother and friends that musket balls had torn holes in his clothing and hit the breech of his gun, but said nothing about a wound. Scammell's justifiable pride in his men was expressed in his Sept. 26 letter to Jonathan Chadbourn.

Poor's description of Arnold, which is in the Jared Sparks Collection at the Widener Library, is quoted by Mintz 194. Arnold had a genius for inspiring controversy, and to this day the extent of his activity in the battle of Sept. 19 is unclear. As John Luzader points out in his comprehensive study of primary sources on this question, he was not persuaded that Arnold "personally led his division against Burgoyne during the First Battle of Saratoga. He may, possibly, have been near the firing line during a part of the battle, although the preponderance of evidence indicates the contrary, and it is certain that he was in the camp at Bemis Heights during a part of the action." Most convincing to me is the evidence offered by Arnold himself. In a letter to Gates written on Sept. 22, he notes that he was ordered to *send out* Morgan and Dearborn, with support, and before the action was over "I found it necessary to *send out* the whole of my Division to Support the attack . . ." (my emphasis). Arnold was not the man to hide his light under a bushel, and I feel certain that if he had been in the middle of the action he would have said so.

Although the quotation in the text describing Arnold's reckless behavior comes from Enoch Poor, Poor goes on to say that he did not see Arnold himself, that his information came from another.

Luzader concludes that the American success in stopping Burgoyne on this day was "due, in large part, to [Arnold's] skillful efforts," but that he was functioning "in the normal capacity of a division commander"—that is, carrying out tactically Gates's strategy. While that is true enough, it is also worth remembering that Arnold had a good deal to do with creating that strategy.

In a letter to Hancock on Sept. 22 Gates reported that Burgoyne had been wounded in the shoulder.

William Hull's recollections of his service in the Revolution were written sometime after the war and were pulled together by his daughter, Maria Hull Campbell, after his death. Even though they were compiled in an effort to salvage his reputation after he was cashiered following his defeats in the War of 1812, they have the ring of authenticity, and certainly there is no doubting Hull's courage and energetic leadership from 1775 until 1784. The events in this chapter are described in his *Life* 92–98.

Hadden xli–xliii and 163–66 tells of his narrow escape and the fortuitous arrival of the 20th Regiment. Stanley gives Phillips high praise for his bravery.

Lamb is quoted in Mintz 195; Digby's praise for Burgoyne is in his *Journal* 274.

Anbury 1:414 describes the shooting of Lieutenant Don; Warren's comment is in his diary 212.

Riedesel's timely arrival is in Specht Sept. 19, Riedesel 1:204fn, and Nickerson 313–15.

Mintz 196 lists British casualties.

Burgoyne's note to Powell is quoted in Nickerson 316–17.

Anbury's appreciation of the rebel achievement is in 1:417.

Joshua Pell is quoted in FTB 1(6):11.

Digby 273 admits what the "victory" cost the British, and Anbury 1:416 praises the Americans.

Glover's letter to his brother and Orne contains his comment; Dearborn's *Journal* Sept. 19 includes his.

Baroness von Riedesel tells of her harrowing experience in her *Journal* 48–50; Anbury 1:426–27 mentions the wounded.

Digby 274, Specht Sept. 19, and Anbury 1:421–22 testify to the suffering of the wounded and the task of burying the dead. Comments about rebel casualties are in Kidder 35, Glover 102, and Mintz 196. For rebel field hospitals see David xxiv–xxvii. Thacher's remarks are in his *Military Journal* 112–14.

Enos Hitchcock's diary Sept. 19 expresses his uncertainty about victory.

Chapter 19
I Will Make a Push in About Ten Days

Scammell's letter of Sept. 22 to Mrs. Andrew Colburn is in the Lemuel Shaw papers at the Massachusetts Historical Society.

John Francis wrote his sister-in-law on Oct. 1.

Specht Sept. 19 states his belief that the Brunswickers were capable of fighting their way into the rebel camp.

Digby Sept. 21 notes the arrival of a message from Clinton.

Clinton's "dumbbell code" is described in *American Heritage*, April 1959, and the message, dated Sept. 12, is in the Clinton *Papers*.

Nickerson 341 notes that it took the transports three months to cross the Atlantic.

Digby mentions the *feu de joie* Sept. 21 and comments on the inaction Sept. 29.

Lincoln summarized his operation in a letter to John Laurens on Feb. 5, 1781.

The Arnold-Brown feud is discussed in "John Brown's Attack, Sept. 18, 1777" in FTB 1(1).

Several letters from Brown are important documents on the raid: to Lincoln Sept. 18; to Gates Sept. 18; to Johnson Sept. 18; and to General —— Oct. 4. Also valuable are FTB 1(1), Thomas Hughes's journal Sept. 18, and Samuel Johnson to his wife Oct. 2.

Brigadier Powell's testy reply to Brown was Sept. 18.

Brown's reception at Diamond Island is described in his Oct. 4 letter to General ——.

Specht Oct. 2 cites Burgoyne's dismay over Brown's raid.

Snell's "Report on the Left Wing . . ." and "Report on the Balcarres and Breymann Redoubts" are extremely valuable descriptions of Burgoyne's defensive works. Specht Sept. 28 mentions the clear-cutting of trees. See also maps in Nickerson, Lossing, Lunt, Brandt.

Bense Sept. 20 complains about the lack of essentials.

Farnum Oct. 1 reports on the troops arriving in camp.

Lady Harriet's *Journal* Sept. 20 has her observations.

Starving horses are mentioned in Digby Sept. 28, and Specht Oct. 4 tells how difficult it was to protect foragers.

State 124 includes Burgoyne's notation on his overworked officers; his Orderly Book 127 and Specht's *Journal* Sept. 28 speak of precautions taken to protect pickets.

Boardman Sept. 2 and Oct. 6 tell of deserters and prisoners coming into the rebel lines, and the fate of the Tory.

The British army's suffering is recorded in Hadden 325–26, Digby Oct. 4, and Stone's *Revolutionary Letters* 119.

Events from Oct. 3 to 6 are well described in Specht's *Journal*.

Burgoyne's appeal to Clinton is dated Sept. 21.

The incident of the silver ball and the unfortunate messenger is in Scheer and Rankin 278.

The Clinton *Papers* include the letters and messages between Burgoyne and Clinton between Sept. 10 and Oct. 23. The fullest account of Clinton's strike against the Highlands appears in Nickerson 341–53. General George Clinton's account of the episode appears in *Quarterly Journal of the New York State Historical Association* 12(2) (April 1931).

The quotation from Sir Henry Clinton about Howe's decision to abandon the Highlands is in Mackesy *War* 144.

Arnold's request to return to Washington's army was made on Sept. 22. Gates's dispatch to Hancock, Arnold's next letter to Gates, and the general's reply were all written on Sept. 23.

On Sept. 22 Gates wrote his wife, saying this would be his final campaign.

Specht Oct. 7 reports Riedesel's objection to Burgoyne's plan of attack.

Burgoyne's shocked realization that his campaign had been no more than a diversion is in *State* xlvii, in a letter to Germain. The same dispatch includes his revised plan to make a reconnaissance in force. For a further discussion of this see Nickerson 356–59.

Chapter 20
They Poured Down Like a Torrent from the Hill

The deserter was an artilleryman, according to Digby 287.

Wilkinson's Oct. 7 letter to St. Clair is in the latter's *Papers* 444.

Baroness Riedesel paints a vivid picture of that morning in her *Journal* 48–51.

Major Williams is discussed in Digby Oct. 7 and in Stone's *Revolutionary Letters* 121.

The number of Captain Fraser's rangers and Indians is from Snell "Report on the Strength of the British Army ..." 99, and Burgoyne's instructions are in *State* 1.

Specht Oct. 7 indicates that Burgoyne's three senior generals were the only ones in on the mission's purpose.

As for the number of troops: Burgoyne, in his Oct. 20 letter to Germain, *State* 1, gives 1,500 for the main body; Specht 89 and Anburey 435 have the same number; Napier 321 says 1,400; Pell 12 says 1,700. I have chosen to follow Snell 99, which gives a total of 1,723, plus general staff and a few Indians. Pell 12 describes the disposition of the three elements; also see Specht 90, Lunt 242.

Comments on the "miserable position" are in Riedesel 1:205, Pell 12, and Lunt 244.

Wilkinson's scouting mission and Gates's orders for Morgan are quoted in Scheer and Rankin 280. That volume 281 has a quotation from Colonel John Brooks, who was with Gates and his officers at the table on this occasion.

Stone, quoting Ebenezer Mattoon in his *Campaign of General John Burgoyne* 371–72, has the angry exchange between Gates and Arnold.

The deployment of rebel troops is given in Ward 526.

Ephraim Squier's diary contains some interesting observations of the battles of September 19 and October 7, along with their aftermath. He was thirty years old at the time and lived to the age of ninety-four.

Snell's work on the British army 98 and Gates's army 19–20 make clear the disparity in numbers, and Stanley 159 has figures on British strength.

Several accounts of the battle are very helpful, among them Stanley 159–60, Digby 287, Pausch quoted in Mintz 209, and Wilkinson in Commager and Morris in *Spirit of 'Seventy-Six* 593.

Snell, in his estimates of Gates's army 19, gives Ten Broek's strength.

Kidder 22–24 has the story of Colonel Cilley's actions.

Wilkinson's account of rescuing Acland is printed in Commager and Morris 592. Anburey 1:445 has a somewhat different version of the incident, including the statement that Acland offered retreating British soldiers fifty guineas to carry him to safety.

The breakthrough by Morgan's and Dearborn's commands is in Dearborn's *Journals* 108, his letter to Wilkinson 7–8, and Wilkinson in Commager and Morris 592.

Arnold's wild exodus from camp is related by Woodruff in Dann 102, and Mintz 209 describes him meeting his Connecticut friends.

The characterization of Arnold as a madman is by Woodruff in Stone *Burgoyne's Campaign* 325.

The attack on Speth's troops is related in Specht 90–91, Ebenezer Mattoon's Oct. 7, 1835, letter to General Philip Schuyler (Jr.) in Commager and Morris 594–95, and Ward 528–29.

State 125 mentions Burgoyne's narrow escapes.

The shooting of Fraser is told by Woodruff in Neilson 254–257, *State* 125, Stone *Burgoyne's Campaign* 249, and Ward 2:529. Anburey 1:439–40 states that the shot that wounded Fraser entered his chest and came out near his backbone. However, this does not jibe with the account by Baroness Riedesel.

How Fraser's loss affected the outcome is in Digby 288.

Anburey's account of Fraser's condition is in his *Journal* 1:439–40.

Pausch's heroic action is recounted in his *Journal* 166–72.

The entry in Warren's diary is on 215; casualties are in Snell *Gates's Army* 69; and Specht Oct. 7 notes Breymann's death. Enos Hitchcock Oct. 8 speaks of scavengers.

Arnold's act of clemency is in Lunt 248, Nickerson 366–67, and Ward 529–30.

Woodruff in Dann 103 tells how Arnold was carried to the field hospital and discusses his own work as a Good Samaritan during the night.

Snell's paper on the British army has casualty figures; Thacher estimates the rebel losses.

The last moments of the fight are noted in Anburey 1:441–46 and Specht 91.

Baroness Riedesel's *Journal* 52 has the account of Lady Harriet and the firing of the baroness's new house; Anburey 1:448 mentions his sense that the rebels were reluctant to continue; *State* 125 is helpful; and Major William Hull, quoted in Mintz 214, speaks of Gates playing a waiting game.

Fraser's funeral is described in Anburey 1:448–49 and *State* 55, 82, and 126.

Wilkinson's memoirs 269–70 relate the Gates-Clerke exchange.

Details on Burgoyne's decision to retreat—and the timing of that maneuver—are in Baroness Riedesel's *Journal* 53, *State* 126, and Gates's letter to Hancock Oct. 12.

Chapter 21
All Remains Still Like Sunday

Baroness Riedesel's *Journal* is a prime source of information on the retreat to Saratoga and subsequent events there. Harnage's warnings, her disbelief at Burgoyne's delays, the maid's hysteria, and her talk with Lady Harriet appear on 53–55.

Specht Oct. 8 also expresses dismay over the delay; Burgoyne explains his reasons in *State* 126. The same source 123 has his complaint about lack of intelligence about the enemy.

Bense Oct. 9 provides a vivid picture of the troops' misery on the retreat.

Hadden xlix and *State* 128–29 note the circumstances of Lady Harriet's departure, and Burgoyne's Oct. 9 letter to Gates explains why she was permitted to leave. More details about her remarkable journey are in Dearborn's long letter to Wilkinson Dec. 15, 1815, and the Acland *Journal* 32–33 relates the couple's experience in Albany and New York.

The baroness's conversation with Phillips appears in her *Journal* 55–56.

Pell 14 notes the position taken by Fellows's men.

Blake's journal for Oct. 8 is in Kidder 37, and Warren 216 has more on Gates's leisurely pursuit.

A sketch of Sutherland appears in Hadden 556. His assignment is covered in Stanley 164; see also Specht Oct. 10. Information about the burning of Schuyler's buildings is in Major Kingston's memorandum of a message from Burgoyne to Gates.

Benjamin Warren 216 comments on the men and equipment left behind in Burgoyne's retreat.

The episode of the British outpost under fire by Morgan's riflemen is detailed in the Nov. 17, 1777, entry of "Letters of a British Army Officer . . ." in the manuscript collections of the New England Historic Genealogical Society.

Glover 103–4 has the account of what was nearly a costly error by Gates.

Specht Oct. 11 mentions Sutherland's outburst.

Baroness Riedesel 57 discusses her appeal to Petersham.

Descriptions of the artillery barrage and its effects are in Stanley 164–65 and Lamb 166, quoted in Ward 535.

The shortage of water is mentioned in "Letters of a British Officer . . ." Nov. 17. The baroness's experiences in the cellar of a house are in her *Journal* 57–62.

Ward 534–35 tells of General Riedesel's frustrated attempt to break out of the trap, and the baron's remarks are in Riedesel 1:174.

The incident of the nursing foal that had to be destroyed is in "Letters of a British Officer . . ." Nov. 17.

Burgoyne's council of war is recorded in Specht Oct. 13. The letter from Burgoyne to Gates was dated Oct. 13; the response came the same day.

Oliver Boardman's journal Oct. 12–16 recounts some of the rumors that spread through camp and reports on the exchanges of letters between Gates and Burgoyne.

Nickerson 105 describes the meeting between Gates and Kingston. The letter carried by Kingston from Burgoyne was dated Oct. 14; Gates's astonishing reply bore the same date.

Mintz 221 and Nickerson 387–89 state that Gates was bluffing and discuss the rancorous exchange of notes. Specht Oct. 14 has further details and Burgoyne to Gates Oct. 14 has the former's rejection of terms.

Disagreements between Germans and British are mentioned in Riedesel 1:183–84, *State* 83 and lx, and Pell in FTB 1(6):14.

Burgoyne's own terms are in a letter of Oct. 14, which bears Gates's marginal comments. The next day he wrote again, saying more time was needed for discussion. On the same date Craig sent a note to Wilkinson stating the desire to change "capitulation" to "convention."

The final exchanges of letters between the two commanders in chief occurred on Oct. 16, when Gates issued his ultimatum.

Wilkinson's account of his meeting with the British general is in his *Memoirs* 1:311–16.

The last council of Burgoyne's officers is described by Specht Oct. 16; extracts from the proceedings are in *State* lx.

Chapter 22
The King Fell into Agonies

Wild's journal Oct. 17 describes the weather.

Digby 317–19 depicts the pitiful condition of the horses and speaks of Burgoyne's emotional remarks to his officers.

Riedesel 1:187–88 tells how the regimental flags were saved.

The breakup of the advance corps is mentioned by Napier 324.

Lamb's *Journal* 183 has his flattering comments on Burgoyne.

The march of the regiments toward the river and his own feelings on the occasion are described by Digby 317–21.

Stone's *Burgoyne's Campaign* 115 has the account of the troops' laying down their arms, and Wilkinson's conversation with the British general is in the same volume 117.

Farnum Oct. 17, Pillsbury 78, and Stone *Burgoyne's Campaign* 129fn describe the scene.

Mintz 1–2 contrasts Burgoyne and Gates.

The words exchanged by the two generals is from Mattoon's reminiscence in Stone *Burgoyne's Campaign* 379.

Ephraim Squier's comment is from his diary Oct. 17.

Stone's *Revolutionary Letters* 128–31 and Specht Oct. 17 include numerous German comments about the American soldiers.

The scene at the marquee and the march of the beaten army are described in the *Continental Journal and Weekly Advertiser* of Jan. 14, 1770, quoted in Lunt 269–70; Stone *Burgoyne's Campaign* 120–24; Specht Oct. 17; and Hitchcock Oct. 17.

Madame Riedesel relates the kindness of Philip Schuyler, and Burgoyne's reception at the American general's Albany home is mentioned in Stone *Burgoyne's Campaign* 124.

The letter from Burgoyne to Germain is dated Oct. 20. It was published in *The Gentleman's Magazine and Historical Chronicle*, vol. 47 (1777), and appears in *State*. Two other letters from the general—to Phillipson and his nieces—were also written on Oct. 20.

Boatner 275 summarizes the travails of the Convention Army. Lamb's comment is from his *Journal* 252. Jefferson's March 27, 1779, letter was to Patrick Henry and is in the Jefferson *Papers* 2:235.

Gates's triumphant message to his wife and son Bob was written on Oct. 20; quoted in Moore 1:511.

Recognition for what St. Clair achieved by his skillful retreat from Ticonderoga is in Baldwin's letter to St. Clair Oct. 17.

Gratitude and a sense of awe at the magnitude of the victory are expressed by Boardman 235–36, Cross Oct. 17, and Hodgkins in a letter to his wife Oct. 17. Sewall's appreciation of the military achievement and the number of prisoners taken are in his diary Oct. 17–18. More on the departure of rebel units is in Greenleaf, Wild, and Specht, all on Oct. 18.

Brandt's *An American Aristocracy* 121–22 describes the Livingston properties burned by Vaughan. Nickerson 405 has an account of the episode.

Peters's account is in the Toronto *Daily Globe* July 16, 1877.

Glover wrote to "Jer'h" Powell on Oct. 22 stating his needs.

Manasseh Cutler's *Journal* Oct. 22 reports arrival of news of the surrender.

Parker's letter to Page bears no date; Patrick Henry's act is recorded in the Robert Honyman diary 179.

The march south and the army's destination are chronicled in Dearborn Oct. 19–Dec. 1, 112–14, and Flexner's *George Washington in the American Revolution* 251–52 and 260.

Material on the Foreign Affairs Committee's communications is drawn from letters of Oct. 6, 18, and 31.

Footnotes on 318 and 321 in Digby's *Journal* quote Walpole and the disgusted New York loyalist who blamed the surrender on Howe.

Howe wrote to Germain on Oct. 22 saying he wanted to resign.

Fox's attack on Germain and Walpole's comments are in the latter's letters of Sept. 18, Oct. 8 and 26, Nov. 7, and Dec. 4, 5, and 11.

Franklin's *Papers* 24:28–29 includes his description of his situation in Passy and, on 552, the letter from a Swiss friend. See also his letter of Oct. 5 to Jane Mecom, Van Doren 576, and Moore 1:504.

Franklin *Papers* 24:100–2 has the Oct. 25 memorandum by Arthur Lee of his conversation with Franklin.

An account of Austin's mission is in Franklin *Papers* 24:234.

The commissioners' report to Congress was made on Dec. 18; see also Van Doren 588.

Notification to Vergennes appears in Franklin *Papers* 25:234–37.

The commissioners' joyful message to Congress was written on Dec. 18, the same day Ralph Izard reported to the Foreign Affairs Committee.

Ralph Izard's message to the Foreign Affairs Committee was written on Dec. 18, 1777.

Van Doren 587–95 and Nickerson 409–14 have accounts of Louis XVI's reception of the American commissioners.

Hollister 13 prints Ebenezer Allen's extraordinary letter about Dinah Mattis. It is worth noting that it was written four score and six years before Abraham Lincoln issued the Emancipation Proclamation.

Acknowledgments

During the years I spent researching and writing this book I came to appreciate once again the extraordinary generosity of the people on whom the historian depends for help delving into the past. That generosity takes many forms, but I think it fair to say that almost everyone I approached for assistance or information supplied what I wanted cheerfully and in many cases went the extra mile, going out of his or her way to look further or suggest other avenues for me to pursue.

I can't vouch for what goes on in other fields, but I have learned through past experience that one of the joys of writing about America's history is that so many doors are thrown open to the serious inquirer. The list that follows includes the many men and women (all of them, I hope) who have provided assistance of one kind or another. If I have omitted anyone, I apologize. It goes without saying that no one named here bears responsibility for faults within the book—those are mine, and mine alone.

From the beginning, Robert and Polly Maguire have shown me every kindness, and he has made invaluable suggestions of sources. Nardi Reeder Campion and Noel Perrin made certain that I found my way to that remarkable institution known as the Baker Library at Dartmouth, and thanks to them I met Robert Jaccaud and Philip Cronenwett, who have been extremely helpful. Judge Eugene H. Nickerson kindly investigated the possibility that his father's papers might contain notes on sources for his splendid study of the Burgoyne campaign (alas, they did not). Dorothy Offendsen gave me the benefit of her years of study of the Revolution in and around Pawlet, Vt. Cynthia Van Vlaanderen assisted me in locating the files of British regiments that served with Burgoyne. She and Corinna Wildman even went so far as to write drafts on London banks so that I could reimburse several British institutions in pounds sterling, and Mrs. Wildman helped me to navigate the mysterious waters of *Debrett's Handbook*, that guide to titled Britons. George Billias, Professor Emeritus at Clark University, and Noble Smith kindly lent me books I had been unable to locate. To Thomas O'Brien, Louise Ransom, and Dr. Marshall Wolf I owe thanks for prodding me to get on with the project.

Several individuals aided me with research. Michael Robinson doggedly tracked down a huge number of documents from repositories in and around New York, New Jersey, and Pennsylvania and managed to decipher a number of manuscripts that appeared to be undecipherable. Heidi Hutchins accommodated a large number of my requests along with her own investigations at the Library of Congress, copying the information and providing provenance. Sydney Stokes, Jr., a Jefferson scholar, located a number of useful Jefferson references for me. Lion Miles, who has made an exhaustive study of the Bennington battle, the Brunswick troops, and the Convention Army, shared his outstanding paper on the battle and helped correct certain misconceptions I had. Dr. Ronald Kingsley, who has been investigating the German forces in the campaign, Sir Francis Carr Clerke, and other related topics, made available his excellent bibliography. Giovanna Peebles introduced me to a number of extremely helpful studies on underwater archaeology in Lake Champlain. Laurie Platt Winfrey of Carousel Research located illustrations expeditiously and efficiently. To the copy editor Edward Johnson I am indebted once again for a splendid job. And Mary Lee Burd at Henry Holt has been helpful in many ways.

Nicholas Westbrook, director of Fort Ticonderoga, read several chapters, let me know where I had erred, made invaluable suggestions, and put the splendid research facilities of the fort at my disposal. Bruce Moseley, former curator at Fort Ticonderoga, answered a barrage of questions with unfailing courtesy and patience, led me through the archives, and put his hand on information when I needed it.

Donald Wickman, an authority on Mount Independence, allowed me to make use of his fine master's thesis and helped in numerous other ways—reading and commenting on several chapters, passing along copies of documents and nuggets of information, and giving me a better understanding of the engagement at Hubbardton.

Helga Doblin has been a mine of information on the German forces under Burgoyne. Her translations of officers' journals, noted elsewhere in the chapter notes and bibliography, are an incomparable resource, and she has graciously shared ideas and information. When confronted with the question of whether Riedesel's troops marched into battle singing hymns, she wrote to the Niedersächsisches Staatsarchiv for advice, paraded through her house singing "A Mighty Fortress Is Our God" and found it a very inspiring tune, produced the cover page of the *Complete Braunschweig Hymnal*, and concluded that all hymns in 4/4 time could provide the proper beat. She and I decided that the Brunswickers were indeed singing.

Carl Fuller and Lennox Lumsden at the Hubbardton, Vermont, battlefield took me on a tour, reviewed my description of the engagement, and gave me a number of very helpful suggestions.

At the Saratoga National Historical Park, S. Paul Okey guided me around the battlefield and immediate environs and shepherded me through the archives there, and he and Joseph Craig read and commented on my chapters dealing with the conclusive battles of the campaign.

A number of libraries and historical societies were absolutely essential to my inquiries, and I include with this list of institutions the names of individuals in each of them who went out of their way to be helpful. I should preface this with special thanks to those responsible for the remarkable collections at the Massachusetts Historical Society in Boston, a mine of information and a delightful place to work. Dr. Louis Tucker, Peter Drummey, Virginia Smith, and Brenda Lawson answered countless questions and assisted in many other ways. Others who provided guidance and assistance are Thomas Knoles at the American Antiquarian Society in Worcester, Mass.; Rita Dockery at the American Philosophical Society in Philadelphia, Pa.; Joseph Parks and his successor, Tyler Resch, at the Bennington (Vt.) Museum; the immensely capable staff at the Boston (Mass.) Athenaeum; Roberta Zonghi in the Rare Book Room at the Boston (Mass.) Public Library; Susan M. Swasta at the William L. Clements Library at the University of Michigan, Ann Arbor, Mich.; Kevin P. Kelly at Colonial Williamsburg (Va.); Martha H. Smart at the Connecticut Historical Society in Hartford, Conn.; Robert D. Jaccaud and Philip Cronenwett at the Dartmouth College Library in Hanover,

N.H.; David J. Fowler at the David Library of the American Revolution in Washington Crossing, Pa.; Gail Bumgardner at the Dorset (Vt.) Library; the staff at the Houghton Library Reading Room and Denison Beach at the Houghton Library at Harvard University in Cambridge, Mass.; the Library of Congress in Washington, D.C.; Jennifer A. Bryan at the Maryland Historical Society in Baltimore, Md.; Mark Bisaillon at the National Archives in Ottawa, Ontario, Canada; Stephanie Betancourt at the National Museum of the American Indian in New York, N.Y.; Mary Ellen Yee, Neil Todd, and Ed Johnson at the New England Historic Genealogical Society in Boston, Mass.; James W. Campbell at the New Haven Colony Historical Society in New Haven, Conn.; the New-York Historical Society in New York, N.Y.; the New York Public Library, New York, N.Y.; Jane E. Ward at the Peabody Essex Museum in Salem, Mass.; Margaret M. Sherry at the Princeton University Library in Princeton, N.J.; Richard D. Stattler at the Rhode Island Historical Society Library in Providence, R.I.; the Rutland (Vt.) Free Library; Karen Ufford Campola at the Saratoga (N.Y.) Historian's office; S. Paul Okey and Joseph Craig at the Saratoga National Historical Park in Stillwater, N.Y.; Gail Rice at the Mark Skinner Library, Manchester, Vt.; Nicholas Westbrook and Bruce Moseley and the staff at Fort Ticonderoga in Ticonderoga, N.Y.; Paul Carnahan and Barney Bloom at the Vermont Historical Society in Montpelier, Vt.; Kevin Graffagnino and Karen Stites Campbell at the University of Vermont's Bailey/Howe Library, Burlington, Vt.; Ann L. S. Southwell at the University of Virginia Library in Charlottesville, Va.; Janet B. Schwarz at the Virginia Historical Society in Richmond, Va.; and Lee Dalzell at the Williams College Library, Williamstown, Mass.

In the United Kingdom a number of organizations and individuals answered my appeals for advice and assistance. I am greatly indebted to several members of the Acland family—Mrs. Nicholas Acland, Sir Anthony Acland, Sir John Acland—and to Lord Carnarvon for their generous help in obtaining the journal of Lady Harriet Acland. Everything I read about Lady Harriet convinced me that she must have kept a diary of some sort, and by extraordinary coincidence my search for such a document was no sooner begun than the journal came to light and was published by the Hampshire County Council in Winchester. I also benefited greatly from the kind assistance of Jennifer Thorp, archivist at Highclere Castle, who edited the document so skillfully, and Sarah Lewin at the Hampshire County Council, who was in charge of its publication. Unfortunately my efforts to locate surviving letters from Lady Harriet to her parents hit a dead end: the present Earl of Ilchester is not aware of the existence of any such correspondence. To Sir John Acland I am most grateful for permission to reproduce the portraits of John Dyke Acland and Lady Harriet Acland.

The Earl of Crawford has my deepest appreciation for permission to study certain papers of his ancestor Alexander Lindsay, 6th Earl of Balcarres. Kenneth Dunn at the National Library of Scotland was also very helpful. Balcarres evidently intended to write the memoirs of his varied and interesting life, and his papers include a number of "Anecdotes" to be used for that purpose; these and a number of his letters to family members shed light on several aspects of the Burgoyne campaign.

Peregrine Pollen was extremely helpful, putting me in touch with several people who knew the whereabouts of certain materials I sought. The Marquess of Abergavenny endeavored to locate some Simon Fraser correspondence for me.

I am also indebted to James Collett White at the Bedfordshire County Council in Bedford, England; General Sir James Eyre; Kenneth Dunn at the National Library of Scotland in Edinburgh; Major J. McQ. Hallam, the Fusiliers' Museum, Bury, Lancashire; D. L. Prior of the Record Office, House of Lords, London; Marion Harding and Claire Wright of the National Army Museum, London; Adam Rodgers, Norfolk Museums Service, Norfolk; Major V. J. Meeson, The Queen's Lancashire Regiment, Preston; Major P. J. Ball, The Royal Gloucestershire, Berkshire and Wiltshire Regiment Museum; Major W. Shaw, The Royal Highland Fusiliers, Glasgow; Major Boris Mollo, Shropshire Regimental Museum, Shrewsbury; M. J. Everett, Regimental Museum of the South Wales Borderers and Monmouthshire Regiment of the Royal Regiment of Wales, Brecon, Powys.

Writing a book often demands periods of total immersion, or at least complete involvement, in the subject, which means that certain chores around the house (and in our case, a farm) have to be handled by others. For their cheerful and helpful assistance, I am very grateful to Robert Matteson, Pauline Dunbar, Daniel O'Leary, and Matthew Tobin.

Special thanks go to my agent Carl Brandt, whose enthusiasm for the project, unflagging good humor, and good advice have meant so much. My editor William Strachan made many valuable suggestions, and I am especially grateful for the care and close scrutiny he devoted to my manuscript.

My wife, Barbara Bray Ketchum, has been with me every step of the way on this expedition, as on past projects. I have benefited as always from her wise counsel and incisive suggestions, including reminders not to sit too long without getting up to stretch.

Index